Economics

FOURTH EDITION

Walter J. Wessels
Professor of Economics
Department of Economics and Business
North Carolina State University

BARRON'S

All inquiries should be addressed to:
Barron's Educational Series, Inc.
250 Wireless Boulevard
Hauppauge, New York 11788
http://www.barronseduc.com

Library of Congress Catalog Card Number 2005058924

ISBN-13: 978-0-7641-3419-7
ISBN-10: 0-7641-3419-1

Library of Congress Cataloging-in-Publication Data

Wessels, Walter J.
    Economics / Walter J. Wessels. — 4th ed.
        p. cm. — (Business review books)
    Includes index.
    ISBN-13: 978-0-7641-3419-7
    ISBN-10: 0-7641-3419-1
        1. Economics.   I. Title.   II. Series.

    HB171.5.W43 2006
    330—dc22   2005058924

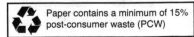

CONTENTS

MICROECONOMICS: CONSUMER AND COST

MICROECONOMICS: COMPETITION AND MONOPOLY

MICROECONOMICS: GOVERNMENT AND THE ECONOMY

INTERNATIONAL TRADE

APPENDIX

PREFACE

The goal of this text is singular: to help you understand economics so that you will do better in class and in business, and to do this as clearly and concisely as possible. The strong positive response from the previous editions shows that this goal was achieved. We have revised this text to bring you up-to-date with current economic understanding. Some of the new topics covered are game theory, real business cycle models, international capital markets, the random walk model of the stock market, and the economic role of financial markets.

Both *students* taking economics who want to do better in economics class and *business professionals* who want to understand better the economic environment they compete in will find this book beneficial. Unlike most texts, we test your understanding throughout each chapter with problems and answers, so that small misunderstandings do not grow. And unlike most study guides, we give you complete explanations and useful examples to help you do these problems.

Throughout this guide, you will find it easy to learn the essentials of economics, especially if you follow the procedure outlined:

1. ***Learn the Definitions and Main Points.*** Each chapter begins with *Key Terms* discussed throughout the unit. This is followed by *You Should Remember,* which summarizes main points taught.

2. ***Work Each Example and Graph.*** As you read the chapters, be sure you work out each example. In addition, because using graphs is essential to understanding economics, be sure you understand each graph before going on to new material. One way to assure this is to redraw each graph and see how it matches the explanation given in the text.

3. ***Do All Problems.*** *Do You Know the Basics* tests your understanding of the basic concepts of economics. *Practical Application* tests your ability to apply the economic tools you have learned. Answers are provided for both. Don't skip either of these sections!

4. ***Understand the Assumptions Being Made.*** Economists use economic models to understand the world. Once you understand an economic model's *assumptions*, the *results* will follow logically. In this text, the assumptions of Keynesian, monetarist, and rational-expectations models are presented in separate chapters so that you can focus on each and thus understand how and why each model works the way it does.

An understanding of economics is essential for understanding the economic events that affect us all. Carefully studying this book in the way I have outlined will help you gain that understanding.

1
WHAT IS ECONOMICS ALL ABOUT?

KEY TERMS

economics study of how people choose among alternative uses of their scarce resources.

marginal analysis evaluating the costs and benefits of a *small* increase in a variable (such as output). If increasing the variable adds more to total benefits than to total costs (that is, if marginal benefit exceeds or equals marginal cost), the variable should be increased.

normative statement a statement about how things *should be* in a moral sense.

opportunity cost value of the best alternative that had to be forgone in order to undertake a given course of action.

positive statement a statement about what *really is* and that can be observed as true or false.

production possibility curve (or frontier) a graph showing combinations of goods that an individual, a firm, or an economy is capable of producing.

scarcity a condition that exists when current resources are inadequate to provide for all of people's wants. A good is scarce if another unit of the good would benefit someone. Another test: The good is scarce if when price of the good is zero (it is free), the quantity people demand (want) exceeds its supply. For example, a cave person considers fresh air to be a free good. In Los Angeles, fresh air is scarce.

WHAT IS ECONOMICS ABOUT?

The social sciences seek to describe how people will act. What makes economics different from the other social sciences is the models economists use. Economic models assume people are rational (with well-ordered preferences), want to maximize something (such as profits or satisfaction), and then do the best they can given their scarce resources.

Consider a simple economic model. We are at a grocery store that has several checkout lanes open. It is a crowded day, and people are in every line. We want a model predicting how many people will be in each line. An economist would likely assume that people know how fast each line is moving and that people seek to spend the least time in line. If the waiting time in one line is less, people will change lines. This will continue until all lines have the same expected wait time. This is the key prediction of the model. It also predicts that slower clerks will have shorter lines.

The prediction of equal waiting time is a *positive statement*. A positive statement is a claim about what *really is*. A positive statement can be tested. We could, for example, find the wait time in a grocery store. Most likely, we would find only an average wait time. However, the results could be wrong because the assumptions may be wrong (people may not have sufficient information or they may care about more things than just the wait time). Thus, a positive statement is a statement that can be demonstrated to be true or false.

Another type of statement is a *normative statement*. A normative statement makes a moral claim about *what should be*. For example, some customers might say, "Some customers have to wait longer than others, and that is not fair." Without making a moral judgment, no way exists to say that such a statement is *right*.

THE BASIS FOR ECONOMICS

Economics is the study of how people choose to allocate their scarce resources. Economists study these choices with models like the one above. Most economic models have three common elements: scarcity, cost, and marginal analysis. Typically, something is scarce (for example, time or money). This results in costs (doing one thing means giving up doing something else). Therefore, the best way of finding out how to get the most of what one wants is by marginal analysis. These three concepts–scarcity, cost, and marginal analysis–form the base upon which economics is built.

SCARCITY

Most people want far more than their current resources allow them to have. This is **scarcity:** people wanting more than can be satisfied with available resources.

Don't confuse scarcity with poverty: Even the rich want more! And remember, the fact that there is only a small quantity of a good (such as castor oil cola) does *not* make it scarce: It must also be desirable.

Test for Determining Scarcity of a Good: A good is scarce if another unit of the good would benefit someone. An alternative test is if the price of the good is zero (it is free), then the demand for the good exceeds its supply. For example, a cave person considers fresh air to be a free good. In Los Angeles, fresh air is scarce.

• *CHOICE*

Scarcity forces people to make choices. When a good is scarce, people are forced to choose between which uses will be fulfilled and which will not be fulfilled. As a consequence, people face a **trade-off:** To satisfy *more* of one need means satisfying *less* of another. For example, when people save their money by putting it into a savings account, they are trading off spending that money today in order to have more to spend in the future.

OPPORTUNITY COST

When a good is scarce, choosing to use the good in one way means giving up some other use. The value of the use people give up is the **opportunity cost** of this choice. Opportunity costs can also be defined as the "value of the best forgone alternative use." This emphasizes that had people *not* made the choice they did, they would have then chosen the next best alternative.

Example: How Opportunity Costs Are Measured

PROBLEM   An owner of a small firm needs to hire some managers. Assume that each manager has time to do only one task. Task A is worth $100,000 to the owner, Task B is worth $75,000, and Task C is worth $50,000. The owner hires only two managers, having one do Task A and the other do Task B. What is the opportunity cost of Task B?

SOLUTION   The opportunity cost of Task B is the value of the forgone task that otherwise would have been accomplished, which in this case is Task C. So the opportunity cost of Task B is $50,000. Note that the opportunity cost of Task A is also $50,000 since, with two managers, Task C is forgone, given up to do Task A.

Example: How the Value of a Good Is Measured

PROBLEM   In the above problem, assume the firm still has only two managers. Assume further that each manager can do the other's task with the same efficiency. What is the value of the second manager (i.e., what would the firm lose if it fired [and did not replace] the second manager)? What is the value of the first manager (when the second is still employed)?

SOLUTION   If the second manager is let go (and not replaced), Task B will not be done. So the second manager's value is $75,000. If the first manager is let go but the second remains, the second manager will take over Task A, leaving Task B undone. So the first manager is also worth $75,000.

This illustrates a basic principle of rationality: When the units of a good or resource are *interchangeable,* people value each and every unit of the good by the good's least valued use (of its current uses). In economic terms, this is the good's marginal value: the value of the good's least important use, which people would forgo if they had one less unit.

YOU SHOULD REMEMBER

1. *Scarcity* occurs whenever people desire more of a good than exists. When a good is scarce, people have to choose among its uses. Scarcity is the source of all choice.

2. A good is a *free good* if it is not scarce. More units of a free good would not make anyone better off.

3. *Opportunity cost* is the highest-valued alternative people have to sacrifice because of the decisions they make. The concept of opportunity costs implies making trade-offs. Getting more of one thing means getting less of another.

4. When the units of a good are interchangeable, each unit should be valued by the good's *marginal value*—the value of the use that would be forgone if there were one less unit of the good.

• *PRODUCTION POSSIBILITY CURVE*

To illustrate the trade-offs faced by a person, firm, or economy, economists use **production possibility curves.** These curves show the *trade-offs* (or *opportunity costs*) people face because of the scarcity of resources. Table 1–1 shows the trade-offs a worker might face when the worker has only four hours in total to produce two goods: chairs and benches. In this example, time (the four hours) is the source of scarcity. The more time the worker spends making chairs, the less time he can spend making benches. Table 1–1 shows this trade-off as the worker spends more time making chairs.

Table 1–1. Detemining Trade-Offs Because of Resource Scarcity

CHAIRS		BENCHES	
Time Spent (in hours)	Product Made	Time Spent (in hours)	Product Made
0	0	4	20
1	4	3	18
2	7	2	14
3	9	1	8
4	10	0	0

Figure 1–1 shows the production possibility curve derived from these numbers. If the worker devotes all four hours to making benches, 20 benches and no chairs will be produced (at Point *A*). One hour spent making chairs (and one *less* hour spent making benches) results in 4 chairs and 18 benches being produced (at Point *B*). Two hours on each results in 7 chairs and 14 benches (at Point C).

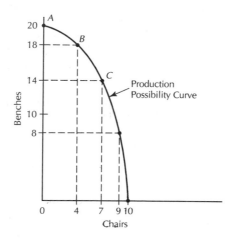

Figure 1–1. Law of Increasing Relative Cost Shown by Production Possibility Curve

Given this information, how do we measure opportunity cost?

Note: If you have trouble with graphs such as that in Figure 1–1, turn to Chapter 2.

Key Procedure for Calculating Opportunity Cost Per Unit for a Production Possibility Curve

1. Start with any *increase* in production of one good, and let this be the *gain*.

2. Measure the *loss* (the decrease in the other good's production necessary to get the gain).

3. Opportunity cost per unit of the good gained is the *loss* divided by the *gain*.

For example, a third hour added to chair making has a gain of 2 chairs (from 7 to 9) and a loss of 6 benches (from 14 to 8), so the opportunity cost per chair over this range is 3 benches per chair (6/2).

Example: Measuring Opportunity Cost

PROBLEM   The worker is currently spending one hour making chairs and three hours making benches. What is the opportunity cost per chair of spending a second hour in chair making (assuming the worker is still limited to four hours)? What is the dollar value of this opportunity cost if benches sell for $12? If chairs sell for $25, how many hours should be spent making chairs?

SOLUTION   By working the second hour on chairs, 3 more chairs are made *but* 4 fewer benches. So the opportunity cost per chair during the second hour is four-thirds of a bench. In dollar terms, this is $16 (4/3 × $12). That is, in the second hour, for every chair made, the worker gives up making four-thirds of a bench. The dollar opportunity cost per chair of a third hour added to chair making is $36 (3 × $12) and for a fourth hour added to chair making, $96 (8 × $12). The worker should spend two hours making chairs; up to and including the second hour, each chair adds more ($25) than is given up. However, the opportunity cost per chair during the third and fourth hours ($26 and $96) exceeds the $25 dollar gain from making the chairs. These are better spent making benches.

LAW OF INCREASING RELATIVE COSTS

In our example, each additional hour spent in chair making had a higher opportunity cost per chair than did the preceding hour. (The first hour's cost per chair was one-half a bench, the second hour's cost was one and one-third benches, the third hour's cost was three benches, and the fourth hour's cost was eight benches.) This *increase* in opportunity cost is shown by the production possibility curve becoming *steeper* as we move right in Figure 1–1.

This example illustrates the **law of increasing relative costs:** As more of a good is produced, its opportunity cost rises. Note that the law refers to "relative cost." In this example, relative cost is the good's opportunity cost. When individuals, firms, or economies face increasing relative costs, their production possibility curves *bow out* as in Figure 1–1.

Reasons for Increasing Relative Costs

1. ***Diminishing returns,*** condition where added inputs increase output by less than what the same increase in inputs previously added to output. For example, a firm adds a worker who adds four chairs to its total production. The firm is experiencing diminishing returns if the next worker it hires adds two more chairs (or any number less than four). If a worker costs $40, the first four chairs cost $10 each and the next two chairs cost $20. Diminishing returns means increasing costs per unit output.

2. ***Differing suitability of inputs,*** which occurs when some workers are better at producing Good A, others Good B. Economically, the first set of resources an economy should devote to producing Good A will be those best suited for A's efficient production. As more and more of Good A is produced, it is likely that resources less and less suited to its efficient production will eventually be used, and the result will be an increase in the relative cost of Good A. A major reason why inputs may differ in suitability is specialization (e.g., a worker who specializes in producing Good A may not know how to produce Good B).

YOU SHOULD REMEMBER

1. The trade-offs and opportunity costs caused by scarcity are illustrated with the *production possibility curve.* It shows a menu of possible outputs of goods (usually of two goods) that can be produced.

2. The *absolute slope* (the slope stated as a positive number) shows the opportunity cost of the good on the horizontal (bottom) axis. For example, in Figure 1–1, an absolute slope of 2 means that one more chair costs two benches. (See Chapter 2 for the definition of *slope.*)

3. The *slope of the production possibility curve becomes steeper as one moves along it to the right. This shows the law of increasing cost.* The opportunity cost of each added chair (the benches not made) increases. This can be due to diminishing returns or to differences in suitability of inputs.

EFFICIENCY

The production possibility curve is drawn assuming that (1) the economy has a fixed amount of resources (including labor, materials, and capital), (2) the economy is using these resources efficiently, and (3) the state of technology remains unchanged.

Figure 1–2 shows different combinations of consumption goods (such as food and toothpaste) and investment goods (such as factories and machinery). At Point A, the economy is *not* using its resources efficiently since it could have more of both goods. An economy could be at Point A because of excessively high unemployment or because of laws and taxes that discourage efficiency. Only when an economy is at a point on its production possibility curve is it using resources efficiently (one such point is Point B).

The Test for Efficiency: To produce more of one good, must the economy produce less of the other? If the answer is yes, then the economy is producing efficiently and is on its production possibility curve.

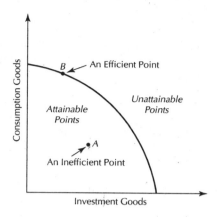

Figure 1–2. Test of Efficiency Shown by Production Possibility Curve

ECONOMIC GROWTH

The production possibility curve can also be used to show the causes and effects of economic growth. Figure 1–3 begins by reproducing Figure 1–2. A society at Point *B* produces 80 units of investment goods and 200 units of consumption goods. Investment goods, such as new plants and equipment, give workers more and better tools to work with so they will be more productive in following years. So next year, the society faces a new production possibility curve (*CC′*). People can have more of both consumption and investment goods (e.g., 100 units of investment goods and 250 units of consumption goods). This upward and outward shift of the production possibility curve illustrates the impact of economic growth.

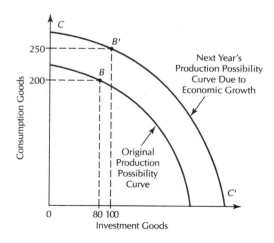

Figure 1–3. Impact of Economic Growth Shown by Production Possibility Curve

Factors That Cause Economic Growth

1. *Increase in investment* since more investment goods make workers more productive. In order to invest more, people have to reduce their current consumption and save more so that their savings are available for investment.

2. *Innovation,* which occurs when someone discovers a way to produce more output from the same amount of inputs. Innovations in technology, in management, and in marketing can all contribute to economic growth.

3. *Increased division of labor,* which over the past two centuries has allowed workers to become more productive in their areas of specialization. Increased division of labor also means that workers are producing not for themselves but for other people. Thus, specialization and trade go together.

4. *Increase in inputs,* e.g., more workers, more machines, and more land. An increase in the number of inputs leads to more output and to economic growth.

YOU SHOULD REMEMBER

1. Only when an economy is on its production possibility curve is it being efficient. If the only way to produce more of one good is to produce less of another, then the economy is producing efficiently.

2. Growth allows an economy to have more of everything. The main ways to have growth are to invest more, innovate, increase specialization, and increase inputs.

3. The points inside the production possibility curve are attainable by society but are inefficient since with its resources, the economy could have more of both goods. The points outside the production possibility curve are unattainable.

MARGINAL ANALYSIS

How should people allocate their scarce resources to get the most value? To answer this question, economists use **marginal analysis:** the analysis of the benefits and cost of the marginal unit of a good or input. This technique is widely used in business decision making and ties together much of economic thought.

In any situation, people want to maximize net benefits:

$$\text{Net Benefits} = \text{Total Benefits} - \text{Total Costs}$$

To do this, they can change a variable, such as the quantity of a good they buy or the quantity of output they produce. This variable is the *control variable.*

Marginal analysis focuses upon whether the control variable should be increased by one more unit.

Key Procedure for Using Marginal Analysis

1. Identify the control variable.

2. Determine what the increase in total benefits would be if one more unit of the control variable were added. This is the **marginal benefit** of the added unit.

3. Determine what the increase in total costs would be if one more unit of the control variable were added. This is the **marginal cost** of the added unit.

4. If the unit's marginal benefit *exceeds* (or equals) its marginal cost, it *should be added*.

Remember to look only at the *changes* in total benefits and total costs. If a particular cost or benefit does not change, ignore it.

Why does this work?

Because: Marginal Benefit = Increase in Total Benefits

Marginal Cost = Increase in Total Cost

So: Change in Net Benefits = Marginal Benefit – Marginal Cost

When marginal benefits exceed marginal cost, net benefits go up. So the marginal unit of the control variable should be added.

Example: Should a Firm Produce More?

A firm's net benefit of being in business is its profits. The following formula illustrates how profits are calculated:

$$\text{Profits} = \text{Total Revenue} - \text{Total Cost}$$

(Note that total revenue is the same thing as total sales; do not confuse "revenue" with "profit.")

The firm's control variable is the output it produces.

PROBLEM   International Widget is producing 50 widgets at a cost of $50,000 and is selling them for $60,000. If it produces a 51st unit, its total sales will be $62,000 and its total cost will be $51,500. Should the firm produce the 51st unit?

SOLUTION   Yes. The 51st unit's marginal benefit is $2,000 and its marginal cost is $1,500. It should be produced. It adds $500 to profit ($2,000 − $1,500).

Example: Should a Better Worker Be Hired?

The following problem emphasizes the importance of looking only at the change in total benefits and costs.

PROBLEM   Acme Manufacturing has trained Worker A at a cost of $30,000, and Worker A is worth $70,000 to Acme. A worker's worth to a firm refers to how much the firm presently values all the future profits it expects to make from the worker, these profits being the revenues produced by the worker less wages and fringe benefits. Later, Acme has the opportunity to hire Worker B. Worker B would cost $30,000 to train but would be worth $90,000. However, to hire Worker B, Acme must fire Worker A. Should Acme hire Worker B?

SOLUTION   No. Hiring Worker B and getting rid of Worker A adds $20,000 in increased worth (so the marginal benefit of this decision would be $20,000). The marginal cost of doing this is $30,000 in added costs for training Worker B. Since the marginal cost exceeds marginal benefit, Acme should not hire Worker B.

What about Worker A's $30,000 training cost? We ignore it, because firing A and hiring B neither increases nor reduces this cost, since it has already been incurred.

YOU SHOULD REMEMBER

1. Marginal analysis forms the basis of economic reasoning. To aid in decision making, marginal analysis looks at the effects of a small change in the control variable. Each small change produces some good (its marginal benefit) and some bad (its marginal cost). As long as there is more "good" than "bad," the control variable should be increased (since net benefits will then be increased).

2. The change in net benefit equals marginal benefit minus marginal cost. If the marginal benefit of an action exceeds its marginal cost, then taking the action causes net benefits to go up.

KNOW THE CONCEPTS

DO YOU KNOW THE BASICS?

1. How do scarcity and poverty differ?
2. Why can't opportunity costs exist without scarcity?
3. Does an economy that is inside its production possibilities curve face any trade-offs?
4. How can a good be costly yet not scarce?
5. What factors cause the production possibilities curve to bow out? And when the curve is bowed out, how does the opportunity cost of each good change if more of the good is produced?
6. What will cause an economy's production possibility curve to shift out and to the right?
7. How are trade and the division of labor related?
8. If the marginal cost of an action exceeds its marginal benefit, why will net benefits fall?
9. Why do people value each unit of a good by its marginal value?
10. Why is the opportunity cost of an option equal to the value of the best of all the alternatives that had to be forgone?

TERMS FOR STUDY

control variable
division of labor
efficiency
growth
investment
marginal analysis
marginal benefit
marginal cost

net benefits
normative analysis
opportunity cost
positive analysis
production possibility curve
scarcity
specialization
trade-off

PRACTICAL APPLICATION

1. The following shows the production possibilities for a plant that can manufacture iron or steel. Columns A–D show the number of tons of each metal that can be produced for each alternative.

	POSSIBLE ALTERNATIVES			
	A	*B*	*C*	*D*
Steel	0	6	10	12
Iron	18	12	6	0

a. Draw the production possibility curve for this plant. Label the curve *EE´*. Does the curve show constant costs or increasing costs?

b. Suppose the firm increases steel production from Alternative B to Alternative *C*. What is the opportunity cost of each ton of steel in terms of iron? Suppose iron sold for $50 a ton. What would be the dollar opportunity cost of a ton of steel? Is this the minimum or maximum price the firm would have to charge in order to produce steel?

c. Suppose new technology allows the firm to produce twice as much steel as shown above but does not affect its iron production. Draw the new production possibility curve and label it *FF´*. Will this raise or lower the opportunity cost of producing twelve tons of steel?

2. On an island, a worker, in an hour, can produce one fish *or* two baskets.

a. What is the opportunity cost of a fish?

b. Suppose the worker becomes twice as efficient, producing in an hour two fish *or* four baskets. How has the opportunity cost of a fish changed?

c. What would cause the opportunity cost of a fish to increase?

3. You have ten workers who are all equally skilled and who can do each other worker's job with the same efficiency. The first worker does a task worth $100, the second, $90, the third, $80, and so on until the last, whose task is worth $10. Worker number one comes to you, demands a raise, and threatens to quit if the raise is not forthcoming. How much at most should you be willing to pay worker number one?

4. On Monday, John B. Burr paid $50 for a ticket to concert A on Tuesday night: This concert gives John a benefit of $60. The ticket is nonrefundable and cannot be sold. On Tuesday morning, John learns that there is another concert B at the same time that will give him a benefit of $70 and costs $45 for a ticket. What is John's opportunity cost of going to concert A? Concert B? Which one should he go to?

    Note: All "benefits" are pure benefits and not net of the ticket price.

5. What is wrong (from an economic point of view) with the following argument? "Marketing is vitally important. After all, without marketing, we wouldn't sell anything and our firm would be bankrupt. Therefore, our firm should spend more on marketing."

6. If a firm faces the following costs and benefits, how many plants should it build? Use marginal analysis.

Plants	Total Revenues	Total Costs
1	$10,000,000	$ 5,000,000
2	18,000,000	12,000,000
3	24,000,000	20,000,000

7. Currently, our military is voluntary; the armed forces sets its wages and benefits so it can attract an adequate and presumably skilled body of soldiers. In the past, our nation has used the draft, forcing people into military service at low pay. If we were to return to a draft, how would the opportunity cost of maintaining our military be affected?

8. How will the following events affect the production possibility curve of an economy?

    Event A: A large fraction of the work force becomes unemployed.

    Event B: The productivity of all workers doubles.

    Event C: The government requires dairy farmers to destroy part of their herds.

9. An economy produces two goods, A and B. Then there is technological progress but in Good A only. Can the economy then consume more of *both* goods?

10. The FDA (Food and Drug Administration) can require drug companies to spend more time and money testing the safety of new drugs. With

more testing, fewer bad drugs (drugs that do not work or have harmful effects) will be permitted to be sold in the United States. However, with more testing, fewer good drugs (drugs that save lives and improve health) will be introduced as quickly. Draw the production possibility curve facing the FDA (with "Lives saved with good drugs" on the vertical axis, and "Lives saved by preventing bad drugs" on the horizontal axis). Which way does the FDA move when it requires more extensive testing? Are the following statements normative or positive: (a) "Requiring more extensive testing kills ten people (by preventing good drugs) for every one person saved (by preventing bad drugs)," (b) "This is too high a cost, so the FDA should reduce extensive drug testing"?

ANSWERS

KNOW THE CONCEPTS

1. Poverty is having few goods. Scarcity is having more wants than goods with which to satisfy them, even if one has many goods.

2. Without scarcity, there are no alternatives that have to be given up, and thus there are no opportunity costs.

3. No. It can have more of all goods.

4. If a costly good is not desirable, it will not be scarce.

5. Diminishing returns and the fact that some inputs are more suitable than others for producing certain goods cause the bowing out of the production possibility curve. When the curve bows out, as more of any good is produced, its opportunity cost goes up.

6. More investment. Innovation. Increased division of labor. Additional inputs.

7. The division of labor means that workers specialize. They must then trade what they produce to get the goods they want to consume.

8. When marginal costs exceed marginal benefits, more is being added to total costs than to total benefits, so net benefits must fall.

9. People value a unit of a good by what would be lost if they didn't have the unit. By interchanging units of the good, a person would have to lose only the least-valued use a unit of the good is being put to, i.e., its marginal value.

10. The opportunity cost of a decision is the value of what the person would have done otherwise. If the person is rational, he or she would otherwise have chosen the most valuable of the alternative options.

PRACTICAL APPLICATION

1. a. The curve is shown below. The curve shows increasing costs.

   b. By going from Alternative *B* to Alternative *C*, represented on the graph by Points *B* and *C*, Acme gets 4 more units of steel but 6 less units of iron. So the opportunity cost per ton of steel is 6/4, or 1.5 tons of iron per ton of steel. In dollars, this iron could sell for $75 (1.5 × $50), so the firm would want $75 at a minimum for a ton of steel (in this range of production) to cover its opportunity costs.

   c. The new production possibility curve will show that the opportunity cost of steel has gone down while the opportunity cost of iron has gone up. Before, 12 tons of steel required giving up 18 tons of iron; now 12 tons require giving up only 6 tons of iron.

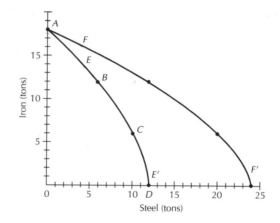

2. a. The opportunity cost of a fish is two baskets.

   b. The opportunity cost of a fish remains at two baskets.

   c. For the opportunity cost of a fish to increase, the worker must become *relatively* more efficient at producing baskets. For example, if the worker could produce two fish or six baskets in an hour, then the opportunity cost of a fish would go up to three baskets. The same result would occur if, instead, the worker could produce one-half fish or one and one-half baskets in an hour. You can see why opportunity cost is also called *relative cost*.

3. If worker number one quit, the other workers could be reassigned tasks and you would be worse off by only $10. So, worker one should be paid no more than $10.

4. The opportunity cost of going to concert A is $35, the foregone net benefit of going to concert B (net benefit of concert B = the benefit of going to concert B minus its cost = $75 – $45). Notice that the cost of A's ticket does not enter the calculation as it already has been paid for. Only costs that change as a result of John's actions are included in opportunity costs. The opportunity cost of going to B is the foregone benefit of going to A: $60. Once again, John should only count the changes due to his current choice. He should not count the cost of A's ticket as he has paid for it even if he does not go to the A concert. Thus, if he chooses B over A, he will forego $60. John should choose to go to concert A: He gains $60 at a foregone cost of $35. Had John gone to B, he would gain $35 but at a great foregone cost of $60.

5. This argument tries to measure the value of an additional expenditure on marketing not by its *marginal* contribution but rather by the total value of *all* marketing. The correct way to evaluate the issue is to ask if the additional money spent on marketing is matched or exceeded by its additional or marginal benefit.

6. The firm should build two plants. The third plant's marginal cost is $8 million while its marginal benefit is only $6 million. Therefore, the third plant should not be built.

7. The cost of maintaining our military forces is the opportunity cost of what the people in the military would have been doing otherwise. With a pay system, only those people whose opportunity cost falls below what the armed forces pays will join. However, with a draft, persons with higher opportunity costs will likely be forced into service. Thus, the total opportunity cost of a draft will be higher.

8. *Event A:* This event has no effect. Rather, it would be illustrated by a movement to inside the production possibility curve (such as Point *A* in Figure 1–2). Recall that all inputs are fully employed when the economy is on its production possibility curve.

    Event B: This event moves the curve up and to the right so that more of all goods can be produced.

    Event C: This event shifts the curve down and to the left.

9. Yes. To produce the "old" amounts of Goods A and B takes fewer inputs; the leftover inputs can then be used to produce more A and B. The old and new production possibility curves look like the answer to Practical Application, Question 1, where steel is Good A.

10. The production possibility curve will look like Figure 1–3. More testing moves the economy along the curve, down and to the right: More lives will be saved by preventing bad drugs, but fewer will be saved by good drugs (as fewer good drugs will be introduced and those that are will

be delayed). Statement (a) is positive, as it can be tested (one study suggests that it is true). Statement (b) is a normative statement, as it says ten lives saved from allowing more good drugs are worth more than one life lost from allowing bad drugs.

2
HOW TO USE GRAPHS IN ECONOMICS

READING GRAPHS

A **graph** tells a story. The story a graph tells us is how two variables are related to each other. One of the variables is measured along the bottom of the graph, and it increases in value as we move from left to right. The other variable is measured along the left side of the graph, and it increases in value as we move from bottom to top. For example, Figure 2–1 shows the profits of a firm at different levels of output. Output is measured along the bottom, and as we move from 0 to the right, output is increasing. The bottom line is the **horizontal axis.** Profits are measured along the side, and they increase as we move up from 0. The side line is the **vertical axis.**

Graphs are read like a page, *from left to right.* Usually, we think of the variable on the horizontal axis as the *cause* of the changes that occur in the variable on the vertical axis.

In Figure 2–1, we begin to read the graph at its left. When output is 0, profits equal 0. As output increases, we follow the graph and see that profits are increasing. For example, at output level A, profits reach Point D. As output continues to increase, profits continue to climb until we reach output level B. As the graph illustrates, we have reached the "top of the hill." Profits have reached their highest level (E) at output level B. Increasing output beyond B causes profits to fall, until they reach 0 at output level C.

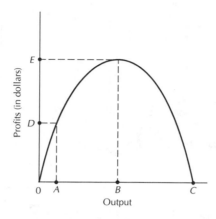

Figure 2–1. Determining Profits Based Upon Different Levels of Output

HOW TWO VARIABLES ARE RELATED

Figure 2–2 shows four different ways two variables, X and Y, can be related:

1. *Panel A* shows that X and Y are **positively related.** When X goes up, Y goes up, and when X goes down, Y goes down. For example, X could be workers hired and Y, output.

2. *Panel B* shows that X and Y are **negatively (or inversely) related.** When X goes up, Y goes down, and when X goes down, Y goes up. For example, X could be the amount of safety equipment a firm installs and Y could be the firm's accident rate.

3. *Panel C* shows that X has no effect on Y. No matter how large or small X is, Y remains the same. Y could be the size of the moon and X, pencil production.

4. *Panel D* shows that Y has no effect on X. No matter how large or small Y is, X remains the same. Y could be the price of a dead artist's paintings and X could be the world supply of the artist's paintings.

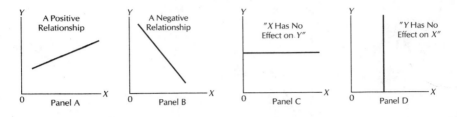

Figure 2-2. Determining Variable Relationships

YOU SHOULD REMEMBER

1. Read graphs from left to right.

2. Think of the variable on the horizontal axis as "causing" the other variable (on the vertical axis) to change.

3. Two variables are positively related to each other if they move together (both going up or both going down).

4. Two variables are negatively related if when one increases, the other decreases.

PLOTTING GRAPHS

To plot a graph, for each value of the variable on the horizontal axis, plot above it the value of the variable on the vertical axis that corresponds to it.

Example: Plotting a Budget Constraint

One type of graph used in economics is the "budget constraint," which shows the different combinations of goods a person could buy on a fixed budget.

PROBLEM Susan has a weekly budget of $10 and can buy sodas at $1 each or hamburgers at $2 each. Plot a graph showing what she could buy over the week, assuming she spends all of the $10. Put hamburgers on the horizontal (or bottom) axis.

SOLUTION If Susan buys no hamburgers, then she can buy ten sodas. So we plot this at Point *A* in Figure 2-3. If she buys one hamburger, she can buy eight sodas. This is Point *B*. We continue until she buys five hamburgers and no sodas (Point C). We connect these points with a smooth line to have the budget constraint shown in Figure 2–3. Note that we have plotted a negative relationship: As Susan buys more hamburgers, she has less money to buy sodas.

MEASURING THE SLOPE

Slope shows how two variables are related. Let X be the variable on the horizontal axis and Y the variable on the vertical axis. Slope is "rise over run." When starting at some X, X_0, let X increase to X_1. The change in X ($X_1 - X_0$) is "the run." Plotted vertically above X_0 is a corresponding value of Y that we will call Y_0. Above X_1 is Y_1. The change in Y ($Y_1 - Y_0$) is "the rise." If Y decreases as X goes up, the rise will be a negative term. To get the slope, divide the rise by the run (divide $Y_1 - Y_0$ by $X_1 - X_0$). Thus, if X increases from 5 to 7 while Y increases from 20 to 24, the slope is 2 (4/2). Instead, if X increases from 7 to 8 and Y decreases from 24 to 20, the slope is –4 (–4/1).

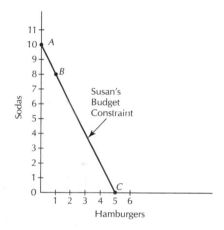

Figure 2–3. Measuring the Slope of a Straight Line

In Figure 2–3, the slope is –2. (Note: for every added hamburger, Susan has to buy two fewer sodas.)

A positive slope (as in Panel A of Figure 2–2) shows a positive relationship. A negative slope (as in Panel B of Figure 2–2) shows a negative relationship. A zero slope (as in Panel C) shows no relationship.

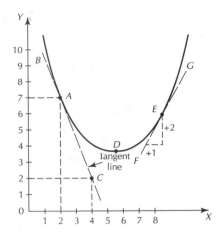

Figure 2–4. Measuring the Slope of a Curved Line

A straight line has the same slope at every point on the line. However, the slope of a curved line constantly changes as one moves along the curved line. To find the slope of a curved line at one of its points, just draw a tangent line through that point. A **tangent line** is a straight line that matches the direction of curve at that point and "touches" the curve just once. Line *BC* in Figure 2–4 is such a tangent line: It measures the slope of the curve at Point *A*. From the figures supplied, you should verify that the slope is –5/2 (or –2.5). At Point *E*, the curve has a slope of 2/1 (or +2). At Point *D*, the curve has a slope of 0.

YOU SHOULD REMEMBER

1. To calculate the *slope of a straight line,* divide the "rise" by the "run," or the change in *Y* by the change in *X,* where *X* is the variable on the horizontal axis.

2. The *slope of a curved line* at a particular point is the slope of the tangent line through that point.

3. Change in *Y* = Slope × Change in *X*.

KNOW THE CONCEPTS

DO YOU KNOW THE BASICS?

1. In Figure 2–1, what is the slope of the curve at output level *A*? Between levels *B* and *C* ? At output level *B*?
2. What are the four possible relationships two variables can have?
3. If *X* and *Y* are positively related, when *X* decreases, what will happen to *Y* ? (In these questions, *X* is the variable on the horizontal axis.)
4. What do Points *A* and *C* represent in Figure 2–3?
5. What is true about all points along Line *AC* in Figure 2–3? What about all points to the left and inside?
6. If *X* and *Y* are negatively related, when *X* decreases, what will happen to *Y* ?
7. If the slope of *Y* with respect to *X* is –3 over a given range, what will happen to *Y* if *X* increases from 7 to 9?
8. Answer question 7 when the slope is +5.
9. If a curve smoothly increases, levels out, and then decreases, what is its slope at its highest point?
   Hint: See Figure 2–1.
10. When *X* goes from 10 to 15, *Y* decreases from 20 to 10. What is the slope of this relationship over this range (assuming that it's a straight-line relationship)?

TERMS FOR STUDY

horizontal axis	slope
negative relationship	tangent line
positive relationship	vertical axis

PRACTICAL APPLICATION

1. Indicate which panel in Figure 2–2 best represents the relationships below. Assume that the first term is the *X* variable on the horizontal axis (such that *X* is the cause and *Y* is the effect).
   a. Population of a city and the cost of a home.
   b. The amount of wheat grown on a small farm and the world price of wheat (i.e., how will the world price of wheat change when the small farm grows more wheat).

   c. The fine for speeding and the fraction of the population that speeds.

   d. The pay for teachers and the number of people who want to become teachers.

2. Plot the following production possibility schedule:

Combinations	Houses	Food
A	0	16
B	4	12
C	7	8
D	9	4
E	10	0

Put houses on the horizontal axis. Give the slope between *A* and *B*, *B* and *C*, and so forth. What does the slope represent? Is this cost increasing or decreasing?

Hint: The slope shows an opportunity cost.

3. Plot the following table, with the number of workers on the horizontal axis. The table shows the output of a small chair workshop as workers are added.

Output	0	5	9	12	14	15	15	13	10
Workers	0	1	2	3	4	5	6	7	8

Give the slope for each worker added. What is the meaning of the slope in this case?

4. Draw a line that starts at the origin (at 0) and begins to rise with a slope of 1. What does this line mark off?

5. Draw a curve relating the tax rate (from 0 to 100 percent) to the total tax revenues that are collected. Put the tax rate on the horizontal axis. The curve should describe the following statement: "At a tax rate of zero, no taxes are collected. As the tax rate increases, total tax revenues rise. But once the tax rate becomes high enough, total tax revenues begin to fall as taxpayers take advantage of more loopholes in the tax law or work less because with taxes so high, the reward for working becomes too low. At a 100 percent tax rate, everyone evades taxes or leaves the country, so no tax revenues are collected."

6. a. Draw a curve showing the following situation. As a firm hires more workers (*X*), its total revenue (*Y*) increases. However, total revenue increases at a decreasing rate such that each worker adds less to total revenue. Label the total revenue curve *TR*.

   b. How is the slope of the total revenue curve related to the marginal benefit of hiring another worker?

c. Draw a curve showing the following situation. As a firm hires more workers (X), its total labor cost (Y) increases at a constant rate, each worker adding the same amount to total cost. Assume the firm's only cost is labor cost. Label the total wage cost curve *TWC*.

d. How is the slope of the total cost curve related to the marginal cost of hiring another worker?

e. If, at a given X, the slope of the total revenue curve is larger than the slope of the total cost curve, should the Xth worker be hired?

7. Draw a curve showing the following relationship: "As a manager spends more hours supervising workers, the total output of the workers being supervised goes up. However, each additional hour of supervision increases total output less than the previous hour." Plot hours of supervision on the horizontal axis. Does this statement describe a positive or negative relationship? What is happening to the slope as hours of supervision increase?

8. Assume that the manager from Question 7 takes a course that improves his or her skill in dealing with workers. As a result, for any given number of hours of supervision, workers are more productive than before. Otherwise, the relationship described above is the same. How will the new curve compare with that in Question 7?

9. When demand and supply curves were developed by economists, the convention that the "cause" be on the horizontal axis had not yet been established. As a result, for demand and supply curves, the cause is on the *vertical* axis. The cause is *price*. Draw the curve that describes the following: "As oil prices fall, consumers buy more oil." Place the cause ("oil prices") onto the vertical axis and the result ("quantity of oil bought") onto the horizontal axis.

10. Draw the curve that describes the following relationship: "As oil prices go up, oil companies produce and sell more oil." Put the cause ("oil prices") on the vertical axis. Why does this curve have a different slope than that in Question 9?

ANSWERS

KNOW THE CONCEPTS

1. Positive. Negative. Zero.
2. Figure 2–2 shows the four possible relationships.
3. Y will decrease.
4. Point A represents Susan's consumption if she consumes only sodas. Point C: only hamburgers.

5. Along Line *AC*, Susan is spending all of her budget ($10). At all points to the left and inside her budget constraint *AC*, she is spending less than $10.

6. *Y* will increase.

7. *Y* will decrease by 6 (–6 = –3 × Change in *X*, which is 2).

8. Y will increase by 10 (10 = 5 × 2).

9. Zero.

10. –2 (–2 = –10/5).

PRACTICAL APPLICATION

1. **a.** Panel A. (Houses usually cost more in large cities.)
   b. Panel C. (One small farm will have no discernible effect on world wheat prices.)
   c. Panel B. (Higher fines discourage speeding.)
   d. Panel A. (Higher wages attract more people into teaching.)

2. At zero houses, the curve begins at 16 units of food and then falls until, at 10 houses, there is no food. The slope between *A* and *B* is –1, between *B* and *C* is –4/3 or –1.333, between *C* and *D* is –2, and between *D* and *E* is –4. Stated as a positive number, this is the opportunity cost of each home (in terms of sacrificed food). The opportunity cost of homes is increasing. See figure below, left.

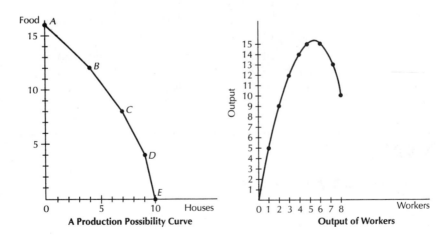

A Production Possibility Curve

Output of Workers

3. See the figure above, right. Going from 0 to 1 worker, the slope is 5, from 1 to 2, it's 4, and then it's 3, then 2, then 1, and between 5 and 6

it's 0, then –2, and finally –3. The slope represents how much each additional worker added to total output.

4. It marks off points where the variables on each axis have equal values (where $X = Y$). See figure on next page.

5. This is the famous Laffer Curve and looks like Figure 2–1 with the tax rate on the horizontal axis. At Point 0 and Point C (which represents the 100 percent tax rate), no taxes are collected. Maximum tax revenues are collected at tax rate B.

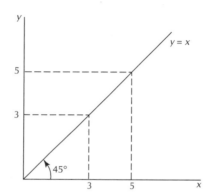

6. The figure on page 30 illustrates the curves.

   a. The *TR* curve rises but the slope becomes smaller as X (labor) increases.

   b. The slope of the *TR* curve is the increase in total revenue divided by the increase in labor hired. This increase in total revenue is the marginal benefit to the firm of hiring the added labor. For example, if the eighth worker adds $15 to total revenue, the slope would be $15. In the figure on page 28, the slope of the tangent line *T* would be $15.

   c. The *TWC* curve is a straight line with the same positive slope at all points.

   d. The slope of the *TWC* curve is the increase in total wage cost divided by the increase in labor. This increase in total wage cost is the marginal cost to the firm of hiring the added labor. For example, if each worker's wage is $10, the slope would equal $10.

   e. Yes. The worker is adding more to total revenue than he or she is adding to total wage cost, so profits are increasing. Recall that Change in Profit = Marginal Benefit – Marginal Cost. Graphically, Change in Profit = Slope of *TR* Curve – Slope of *TWC* Curve. In the figure on page 28, the eighth worker should be hired because the *TR* curve rises faster than the *TWC* curve. For example, if the eighth worker adds $15 to total revenue and $10 to total wage cost, the worker adds $5 to profits.

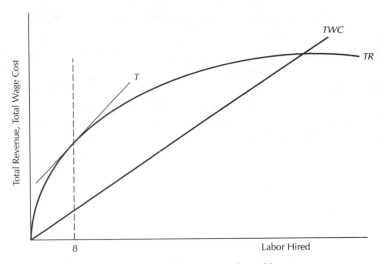

Total Revenue and Total Wage Cost for Problem 6

7. The curve should show a positive relationship and therefore have a positive slope. As hours of supervision increase, the positive slope should become smaller. Mathematically, this curve is described as "increasing at a decreasing rate." See figure below.

8. The new curve will be above the old one and will have the same general shape. See figure below.

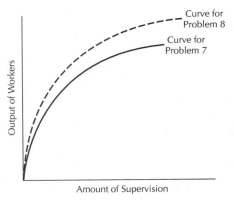

A Curve Increasing at a Decreasing Rate

9. The graph should look like Panel B in Figure 2–2. This curve is a demand curve because it describes the effect that price has on the quantity demanded. Its slope is negative.

10. The graph should look like Panel A in Figure 2–2. This curve is a supply curve because it describes the effect that price has on the quantity supplied. Its slope is positive. It has a different slope than Question 9 because it is describing the behavior of sellers (who respond to higher prices by selling more), while the demand curve in Question 9 describes the behavior of buyers (who respond to higher prices by buying less).

3

SUPPLY AND DEMAND: PART ONE

KEY TERMS

equilibrium price (market clearing price) price at which the quantity demanded equals the quantity sold.

law of demand quantity demanded and price are inversely related—more is demanded at a lower price, less at a higher price (other things being equal).

law of supply quantity supplied and price usually are directly related—more is supplied at a higher price, less at a lower price (other things being equal).

quantity demanded maximum quantity of a good that buyers are willing to buy at a given price (over a fixed period of time).

quantity supplied maximum quantity of a good that sellers are willing to supply at a given price (over a fixed period of time).

HOW TO STUDY SUPPLY AND DEMAND

To understand supply and demand better, you should remember:

1. *Supply and demand is about trade.* Buyers purchase goods with money, and sellers get money for selling goods. However, behind this exchange of monies is the exchange of goods: Buyers are in effect trading what they make (and sell) for the goods they buy.

2. *Suppliers and demanders are different.* It is important to separate the **buyers (demanders)** from the **sellers (suppliers)** of a good. This is

because they react in different ways to changes in the price as well as to changes in other variables. For example, a higher price reduces the quantity of the good that demanders want to buy but increases the quantity sellers want to sell. It is important, therefore, to understand which variables each group reacts to and how it reacts.

3. *Events caused by price changes differ from those that cause price changes.* Events caused by price changes are covered in this chapter, and events that cause price changes are addressed in Chapter 4. Events *caused* by price changes are shown by a demand or supply curve; events that *cause* the price to change are shown by a *shift* from an old to a new demand or supply curve.

4. *The quantity of a good actually bought and sold need not equal the quantity demanded and supplied.* Demand refers to how much buyers would like to buy at various prices. Supply refers to how much sellers would like to sell at various prices. Just because they would *like* to buy or sell a certain amount does *not* mean they can. For example, if Cadillacs sold for $5, most of us would like to buy several. But this does *not* mean that we can. So quantity demanded need not equal the quantity bought.

PRICE

The pertinent price of a good is its **relative price:** its price relative to the price of other goods. The relative price of Good A tells how much of Good B must be given to get one more unit of Good A.

Example: Calculating Relative Prices from Money Prices

PROBLEM   If a TV's price is $200 and a personal computer's is $2,000, what is the relative price of the TV? Of the computer?

SOLUTION   Divide the price of the good in question by the price of the good given up. The relative price of one TV is one-tenth of a computer, and the relative price of one computer is ten TVs.

When economists say that supply and demand responds to price changes, they are talking about changes in *relative* prices. What if *all* prices doubled (including wages and income)? Then relative prices would be unchanged: Neither demand nor supply would change.

YOU SHOULD REMEMBER

The relevant price is the relative price of a good. The relative price of Good A is the quantity of the other good(s) sacrificed to get one more unit of Good A. It is calculated by dividing the price of Good A by the price of the other good(s).

DEMAND AND THE LAW OF DEMAND

At each price, the **quantity demanded** is the maximum quantity buyers want to buy at that price. The quantity demanded is not necessarily the amount bought. Millions of Americans would want to buy a new Mercedes-Benz if its price were only $100, but none could be bought at $100! The **demand price** for a given quantity of a good is the highest price buyers would be willing to pay for the last unit of that quantity. If the demand price for 1,000 oranges is $1, then buyers are willing to pay at most $1 for the 1,000th orange. The demand price reflects *marginal benefit.* That is, the 1,000th orange is worth $1 to buyers and this is the most they would pay for it.

The **law of demand** states that *when price increases, the quantity demanded decreases—assuming other things do not change.* These other "things" are the *nonprice determinants of demand* and include such factors as income and tastes. When these other things do not change, we say that the quantity demanded and price have an *inverse* (or *negative*) relationship. If the price goes up, the quantity demanded goes down, and when price goes down, the quantity demanded goes up.

Why the Law of Demand Holds

1. The *added buyer effect.* A lower price attracts new buyers.

2. The *income effect* of a lower price. A lower price allows buyers to buy the same number of goods with less money. The money left over is like having more income. Some of this income may go for buying more units of the good.

3. The *substitution effect* of a lower price. A lower relative price means that the consumer gives up less of other goods to buy the good for which the price has decreased. This encourages buyers to "substitute toward" the good.

YOU SHOULD REMEMBER

1. The *quantity demanded* is the maximum quantity buyers want to buy at a given price. It need not equal the amount actually bought at the price: Less, but not more, could be bought.

2. The *law of demand* works because of the added buyer effect, the income effect, and the substitution effect.

3. The *demand price* for a good reflects its *marginal benefit* to buyers. It is the highest price buyers would pay for the last (or marginal) unit of the particular quantity of the good.

THE DEMAND CURVE

The **demand curve** shows the quantity demanded of a good at various prices, assuming that the nonprice determinants of demand, such as consumers' income, don't change. Table 3–1 shows a demand schedule for wheat. At 90¢, buyers will buy up to forty-five bushels but no more. When the price is reduced to 85¢, they will buy up to sixty-five bushels. We say that "the quantity demanded has increased" by twenty bushels as a result of this price change. We do *not* say "demand has gone up" by twenty bushels because "demand" (i.e., the demand curve) has not changed. We also say that the marginal benefit of the eighty-fifth bushel of wheat is 80¢ and of the 105th bushel, 75¢.

Table 3–1. Determining Demand Based Upon Price

The Demand for Wheat*		
Price (cents per bushel)	Quantity Demanded (bushels per month)	Point on Figure 3–1
90	45	A
85	65	B
80	85	C
75	105	D
70	125	E

*Hypothetical Data

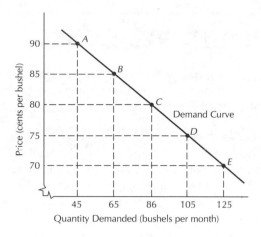

Figure 3–1. Law of Demand Shown by Demand Curve

Key Procedure for Plotting Demand Curves

1. Start at any price on Table 3–1. Locate the price on the vertical axis of Figure 3–1. Go horizontally to the right until the quantity on the horizontal axis agrees with the price quantity in Table 3–1. Mark that point.

2. Do this for each price.

3. Connect the points with a smooth line or curve.

Points to Note About Figure 3–1

1. The demand curve is a straight line with a slope of –1/4 (with a rise of –5, over a run of 20). Every 1¢ decrease in wheat prices increases the quantity of wheat demanded by 4 units.

2. Not all demand curves are straight lines, but all should have negative slopes.

3. The total revenue from wheat equals price times quantity (assuming suppliers supply the quantity demanded!). For example, at Point *C*, total revenue = $0.80 × 85 or $68 (per month). At Point *D*, total revenue equals $78.75. Total revenue is the area of the rectangle under the demand curve.

4. The 105th unit of wheat has a marginal benefit of 75¢ to consumers. Therefore, if consumers already have 104 units of wheat, they would pay at most 75¢ to get one more unit. The demand price equals the good's marginal benefit.

5. At 85¢, demanders would buy at most 65 units of wheat (in a month). They might actually buy less because of limited supply. However, they will never buy more than 65 units at a price of 85¢ per unit.

YOU SHOULD REMEMBER

The demand curve shows the effect of price on the quantity buyers want to buy (with the nonprice determinants of demand being held constant so that the focus is on the effects of changing the price). As we move down along the demand curve, the *quantity demanded* goes up as the price goes down. However, *demand* (i.e., the demand curve) remains unchanged.

SUPPLY AND THE LAW OF SUPPLY

The **quantity supplied** at any given price is the maximum quantity sellers want to sell at that price. The quantity supplied is not necessarily the amount sold. For example, for $1 million a car, Ford would gladly sell triple its current output, but few Fords would actually be sold. The **supply price** for a given quantity is the *lowest* price sellers would be willing to sell the last unit of that quantity for. *Supply price* reflects marginal cost. If the marginal cost of the 1,000th unit of output is $2, the supply price of 1,000 units is $2. It is the lowest price sellers would be willing to produce that and all other 999 units at. (This assumes marginal cost is constant or rising.)

The **law of supply** states that the *quantity supplied will increase when the price is raised and will decrease when the price is reduced*. Price and the quantity supplied have a direct (or positive) relationship: When one goes up, the other goes up also, and when one goes down, so does the other. For any supply curve, the nonprice determinants of supply, such as technology and wages of workers, are held constant.

A higher market price usually elicits a greater quantity supplied for two reasons:

1. The higher price increases the profits of existing sellers, causing them to want to sell more and

2. The higher price attracts new suppliers.

YOU SHOULD REMEMBER

1. The *quantity supplied* is the maximum amount sellers want to sell at a given price. It need not be the actual amount they do sell at that price: Less but not more could be sold.

2. The *law of supply* states that the quantity supplied goes up when the price goes up and goes down when the price goes down.

3. *Supply price* reflects marginal cost.

THE SUPPLY CURVE

The **supply curve** shows the quantity supplied at various prices, holding the nonprice determinants of supply constant. Table 3–2 shows a supply schedule for wheat. At 80¢, sellers at most want to sell eighty-five units. However, at 85¢, they will want to produce fifteen additional units. We say the "quantity supplied has increased" by fifteen bushels. We do not say "supply has increased" because supply (i.e., the supply curve) has not changed. The marginal cost of the eighty-fifth unit is 80¢. This is the lowest acceptable price to sellers, as it just covers their marginal cost.

Table 3–2. Determining the Quantity Supplied Based Upon Price

The Supply of Wheat*		
Price (cents per bushel)	Quantity Supplied (bushels per month)	Point on Figure 3–2
90	115	A
85	100	B
80	85	C
75	70	D
70	55	E

*Hypothetical Data

Figure 3–2 shows the graph of the supply schedule shown in Table 3–2. At Figure 3–2, plot the supply curve by following the same procedure used for plotting the demand curve at Figure 3–1.

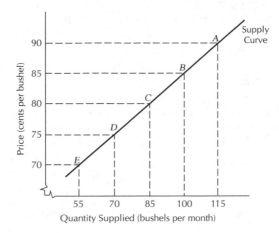

Figure 3–2. Law of Supply Shown by Supply Curve

Points to Note About Figure 3–2

1. The supply curve is a straight line with a slope of +1/3 (the rise of +5 is over the run of +15). Supply curves need not be a straight line, but they usually have a positive slope.

2. The most units suppliers would provide at 80¢ is 85 bushels a month. The marginal cost of producing the 85th bushel is 80¢. If the price were less, supplying the 85th unit would not be profitable. The 100th unit's marginal cost is 85¢. The positive slope shows that marginal cost, the added cost of producing another unit of the good, is rising.

YOU SHOULD REMEMBER

The *supply curve* shows the effect of price on the quantity sellers want to supply. The nonprice determinants are held constant so the effects of price changes alone are shown. When the price goes up, the quantity supplied goes up. However, supply (i.e., the supply curve) remains unchanged.

MARKET EQUILIBRIUM

Equilibrium occurs in a market when the price has no tendency to change. This occurs at the price at which the quantity demanded equals the quantity supplied. Only at the **market equilibrium price** do buyers buy the quantity they want *and* sellers get to sell the quantity they want. No one wants to buy or sell more.

Table 3–3 shows how markets get to equilibrium. The numbers in Table 3–3 come from Tables 3–1 and 3–2.

Table 3–3. How Markets Get to Equilibrium

Demand and Supply of Wheat				
Price (cents per bushel)	Quantity Demanded (bushels per month)	Quantity Supplied (bushels per month)	State of Market	Tendency for Price Change
90	45	115	Surplus of 70 units	Decreases
85	65	100	Surplus of 35 units	Decreases
80	85	85	Equilibrium	Stays same
75	105	70	Shortage of 35 units	Increases
70	125	55	Shortage of 70 units	Increases

The **market equilibrium price** is 80¢. The quantity demanded (eighty-five) equals the quantity supplied (eighty-five) at that price.

At any price *higher* than the equilibrium price, there will be a **surplus:** Sellers will want to supply more goods than buyers want to buy. At 90¢, the surplus is seventy units (70 = 115 – 45). The market is not in equilibrium because the sellers who cannot sell all they want will seek buyers by lowering the price.

At any price *lower* than the equilibrium price, there will be a **shortage:** Buyers will want to buy more goods than sellers want to sell. At 75¢, there is a shortage of thirty-five units (35 = 105 – 70). The market is not in equilibrium: Buyers who cannot purchase all they want will seek to induce sellers to supply more by bidding the price up.

At 80¢, the market **clears:** Buyers are actually buying the most they intend to at that price and sellers are actually selling the most they intend to at that price. The quantity demanded equals the quantity supplied. Since everyone is actually buying or selling what they want to at 80¢, no one has any incentive to change the price. So at 80¢, the market is in *equilibrium.*

All eighty-five bushels sell at 80¢ each. This reflects the **law of one price:** In any given market, *all units tend to trade at the same price.* Sellers who try to charge more lose business. Any buyers who try to buy for less will not find willing sellers. So all buy and sell at the market clearing price.

Figure 3–3 uses the numbers from Table 3–3 to plot the supply and demand curves.

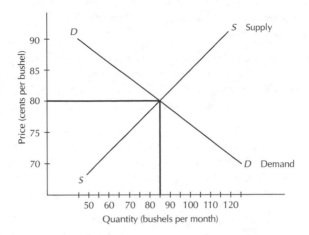

Figure 3–3. Demand and Supply in Equilibrium

The supply curve is labeled *SS*, and the demand curve is *DD*. The equilibrium price of 80¢ and the equilibrium quantity of eight-five bushels of wheat are drawn in with a dark line. Equilibrium occurs when the two curves cross.

Key Procedure for Reading Supply and Demand Diagrams

1. At any given price, draw a line horizontally across the graph.

2. The point at which this line intersects the supply curve is the quantity supplied at that price. The point at which it intersects the demand curve is the quantity demanded at that price.

3. When the quantity supplied exceeds the quantity demanded, the excess supply shows the *surplus*. For example, at 85¢, a surplus of thirty-five units exists.

4. When the quantity demanded exceeds the quantity supplied, the excess demand shows the *shortage*. For example, at 75¢, a shortage of thirty-five units exists.

5. When quantity demanded equals quantity supplied, the market is in *equilibrium*.

STUDYING DEMAND AND SUPPLY CURVES

Learn to look at demand and supply graphs both across (horizontally) and up and down (vertically). Keep these points in mind when studying demand and supply graphs:

1. Going across, the demand curve shows the most buyers willing to buy (if they can!) at the current price. Going up and down, the demand curve shows the most buyers are willing to pay for that unit of the good, assuming they already have all the previous units: This is that unit's marginal benefit.

2. Going across, the supply curve shows the most sellers are willing to sell (if they can!) at the current price. Looking at the supply curve vertically, the supply price shows the lowest price for which sellers are willing to produce and sell one more unit of the good: This is that unit's marginal cost.

3. Going across, the market is in equilibrium only at the price where the quantity demanded (the most buyers are willing to buy) equals the quantity supplied (the most sellers are willing to sell). At this market clearing price, the quantity demanded equals the quantity supplied.

4. When you buy a good, by definition, someone else has sold it. Thus, the quantity bought of a good always equals the quantity sold. However, only at the market clearing price does the quantity demanded equal the quantity supplied.

5. When the price differs from the market clearing price, trade occurs at the smaller of the quantity demanded or the quantity supplied (barring government subsidies or intervention). If the price is above the market clearing price, the quantity bought and sold equals the quantity demanded. There is a surplus because sellers want to sell more than demanders are buying. If the price is below the market clearing price, the quantity bought and sold equals the quantity supplied. There is a shortage because demanders want to buy more than sellers are selling.

6. Vertically, the market is in equilibrium at the quantity whose demand price equals its supply price. At a smaller quantity, buyers are willing to pay a price exceeding the good's marginal cost (supply price), giving incentives to sellers to produce more. At a larger quantity, buyers are not willing to pay a price that covers the good's marginal cost: These units will not be produced.

7. The demand and supply curves show how changing the price affects the quantity buyers want to buy and the quantity sellers want to sell. Changing the price down to zero or up to a trillion dollars does not shift either curve. They *already* show the effects of price. The one thing that *never* shifts the demand curve or supply curve for a good is the good's price! Never! Remembering this point will steer you away from most of the mistakes made with demand and supply curves.

YOU SHOULD REMEMBER

1. Market equilibrium occurs at the price at which the quantity supplied equals the quantity demanded. The price does not tend to change (as long as the nonprice determinants of demand and supply remain unchanged).

2. If the price is above the market equilibrium price, a *surplus* will occur. Quantity supplied exceeds quantity demanded. The market price will tend to fall.

3. If the price is below the equilibrium price, a *shortage* will occur. Quantity demanded exceeds quantity supplied. The market price will tend to rise.

PRICE FLOORS

A **price floor** is a restriction imposed by the government that prohibits the price from falling below a certain level. If the price floor is below the market equilibrium price, the floor has no effect. However, if the price floor is above the market price, it causes a *surplus*: At least some sellers will not be able to find buyers for all they want to sell.

Figure 3–4 shows the effect of a particular floor: a minimum wage that must be paid for the labor of teenagers.

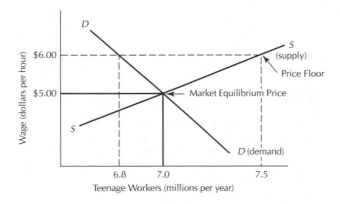

Figure 3–4. Determining the Effect of a Price Floor

DD is the demand curve for teenage employment. At the lower wage shown on the graph, employers are willing to hire more teenagers. *SS* shows the supply curve. At the higher wage, more teenagers are willing to work.

The market clearing wage is $5.00, and the market clearing quantity employed is 7 million. If the government imposes a minimum wage of $6.00, employers are only willing to hire 6.8 million teenagers, while 7.5 million teenagers want to work. There will be a surplus of 0.7 million teenagers (0.7 = 7.5 – 6.8). The 0.7 million surplus comes partly from the reduction in the quantity demanded (0.2 million lost jobs at the higher wage) and partly from the increase in the quantity supplied (0.5 million more teenagers want to work at the higher wage). If a minimum wage is set above the market clearing wage, it causes employment to fall and the number of persons wanting jobs to rise.

PRICE CEILINGS

A **price ceiling** is a restriction imposed by the government that prohibits a price from going above a certain level. If the price ceiling is below the equilibrium price, shortages are created. Shortages are not just the scarcity of goods; all goods are scarce, but only those with price ceilings have chronic shortages.

Figure 3–5 shows the effect of a price ceiling on gasoline. With a ceiling price of $1.00 per gallon, there is a shortage of 40 million gallons. The gasoline shortages in the 1970s, for example, were caused by our government's price ceiling on the price of gas. OPEC made gasoline more scarce, but it didn't create the shortages.

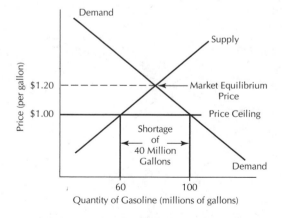

Figure 3–5. Determining the Effect of a Price Ceiling

EFFECTS OF PRICE CEILINGS AND FLOORS

When lawmakers try to force the price away from its equilibrium level, the quantity bought and sold is *reduced*. The quantity actually bought and sold is the *smaller* of the quantity demanded and the quantity supplied. This reflects the basic freedom inherent in markets: No one is forced to buy or sell more than they want—so the smaller of the quantity demanded and supplied is the quantity actually bought and sold. This quantity (the smaller of demand and supply at each price) is called **locus of trade.**

Other consequences of price floors and ceilings are:

1. ***Nonprice Rationing:*** This is any method of equating supply and demand other than price. Two main methods of rationing without prices are:

   a. *Waiting lines,* such as the high unemployment caused by the minimum wage law or the waiting lines of customers at gas stations caused by the ceiling on gas prices; and

   b. *Discrimination*—for example, the discrimination caused by the minimum wage law. The law resulted in a surplus of applicants, so employers can be selective as to whom they hire. In the past, faced with a surplus of applicants, employers have hired mainly whites: The result is that black teenagers have had at least twice the unemployment rate of whites.

2. ***Changes in Quality:*** With a price *ceiling*, sellers, to save on costs, will cut back on quality. For example, the rent controls in New York City have produced some of the most run-down apartments and unresponsive landlords in the country.

   With a price floor, sellers try to attract buyers by offering better quality (since they cannot lower the price). For example, when government regulations allowed airlines to set a price floor on ticket prices, airlines competed by offering many extras, such as better food and wider seats.

3. ***Black Markets and Violation of the Law:*** To get around a price ceiling, the buyers who cannot buy what they want at the ceiling price will seek out sellers who are willing to sell at illegal prices (which usually are higher than the market equilibrium price).

4. ***Effect of price ceilings and price floors.*** A price ceiling is usually imposed to help buyers. But it helps only the buyers who are able to buy the good at the low price. The existence of a shortage means that there are many buyers who are not able to buy what they want. These buyers are hurt by price controls. Similarly, a price floor is usually imposed to help sellers. But it helps only the sellers who are able to sell the good at

a higher price. The existence of a surplus means that many sellers are not able to sell their goods. These sellers are hurt by the price floor.

YOU SHOULD REMEMBER

1. A price *ceiling* set *below* the equilibrium price results in a *shortage* of the good. A price *floor* set *above* the equilibrium price results in a *surplus*.

2. Price controls (either ceilings or floors) lead to nonprice rationing (including waiting lines and discrimination), changes in quality, and black markets.

ON THE NATURE OF THE PRICE SYSTEM

The creation of money and the price system stands with the invention of language and the alphabet as one of the great social inventions of mankind. Like language, the price system summarizes and communicates information. For example, people do not need to know that a mine cave-in in Chile has reduced the world's supply of copper; they need only know that copper wire has gone up in price so that they will have to cut back on its use. Thus, the price system saves on information costs. With prices, no one has to tell businesses which goods consumers want them to produce or tell consumers which goods are too expensive to consume.

In competitive markets, the demand curve for a good is also the good's *marginal benefit schedule*, and the supply curve is the good's *marginal cost schedule*. This is because at any given level of output, (1) the price that demanders are willing to pay reflects the marginal benefit they derive from the last unit of the good and (2) the price at which suppliers are willing to sell reflects their marginal cost. Marginal analysis tells us that a good's supply should be increased as long as its marginal benefit exceeds its marginal cost. Doing this maximizes net benefits. So when sellers sell until the quantity demanded equals the quantity supplied ("where demand equals supply"), society is achieving its maximum net benefit.

KNOW THE CONCEPTS

DO YOU KNOW THE BASICS?

1. Is the quantity demanded the same as the quantity bought?
2. Is the quantity supplied the same as the quantity sold?
3. What is the difference between scarcity and shortage?
4. Can there be a surplus of a scarce good?
5. How can a merchant tell whether his or her price is too low? Too high?
6. Does demand change when the price changes?
7. When there is a shortage, how will the price change? What will happen to the quantity demanded and supplied?
8. Why does an individual usually buy more of a good when its price falls? Give two reasons.
9. How do you find in a demand and supply diagram the quantity that will be bought and sold at each price?
10. How will some demanders be hurt by a price ceiling?

TERMS FOR STUDY

law of demand
law of one price
law of supply
locus of trade
market clearing price
market equilibrium
nonprice rationing

price floors and ceilings
quantity demanded
quantity supplied
relative price
shortage
surplus

PRACTICAL APPLICATION

1. The table below shows the demand and supply of coats in Small Town.
   a. What is the equilibrium price of coats? Will a shortage or surplus of coats occur?
   b. At what price will the most coats be sold?
   c. The mayor of Small Town, in order to "help the poor by making coats cheaper," imposes a price ceiling of $40. How many coats will be bought and sold? Will a surplus or shortage of coats occur?

d. The mayor of Small Town, in order to "help protect our coat industry," imposes a price floor of $80 instead. How many coats will be bought and sold? Will a shortage or surplus of coats occur?

Price	Quantity of Coats Demanded (per day)	Quantity of Coats Supplied (per day)
$80	50	110
$70	60	90
$60	70	70
$50	80	50
$40	90	30

2. Is the following statement correct? "Home prices are so high there is a shortage of homes. Not everyone who wants a home will be able to buy one."

3. Suppose a rent control law forces rents below the market level of rents. How might owners of apartment buildings offset the effects of rent control laws on their profits?

4. Over a two-year period, the price of TVs went up 5 percent and the price of all other goods went up 12 percent. During the same period, more TVs were sold. Does this support or contradict the law of demand?

5. If each person demands one movie a month when one movie ticket costs $6, two movies a month when each costs $4, and three when each costs $2, what will the total demand be for 100 people for each price?

6. Price ceilings can result in such long waiting lines that the effective cost of the good stays the same or even increases. For example, on a large college campus, the opportunity cost of an hour waiting in line is $10 an hour for all students. The college allocates 1,000 seats at the home games to students. If sold in a competitive market to college students, the equilibrium price of the tickets would be $40. However, the college gives the tickets away free and mandates that they not be resold (this results in an effective price ceiling of $0). The college gives the tickets away, one to each person waiting in line. How long will the line be and how many hours will people have to wait in line if the demander of the 1,000th seat "pays" in time cost the benefit to them of a seat at the game?

7. How would you expect a minimum wage (that is above the market clearing wage) to affect the working conditions and the on-the-job training supplied by employers?

8. There are 100 demanders, each of whom would pay up to $1,000 for one widget (none needs a second widget). There are 200 sellers; 150 of them can produce and sell a widget at $50 per unit, the other 50 at $100. What will the market price for widgets be? How is this efficient?

9. Suppose that employers dislike hiring blue-eyed workers and suffer a loss in their personal satisfaction equivalent to 50¢ an hour for each hour they employ a blue-eyed worker. How could a blue-eyed worker then get a job with an employer? In this case, what would be the effect of a minimum wage law that pushed blue-eyed workers' wages up by 50¢?

10. When John earned $10, he bought four hamburgers at $2 each and two sodas at $1 each. In the following month, he earned $20, but the price of hamburgers had risen to $3 and the price of sodas had risen to $4. So if John wanted to, he could still buy four hamburgers and two sodas. Will he?

   Hint: What has happened to the relative price of sodas?

ANSWERS

KNOW THE CONCEPTS

1. No. When the market price is below the market clearing price, the quantity bought will be less than the quantity demanded. For example, if the price of a luxury home was $1,000, buyers will demand many more than sellers are willing to sell. As a result, the quantity demanded will exceed the quantity bought (and sold). At the market price (or above), the quantity demanded will equal the quantity bought.

2. No. When the market price is above the market clearing price, the quantity supplied will be greater than the quantity sold. For example, if the price of this book was $1,000, the quantity supplied would be great but few copies would be sold. At the market price (or below), the quantity supplied will equal the quantity sold.

3. Scarcity is when there are not enough units of a good to satisfy all of everyone's wants when the price of the good is zero. A shortage is when there are not enough units sold *at a given price* to satisfy what people want to buy *at that price*.

4. Yes; just impose a price floor above the equilibrium price.

5. If the price is too low, there is excess demand for the merchant's goods. If it is too high, there is excess supply.

6. No. The *quantity demanded* changes when the price changes.

7. The price will rise; the quantity demanded will decrease, while the quantity supplied will increase.

8. Income effect and substitution effect.

9. In a demand and supply diagram, pick a price. Then go directly right until you reach the first curve (either the demand or supply curve). This will be the amount bought and sold at this price. Why? Do this for all prices and you have the locus of trade.

10. Suppose the market price is $10. A price ceiling of, say, $8 means less will be sold. Some buyers may not get any, or very little, when compared with what they were buying at $10. So they lose. For example, a buyer who would have paid $30 and did pay $10 loses $20 if she cannot buy it.

PRACTICAL APPLICATION

1. **a.** $60. At the equilibrium price, neither a shortage nor a surplus of coats will occur. Demanders want to buy 70 units, and suppliers want to supply 70 units. Buyers *and* sellers get what they want.

   b. $60. Buyers will buy less at any higher price. Sellers will sell less at any lower price. The market-clearing price maximizes trade.

   c. 30 coats will be bought and sold. Demanders want to buy 90 coats, but sellers want to sell only 30. Trade takes place at the smaller of the two numbers. So a shortage of 60 coats (90 – 30) will occur.

   d. 50 coats will be bought and sold. Demanders want to buy 50 coats, while sellers want to sell 110 coats. Trade takes place at the smaller of the two numbers. So a surplus of 60 coats (110 – 50) will occur.

2. The statement is incorrect. At the equilibrium price, there will be no shortages since all buyers who want homes at *prevailing* prices will get them. If there were a shortage of homes, the price would *rise* until the housing market reached equilibrium.

3. Rent controls create a shortage of apartments, so owners can cut back on maintenance and service without losing renters. Apartment owners may also seek ways to charge renters for "extra" services, even if these ways are illegal. For example, some apartment owners have allegedly used these methods to reduce the adverse impact of rent controls: (1) "key money" for the key to the apartment, (2) kickbacks from rental brokers who get paid to find apartments for their clients, and (3) lower pay to the apartment's superintendent, who then collects "tips" from renters.

4. The *relative* price of TVs went down over the two-year period (by 7 percent) and more TVs were demanded. So this supports the law of demand.

5. The market demand is the sum of the individual's demand at each price. At $6 per movie ticket, 100 tickets will be sold. At $4, 200 tickets, and at $2, 300 tickets.

6. Since the equilibrium price is $40, the demander of the 1,000th ticket values it at $40 and is willing to wait 4 hours in line for it (paying $40 in time cost for it). So 1,000 people will wait in line 4 hours or more.

7. A minimum wage prevents employers from offering lower wages in exchange for training and good working conditions. As a consequence, employers faced with a minimum wage above what they would otherwise pay will cut back on training (by hiring only experienced workers) and be less concerned with working conditions. One study found that minimum wages actually caused many workers to lose more, in training and working conditions, than they gained from higher wages.

8. The market clearing price is $50. At higher prices, there will be sellers who can't find a buyer and who will bid the price down. At $50, no further price cutting takes place. This result is efficient, as the *lowest*-cost sellers are those that *do* sell.

9. Blue-eyed workers can get a job with employers if they work for 50¢ less per hour than do other workers. This will compensate the employers for their dislike of blue-eyed workers. A minimum wage that prevents blue-eyed workers from accepting lower wages in order to get work will reduce their employment.

10. The relative price of sodas has gone up from one-half ($1/$2) to four-thirds ($4/$3) of a hamburger. The substitution effect predicts that John will substitute "away" from sodas "toward" hamburgers.

4

SUPPLY AND DEMAND: PART TWO

THE DIFFERENCE BETWEEN ECONOMIC *SHIFTS* AND *MOVEMENTS*

One of the most important distinctions in economics is between:

1. **Movements *along*** the demand curve. This refers to moving along a given demand curve, tracing out the effects that different prices have on the quantity of goods people want to buy. (See Chapter 3.)

2. **Shifts *in*** the demand curve. This refers to changing the demand curve, i.e., shifting it left or right, because some variable other than price has changed. Again, note that some texts refer to a "shift in demand" as a "change in demand." This chapter focuses on shifts in demand and supply.

Another key distinction is between demanders and suppliers. Their different reaction to price is shown by the demand and supply curve. It may help you to think of demanders and suppliers as being in separate rooms. An auctioneer asks each room how much they will buy or sell at each price. The demand and supply curves trace out the answers. The price is set where demand equals supply. Then some event occurs and changes the answers from one or both rooms. Demanders' answers are affected by events changing their willingness to pay for the good. Suppliers' answers are affected by events changing the cost of producing the good. After the event, the auctioneer again asks both rooms how much they will buy or sell at each price. The result is a new curve (or curves) and a new market clearing price.

FACTORS SHIFTING DEMAND

When we constructed the demand curves in the previous chapter, we were holding the *nonprice determinants of demand* constant. What will happen when they change?

Key Procedure for Shifting the Demand Curve

1. Draw a supply and demand diagram, and indicate the equilibrium price and output by drawing a **price line** (a horizontal line drawn from the intersection of the demand and supply curves to the vertical axis: for example, Line *AF* in Figure 4–1) and **output line** (a vertical line drawn from the intersection to the horizontal axis: e.g., line *AG* in Figure 4–1).

2. While holding the price constant, ask yourself whether a specific event will increase or decrease the quantity people want to buy. If the event will increase the quantity demanded, draw a new demand curve to the right of the old one, as in Figure 4–1. If the event will decrease the quantity demanded, draw a new demand curve to the left, as in Figure 4–2).

3. Find the new intersection, and indicate the new equilibrium price and output as in Step 1 (e.g., with Line *BH* and Line *BI* in Figure 4–1).

Table 4–1 lists the main factors that shift the demand curve and describes their effects. **Normal goods** are goods whose demand goes up when income goes up (most goods "normally" act this way). **Inferior goods** go down in demand when income goes up (low-quality products often fit this category). **Substitutes** are goods that compete with one another, such as

Shell and Exxon gas. **Complements** are goods that go together, such as hot dogs and mustard or gas and cars. Note that consumers determine which goods are substitutes and which are complements. (For example, if all consumers wanted to wear right but not left shoes, they would not be complements.) **Future price expectations** are what buyers expect the future prices of the good will be. If they expect the price will go up in the future, they will buy more now. If they expect the price will go down in the future, they will delay their purchases and buy less now. This mainly applies to goods that can be stored.

Table 4–1. Main Factors That Shift Demand

Factor	Change in Factor	Effect on Demand
Consumer income		
Normal good	Income up	Increase (right)
	Income down	Decrease (left)
Inferior Good	Income up	Decrease
	Income down	Increase
Price of substitutes		
(*P-S*)	*P-S* up	Increase
	P-S down	Decrease
Price of complement		
(*P-C*)	*P-C* up	Decrease
	P-C down	Increase
Population		
(of buyers)	Population up	Increase
	Population down	Decrease
Tastes		
	Toward good	Increase
	Away from good	Decrease
Future price expectations		
	Future price up	Increase
	Future price down	Decrease

YOU SHOULD REMEMBER

To determine how an event shifts the demand curve, ask yourself how the event will change the quantity demanded if the price does *not* change. An event that *increases* demand shifts the demand curve to the *right;* an event that *decreases* demand shifts the curve to the *left.*

• *EFFECTS ON SHIFTS IN DEMAND*

Figure 4–1 shows the effect of an *increase in demand*. When demand increases, at any given price people want to buy more of the good. The demand curve shifts outward and to the right.

Figure 4–1 shows the demand and supply for cheese. Initially, the demand curve is *DD* and the supply curve is *SS*. The equilibrium price is $1.30, and the equilibrium quantity is 90 tons (at Point *A*). Now suppose some event causes people to buy more cheese at every price (e.g., people come to believe that cheese cures cancer). At $1.30, they previously demanded 90 tons of cheese, but now they want 120 tons at that price (at Point *C*). Similarly, at $1.50, they previously wanted 80 tons but now they want 110 tons. The new demand curve is *D´D´*.

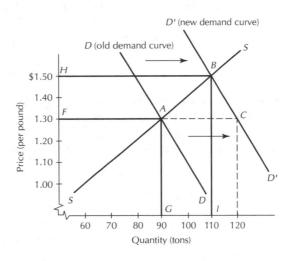

Figure 4–1. Effects of a Demand Increase

If after this event the price stays at $1.30, there will be a 30-ton shortage of cheese (with a quantity demanded of 120 tons and a quantity supplied of 90 tons). So the price will be bid up. The shortage will be eliminated at $1.50. The equilibrium output will have increased from 90 tons to 110 tons. The new equilibrium will be at Point B.

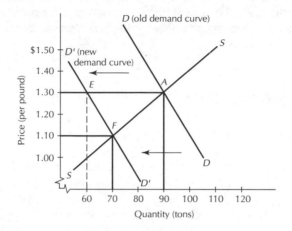

Figure 4–2. Effects of a Demand Decrease

Figure 4–2 (on page 52) shows the effects of a *decrease in demand.* When demand decreases, people buy less at each price. While beginning with the same equilibrium (90 tons of cheese and a price of $1.30), suppose some event decreases demand (e.g., people come to believe that cheese causes heart attacks). At each price, people want to buy less, so the demand curve shifts inward and to the left. At $1.30, for example, people want 30 fewer tons of cheese than before (from 90 to 60 tons, at Point E). If the price remained at $1.30, there would be a 30-ton surplus of cheese. So the price falls. The new equilibrium price is $1.10 and the new equilibrium output is 70 tons (corresponding to the new intersection of demand and supply at Point F).

Key Results of Shifts in Demand

1. If an event *increases* demand, the demand curve will shift outward and to the *right*. If the supply curve is not affected, the equilibrium *price* and *quantity* will *increase*.

2. If an event *decreases* demand, the demand curve will shift inward and to the *left*. If the supply curve is not affected, the equilibrium *price* and *quantity* will *decrease*.

FACTORS SHIFTING SUPPLY

Supply is affected by a different set of factors than is demand. Basically, supply is affected by those factors that affect the unit cost of production. The effect of the main factors is shown in Table 4–2, when P = price, I = input, SP = substitute products, and JP = joint products. An **input** is something used to produce the good, such as labor or materials. A **substitute product** is one that could be produced with the same (or very similar) set of inputs. A substitute product for gasoline is heating oil and a substitute product for wheat is corn. When the price of a substitute product of a good goes up, the opportunity cost of producing the good goes up. **Joint products** are goods that are almost always produced together because it is difficult to produce them separately. Examples include leather and beef or lumber and wood shavings. **Future price expectations** are what sellers expect the future prices of the good will be. If sellers expect the price to go up, they will supply less now (holding back on some of their stock to resell in the future). If sellers expect future prices to go down, they will sell more now. This mainly applies to goods that can be stored.

Key Procedure for Shifting the Supply Curve

1. Draw the supply and demand curves as they appear before the event, and draw in the price and output lines from the intersection of demand and supply.

2. While holding price constant, ask yourself if the event would increase or decrease the quantity supplied at the price level in step 1. If the event would increase the quantity supplied, draw the new supply curve to the right of the old, as in Figure 4–3. If the event would decrease the quantity supplied, draw the new curve to the left, as in Figure 4–4.

   Graphing changes in supply is often easier by holding quantity constant. If the event (say a rise in wages) increases marginal cost, draw the new supply curve *vertically* higher. If the event lowers the unit's cost (for example, due to greater efficiency), draw the new supply curve *vertically* lower. The vertically lower curve means that the quantity supplied has increased.

3. Identify the new intersection of demand and supply by drawing in the new price and output lines.

Table 4–2. The Main Factors That Shift Supply

Factor	Change in Factor	Effect on Supply
Technology		
	Greater efficiency	Increase
	Less efficiency	Decrease
Price of inputs		
(P-I)	P-I up	Decrease
	P-I down	Increase
Number of firms		
	Number up	Increase
	Number down	Decrease
Price of substitute products		
(P-SP)	P-SP up	Decrease
	P-SP down	Increase
Price of joint products		
(P-JP)	P-JP up	Increase
	P-JP down	Decrease
Future price expectations		
	Future price up	Decrease
	Future price down	Increase

YOU SHOULD REMEMBER

To determine how an event will affect supply, ask yourself how the quantity supplied will change if the price is held constant. Alternatively, while holding output constant, ask yourself if the supply price will go up or down. If it will go down, supply will increase; if it will go up, supply will decrease. An event that *increases* supply shifts the supply curve to the *right*. An event that *decreases* supply shifts the curve to the *left*.

• EFFECTS OF SHIFTS IN SUPPLY

Figure 4–3 shows the effects of an *increase in supply*. Initially, equilibrium is at Point A, where the price is $1.30 and output is 90 tons of cheese. Then some event increases the supply of cheese (e.g., the wage of cheese workers falls). The new supply curve is $S'S'$. At $1.30, for example, suppli-

ers are willing to supply 110 tons (at Point *C*), 20 more tons than previously. If the price were to remain unchanged, there would be a surplus. So the
price will fall. The new equilibrium will be at Point *H*, with a new equilibrium price of $1.10 and output of 100 tons.

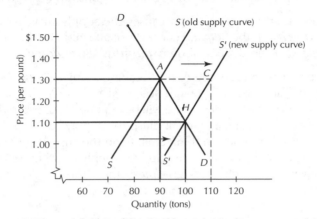

Figure 4–3. Effects of a Supply Increase

Figure 4–4 shows the effect of a *decrease in supply*. The initial equilibrium is at Point *A*. Then some event decreases supply, shifting the supply
curve left from *SS* to *S´S´*. At $1.30, suppliers now will supply only 70 tons,
compared with the 90 they would have supplied before the event. If the
price remained at $1.30, there would be a shortage. So the price rises. The
new equilibrium is at Point *I*, with a price of $1.50 and an output of 80 tons.

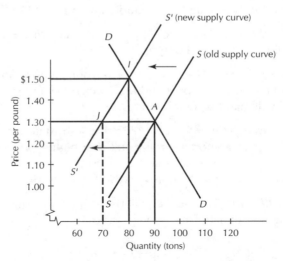

Figure 4–4. Effects of a Supply Decrease

Key Results of Shifts in Supply

1. An event that *increases* supply causes the supply curve to shift outward and to the *right*. If the demand curve is not affected, then the equilibrium *price* will decrease and the equilibrium *quantity* will go *up*.

2. An event that *decreases* supply causes the supply curve to shift inward and to the *left*. If the demand curve is not affected, the equilibrium *price* will *increase* and the equilibrium *quantity* will go *down*.

3. An event that reduces the cost of making a unit will cause the supply curve to shift vertically down. (Note that this is an increase in supply because at the same price, more will be supplied.) An event that increases the cost of making a unit will cause the supply curve to shift vertically up. It is often easier to think of shifts in the supply curve in terms of its vertical shift: If Unit costs go *up*, the supply curve moves *up* vertically; conversely, if unit costs go *down*, the supply curve moves *down* vertically.

HOW TO AVOID MISTAKES IN ANALYZING SUPPLY AND DEMAND

Remember the following to avoid most common mistakes: A change in the price will *never* shift a demand or supply curve! The curves show *all* of the effects of the changing price. Use the procedure below to show correctly how events affect demand and supply.

Key Procedure for Analyzing Supply and Demand

1. *Initial Equilibrium*. Draw the supply and demand diagram. Label the initial equilibrium price and output.

2. *Event and Shift*. Some event occurs. Ask yourself how demand and supply would change if the price did *not* change from its initial level. Draw in the new demand or supply curve.

3. *Allow the Price to Change*. At the old price, a shortage or a surplus of the good will occur. A shortage will result in a higher price. A surplus will result in a lower price. Since a change in the price never shifts either curve, do not draw in any more curves!

4. *New Equilibrium*. The new equilibrium price and quantity will occur where the new demand and supply curves cross.

Example: Effect of Higher Consumer Income

PROBLEM   How will the price and quantity of new cars be affected if the income of consumers goes up? Remember that cars are a "normal" good.

SOLUTION   1. *Initial Equilibrium.* We begin with the car market being in equilibrium.

2. *Event and Shift.* Then consumer income goes up. If the price were unchanged, consumers would buy more cars. So we draw the new demand curve to the right of the old one, as in Figure 4–1.

3. *Allow the Price to Change.* At the initial price there is now a shortage of new cars. As a result, the price will rise.

4. *New Equilibrium.* As shown in Figure 4–1, at the new equilibrium (where the new demand curve crosses the supply curve), the price and quantity of cars will be higher.

By drawing the demand and supply curves, an added insight you will have is that if *both* the demand and supply curves shift, you cannot tell how *both* output and price will change. You can only tell how one will change. See Practical Application, Question 3.

KNOW THE CONCEPTS

DO YOU KNOW THE BASICS?

1. Why do we hold price constant when we talk about increasing or decreasing demand?

2. Is it the same when people are willing to (1) buy more at each price and (2) pay a higher price for each quantity?

3. If consumers buy fewer burner covers for their stoves when their income goes up, are burner covers a normal good or an inferior good?

4. When the price of a good's complement goes up, what happens to the demand for the good?

5. How does the supply curve move vertically when supply increases or "goes up"? What do *up* and *down* refer to in demand and supply diagrams?

6. A new higher demand curve causes the price to increase. How will the higher price shift the demand curve?

7. Does an increase in both price and output violate the law of demand?

8. If the cost of production goes up, does the supply curve shift to the left or to the right?

9. What is the only factor that changes the quantity demanded (and supplied) but not demand (and supply)?

10. If world demand for wheat goes up and at the same time farmers find a cheaper way to grow wheat, what will happen to wheat prices and output?

TERMS FOR STUDY

complements
increase and decrease in demand
increase and decrease in supply
inferior goods
inputs

joint products
normal goods
shift in demand and supply
substitute products
substitutes

PRACTICAL APPLICATION

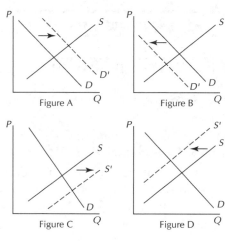

Figure A

Figure B

Figure C

Figure D

D = Old Demand Curve
D' = New Demand Curve
P = Price
Q = Quantity
S = Old Supply Curve
S' = New Supply Curve

1. Refer to Figures A, B, C, and D on page 62. Select the figure that best illustrates the likely effect of the following events. The dotted line shows the shift caused by the event.

   Event A: Computer chips, used to make personal computers, go down in price. Which figure illustrates the effect on the market for personal computers?

   Event B: Consumers' income falls during a recession. Which figure illustrates the effect on the market for vacation travel (which is a normal good)?

   Event C: The price of margarine rises. Which figure illustrates the effect on the butter market (a substitute for margarine)?

   Event D: Building firms can build office buildings or school buildings. The price of office buildings falls (due to a national recession), while the demand for school buildings is unaffected. Which figure illustrates the effect on the market for school buildings?

   Event E: The price of compact discs goes down. Which figure illustrates the effect on the market for compact disc players (a complement to compact discs)?

2. Assume markets are initially in equilibrium. Then the following events occur. Beside each of the events, place a +, –, or 0 to indicate the shift in the demand and supply curves and the change in price and quantity from their initial value.

   Event A: Consumer income rises. Effect on eating out (a normal good)? $S\_\_D\_\_P\_\_Q\_\_$

   Event B: New management techniques allow cars to be produced at a lower cost. Effect on car market? $S\_\_D\_\_P\_\_Q\_\_$

   Event C: Government regulations increase the cost of building homes. Effect on the market for new homes? $S\_\_D\_\_P\_\_Q\_\_$

   Event D: National income goes down. Effect on fishing rods (an inferior good)? $S\_\_D\_\_P\_\_Q\_\_$

   Event E: Bakeries can make cookies or pies. The demand for pies goes up. Effect on market for cookies? $S\_\_D\_\_P\_\_Q\_\_$

3. Fill in the following table with +, –, 0, and ? to describe the effect of the combination of events. The + sign is for increase, – for decrease, 0 for no change, and ? for uncertain. For example, in the first row and the first column, indicate how price and quantity will change if both demand and supply increase.

	Supply +	Supply –	Supply 0
Demand +	P__Q__	P__Q__	P__Q__
Demand –	P__Q__	P__Q__	P__Q__
Demand 0	P__Q__	P__Q__	P__Q__

4. In the 1990s, the price of new homes (adjusted for inflation) increased and the quantity built also increased. If only one curve shifted to cause this result, which one was it: demand or supply? How did it shift, and what reasons might have caused this shift?

5. Draw a supply and demand diagram for Good *A*—a free good and for Good *B*—a good too costly to produce.

6. By using demand and supply diagrams, show the effect of the following events on the market for sport utility vehicles (SUVs). SUVs are a substitute for cars.

   a. Government regulations, applied only to cars, require that cars weigh less. As a result, when a car and an SUV crash, the car's occupants are more likely to be injured or killed than those in the SUV.

   b. More car companies build and supply SUVs.

   c. Higher gasoline prices raise the cost of driving SUVs more than the cost of driving cars because SUVs get fewer miles per gallon.

   d. The government imposes a tax on suppliers for each SUV they sell.

7. The market for air-conditioning systems is in equilibrium. A long heat wave then causes each demander to increase the price he or she is willing to pay for an air-conditioning system by $500. Will the price for air-conditioning systems go up $500? What would happen if the supply curve is perfectly flat (horizontal)?

8. As an application of Table 4-2, consider the effect of a freeze that reduces the supply of corn. Choose the correct italicized choices:

   a. Because of the freeze, the price of corn will go [*up or down*].

   b. Because corn is an input in cattle raising (since the cows are fed corn), there will be [*an increase or a decrease*] in the supply of cows once cattle farmers adjust their herds.

   c. The price of beef will go [*up or down*].

   d. If corn prices are expected to remain high, wheat farmers may convert some of their land to corn. Corn and wheat are substitute products, and the price of wheat will go [*up or down*] as its supply is [*increased or reduced*].

   e. If there is a sudden fad to wear leather boots, increasing both the demand for leather and the price of leather, beef (a joint product of leather) prices will go [*up or down*].

9. In Yorkville, rent controls have created a shortage of apartments. If rent controls (which impose a price ceiling on rents) were removed, what would happen to the quantity of apartments demanded? To the quantity supplied? To the number of apartments rented?

10. Burr's Burgers keeps its meat frozen. A hurricane cuts off electricity to Burr's freezer. Burr will lose $3,000 in meat without electricity. Electric generators (of the type that would help Burr) usually sell at a market clearing price of $1,200. But because of the storm, the market clearing price rises to $2,000. Suppose the governor of the state outlaws "price gouging" and imposes a price ceiling of $1,200 on electric generators. Will Burr be better off because of the law?

ANSWERS

KNOW THE CONCEPTS

1. We hold price constant to avoid confusing an event that *causes* a shift in demand while holding price constant with the events *resulting* from price changes.

2. Yes. Both show an increase in demand.

3. An inferior good.

4. It shifts to the left and down (e.g., a decrease in demand).

5. When supply "increases" or "goes up," the quantity supplied at each price goes up. But be careful: When supply "goes up," the supply curve moves to the *right* but it also moves vertically *down*. Similarly, when supply goes "down," the quantity supplied at each price goes down, which means the supply curve moves to the left and vertically *up*.

6. The higher price will not shift the new demand curve. A change in the price will never shift a demand or supply curve!

7. No. The event occurs when the demand curve shifts to the right (e.g., when there is an increase in demand).

8. To the left (e.g., a decrease in supply). In analyzing cost, it is usually easier to think vertically. When the cost of making a good goes up, the supply curve shifts vertically up (horizontally, this is a decrease in supply). When cost goes down, the supply curve goes vertically down (horizontally, this is an increase in supply).

9. Price.

10. Wheat prices: effect is uncertain.
Wheat output: up

PRACTICAL APPLICATION

1. *Event A:*   C
   Event B: B
   Event C: A
   Event D: C
   Event E: A

2. *Event A:*   0, +, +, +
   Event B: +, 0, −, +
   Event C: −, 0, +, −
   Event D: 0, +, +, +
   Event E: −, 0, +, −

3. *First Row:* Column 1: ?, +. Column 2: +, ?. Column 3: +, +.

   Second Row: Column 1: −, ?. Column 2: ?, −. Column 3: −, −.

   Third Row: Column 1: −, +. Column 2: +, −. Column 3: 0, 0.

4. When price and quantity change in the same direction, it is due to a shift in the demand curve (moving along the unchanged supply curve). This event was caused by an increase in demand, resulting in a higher price and quantity. The most likely cause was the rise in income due to the economic expansion (new homes being a normal good).

5.

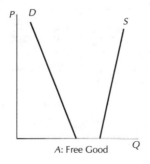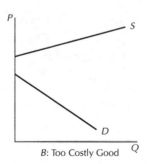

A: Free Good   B: Too Costly Good

D = Demand
P = Price
Q = Quantity
S = Supply

6. **a.** The demand for SUVs will increase. The price and quantity of SUVs will increase (as in Figure A of Practical Application 1).

   b. The supply of SUVs will increase. The price of SUVs will decrease while the quantity will increase (as in Figure C of Practical Application 1).

   c. The demand for SUVs will decrease. The price and quantity of SUVs will decrease (as in Figure B of Practical Application 1).

   d. The supply of SUVs will decrease. The price of SUVs will increase while the quantity will decrease (as in Figure D of Practical Application 1).

7. The price will increase by less than $500. The effect of this event is shown by drawing a new demand curve $500 vertically above the old demand curve. If the quantity supplied stayed the same, the price would increase by $500. However, the quantity supplied will increase as the price rises from its old level. The higher quantity supplied will meet the quantity demanded at some price between no price change and a price $500 higher. If the supply curve were a perfectly flat horizontal line, the price would remain unchanged, not rising at all.

8. **a.** Up.

   b. Decrease.

   c. Up.

   d. Up; Reduced.

   e. Down.

9. As rents rise, the quantity demanded will go down while the quantity supplied will go up. This will remove the shortage. The number of apartments rented will go up.

10. With a price ceiling at $1,200, there will be a shortage of electric generators. If Burr is lucky and is able to buy one at that price, he is better off by $1,800. On the other hand, if he cannot get an electric generator, he is worse off by $3,000. Price ceilings often make some buyers somewhat better off and other buyers much worse off.

5
MEASURING NATIONAL OUTPUT

INTRODUCTION

In 2004, the U.S. economy produced $11.7 trillion worth of goods and services. Just how big is $1 trillion? To earn $1 trillion in 20 years, you would have to make over $95,000 a second. If you were to lay $100 bills end to end, $1 trillion would go from the earth to the sun and then some.

In the same year, 2004, per capita income was $39,919. In real terms (using 2000 dollars), it was $36,590. Twenty years before, in 1984, per capita income was $16,638, while in real terms (in 2000 dollars), it was $24,593. To determine how much better off people were in 2004 compared with 1984, we compare real per capita incomes: It grew almost 49 percent in 20 years.

How does the government calculate these amounts? This chapter will explore that topic.

BASIC PREMISES

In order to find out how our economy is doing, our government uses *national income accounting* to *measure national output*. To understand what national income is and how it is measured, it is first necessary to understand two basic identities (e.g., $x + x = 2x$ is the identity; an identity is true by definition).

Identity 1: A dollar spent is also a dollar received. Every dollar spent is received by someone as income. So total spending equals total income.

Identity 2: Each good produced is a good bought (since even goods produced but not sold are counted as being purchased for inventory by the firm producing them). So total output equals total sales.

To make sure these identities work, economists count only final goods and services in measuring our nation's national output. A **final good** is one that is produced but not resold within the year. So if a farmer sells wheat for $1.00 to a miller, who mills the wheat into flour and sells it for $2.50 to a baker, who then sells it as a cake to a consumer for $5.00, *only* the final sale of $5.00 is counted as part of national income. To add in the other sales ($1 and $2.50) in addition to the $5.00 final sale would be double counting, since the other sales are already counted in the $5.00.

Economists want to measure **nominal GDP:** the market value of all final goods and services produced within a nation in a given period of time even if it was produced by foreign citizens and corporations operating within the nation's borders. To do this, they take the final goods and services produced in the nation, value them at the price they were sold at, and then add them together to get nominal *GDP* (also called *GDP in current dollars*).

Related to *GDP* is the nation's **gross national product (GNP):** the total market value of final goods and services produced by a nation's citizens even if it was produced outside the nation. For the United States,

$$GNP = GDP + \text{ Income Receipts from Rest of World}$$
$$- \text{ Income Payments to Rest of World}$$

GDP measures what is produced within the nation, while *GNP* measures what its citizens produce. *GDP* better reflects what a nation produces, while *GNP* better reflects what a nation's citizens earn. For the United States, *GDP* and *GNP* are very close (less than 0.1 percent difference).

Nominal *GDP* changes from year to year because (1) prices change and (2) outputs change. Because a nation's well-being depends on the output of goods and services, we want to remove the effect of changing prices. To do this, economists use a price index (called the *GDP* deflator) to measure how much prices have changed from a "base" year, which currently is 2000. The concept of a price index is relatively simple. Suppose a simple economy produces and consumes only wheat. In 2000, it produced 100 tons of wheat that sells for $50 a ton. The economy's nominal *GDP* was $5,000. In 2005, it produced 100 tons of wheat, but prices rose to $60 a ton. Its nominal *GDP* has increased to $6,000, but its real *GDP* is the same. To show this, we divide the 2005 nominal *GDP* ($6,000) by the 2005 price of wheat ($60): The real GDP in 2005 is 100 tons of wheat. To calculate real *GDP*, we divide the nominal GDP by the price index. When there are more than one good, a price index is created, and its value is set at 100 in the base year. If in the subsequent year prices rise on average 5 percent, the index will rise to 105. To calculate the average rise in prices, the increase in the price of each good is weighted by the expenditure or output share of the good. The output share is chain weighted, reflecting an average of the good's current and previous year's output share.

To calculate real GDP, divide nominal GDP by the price index (moving the decimal point in the price index two places to the left). For example, if nominal GDP is $10 trillion and the price index is 200, real GDP is $5 trillion.

THE CIRCULAR FLOW OF INCOME

The two basic "identities"—income and spending, or the monetary flows, and income and output, or the flows of goods and services—are illustrated in Figure 5–1, which shows the **circular flow of income**. *Households* are defined as the owners of all factors of production in the economy. Households provide the factor services of labor, land, capital, and ownership to businesses. This is Flow A. In return, households get paid wages, rent, interest, and profits. This flow of factor payments is Flow B. *Businesses* provide goods and services to households; this is Flow C. In return, households buy the goods and services; their spending is Flow D.

The identity of income and spending is represented by the equality of Flow B (factor payments) with Flow D (spending). These are the monetary flows in the economy. The identity of income and output is represented by

Flow A (factor services) and Flow C (goods and services). These are the flows of goods and services in the economy.

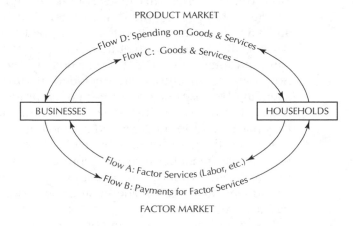

Figure 5–1. The Circular Flow of Income

MEASURING *GDP*

There are two basic ways to measure national income. The first is to measure total spending on goods and services (Flow D). This is the **expenditures approach**. The second method is to measure total income (Flow B); this is the **incomes approach**.

Two Ways to Measure *GDP*

1. **The Expenditures Approach**
   One way to measure *GDP* is to add up the spending on goods and services by households, businesses, governments, and foreigners. The following formula can be used:

$$GDP = C + I + G + NX$$

where C = Household Consumption Spending
It *includes* all household spending on final goods and services. However, it *excludes* the purchase of new homes (because such a purchase is counted as an investment) and the purchase of used goods, such as used cars (because only current output is included in *GDP*).

I = Business Investment Spending
It *includes* all private domestic investment spending: (1) business investment in new plant and equipment,

(2) additions to the inventories of goods businesses hold, and (3) residential construction (or new homes). However, it *excludes* machines sold to foreign nations (because they are counted as exports). The purchase and sale of stocks and bonds are excluded from *GDP* because they represent the trading of property rights in existing capital and not the production of new capital. Additions to inventory are included in investment spending because they represent goods produced but not sold in the year (thus, they are "investment" since they have a cost in this year and a benefit in the future year when they are sold). Subtractions from inventory reduce investment because they represent goods sold in the year but produced in previous years (thus, the investment businesses made in stocking unsold goods has been reduced).

I is gross investment, the total amount of capital goods produced in a year. *Capital* is a nation's stock of productive resources, including plants, equipment, and inventories. Each year, a certain amount of a nation's capital stock *depreciates*, or wears out and becomes obsolete. Gross investment minus depreciation equals net investment. Net investment is how much on net is added to a nation's capital stock.

$G =$ Government Purchases
It *includes* spending on goods and services by local, state, and federal governments. Because most government goods and services are not sold in the open market, the government's output is valued at its cost (including the wages paid to government employees). *G does not include* **transfer payments**, which are government payments not made in exchange for goods or services. Social Security payments and food stamp payments are examples of transfer payments not included in *G*.

$NX =$ Net Exports
It *includes* spending on domestically produced goods by foreigners (exports) minus spending on foreign goods by domestic residents (imports). What the United States sells to foreigners (exports) is clearly part of the final product produced within the nation. So why do we subtract imports? Because *C*, *I*, and *G* all include spending on imports produced in other nations. So to get the amount spent on U.S.-produced goods, imports are subtracted here.

2. The Incomes Approach

Method One: Sum of Factor Payments

One way to measure total income is to sum the incomes of each type of factor. To do this, though, two adjustments must be made.

a. First, *depreciation* is subtracted from *GDP* to take account of the fact that our capital stock wears out a little each year. (Depreciation is also called the *capital consumption allowance*.)

b. Next, *indirect business taxes*, which include sales taxes and any other taxes not based on income, are subtracted. Neither depreciation nor indirect business taxes are an income to any factor of production and, as a result, they are not included in national income.

This yields the formula:

GNP – Depreciation – Indirect Business Taxes = National Income

where National Income = Wages + Rent + Interest + Profits.
It *includes* wages (compensation of employees), rent (rental income), interest (net interest), and profits (corporate profits plus proprietors' income). These are payments to the *factors* of production (land, labor, capital) plus profits. It *excludes* interest payments made by households or the government, because it is assumed that only interest payments by businesses are based upon the production of goods and services. Proprietors' income is the income of the self-employed.

Note: The terms in parentheses are the official *national income accounting* names. Also, *GDP* is used in the formula, as it equals the income earned by U.S. citizens.

Method Two: Sum of Values

This method adds the income created by each business, i.e., the **value added** by each business. Value added is the value of a business's output minus its purchases from other businesses.
For each firm, we have:

Factor Payments = Wages + Rents + Interest Payments

and

$$\text{Profits} = \text{Value of Output} - \text{Factor Payments} \\ - \text{Purchases from Other Firms}$$

But since

Value Added = Value of Output – Purchases from Other Firms

it follows from the definition of profits that:

Value Added = Factor Payments + Profits

For the nation as a whole, then, we have:

Sum of Value Added = National Income
                    = Sum of Factor Payments + Profits

YOU SHOULD REMEMBER

1. Total spending equals total income equals total output.

2. Goods produced but not sold are still counted as sales to the firms producing them.

3. Changes in real *GDP* better reflect changes in output than changes in nominal *GDP* do.

4. *GDP* = *C* + *I* + *G* + *NX* = Total Expenditures.

5. National income equals total factor payments.

6. The total factor payments a firm makes (including its profits) equals its value added. The sum of value added across all firms equals total national income.

7. Because all other sales (of intermediate products that are resold within the year) are reflected in the price of final goods, to add in these other sales would be "double counting"—counting them once as intermediate sales and then counting them again when they are resold in final sales.

8. Changes in real *GDP* reflect changes in real output. Nominal *GDP* changes when prices and/or output changes.

GDP AND NATIONAL WELFARE

GDP should not be confused with national well-being, although it is closely related. Some of *GDP*'s limitations are:

1. *GDP ignores many nonmarket transactions,* such as the value of a person who works in the home but is not paid by his or her spouse. Also, unreported income earned in the "underground economy" is ignored (e.g., some waiters may not fully report their tip income, and some plumbers may not report their cash sales).

2. *GDP ignores the value of leisure.* Leisure includes those activities we would be willing to pay to do, because they bring direct enjoyment to us. Some people feel that Americans are overworked, both in the workplace and at home. So while *GDP* may appear to be high, they claim we are worse off than we were twenty years ago due to lack of leisure time.

3. *GDP ignores the ecological costs* of producing output (including the costs of pollution).

4. *GDP focues on output, but it is consumption that affects our nation's welfare.* For example, if other nations sell us more goods than we sell them, our nation will likely be better off because it can then consume more. But this will reduce *GDP* since net exports will then be negative. Focusing only on output thus gives a distorted view of national welfare.

5. *Government spending is valued at cost, not at its value.* Worthwhile projects are thus undervalued and worthless projects overvalued.

NATIONAL INCOME ACCOUNTING FORMULAS

The specifics of national income accounting, briefly, are as follows:

Basic Formulas

1. **Gross Domestic Product (*GDP*)** $= C + I + G + NX$

2. ***GNP*** $=$ ***GDP*** $+$ Income Receipts from Rest of World $-$ Income Payments to Rest of World

3. **Net National Product (*NNP*)** $= GNP -$ Depreciation

4. **Net Investment** $=$ Gross Investment $(I) -$ Depreciation

5. National Income

(a) National Income = *GNP* – Depreciation – Indirect Business Tax

(b) National Income = *NNP* – Indirect Business Tax

(c) National Income = Sum of Factor Payments

6. Personal Income (*PI*)

(a) *PI* = *NI* – Social Security Contributions – Corporate Income Taxes – Undistributed Corporate Profits + Transfer Payments

(b) *PI* = Household Income

7. Disposable Income (*DI*)

(a) *DI* = *PI* – Personal Taxes

(b) *DI* = After-tax Household Income

(c) *DI* = Consumption Spending + Personal Savings + Interest Payments to Businesses

(d) *DI* = *NI* – Corporate Profits – Taxes (personal, corporate, and social security) + Personal Dividend Receipts + Interest Paid by Government + Transfer Payments by Government and Businesses to Households

where C = household consumption spending

DI = disposable income

G = government spending

GDP = gross domestic product

GNP = gross national product

I = gross investment

NI = national income

NNP = net national product

NX = foreign net export spending

PI = household income

Note: Depreciation is the same as Capital Consumption Allowance.

APPLYING THE NATIONAL INCOME PREMISES

National income equals total income. Because each dollar spent is received as income, national income also equals total spending. If we look at national income as total spending, we have:

$$\text{National Income} = C + I + G + NX.$$

If we look at national income in terms of how it is *allocated* by private households, it is consumed, saved, or taxed:

National Income $= C +$ Private Savings $+$ (Taxes $-$ Transfer Payments)*.

Here is how to think about this equation. Households earn income, and the government takes away taxes but gives back transfer payments. Households then either consume or save the remainder (the savings by households is called *private savings*). By letting Y be national income, we have:

Private Savings $= Y -$ (Taxes $-$ Transfer Payments) $- C$.

Public savings is the amount of tax revenues that the government has left over after its spending outlays:

Public Savings $=$ Taxes $- G -$ Transfer Payments.

When taxes exceed outlays (G plus Transfer Payments), the government has a budget surplus and public savings are positive. When the government spends more than it collects in taxes, the government runs a deficit and public savings are negative.

Total savings (S) is the sum of private and public savings, so we have:

$$S = Y - C - G \text{ or } Y = C + G + S.$$

From the spending side, $Y = C + I + G + NX$. From the allocation side, $Y = C + G + S$. By putting these two sides together, we must have:

$$S = I + NX,$$
where $S =$ National Savings $=$ Private Savings $+$ Public Savings.

We hear about government deficits and trade deficits in the news. These equations show how they are related. First, we have some "minus" relationships (where A $-$ B) you need to remember:

Trade Deficit $=$ Imports $-$ Exports $= -NX$ and
Government Deficit $=$ Taxes $- G -$ Transfer Payments $= -$ Public Savings.

---

* (*Taxes $-$ Transfer Payments*) is in parentheses because this is the *net taxes* the public pays the government. Savings is that part of disposable income that is not consumed. Thus:
Disposable Income (DI) $= C +$ Savings.
In turn,
Disposable Income (DI) $=$ National Income $-$ (Taxes $-$ Transfers).

Next, since *S* equals private plus public savings, $S = I + NX$ can be written as:

Private Savings – Government Deficit = I – Trade Deficit or
I + Government Deficit = Private Savings + Trade Deficit.

The second equation has the following interpretation. On the left-hand side is total borrowing. Businesses borrow to finance investment (I), and the government borrows to finance its deficit. On the right-hand side are the funds they borrowed, including private savings and the net funds borrowed from other nations (which show up as a trade deficit).

A final way to rewrite this identity is:

$I + G + NX$ = Private Savings + (Taxes – Transfer Payments).

On the left-hand side are items that increase total spending (other than *C*). The right-hand side shows the items that lower spending. Some texts refer to items on the left as *injections* into the spending stream, while items on the right are called *leakages*.

YOU SHOULD REMEMBER

1. *GDP* measures national output and not necessarily national welfare.

2. Total Spending is on Consumption (*C*), Investment (*I*), Government Spending (*G*), or Net Exports (*NX*). Total income is allocated either to Consumption, Savings, or Taxes.

3. Since

    Total Income = Total Spending,

    it is also true that

    National Savings = *I* + *NX*,

    I + Government Deficit = Private Savings + Trade Deficit, and

    I + *G* + *NX* = Private Savings + (Taxes – Transfer Payments).

KNOW THE CONCEPTS
DO YOU KNOW THE BASICS?

1. Why are only final goods and services counted in *GDP*?
2. Why do changes in real *GDP* better reflect how total output is changing than changes in nominal *GDP*?
3. What are the two basic national income identities, and how are they pictured in the circular flow of income?
4. What makes *GDP* gross and *NNP* net?
5. Which national income account best reflects total factor payments?
6. Which national income account best reflects the income households receive? The after-tax income that households receive?
7. How do households dispose of disposable income?
8. In a simple economy without international trade or a government, how are investment (*I*) and savings related?
9. With a government sector, how do businesses and the government in a sense compete for savings?
10. Does *GDP* measure national welfare?

TERMS FOR STUDY

businesses	households
circular flow of income	incomes approach
depreciation	investment, gross and net
expenditures approach	net exports
final goods	savings
GDP, NNP, NI, PI, DI	transfer payments
government deficit	value added

PRACTICAL APPLICATION

1. Which of the following are counted in *GDP?*
    a. Purchase of $5,000 of Walt Disney Company stock.
    b. A $5,000 payment to a lawyer to defend yourself in a court case.
    c. A consumer spends $5,000 to buy a used Cadillac.
    d. Another consumer spends $5,000 to purchase a state-of-the-art television system made in Japan.

e. $5,000 is earned by an American in Paris.

f. $5,000 in Social Security is paid to a retired school teacher.

g. A $5,000 computer is produced by a small firm, which cannot sell it.

2. Suppose $GDP = \$12,000$, $C = \$9,600$, $G = \$400$, and $NX = \$320$.

    a. What is I?

    b. If exports equal $1,400, what are imports?

    c. If taxes equal $800 and transfer payments equal $480, what is the government's deficit equal to? What are private savings equal to?

    d. If U.S. citizens earn $1,600 abroad and foreigners (individuals and corporations) working in the United States earn $600, what is GNP?

    e. If indirect business taxes equal $280 and depreciation equals $300, what is the net national product (NNP) and the national income (NI)?

3. What are net exports equal to when $GDP = \$2,000$, $I = \$200$, $C = \$1,200$, and $G = \$300$? If taxes equal $200 and there are no transfer payments, what do savings equal? If imports equal $160, what do exports equal?

4. Indicate how the following affect measured GDP and the national welfare.

    a. The government mandates that employers supply $100 billion of new medical care to workers. Workers value the new medical care at $10 billion. Employment falls as a result.

    b. More women join the labor force. They value wages over the time they gave up to work.

    c. The government builds a sports arena in every town in America. The cost of the arenas far exceeds their value to sport fans.

    d. A business executive quits her job to go back to school and get an M.B.A.

5. Until recently, the U.S. government suffered from what is called the twin deficits. One deficit is the government's deficit (G + Transfer Payments − Taxes), and the other deficit is the trade deficit (Imports − Exports, or $-NX$).

    a. If the United States saves what it invests, how are the two deficits going to be related?

    b. Recently, the U.S. government has been running a surplus while the trade deficit (exports exceeding imports) still exists. What does this say about what has been happening to investment and savings?

    c. One school of economic thought argues that an increase in the deficit means higher future taxes and people saving an equivalent amount now to pay for the higher taxes later. In this case, changes in the government deficit are matched by changes in savings. If this does occur, how would investment and the trade deficit be related?

6. Suppose that private savings are fixed at 15 percent of *GDP*. Also assume that net exports are zero. If the government's deficit equals 5 percent of *GDP*, what percentage of *GDP* is investment?

7. A farmer grows corn, which she sells for $10; a miller buys the corn, grinds it, and sells it as cornmeal for $15; a baker buys the cornmeal and sells it as corn muffins for $22. How much was contributed to *GDP* in these transactions? What was the value added of each person?

8. An economy produces $15 billion in investment goods and $100 billion in consumption goods. All investment goods were sold, but only $90 billion of the consumption goods were sold. There is no government or international trade. What was *GDP*? What was consumption and investment?

9. There are only two firms in an economy. Firm A buys from Firm B and vice versa. What is the value added for each firm? What is *GDP*? Show that total factor income equals *GDP*.

	Firm A	Firm B
Total sales	$1,000	$3,400
Wages, rent, and interest	$ 800	$1,600
Purchases from other firm	$ 100	$1,000
Output	$1,100	$3,400

ANSWERS

KNOW THE CONCEPTS

1. Because all other sales (of intermediate products that are resold within the year) are reflected in the price of final goods.

2. Changes in real *GDP* reflect changes in real output. Nominal *GDP* changes when prices and/or output changes.

3. A dollar spent is a dollar received: Flow D equals Flow B. A good sold is a good bought: Flow A equals Flow C.

4. "Net" refers to subtracting depreciation. "Gross" includes depreciation.

5. *NI*: National Income.

6. *PI*: Personal Income. *DI*: Personal Disposable Income.

7. They consume or save it.

8. I = Private Savings

9. When we added the government sector, we had

$$\text{Investment} + \text{Government Deficit} = \text{Private Savings}$$

Businesses borrow to finance their investment spending, and the government borrows to finance its deficit. Thus, to the degree that savings are fixed in size, the more the government borrows, the less businesses can borrow for investment.

10. No. It is a measure of output and spending.

PRACTICAL APPLICATION

1. Only b and g are included in *GDP*. The other transactions do not reflect the *current* production of goods and services within the United States.

2. a. $I = \$1,680$.

    b. Imports = \$1,080.

    c. Government deficit = \$80, and private savings = \$2,080.

    d. *GNP* = \$13,000.

    e. *NNP* = \$12,700, and *NI* = \$12,420.

3. Net exports = \$300, savings = \$500, and exports = \$460.

4. a. Decrease *GDP* (less output with less employment), decrease welfare.

    b. Increase *GDP*, increase welfare.

    c. Increase *GDP*, decrease welfare.

    d. Decrease *GDP*, increase welfare.

5. Use *I* + Government Deficit = Private Savings + Trade Deficit to answer these questions.

    a. When *I* = Private Savings, then the twin deficits will be equal because Government Deficit = Trade Deficit.

    b. When the government runs a surplus, the government deficit is a negative number. For the trade deficit to be a positive number, investment (*I*) must be larger than savings. Most likely, businesses are borrowing the funds they need for investment from abroad since they cannot get sufficient funds from U.S. savers.

    c. In this case, investment (*I*) and the trade deficit will move together. An increase in investment would be matched dollar for dollar by an increase in the trade deficit.

6. Investment plus the government's deficit equals private savings. So investment equals 10 percent of *GDP*.

7. The final good sold for \$22; this is the contribution of *GDP*. It also equals the sum of the value added: \$10 for the farmer, \$5 for the miller, and \$7 for the baker.

8. *GDP* was $115 billion, the sum of output produced. Consumption was $90 billion (the amount households spent), while investment was $25 billion. $15 billion was for the investment goods produced. The other $10 billion of investment was the increased inventory due to the unsold consumption goods.

9. The value added is the firm's output (recall that unsold output is treated as a sale to the firm) less its purchases from other firms. Firm A's value added is $1,000 and B's is $2,400. So *GDP* equals $3,400. Firm A's profits are $200 (once again, the value of its output is counted as its revenue even if it's not sold). Firm B's profits are $800. So wages, rent, and interest total $2,400 and profits total $1,000, giving us a national income of $3,400.

6
INFLATION AND UNEMPLOYMENT

MEASURING INFLATION

To measure how much prices have risen, economists use price indexes. **Price indexes** measure how prices today compare with those in some selected year (called the **base year**): they express today's cost of a market basket of goods as a percentage of the basket's cost in the base year. For example, the August 2005 Consumer Price Index (CPI) was 196.4. Thus, the cost of a market basket of goods in the CPI was 196.4 percent of its cost in the base period of 1982–1984. Prices had increased 96.4 percent since 1982–1984. (The percentage increase from the base year equals the index's value minus 100.)

Key Procedure for Constructing a Price Index

1. For a base year, determine what goods people bought and how much of each they bought. Calculate the cost of this basket of goods for the base year.

2. Calculate the cost of the basket for Year T.

3. The price index for Year T is shown by the following formula:

$$\frac{\text{Cost of Basket in Year T}}{\text{Cost of Basket in Base Year}} \times 100$$

For example, if the basket costs $6,000 in the base year and $9,000 in 1975, the 1975 price index is 150. Prices have gone up 50 percent. The price index for the base year is always 100.

Example: Calculating a Price Index

PROBLEM   In 1980, Joe, in a typical week, bought ten bottles of wine (at $4 each) and twenty pizzas (at $6 each). In 1985, wine cost $6 and pizza cost $8. What is Joe's 1985 price index, using 1980 as the base year?

SOLUTION   137.5. The 1980 basket cost $160 in 1980 ($4 × 10 + $6 × 20) and would have cost $220 in 1985 ($6 × 10 + $8 × 20). $220/$160 times 100 equals 137.5.

Beginning in 1999, the government started using geometric means to estimate the prices of 60 percent of the goods in the CPI. This method is best shown by example.

Key Procedure for Estimating a Geometric Price Index

1. For each good, divide Year T's price by the good's price in the base year. The result is a ratio.

2. Use the good's share in the consumer's budget in the base year as the exponent of that ratio. If the price ratio is 1.25 and the good represents 30 percent of the consumer's budget, we would have $1.25^{0.30}$ or 1.07. (Note: you will need a calculator that can calculate exponents to do this.)

3. The price index for year T equals the product of the ratios times 100.

Example: Calculating a Geometric Price Index for Joe

PROBLEM   Calculate a geometric price index for Joe using the figures from the problem above. Note that in the base year (1980), Joe spent $40 on wine and $120 on pizza out of a budget of $160.

SOLUTION   The ratio for wine is $6/$4 = 1.5. The ratio for pizza is $8/$6 = 1.333. Wine's share is $40/$160 = 0.25. Pizza's share is $120/$160 = 0.75. So in step 2, for wine, we have $1.5^{0.25} = 1.107$. For pizza, we have $1.333^{0.75} = 1.241$. The price index in 1995 equals $1.107 \times 1.241 \times 100 = 137.3$.

THE THREE MAIN PRICE INDEXES

- ***The Consumer Price Index (CPI).*** The CPI measures the cost of the market basket of goods purchased by urban consumers (who make up 87 percent of the population). This index is usually referred to as the Consumer Price Index. It reflects how prices today compare to those in the base years of 1982–1984. The goods in the baskets were revised to reflect goods and services bought in 2001–2002, but the index still equals 100 in the base period of 1982–1984. The good mix will be updated every few years. The Chained Consumer Price Index for All Urban Consumers (C-CPI-U) is similar to the CPI-U, but it is calculated another way. It uses a chained index that accounts for the ability of consumers to achieve the same standard of living from alternative sets of goods and services. In contrast, the CPI assumes people want to purchase the same relative number of each good and service as they did in the base year.

- ***The Producer Price Index (PPI).*** The PPI measures the cost of a basket of goods produced by firms, mainly in manufacturing. This index often acts as an early indicator of inflation.

- ***The GDP Deflator.*** The *GDP* Deflator measures the price of all goods and services produced in the United States. This basket is constantly being updated to reflect current spending patterns (unlike the CPI, whose basket is based on 2001–2002 spending patterns). Economists use the *GDP* Deflator to measure inflation. It covers more goods than either the CPI or the PPI and better reflects current spending patterns.

PROBLEMS WITH PRICE INDEXES

Price indexes often do not accurately measure the change in prices, because of two major problems:

1. *Price indexes do not fully account for changes in quality.* To the degree that price indexes do not take account of improvements in quality, they *overstate* how much prices have risen. For example, suppose 1998 prices were 10 percent higher than 1997 prices but 1998 goods were 10 percent better. While consumers in 1998 were paying 10 percent more in higher prices, they were also getting (in terms of better quality) 10 percent more,

so the true cost of living had not changed. A price index showing a 10 percent increase in prices would overstate the increase in the cost of living.

2. *The major price indexes (such as the CPI) ignore changes in consumption patterns.* Due to the law of demand, consumers buy less of those goods whose prices have gone up more. In this way, consumers partially offset some of the impact of higher prices on their cost of living. Because the CPI ignores this, it overstates the increase in the cost of living. This problem is called "the index number problem." See Practical Application, Question 7.

THE MEANING OF INFLATION

Inflation is a rise in the general price level of goods and services. The **inflation rate** is the percent change in the general price level over a year.

Key Procedure for Measuring the Inflation Rate

1. Let P (*Year T*) be Year T's price index and P (*Year T–1*) be the prior year's price index.

2. The *rate of inflation in Year T is:*

$$\frac{P \ (Year \ T) - P \ (Year \ T{-}1)}{P \ (Year \ T{-}1)} \times 100$$

YOU SHOULD REMEMBER

1. *Price indexes* measure the cost of a market basket of goods, expressed as a percent of its cost in some base year. Price indexes overstate the rise in prices when they ignore improvements in quality and shifts in spending away from goods whose prices have increased more.

2. The *measured inflation rate* is the percent increase in the price index in a year.

HOW INFLATION AFFECTS REAL INCOME

To understand the effect of inflation fully, it is necessary to understand two key concepts. The first is *nominal:* it refers to the actual money amount. For example, in many years, workers get substantial increases in their nominal wage. Yet, when inflation is taken into account, their real wage has increased little. To calculate how much better off workers are, economists use price indexes to convert nominal amounts into real amounts.

Key Procedure for Using Price Indexes to Calculate Real Values

1. Convert the price index from its percent form to a decimal form by moving its decimal point two places to the left.

2. Divide the nominal amount by the price index to derive its real value.

Example: Using the CPI to Calculate Changes in Real Wages

PROBLEM   In 1994, the average hourly earnings were $11.32. By 2004, it had risen to $15.67. In the same period, the CPI rose from 148.2 to 188.9. What was the real wage in each year, and by how much did it change?

SOLUTION   The real hourly wage in 1994 was $7.63 ($11.31/1.482). In 2004, it was $8.30 ($15.67/1.889). Real wages had risen 8.8 percent.

To show how inflation affects real income, assume for the moment that workers consume only bread. If they are paid $4 an hour and can buy a loaf of bread for 50¢, their nominal wage is $4 and their real wage is eight loaves of bread. But suppose the price of bread rises to $1. Their real wage will fall by 50 percent to four loaves. They will be worse off because they did not anticipate the rise in prices. Suppose both employers and workers alike anticipate that prices will double. Since the price of what workers produce has doubled, the dollar value of each hour of work will double from $4 to $8. So employers will be willing to pay a wage of $8. Similarly, workers will demand a wage of $8, which will give them the same real wage (eight loaves) as before. In this case, the wage will rise to $8 and workers will not suffer any loss in real income. Inflation harms people mainly when they do not anticipate and adjust to it.

Inflation also affects the real income earned from investments. The nominal interest rate is the money paid on bonds and investments, expressed as a percent per year. The **real interest rate** is the amount of goods and services paid on bonds and investments, expressed as a percent per year. The *approximate* relationship between these is:

Real Interest Rate = Nominal Interest Rate – Inflation Rate.

Suppose, for example, you buy a one-year treasury bill paying 10 percent for $1,000. In one year, you'll get $100 in interest plus the $1,000 back. You will have earned a nominal interest of 10 percent. Suppose consumer prices go up 4 percent over the year. In real terms, you will get back $1,100/1.04, or $1,058. So you will have earned a real rate of interest of 5.8 percent. (Note that the formula above is a little off, as it calculates the real interest rate as being 6 percent.)

THE ECONOMIC COSTS OF INFLATION

Now let us consider the costs of inflation to an economy before and after people come to anticipate inflation.

• *UNANTICIPATED INFLATION*

It has often taken years for people to anticipate and adjust to inflation fully. During the period before people fully adjust, inflation's main effect is to harm those with long-term contracts that pay them a fixed dollar amount over several years. For example, savers who bought a 20-year bond that pays them a fixed amount of money each year for 20 years will find that inflation erodes the real value of their returns.

Just as there are losers from inflation, there are winners: those with long-term contracts that have to pay out fixed amounts of money per year. Winners include employers with long-term contracts paying fixed money wages to workers and borrowers paying back fixed interest payments on loans. These winners benefit from lower real costs.

• *ANTICIPATED STEADY INFLATION*

Even if inflation comes to be fully anticipated and persists year after year at a constant rate, it still has costs. However, once anticipated, there usually is not the redistribution of wealth as described above. For example, unions will seek to protect workers by putting cost-of-living adjustments (called COLAs) into their contracts. And nominal interest rates will likely rise to off-set the loss in purchasing power. In particular:

Nominal Interest Rate = Real Interest Rate + Expected Rate of Inflation

For example, if savers want a real return of 4 percent and expect a 10 percent rate of inflation, they will want a 14 percent nominal interest rate.

The Two Main Costs of Steady *Anticipated* Inflation

1. *Excessive Cash Management.* Inflation acts like a tax on money holdings. For example, suppose your money holdings equal $1,000. An inflation rate of 10 percent will reduce the value of your holdings. In order to maintain the real value of your money holdings, you will have to increase your holdings by 10 percent, or in this case $100. This $100 in added cost is like a 10 percent tax on money holdings. The higher the rate of inflation, the more expensive it becomes to maintain the real value of one's money holdings. The result is that *inflation causes people to reduce their real money holdings*.

But smaller real money holdings result in inconveniences for people. For example, if people carry less cash in their pocket, they may have to go to the bank more often to get cash. The added cost of more frequent financial transactions due to inflation is called the "shoe leather cost" of inflation (the "shoe leather cost" being the wearing out of one's shoes due to the more frequent trips to the bank). In this way and others, inflation raises the cost of cash management.

2. ***More Frequent Posting of Prices.*** The greater the rate of inflation, the more often businesses have to post new prices. Menus have to be changed, advertising increased, and catalogs revised.

• *VARYING INFLATION WHOSE AVERAGE RATE IS ANTICIPATED*

Suppose people have come to anticipate the average rate of inflation. However, inflation varies, sometimes being above and other times below its average rate.

The Three Main Costs of Anticipated but Varying Inflation

1. *Compensating for Uncertainty.* Suppose workers' nominal wages are set by a long-term contract to increase with the average rate of inflation. On average, then, their real wages will be unchanged. However, as inflation goes above and then below its average level, their real wages will go below and then above its anticipated average level. Because of the uncertainty as to what their actual real wages will be, workers who sign long-term contracts will demand extra compensation. Real wages will increase. The result will be higher real wages and a fall in employment.

2. *Destroyed Information.* When inflation varies, knowing what a good price is or how to shop wisely becomes difficult. It is like the *Twilight Zone* episode in which a man finds that the meaning of words is constantly changing. Just to converse, he must constantly relearn his language. Similarly, varying inflation forces people to relearn prices constantly.

3. *Increase in Tax Rates.* Inflation increases nominal income relative to real income. In many cases, the U.S. tax codes do not take this into account. The result is that as inflation goes up, so do tax rates, particularly on profits and capital gains (see Questions 9 and 10). For example, in 1979, with its high inflation rate of 11 percent, the effective tax on business investment reached 95 percent. As a result, investment fell, with a resulting decline in output and growth.

YOU SHOULD REMEMBER

1. The *nominal value* of a payment is its dollar amount; its *real* value is expressed in terms of the goods and services it can buy.

2. Unanticipated inflation hurts lenders and those on fixed incomes. It helps borrowers and those whose costs are fixed in nominal terms.

3. When inflation is fully anticipated and steady, it still costs the economy in added cash management costs, in more frequent posting of prices, and in increased taxes.

4. When inflation's average rate is anticipated but it varies around that rate, it brings the added costs of greater uncertainty and a higher cost due to destroyed information.

5. Nominal interest rates equal the real rate *plus* the expected rate of inflation (as compensation for lost purchasing power).

MEASURING UNEMPLOYMENT

Every month, the Department of Labor (DOL) interviews 60,000 households that have been randomly selected to represent the whole U.S. population. Based upon their answers, all people aged 16 or older are put into one of the following three categories.

Labor Force Categories

1. *Employed.* A person is **employed** if the person (1) has done any work in the week prior to the interview or (2) has a job but is absent because of illness, a strike, or vacation.

2. *Unemployed.* A person is **unemployed** if the person (1) did not work in the previous week but has made specific efforts to find a job in the last four weeks, (2) has been laid off and is waiting to be recalled in the next 30 days, or (3) is waiting to report to a new job in the next 30 days.

3. *Not in the Labor Force.* The **labor force** is all those who are employed or unemployed; the rest of the population is **not in the labor force.** This includes people who are full-time students, nonworking spouses, or retired. It also includes "**discouraged workers**," persons who want to work but have given up looking for employment.

The **rate of unemployment** is the percent of the *labor force* that is unemployed. So if there are 100 million employed persons and 20 million unemployed persons, the unemployment rate will be 16.7 percent (20/120 × 100).

Figure 6–1 shows the flows in the labor market. People leave unemployment either by finding jobs or by becoming discouraged and leaving the labor force. On average, half leave each way. After a few months, most discouraged workers will reenter the labor force. Of those entering unemployment, 50 percent are job losers (having either been fired or being put on indefinite layoff), 25 percent are reentrants, and the rest are evenly divided between job leavers (quitting to seek better work) and new entrants.

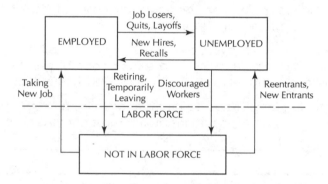

Figure 6–1. Labor Force Flows

THE EFFECT OF RECESSION

The economy is in a **recession** when total output falls. A recession increases the unemployment rate in two main ways. First, there is an increase in the number of workers losing their jobs: This increases the "flow" into unemployment. Second, it takes longer to find a job during a recession: This reduces the "flow" out of unemployment. The number unemployed thus swells during a recession.

THE TYPES AND COSTS OF UNEMPLOYMENT

The Three Types of Unemployment

1. *Frictional unemployment* is due to the normal workings of an economy. Frictional unemployment occurs because (a) workers quit to find better jobs, (b) employers fire workers and look for better ones to replace them, (c) consumers change the goods they buy, thereby reducing jobs previously available in producing the goods they no longer want

but increasing jobs elsewhere, and (d) technological progress makes the skills of some workers obsolete.

2. ***Structural unemployment*** occurs if cause (c) or (d) above seriously affects certain industries, occupations, or areas of the country so that only with very high costs can workers relocate and/or retrain for new careers.

3. ***Cyclical unemployment*** is due to downturns in the economy. When economists say the economy is at **full employment,** they mean that there is no cyclical unemployment. However, both frictional and structural employment can and do exist when the economy is fully employed. The unemployment rate at full employment is about 5 percent to 6 percent.

Frictional unemployment, while costly to those losing their jobs, benefits the economy. Because it exists, the economy can better match workers with the employers and can shift output toward those goods consumers want. *Structural unemployment* has a net social benefit if the benefits of retraining (and/or relocating) the unemployed workers exceed the cost. *Cyclical unemployment* is costly mainly because it is associated with the cost of lost output. This cost is the difference between the value of the output and the opportunity cost of producing it. So if output falls by $100 billion and this output would have cost $40 billion to produce, the social loss is $60 billion.

Unemployment is linked to real *GDP* by what is called **"Okun's Law."** The law states that for every 2 percent that real *GDP* is below its potential full-employment level over a year's time, the unemployment rate will increase by 1 percent. (Some studies put this ratio at 2.5 to 1 rather than 2 to 1.) Since potential full-employment *GDP* usually grows at 3 percent a year, if real *GDP* grows at 3 percent, the unemployment rate should remain unchanged. If it grows at 5 percent over a year, the unemployment rate should fall by 1 percentage point (e.g., from 5 percent to 4 percent). And if real *GDP* does not grow at all, the unemployment rate should rise 1.5 percent (e.g., from 5 percent to 6.5 percent).

Be careful to note that Okun's Law is an observed regularity of how changes in *GDP* affect unemployment. It does not say that decreasing unemployment (e.g., by a government program to train the unemployed) will cause *GDP* to rise.

The official unemployment rate does not necessarily capture the full extent of the misery caused by a recession. It fails to count (1) discouraged workers who have dropped out of the labor force because they cannot find a job and (2) the **underemployed,** part-time workers who want to work full-time.

YOU SHOULD REMEMBER

1. The unemployment rate is the percentage of the labor force that is unemployed.

2. Unemployment goes up in a recession because more people lose jobs and find that it takes longer to find new jobs.

3. Okun's Law states that every 2 percent increase in the real *GDP* growth rate above its potential level, if sustained for a year, results in a 1 percent decrease in the unemployment rate.

4. Cyclical unemployment is costly because of the lost output associated with it.

5. At full employment, both frictional and structural unemployment will be present; only cyclical unemployment will be zero.

KNOW THE CONCEPTS

DO YOU KNOW THE BASICS?

1. How does inflation hurt those on fixed incomes?

2. How can savers protect themselves from inflation?

3. Why do interest rates eventually go up during a period of inflation?

4. When inflation causes greater uncertainty in the economy, workers often demand higher real wages as compensation for the higher uncertainty. How does this hurt the economy?

5. If real *GDP* is constant while the *GDP* Deflator increases, what will happen to nominal *GDP*?

6. What does a price index of 180 mean? How much have prices risen since the base year?

7. Why does an improvement in quality cause a price index to overstate how much prices have gone up?

8. What are the different ways someone can become unemployed?

9. If the unemployment rate is 10 percent and 90 million workers are employed, how many are unemployed?

10. What is the main cost associated with cyclical unemployment?

TERMS FOR STUDY

discouraged worker
employed, unemployed
frictional, structural, and
   cyclical unemployment
inflation
inflation rate
labor force
Okun's Law

real interest rate,
   nominal interest rate
real, nominal
real wages, nominal wages
steady inflation and varying
   inflation
unanticipated inflation and
   anticipated inflation

PRACTICAL APPLICATION

1. Bill retires and invests $300,000 at 7 percent, earning $21,000 a year. If inflation is 3 percent, what is Bill's real rate of return? If Bill consumes all $21,000 each year, what will happen to the real value of his investment and his income? How might he have prevented this? (Assume he can earn 7 percent on any added investments.)

2. Fill in the missing numbers in this table for the mythical country of Rulgria. The price index used is the *GDP* Deflator.

Year	Real *GDP*	Price Index	Nominal *GDP*
1970	100	50	—
1980	300	—	300
1990	—	200	1,400
2000	1,000	—	3,000

Hint: Real *GDP* equals nominal *GDP* divided by *GDP* Deflator, stated as a decimal number.

3. If inflation continues for 20 years at a 6 percent rate, by how much will prices increase?

4. From the following figures, calculate the price index for this worker, using 1995 as the base year. How much did prices go up? What is the real income in each year? (Assume that the worker spent all of his or her income in each year.)

Item	Price and Quantity			
	2000		2005	
Food	$1	2,000	$2	1,250
Housing	$500	4	$1,500	3
Clothing	$50	40	$80	50

5. The percent change in the CPI is equal to the sum of the percent change in its components, each weighted by its share in the base-period budget. For example, housing represented 42.6 percent of budget. If housing costs go up 10 percent, what will this contribute to the inflation rate, as measured by the CPI? Medical care constitutes only 4.8 percent of the budget. If medical costs go up 10 percent, what is its contribution to the inflation rate?

6. Indicate the labor force status of the following persons:

   a. A doctor who is too sick to work.

   b. A mechanic who could not find a job needing his skills and is waiting for the economy to improve before he looks for work again.

   c. A full-time student.

   d. A laid-off steel worker waiting to return to work.

   e. A laid-off executive who is making ends meet by working at a car wash.

   f. An executive given a year off to have a baby.

7. This example illustrates the index number problem. Suppose John consumes only bread. In Year 0, John buys four loaves of white bread and four of dark bread, all at $1 each. John likes both equally. In Year 1, white bread costs $2 but dark bread still costs $1. So John switches to dark bread.

   a. What has happened to John's cost of living?

   b. What will the values be for a price index using Year 0 as the base year? Does it overstate or understate the true increase in John's cost of living?

8. Historically, 30-year U.S. Treasury bonds have paid a real rate of interest of 4 percent. If these bonds pay an interest rate of 7 percent, what inflation rate do savers expect, assuming they plan to get a 4 percent real rate of return? Historically, one-year U.S. Treasury bills have paid a real rate of return of 0 percent. If they are paying 4 percent, what does this imply savers expect?

9. Mr. Jones buys 100 shares of XYZ stock in 1990 for $1,000. In 1999, he sells it for $1,820. In 1999, he paid a 40 percent combined state and federal tax rate on his $820 profit. During that time, the CPI went from 100 to 130. How much in real value did his stock go up? What percentage of his real profits was taxed? How could the government prevent inflation from making this tax rate so high?

10. This problem illustrates how inflation combined with our tax code increases the tax rate on profits. (A related fact is that stock prices and inflation have been negatively related in recent years.) In Year 0, the XYZ Corporation buys a $100,000 machine, which will have to be replaced every five years. So it writes off a fifth of the value of the

machine each year as depreciation. The following table illustrates its profits in Year 4, assuming there is no inflation.

	Sales	$40,000
−	Factor Costs	$10,000
−	*Depreciation*	*$20,000*
	Profits	$10,000
−	*Taxes (50%)*	*5,000*
	After-tax Profits	$ 5,000

Now suppose there is inflation, so all prices double (including the replacement cost of the machine, sales, and costs). But the government allows depreciation to be written off at only historical cost (i.e., $20,000). What is the new profit statement in Year 4? What is the effective tax on profits?

ANSWERS

KNOW THE CONCEPTS

1. It reduces their *real* income.

2. They can demand a higher nominal interest rate. Some savers have been demanding a variable interest rate based upon short-term interest rates, which usually reflect current inflation rates.

3. As savers come to expect higher rates of inflation, they demand higher nominal interest rates to compensate them for their loss in purchasing power.

4. By applying the laws of demand and supply to labor, this event causes the supply curve of labor to shift left. As a result, employment falls. With less employment, output and *GDP* fall.

5. Nominal *GDP* will increase.

6. The cost of a basket of goods is 180 percent of its base-year cost. Prices have risen 80 percent since the base year.

7. An improvement in quality gives the consumer more value per dollar, so that even if the price of the item is unchanged, its cost-per-unit value is reduced.

8. A person can quit, be fired, or be laid off. Also, a person can be an entrant or reentrant into the labor force.

9. 10 million.

10. The loss due to decreased output.

PRACTICAL APPLICATION

1. The real rate of return is 4 percent (7 percent – 3 percent). If Bill consumes $21,000 a year, the real value of his investment will go down 3 percent a year. To prevent this, he will have to increase his investment by 3 percent each year. In the first year, he would have to reinvest $9,000 (3 percent of $300,000), leaving him $12,000 to consume. If he continues to reinvest the inflation part of the interest rate, the real value of his income and investment will stay the same (at a real value of $12,000). That is why economists say he is really earning 4 percent on his investment (note that $12,000 is 4 percent of $300,000). It is the real amount he can continue to consume. Many retired people are fooled by inflation into consuming all their interest income only to find their standard of living has fallen.

2. $50 for 1970, 100 for 1980, $700 for 1990, and 300 for 2000. 1980 is the base year.

3. If the price level starts at 1, then at the end of one year, it will be at 1.06. Then prices will grow 6 percent more, or 1.06 times 1.06, to 1.1236 by the end of the second year. By the end of 20 years, the price level will grow to 1.06 times itself 20 times, or to 3.21. Prices will have risen 221 percent.

4. The cost of the 2000 basket was $6,000 in 2000. The same basket (with 2000 quantities) cost $13,200 at year 2005 prices. The price index using 2000 as the base year is by definition 100 in 2000. So the price index in the year 2005 is 220 (from $13,200/$6,000 times 100).

   When using the 2000-based basket, real income in 2000 was $6,000 ($6,000/1.00) and $5,000 in 2005 ($11,000/2.20).

5. Housing's contribution will be 4.26 percent (= .426 times 10 percent). Medical costs will contribute only 0.48 percent to the inflation rate. If these are the only two items whose price went up, the inflation rate will be their sum, 4.74 percent.

6. **a.** The doctor is employed.
   b. The mechanic is not in the labor force (and is a discouraged worker).
   c. The student is not in the labor force.
   d. The steel worker is unemployed.
   e. The laid-off executive is employed.
   f. The executive having a baby is not in the labor force.

7. **a.** John's cost of living remains unchanged since John has avoided the price rise by changing his consumption pattern.

b. The calculated price index will be 100 in Year 0 and 150 in Year 1, showing a 50 percent increase in the general level of prices. So the rise in the calculated price index overstates the true increase in the cost of living (which in this case didn't go up at all).

8. They must be expecting an annual inflation rate of 3 percent *over the next 20 years*, and a 4 percent rate of inflation next year.

9. He bought the stock for a real value of $1,000 and sold it for a real value of $1,400. His *real* profit was only $400. However, he paid $328 in taxes on his *nominal* profit of $820. So taxes equal 82 percent of his real profit! To eliminate this disincentive to invest, the government could allow taxpayers to calculate real profits and pay taxes on only that.

10. According to the government, this firm's profits will be $40,000 ($80,000 in sales minus $20,000 in factor costs and $20,000 in depreciation). So the government will impose a tax of $20,000. But the firm's *true* profits (taking into account the fact that depreciation has gone up to $40,000 because the machine is now more costly to replace) will be only $20,000. The firm's after-tax profits are calculated as follows:

	Sales	$80,000
−	Factor Costs	$20,000
−	*Depreciation*	*$40,000*
	Profits	$20,000
−	*Taxes*	*$20,000*
	After-tax Profits	$0

The effective tax rate went from 50 percent to 100 percent. In 1979, some economists estimated that the high inflation in that year raised the effective tax rate on corporate profits to as high as 95 percent.

7

INTRODUCTION TO MACRO-ECONOMICS: OUTPUT, GROWTH, AND CAPITAL

KEY TERMS

bond a certificate of indebtedness.

capital the stock of equipment and structures used to produce goods and services.

human capital the knowledge and skills that make people more productive.

macroeconomics the study of the whole economy, including the study of inflation, unemployment, economic growth, and the business cycle.

market for loanable funds where savers and borrowers get together, savers supply their savings—the *loanable* funds—to borrowers, and borrowers demand the funds.

stock a claim to partial ownership in a firm.

technological progress (or improvement) the change in technology resulting in more output from the same quantity of inputs.

WHAT IS MACROECONOMICS?

Macroeconomics studies the economy as a whole. Microeconomics is the study of the economic actions of individuals, including individual households and individual firms. For example, while microeconomics studies how demand and supply determine a good's price, macroeconomics studies what determines the price level of all goods. While microeconomics studies how many workers a firm employs, macroeconomics studies how many workers an economy employs. Macroeconomics also studies economic growth.

RECESSIONS

An economy operating at its potential level is said to be at full employment. At full employment, some unemployment occurs. This is consistent with the shifting of workers between jobs due to changing tastes and technology.

A recession occurs when *GDP* falls significantly below its full employment level. The Department of Commerce defines a recession as when real *GDP* declines for two consecutive quarters.

Two types of recessions occur. First, output can fall if the economy is operating at below its potential (full-employment) level. Second, output can fall if the economy's potential level of output falls.

The first type of recession occurs when output falls significantly below its full-employment level in a recession. Unemployment grows as a large number of workers cannot find work. The most dramatic recession of this type in our nation's history is the Great Depression, where 25 percent of the workforce was unemployed and real output fell more than 30 percent. This type of recession usually occurs when consumers and investors reduce their aggregate spending.

The second type of recession occurs when the economy's potential output falls. For example, a nation that passed a minimum wage of $2,000 per hour will likely experience massive unemployment and a recession. Its potential output has decreased. As another example, a decline in efficiency (perhaps due to higher taxes) or a decline in technological progress could cause output to fall. Even if unemployment rises, the economy may still be fully employed in the sense that employers are fully hiring all the workers they can.

The difference between a decline due to output falling below its full-employment level and a decline due to full-employment output falling is crucial. The first type of decline fits recessions described by Keynesian and monetary economists (each giving different reasons for the decline in spending). The second type fits recessions described by rational expectations economists (who give different reasons for the decline in full-employment output).

YOU SHOULD REMEMBER

1. A recession occurs when real output falls in two consecutive quarters.

2. Output is said to be at its potential or full-employment level when labor and other inputs are being fully utilized, given the laws and institutions of the economy.

3. A recession can occur because output falls below its potential level or because its potential level decreases.

WHY RECESSIONS OCCUR

Two startling facts exist about modern capitalistic economies. The first is that they have recessions. The second is that most of the time they are not in a recession. This suggests that some cause occasionally derails the economy. Yet, over time, the economy rebounds to full employment. What could the cause be? How does the economy recover?

Three main schools of thought try to answer these questions:

1. *Monetary Economists* (also called classical economists or neoclassical economists). This school observes that sudden and large decreases in the money supply (or decreases in the rate of monetary growth) usually precede recessions. While the economy naturally tends to be fully employed, sudden unexpected declines in the money supply will decrease total spending, depressing the economy until people and prices can adjust to having less cash.

2. *Keynesian Economists* (or neo-Keynesian economists). John Maynard Keynes emphasized the importance of total spending and the components of total spending (consumption, investment, government spending, and net exports). In particular, he felt that when people reduced consumption spending to save more, financial markets in times of uncertainty would be unwilling to spend the new savings on investments. The result would be a decrease in total spending. Keynes also believed that prices are sticky—resistant to changes (he believed workers would be reluctant to renegotiate for lower wages). The mix of less spending and fixed prices means lower output and a recession. Keynesians today put a

similar emphasis on total spending and the rigidity of prices for explaining the business cycle.

3. *Rational Expectations Economists.* This school emphasizes that people will optimally use all the information they have. Consequently, a recession, which people want to avoid, cannot be caused by factors known in advance. A corollary is that unpredicted events will cause recessions. Rational economists tend to emphasize factors that reduce the full-employment level of output. (For this reason, they are also called real business cycle economists). For example, during the Great Depression, the government raised taxes and tariffs dramatically, passed laws aiding the spread of unions, passed massive new regulations limiting what firms could do, and tried to monopolize every major industry. Each of these had the effect of cutting output. Finally, rational expectations economists argue that prices and wages are not sticky. Instead, mistakes by firms and workers could cause them to not adjust wages even if adjusting wages led to full employment.

YOU SHOULD REMEMBER

1. Monetarists say that declines in the money supply (or declines in money's rate of growth) caused most recessions.

2. Keynesians say that decreases in aggregate spending, due to less investment spending and more savings (leading to less consumption spending), caused most recessions.

3. Rational expectations economists attribute most recessions to unforeseen changes, since foreseen changes would have been anticipated and reflected in current output. They emphasize factors such as technological change and taxes.

FULL-EMPLOYMENT OUTPUT

This section will assume the economy is at full employment and that actual output equals potential output. Two issues, often confused, are (1) what determines the level of national output and (2) what determines the rate of economic growth (what percent output grows each year). Separating these issues is important! For example, a minimum wage may lower the level of national output, but it does not necessarily lower economic growth continually. As another example, an economy that sets aside a large fraction of its resources for research will have less output now, but it will grow faster.

THE LEVEL OF CURRENT OUTPUT

Output is produced with the inputs of labor, physical capital, human capital, natural resources, and technological knowledge. The more inputs, the more output. In more detail,

- *Output* is the total goods and services produced per period (*GDP*).

- *Labor* is work hours per period and is the product of the number of people working times the hours worked. Labor can be increased by increasing the number of people working or by increasing the hours each works.

- *Physical capital* is the stock of equipment and structures used to produce goods and services. It includes machines, tools, plants, stores, highways, and the many other inputs used in the production process.

- *Human capital* is the knowledge and skills that make people more productive. Human capital is created by education, on-the-job training, learning by doing, and natural ability.

- *Natural resources* are the productive inputs provided by nature, such as land, minerals, and water. When the waterwheel was discovered as a source of energy, rivers became a valuable natural resource.

- *Technological knowledge* is knowledge of the best ways of producing goods and services. *Technological progress (or improvement)* occurs when more output can be produced from the *same* quantity of inputs. When stated another way, technological progress occurs when the same output can be produced with *fewer* inputs. Technological progress can occur when scientists discover new knowledge, when firms introduce new innovations, when managers find new ways to cut costs, and when workers discover new ways of doing things better. Technological knowledge differs from the other inputs in a very fundamental way. Once a machine is built, if another one is needed, another machine has to be built at a similar cost. On the other hand, once the knowledge of how to do something is created, that knowledge can be used again and again at no additional cost. Knowledge is the only freely reproducible resource.

Besides total output, we are interested in the output per person, or per capita output. For a nation, output per person is the same thing as the real income per person (subtracting out income from other nations). A nation that wants a higher per capita income has to produce more per person.

A related concept is labor productivity[1] (or average productivity): the output per hour worked. *Labor productivity* equals total output divided by total work hours. Labor productivity goes up when, per work hour, there is more capital, more human capital, more natural resources, and better technological knowledge.

PROBLEM   Describe how the following events will affect total output, output per hour worked (that is, labor productivity), and output per worker. Assume that the law of diminishing returns applies such that when labor hours increase, output goes up but at a diminishing rate, causing labor productivity to fall.

Event A: A nation mandates that no worker work over 35 hours a week (most are currently working 40 or more hours). Assume the number of workers stays the same.

Event B: A nation sets aside 95 percent of its land as a natural habitat for earthworms.

Event C: The Black Plague wipes out most of the population but leaves capital and other inputs unaffected.

Event D: A new management technique allows firms to produce their current output with fewer inputs.

SOLUTION   *Event A:*   Less total hours means less total output. The law of diminishing marginal product means that less labor increases output per work hour (so labor productivity increases). However, output per worker goes down. Output per worker equals total output divided by the number of workers. In this case, the denominator is going down while the numerator stays the same.

Event B: Less land available for production means less inputs, and less inputs means less total output. Output per work hour and output per worker will fall.

Event C: Less inputs means less output. However, the event increases capital per worker and natural resources per worker, so output per worker hour (and per work hour) will increase. The Black Plague in Europe dramatically increased per capita income—a good deal, if you survived.

---

[1] A related concept is total factor productivity. Total factor productivity equals total output divided by a quantity index of all inputs. The quantity index multiplies the base period price of each input with its current quantity. Total factor productivity is a better measure of an economy's productivity.

> *Event D:* Same output but less inputs implies that with the same inputs, firms can produce more output. Since, for the economy, total inputs remains the same, total output will increase. Output per worker hour and output per worker will increase.

Governments sometimes pass laws that reduce potential output by reducing inputs. For example, very generous welfare payments will cut back the number of persons who want to work, reducing potential output. Similarly, some European governments impose stiff fines on firms for laying off workers. As a result, firms hire fewer workers, knowing that weeding out the less productive ones will be hard. Consequently, output falls.

Many countries of the world have lower output because they have corrupt governments where officials extort bribes from business owners in exchange for letting them stay in business. Corruption of this type discourages the entry of new firms. It also discourages investment by current firms, because they know that if they invest, much of the investment's profits will be taken away by corrupt government officials. Reduction of corruption with the establishment of property rights and the rule of law increases economic growth.

GROWTH ACCOUNTING

Growth accounting studies the causes of economic growth. A key concept often used in growth accounting is that the market value of inputs can be used to evaluate the importance of the inputs in the production process. To illustrate, suppose that 80 percent of national output (*GDP*) is paid out in the form of wages, then a 10 percent increase in the labor supply will increase output by 8 percent (0.80 of 10 percent). Next suppose that the only other input is capital: Its share of output must be 20 percent. Thus, a 10 percent increase in capital should increase output by 2 percent (0.20 of 10 percent). So if labor increases by 20 percent and capital increases by 10 percent, output should increase by 18 percent (0.80 × 20 percent + 0.20 × 10 percent). But what if output goes up 21 percent? The extra 3 percent is said by growth accounting to be due to technical change. When technical change is positive, it means that even if inputs had remained the same in quantity, new technology (including new management methods and better marketing) would have increased output. Viewed this way, technical change is the same thing as total factor productivity.

The fundamental equation of growth accounting is

Percent Growth in Output =
Labor's Share of National Income × Percent Growth in Labor

plus

Capital's Share of National Income × Percent Growth in Capital

plus

Technical Change

Because the growth in per capita income closely matches the growth in output per worker (or labor), economists are interested in what causes the growth in output per labor. The growth in output per labor equals the growth in output minus the growth in labor. Rearranging the above equation, we have

Percent Growth in Output per Labor = Capital's Share ×
(Percent Growth in Capital – Percent Growth in Labor) +
Technical Change

The two main causes of an increase in output per labor (and often of an increase in per capita income) are

1. *Increase in Capital Invested per Labor.* The growth in capital per labor (or in the capital/labor ratio) equals the percent growth in capital minus the percent growth in labor. Thus, the more invested in each worker, the more each worker produced. Investment can include investment in human capital (by education and on-the-job training) and investment in physical capital (such as more plant and equipment). Investment is financed by savings, thus the ability of a nation to save domestically and attract capital from other nations is important for economic growth.

2. *Technical Change.* New technology raises total factor productivity. Research and development, new inventions, new managerial methods, and new marketing methods are all ways that can increase total factor productivity. Technical change can be any source of growth, even if it is not strictly technical in nature. For example, Adam Smith, in *The Wealth of Nations*, attributed economic growth in large part to the division of labor. Division of labor breaks production down so that each worker specializes in doing one task. As a result, each worker needs less training and skill to become productive. This makes less-skilled workers more productive and increases the productivity of the whole population. Another form of the division of labor occurs when people become expert in doing narrow but valuable tasks (such as brain surgery). What allows for

the division of labor? Large markets for goods and services are needed. For example, in rural areas, most doctors are general practitioners. In urban areas, with a larger market, many doctors specialize. For a nation, international trade creates large markets, which in turn allow the division of labor that makes workers more productive and produces higher rates of economic growth. Economies of scale are another source of economic growth. Some tasks, when done on a large scale, become more than proportionately more productive. Doubling the size of tractor might, over a certain range, triple output. A railroad is not productive at all until its track reaches a certain length. In the past century, doing things bigger has often meant doing them better.

Growth accounting usually uses the market value of inputs to evaluate the importance of factors in explaining economic growth. If possible, actual empirical estimates of the importance of factors are used.

PROBLEM   Real *GDP* growth in Nation X equals 3.5 percent per year. Labor has been growing at 2 percent a year while capital has been growing at 4 percent a year. Labor earnings equal 75 percent of *GDP*, and capital earnings equal the remaining 25 percent. What is the rate of technical change in Nation X? What is the percent growth in output per labor?

SOLUTION   Using the equation of growth accounting, we have

3.5 percent = 0.75 × 2 percent + 0.25 × 4 percent + Technical Change

Solving the equation for technical change, we get the rate of 1.0 percent per year. The percent growth in output per labor equals the percent growth in output minus the percent growth in labor: 1.5 percent per year.

PROBLEM   Suppose there are three inputs: labor, capital, and land. Labor's share of national income is 70 percent, capital's share is 20 percent, and land's share is 10 percent. Both labor and capital grow by 10 percent. Land remains unchanged. If there is no technical change, what will happen to output? To output per labor?

SOLUTION   Output will grow by 9 percent (0.70 × 10 percent + 0.20 × 10 percent). Output per labor will fall by 1 percent (9 percent − 10 percent).

CREATION OF CAPITAL

The creation of capital plays a central role in economic development. Physical capital (usually called capital) is the equipment and structures (such as drill presses, factory buildings, and railroads) used to produce goods and services. Human capital is the knowledge and skills that make workers more productive.

Savings create capital. In turn, people save by foregoing consumption. Why do people save? People save—give up current consumption—to get more future consumption. For example, going to college creates human capital. It also means giving up consumption now. In exchange, students hope to earn (and consume) more in the future. The same process occurs with the creation of physical capital, but it is more difficult to see because two groups are involved. The first group are the savers. Savers might buy a *bond*, a certificate of indebtedness. A bond typically promises to pay interest for a certain number of years and then, at the date the bond matures, to pay back the face value of the bond. Alternatively, savers may buy a *stock*, a claim to partial ownership in a firm. The second group involved are borrowers. Borrowers include firms issuing stocks and bonds to finance the building of physical capital. Selling bonds to raise money is called *debt financing* and selling stocks is called *equity financing*. Borrowers take the savings and use it to build physical capital. In turn, the physical capital increases future output and future consumption.

Economists call borrowers the investors because they are making the actual purchase of capital. In this sense, savers do not invest—only borrowers invest. This is an important distinction, especially in the Keynesian model where what is saved by savers is not always invested.

A third group often entering between savers and investors are the financial intermediaries. They include banks, mutual funds, and financial bankers. Financial intermediaries collect the funds from savers and then give them to borrowers in exchange for stocks, bonds, and other forms of indebtedness (such as a loan). The borrowers create the actual physical capital.

At the national level, when people consume less, this frees up workers and other inputs to be used to produce capital. However, how do we know that savings will equal investment? We turn to that question now.

CAPITAL MARKETS

Financial assets, such as stocks and bonds, are claims to future incomes. These future claims are paid from the physical (and human) capital financed by the sale of the financial assets.

Another term for financial assets is loanable funds. *The market for loanable funds* is the market that brings savers and borrowers together. Savers supply the loanable funds. For example, when savers buy a bond, they are supplying loanable funds to the institution issuing the bond. The institution can be a firm or a government. Borrowers demand loanable funds. For example, when an institution sells a bond, it is demanding loanable funds.

Equilibrium occurs in the loanable funds market when savings equal investment:

National Savings = Domestic Investment + Net Foreign Investment

or

$$S = I + NFI$$

When a nation saves S, it invests domestically in I or abroad in NFI. S is national savings and is the *sum* of private savings (created by households) and public savings (created by governments when they collect more taxes than they spend). When the government runs a deficit, it is more useful to write this equation as:

Private Savings = Domestic Investment + Government Deficit + NFI.

This equation focuses on private savers. Their savings finance domestic investment, net foreign investment, and the government's deficit.

The price that brings the loanable funds market into equilibrium is the real interest rate. The nominal rate of interest is the actual interest rate without any correction for inflation. The real rate of interest equals the nominal interest rate minus the expected rate of inflation. If inflation is expected to be 3 percent over the life of the bond, then an 8⟨percent bond is paying a real interest rate of 5 percent. The real rate is what matters to savers and borrowers.

Suppliers of loanable funds (savers) supply more loanable funds (save more) when the real interest rate increases. Demanders of loanable funds (borrowers) demand less loanable funds when the real interest rate increases. Figure 7–1 shows the domestic market for loanable funds.

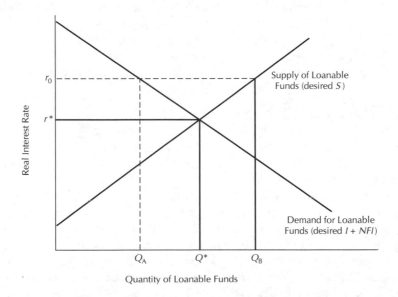

Figure 7–1. The Market for Loanable Funds

Points to Note About Figure 7-1

1. The real interest rate, not the nominal interest rate, is on the vertical axis because savers and borrowers care about the real return.

2. Higher interest rates make people save more. When the real interest rate goes up from r^* to r_0, desired savings go from Q^* up to Q_B.

3. Higher interest rates make borrowing more expensive, so borrowers borrow less. When the real rate increases from r^* to r_0, desired borrowing decreases from Q^* to Q_A.

4. The market clears at r^*; Q^* is the quantity of loanable funds borrowed and saved.

5. The supply of loanable funds is from domestic savers only.

6. The demand for loanable funds includes domestic borrowers (for I) and foreign borrowers (for NFI). Borrowers use the money for investment.

7. At $r^*, Q^* = S = I + NFI$.

Table 7–1 shows the factors shifting the demand and supply curves. The results of the last two rows (World confidence in domestic currency and Foreign investors want to invest more in U.S.) may seem illogical. To understand them, recall that for the U.S. net foreign investment:

$$NFI = \text{Investment Abroad by U.S. Citizens} - \text{Investment in the United States by Foreigners.}$$

An event that increases investment in U.S. assets by foreigners decreases NFI! For example, if foreigners become more confident in the U.S. currency (meaning they think its value will appreciate), they will invest more in the United States, decreasing NFI.

The supply curve is desired domestic private and public savings. When income increases, most people save more at any given interest rate, so the supply curve shifts right. When the government runs a surplus, this adds to public savings, so the supply curve shifts right. However, when the government runs a deficit, this decreases public savings, shifting the supply curve to the left.

The demand curve can be regarded as a menu of investment projects. It goes from the projects with the highest returns on the left to projects with lower and lower returns as we move to the right. Anything that increases what a given investment pays (such as lower taxes, reduced costs, higher prices, and new technology) shifts the demand curve to the right and vertically up. Anything that makes foreign investment relatively more attractive (such as higher returns abroad, greater confidence in the stability of foreign govenments, and greater confidence in foreign currency) also shifts this curve vertically up and to the right. On the other hand, anything that makes domestic investments appear more attractive to foreigners will shift this curve to the left. (Recall that *NFI* is the *difference* between domestic investment abroad and the investments by foreigners in the United States).

The loanable funds model presented here is a simplification. For example, we assume that all private borrowing is for investment in capital goods. However, many people borrow to finance current consumption. In addition, many businesses invest in marketing, research, and other forms of capital other than physical plant and equipment.

Table 7–1. Factors Shifting Demand and Supply Curves for Loanable Funds

Factor	Change in Factor	Effect on Supply
Supply Curve of Loanable Funds (Desired *S*)		
Income	Income up Income down	Shift right Shift left
Government surplus	Surplus up (deficit down) Surplus down (deficit up)	Shift right Shift left
Desire to save	Up Down	Shift right Shift left
Demand Curve for Loanable Funds (Desired *I* + *NFI*)		
Rate of return on domestic investments	Up Down	Shift right Shift left
Rate of return on foreign investments	Up Down	Shift right Shift left
World confidence in domestic currency	Up Down	Shift left Shift right
Foreign investors want to invest more in U.S.		Shift left (*NFI* down)

PROBLEM   How will the following events shift demand and supply for loanable funds? What will the effect be on the equilibrium real interest rate?

Event A: The government runs up a larger than expected deficit (private savings remain unaffected).

Event B: Rates of return in other countries unexpectedly decline.

Event C: The corporate income tax increases.

Event D: Savers want to save more than before.

Event E: Foreign investors suddenly begin to worry that the United States will devalue its currency (reducing the effective return on their U.S. investments).

SOLUTION   *Event A:* Shifts the supply curve to the left (as public savings become more negative), r^* up.

Event B: Shifts the demand curve to the left (*NFI* down), r^* down.

Event C: Shifts the demand curve to the left (as any given investment now pays a lower after-tax return than before), r^* down.

Event D: Shifts the supply curve to the right, r^* down.

Event E: Shifts the demand curve to the right (foreign investors in the U.S. economy reduce their investment, making *NFI* larger), r^* up.

YOU SHOULD REMEMBER

1. The loanable funds market brings together savers (private savings plus public savings) and borrowers (borrowing for domestic investments and net foreign investment). Savers supply loanable funds. Savers want to save more when the real interest rate increases. Borrowers demand loanable funds. Borrowers want to borrow more when the real interest rate decreases.

2. Net foreign investment equals the value of foreign investment by domestic citizens minus the value of domestic investment by foreigners.

3. The loanable funds market clears when $S = I + NFI$.

WILL SAVINGS BE INVESTED?

In classical economic models (those existing before 1930), interest rates would change until the loanable funds markets cleared and saving equaled investment. John Maynard Keynes disagreed. His interpretation of the Great Depression was that the uncertainty and fear created by the stock market crash caused people to want higher savings. The same uncertainty and fear also caused borrowers (investors) to want to borrow less. Interest rates could not fall enough to clear the loanable funds market. Instead, as people consumed less in order to save more, total spending fell, firms went bank-rupt, and investors wanted to borrow even less. The process fed on itself, reducing output, making people more fearful, and so forth. In his model, the loanable funds market cleared by having national income fall so much that savings decreased down to the small amount investors were willing to invest. In other words, falling income, not falling interest rates, clear the loanable funds market in a recession (at full employment, Keynes felt the classical model applied).

Neoclassical economics (the dominant view of economists) emphasizes how markets achieve equilibrium when people are rational, are well-informed, and seek to maximize their net benefit (consumers maximize util-ity, and producers maximize profits). In neoclassical models, the market works well when people have the right expectations about prices and inter-est rates. In these models, markets fail—causing recession or unhealthy expansion—only when people's expectations are wrong (for example, if unions expect higher prices next year than actually will exist and, as a result, set wages too high, then workers may lose jobs). In the neoclassical model, interest rates will let savings equal investment. However, incorrect expecta-tions in the neoclassical model (for example, investors being incorrectly pes-simistic) can still cause a recession.

The rational expectation model modifies the neoclassical model with peo-ple having expectations based on the best information available. Thus, in a rational expectation model, if people choose to save, they are planning to consume more in the future. Financial intermediaries (investors) know this and finance the capital construction producing the future consumption goods needed to pay off the savers. Unspent savings represent a profit opportunity for financial intermediaries and, assuming rational behavior, will be invested. In other words, savers demand more consumption in the future, and financial intermediaries supply it. Thus, the economy stays fully employed. The only time the economy will not be fully employed is when people make mistakes (for example, if investors make a mistake about future consumption). Even though one can predict that mistakes will occur, no rational expectation model can predict when or how mistakes will occur. Suppose such a model existed. Under rational expectations, people would use the model to avoid costly mistakes. Then, the model would be wrong in its predictions.

Neo-Keynesian economists assume rational expectations but also assume that institutional impediments discourage savings being invested. One major model is based on asymmetrical information. Suppose savers make more savings available to banks. Assume that banks, to lend the money, have to lend it to new borrowers at a lower rate. The asymmetrical information is that the banks do not know how risky the new borrowers are (but the bor-rowers do). Most likely, the lower rate will attract risky borrowers as well as worthy ones. However, the banks cannot tell which is which. The result may be that banks will not lend out the savings although worthy investments are available.

KNOW THE CONCEPTS

DO YOU KNOW THE BASICS?

1. What type of price does macroeconomics study and what type of price does microeconomics study?
2. What causes total spending to fall according to monetarists? Keynesians?
3. How is capital created?
4. What is the difference between financial and physical capital?
5. When General Motors sells a bond, is it demanding or supplying loanable funds?
6. If a firm hires more inputs and produces more output, does labor productivity increase?
7. A firm produces the same output as last year but with half the workers and other inputs. Is this technological progress?
8. If the interest rates go from 5 percent to 10 percent and the inflation rate goes from 2 percent to 9 percent, are savers better off?
9. If the government surplus increases, what happens to national savings?
10. Foreign investors want to invest more in the United States. What happens to the demand for loanable funds?

TERMS FOR STUDY

bond	natural resources
capital	nominal interest rate
economic growth	productivity
human capital	rational expectations economics
Keynesian economics	real interest rate
loanable funds	recession
macroeconomics	stock
monetarist economics	technological progress

PRACTICAL APPLICATION

1. How will the following events affect the real interest rate?

Event A: The government deficit grows larger.

Event B: Foreigners suddenly invest more in the United States.

Event C: Savers save less.

Event D: Computers increase the rate of return on all investments by one percentage point.

2. The market for loanable funds clears. The government deficit equals $50, domestic investment is $500, and net foreign investment is $100. What is private savings equal to? Public savings?

3. If the capital stock increases 10 percent next year and capital's income is 15 percent of *GDP*, then by how much will *GDP* grow? If the labor force increases by 10 percent and labor's share of national income is 80 percent, then how much will this increase the output?

4. A new discovery cuts in half the workers needed to produce any given quantity of output. This is true for the whole economy. What will happen to total output, assuming full employment? What is this called?

5. Suppose the government outlaws any worker from working more than 20 hours a week (perhaps to spread the work around). What would the effect be on per worker output (assuming the number of persons working stays the same)? What would the effect be on hourly productivity (assuming diminishing returns)?

6. Which of the macroeconomic schools would likely have written each of the following statements?

Statement A: "Recent optimism in the investment community leads me to predict an upturn in investment spending that will stimulate the economy."

Statement B: "The rapid expansion of the money supply will cause rapid inflation."

Statement C: "Businesses, anticipating that the government will attempt to stimulate aggregate spending, are prepared to raise prices. This will have the effect of neutralizing the impact of the government's stimulus package on the economy."

7. The following greatly simplified problem will give you a sense of rational expectations models. All households in an economy are exactly alike. All want the same consumption year after year and will save or lend to get this. Household income in year one is $40,000, is $50,000 in year two, then it goes to $40,000 in year three, back to $50,000 in year four, and so forth, cycling between $40,000 and $50,000. Assume the interest rate is zero (this is only to make the problem very simple) and households want to consume all of their average income. The only way households can lend or borrow money is from overseas. (Note that when household income is $X, each household produces $X worth of goods.)

    a. What will annual household consumption be?

    b. In good years, what do households do with their savings? How is this reflected in net exports per household?

    c. In bad years, how do households finance their consumption? How is this reflected in net exports per household?

8. Another characteristic of rational expectations economics is that people make good use of all information, including the information provided by economic models. Suppose I propose the following model: "In years divisible by 7, the economy will go into a recession." What is wrong with this model from the rational expectations point of view (assuming people can take steps to avoid the costs of a recession—for example, by lowering wages to prevent unemployment)?

9. Wal-Mart has been accused of causing the loss of jobs in the retail sector and lowering prices. If true, how does this affect economic growth?

10. Suppose that doubling of all inputs doubles output (this is called *constant returns to scale*). Suppose that population, capital, and human capital all double but that natural resources and technology stay the same. What will happen to output per person? What will happen to per capita income?

ANSWERS

DO YOU KNOW THE BASICS?

1. Macroeconomics studies the average price of all goods (for example, the consumer price index). Microeconomics studies the relative price of single goods, that is, the price of the good relative to price of all other goods. This is relevant to individual demanders.

2. According to monetarists, declines in the money supply cause total spending to fall. According to Keynesians, declines in some component of spending (usually investment or consumption spending) cause the decline in total spending.

3. Capital is created by savings. Consumers, by saving, free inputs to move from producing consumption goods to producing capital goods.

4. Physical capital is the actual structure and equipment used to produce goods and services. Financial capital is the ownership claims to the capital (in the case of stocks) or claims to a certain monetary amount of what the capital produces in the future (in the case of bonds).

5. General Motors is demanding loanable funds. It is borrowing money, and in the future, it will have to pay the money back with interest.

6. Not necessarily. Only if output increases relative to labor will productivity increase. For example, if output increases 10 percent and the firm hired 8 percent more labor hours, labor productivity would increase 2 percent. However, if output and labor both increased 10 percent, labor productivity would remain unchanged.

7. This is technological progress because output per unit input is now higher. The freed inputs can be employed to produce new output, raising total output.

8. Savers are worse off. Initially, their real rate of return was 3 percent (5 percent − 2 percent). Then the real rate of interest fell to 1 percent (10 percent − 9 percent).

9. National savings (which equal public savings plus private savings) will increase.

10. Net foreign investment will fall so the demand for loanable funds will fall. Recall that *NFI* equals the value of foreign assets bought by domestic citizens minus the value of domestic assets bought by foreign citizens. The latter is increasing so *NFI* is decreasing.

PRACTICAL APPLICATION

1. *Event A:* Supply of loanable funds (national savings) shifts left. Interest rates rise.

   Event B: *NFI* decreases. The demand curve of loanable funds shifts left. Interest rates fall.

   Event C: The supply curve of loanable funds shifts left. Interest rates rise.

   Event D: The demand curve of loanable funds shifts vertically up (by 1 percent) and shifts right. Interest rates rise (but by less than 1 percent).

2. Private savings equal $650. National savings equal $600.

3. Using the share multiplied by the increase formula, output will grow by 1.5 percent (= 0.15 × 10 percent). When labor grows 10 percent, the growth rate will increase by 8 percent (= 0.80 × 10 percent). The problem illustrates the point that growth in major inputs has more impact than growth in minor inputs.

4. If workers are fully employed, then output per worker, output per worker hour, and per capita income would all be doubled. This is called technological progress. While in the short run, technological progress sometimes causes people to lose jobs, in the long run, it increases income.

5. Labor input would be cut while other inputs would be unaffected (at least initially). Total output would fall and so would output per worker. On the other hand, due to the law of diminishing returns, output per work hour will increase. Therefore, output per hour will increase and hourly productivity will be higher. However, since output per worker is decreasing, per capita income will fall.

6. *Statement A:*　　　　Keynesian economist.

   Statement B:　　　　Monetarist economist.

   Statement C:　　　　Rational expectations economist.

7. **a.** $45,000 (equal to average income).

   b. In good years, each household produces (and earns) $50,000 but only wants to consume $45,000 of it. The $5,000 will be lent to foreigners, who in turn will use the money to buy the $5,000 in excess output from the nation. Net exports per household will equal $5,000.

   c. In bad years, each household produces (and earns) $40,000 but wants to consume $45,000. They borrow $5,000 from foreigners (or call back their loans from good years) and use the money to buy the extra $5,000 worth of goods needed to meet their goal of consuming $45,000 of consumption goods. Net exports per household will equal –$5,000.

8. If people know the prediction of the model and take steps to avoid the recession, then the model will no longer be true. Therefore, the model is inconsistent with rational expectations.

9. This increases economic growth and, in growth accounting, would appear as growth through technical change. Economic growth due to technical change means each worker is producing more output. This usually increases per capita income. Stated differently, economic growth in per capita output means each unit of output requires fewer workers (and capital) to produce. The loss of jobs in the retail sector would be consistent with Wal-Mart making retail workers more productive (just as increased productivity in the farm sector has led to the nation needing fewer farmers). This shows up in the form of lower prices such that those buying Wal-Mart products are getting a higher real wage than they otherwise would have received. Even though there are some losers from economic growth (namely those who lost their jobs), most people are better off because of economic growth (if you do not agree, imagine how well off you would be living with the technology from 1800).

10. If all inputs double except natural resources, output will go up but not quite double. Let L be labor hours and Q be output. Q/L is output per labor hour. The bottom term doubles but the top term does not quite double. The ratio will fall. Output per work hour, output per worker, and per capita income will all fall. Why has this not happened in the past? First, natural resources have become more available as new technologies for extracting them have become available. Second, technological progress has also occurred, more than offsetting the forces of population growth on per capita income.

8

AGGREGATE DEMAND AND SUPPLY: THE KEY TO MACRO-ECONOMICS

Macroeconomics is the study of the economy as a whole, including the causes of the business cycle, unemployment, and inflation. In order to focus on the main factors affecting inflation and unemployment, macroeconomics *aggregates* output (into *GDP*) and prices (into a price index, such as the *GDP* Deflator). Macroeconomics ignores the demand and supply for individual goods and instead looks at the demand and supply for *all* goods.

AGGREGATE DEMAND AND SUPPLY

The main tool of macroeconomics is the *aggregate* demand and supply diagram shown in Figure 8–1. This looks like the demand and supply diagram for an individual good such as those in Chapters 3 and 4, but the quantity on the horizontal axis is the total real output of the whole economy (or real *GNP*), which we label *Q*. Instead of price (i.e., relative price) on the vertical axis, we have the price level *P* (which is the *GDP* Deflator).

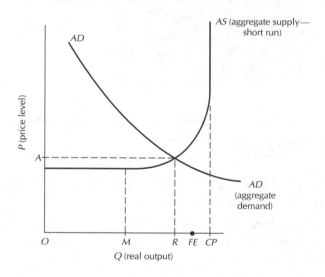

Figure 8–1. Effects of Aggregate Demand and Supply

AD is the aggregate demand curve. **Aggregate demand** is the total output demanded in an economy at a given price level (over a given period of time). It is the total amount of goods people *want* to buy, so it does *not* include the unwanted output that firms produce but cannot sell. (This is in contrast to the practice in national income accounting of counting this unwanted output as part of "sales.") Aggregate demand equals the sum of the consumption, investment, government, and net export expenditures that people want to make. The **aggregate demand curve** shows the aggregate quantity demanded goes up when the price level falls.

AS is the short-run aggregate supply curve. **Aggregate supply** is the total output produced in an economy at a given price level. The **short run** is that period of time over which nominal factor costs do not change (due, perhaps, to workers having long-term contracts that are not easy to change). Nominal factor costs include the dollar wages that workers are paid, the dollar cost of machinery and plants, and the dollar interest payments that firms have to pay on their borrowings to buy plant and equipment. The **short-**

run aggregate supply curve shows the aggregate quantity supplied rises when the price level rises.

In Figure 8–1, the economy will produce where aggregate demand intersects aggregate supply at price level A and output level R. At a *higher* price level, aggregate supply exceeds aggregate demand: Firms will not be able to sell all the goods they produce (and will experience a resulting increase in their inventories). Firms will respond by decreasing their output and lowering their price. At a *lower* price level than the equilibrium price level A, aggregate demand exceeds aggregate supply: Firms will find their inventories running low and will respond by raising prices and output. Only at price level A and output level R will the economy be in equilibrium.

YOU SHOULD REMEMBER

1. The *aggregate quantity demanded* increases when the price level falls and decreases when the price level rises.

2. In the short run, the *aggregate quantity supplied* increases when the price level rises and decreases when the price level falls. The short run is the period over which nominal factor costs (such as wages) do not change.

3. Equilibrium results when firms produce the quantity of goods and services people want (i.e., when the aggregate quantity supplied equals the aggregate quantity demanded).

AGGREGATE DEMAND

The aggregate demand curve shows that as the price level falls, total real demand increases. This result seems to follow from the law of demand, but in fact it does not. Recall that the law of demand states that the quantity of a good demanded goes up when the good's *relative* price falls. However, when the price level falls, such that all prices fall by the same percentage amount, the relative price of all goods remains *unchanged*! So why does a lower price *level* result in an increase in aggregate demand?

The reasons why aggregate demand goes up when the price level falls:

1. *Real Wealth Effect*. Some assets (including money) have a fixed nominal value. For example, a 100-dollar bill will always be worth 100 dollars. When prices fall, these assets can buy more and people feel wealthier. This makes people buy more goods. So aggregate demand goes up as the price level falls because:

Lower Prices→ Higher Real Value of Nominally Fixed Assets→
People Feel Wealthier→ Aggregate Demand Increases

2. *Real Interest Effect.* People usually want to keep enough money on hand
to buy a certain real quantity of goods and services (for example, a person might want enough cash to buy a week's worth of groceries). When
prices fall, people need less cash to buy the same real amount. Some of
their excess cash will be spent (this is part of the real-wealth effect). The
rest of the excess cash may be lent. More lending lowers interest rates,
which in turn spurs more investment spending, which in turn increases
aggregate demand. So aggregate demand goes up as the price level falls
because:

Lower Prices→ Excess Cash→ Some of Excess Cash Lent→
Interest Rates Reduced→ Investment Spending Increases→
Aggregate Demand Increases

3. *Foreign Trade Effect* (exchange rates inflexible). The exchange rate is
the rate at which a person can trade the currency of one country for the
currency of another (for example, 90 yen for one dollar). Suppose prices
fall in the United States and the U.S. exchange rate remains unchanged.
U.S. goods will now be relatively cheaper to citizens of other nations, and
they will buy more U.S. goods. U.S. exports will go up, increasing aggregate demand. So aggregate demand goes up as the price level falls
because:

Lower Prices→ U.S. Goods Cheaper in World Marketplace→
Foreigners Buy More U.S. Exports→ Aggregate Demand Increases

4. *Exchange Rate Effect* (when exchange rates are flexible). When lower
prices result in lower interest rates, the lower interest rates make U.S.
investments less attractive to foreign investors. They will need fewer dollars to buy U.S. investments with, so foreign demand for U.S. dollars will
fall. The dollar will be worth less. The exchange rate for the dollar will fall
(it will buy fewer units of foreign currency). Not only will the exchange
rate fall but the *real exchange rate* (the rate at which U.S. goods trade
for foreign goods) will fall as well. U.S. goods will be relatively cheap,
causing foreigners to buy more U.S. goods. Lower prices will cause
aggregate demand to rise because:

Lower Prices→ Lower Interest Rates→ U.S. Investments Less
Attractive to Foreigners→ Real Exchange Rate Falls→ Foreign
Demand for U.S. Goods Increases→ Aggregate Demand Increases

AGGREGATE SUPPLY (SHORT RUN)

The positive slope of an aggregate supply curve shows real output rising when prices rise. This reflects the fact that increases in aggregate spending usually result in higher levels of national output, at least initially. Economists are not sure exactly why this is so. Some of the theories as to why include:

1. *Sticky-Wage Theory.* Nominal wages are slow to adjust in the short run. One reason might be long-term labor contracts. If nominal (dollar) wages are fixed, then an increase in the price level means more profit for firms. Higher profits encourage firms to produce more. So the aggregate supply curve has a positive slope because:

> Higher Price Level→ Higher Profits Since Nominal
> Wages Fixed→ More Output Produced

2. *Sticky-Price Theory.* Recently, some economists have emphasized that prices may be slow to adjust. This may be due to the *menu cost* of changing prices. In addition, firms may be willing to suffer temporary losses by not raising prices in order to maintain or gain market share. In this case, think of the price level on the vertical axis as the *potential* price level that would exist if firms fully adjusted their prices. Now suppose an increase in aggregate demand increases this potential price level. If firms continue to sell their goods at an unchanged price, then they will sell more. Aggregate supply will increase, at least until prices adjust. In the short run, the aggregate supply curve has a positive slope because:

> Higher Potential Price Level (Aggregate Demand
> Increased)→ Firms Raise Output Instead of Raising
> Prices→ More Output Produced

3. *Misperception Theory.* Supply is a function of relative price: the price of the good relative to the price of inputs. If all prices go up equally—the price of goods and the price of inputs—the relative price of goods would be unchanged and supply would remain unchanged. However, if the price of a good goes up relative to the price of inputs, more of the good would be produced. An increase in all prices leaves output unchanged, but an increase in the relative price of a single good would increase its supply. In the misperception theory, a firm does not initially know if an increase in its price reflects an increase in all prices or in its relative price. As a result, when all prices rise, firms may initially respond by producing more output. The aggregate supply curve in this theory has a positive slope because:

Higher Potential Price Level (Due to an Increase in Aggregate
Demand)→ Confusion About the Increase in the Good's
Relative Price→ Output Increased

4. *Intertemporal Substitution Theory.* Workers (and other input suppliers) know that good times occur and that bad times occur. They are willing to work longer hours during the good times in order to save up for the bad times. Think of the price on the vertical axis as the potential (or long-run) price level. In this effect, aggregate demand goes up, potential price goes up, but actual prices stay the same (or rise less) as workers are willing to work longer hours to get ahead during good times. This effect allows supply to increase in the short run when aggregate demand increases. This theory and the misperception theory are often combined. The aggregate supply curve has a positive slope because:

Higher Potential Price Level (Due to an Increase in
Aggregate Demand)→ Labor (and Other Input) Supply
Increases to Take Advantage of Good Times→ Output Increases

The rest of this chapter will use *the sticky-wage theory.* It will construct and explain the shifts in the aggregate supply curve.

The aggregate supply curve is drawn as a horizontal line over a range of output that is far below the economy's capacity output (this range going from O to M in Figure 8–1). Over this range, there is no shortage of inputs, and firms can increase output without any increase in unit costs (the cost of each unit of output). However, as the economy begins to approach the capacity of what its plants and equipment can produce, it becomes harder and harder to produce extra output, and so unit costs start to rise. The aggregate supply then begins to rise as well, and it rises faster as the economy approaches its capacity (moving from M to CP). When the economy reaches its capacity output (CP in Figure 8–1), the aggregate supply curve becomes vertical since it is impossible to produce any more goods, no matter how high the price level. Because at full employment there is still unemployment, an economy's capacity output level (CP) is above the full-employment output level (FE).

YOU SHOULD REMEMBER

1. Aggregate demand goes up at lower prices because people holding money and bonds are then richer and so buy more.

2. In the short run, dollar factor costs are defined to be constant. So higher prices mean more profits and more output. However, as the economy approaches its capacity, unit costs rise and so it takes higher and higher prices to induce firms to produce more.

THE EFFECTS OF SHIFTS IN AGGREGATE DEMAND AND SUPPLY

• *SHIFTS IN AGGREGATE DEMAND*

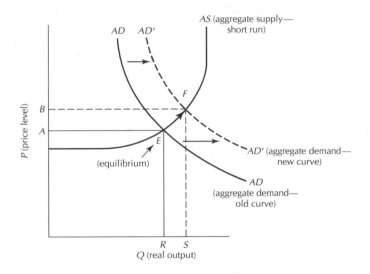

Figure 8–2. Effects of an Increase in Aggregate Demand

The effects of an *increase in aggregate demand* (from *AD* to *AD´*) are shown in Figure 8–2. Aggregate demand increases when, while holding the price level constant, people want to buy more (i.e., the aggregate demand curve shifts right). For example, business firms may want to spend more on capital goods. Equilibrium goes from Point *E* to Point *F*. The output level increases from *R* to *S*, and the price level increases from *A* to *B*. So prices and output will rise. How much prices and output will rise depends upon where the economy was initially on the aggregate supply curve. The closer the economy is to its capacity, the more prices will rise and the less output will rise for any given increase in aggregate demand.

The effects of a *decrease in aggregate demand* are shown in Figure 8–3. Aggregate demand decreases (i.e., the aggregate demand curve shifts left) when, while holding the price level constant, total real spending falls. For example, consumers may decide to buy fewer goods. As a consequence, equilibrium goes from Point *E* to Point *G*. The price level falls to *C*, and the output level falls to *T*. Note that prices and output both fall as a result of a decrease in aggregate demand. For example, from 1929 to 1933, prices fell about 20 percent, while output fell 30 percent.

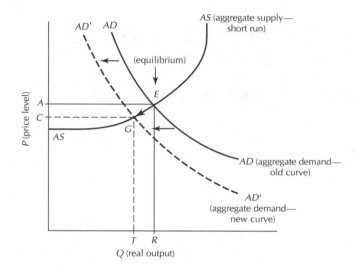

Figure 8–3. Effects of a Decrease in Aggregate Demand

Aggregate demand increases (shifts right) when, at any given price level, more is spent on U.S. goods. This could be caused by an increase in consumption spending (for example, if consumers feel more confident or wealthier), by an increase in investment spending (for example, if businesses feel more confident, if interest rates fall, or if favorable tax legislation is passed), by an increase in government spending, or by an increase in spending by the world on U.S. exports. It could also be caused by an increase in the money supply, which puts more money into people's hands to spend. Aggregate demand decreases (shifts left) when, at any given price level, less is spent on U.S. goods.

• *SHIFTS IN AGGREGATE SUPPLY*

The effects of an *increase in short-run aggregate supply* are shown in Figure 8–4. The price level falls from *A* to *D* while the output level increases from *R* to *U*. Equilibrium shifts from Point *E* to Point *K*. Output increases, and the price falls.

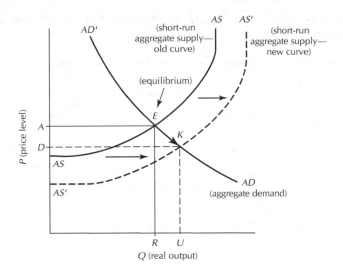

Figure 8–4. Effects of an Increase in Short-Run Aggregate Supply

Aggregate supply will increase (i.e., the aggregate supply curve will shift right) when (1) factor costs fall, (2) a decrease in taxes reduces production costs, or (3) improvements in technology reduce costs.

The effects of a *decrease in short-run aggregate supply* are shown in Figure 8–5. Aggregate supply decreases when, while holding prices constant, firms produce less. The aggregate supply curve shifts left. Equilibrium shifts from Point *E* to Point *H*, the price level rises from *A* to *J*, and the output level falls from *R* to *V*. Price rises and output falls. This undesirable mix of price increases and economic contraction is called **stagflation.** For example, in 1974–1975, real output fell by 5 percent while inflation soared above 12 percent.

YOU SHOULD REMEMBER

1. Shifts in aggregate demand are caused by changes in aggregate real spending, holding the price level constant.

2. Shifts in aggregate supply are caused by changes in factor costs and technology.

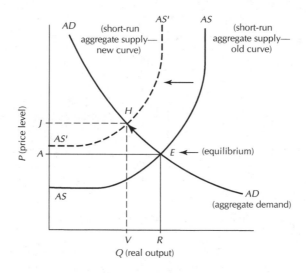

Figure 8–5. Effects of a Decrease in Short-Run Aggregate Supply

AGGREGATE SUPPLY (LONG RUN)

The **long run** is the period of time over which input costs, such as wages, are free to adjust. *Long run* (in macroeconomics) refers to the time it takes the economy to come to a complete full-employment equilibrium. In the long run, all contracts (such as those between employers and workers) can be rewritten so that contracted-for wages reflect the actual price level and so that any false expectations (about price level) that cause unemployment are eliminated. In the long run, workers will set their wages such that they will be fully employed. Thus, output will be at its full-employment level. In Figure 8–6, long-run output will be at *FE* (full employment) no matter what the price level. So we draw the **long-run aggregate supply curve** as a vertical line at *FE*.

The long-run price level will be determined by where the aggregate demand curve intersects the long-run aggregate supply curve (here, at price level B). At this price level, the economy will be at full employment. The level of unemployment that exists at full employment is called the **natural rate of unemployment.** If unemployment is above its natural rate, wages (and thus costs and prices) tend to fall. Alternatively, if unemployment is below its natural rate, wages (and thus costs and prices) tend to rise. Only at price level B (where AD intersects that long-run aggregate supply curve) will the economy be in a *long-run equilibrium*. Chapter 10 shows how the economy reaches full employment in the long run.

It is a basic axiom of macroeconomics that an equal percent increase in all prices (including incomes and costs) will not have any real effect on output or employment in the long run. To understand why, recall that a good's "price" is the good's relative price (its price divided by the prices of other goods). If all prices rise the same percent, the good's relative price stays unchanged, leaving the quantity of goods demanded and supplied unchanged. Also recall that a price to buyers is an income to sellers. Thus, when prices rise, incomes rise with it. When prices and income rise by the same percent, real income does not change. This is why, when aggregate demand goes up, it has no effect on real output in the long run. All it does is raise prices.

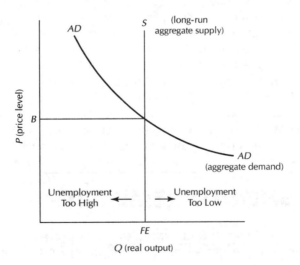

Figure 8–6. Effects of Long-Run Aggregate Supply

YOU SHOULD REMEMBER

In the long run, factor costs can change. Factor costs change so full employment is achieved. As a consequence, the long-run aggregate supply curve is a vertical line at the full-employment level of output.

HOW TO APPLY AGGREGATE DEMAND AND SUPPLY

When the aggregate demand and supply diagram shows prices falling (as in Figures 8–3 and 8–4), it is predicting that prices will be lower than they otherwise would have been. For inflationary times, this means it is predicting that the rate of inflation will fall (say, from 10 percent to 4 percent a year). This is called **disinflation.** If the price level actually falls, it is call deflation. When prices are shown to increase (as in Figures 8–2 and 8–5), it is predicting that the rate of inflation will increase (say, from 4 percent to 8 percent a year).

Similarly, when output is shown to increase (as in Figures 8–2 and 8–4), it is predicting that the growth rate of output will increase (say, from 2 percent to 4 percent a year). A decrease in output (as in Figures 8–3 and 8–5) predicts a decrease in the growth rate of output. A drop in the growth rate of output below its usual 3 percent growth rate is called a **growth recession** (e.g., if output grew at only 1 percent per year). However, when output falls for two consecutive quarters, it is called a **recession.** When output falls steeply for a prolonged period, the economy is in a **depression.**

YOU SHOULD REMEMBER

1. Aggregate demand and supply analysis predicts *changes* in the *rate* of price growth (i.e., in inflation) and in the rate of output growth.

2. Inflation is an increase in the price level. Disinflation is a decrease in the rate of inflation. Deflation is a fall in the price level.

3. A growth recession is when output grows at less than its potential (which is about 3 percent per year). A recession is when output falls for two consecutive quarters.

KNOW THE CONCEPTS

DO YOU KNOW THE BASICS?

1. On the aggregate demand and supply diagram (Figure 8–1), what do output and price represent?
2. How can the price level go up and yet the "price" of each good remain unchanged?
3. How does a lower price level increase the aggregate output demanded?
4. When prices are lower, total dollar spending may fall. Does this contradict the fact that lower prices increase aggregate demand?
5. Does output always go up when prices go up?
6. In the Great Depression, prices and output fell. What shift in aggregate demand and supply would best describe the cause of this event?
7. What changes in wages will cause the short-run aggregate supply curve to shift to the left?
8. How should the government shift the aggregate demand curve if it wants to raise output? What will happen to the price level?
9. How should the government shift the aggregate demand to reduce inflation? What will happen to output?
10. How will wages and other input costs tend to change when unemployment is above its natural rate?

TERMS FOR STUDY

aggregate demand
aggregate supply (long run)
aggregate supply (short run)
disinflation, deflation

natural rate of unemployment
recession, growth recession,
  depression
stagflation

PRACTICAL APPLICATION

1. Select from Figures 8–2 through 8–5 the figure that best reflects each of the following events:

    Event A: Workers cut wages and businesses cut prices. The falling prices encourage consumers to buy more.

    Event B: An improved world economy increases the demand by the rest of the world for U.S. exports.

Event C: Higher taxes cause business firms to cut back on output, leading to higher prices.

Event D: Falling stock market prices reduce the wealth of Americans. As a result, they spend less.

2. Chapter 5 states that total spending always equals total output in national income accounting. So how can aggregate demand be different from aggregate supply in this chapter?

3. Use the table below to answer the following questions.

   a. What is the equilibrium output and price level?

   b. Why will the economy not be in equilibrium at a price level of 160?

   c. Why will the economy not be in equilibrium at a price level of 100?

   d. Suppose money wages are fixed at $10 an hour. What is the real wage at each price level? How does this explain why aggregate supply increases in the short run when the price level is higher?

Price Level	Aggregate Demand	Aggregate Supply (Short Run)
80	2,400	1,500
100	2,200	1,750
120	2,000	2,000
140	1,800	2,200
160	1,600	2,300
180	1,400	2,350

4. An economy produces bread and clothing. In 2000, bread cost $2 a loaf and clothing cost $20 a unit. In the same year, the economy produced 20,000 loaves of bread and 5,000 units of clothing. In 2001, bread cost $1 and clothing $10.

   a. If in 2001 the same quantities of goods were produced, what happened to nominal income? To real income (letting 2000 be the base year)? To relative prices?

   b. Would output be the same in 2001 as it was in 2000 (assuming aggregate demand curve remains unchanged)?

5. In the Great Depression, both real *GDP* and prices fell by over 25 percent. Select from Figures 8–2 through 8–5 the most likely cause of the Great Depression.

6. A recent headline read "Renewed Growth Will Fuel More Inflation." This headline reflects a common notion in the press that a high growth rate in *GDP* causes higher inflation rates. Use the aggregate demand and supply diagram to show when this is incorrect.

7. If aggregate supply shifts to the right each year due to technological progress, then what must the government do to maintain a stable price level?

8. Many economic commentators state that "recessions cause prices to fall." If they mean that reduced output (i.e., reduced aggregate supply) *causes* lower prices, are they correct?

9. Both exports and imports have been rising as a percent of U.S. *GDP*, as the U.S. economy becomes more global. One consequence is that we will be more impacted by events in the rest of the world. Use Figures 8–2 through 8–5 to indicate how these international events might affect the United States. Briefly describe why.

    Event A: The European Community (EC) results in a wealthier Europe. This results in an increased demand for U.S. exports.

    Event B: The European Community erects high tariff barriers, reducing U.S. exports to Europe.

    Event C: The value of the dollar falls, with the result that U.S. goods are cheaper to the rest of the world.

    Event D: Oil prices go up, raising the cost of producing goods in the United States.

10. What will happen if, at the same time, workers demand and get higher wages and consumers decide to increase their real consumption spending?

ANSWERS

KNOW THE CONCEPTS

1. Output is real *GDP* and the price level is the *GDP* Deflator.

2. An increase in the price level that raises all prices an equal percentage amount will leave the *relative* price of all goods unchanged.

3. A lower price level increases the purchasing power of money, bonds, and other nominally fixed assets. This increase in wealth causes people to buy more goods.

4. Aggregate demand refers to total desired *real* spending. So it is possible for total dollar spending to fall, but if prices fall even more, real spending (i.e., the real quantity of goods bought) will go up.

5. No. If aggregate supply decreases, output can fall when prices rise.

6. A decrease in aggregate demand.

7. An increase in wages.

8. The government should increase aggregate demand so that the curve shifts right. Prices will rise.

9. To reduce inflation, the government should decrease aggregate demand so that the curve shifts left. Output will fall.

10. Wages and other factor costs will fall.

PRACTICAL APPLICATION

1. *Event A:*   Figure 8–4.
   Event B: Figure 8–2.
   Event C: Figure 8–5.
   Event D: Figure 8–3.

2. In national income accounting, unsold output is counted as a "sale" to the firm producing it. However, aggregate demand reflects the true quantity demanded and so excludes unsold and unwanted output.

3. **a.** Equilibrium output is 2,000 and price level 120.

   b. At 160, aggregate supply exceeds aggregate demand. Unsold output will cause firms to cut back on production and also to reduce prices in order to boost sales.

   c. At 100, aggregate demand exceeds aggregate supply. Inventories will be drawn down. Firms will increase output and raise prices.

   d. Real wages equal money wages/P, where P is the price index stated as a decimal. By starting at 80 ($P = .8$) and going down, real wages will be $12.50, $10.00, $8.33, $7.14, $6.25, and $5.56. As real wages fall, the real cost of producing output falls, so firms produce more at higher price levels.

4. **a.** In 2000, nominal income was $140,000. With the same output, 2001's nominal income was $70,000 but its real income was still $140,000 ($70,000/.050, where 0.50 is the 2001 price level since prices are one-half of what they were in 2000). Relative prices did not change. For example, the relative price of a loaf of bread was one-tenth of a unit of clothing in both 2000 and 2001.

   b. The lower price level in 2001 increased the real value of people's nominal assets, causing people to demand more. The economy will move down and to the right along its aggregate demand curve.

5. For output and prices to fall, aggregate demand has to fall, as in Figure 8–3.

6. As Figure 8–4 shows, an increase in output (growth) will cause inflation to decrease, not increase. So if the output growth is caused by an increase in aggregate supply, the headline is wrong. However, if the output growth is caused by an increase in aggregate demand (as in Figure

8–2), the higher output will be accompanied by higher inflation, and the headline will be correct. So it is important to know whether output is going up because of an increase in aggregate demand or in aggregate supply. This is the distinction that many economic commentators ignore.

7. If the government does nothing, then prices will fall when output grows (as in Figure 8–4). To keep prices stable, aggregate demand must be increased along with aggregate output (so both shift right by the same amount).

8. No. Reduced aggregate supply will increase the price level (as in Figure 8–5).

9. *Event A:*   Figure 8–2. Historically, as the rest of the world prospers, world spending on U.S. exports goes up, increasing aggregate demand.

   Event B: Figure 8–3. The prospect of protectionism in Europe could seriously hurt the United States.

   Event C: Figure 8–2. The lower value of the dollar ("a weaker dollar") results in more export sales, increasing aggregate demand.

   Event D: Figure 8–5. In the 1970s, higher oil prices resulted in stagflation: higher prices and lower output.

10. The price level will rise. The effect on output cannot be predicted without more information as to how much aggregate demand and supply shift.

9

AGGREGATE DEMAND IN THE PRIVATE SECTOR: THE KEYNESIAN MODEL

KEY TERMS

actual or realized investment total investment spending, including unsold output put into inventory.

consumption spending by households on consumption goods and services.

desired or planned investment total investment spending that businesses *want* to make. It does *not* include unwanted inventory accumulation.

equilibrium in aggregate demand when spending equals income.

marginal propensity to consume (*MPC*) additional consumption spending caused by one dollar being added to disposable income.

savings the unconsumed portion of disposable income.

spending multiplier the number by which an initial increase in spending must be multiplied to get the resulting change in total spending.

This chapter presents the basic Keynesian model. Keynesian economics is based upon the writings of John Maynard Keynes and emphasizes the importance of total spending in determining national income. We make the following assumptions to simplify matters. (Be sure to read assumption 4!)

1. The government and the rest of the world do not exist. So government spending, taxes, transfer payments, and net exports are all zero.

2. All savings are personal savings (i.e., there is no business saving). There is no depreciation.
Note: Assumptions 1 and 2 imply that $GDP = NNP = NI = PI = DI$.

3. Output is far below capacity such that it is on the horizontal section of the aggregate supply curve (see Figure 8–1, O to M). Thus, when aggregate demand goes up, the price level stays unchanged. As a consequence, all changes in spending and income are *changes in real income and spending*.

4. "Spending," "desired spending," and "planned spending" all refer to the same thing: the spending people *want* to do. Unlike national income accounting, we will *not* count unwanted and unsold output (that goes into inventories) as part of spending. Thus, while national income accounting defines spending so that total dollar spending always equals the value of output produced and the income earned, we will now define spending as desired spending. So it is now quite possible that (*desired*) spending equals neither the value of output produced nor the income earned.

THE BASIC KEYNESIAN MODEL

CONSUMPTION FUNCTION

Consumption is the spending on consumer goods over a given period (usually, a year). **Consumer goods** are goods and services that are consumed or used up within the year, such as food and electricity. (In practice, however, many goods counted as consumption goods last longer than a year, such as dresses, cars, and toasters.)

John Maynard Keynes made two key assumptions about what determines consumption spending:

Keynes' Assumptions on Consumption Spending

- *Assumption 1:* People base their consumption spending mainly on their *current* take-home pay (i.e., on disposable income, or *DI*).
- *Assumption 2:* When people get additional income, they do not spend it all.

Table 9–1 shows an example of a Keynesian consumption function. The **consumption function** shows the level of consumption at different levels of disposable income, holding constant the other determinants of consumption (discussed later in this chapter). In the **Keynesian consump-**

tion function, consumption goes up as *DI* goes up but not all of the additional income is consumed. In this example, each additional $1,000 in income adds $800 to consumption. The added consumption due to $1 more of income is the **marginal propensity to consume (*MPC*).** *MPC* equals the addition to consumption *divided* by the addition to disposable income that caused consumption to go up. In this case, *MPC* equals 0.8 ($800/$1,000).

Table 9–1. The Keynesian Consumption Function

Disposable Income (*DI*)	Consumption (*C*)	Savings (*S*)
$ 3,000	$3,400	–$ 400
4,000	4,200	–200
5,000	5,000	0
6,000	5,800	200
7,000	6,600	400
8,000	7,400	600
9,000	8,200	800
10,000	9,000	1,000

Savings is unconsumed income (disposable income minus consumption). At the "break-even" income of $5,000, savings are zero. Below $5,000, there is dissaving (or negative savings). To **dissave**—to consume more than is earned—people can borrow money or draw down their bank accounts. Above $5,000, savings are positive. Every $1,000 added to income adds $200 to savings. The **marginal propensity to save (*MPS*)** is the added savings *divided* by the added disposable income that caused savings to go up. In Table 9–1, *MPS* = 0.2 ($200/$1,000).

Since every added dollar of income is consumed or saved, we have:

$$MPC + MPS = 1.$$

Note that the **average propensity to consume (*APC*),** which is consumption divided by disposable income, does not have to equal the *MPC*. At *DI* = $10,000, for example, *C/DI* = 0.9 while *MPC* = 0.8.

Example: Using MPC

PROBLEM   If *MPC* = 0.75, how much will consumption increase when disposable income goes up by $10,000? What will happen to savings?

SOLUTION   Consumption will go up $7,500 (0.75 × $10,000), and savings will go up $2,500 (0.25 × $10,000).

Figure 9–1 shows both the consumption and savings curves from Table 9–1.

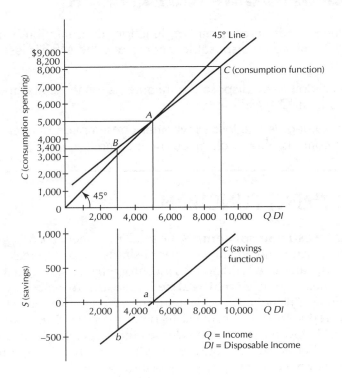

Figure 9–1. The Relationship of Consumption and Savings

The **45-degree line** in Figure 9–1 serves as a valuable reference line. All points on this line have the same value on the vertical and horizontal axes. So at Point *A*, consumption equals income (of $5,000). Since disposable income (*DI*) is on the horizontal axis, for any given level of disposable income, the 45-degree line tells us how far we have to go up vertically to find the same disposable income. For example, Point *B* is above the 45-degree line, so consumption ($3,400) is above income ($3,000). Point *C* is below this line, so consumption ($8,200) is below income ($9,000).

The savings curve is shown on the bottom graph. "Savings" is defined as the difference between income and consumption or the difference between the 45-degree line and consumption.

The slope of the consumption curve is the *MPC* and the slope of the savings curve is the *MPS*.

YOU SHOULD REMEMBER

1. In the Keynesian consumption function, consumption is mainly determined by disposable income and the *MPC* is less than one.

2. Every dollar of disposable income is either consumed or saved: *MPC* + *MPS* = 1.

3. The 45-degree line tells us whether consumption at each level of income is above, at, or below income.

INVESTMENT FUNCTION

Desired investment spending is the total investment spending on such items as new plants and equipment that businesses *want* to make. It does *not* include the unwanted additions to inventory that result when firms cannot sell all their output. **Actual realized investment** is the total investment spending (including unwanted inventory accumulation) and is the investment reported in the national income accounts. When we refer to "investment" below, we mean *desired* investment spending. Since we have assumed that businesses do not save, they must borrow from households the money they need to invest (e.g., by issuing bonds).

Keynes' Assumption on Investment Spending

* *Assumption:* While savings decisions are made by households, the decision to invest those savings is made independently by businesses such that there is no guarantee that businesses will automatically invest what households want to save.

Investment is usually considered by Keynesians to be fixed, no matter what the level of income (as at the left of Figure 9–2), or as increasing very little when income goes up (as at the right of Figure 9–2). In the right graph of Figure 9–2, when income increases from *Y1* to *Y2*, investment stays unchanged at *I0*. In the left graph of Figure 9–2, an increase in income from *Y1* to *Y2* increases investment spending from *I1* to *I2*.

Normally, economists assume that businesses produce what consumers want; e.g., if consumers want more toothbrushes, more toothbrushes will be produced. But this is not the case for the Keynesian investment function. When people save more, they are in effect demanding businesses to invest more, since savings represent a demand for greater consumption in the future, and investment is the way businesses produce the supply for this future demand. However, in the Keynesian investment function, businesses do not invest more when people save more.

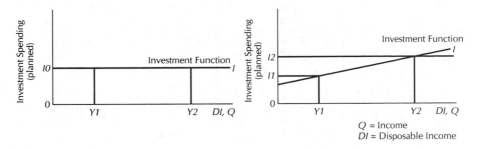

Figure 9–2. Effects of Increased Income on the Investment Function

EQUILIBRIUM IN AGGREGATE DEMAND

The spending side of the economy will be in **equilibrium** when income equals desired spending. Since we are assuming that the economy is on the flat section of the aggregate supply curve, changes in dollar spending will equal changes in real spending *and* output.

Table 9–2 presents the Keynesian consumption and investment functions for a simple economy. Disposable income (DI) (or simply income [Q] when there are no taxes) is in the first column. Consumption (C) is shown to be increasing with an *MPC* of 0.75. Investment (I) is "autonomous," i.e., income does not affect it. The investment spending we are talking about here is the desired or planned investment spending firms really want to make. It does not include unwanted changes in inventories. Total desired spending (D) is in the next column. The change in inventories (output – sales) is next. How producers will change their output given their current sales is shown in the last column.

When income is below $6,000, spending exceeds output, and businesses find their inventories unintentionally falling below the level they want to maintain. They will respond to the shortage of goods by increasing output. At an income of $3,000, for example, $3,000 is produced but $3,750 is spent. Businesses will respond by producing more. Note that realized investment (equal to $1,500 plus the change in inventory of –$750) equals savings ($750) but that desired (or planned) investment ($1,500) exceeds savings ($750 = $3,000 – $2,250). In this case, businesses want to invest more ($1,500) than what households want to save ($750).

Table 9–2. Reaching Equilibrium in Aggregate Demand

Q or DI Income	C	I	D (C + I)	Change in Inventories (Q – D)	Output Response by Businesses
$ 1,000	$ 750	$1,500	$2,250	– $1,250	Increase
2,000	1,500	1,500	3,000	– 1,000	Increase
3,000	2,250	1,500	3,750	– 750	Increase
4,000	3,000	1,500	4,500	– 500	Increase
5,000	3,750	1,500	5,250	– 250	Increase
6,000	4,500	1,500	6,000	0	NO CHANGE
7,000	5,250	1,500	6,750	+ 250	Decrease
8,000	6,000	1,500	7,500	+ 500	Decrease
9,000	6,750	1,500	8,250	+ 750	Decrease
10,000	7,500	1,500	9,000	+ 1,000	Decrease
11,000	8,250	1,500	9,750	+ 1,250	Decrease

C = Consumption   DI = Disposable Income   I = Investment
D = Spending   Q = Income

When income is above $6,000, output exceeds spending, and businesses will find their inventories unintentionally rising above the level they want to maintain. They will respond to the surplus of goods by decreasing output. For example, when Q equals $11,000, spending equals $9,750. Realized investment (equal to $1,500 plus the increase in inventory of $1,250) equals savings ($2,750 = $11,000 – $8,250), but savings ($2,750) exceeds desired investment ($1,500). In this case, businesses want to invest less ($1,500) than what households want to save ($2,750).

When income equals $6,000, the economy is in equilibrium. Spending ($6,000) equals income. Only in equilibrium do savings equal desired investment (in this case, each equals $1,500). There is no unintended change in inventories, nor are there any shortages or surpluses of goods.

Figure 9–3 illustrates Table 9–2. Figure 9–3 is referred to as the **income-expenditure diagram** (or the output-expenditure diagram). Curve D is the **total spending curve**; it shows the total *desired* spending (consumption plus desired investment spending) at each level of income. This curve is derived by adding the consumption and investment spending at each level of income.

YOU SHOULD REMEMBER

1. When desired spending exceeds income, inventories fall and firms respond by producing more. When income exceeds spending, inventories rise and firms cut back on output. Only when income equals spending will output remain unchanged (i.e., equilibrium will be reached).

2. At all income levels, savings always equal realized investment. Only at equilibrium do savings equal planned or desired investment.

3. In the income-expenditure diagram, equilibrium occurs where the total spending curve crosses the 45-degree line (where spending equals income).

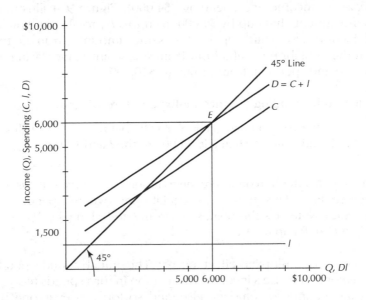

Figure 9–3. Income-Expenditure Diagram Showing Equilibrium: Spending Equaling Income

Equilibrium occurs when total spending equals income *or* where the total spending curve D intersects the 45-degree line (at Point E). (Recall that the 45-degree line tells us how far up we must go to have the same number that is on the horizontal axis. So when D crosses the 45-degree line at Point E,

income equals spending.) To the right of Point *E*, the economy has inadequate demand to support its income. To the left of Point *E* is excess demand.

APPLYING THE KEYNESIAN MODEL
SHIFTS IN INVESTMENT

To show the effect of an increase in investment spending, go back to Table
9–2 and increase investment spending to $2,500 at each level of income.
How will this affect *equilibrium* income? First, we can see that at each level
of income, total spending (*D*) goes up $1,000. Now, *equilibrium* total
spending will equal income at $10,000. (Be sure you verify this by rewriting
the *D* column.) So an increase in investment spending of $1,000 increases
income and total spending by $4,000. This illustrates the **spending multi-
plier** effect. In this case, the spending multiplier is 4: it equals the amount
by which the initial increase in spending ($1,000) has to be multiplied to get
the increase in income and spending ($4,000). Figure 9–4 illustrates this
case. As investment shifts up by $1,000 from *I* to *I´*, total spending at each
level of income also shifts up by the same amount (from *D* to *D´*).
However, the equilibrium shifts from Point *E* to Point *F*, increasing equilibrium income and spending from $6,000 to $10,000.

Hints for Understanding the Income-Expenditure Diagram

1. Be sure that you compare Table 9–2 with Figure 9–4. This will give you
   the *I*, *C*, and *D* lines. Then add $1,000 to the *I* and *D* lines to get *I´* and
   D´.

2. Focus your attention on where the total spending curve *D* crosses the 45-
   degree line. This represents equilibrium (where spending equals
   income). Note how this point shifts from *E* to *F* along the 45-degree line
   when *D* shifts up to *D´*.

Why does this multiplier effect occur? The initial added spending is
received as someone else's income. This person in turn spends more, which
again means income to someone else, and so forth. If everyone has the
same *MPC*, then each added dollar of spending will eventually result in an
increase in total spending according to this formula:

$$\text{Spending Multiplier} = 1/(1 - MPC)$$

Table 9–3. The Spending Multiplier Effect

"Round"	Received Income	Spending	
1	—	$1,000	Autonomous Spending
2	$1,000	$800	Induced Spending
3	$800	$640	Induced Spending
4	$640	$512	Induced Spending
⋮	⋮	⋮	⋮
Sum of Remaining Rounds	$2,560	$2,048	Induced Spending
Total	$5,000	$5,000	

Table 9–3 illustrates the case for an *MPC* of 0.8. The multiplier is 5 (1/.2), so an increase in investment spending of $1,000 results in an eventual increase in total spending of $5,000. In the first round, $1,000 is spent. In the second round, 80 percent of the $1,000 in added income is spent, so $800 is spent and then received as income. Then $560 is spent and earned, and so forth. The sum of the infinite series of $1,000 times $(1 + .8 + .8^2 + ...)$ is $1,000/(1 − .8) (which equals $1,000/.2, or $5,000).

A major source of confusion usually arises at this point. It involves the failure to distinguish between (1) the initial shift in spending that occurs at a given level of income (which economists call the change in autonomous spending) and (2) the secondary consumption respending caused by the change in autonomous spending (which economists call the induced change in spending). In the multiplier formula, the total change in spending is divided by the change in autonomous spending (i.e., $5,000 is divided by $1,000). In general, we have for any increase in autonomous spending:

$$\text{Change in National Income} = \frac{\text{Spending}}{\text{Multiplier}} \times \frac{\text{Increase in Autonomous}}{\text{Spending}}$$

In terms of Figure 9–4, the increase in autonomous spending equals the *vertical* shift in the total spending line (*D*). The resulting increase in equilibrium spending and income is the *horizontal* shift in equilibrium income (where *D* intersects the 45-degree line). The multiplier is the ratio of the horizontal shift over the vertical shift.

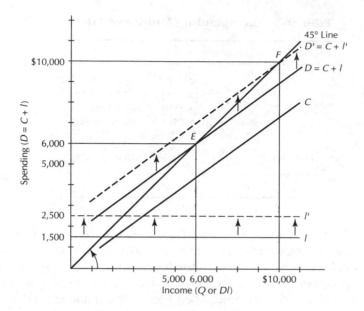

Figure 9–4. The Spending Multiplier Effect Showing the Outcome of Increased Investment

---

YOU SHOULD REMEMBER

1. An increase in autonomous spending is the increase in spending (holding income constant).

2. An increase in autonomous spending increases equilibrium income by some multiple of itself. This multiplier process occurs because the initial addition to spending becomes income, part of which is spent and earned and then spent again, and so forth.

3. The spending multiplier equals the total change in spending (or income) divided by the change in autonomous spending. In our simple case, it equals $1/(1 - MPC)$.

Example: Calculating the Effects of Changes in Investment Spending

PROBLEM   Businesses become more optimistic about the future and increase their desired investment spending by $5 billion. If the *MPC* is 0.9, by how much will equilibrium income increase?

SOLUTION   The spending multiplier is 10 (1/0.1). So the $5 billion increase in investment spending increases national equilibrium income by $50 billion (10 × $5 billion).

Example: Using the Spending Multiplier

PROBLEM   The economy is in equilibrium at an income of $200 billion. At this level of income, households suddenly decide to increase their consumption spending by $10 billion. If the *MPC* is 0.8, how much will equilibrium national income increase? What is the change in autonomous consumption spending? What is the induced increase in consumption spending?

SOLUTION   The increase in autonomous consumption spending is $10 billion. Since the spending multiplier is 5 (1/0.2), equilibrium national income will increase by $50 billion. Since investment spending in this example does not change, spending and thus total autonomous consumption spending goes up $50 billion. The induced increase in consumption spending (caused by the multiplier process) is $40 billion (change in induced consumption = *MPC* × change in equilibrium income, or 0.8 × $50 billion).

DETERMINANTS OF CONSUMPTION

The following are variables (other than disposable income) that affect the level of consumption spending at any given income level.

1. *Wealth:* **Wealth** is the net value of all the assets that a person owns (including the value of the person's skills, i.e., the value of all future earnings). When income is held constant, wealthier persons consume more. All of the determinants below affect consumption because they affect wealth.

2. *Price Level:* A lower price level makes people wealthier because their *real* money holdings are now worth more, and so they consume more. A major confusion occurs at this point between real consumption (which increases when the price level falls) and nominal or dollar consumption spending (which falls at a lower price level). The income-expenditure diagram, the consumption function, and the total spending curve are all in *real terms*. So a lower price level shifts them *up*, with a resulting increase in output and real spending.

   The price level affects debtors and lenders differently. Suppose you borrow $1,000 and agree to pay back $1,100 next year. If the price level stays the same, you owe $1,100 in real dollars (that is, in real consumption given up next year to pay back the debt). However, if the price level goes up 10 percent, you will have to pay back only $1,000 in real dollars. The higher price level makes you, the debtor, better off, and so you can and probably will consume more. However, it makes the lenders worse off, and they probably will consume less.

3. *Future Income Prospects:* When people expect to earn more in the future, they are likely to consume more in the present. This is the fundamental idea behind the **permanent-income hypothesis. Permanent income** is one's expected average future earnings. The permanent-income hypothesis assumes that a person's consumption spending will be a constant fraction of the person's permanent income. The **life cycle model of consumption** modifies this basic idea by taking into account people's ages, when they expect to retire, and how many retirement years they expect to have. For example, older workers nearing retirement typically save more of their income.

A major implication of the permanent-income hypothesis is that consumption will increase very little (if at all) when an increase in income is expected to last only a short time. Thus, it would follow that a one-year tax rebate, for example, could not stimulate consumption spending very much (as in fact it did not in 1975).

DETERMINANTS OF INVESTMENT

Some of the main variables that affect investment spending:

1. *Future Expected Profits:* When businesses expect future profits to be higher, they are willing to invest more.

2. *The Real Interest Rate:* Businesses usually borrow to finance their investment spending. The real interest rate reflects the real cost of this borrowing. The higher the real borrowing cost, the lower investment spending will be.

3. *Optimism About the Future:* When businesses are optimistic about the future, they speed up their investment spending. And when they are pessimistic, they postpone investments.

4. *The Accelerator Effect:* Capital produces goods and services (Q). So the demand for new capital depends upon *new* Q, i.e., the increase in Q. Therefore, changes in output can increase investment. This is termed the accelerator effect. (See Practical Application, Question 8.)

5. *The State of the Capital Stock:* During a recession, capital improvements and additions are postponed. Once the recession is over, they are speeded up. Thus the state of the capital stock can affect how much new investment will be needed.

FACTORS SHIFTING THE TOTAL SPENDING CURVE

Any factor that increases spending at a given level of income will shift the total spending curve, which in turn will increase equilibrium spending and income. Table 9–4 summarizes these factors.

Table 9–4. Factors Shifting The Total Spending Curve

Factor	Change in Factor	Shift in Total Spending Curve
Affecting Consumption		
Wealth	Up	Up
	Down	Down
Price Level	Up	Down
	Down	Up
Permanent	Up	Up
Income	Down	Down
Affecting Investment		
Future	Up	Up
Profits	Down	Down
Real	Up	Down
Interest	Down	Up
Rate		
Optimism	Up	Up
	Down	Down

PLOTTING AGGREGATE DEMAND

The income-expenditure diagram (Figure 9–5) can be used to derive the aggregate demand curve (which relates the price level to aggregate demand) in five steps:

- **Step 1:** Start out with Price Level –0 and show the initial equilibrium in the income-expenditure diagram. The left panel of Figure 9–5 shows that the economy initially is in equilibrium at Price Level –0, with the total spending curve D (Price Level –0) crossing the 45-degree line at Point E and output level Q.

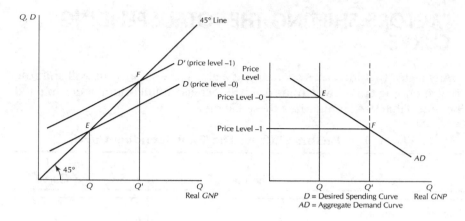

Figure 9–5. Plotting Aggregate Demand

- **Step 2:** Plot the equilibrium output Q and Price Level –0 as Point E in the right panel. This is a point on the aggregate demand curve.
- **Step 3:** Show the effects of a *lower price level* in the income-expenditure diagram. Let the price level fall to Price Level –1 (exactly why the price level is falling does not matter at this point). Due to the real balance effect, the total spending curve will shift upward as shown in the panel on the left as the total spending curve D (Price Level –1). The new equilibrium is at Point F with output at level Q'.
- **Step 4:** Plot the new Price Level –1 and output Q' in the panel on the right as Point F. This gives us a second point on the aggregate demand curve.
- **Step 5:** Continue changing the price level, which in turn changes the total spending curve, which in turn changes the equilibrium level of output. This output, when plotted with the price level, gives the aggregate demand curve AD. Thus, along the AD curve, income equals spending.

THE KEYNESIAN MODEL

Keynesians focus on total spending and the willingness of people to spend. When you read an economic forecast emphasizing how different groups—consumers, investors, and governments—will be spending, you most likely are reading a Keynesian forecast. Even though the multiplier process as taught in this chapter is very mechanical, the model captures a key feature of the Keynesian model: how changes in the national mood can reinforce itself. If the public becomes pessimistic and cuts back on spending, this in turn could cause a loss of jobs and make people even more pessimistic. Left unchecked, this could lead to a recession. Similarly, if the public becomes optimistic and increases spending, this in turn could cause an increase in jobs, and people could become even more optimistic. Left unchecked, it could lead to wasteful investments and a future downturn in the economy if and when the stock market crashes.

KNOW THE CONCEPTS

DO YOU KNOW THE BASICS?

1. In the Keynesian consumption function, if people receive $1,000 in additional income, will they increase their consumption spending by $1,000, more than $1,000, or less than $1,000?

2. When the economy is in equilibrium, how are spending and income related? Investment and savings?

3. What does the 45-degree line represent? How does it help you find equilibrium?

4. What is the difference between a change in autonomous spending and an induced change in spending?

5. How can spending go up if the price level falls?

6. When people save more, why do investors not invest the added savings in the Keynesian model?

7. What is the main variable that changes in the Keynesian model to ensure that the economy reaches equilibrium?

8. How will an increase in wealth shift the total spending curve?

9. How will an increase in the real interest rate shift the total spending curve?

10. How will an increase in the price level shift the total spending curve?

TERMS FOR STUDY

autonomous changes in spending
consumption function
desired investment, actual
    investment
equilibrium
induced changes in spending
inventory changes

marginal propensity to
    consume, to save
permanent income
savings
spending multiplier
wealth

PRACTICAL APPLICATION

1. Use the following table to answer these questions:
   a. What is the equilibrium level of income?
   b. What is the *MPC*? The *MPS*?
   c. If $10,000 of goods are produced, what will happen to inventories? What is actual investment? How is actual investment related to desired investment and savings?
   d. Answer (c) again for $15,000.
   e. If investment spending goes up by $100, how much will equilibrium income go up? What is the multiplier?
   f. If, instead, at all levels of *Q*, consumption spending goes up by $100, how much will equilibrium income go up? What is the multiplier? How much will consumption spending go up?

Income (Q)	Consumption (C)	Desired Investment (I)
$10,000	$ 8,300	$2,000
11,000	9,200	2,000
12,000	10,100	2,000
13,000	11,000	2,000
14,000	11,900	2,000
15,000	12,800	2,000

2. Fill in the blanks in the following table:

MPC	Multiplier	Change in Q Caused by Autonomous Increase of Spending by $1,000
0.9	___	___
	5	___
0.75	___	___
	___	$2,500
	2	___
0.25	___	___

3. If desired investment spending is $2,000 no matter what output is, what *must* savings be when the economy is in equilibrium? What must output be if the marginal *and* average propensity to consume is 0.80 (that is, people save 20 percent of their income no matter what their level of income is)?

4. How will the following events affect *real* consumption spending?

   Event A: A rise in the general price level.

   Event B: The real values of homes increase.

   Event C: Taxes are increased.

5. Other things being equal, in which case would investment spending be highest?

Case	Nominal Interest Rate	Expected Rate of Inflation
A	5	0
B	10	8
C	9	3
D	20	15

6. Suppose the *MPC* is 0.6. If at each level of income, people want to consume $2,000 more, how will income change? How will consumption change (break *C*'s change into its initial autonomous increase and the induced secondary consumption respending)? Assume *I* is fixed.

7. Suppose the *MPC* is 0.75. By how much must investment spending increase for *GDP* to go up $50 billion?

8. This question illustrates the accelerator effect. Let *WQ* equal the number of widgets consumed in a year. Every 1,000 widgets require a widget-making machine to produce them. Let *WMMQ* be the number of machines. These machines are well built and last forever. Fill in the following table, and explain how the table illustrates the accelerator effect.

Year	WQ	WMMQ	New Machines Built
1	20,000	20	0
2	22,000	22	2
3	25,000		
4	29,000		
5	30,000		
6	30,000		

9. This question explores how international trade affects the multiplier. Assume initially that a country is isolated from the world and its *MPC* is 0.8. What is the multiplier? Now assume it opens up its borders and people still spend 80¢ of every new dollar earned on consumption. However, 50¢ is spent on domestically produced consumption goods and 30¢ on imported consumption goods. What is the multiplier now?

10. Keynes assumed that when interest rates are very low, people do not care whether their savings are invested (and earning interest) or kept in cash. This problem illustrates what happens if this is not true. Suppose an economy is in equilibrium at $Q = \$10,000$. At this income, people want to hold $1,000 in cash, no more and no less. $MPC = 0.8$. What will happen if planned investment spending increases by $100?

ANSWERS

KNOW THE CONCEPTS

1. Less than $1,000, since $MPC < 1$.
2. Spending = Income and Investment = Savings.
3. The set of points at which the values on the vertical and horizontal axes are equal. Since income is on the horizontal axis and spending is on the vertical axis, it crosses the point on the total spending curve at which spending equals income.
4. A change in autonomous spending is the change in spending if income does not change. Induced changes in spending occur because income changes.
5. When the price level falls, the real balance effect causes an increase in *real* spending. So even if nominal spending falls (such that fewer dollars are spent), more real dollars will be spent.
6. Investors may be uncertain about the future of the economy and not want to invest more, even if interest rates are low. In an extreme case, investment spending is autonomous and totally unresponsive to changes in the interest rate. The basic insight of Keynes is that the same uncertainty causing households to save *more* may also cause investors to invest *less*. The second insight states that when desired savings exceed investment, equality is achieved by reducing national income, which, in turn, reduces desired savings (this is the process he believed to cause the Great Depression).
7. Income (and output). Keynes assumed that businesses facing inadequate demand would reduce their output and employment (and thus reduce the income they pay out) instead of reducing their prices.
8. The total spending curve will shift up and to the left.
9. Investment spending will fall. The total spending curve will shift down and to the right.
10. The real balance effect will reduce real consumption spending. The total spending curve will shift down and to the right.

PRACTICAL APPLICATION

1. a. $13,000 (where $Q = C + I$).

   b. $MPC = 0.9$. $MPS = 0.1$.

   c. Inventories will fall by $300 as spending ($10,300) exceeds output ($10,000). Actual investment ($1,700) equals investment spending ($2,000) plus the change in inventories (–$300). This equals savings ($1,700). However, actual investment falls short of desired investment savings. The economy will tend to expand.

   d. Inventories will rise by $200 as output ($15,000) exceeds spending ($14,800) by $200. Actual investment equals $2,200. It equals savings but exceeds desired investment. The economy will tend to contract.

   e. Equilibrium income will go up by $1,000. Now, $C + I$ equals Q at $14,000, where $I = \$2,100$ and $C = \$11,900$. The multiplier is 10 (= $1/(1 - MPC) = 1/0.1$).

   f. Equilibrium income will go up by $1,000 as in (e), with a multiplier of 10. Consumption spending will be $12,000, an increase of $1,000. $100 of this increase is the autonomous increase in consumption; the other $900 is induced by the $1,000 increase in income. In both (e) and (f), in terms of Figure 9–4, the total spending line shifts up by $100 and equilibrium shifts right by $1,000.

2.

0.9	10	$10,000
0.8	5	$ 5,000
0.75	4	$ 4,000
0.6	2.5	$ 2,500
0.5	2	$ 2,000
0.25	1.333	$ 1,333

3. In equilibrium, $I = S$, so savings must equal $2,000. In the Keynesian model, income will go up or down until savings equals investment. When people save 20 percent of their income, income must equal $10,000.

4. *Event A:* Decreases consumption spending by reducing the real value of money holdings.

   Event B: Increases consumption spending by increasing wealth.

   Event C: Decreases consumption spending by decreasing disposable income.

5. Case B, where the real interest rate (i.e., the real borrowing cost) is lowest (only 2 percent).

6. The multiplier is 1/0.4 (or 2.5), so income goes up by $5,000. Total consumption goes up by $5,000. This is the sum of the $2,000 initial autonomous increase and the induced $3,000 consumption respending (*MPC* times increase in income).

7. The multiplier is 4 (1./0.25). So 4 times the increase in *I* should equal $50 billion. The increase in *I* needed is $12.5 billion.

8.

Year	WQ	WMMQ	New Machines Built
1	20,000	20	0
2	22,000	22	2
3	25,000	25	3
4	29,000	29	4
5	30,000	30	1
6	30,000	30	0

The demand for *new* machines (i.e., investment demand) depends on the *change* in widget demand, not the level of widget demand. So even though widget demand does not decline, the demand for new widget-making machines falls when widget demand levels off. For the economy, the accelerator effect states that investment spending goes up when consumption spending accelerates and falls when consumption spending decelerates and levels off.

9. International trade tends to reduce the multiplier. In this case, it goes from 5 (= 1/.2) to 2 (= 1/.5).

10. We answer this question by asking how businesses can get the $100 when income is still equal to $10,000. Since the economy is at equilibrium, all savings are invested. The only source of cash is from money holdings, but by assumption, people will not reduce (or lend out) these holdings. So businesses will be trying to borrow more than people want to lend them. The interest rate will go up, causing businesses to reduce their planned investment spending back to its original level. The actual multiplier is 0, not 5 as it would be in the Keynesian model.

10

AGGREGATE SUPPLY AND GETTING TO FULL EMPLOYMENT

KEY TERMS

***GDP* gap** gap between actual output and potential output. When output is above its potential level, there is an "inflationary" or "expansionary" gap; when it is below, there is a "recessionary" or "contractionary" gap.

potential real *GDP* the level of *GDP* that can be produced when all resources are fully employed, such that demand and supply for labor (and other factors) are equal, there being neither a shortage nor a surplus of workers. Also called the "full-employment level of output."

self-correcting mechanism the means by which an economy gets to its potential level without governmental intervention.

Chapter 9 showed you how to construct the *aggregate **demand** curve*. Now we will construct the *aggregate **supply** curve* to show how the economy gets to full employment and its potential level. First, a short review.

1. *Aggregate demand* is the total output demanded. Along the aggregate demand curve, spending equals income. Aggregate demand is higher at lower price levels.

2. *Aggregate supply* is the total output supplied. In the short run, factor costs (especially wages) are fixed in money terms. A higher price level causes firms to produce more: The short-run aggregate supply is larger at higher prices. In the long run, factor costs adjust freely until the economy is at full employment and at potential real *GDP*.

CONSTRUCTING THE AGGREGATE SUPPLY CURVE TO GET TO FULL EMPLOYMENT

LONG-RUN EQUILIBRIUM

Figure 10–1 shows the economy at its **long-run equilibrium** level. This is where the economy, left undisturbed, will eventually go. Actual *GDP* is at **potential real** *GDP* or its full-employment level (*FE* in Figure 10–1). Potential *GDP* is the level of output the economy can produce given its resources, institutions, and laws. When the economy is producing at its potential level, workers are getting the wages they expected, investors are getting the returns they expected, and job searchers (the unemployed) are finding jobs that meet what they expected. "Expected" wages, returns, and jobs do not mean high wages, good returns, or great jobs. Instead, it means that people are getting what is reasonable to expect given what the economy is currently capable of offering. For example, some nations where unions are very powerful have a high number of people out of work. Yet such economies could be producing at their potential full-employment *GDP* if employers are fully employing all the workers at the union's high wage and unions are setting wages so they are getting the high real wage level they desire.

First look at the top panel. Equilibrium is at Point *E*, with output at *FE* (its full-employment level). The short-run aggregate supply curve (*AS*), the long-run aggregate supply curve (*S*–Long Run), and the aggregate demand curve (*AD*) all intersect at Point *E*. The *AS* curve is drawn with costs fixed at the level consistent with price level *A*.

The bottom panel shows the spending side of the economy (from Chapter 9). The total spending curve (*D*) is constructed assuming the price level is at *A* (in the top panel). Total spending equals income at point *E′* on the 45-degree line at the potential, full-employment level of output. *E′* plots into the top panel at Point *E′* on the *AD* curve.

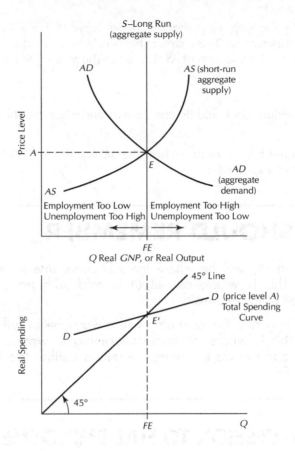

Figure 10–1. An Economy at Full Employment

Three Conditions for Full-Employment Equilibrium

1. *Spending equals income.* This is shown in the bottom panel, where D, the total spending curve, crosses the 45-degree line at point E´. *All* points on the aggregate demand curve (AD) satisfy this condition.

2. *All output is bought.* This is shown in the top panel by the intersection of the short-run aggregate supply curve (AS) and the aggregate demand curve (AD).

3. There is *full employment,* and the economy is at *potential real GDP.* Workers are fully employed in the sense that the demand for workers equals the supply of workers. Unemployment is neither too high nor too low but at its natural level consistent with the turnover that is normal in a growing and changing economy. The economy will always be at the point at which the AS and AD curves intersect. However, this need not be at full employment! Only if they intersect at potential GDP (FE), as

shown by the long-run aggregate supply curve (S–Long Run), will there be full employment. This chapter shows how and why the *AS* curve shifts to move the intersection of *AS* and *AD* to the *S*–Long Run curve.

Study Hint

1. Redraw Figure 10–1, and determine why and where all three conditions are met.

2. Go back to Chapter 9 and see how the *AD* line in the right-hand panel of Figure 9–5 was derived.

YOU SHOULD REMEMBER

1. The economy will be where the *AD* curve intersects the *AS* curve. This is where all output is sold with no unwanted changes in inventories.

2. In the long run, the economy will always be at full employment. This is where all workers wanting to work at current wages can get work. Unemployment is neither too high nor low at *FE*.

FROM RECESSION TO FULL EMPLOYMENT

What happens when *AD* and *AS* curves intersect at a level of output other than the full-employment level? Basically, because condition 3 is *not* satisfied, wages and other factor costs change to shift the *AS* curve toward full employment.

Suppose the economy is in a recession. How can the economy get back to full employment? Figure 10–2 shows an economy in a recession. The economy will always be where the *AD* curve intersects the *AS* curve: at Point *F*, with prices at level *B* and output at level *R*. At price level *B*, aggregate demand equals *R*, as shown in both the top and bottom panels.

Conditions 1 and 2 are satisfied at Point *F*. However, output is below the full-employment level. Unemployment is too high, and condition 3 is *not* satisfied. The economy has a **recessionary gap** of *FE* – *R*.

The Sequence from Recession to Full Employment

1. *Unemployment is too high.* Output (*R*) is below its full-employment level (*FE*) in Figure 10–3.

2. *Nominal wages will fall.* The surplus of workers causes wages to fall. (*Note:* Saying there is a surplus of workers is the same as saying the unemployment rate is too high.)

3. *Aggregate supply will shift right.* Lower wages (and other factor costs) plus competition between firms causes prices to fall, shifting the aggregate supply curve down and outward from *AS* to *AS´* in Figure 10–3.

4. *Lower prices stimulate aggregate demand.* The lower price level makes consumers richer, since their money holdings now buy more. The bottom panel in Figure 10–3 shows the lower price level shifting up the whole total spending curve from *D* to *D´*. The top panel shows total real spending increasing as the economy shifts *along* the aggregate demand line (*AD*) from Point *F* to Point *E*.

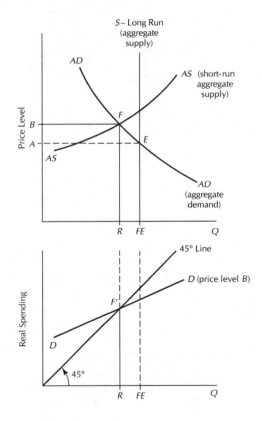

Figure 10–2. An Economy in Recession

5. *The economy moves to full employment.* Wages and prices fall until workers are fully employed at *FE*. The *AS* curve shifts and slides down along the *AD* curve until the economy reaches full employment and potential *GDP*.

How long will an economy need, once in a recession, to return to full employment? Keynesian economists typically feel that an economy's **self-correcting mechanism,** the means by which it reaches *FE* without government intervention, is too slow (and usually recommend governmental action to increase aggregate demand).

Study Hint

1. Redraw the Figure 10–3 graph yourself. First draw the *AS* and *AD* curves so that they intersect at less than full employment.

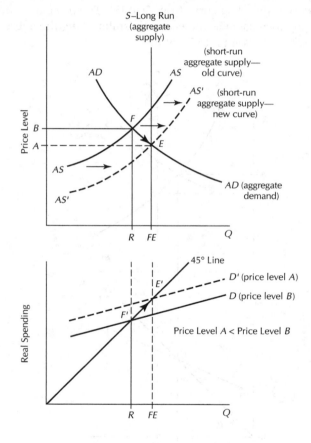

Figure 10–3. An Economy Recovering from Recession

2. Next, visualize the *AS* curve slowly falling as wages and prices fall. Trace how its intersection with *AD* moves the economy toward full employment (*FE*). Once full employment is reached, prices stop falling and the economy is in equilibrium.

FROM TOO LITTLE UNEMPLOYMENT TO FULL EMPLOYMENT

Too little unemployment sounds like having too much money—most of us could live with it. However, too little unemployment is the same thing as too much work. Workers find themselves working too long for too little as firms push output beyond its full-employment level.

Figure 10–4 shows such an "overemployed" economy. The economy is at Point *G*, with output at level *V* and price at level *C*. It has an expansionary gap of *V – FE*.

The Sequence from Too Little Employment to Full Employment

1. *Unemployment is too low* since output (*V*) exceeds its full employment level (*FE*).

2. *Wages will rise* since a shortage of workers exists.

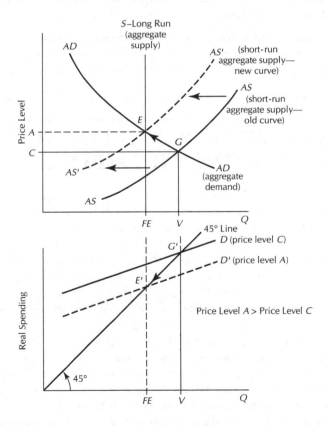

Figure 10–4. An Economy Going from Overemployment to Full Employment

3. *The aggregate supply curve will shift left* as costs are pushed up from *AS* to *AS´* in Figure 10–4.

4. *Aggregate demand is dampened* by the rise in prices. In the bottom panel, the total spending curve shifts down from *D* to *D´*. In the upper panel, the *AS* curve shifts up *along* the *AD* curve from *G* to *E*.

5. *The economy reaches full employment* at output level *FE*.

YOU SHOULD REMEMBER

1. The aggregate supply curve (*AS*) shifts so as to bring the economy to full employment.

2. When output is less than its full-employment level, wages and prices fall until the *AS* curve shifts down along the aggregate demand curve (*AD*) enough for output to reach its full-employment level.

3. When output exceeds its full-employment level, wages and prices rise until the *AS* curve shifts up and along the *AD* curve enough for output to reach its full-employment level.

THE EFFECTS OF EMPLOYMENT ON THE SPENDING MULTIPLIER

In Chapter 9, the effect of more spending was to increase total output by some multiple of itself. However, we assumed that the economy was producing at far below its capacity, so that the price level was not increased when aggregate demand increased. As a consequence, increases in aggregate demand caused equal increases in real income. However, what happens if the economy is close to capacity? As you will see, the spending multiplier will be smaller than that suggested in Chapter 9.

The economy begins at its long-run full-employment equilibrium in Figure 10–5. The solid lines (*AS*, *AD*, and *S*–Long Run) show where the economy starts out. They intersect at Point *E*, at price level *A* and output level *FE*.

Now suppose investment spending at each level of output goes up $1,000 and that the marginal propensity to consume (*MPC*) is 0.8. According to the spending multiplier, total spending will increase by $5,000. So the horizontal shift in aggregate demand from Point *E* to Point *F* will be $5,000. This would also be the increase in output if prices remained unchanged. However, prices *do* rise as output expands. In the short run, the economy goes from Point *E* to Point *G*. (The solid *AS* curve still holds since costs have not changed, but *AD ′* is the new aggregate demand curve.) So the short-run increase in output (from level *FE* to level *S*) is smaller than the increase suggested by the multiplier (from level *FE* to level *T*).

In the long run, the economy will return to full employment as the *AS* curve shifts up to *AS ′*. The long-run multiplier will be zero since output is unchanged. (Note, however, that this is true only when we start at level *FE*; at less than *FE*, increased spending can increase output in the long run).

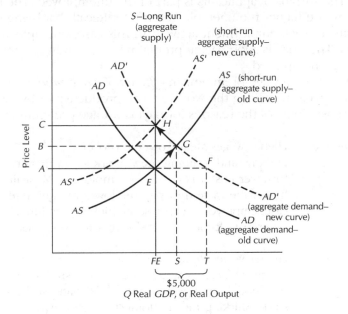

Figure 10–5. The Effects of Output on the Spending Multiplier

THE NATURAL RATE OF UNEMPLOYMENT

The natural rate of unemployment is the rate when the economy is at full employment. It is the normal rate of unemployment around which the actual rate fluctuates. When the economy is in a recession, the unemployment rate exceeds the natural rate. When the economy is in an expansion, the unemployment rate falls below its natural rate.

What determines the natural rate of unemployment? The simple answer is people changing their minds. First, consumers change their minds. For example, when they switch from eating meat to eating vegetables, jobs are lost in the meat industry while jobs are gained in the vegetable industry. Even if the total number of jobs stays the same, workers will be unemployed until they find a new job. Second, employers change their minds. They may find that some workers are not as productive as they hoped and so fire them. Third, employees change their minds. They may discover their jobs do not provide the mix of wages and amenities that they want and so quit. All these events lead to job turnover. Even in good times, the average job in the United States has an annual turnover rate of 30 percent.

The question, "Why is there unemployment?" may have a more complex answer also. Unemployment occurs because firms pay a wage premium (a wage higher than the minimum they could pay), which attracts a surplus of applicants. The surplus of applicants is part of the unemployed. The higher the premium, the higher the unemployment rate. Recall that being unemployed means to seek employment actively. In this case, unemployment is like a lottery. The prize is a job paying premium wages, and the cost of the ticket is being unemployed.

Why do firms pay a wage premium? In *efficiency wage models*, a higher wage pays for itself by making the worker more productive or by lowering some other cost. Some of the reasons for paying a wage premium include:

Reason One: Higher Wages Mean Lower Turnover
Finding and training new workers (a major part of turnover costs) is costly for employers. Most likely, the higher the wage they pay, the lower the quit rate. In this case, employers will pay some higher premium if the premium pays for itself by reducing turnover costs.

Reason Two: Higher Wages Reduce Shirking
Another efficiency wage model is the shirking model. In this model, employers want to motivate workers not to shirk. Shirking means doing less than expected on the job. Shirking includes not working hard enough, taking longer-than-expected lunch breaks, and stealing too many office supplies. Workers benefit from shirking (if they did not, they would not shirk). Therefore, employers have to make shirking costly for workers. One way is to (1) fire workers caught shirking plus (2) pay a wage premium so that being fired makes the fired worker worse off. If the premium is high enough, workers will not shirk to avoid getting caught and fired.

Reason Three: Higher Wages Raise Worker Quality
Higher wages may lead a better quality of worker to apply, which in turn raises the productivity of the workforce. Lower-quality workers may not apply to better-paying jobs, knowing that they are likely to be fired. Thus, even if higher-paying employers cannot initially tell who the better workers are, they will get a mix of better workers.

Job search models are another set of models describing unemployment. In these models, unemployed workers take time to seek out jobs and find the best wage offers. Similarly, employers seek the workers who best fit their jobs. The process is one of seeking and sorting workers among employers. This takes time and creates a pool of the unemployed. The more important matching the right worker with the right job is, the longer the sorting and matching will take and the more unemployment there will be.

Another name for the natural rate of unemployment is NAIRU, the Non-Accelerating Inflation Rate of Unemployment. At this rate of unemployment, there is no pressure for the rate of inflation to change. If unemployment is higher than NAIRU, it is argued that inflation will go down because there is excess supply in the economy. On the other hand, when unemployment falls below NAIRU, it is argued that inflation will accelerate because the labor markets are tight and that the economy has excess demand. NAIRU is a short-run concept because, in the long run, any rate of inflation (as long as it is predictable and so high as to reduce output) is consistent with full employment).

Is unemployment a reliable indicator of the state of the economy? To answer this, be sure you do not confuse unemployment with the loss of employment. Unemployment is the fraction of the labor force actively searching for a job. Unemployment can go up because people are optimistic about the state of the economy and want to work while wages are high. In this case, the higher unemployment rate reflects a robust economy. Also, in theory, if people fully anticipate future rates of inflation, the economy can experience accelerating rates of inflation without any change in unemployment. The usefulness of unemployment as an indicator of the state of the economy is an empirical one, and, in the short run, it has often proved to be a useful indicator.

PROBLEM   If an employer pays a wage of $20,000 a year, 10 percent of the workers will quit in a year. If the same employer pays a wage of $22,000 a year, 4 percent of the workers will quit. If a worker quits, replacing that worker costs the firm $40,000. Which wage should the employer pay (assuming the employer can pay only one or the other)?

SOLUTION   The annual turnover cost per job position will be the turnover rate (stated as a decimal) times the turnover cost (here, $40,000). If the employer pays a wage of $20,000, the annual turnover cost will be $4,000 (0.10 times $40,000) per position. The total annual cost per position will be $24,000 ($20,000 plus $4,000). If the employer pays a wage of $22,000, the annual turnover cost will be $1,600 (0.04 times $40,000): the annual cost per position will be $23,600. Paying an annual wage of $22,000 is cheaper. The wage is $2,000 higher but the turnover cost is $2,400 lower, saving on net $400.

PROBLEM   Which wage (of the two) should the employer pay if the employ-er does not intend to replace the worker, as might be the case in a recession?

SOLUTION   If a worker is not replaced, no turnover costs accrue. The lower wage of $20,000 would keep its costs down.

YOU SHOULD REMEMBER

1. The natural rate of unemployment is the rate that occurs at full employment.

2. In efficiency wage models, employers pay a higher wage than needed because the higher wage lowers some other costs by even more (including turnover costs and shirking costs) or makes workers more productive.

3. In the efficiency wage models, the higher the premium, the higher the number of unemployed workers seeking the premium and the higher the unemployment rate.

4. In job search models, unemployment is part of the process of workers and employers sorting themselves out to find the best match. The more important matching the right worker with the right job is, the longer this sorting will take, resulting in higher unemployment.

KNOW THE CONCEPTS

DO YOU KNOW THE BASICS?

1. Along the aggregate demand curve (*AD*), what is true about spending and income?

2. Why does the *AD* curve have a negative slope?

3. Can too much employment occur?

4. Where will output always be in the long run?

5. If an economy produces less than its full-employment level of output (*FE*), what will happen to wages and prices? How will this bring the economy back to full employment?

6. If an economy produces more than its full-employment level of output, what will happen to wages and prices? How will this bring the economy back to full employment?

7. How will prices change when the economy is underemployed?

8. (*Assume in this question as well as in Questions 9 and 10 that the economy is at full employment, that the following event then occurs, and that the government does not aid the economy's return to full employment.*)

   In 1981–1982, the U.S. government took steps that shifted the aggregate demand curve inward and to the left. Describe what happened and how the economy recovered.

9. In the 1960s, the U.S. government shifted the aggregate demand curve outward and to the right. Describe what happened and how the economy recovered.

10. In the mid-1970s, high oil prices shifted the aggregate supply curve to the left. Describe what happened and how the economy recovered.

TERMS FOR STUDY

aggregate demand, aggregate
  demand curve
aggregate supply, aggregate supply
  curve (short and long run)
employment

overemployment
potential real *GDP*
self-correcting mechanism
underemployment
unemployment

PRACTICAL APPLICATION

1. Use the table below to answer the following questions. The table shows short-run aggregate supply schedule (*AS*) for various nominal wages. Each entry shows the real level of output (*Q*) firms will produce. Note how higher wages reduce *AS* at each price level. The last column shows aggregate demand (*AD*) at each price level.

   a. What is the short-run equilibrium price level and wage when the nominal wage (*W*) is $10? $14? $18?

   b. Suppose full employment occurs at the real output level of 2,000. What happens when initially *W* = $10? *W.* = $18?

Price Level (P)	AS if W = $10	AS if W = $14	AS if W = $18	AD
80	1,800	1,200	700	2,400
100	2,200	1,700	1,100	2,220
120	2,400	2,000	1,500	2,000
140	2,500	2,300	1,800	1,800
160	2,500	2,500	2,100	1,600

2. The unemployment rate that exists when *GNP* is at its potential level is called the **natural rate of unemployment.** This is the rate consistent with workers changing jobs to find better ones, with consumers changing which goods they buy (which results in lost jobs in some sectors of the economy while other sectors expand), and with the search by employers for the best workers. How will the following events affect the natural rate of unemployment?

Event A: A growing fraction of the workforce becomes willing to quit when their job is unsatisfactory.

Event B: Employers, to maintain their competitiveness, become more willing to fire unproductive workers.

Event C: Consumers become more conservative, changing fashion and brands less often.

Event D: The government makes it expensive for employers to fire workers, making them go to court to prove the worker was unproductive.

3. Suppose the economy is initially in a long-run full-employment equilibrium. The aggregate demand increases, shifting the *AD* curve to the right.

   a. What will happen in the short run to employment? To real wages?

   b. What will happen in the long run?

4. During the Great Depression, Congress actively attacked business in congressional hearings, passed higher taxes, and passed legislation that made unions stronger. Did this help or hinder the recovery of the economy?

5. How will an economy's recovery time be affected if workers become less militant, such that they are willing to negotiate for lower wages when hard times hit?

6. State and local planners often claim that a plant being located in their area has a "multiplier" effect. The area's residents will benefit, it is claimed, by the spending and employment the new plant adds to the community. Will this be true if the state's resources are fully employed?

7. In the following table, what is the multiplier, holding the price level constant? (Note: I = investment spending.) What is the multiplier once price increases are taken into account? Each entry shows the real aggregate output (Q) demanded or supplied.

Price Level (P)	AD I = 130	AD I = 140	AS
100	2,210	2,310	2,110
110	2,205	2,305	2,155
120	2,200	2,300	2,200
130	2,195	2,295	2,245
140	2,190	2,290	2,290
150	2,185	2,285	2,335

8. Assume that at full employment, the demand for workers equals supply at a real wage of $10; the quantity demanded and supplied is 100 million. The money wage is fixed in the short run at $10, and the price level at full employment is 100. The solid lines in the following graph show this. The graph on page 164 shows that as *real wages* go down, firms demand more workers but fewer workers want to work. Assume that employment equals the employers' demand for workers in the short run because the workers are under contract to work the hours the employers demand. Where will the economy be on the graph if the price level falls to 80? Rises to 120?

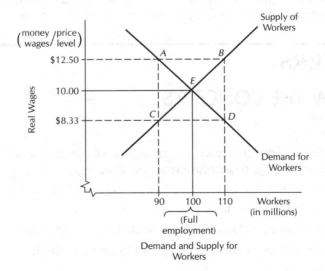

Demand and Supply for Workers

9. Using the same set of circumstances used in Question 8, label the price levels for the aggregate supply curve when the real money wage is $10. Assume that 90 million workers produce a *GDP* of $500 billion, 100 million produce a real *GDP* of $600 billion, and 110 million produce a real *GDP* of $650 billion, all three amounts being in real dollars.

10. If workers in Question 8 had expected a price level of 120, what nominal money wage would they have demanded? Draw the short-run aggregate supply curve for this wage in the graph for Question 9.
    Hint: The *AS* curve there is drawn for an expected price level of 100.

11. This problem illustrates the shirking model of efficiency wages. In this version of the model, if workers shirk, nothing gets produced. The employer must pay a wage high enough to keep workers from shirking. Let $20,000 be the wage other employers are paying. Workers value a year's worth of shirking at $5,000 (for example, this might be their value of sleeping on the job). If the workers shirk, they have a 20 percent chance of getting caught and fired. If fired, they lose the present value of all the future wage premiums they would have earned had they stayed with the firm. Assume that the present value of the job equals 10 times the wage premium. Since the worker has only a 20 percent chance of suffering this loss, the expected value of this loss is 0.20 times the present value of the wage premium.
    a. What is the lowest wage the firm can pay and not have workers shirk?
    b. What will happen to the wage if the firm begins to monitor workers more closely, increasing the chance they will catch shirking workers?
    c. What will happen if a worker does not plan to stay with the firm long, such that the present value of any premium decreases?

ANSWERS

KNOW THE CONCEPTS

1. They are equal.
2. A lower price level increases the real value of nominal assets, which in turn causes people to increase real spending.
3. Yes, when a shortage of workers forces wages and prices up.
4. At its full-employment level (*FE*).
5. Wages and prices will fall, shifting the *AS* curve to the right.
6. Wages and prices will rise, shifting the *AS* curve to the left.
7. Prices will fall.

8. In the short run, output and prices fell.
   In the long run, output returned to its full-employment level as prices fell further.

9. In the short run, output and prices rose.
   In the long run, output fell back to its full-employment level as prices rose further.

10. In the short run, prices rose and output fell.
    In the long run, output rose back to its full-employment level as prices fell back to their original level.

PRACTICAL APPLICATION

1. **a.** At $W = \$10$, equilibrium Q is 2,200 at $P = 100$. At $W = \$14$, 2,000 and 120. At $W = \$18$, 1,800 and 140.

   b. In the long run, $W = \$14$, $P = 120$, and equilibrium $Q = 2,000$. At $W = \$10$, the economy is overemployed at $Q = 2,200$. Wages will rise, shifting the AS schedule "up" to the second column. At $W = \$18$, the economy is underemployed, so wages will fall. AS schedule shifts "down" to the middle column.

2. *Event A:* Increase the natural rate of unemployment due to increases in turnover.

   Event B: Increase the natural rate of unemployment.

   Event C: Decrease the natural rate of unemployment.

   Event D: Uncertain effect: In Europe, where there are strict employment laws, the long-run effect has been much higher unemployment as firms are reluctant to hire new workers.

3. **a.** Output will increase and prices will rise. Since money wages are constant in the short run, *real* wages will fall as prices go up. Employment will increase as employers find their real costs reduced. Workers will not like working for lower real wages, but they may be locked in to a long-term contract.

   b. Workers will demand and get higher real wages. Employment will fall back to its full-employment level. Output will fall. Prices will rise even further than in the short run.

4. These activities were in large part responsible for hindering the recovery, as they discouraged investment spending and made workers more militant against reducing wages. As a result, the Great Depression lasted more than ten years.

5. This will speed up the recovery time, as the AS supply curve will then shift down faster, bringing GNP to its potential level sooner.

6. No. At full employment, the resources used by the plant (including land and labor) must come from other uses. To get these resources, the

plant (and its employees) must bid them away from others in the area by offering higher prices for them. The effect will be higher prices and a lower real income for those not directly benefited by the plant. The area as a whole will benefit only to the degree the plant *on net* adds resources to the area.

7. At a given price level, an increase in investment spending of $10 increases aggregate demand by $100. So the spending multiplier is 10. However, at $I = 130$, $AD = AS$ at $P = 120$ and $Q = 2,200$, increasing I to 140, $AD = AD$ at $P = 140$ and $Q = 2,290$. An increase in I of $10 increases Q by $90 once price increases are taken into account, giving a smaller multiplier of 9.

8. At a price level of 80, real wages rise to $12.50 ($10/0.8). The economy will be at Point *A*, and employment will be at 90 million workers. The economy will have less than full employment.

   At a price level of 120, real wages fall to $8.33 ($10/1.20). Employment rises to 110 million as the economy will be at Point *D*. The economy will have more than full employment.

9. To answer this question, you have to find the price level that converts the nominal wage of $10 into the real wages at each level of employment in Question 8. The real wage of $12.50 is associated in Question 8 with an employment level of 90 million and thus an output level of 500 billion: The price level must be 80 (real wage is $12.50 = $10/0.80). 100 is the price level associated with 100 million employed and output 600 billion, with a real wage of $10. 120 is the price level associated with output of 650 billion (and a real wage of $8.33). This corresponds respectively to underemployment (Point *A* in the graph for Question 8 and *A′* here), full employment (Points *E* and *E′*), and overemployment (Points *D* and *D′*). As real wages fall, employment expands.

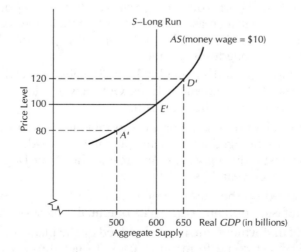

10. Workers, to be fully employed, will demand a nominal wage of $12, giving them the real full-employment wage of $10 ($12/1.20). The new aggregate supply curve (for a nominal wage of $12) will be *above* the *AS* curve for Question 9 and will intersect the full-employment long-run supply curve at price level 120.

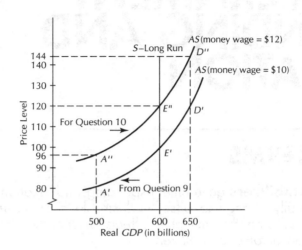

11. a. $22,500. The workers will not shirk if they expect to lose more by shirking—the expected cost of losing the job—than they gain by shirking ($5,000), or

0.20 × Present Value of Wage Premium ≥ $5,000 or
0.20 × 10 × Wage Premium ≥ $5,000

The lowest wage premium is from the equation:

0.20 × 10 × Wage Premium = $5,000

The lowest wage premium that will keep workers from shirking is $2,500. The firm should pay a wage of $22,500.

b. The wage will decrease. For example, if the firm in the above example has a 50 percent chance of catching the worker, the firm needs to pay only $21,000.

c. The wage the firm needs to pay will increase. This is why firms do not like to announce that they will be shutting down a factory—without a higher wage, more workers are going to shirk.

11

FISCAL POLICY: GOVERNMENT SPENDING AND TAXATION

KEY TERMS

built-in stabilizers government spending and taxation, which automatically change to offset undesirable changes in *GDP*, thereby reducing the multiplier effects of spending changes. Also called *automatic stabilizers*.

government debt the total amount the government owes.

government deficit excess of government spending over taxes collected (for a year).

government surplus the excess of taxes over government spending.

marginal tax rate amount of taxes paid on the last dollar of income earned.

tax multiplier number that a tax change must be multiplied by to get the resulting change in *GDP*. A tax multiplier of –5 implies that a $200 increase in taxes will reduce *GDP* by $1,000.

In Chapter 10, we saw that an economy can get out of a recession by itself. However, many economists consider this process to be too slow and thus recommend that the government stimulate the economy by increasing aggregate demand. This chapter discusses how the government may do this (according to the Keynesian model) through its **fiscal policy,** which involves changing government spending and taxation.

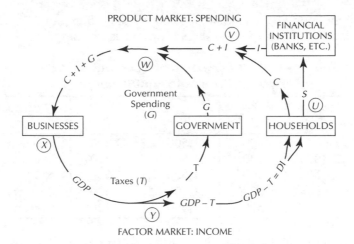

Figure 11–1. The Circular Flow of an Economy—with Government

Figure 11–1 shows the circular flows in an economy with a governmental sector. When beginning at Point U, households either consume (C) or save (S) their disposable income. Savings go into the financial system (e.g., into bank accounts, mutual funds, or pension plans) and come back into the spending stream as investment spending at Point V. Then, at Point W, we add government spending (G). Total spending (and GDP) equals $C + I + G$. Businesses pay out as total income the GDP at Point X. The government collects taxes (T) at Point Y, leaving disposable income (DI) equal to $GDP - T$.

Note: We are ignoring transfer payments from the government to households.

WHAT FISCAL POLICY IS

THE EFFECT OF SPENDING

Government *adds* spending but it *takes away* dollars from the economy in the tax revenues it collects. We will examine the effect of spending first, holding tax revenues constant. Then, we will examine the effect of changing taxes, holding government spending constant. To get the combined effect, we just add these two effects together.

Return to the Keynesian model of aggregate demand as described in Chapter 9. We assume that the economy is on the horizontal section of the AS (aggregate supply) curve so that more output will not raise prices.

Government spending is just like investment spending and has identical effects. Table 11–1 shows the spending at various levels of real *GDP* (*Q*).

Table 11–1. Total Government Spending and the Effect on Economic Equilibrium

Q	C	I	G	D	Output Response
3,000	1,800	500	1,500	3,800	Increase
4,000	2,400	500	1,500	4,400	Increase
5,000	3,000	500	1,500	5,000	NO CHANGE
6,000	3,600	500	1,500	5,600	Decrease
7,000	4,200	500	1,500	6,200	Decrease

When output equals $5,000, total spending equals income and the economy is in equilibrium. Note that *Q*, real output, is also real income.

Figure 11–2 illustrates Table 11–1. Equilibrium occurs where spending equals income or where the total spending curve (*D*) crosses the 45-degree line (at Point *E*). Note that *D* (total spending) is derived by adding *C*, *I*, and *G* at each level of output.

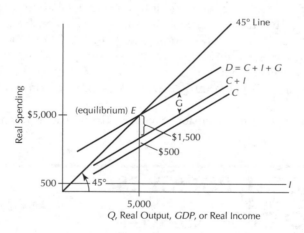

Figure 11–2. A Visual Look at Total Government Spending and the Effect on Economic Equilibrium

Since government spending is like investment spending, it has the same *spending multiplier*. A new dollar of government spending is spent and earned as income, *MPC* of it is respent and earned, and so forth. The total increase in equilibrium spending (and income) will be determined by

$$\text{Spending Multiplier} = \frac{1}{1 - MPC}$$

Example: Effect of Government Spending

PROBLEM $MPC = 0.6$ and government spending (G) increases by $800. What will happen to equilibrium income?

SOLUTION The spending multiplier is 2.5 (1/0.4), so equilibrium income and spending will increase by $2,000.

YOU SHOULD REMEMBER

1. Without international trade, total spending equals $C + I + G$.

2. Every dollar increase in government spending increases *GDP* by the spending multiplier.

THE EFFECT OF TAXATION

When holding government spending constant, how will a change in taxes affect aggregate demand? Remember that taxes affect total spending *only through their effects on consumption spending*! If a person's taxes go up by $1, the person's disposable income is $1 lower. If *MPC* is 0.8, the person will then reduce consumption spending by $0.80. This initial $0.80 reduction in consumption *then* has a spending multiplier effect on the economy. The tax multiplier is thus:

$$\text{Tax Multiplier} = -MPC \times \text{Spending Multiplier.}$$

Example: Effect of Taxes

PROBLEM $MPC = 0.8$ and taxes go up by $1,000. What will happen to equilibrium income?

SOLUTION Consumption initially falls by $800 (Change in $C = -MPC \times$ change in taxes). The spending multiplier is 5(1/0.2). So equilibrium income falls by $4,000 ($-5 \times$ $800). The tax multiplier is -4 (-0.8×5).

So far, we have treated taxes as if they were a lump sum, meaning they do not change when income changes. In fact, more taxes are paid as income goes up. When taxes go up with income, the spending multiplier will be smaller. To see why, recall the "rounds" of spending, earning, and respending that take place in the multiplier process. (See Table 9–3.) Because earnings are taxed, *less* disposable income is available for respending on each round. The result is that total secondary consumption respending will be smaller.

YOU SHOULD REMEMBER

1. The tax multiplier is –MPC/(1 – MPC).

2. When taxes go up with income, the spending multiplier becomes *smaller*.

• *SUPPLY-SIDE ECONOMICS*

1. People supply less labor, capital, and other factors when taxes increase.

2. The decision to supply more or less of a factor is determined by the **marginal tax rate** (the rate of taxes people pay on their last dollar earned).

3. When *marginal* tax rates go up, aggregate supply goes down. The *average* tax rate does not matter.

4. This shift in aggregate supply is more important for predicting what taxes will do than is the shift in aggregate demand.

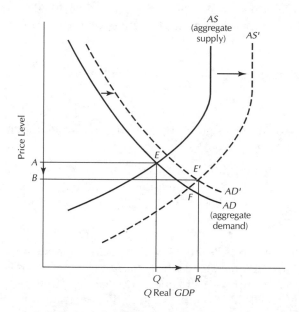

Figure 11–3. The Effect of a Tax Cut Shown by Supply-Side Economic Model

Figure 11–3 illustrates these assumptions. When taxes decrease, aggregate demand and aggregate supply increase, but according to the last assumption, the *AS* curve shifts out more. The economy goes from Point *E* to Point *E′*. Output increases (from level *Q* to level *R*), and prices fall (from level *A* to level *B*). In this case, it is possible to stimulate the economy out of a recession without higher rates of inflation.

In our progressive tax system, as people earn more, each addition to earnings is taxed at a progressively higher tax rate. By going to a less progressive tax structure, it is possible to collect the same average tax but have a lower marginal tax rate (at least for most people). Thus, if the government lowered the marginal tax rate but left the average tax rate the same, aggregate supply would shift out and right, but aggregate demand (which depends on total tax revenues) would not shift. The economy would go from Point *E* to Point *F* in Figure 11–3. This is the theory behind the 1986 tax reform.

A related part of supply-side economics is the **Laffer curve,** which is illustrated in Figure 11–4. The tax rate is on the vertical axis. Total tax revenues are on the horizontal axis. At a tax rate of 0 or 100 percent, no taxes will be collected (at 100 percent, no one will work). These rates are represented by Points *A* and *B*, respectively. As the tax rate increases from 0 percent, total tax revenues go up but people begin to work and earn less, so *GDP* falls. At first, the tax rate goes up more than the amount by which the *GDP* falls. At point *C*, however, the rise in the tax rate is exactly offset by a fall in income (*GDP*), so *on net* tax revenues do not change. *T* is the most taxes the government can ever collect. At a higher tax rate, income (*GDP*) falls by more than the tax rate increases, so total tax revenues fall. Above the tax rate *C*, to increase tax revenues, the government should reduce the tax rate. Some studies suggest that a marginal tax rate above 40 percent reduces tax collections.

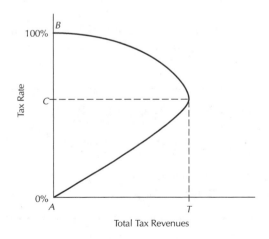

Figure 11–4. The Laffer Curve

THE OVERALL EFFECTS OF SPENDING AND TAXATION

When government spending (G) and taxes (T) both change, just add their separate effects together. One important combination occurs when G and T both increase by the same amount. The **balanced-budget multiplier** is the number the increase in G is multiplied by to get the increase in equilibrium income when T increases by exactly the same amount as G. One more dollar of G increases equilibrium income by $1/(1 - MPC)$, while one more dollar of T decreases equilibrium income by $-MPC$ times $1/(1 - MPC)$. When adding these two effects together, the balanced-budget multiplier is just 1:

$$\frac{1}{1 - MPC} + \frac{-MPC}{1 - MPC} = \frac{1 - MPC}{1 - MPC} = 1$$

For example, if government spending and taxation both increase by $2,000, equilibrium income goes up by $2,000.

LIMITS OF AN ACTIVE FISCAL POLICY

While fiscal policy sounds easy, economists often do not know whether it is needed or exactly when and how much it is going to affect the economy. As an analogy, suppose your car's gas pedal and brake worked with a variable time lag, sometimes working immediately, sometimes working 30 to 60 seconds after you press them. Suppose that for a given push, they resulted in varying degrees of acceleration or braking. Most likely your driving policy would be to hold a "steady course." So it is with fiscal policy when the timing and degree of its effects are uncertain.

YOU SHOULD REMEMBER

1. The balanced-budget multiplier equals 1.

2. The case for an active fiscal policy is weakened when its effects are uncertain in timing and degree.

THE EFFECT ON AGGREGATE SUPPLY AND DEMAND

Up to this point, we have assumed that fiscal policy does not affect prices. However, near full employment, it will. To take this into account, we must return to the aggregate demand and supply analysis from Chapter 10 and Figure 10–5. Assume the economy is in equilibrium at price level A and full-employment output *FE*. Then government spending goes up $1,000 when the *MPC* is 0.8. Equilibrium income will go up $5,000 *if the price level does not change*. In Figure 10–5, this $5,000 increase is shown by the horizontal outward shift of the aggregate demand curve from Point E to Point F. If the price level did *not* change, output would also increase, from level *FE* to level T. However, in the short run, the economy moves up the *AS* curve to G, where prices are higher (B > A) and output smaller (S < T). So the true short-run multiplier will be smaller than 5. In the long run, wages will increase, shifting the *AS* curve up and to the left. Prices will rise still more (from B to C), and output will fall back to its full-employment level. Thus, at full employment, more government spending and lower taxes raise prices, not output. The modified multiplier is zero.

DEFICITS: DO THEY MATTER?

Because the government deficit equals government spending minus taxes $(G - T)$, we can also write:

$$G = T + \text{Deficit.}$$

That is, government spending is financed either by taxes *or* by the government borrowing money (by issuing government bonds) to cover its deficit.

Some economists believe that "deficits do not matter"; i.e., equilibrium income will be the same whether government spending is paid for with taxes or borrowings. In contrast with this is the Keynesian result derived above, which suggests that *lower* taxes (and thus higher deficits) will increase equilibrium income (assuming G remains unchanged).

To see why deficits might not matter, assume that government spending is fixed. The only issue is how to pay for G: pay taxes now and run a deficit. However, deficits are just delayed taxes that the public will have to pay later. If the public knows this, it may regard a $150 billion deficit the same as $150 billion more in taxes since the money will eventually have to be paid anyway. (This theory is called the Ricardian Tax Equivalence Theorem, after David Ricardo, a famous nineteenth-century economist.)

If this is the case, then "deficits do not matter." What will happen? Suppose taxes go down by $1,000 (and G stays the same so the government has to borrow $1,000). Disposable income (*DI*) will go up by $1,000. Households, knowing they will have to pay the $1,000 eventually, save the $1,000 in added disposable income. Consumption spending (*C*) will be *unchanged*! Therefore, because *C* is unchanged (and so are *G* and *I,* investment spending), total spending (*C + G + I*) is unchanged. The deficit will *not* change equilibrium income.

There is a considerable body of evidence that supports this point of view. Economic data suggest that once the effects of government spending are accounted for, deficits have no (or very little) effect on output, interest rates, private investment, or foreign exchange rates. Further, higher deficits do seem to increase savings but not as fully as the theory implies. A possible problem with the "deficits do not matter" theory is that it may be true only up to a point. At some high level of debt, the public comes to doubt the willingness and ability of the U.S. government to continue paying the interest on its debt. At this point, a crisis could develop with real and negative effects.

• *BUILT-IN STABILIZERS*

Fiscal policy involves (1) active programs designed to influence the economy (such as special spending programs and changes in the tax breaks) and (2) automatic programs, which respond to changes in the economy without explicit orders from our political officials. Programs that are automatic are called **built-in stabilizers.** They include (a) unemployment insurance and welfare programs and (b) our tax system. When *GDP* goes down and unemployment up, (a) increases transfer payments automatically while (b) reduces taxes (since people pay less taxes at lower incomes). This *reduces* the amount by which disposable income decreases when *GDP* goes down. In turn, this reduces the decrease in consumption spending when *GDP* falls. Built-in stabilizers thus "dampen" the multiplier process and the resulting change in *GDP*.

• *THE HIGH-EMPLOYMENT DEFICIT*

How active is fiscal policy? To find out, many economists look at what the deficit *would be* if the economy were at full employment: the **high-employment deficit** (also called the "active" or "structural" deficit). By looking at the high-employment deficit instead of the actual deficit, the cyclical effects of the automatic stabilization programs are removed and only the *active* component of fiscal policy remains. The high-employment deficit (or surplus) tells economists how much fiscal policy is actively working to affect the economy: A higher high-employment deficit indicates a shift toward a greater stimulation of the economy.

• *BURDEN OF THE DEBT*

The federal **government's debt** equals the government's total indebtedness and now exceeds 8 trillion dollars. The government's deficit is how much it must borrow in a given year. The government's *debt* is the total of all it has borrowed and not paid back over all past years. The deficit is, then, what is added annually to the government's total debt. In 2004, the federal government's deficit was $413 billion, and the government continues to run deficits so that in 2005 the federal government's debt surpassed $8 trillion (about $27,000 per person). To pay the interest on this portion of the debt, the government has to raise tax revenue or reduce spending. To pay interest on the debt it holds, the government needs to make only two book-keeping entries: pay and paid.

Does this debt represent a burden to the economy? Economists make the following conclusions:

1. A deficit that stimulates the economy out of a recession into full employment will be a benefit, not a burden.

2. Deficits incurred when the economy is near full employment can be harmful. To see why, recall the injections = leakages equation:

$$I + \text{Government Deficit} = S + \text{Trade Deficit}$$

When the government deficit goes up when the economy is fully employed, then either private investment (I) must go down, savings (S) go up, or the trade deficit ($-NX$) go up. If savings go up, there will be no burdens from deficits (this is the outcome of the "deficits do not matter" point of view). If savings do not go up, then the government can get more only (1) by **crowding-out** private investment (I will go down) or (2) by borrowing from foreigners (which shows up as a higher trade deficit for reasons we will discuss in Chapter 15). (2) increases the indebtedness of the United States to foreigners. If the money borrowed is invested wisely (for example, in education and scientific research), resulting in more U.S. economic growth, this will not be a problem. However, if it is wasted, future generations will have to lower their consumption levels either (1) because more productive private investment was crowded out or (2) because we must pay the debt's interest to the rest of the world. Another way to finance the deficit is to **monetize** the debt. In effect, the government pays for the deficit by printing more money. This leads to inflation, with all its social costs.

YOU SHOULD REMEMBER

1. Deficits help the economy if lower taxes cause *GDP* to expand.

2. Deficits harm the economy when they (a) do not stimulate the economy and (b) reduce private investment, thereby reducing growth.

KNOW THE CONCEPTS

DO YOU KNOW THE BASICS?

1. Why is government spending the same as investment or consumption spending?
2. Why does a decrease in taxes have a smaller multiplier effect than the same increase in government spending?
3. If the government wants to spend more *without* increasing equilibrium income, by how much must it increase taxes (as compared with the increase in government spending)?
4. How does the income tax affect the size of the spending multiplier?
5. Why is the actual deficit not a good guide to how active the government's fiscal policy is?
6. If government borrowing reduces business borrowing, how does this affect our economy's growth?
7. If the public anticipates having to pay the future taxes implicit in any deficit, why will a lower tax not increase consumption spending (and aggregate demand)?
8. Why is government spending (G) an injection? Why are taxes (T') a leakage?
9. Will the multiplier effect of more government spending be larger or smaller when prices go up as output increases?
10. How do built-in stabilizers help stabilize the economy?

TERMS FOR STUDY

automatic fiscal policy	high-employment deficit (and
balanced-budget multiplier	surplus)
built-in stabilizers	spending multiplier
"deficits do not matter"	supply-side economics
discretionary or active fiscal policy	tax multiplier

PRACTICAL APPLICATION

1. Fill in the following table and answer these questions based on:

$$MPC = 0.6, I = \$500, G = \$700, \text{ and } T = \$500$$

   a. What is the equilibrium income?

b. What are the injections $(G + I)$ and leakages $(S + T)$ at this income?

c. What will happen to equilibrium *GDP* if government spending goes up $400? If *I* goes up $400 instead?

Q	DI	C	D = C + I + G
$2,000	1,500	1,200	2,400
3,000	_____	_____	_____
4,000	_____	_____	_____
5,000	_____	_____	_____
6,000	_____	_____	_____

2. **a.** When *MPC* = 0.75, if *G* and *T* both increase by $1,000, what will happen to equilibrium income?

b. By how much must *T* be increased (assuming *G* is increased by $1,000) so that equilibrium income does *not* increase?

3. If the government wants to increase equilibrium income by $4,000 when *MPC* = 0.8, how much must it increase *G*?

4. If the government wants to increase equilibrium income by $4,000 when *MPC* = 0.8, by how much must it reduce *T*?

5. Assume in a small closed country that all citizens earn $10,000 a year, the government spends $1,000 per citizen, and each citizen spends $9,000 on consumption. There is initially no savings, no net investment, and the real interest rate is zero. The government had been collecting $1,000 per citizen to pay for its spending. Then it decides for only one year to issue $1,000 per citizen in bonds, which are paid back next year. So, in per capita terms, the new tax looks like:

Year 0   No taxes but $1,000 in bonds

Year 1 $2,000 in taxes (includes $1,000 to pay back bond)

Year 2+ $1,000 in taxes

In the Keynesian model, what would happen? If people foresaw what was going to happen and wanted to maintain $9,000 in annual consumption, what would happen?

6. If "deficits do not matter," then what does in fiscal policy?

7. If the economy is at or near full employment, what will be the main impact of a reduction of government spending on real *GDP* and prices?

8. Households decide to save $10,000 more. By how much must the government increase *G* if it wants to maintain the same level of national income?

Hint: *C* is going down by $10,000.

9. If "deficits do not matter," what will happen to *DI, C,* and *S* when *T* goes down $5,000?

10. If *G* goes up $1,000 and equilibrium income goes up $4,000, what is the *MPC*?

ANSWERS

KNOW THE CONCEPTS

1. Because *C, G,* and *I* all directly enter the spending stream and are received as income.

2. Because a decrease in *T* initially increases *C* by a smaller amount (since *MPC* < 1). The resulting change in total spending is smaller.

3. It would have to increase *T* more than *G*.

4. It makes the spending multiplier smaller.

5. The size of the actual deficit in a recession will be larger because of the effects of the automatic stabilizers. To measure the active component of fiscal policy, these effects must be removed.

6. It reduces future growth.

7. Because households will regard less taxes now as *more* taxes later, they will save an amount equal to the delayed tax. *C* will be unchanged.

8. *G* adds to total spending, while *T* represents an allocation of income away from spending.

9. Smaller.

10. They reduce the multiplier effects of changes in autonomous spending.

PRACTICAL APPLICATION

1. **a.** $3,000.
   b. Injections (*I* + *G*) equal $1,200. At $3,000, *S* = $700 (*S* = *DI* – *C*). Leakages (*S* + *T*) equal $1,200.
   c. The spending multiplier is 2.5. Equilibrium income will increase by $1,000 in either case.

2. **a.** The balanced-budget multiplier is 1, so equilibrium income will go up $1,000.
   b. To not change equilibrium income, the increase in taxes must reduce *C* by the amount *G* goes up so that total spending is unchanged. To decrease *C* by $1,000, *DI* must fall by $1,333.33: *T* must increase by $1,333.33. To get the $1,333.33 figure, solve the equation: Change in

C equals – *MPC* times increase in taxes. (In this case, the change in *C* is –$1,000.)

3. *G* must increase by $800 (the spending multiplier is 5: 5 × 800 = $4,000).

4. *T* must be reduced by $1,000 (the tax multiplier is –4).

5. In the Keynesian model, consumption is based on current disposable income and not on wealth. So in year 0, people would increase their consumption. The $1,000 in bonds would be paid for by selling off assets, thereby depreciating the nation's capital stock. In the next year, the people would reduce consumption well below $9,000. With foresight, they would buy the bonds with the tax savings and then sell the bonds to pay off next year's higher taxes. This would allow them a constant consumption stream of $9,000 a year, every year. This corresponds to the "deficits do not matter" result.

6. The two things that matter are (1) government spending and (2) the efficiency of the tax system. Some evidence suggests that higher levels of government spending reduce real *GDP* growth (with the exception of government spending on education, research, and on the nation's infrastructure). It may also be that when (and *only* when) the economy is in a recession, any kind of government spending may stimulate the economy. A tax system is more inefficient the more it discourages productive economic decisions, including the decisions to work, save, and invest.

7. The *AD* curve will shift left by the change in *G* times the spending multiplier. In the short run, with the *AS* curve unchanged, prices will fall as output falls. Unemployment will go up. In the long run, wages (and thus prices) will fall, shifting the *AS* curve down and right, causing output to return to its full-employment level but pushing the price level down below its short-run level.

8. By $10,000.

9. *DI* goes up $5,000, savings (*S*) go up $5,000, *C* remains unchanged (*C* = *DI* – *S*).

10. *MPC* = 0.75.

12
THE SUPPLY OF MONEY

KEY TERMS

asset physical property or intangible right (e.g., plant, equipment, patents, money, or bonds) that has economic value.

liquidity the ease with which an asset (such as a stock or bond) can be converted into cash. Cash is the most liquid asset. Bonds are relatively liquid, and land is usually illiquid.

money the medium of exchange; what people use to pay for goods and services.

WHAT IS MONEY?

An increase in the money supply can dramatically increase aggregate demand, as later chapters illustrate. This chapter, however, covers what causes the money supply to change.

Money is an asset with which people buy and sell goods. Hence, it is defined as the medium of exchange. Coins, currency (such as dollar bills), and checking accounts all serve as money.

Trade without money is **barter**. In barter, you have to find someone who (1) wants what you have and (2) has what you want. When such a person is found, it is called a double coincidence of wants since both (1) *and* (2) have to be true for barter to occur.

With money, trade takes place just by having people (1) sell what they have for money and then (2) use the money to buy what they want. Money therefore does not require a double coincidence of wants and thus expands the range of mutually advantageous trades people can make.

At times, gold and other goods served as **commodity money**, i.e., a widely traded good that was valued both for its use as a medium of exchange and for its intrinsic value. Currently, all major currencies of the world are fiat, not backed by gold or any other valuable material. The United States dollar is a fiat money.

Unfortunately, the term "money" is commonly used in other ways that are confusing. Money is *not* "savings," "income," or "borrowings." These terms refer to real goods and services. (For example, income is the real goods and services a person earns.) They are not money. Just as a picture of a house is not the house, money is a measure of the value of goods and services; it is not the goods and services themselves.

The Functions of Money

1. *Separate sales from purchases:* Money allows people to avoid the double coincidence of wants.

2. *Unit of account:* Money allows people to put a price on all goods.

3. *Standard of deferred payment:* In almost all contracts, when people agree to be paid in the future, it is usually in money. (The alternative is to be paid in goods.)

4. *Store of value:* People "store" their savings by setting aside an amount of money (often in a bank account).

HOW MONEY IS MEASURED

The more easily and more quickly one can trade an asset for goods without taking a loss, the more liquid the asset. Money is the most liquid asset; a bond is less liquid since it takes some time and effort to trade it for most goods. Land is illiquid.

Many different measures of the money supply exist. What economists categorize as money depends on what assets they think are liquid enough to be considered money.

Classifications of Money Measurement

1. **M1:** The most liquid measure of money, consisting of assets easily exchanged for goods and services: coins and paper currency (held by the public), traveler's checks, demand deposits (checking accounts), and other checkable deposits. Other checkable deposits include NOW (Negotiable Orders of Withdrawal) accounts and ATS (Automatic Transfer Service) accounts. Both NOW and ATS accounts are effectively checking accounts that pay interest.

2. **M2:** The next most liquid measure of money, adding assets easily converted into M1. It consists of M1 plus household savings deposits, time deposits, and retail money market mutual funds.

3. **M3:** M3 consists of M2 plus institutional money funds, large time deposits, repurchase agreements, and Eurodollars.

In 1999, M1 was nearly 1,100 billion dollars, M2 was 4,500 billion dollars, and M3 was 6,200 billion dollars. To put these numbers into perspective, *GDP* was nearly 9,000 billion dollars in 1999, so M1 is about 12 percent of *GDP*, M2 is about 50 percent, and M3 is nearly 70 percent.

Most economists use either M1 or M2.

THE FEDERAL RESERVE

The Federal Reserve System, often referred to as the Fed, is the central bank of the United States. Its main job is to control the money supply. It is overseen by the seven-member Board of Governors, headed by the Chairman of the Federal Reserve. The Board of Governors set the discount rate (the rate private banks pay when borrowing from the Fed) and the reserve requirements backing bank deposits (which will be discussed in the next section). Members of the Board of Governors are also members (along with 5 heads from the 12 regional Federal Reserve Banks) of the important Federal Open Market Committee (FOMC). The FOMC buys and sells government bonds with the goal of controlling the money supply and influencing interest rates. A model describing the FOMC is presented at the end of this chapter.

YOU SHOULD REMEMBER

1. Money is the medium of exchange; using money for trade means people do not have to seek a double coincidence of wants.

2. Money serves as a unit of account, as a means of deferred payment, and as a store of value. It serves all these functions because it separates sales from purchases.

3. Savings, income, and borrowing all are real physical goods and services; they are not money.

4. M1 is currency (held by the public) and checkable deposits. It represents transaction monies. M2 adds savings accounts and checkable money market accounts to M1.

BALANCE SHEETS AND BANKS: FEDERAL AND COMMERCIAL

Table 12–1 shows a partial balance sheet for the U.S. banking system for early 1986. **Assets** are what people own or what other people owe them. **Liabilities** are what people owe others.

The top panel shows the balance sheet for the **Federal Reserve System** (Fed). The Fed is the nation's main banking regulatory agency. It controls the money supply. It also serves as a "lender of last resort" to banks needing funds (see 1 and 11 on the Balance Sheet. When referring to the assets column, the Fed's assets include loans to banks, which it lends at an interest rate called the "discount rate" (1), government securities, which are part of the open market operations discussed below (2), and gold (3). Its liabilities include Federal Reserve notes, which in effect are all of the U.S. paper currency held either by the public or the banks (4) and deposits of commercial banks at the Fed (5).

The assets of all commercial banks (see bottom panel) include their deposits at the Fed (6A) and their vault cash, i.e., the cash and coin banks keep on hand to meet daily cash withdrawals (6B). Banks lend money either to the public (7) or to the government (8). The funds needed to make these loans come from the liability side of the commercial banks' balance sheet. The sources of funds include checkable deposits (9), other deposits, which are mainly time and savings deposits (10), and money borrowed from the Fed (11).

Table 12–1. Partial Balance Sheets of the U.S. Banking System

The Balance Sheet of the Federal Reserve Bank (in billions of dollars)	
Assets	Liabilities
1. Loans to banks . . . . . . $ 1	4. Federal Reserve notes
2. Government securities . . $ 266	A. Currency held by the
3. Gold and other assets . . $ 66	public $268
	B. Vault cash of banks . . . . . . $ 34
	5. Deposits of banks at Fed . . . . $ 29

The Balance Sheet of Combined Commercial Banks (in billions of dollars)	
Assets	Liabilities
6. Reserves	
A. Deposits at Fed . . . . $ 29	9. Checkable deposits . . . . . . $ 644
B. Vault cash . . . . $ 34	10. Other deposits $1,805
7. Loans to public $2,668	11. Loans from Fed . . . . $ 1
8. Government securities . . . $ 704	

Note that 1 matches 11, 4B equals 6B, and 5 equals 6A. These are the assets and liabilities that banks and the Fed owe each other.

M1 equals (4A), the currency held by the public plus (9), checkable deposits, plus traveler's checks ($8 billion), so M1 equals $920 billion. The Fed limits how much banks can loan by requiring them to place a certain fraction of their deposits at the Fed (this fraction is called the required reserve ratio); banks place (5) at the Fed, and the Fed owes them (6A).

HOW MONEY IS CREATED

For the rest of the chapter, we will define money as M1, or money = currency (held by the public) + checkable deposits. We will follow how money is created step-by-step. To simplify our analysis, assume that: (1) banks lend all their excess reserves and (2) the public redeposits all lent money into the banking system.

Steps by One Bank

Step 1: Suppose the Fed somehow causes $1,000 in new money to be deposited at a bank. The bank puts the $1,000 into reserves. Let us assume that the Fed has a required reserve ratio of 10 percent. So the bank puts $100 into deposits at the Fed (its required reserves) and puts its excess reserves (the reserves a bank holds over what the Fed requires of it) of $900 into its vault. Here is how the balance sheet looks:

Combined Commercial Banks' Balance Sheet	
Assets	Liabilities

6. Reserves
    A. Deposits at Fed   +$100
    B. Vault cash   +$900
	9. Checkable deposits +$1,000

So far, the money supply has increased only by the $1,000 the Fed has added. Note that the currency held by the bank is defined to not be a part of the money supply.

Step 2: The bank lends out its excess reserves of $900. It does this by creating a new $900 checkable deposit in the borrower's name. So instead of +$1,000 in checkable deposits, there is +$1,900.

Combined Commercial Banks' Balance Sheet	
Assets	Liabilities
6. Reserves	9. Checkable deposits +$1,900
A. Deposits at Fed +$100	
B. Vault cash +$900	
7. Loans +$900	

Now the money supply has increased by $1,900! The right given to banks by the government to lend money it owes its depositors is called **fractional reserve banking.** It is this right that allowed this bank to create the added $900.

Steps by the Banking System

Step 3: The borrower of the $900 spends it, and the people getting the $900 deposit it *at another bank.* Nothing has changed from above, except that the other bank now holds the $900 as deposits at the Fed and as vault cash.

Step 4: The new bank getting the $900 will put 10 percent of it ($90) into required reserves and lend the remainder ($810) by putting $810 into some other borrower's checking account. Now the balance sheet will look like this:

Combined Commercial Banks' Balance Sheet	
Assets	Liabilities
6. Reserves	9. Checkable deposits +$ 2,710
A. Deposits at Fed +$ 190	
B. Vault cash +$ 810	
7. Loans +$1,710	

By this step, the initial $1,000 deposit has increased the money supply by $2,710 (the increase in checkable deposits). As long as there are excess reserves and as long as banks lend these reserves out, this process will continue *until all of the initial cash is deposited at the Fed* as required reserves.

Step 5: When all of the $1,000 goes for meeting the 10 percent reserve requirement, banks will stop this process of lending and relending. The last balance sheet will look like this:

Combined Commercial Banks' Balance Sheet	
Assets	Liabilities
6. Reserves	9. Checkable deposits +$10,000
A. Deposits at Fed +$1,000	
B. Vault cash + 0	
7. Loans +$9,000	

Now the $1,000 is all in required reserves; it equals 10 percent of total added deposits, $10,000. The money supply has increased by $10,000 (the added deposits). In general, if R is the required reserve ratio, we have:

$$\text{Increase in the Money Supply} = \frac{\text{Initial Cash Added}}{R}$$

$1/R$ is the money supply multiplier. It tells us by how much an added dollar in banks' reserves (no matter what the source) will increase the money supply. The higher the ratio, the smaller the multiplier.

Mathematically, let "f" be the fraction of each dollar deposited that is lent *and* redeposited. When a dollar is added to the banking system, it is lent and relent such that the increase in the money supply is:

$$1 + f + f^2 + \ldots = 1/(1-f)$$

In our simple case, $1 - f = R$, so the money multiplier is $1/R$.

The *actual* money multiplier is smaller than $1/R$ for two reasons: (1) banks like to keep some vault cash to meet their daily needs to cash checks and provide change; (2) the public does not redeposit all the money that is lent—it holds some fraction of it out as cash. When new money is introduced into the banking system, both of these factors *reduce* the amount redeposited in each step, resulting in a smaller f and a *smaller multiplier*. For example, the reserve ratio for checking accounts is 12 percent, which would imply a simple money multiplier for M1 of 8.33 (1/.12). In fact, M1's actual money multiplier is currently near 2.7, a far smaller number.

YOU SHOULD REMEMBER

1. Banks mainly put their deposits and loans from the Fed into their reserves, loans to the public, and government securities.

2. Banks create money by lending out their excess reserves. They do this by increasing the borrower's checking account by the amount lent.

3. The simple money multiplier is $1/R$, R being the required reserve ratio (the fraction of deposits that banks must deposit at the Fed). A dollar of new reserves will increase the money supply by, at most, $1/R$ dollars.

4. The actual money multiplier is less than $1/R$, because banks do not lend all their excess reserves and the public does not redeposit all it borrows from banks.

HOW THE FED CONTROLS THE MONEY SUPPLY

The Fed has direct control over the **monetary base** (also called *high-powered money*). The monetary base is essentially all the cash in the economy: It is the sum of bank reserves and currency held by the public (in Table 12–1, 4 + 5). It represents the total cash the banking system *could* use as reserves (and would be used if the public deposited all its cash into banks).

The Fed can affect the *actual money multiplier*: The actual money multiplier takes into account the fact that banks do not lend out all their excess reserves and the public does not deposit all its money in banks. We have:

M1 = Actual Money Multiplier × Monetary Base

Table 12–2. Major Methods of Money Control

Method	Effect		
	On Monetary Base	On Money Multiplier	On Money Supply
1. Required reserve ratio			
Increase	None	Decrease	Decrease
Decrease	None	Increase	Increase
2. Open market operation			
Fed Buys Bonds	Increase	None	Increase
Fed Sells Bonds	Decrease	None	Decrease
3. Discount Rate			
Increase	Decrease	None*	Decrease
Decrease	Increase	None*	Increase

*Note: A higher discount rate will discourage banks from keeping excess reserves and therefore will reduce the money multiplier. A lower rate will increase the money multiplier. This effect is so small, though, that "none" is closer to reality as an answer.

How the Methods of Money Control Actually Work

Method 1: Change the reserve requirement. If our simple money multiplier (1/R) held, then an increase in R from 10 percent to 15 percent (0.10 to 0.15) would decrease the money multiplier from 10 to 6.67. For a given monetary base of, say $50 billion, this would decrease the money supply from $500 billion to $333.3 billion.

Method 2: Add or subtract new reserves by buying and selling government securities. This is called an open market operation and is carried out by the Federal Open Market Committee (FOMC). This is the method the Fed uses most often to change the money supply.

If the FOMC buys securities from banks, it pays for the bank's government securities (8 in Table 12–1) by adding to the bank's reserves at the Fed (6A). This increases the monetary base and thus the money supply. By selling government securities, the Fed has the opposite effect. It reduces the monetary base and the money supply by taking money in exchange for the bonds it sells.

Method 3: Add new reserves by lending to banks. When banks borrow from the Fed, the Fed charges banks a rate of interest called the discount rate. A reduced discount rate encourages banks to borrow. When banks borrow, the Fed increases 5 (and banks increase 11 and 6A). This increases the monetary base and thus the money supply. Actually, banks borrow very little from the Fed, and thus changes in the discount rate have very little impact on the money supply. Nevertheless, the changes are widely watched, because they often signal changes in Fed policy.

Other Methods: The Fed also sets the minimum percentage of a stock purchase that must be paid for in cash (the **stock margin requirement**). The higher the margin, the harder it is to buy stocks on credit. Also, the Fed has at times restricted the credit conditions for home mortgages and consumer loans. By limiting credit, the Fed makes it harder for people to buy homes and expensive consumer goods. Neither of these methods directly impacts the money supply unless it reduces what banks lend. One last method the Fed uses is **moral suasion**, or "jawboning," to get banks to do what it wants (e.g., it may encourage or discourage banks to lend to foreign governments).

YOU SHOULD REMEMBER

1. The Fed *increases* the money supply by reducing the required reserve ratio (R), by buying government securities, and by lowering the discount rate.

2. The Fed *decreases* the money supply by raising R, by selling government securities, and by raising the discount rate.

3. The monetary base is at the base for all the loans that the banking system can make. It includes the currency held by the public plus all bank reserves.

4. M1 equals the actual money multiplier times the monetary base.

TAYLOR'S RULE: WHAT DOES THE FEDERAL RESERVE DO?

Central banks usually seek to stabilize the rate of inflation. In addition, some seek to keep the economy at full employment. To do this, they usually focus on controlling an intermediate target. In the past, the intermediate target has often been the money supply.

Currently, most central banks focus on influencing interest rates. Interest rates provide an instant feedback. The interest rate that central banks do (and should) care about is the real interest rate (the nominal rate less the rate of inflation). If, instead, the central bank focused on maintaining a particular nominal rate, it could lead to wide swings in the money supply. To illustrate, suppose the central bank targets a certain nominal interest rate, say 4 percent. To do this, say it increases the money supply. In the short run, rates will fall to 4 percent. But then inflation starts to grow and the interest rates start to rise: The central bank would then increase the money supply even more! The result would be run-away inflation. To avoid this, the central bank should focus on real rates of interest. When inflation starts to rise, real rates are likely to fall, correctly indicating that the economy is being stimulated. Should the central bank keep increasing the money supply, inflation will get worse.

Many countries use inflation targeting. With inflation targeting, the central bank announces an explicit inflation rate it wants to achieve, and it commits itself to achieving this rate. In these countries, the central bank is free to set interest rates which in turn affect aggregate demand and inflation. It is important that the central bank be free of political influence because, when it is not, some politicians with their short time horizon (the next election) often push for more inflation. A central bank using inflation targeting will issue frequent forecasts of where it thinks the economy, interest rates, and inflation will be going. It is important that the central bank let people know what it is doing (this is called transparency) because the economy is more stable when people know what to expect.

Although the Federal Reserve Bank, the central bank in the United States, seeks price stability, it does not currently use inflation targeting. Instead, the Fed (as well as other central banks such as the European Central Bank) often appears to be following what is called Taylor's rule (named after John Taylor who first proposed the rule). The rule predicts how the Fed determines the federal funds rate (the rate private banks charge other private banks to borrow money). To illustrate the rule, assume that if the economy is at full employment, the real federal funds rate (the federal funds rate minus the rate of inflation) would be 2 percent. Next, assume the Fed wants the inflation rate to be 3 percent. According to Taylor's rule, the Fed *might* set the target federal funds rate (r) so that it equals:

$$\text{target r} = 2 \text{ percent} + \text{Rate of Inflation} + 0.5 \text{ (Rate of Inflation} - 3 \text{ percent)} + 0.5 \text{ (Real } GDP \text{ Gap)}$$

The real *GDP* gap is the percent difference between real *GDP* and the full-employment level of *GDP* (the level of *GDP* consistent with a stable inflation rate). If the Fed was interested only in controlling inflation (i.e., inflation targeting), the weight on the real *GDP* gap would be zero. If the Fed was interested only in keeping the economy at full employment, the weight on the (Rate of Inflation – 3 percent) term would be zero.

In this example of Taylor's rule, the Fed is seeking to keep the real interest rate at 2 percent as long as inflation is at its targeted level and *GDP* is at its full-employment level. When the economy is "overheated" with inflation growing and output exceeding its full-employment level, the Fed will target a higher real rate of interest. It will try to raise interest rates by selling bonds: The increase in the supply of bonds will lower the price of bonds and raise interest rates. Selling bonds decreases the money supply (when the Fed sells bonds, it gets in return money, which it, in effect, destroys). This (along with the higher real interest rates) dampens the growth in aggregate demand. When the economy is in a recession with inflation falling and output falling short of its full-employment level, the Fed will target a lower real rate of interest. It will try to decrease interest rates by buying bonds: The increase in the demand for bonds will raise the price of bonds and lower interest rates. Buying bonds will increase the money supply (because the Fed effectively creates money to pay for the bonds). This (along with the decrease in real interest rates) stimulates the growth in aggregate demand.

To illustrate Taylor's rule, suppose the economy is at full employment but the rate of inflation is too high at 5 percent. Taylor's rule predicts that the Fed will set the target federal funds rate at 8 percent (= 2 percent + 5 percent + 0.5 (5 percent – 3 percent)). The target real funds rate is equal to 3 percent (= 8 percent – 5 percent). To raise the real interest rate above its full-employment level (2 percent), the central bank will sell bonds (which decreases the money supply). Increasing the supply of bonds decreases the price of bonds. Interest rates and the price of bonds are inversely related. Thus, selling bonds increases the interest rate. The decrease in the money supply along with the increase in real interest rates will reduce aggregate demand and inflation. Next, suppose the inflation rate is on target at 3 percent but real *GDP* is 4 percent below its full-employment level. The Fed is predicted to set the target federal funds rate at 3 percent (= 2 percent + 3 percent + 0.5 (–4 percent)). This makes the target real federal funds rate equal to 0 percent. To lower real interest rates to this level, the central bank will have to buy bonds and increase the money supply. The increase in the money supply along with the reduced real interest rate will stimulate the economy and bring *GDP* back to full employment.

Taylor's rule describes what central banks do. It can also describe what central banks should do. Simulations show that with the correct weights and targets, the rule does well.

KNOW THE CONCEPTS

DO YOU KNOW THE BASICS?

1. How does money make it easier for people to trade?
2. Why is income not money?
3. What is it that is really "borrowed" when people borrow "money"?
4. Are credit cards money?
5. How does the lending of excess reserves by banks create money?

6. If the legal reserve requirement is 20 percent, what is the most the banking system can lend out if an individual deposits $1,000?

7. How does the Fed's buying government securities add to the monetary base? How does this change the money supply?

8. Why does lowering of the discount rate add to the monetary base?

9. What factors make the actual money multiplier smaller than $1/R$?

10. How does increasing the monetary base change the money supply?

TERMS FOR STUDY

checkable deposits

commodity money

discount rate

double coincidence of wants

excess reserves

fiat money

inflation targeting

liquidity

M1

M2

monetary base

money

open market operation

required reserve ratio (R)

Taylor's rule

PRACTICAL APPLICATION

1. In a barter economy, how would an economics professor survive?

2. Assume the required reserve ratio is 20 percent.

    a. If a single bank in the banking system has $10 million in excess reserves, how much new money, at most, could it create by itself?

    b. If the whole banking system has $10 million in excess reserves, how much new money, at most, could it create?

3. Fill in the following table. Assume that banks keep 20 percent of their deposits backed by reserves and that the public redeposits all the money it is lent. Show the effect of $1,000 in new reserves being deposited at Bank A, Bank A lending its excess reserves, the money from the loan being spent and deposited at Bank B, and so forth.

	Increase in Deposits	Increase in Loans	Increase in Reserves
Bank A	$1,000	$800	$200
Bank B	_____	_____	_____
Bank C	_____	_____	_____
. . .			
Total	_____	_____	_____

4. Indicate whether the following events will increase or decrease the money supply:

   Event A: The Fed buys government securities from the public.

   Event B: Because more people are defaulting on their loans, banks decide to hold more excess reserves.

   Event C: Because of the convenience of credit cards, the public holds less cash than before.

   Event D: The Fed raises the discount rate.

   Event E: The Federal Funds Rate is the rate of interest banks charge one another to borrow money. The Federal Funds Rate goes up.

   Event F: The Fed lowers the required reserve requirement for backing demand deposits.

5. Jane withdraws $1,000 from her checking account and puts it into a cookie jar. How much, at most, could the money supply fall if the required reserve ratio is 10 percent?

6. Suppose the Fed is using Taylor's rule. It wants an inflation rate of 2 percent and a full-employment real funds rate of 3 percent. It weights excess inflation by 0.5 and the *GDP* gap (the percent gap between real *GDP* and the full-employment level of *GDP*) by 0.5. If inflation is running at 5 percent and real *GDP* is 4 percent above its full-employment level, what real federal funds rate will the Fed target? If the rate is below this level, will it buy or sell bonds to achieve this target level? What if the rate is above this level?

7. If the public suddenly wanted to hold all its money in the form of cash (withdrawing all its money from checking and savings accounts), what would happen to the money supply?

8. If banks could not find anyone willing to borrow funds at the interest rate they charge, what would happen to the money supply?

9. A "run on the bank" refers to the situation when most of a bank's depositors withdraw their deposits from their bank. What does the bank multiplier process tell us will be the outcome of this process? In 1934, the Federal Deposit Insurance Corporation (FDIC) was set up to guarantee bank deposits. Before that time, if a bank failed, its depositors could lose all their savings. Now, the FDIC insures these deposits (up to $100,000). How does this reduce the likelihood of runs on the bank? How does this reduce the impact of runs on the bank?

10. In the Great Depression, the money base remained the same but the money supply fell by over 30 percent. This occurred without any direct intervention from the Fed. What did the public do to cause this to occur?

ANSWERS

KNOW THE CONCEPTS

1. With money, people do not have to sell their goods and services only to those who have goods and services they want.
2. Income is the goods and services one earns; money is only a measure of its value.
3. A borrower is actually borrowing real goods and services.
4. No. Credit cards are a means of spending money. Money is what people use to pay their credit card bills.
5. The lending of excess reserves creates money (1) instantly when the borrower's checkable deposit is increased (this is how banks give people loans) and (2) later, when the lent money is redeposited by the people from whom the borrower buys goods and services, and this is relent and so on.
6. $4,000.
7. This increases the monetary base, and through the money multiplier process, the money supply is increased even more.
8. A lower discount rate encourages banks to run down their excess reserves since it is then cheaper to get some extra cash from the Fed when needed. Banks run down their excess reserves by lending them: This creates money.
9. The two main factors are (1) banks do not lend all their excess reserves and (2) the public does not redeposit all the funds it has been lent.
10. The bigger the monetary base, the more money that can be created through the money multiplier process.

PRACTICAL APPLICATION

1. The professor would have to find students that wanted economic lessons *and* had something the professor wanted (such as food, housing, and clothing). Obviously, there are not too many professors of economics in barter economies. Indeed, there is very little specialization in barter economies, since most people produce only goods that are in common demand.
2. **a.** $8 million.
   b. $40 million (5 × $8 million).

3. Bank B: $800, $640, $160. Bank C: $640, $512, $128. Total: $5,000 (1/.2 × $1,000), $4,000 (80 percent of $5,000), and $1,000 (20 percent of $5,000 and the initial increase in reserves).

4. *Event A:* Increase (mainly due to bigger monetary base).

    Event B: Decrease (smaller multiplier).

    Event C: Increase (larger multiplier because more of the money lent is redeposited).

    Event D: Decrease (smaller base when banks borrow less from Fed).

    Event E: Decrease (smaller multiplier as banks hold larger excess reserves, either to lend or to avoid having to borrow at the higher rate).

    Event F: Increase (larger multiplier).

5. $9,000 (checking deposits will fall $10,000 but currency held by the public will go up $1,000).

6. The formula will be:

r = 3 percent + 2 percent + 0.5 (5 percent – 2 percent) + 0.5 (4 percent)

Thus, the Fed will target a federal funds rate of 8.5 percent. If the current rate is below this, it will sell bonds, lowering the price of bonds and raising interest rates. This will decrease the money supply. If the current rate is above this, it will buy bonds, increasing the price of bonds and lowering interest rates. This will increase the money supply.

7. The money supply would shrink back down to the size of the monetary base.

8. The money supply would shrink, because banks could not lend and relend.

9. Runs on banks cause the money supply to shrink. As citizens try to get cash, banks call in loans, forcing businesses to draw down their deposits, which in turn forces more loan liquidation, and so forth. The net result is a dramatic decrease in the money supply and an inevitable decline in economic activity. The FDIC makes depositors less nervous and so reduces the likelihood of runs on banks. However, even in those cases where banks have failed, it replaced lost deposits with new money, thus keeping the effects of the bank failure from spreading to other banks. This kept the money supply from shrinking.

10. Falling stock prices and the decline in *GDP* led to rising defaults on loans. In turn, many banks went out of business. At the time, there was no government insurance to protect depositors. So, may people lost their savings. This made others withdraw money from banks and keep their savings in cash. As a result, the money multiplier decreased dra-

matically. Adding to this decrease was the fact that the remaining banks kept larger excess reserves to offset bad loans and protect themselves from runs on the bank. Had the Fed intervened, as it was supposed to, it could have prevented what was a recession from turning into a depression.

13
MONEY AND AGGREGATE DEMAND

KEY TERMS

equation of exchange ($MV = PQ$) money $\times$ velocity equals price $\times$ output.

long-run neutrality of money theory that changes in the money supply have no real effects on output or employment in the long run.

nominal money (M) dollar amount of money.

quantity theory of money theory that uses the equation of exchange to make predictions by assuming that the annual change in velocity is small and predictable.

real money (M/P) money in terms of what it can buy.

velocity the number of times an average dollar is used in a year to buy final goods and services (also called *income velocity*).

How does money affect aggregate demand? Most economists agree that the *quantity theory of money* accurately describes the long-run effects of money. In this model, money affects only prices and not output in the long run. On the other hand, economists disagree about the short-run effects of money. Keynesians emphasize the effects of money on credit markets and investment spending while Monetarists emphasize the effects of money on all spending.

MONEY DEMAND

Money is anything widely used for making transactions. While money includes many things, thinking of money as cash is easiest. Ignore for now credit cards, checks, and all other forms of credit. By using the cash-only definition, the demand for money is the demand for cash. To hold more cash, you have to forego spending. For example, if between now and next year, you wanted to add $1,000 to your cash on hand, you would have to give up $1,000 of spending. The cost of holding more cash is the value of foregone spending.

Holding cash has benefits. Some of the reasons people demand money include:

- **Transaction Demand for Money:** People have money holdings because this allows people to buy and sell goods easily (the alternative is barter).
- **Precautionary Demand for Money:** Larger money holdings allow people to meet unforeseen expenses. For example, having money on hand could allow you to take advantage of a bargain price that you otherwise would have to pass up.
- **Speculative Demand for Money:** People may hold money because they feel money is safer than other assets. Stocks, bonds, and real estate all fluctuate in price. A dollar, on the other hand, is always worth a dollar. Keynes argued that if people expected bond prices to fall, they would try to sell the bonds and build up their money holdings.

THE QUANTITY THEORY OF MONEY

Consider the following thought experiment. Suppose you awoke tomorrow and were told that there was some good news and some bad news. The good news is that your wages, income, and wealth had doubled, right down to the change in your wallet. The bad news is that all prices had doubled. At first, you think, "Wow, I am twice as rich." Next, when you see that prices have doubled also, you realize that nothing has really changed. Your real wage and real income are still the same. You can buy no more than you could before. This leads to an important insight: the real value matters. So if all the dollars in the economy doubled and all dollar prices (including wages, interest payments, and so forth) doubled, then once people adjusted, real output and all other real magnitudes would remain unaffected. In the long run, money does not matter.

The insight that money has no real effects in the long run is captured in the quantity theory of money. The basic assumptions of the quantity theory include:

1. People want to hold a fixed ratio of income, k, in money holdings. For example, if k is 0.1, a person with an annual income of $50,000 will want to hold $5,000 on average in money (in the form of cash and bank deposits). The fraction k is called the Cambridge k.

2. Money supply (MS) is determined by the Federal Reserve Board (the Fed).

3. In the long run, the economy is at full employment. Let Q be the level of national output at full employment. We will measure Q in the number of baskets of goods produced. Let P be the price level of a basket of goods. Nominal gross national product ($\$GDP$) equals $\$GDP = P \times Q$. The nation's demand for money (MD) is:

$$MD = k\ \$GDP = kPQ.$$

If money demand equals money supply, we can write:

$$MS = kPQ.$$

This equation is the quantity theory of money. In the long run, k is fixed and Q is at its long-run level. Thus, if the money supply doubles, prices will double.

PROBLEM   Use the quantity theory of money to solve for the price level and nominal income. In Country X, people want to hold 10 percent of the income in money holdings. Full-employment output is 2,000 baskets of goods. The money supply is $400.

    a. What is the long-run price level (P) and nominal *GDP*?

    b. If the money supply rises to $800, what is the long-run price level (P) and $\$GDP$?

    c. What has happened to the real money holdings (MS/P) of people in **a** and **b**?

SOLUTION   **a.** $P = MS/(kQ) = \$400/200 = \$2.$ $\$GDP = PQ = \$4,000.$

    b. $P = \$4$ and $\$GDP = \$8,000.$

    c. In case **a**, real money holdings $= MS/P = \$400/\$2 = 200.$
    In case **b**, real money holdings $= MS/P = \$800/\$4 = 200.$
    Real money holdings are the same because all real magnitudes are unaffected by money (nominal money!) in the long run!

How does the quantity theory work? Suppose we start out with case A in the problem above ($MS = \$400$, $k = 0.1$, $P = \$2$, and $Q = 2,000$). People are holding enough money to buy 200 baskets of goods (this being their desired real money holdings). Now suppose the money supply rises to $800 (as it did in case **b**). If prices stay at $2, people find they are holding more money ($800) than they want ($400). To reduce their money holdings, they will try to spend it. One person can get rid of cash. However, everyone together cannot. Society will always have $800. So if everyone wants to hold less cash but this is impossible, what will happen? Instead, as people spend more to reduce their money holdings, prices and nominal incomes will go up (recall that spending = income for the economy). In nominal terms, prices will rise until the nominal demand for money ($MD = kPQ$) rises to equal the nominal supply of money ($800): P = $8. In real terms, prices will rise until real money supply (*MS/P*) equals real money demand (*kQ*) of 200 baskets of goods.

Often, economists refer to money's velocity (*V*) instead of the Cambridge *k*. Velocity, *V*, is the number of times the average dollar is spent in a year. Since *$GDP* is total spending and *MS* is the number of dollars, $V = \$GDP/MS$. With *MS* = *MD*, we can see that *V* = 1/*k*, as *k* = *MD/$GDP*. For example, if the money supply is $100 and *k* = 0.10, then aggregate spending and income equal $1,000. This means that each of the 100 dollars has to be spent on average 10 times in the year. Hence, velocity equals 10, the inverse of 0.1.

By using velocity, the quantity theory of money can be restated as the more commonly used *equation of exchange*:

$$MS \times V = P \times Q.$$

This gives us a very simple equation for aggregate demand:

$$\$GDP = MS \times V = MS/k.$$

Figure 13-1 (see page 201) shows the long-run aggregate demand curve in an economy where the money supply equals $400 and *k* = 0.05 (or *V* = 20). Aggregate demand equals $8,000 (= *MS* × *V* = $400 × 20). As a result, the area under the aggregate demand (*AD*) curve is always $8,000.

Points to Note About Figure 13–1

1. The area under the aggregate demand curve is always $8,000. When output is 4,000 and each unit sells for $2, total spending is $8,000. When output is 8,000 and the price level is $1, total spending is $8,000.

2. The nominal money supply is the same all along the aggregate demand curve. A higher money supply would correspond to a higher aggregate demand curve.

THE LONG-RUN NEUTRALITY OF MONEY

The quantity theory of money predicts that in the long run, the quantity of money will not affect anything real. This result is called *the long-run neutrality of money*. Figure 13–1 (see page 213) illustrates this proposition. Suppose that people want to hold 5 percent of their income in money holdings, that the long-run real level of output is 4,000, and that the money supply is $400. Aggregate demand will be $8,000, and the price level will be $2. If the money supply increases to $800, aggregate demand will be $16,000. At the full employment output of 4,000, the price level will double to $4. Nothing real has changed; only all prices and all incomes have doubled in their dollar amounts.

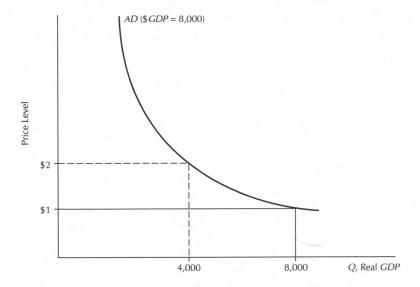

Figure 13–1. Long-Run Aggregate Demand with Quantity Theory

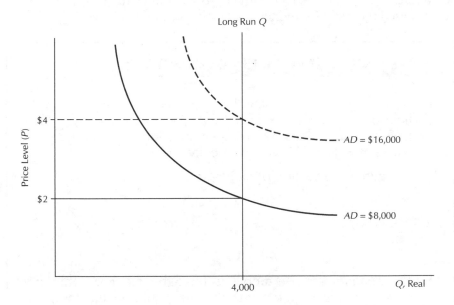

Figure 13–2. Long-Run Neutrality of Money

Points to Note About Figure 13–2

1. Total spending is $8,000 at all points on the AD = $8,000 curve. Along this curve, the money supply is $400 and velocity is 20 ($k$ = 0.05).

2. Total spending is $16,000 at all points on the *AD* = $16,000 curve. Along this curve, the money supply is $800 and velocity is still 20.

3. Velocity stays unchanged in the quantity theory of money.

4. Doubling the money supply from $400 to $800 doubles the price level from $2 to $4.

5. The price level can be found by dividing aggregate demand by *Q*.

One way to understand the quantity theory is to realize that while the Fed can change the nominal money supply, in the long run, it has no effect on the real money supply. For example, in Figure 13–2, at full employment, whatever the nominal money supply is, the real money supply will always be 5 percent of real output (*MS/P = kQ*) or 200. The 200 stands for the output that money holdings can buy (200 baskets of goods). Another way to understand the quantity theory is that, in the long run, increase aggregate demand (total dollar spending) can be increased in only two ways. One is to increase the money supply. The other is to decrease *k*, the fraction of income people want to hold in money balances (note that decreasing *k* is the same thing as increasing velocity). For example, the introduction of credit cards most likely decreased the need for money holdings, resulting in a lower *k*.

YOU SHOULD REMEMBER

1. According to the quantity theory of money, people want to hold a certain fraction (k) of their income in money ($MD = k\$GDP$). Each dollar will be spent on average V times a year, where $V = 1/k$. V is called velocity.

2. The quantity equation of money is:

$$MS \times V = P \times Q$$

or

$$MS = k \times P \times Q$$

3. The nominal money supply is fixed by the Fed. The real money supply is determined by the public in the long run ($MS/P = kQ$).

4. Aggregate demand ($\$GDP$) = $MS \times V = MS/k$.

5. In the long run, changes in the money supply affect only prices, not output.

HOW TO PREDICT INFLATION

To predict inflation with the quantity theory, economists put the quantity theory into its percent form:

$$\%\Delta P = \%\Delta MS - \%\Delta Q + \%\Delta V$$

or

$$\%\Delta P = \%\Delta MS - \%\Delta Q - \%\Delta k$$

$\%\Delta$ stands for *the percent change*. The percent change in prices ($\%\Delta P$) is the rate of inflation. $\%\Delta MS$ is the growth rate in the inflation rate. $\%\Delta Q$ is the growth rate in real *GDP*. For example, if the money supply grows at 7 percent, output grows at 3 percent, and velocity (V) grows at 1 percent, the inflation rate will be 5 percent. For many years, the velocity of M2 grew at a steady 1 percent rate, making the equation remarkably accurate when applied to long periods of time. In recent years, velocity has become less stable, making the equation less useful.

We get the following predictions from this equation (each prediction holding the other variables unchanged):

1. The rate of inflation will increase when the money supply grows at a faster rate. If growth rate in the money supply goes up by 5 percent, inflation will increase 5 percent.

2. The rate of inflation will go down when output grows faster. If the *GDP* growth rate jumps from 1 percent a year to 3 percent a year, the inflation rate will be 2 percent lower.

3. High rates of inflation are always caused by the money supply increasing. Changes in Q and V are just too small to explain inflation rates exceeding 6 percent.

At the peak of an expansion, commentators often say that rising output will fuel more inflation. Instead, as we can see, rising output douses inflation. The commentators are confusing cause and effect. A rising aggregate demand increases total output in the short run, but in the long run, it leads to more inflation. The rise in output does not cause the higher prices; the rise in aggregate demand causes output and then prices to rise. Had output expanded more, inflation would have been less!

> # YOU SHOULD REMEMBER
>
> **1.** High rates of inflation are always caused by increases in the money supply.
>
> **2.** Inflation will be higher (a) the faster the money supply grows, (b) the slower output grows, and (c) the faster *V* increases.
>
> **3.** Inflation will be lower (a) the slower the money supply grows, (b) the faster output grows, and (c) the slower *V* increases.

THE GERMAN HYPERINFLATION

In the 1920s, Germany started printing money to finance government spending. Prices rose sixfold from mid-1921 to mid-1922. In the next 12 months, prices rose 180 times. However, that was only the beginning. In the subsequent year, prices rose another 8,540,000,000 times! During the peak of the inflation, workers were paid hourly, giving their earnings to their spouses to spend before it became worthless. The German government ran the printing presses day and night, printing money in higher and higher denominations. It blamed profiteers for the inflation and claimed it was printing more money only so people could afford to pay the higher prices. Of course, the government itself was the profiteer causing the higher prices by printing money. One story is about two brothers, one who worked hard and saved and the other who drank all the time. The frugal bother was impoverished when his savings were made worthless by the German hyper-inflation. The drunken brother collected his used bottles and had more wealth! The German hyperinflation destroyed the German middle class and undermined morals. In many ways, it created the conditions for Hitler to come to power.

THE SHORT-RUN EFFECTS OF MONEY: THE MONETARIST MODEL

All economists agree that the quantity theory describes the long-run effects of money. Where they disagree is how and when money affects the economy in the short run. We will begin with monetarism since it is most closely linked to the equation of exchange.

The basic premises of monetarism are:

1. *People hold money for different reasons than they save.* Bonds (and other forms of saving) do not act as close substitutes for money.

2. The main factor determining the money people want to hold is their income, not the interest rate.

3. Money has its main impact on aggregate demand through its effects on total spending. An excess supply of money is spent on goods (and not on bonds as in the Keynesian model).

The basic steps in the monetarist model are:

$$MS \text{ Up} \rightarrow \text{Excess Money Supply} \rightarrow \text{Spending Up} \rightarrow$$
$$AD \text{ Up} \rightarrow P \text{ and } Q \text{ Up.}$$

The following will review these steps one at a time.

Step One: Monetarists regard the equation of exchange (with the Cambridge k) as a demand function for money:

$$MD = kPQ.$$

k is the fraction of income people want to hold in money balances. It determines the demand for money (given income). While monetarists recognize that interest rates and other factors affect the size of k, they regard k as relatively stable.

Suppose people are holding the money—the cash and bank deposits— they want ($MS = MD$). Then the Fed increases the money supply.

Step Two: Initially, people have more money than they want ($MS > MD$). If I gave you \$10,000 in cash and told you to get rid of it, what would you do? Most likely, you would, for a while, spend more than you earn. Similarly, people with excess cash try to spend more than they earn. However, for a whole economy, this is impossible. Every dollar spent is a dollar earned. Similarly, the economy cannot reduce money holdings. While you can get rid of the \$10,000 in cash, other people will end up with it! So what will happen as people try to spend more?

Step Three: Total dollar spending and total dollar income will increase: aggregate demand will rise. As nominal income ($P \times Q$) rises, money demand ($MD = kPQ$) will also rise until the demand equals the supply of money ($MD = MS$).

The quantity theory of money is useful if velocity can be accurately estimated. In the 1960s and 1970s, it did remarkably well compared with the Keynesian models of the time. In the early 1980s, the United States underwent a financial revolution with credit cards, money market accounts, interstate banking, and many other changes. Since then, velocity has been far less predictable, and the relationship between monetary growth and inflation has been harder to discern.

YOU SHOULD REMEMBER

1. Monetarists use the quantity model to describe the short-run effects of money on aggregate demand.

2. In their model, money directly affects aggregate demand.

KEYNESIAN MODEL OF THE SHORT-RUN EFFECTS OF MONEY

The basic premises of Keynesians are described in the following:

1. Savings can be put into money holdings or into other assets that pay interest (the latter we will lump together as bonds). Bonds and money holdings are considered close substitutes.

2. The choice of where to put one's savings is determined by the interest rates bonds pay. The higher the interest rates, the less attractive money holdings are and the less money people will try to hold. The lower the interest rates, the less attractive bonds are and the more money people will try to hold.

3. Money has its main impact on aggregate demand through its impact on investment spending. The process is as follows:

$$MS \text{ Up} \rightarrow \text{Savings Up} \rightarrow \text{Interest Rate Down} \rightarrow$$
$$\text{Investment Spending Up} \rightarrow AD \text{ Up} \rightarrow P \text{ and } Q \text{ Up.}$$

We will now look at this process in detail.

Step One: To make the analysis simple, assume that people can put their savings into only two financial assets:

- Money, which can be cash or checking accounts. Money does not pay any interest (or, on some bank deposits, very little compared with bonds).

- Bonds, which are IOUs issued by borrowers promising to pay fixed amounts of money on specified dates. If a bond paid a fixed annual payment year after year, forever, its interest rate would be

$$\text{Interest Rate} = \frac{\text{Fixed Annual Payment}}{\text{Price of Bond}} \times 100$$

For example, a bond paying interest of $500 a year, year after year, forever, selling for $4,000, has an interest rate of 12.5 percent. A bond that pays interest forever is called in perpetuity. These are very rare. Most bonds pay interest for a fixed number of years and then pay back their face value. We will discuss the value of bonds later in this chapter. The essential point is that a higher interest rate means a lower bond price.

In the Keynesian model, money and bonds are close substitutes. The main cost of holding money in the Keynesian model is the foregone interest one could have earned by holding a bond of the same value. When interest rates increase, the quantity of money demanded decreases. When interest rates fall, the quantity of money demanded increases. The more readily the public is willing to substitute bonds for money (and money for bonds), the more the quantity of money demanded will increase when interest rates fall. Figure 13–3 shows the relationship between money demand and interest rates.

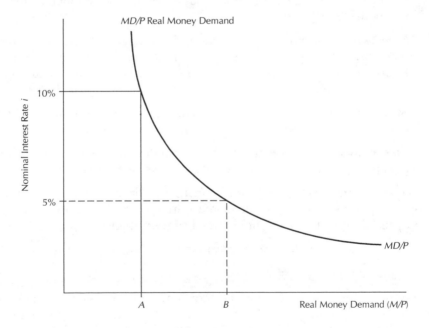

Figure 13–3. The Effect of Interest Rates on Money Demand

Points to Note About Figure 13–3

1. Nominal interest rates paid by bonds are on the vertical axis. The nominal interest rate is also the opportunity cost of holding money.

2. Money demand is real money demanded—the purchasing power of money that people care about (MD/P).

3. As the interest rate—the opportunity cost of holding money—falls from 10 to 5 percent, the quantity of real money demanded goes up from A to B.

4. A monetarist would likely draw the demand curve as being very steep, almost vertical, indicating that k is insensitive to interest rates.

5. Keynes argued that at a low-enough interest rate, the money demand curve becomes flat since people have little incentive to hold bonds rather than money when interest rates are low. He called this the *liquidity trap*, which we will examine below.

Assume that money demand equals money supply (say at an interest rate of 10 percent and a real money supply of A). The Fed then increases the money supply.

Step Two: People now have more money holdings than they need. Rather than spend it, they buy bonds with it. This causes bond prices to rise. Higher bond prices means the interest rate has fallen (see the interest rate formula in step one above).

Step Three: In the loanable funds model, this increase in savings and the lower interest rates will cause investment spending to increase.

Step Four: The increase in investment spending will be magnified by the multiplier process into an even greater increase in aggregate demand.

What makes monetary policy more effective, such that an increase in the money supply results in a greater increase in aggregate demand curve? In the Keynesian model, money supply has a **bigger** impact:

- investment spending increases more when interest rates fall, and

- the multiplier is bigger.

If interest rates are very low and the economy is in a recession, Keynes felt there could be a *liquidity trap*. In a liquidity trap, money supply has no impact at all on aggregate demand. This occurs because all increases of the money supply go into money holdings. None of it goes to buy bonds because they pay too little. None is spent because people want to build up their savings due to uncertainty. For example, in the recent Japanese recession, interest rates fell below 1 percent on Japanese bonds, making them a very risky investment (even a slight increase in interest rates would send their price falling). At the same time, Japanese financial intermediaries as well as the public appeared to be saving rather than spending the extra money the government printed. Keynesians recommended more government spending, rather than an expanding money supply, to stimulate the economy.

YOU SHOULD REMEMBER

1. In the Keynesian model, savings can be put into bonds (investments) or into money holdings. The higher the interest rate that bonds pay, the less people put into money holdings.

2. In the short run, an increase in the money supply mainly goes to buy bonds, which lowers interest rates, which increases investment spending, which increases aggregate demand through the multiplier process.

3. Keynesians regard money holdings as a close substitute for savings; monetarists regard money holdings as a poor substitute for savings.

THE LONG-RUN EFFECTS OF MONEY SUPPLY ON INTEREST RATES

Money is neutral if we are talking about a one-time increase in the money supply. However, money has real effects if the money supply grows at a constant higher rate. Suppose the growth rate in the money supply increases from 1 percent a year to 10 percent a year. Inflation rates will increase by 9 percent (say from 3 percent to 12 percent). The nominal interest rate will increase 9 percent (to compensate savers for lost purchasing power). This is called the *inflationary premium effect*. The higher nominal interest rate means that the real money supply will be lower in the long run. More nominal money means less real money! Real output will also be lower, decreasing by a small amount due to the added shoe leather cost and menu costs of the higher inflation.

YOU SHOULD REMEMBER

1. An increase in the growth rate of the money supply leads to a higher rate of inflation.

2. If people expect a higher rate of inflation, the nominal interest rate will go up (by the increase in the expected rate of inflation).

3. In the long run, a larger nominal money supply will increase neither real investment spending nor real aggregate demand, even in the Keynesian model.

THE SPENDING MULTIPLIER AND FISCAL POLICY

The spending multiplier (and thus fiscal policy's impact) is smaller when the effects of money demand are taken into account. Suppose government spending increases but the money supply is held constant. Further, assume prices do not change. Initially, total aggregate demand will increase according to the spending multiplier. However, the corresponding increase in income will increase money demand. People with higher incomes typically want higher money balances (a 10 percent increase in real income increases real money demand by between 7 percent and 10 percent). The higher money demand creates an excess money demand, resulting in people trying to sell their bonds to get money. The price of bonds will fall, and interest rates will rise. Investment spending will fall. (Economists say that investment spending has been **crowded out** by government spending.) This decrease in investment spending will partially offset the impact of higher government spending. We will have:

G up → AD, GNP up → M demand up → i up → I down (offset G up)

For further information on how to solve for national output in the Keynesian model, see the Appendix, page 589.

BONDS: INTEREST RATES AND PRICES

Bonds usually pay yearly or semiannual payments for a fixed number of years and then pay back their face value (usually $1,000) when they are retired. To calculate what you should pay for a bond, ask the question, "What would I have to save at the interest rate I earn on my other savings in order to get the same return?" The answer will be the bond's present value. Your current interest rate is the best rate you can earn on other assets of similar risk (and are willing to lend at). For example, suppose you can earn 10 percent on your savings. A dollar saved today would yield $1.10 a year from now. So what would you be willing to pay for a treasury bill (a short-term U.S. government bond) that pays back $1,000 in one year? You should be willing to pay $909.09 or $1,000/1.10). By dividing by 1.10, you find out how many dollars you need to invest today to get $1,000 back in one year. If the treasury bill sells for more than this, do not buy it (as you can do better elsewhere at 10 percent). If it sells for less, buy it (because it is paying better than 10 percent. The **yield** on any bond is the interest rate that makes its actual price equal to its present value. For example, if the above treasury bill sold for $892.86, its yield would be 12 percent.

If you save a dollar for two years at 10 percent per year, the dollar will grow to $1.21 in two years. In one year, it is worth 10 percent more ($1.10) and in the next year, the $1.10 is worth 10 percent more, or $1.21 ($1.10 × 1.10). In the second year, not only does the original dollar earn interest, so does the interest (of $0.10) earn interest. This phenomenon is called **compound interest.**

In general, in N years, $1.00 will be worth $(1 + i)^N$ dollars, where i is the interest rate stated as a decimal number. To find the present value (PV) of an N-year bond, economists use the formula:

$$PV = \frac{C1}{(1+i)} + \frac{C2}{(1+i)^2} + \frac{C3}{(1+i)^3} + \ldots + \frac{\text{Face Value}}{(1+i)^N}$$

$C1$ is the coupon or payment in the first year, $C2$ the second year's payment, and so on. Each C is divided by what a dollar saved today would be worth at i percent interest by the year that the C is paid. For example, $C2/(1 + i)^2$ is what one would have to save today at i percent to get $C2$ in two years. So PV is what one would have to save today to get the same payments the bond makes.

If all the coupon payments are equal, a bond that pays C forever is worth:

$$PV = C/i$$

A bond that pays C for N years and then stops (with no return of face value) is worth:

$$PV = C/i \times (1 - 1/(1 + i)^N)$$

When the bond pays back its face value, we just add the face value's present value to this term. Note that as N gets large, the value of the bond gets very close to C/i, its value when it pays C forever.

Example: Calculating Present Value

PROBLEM   When the interest rate is 10 percent, what is the present value of a ten-year bond paying $80 a year for ten years and, in the tenth year, an additional $1,000?

SOLUTION $887.11. $80 a year for ten years is worth $491.57 (letting $N = 10$ in the equation above). $1,000 in ten years is worth $385.54 ($1,000 divided by 1.10 to the tenth power).

An important point to remember when investing in bonds is that the price of long-term bonds changes far more when interest rates change than does the price of short-term bonds. This point can be demonstrated by using the formulas above. Suppose the market interest rate is 10 percent. Bond A pays $1,100 in one year. Bond B pays $100 a year forever. According to our formulas, both have a present value of $1,000. This will also be the price at which they will sell. Now suppose the interest rate goes up to 20 percent. Bond A's price (and PV) will fall to $916.67, while Bond B's price will fall to $500. Thus, the price of the longer-term bond (Bond B) changes more when the interest rate changes. In general, the value of short-term bonds is far less volatile than that of long-term bonds, and thus short-term bonds are a safer investment. On the other hand, long-term bonds usually pay a higher interest rate to compensate bond buyers for the higher risk.

THE DIFFERENCES BETWEEN KEYNESIAN AND MONETARIST VIEWS

Most texts lise the disagreements between Keynesians and monetarists. Typically on these lists are the following issues:

- *How fast will the economy recover on its own from a recession?* Monetarists generally believe that the economy will usually be at full employment unless the government acts to destabilize the economy. In addition, monetarists believe in a faster recovery time than Keynesians.

- *What causes recessions?* Monetarists believe that most recessions have been caused by sharp decreases in the growth rate of the money supply. They point to the Great Depression (when the money supply was cut by one-third) and to the 1981–1982 recession (when the money growth rate was cut by one-half). Keynesians believe that changes in investment spending (and consumer durable spending) have caused our recessions. They point to the dramatic decline in investment that has preceded most of our recessions.

- *Should the government actively try to keep the economy at full employment?* Economists have identified several key "lags" in using economic policy to affect the economy actively (which is called **discretionary economic policy**). Suppose the economy is in a recession. The first lag is the **recognition lag:** It takes time for the government to recognize that something is wrong with the economy. The second lag is the **implementation lag:** It takes time for the government to implement its policy and take action. The final lag is the **effectiveness lag:** It takes time for government action to affect the economy. If these lags are too long and if their length is uncertain, the effect of discretionary policy can be for the government to do the wrong thing at the wrong time. For example, a policy to dampen inflation may impact the economy later when it is in a recession, making the recession worse. Monetarists believe the government should steer a steady course by following a set of fixed rules (such as increasing the money supply at a steady 4 percent). Keynesians, on the other hand, more readily advocate discretionary policy action, although many now reject trying to "fine-tune" the economy with continual discretionary policy action.

- *How productive is government spending?* Keynesians believe that government spending can have a strong positive effect on our economy. Investments in basic research, in highways, and in related projects have produced very good results. Monetarists tend to doubt that most added government programs will be efficient.

- *How harmful are higher taxes?* Keynesians believe that if government spending is productive, then the higher taxes needed to support the government spending will not harm the economy. Supply-side economists and monetarists believe that taxes reduce aggregate supply and slow the growth rate of output.

- *How steep is the aggregate supply curve and how fast does it shift up when prices go up?* Keynesians tend to believe the AS curve is flat (especially when the economy is in a recession) and is slow to shift up when prices increase. Monetarists tend to believe that the AS curve is steep and that it will shift up quickly when prices increase.

- *Is investment spending insensitive to changes in the interest rates?* Some texts set forth the position that investment spending is insensitive to changes in the interest rate as Keynesian, which it is, but some texts then ascribe the opposite belief to monetarists. They state this in the context of the model in the section of this chapter relating to "The Keynesian Model of the Short-Run Effects of Money," where money supply affects aggregate demand only through changing the interest rate and investment spending. However, monetarists do not believe this is the main way monetary policy affects the economy (except perhaps in the short run). Monetarists believe that more money causes people to spend more *even if the interest rate does not change!*

So who is right? Over the years, monetarists and Keynesians, by studying real-world data, have come closer in their beliefs about the economy. Almost all economists, for example, believe that very high rates of inflation can be caused only by high rates of monetary growth. Most monetarists acknowledge that fiscal policy can affect the interest rate (and thus V) and that increases in government spending have stimulated the economy in the past. Finally, most economists will predict a recession when the money supply's growth rate is decreased dramatically.

KNOW THE CONCEPTS

DO YOU KNOW THE BASICS?

1. What two variables determine aggregate demand in the quantity theory of money?
2. What variable mainly affects money demand in the monetarist model? In the Keynesian model?
3. How will inflation and economic growth be related (when the growth rate in the money supply and velocity remain unchanged)?
4. Why, in the long run, does a change in the money supply not affect anything real, including real output and the real money supply?
5. What causes a difference between desired spending and income in the monetarist model? In the Keynesian model?
6. Why is the opportunity cost of holding money the nominal interest rate that a bond pays?
7. Why does the quantity of money people want to hold go up when the interest rate falls?
8. If the government runs a deficit and sells bonds to finance the deficit, how might this stimulate the economy in the quantity theory of money?
9. When will an increase in the money supply result in higher, not lower, interest rates?
10. Why is the spending multiplier weaker when we consider the effects of higher income on money demand?

TERMS FOR STUDY

bonds
Cambridge k
crowding out
equation of exchange
inflation premium effect

interest rate
liquidity effect

neutrality of money
nominal income
precautionary demand for money
quantity theory of money
quantity theory of money
(percent change form)
speculative demand for money
transaction demand for money
velocity

PRACTICAL APPLICATION

1. When using the quantity theory, how will the following events affect the money supply, V, and nominal income (or $\$GDP$)?

   Event A: Because of widespread bank failures, the public increases its cash holdings.

   Event B: Credit cards become widely used.

   Event C: The money supply is reduced.

   Event D: The nominal interest rate rises.

2. If money demand equals 5 percent of income, the money supply is $60, and real *GDP* is 1,000 units of output, what will the price level be? What will the price level be if the money supply is $120? What happens to nominal income? To real money holdings?

3. A small country produces 5,000 units of output and has a money supply of $2,000. Its citizens want to hold 10 percent of their income in money ($k = 0.10$).

   a. What are V, $\$GDP$, P, and the real money supply (MS/P)?

   b. If the money supply doubles to $4,000 but real output and V stay the same, what will $\$GDP$, P, and the real money supply be?

4. The simple quantity theory makes it appear that increases in the money supply show up right away in more spending. However, monetarists recognize that there are significant and long lags in this transmission process. One prominent version assumes that people, getting new money, first use it to buy financial assets, such as stocks and bonds. Only over time does this new money make its way into new spending. To see how, suppose everyone is alike: they hold $2,000 in cash and want 20 percent of their income in cash (there are no demand deposits in this economy). So everyone's money income is $10,000. Real output

per person is at its potential level of 10,000 units, so the price level is $1. Then, one morning, they wake up and find $1,000 in new cash under their pillows. Assume there is only one other asset: stocks. How do you think they will react? How will this money eventually get into the spending stream?

5. A firm has the following menu of projects, listed in no particular order: project A, with a yield of 12 percent and a cost of $100,000; project B, with a yield of 8 percent and a cost of $200,000; project C, with a yield of 10 percent and a cost of $300,000; and project D, with a yield of 15 percent and a cost of $250,000. How much will this firm borrow and invest when the interest rate is 12 percent? 10 percent? 8 percent?

6. While using the Keynesian model, describe the effect of a $40 billion increase in the money supply under these conditions: (a) a $40 billion increase in the money supply reduces the interest rate by 1 percent, (b) a 1 percent decrease in the interest rate increases investment spending by $60 billion, (c) the spending multiplier is 2.5, and (d) the economy is on the horizontal segment of its aggregate supply curve, so prices do not rise when aggregate demand increases.

7. If the Fed increases the money supply by $40 billion, will it have a bigger or smaller impact on _GDP_ than in Question 6 above when we make the following changes? (Treat each change as if it is the only change in Question 6's conditions.) For each of the changes, calculate the increase in _GDP_.

Change A: A $40 billion increase in the money supply reduces the interest rate by 1/2 percent.

Change B: A 1 percent decrease in the interest rate increases investment spending by $80 billion.

Change C: The spending multiplier is 2.0.

Change D: Prices do rise when aggregate demand increases.

8. While using the Keynesian model, select the correct term from the italicized choices. An increase in the money supply will increase real _GDP_ more when:

   a. It decreases the interest rate [_more/less_].

   b. Investment spending responds [_more/less_] to changes in the interest rate.

   c. The multiplier is [_bigger/smaller_].

   d. The aggregate supply curve is [_flatter/steeper_].

   e. Money demand increases [_more/less_] when the interest rate changes.

9. It is commonly asserted that low interest rates mean the Fed is following an "easy," expansive monetary policy, while high interest rates imply a "tight," contractive monetary policy. If monetary policy had only a

liquidity effect, then what would interest rates tell us about monetary policy? If monetary policy had mainly the inflationary premium effect, what would interest rates tell us about monetary policy?

10. This problem analyzes why investment spending depends on the *real* interest rate, not the nominal interest rate. To show this, consider a very simple example.

Case 1: There is no inflation. Axel Widget Company has to pay $10,000 in advance to buy a machine. Axel gets it one year later and produces 1,000 widgets with it, and then the machine falls apart and is worthless. Each widget sells for $11. What are the real and nominal rates of return on this machine?

Case 2: There is a 20 percent rate of inflation expected over the year. Axel expects widgets to sell for 20 percent more ($13.20 each). What are the real and nominal rates of return on the machine?

11. The theory in this chapter ignores international capital markets. To see what impact they will have, suppose that foreign capital is available to all U.S. businesses at an interest rate of 8 percent, no matter how little or how much is borrowed. Describe how the following events will affect interest rates, investment spending, U.S. savings, and aggregate demand (using the Keynesian model).

Event A: The Fed buys government bonds in an open-market operation.

Event B: The public's demand for money increases.

Event C: Government spending increases.

ANSWERS

KNOW THE CONCEPTS

1. Velocity (V) and the money supply (M). Aggregate demand $= V \times M$.

2. In the monetarist model, income is the main variable affecting money demand. As people earn and spend more dollars, they need more dollars in their money holdings. In the Keynesian model, the interest rate plays a leading role. As interest rates rise, people demand less money. They substitute bonds (and other assets) for money.

3. Nominal income ($\$GDP$) grows at a rate equal to $\%\Delta MS + \%\Delta V$. This, in turn, equals $\%\Delta P + \%\Delta Q$ ($= \%\Delta\$GDP$). So when the growth rate of output ($\%\Delta Q$) increases 1 percent, inflation ($\%\Delta P$) will fall by 1 percent.

4. In the long run, relative prices will return to the levels that clear all markets, and output will be at its full employment level. Real output will remain unaffected and the real money supply (which equals $k \times Q$) will remain unaffected.

5. In the monetarist model, a difference between desired spending and income is caused by either an excess demand for money ($MD > MS$) or an excess supply of money ($MS > MD$). An excess demand for money reduces desired spending, and an excess supply increases it. In the Keynesian model, changes in desired spending (particularly in desired investment spending) cause the difference.

6. Holding cash pays nothing. Holding a bond (or an interest-bearing bank account) pays interest. So holding cash (and most other forms of money) means giving up the interest that a bond of the same value would have paid.

7. The higher the interest rate, the less people want to hold money (since the foregone cost of holding money is up). V will increase since k is decreasing.

8. Government sells bonds to:

Finance deficit $\rightarrow$ Increases interest rate $\rightarrow$ People want to hold less money $\rightarrow$ V up (as k is down) $\rightarrow$ $M \times V$ up $\rightarrow$ Aggregate demand up.

9. If the increase in the money supply is expected to increase prices (and inflation), interest rates will rise.

10. As people earn more, they increase their money holdings. This reduces the amount of money respent, which in turn reduces the spending multiplier.

PRACTICAL APPLICATION

1. *Event A:* MS down, V down, $\$GDP$ down. (This happened in the Great Depression.) Note that the change in $\$GDP$ is also the change in aggregate demand.

   Event B: MS unchanged, V up, $\$GDP$ up.

   Event C: MS down, V unchanged, $\$GDP$ down.

   Event D: MS unchanged, V up, $\$GDP$ up.

2. $P = MS/kQ$. k is 0.05 and $V = 20$. In the first case, P equals $1.20. In the second case, $2.40. $\$GDP$ equals V times MS, increasing from $1,200 to $2,400. Note that P also equals $\$GDP/Q$. The real money supply (MS/P) equals 5 percent of real income, or $50 (in real dollars). In the first case, it is $60/1.20; in the second, $120/2.40.

3. **a.** $V = 10$. $\$GDP = \$20,000$. $P = \$4.00$. $MS/P = 500$.
   b. $\$GDP = \$40,000$. $P = \$8.00$. $MS/P = 500$.

4. While surprised by the new money but not wanting to spend it right away, people will probably first buy stocks. Stock prices will rise. However, the $1,000 in cash is still in people's hands. For some time, people may use the new money to buy and trade stocks in the rising stock market, with no effect on spending, output, or prices. Next, business firms will issue new stock with which to buy capital goods. Aggregate demand will go up. Prices will likely stay constant, as the capital-goods sector usually keeps large inventories, as well as excess workers and capacity, to meet new demand. This allows them to increase output without having to raise prices. As people feel wealthier, they will buy more consumer goods, which will push prices up. We then follow the expansion-contraction scenario described in Chapter 10 under "From Too Little Unemployment to Full Employment." Output returns to 10,000 units per person, the price level rises to $1.50, and stock prices fall back to their old real level. A recession may even result as excess capital was produced. So the production of new capital goods has to fall for a while below their potential level, with resulting unemployment in the capital-goods sector as the excess is worked off.

5. At 12 percent, project A just covers its costs, and project D makes 3 percent net rate of profit. The firm will invest $350,000. At 10 percent, it invests in projects A, C, and D, at a total cost of $650,000. At 8 percent, it invests in projects A, B, C, and D, at a total cost of $850,000.

6. *GDP* will be increased by $150 billion.

7. *Change A:* The increase in *GDP* will be smaller (a $75 billion increase as opposed to the $150 billion increase in Question 6).

   Change B: The increase in *GDP* is bigger: $200 billion.

   Change C: The increase in *GDP* is smaller: $120 billion.

   Change D: The increase in *GDP* is smaller: When prices go up, the increase in real *GDP* is smaller.

8. (a) more, (b) more, (c) bigger, (d) flatter, (e) less, (e) needs further explanation. When money demand is less sensitive to changes in the interest rate, then the money demand curve in Figure 13–3 is *steeper*. That means when the money supply goes up, interest rates must fall *more* to increase the quantity of money demanded to equal the new supply.

9. With the liquidity effect only, an increase in the money supply will lower interest rates, while a decrease will raise interest rates. In this case, changes in the interest rates do tell us if the money supply is expanding or contracting. However, this is true only in the short run, if at all. In the long run, expanding the money supply raises total spending *and* the inflation rate. This raises nominal interest rates! So, in the short run more money lowers interest rates, but in the long run, it raises them. So do not look at interest rates to determine the expansiveness or tight-

ness of the money supply. Most economists look instead at the growth rate of M2 and the monetary base.

10. In Case 1, the real and nominal rates of return are the same, since there is no inflation. The rate is 10 percent. An investment of $10,000 today grows in worth by 10 percent to $11,000 (the revenues from selling 1,000 widgets at $11).

In Case 2, the nominal return is 32 percent. The real return is still 10 percent. (The real value of $13,200 in sales one year from now is $13,200/1.20, or $11,000. We divide by 1.20 since goods costing $1 today will cost $1.20 in one year.)

11. In all these cases, capital will flow into or out of the country, with the result that interest rates remain at 8 percent. So neither interest rates nor bond prices are affected.

Event A: Increases money supply, causes excess money supply. People buy bonds to get rid of excess money. Bonds are bought from the rest of the world (as at 8 percent, no more U.S. bonds are available). The rest of the world uses dollars from bond sales to buy U.S. exports. So aggregate demand goes up. The increase in aggregate demand increases money demand and returns the money market to equilibrium at 8 percent interest rate.

Event B: Causes excess money demand. People sell bonds to get more money. Since the best deal is the 8 percent offered by the rest of the world, they sell U.S. bonds to the rest of the world. U.S. citizens use foreign money from bond sales proceeds to buy imports (rather than domestic goods). So aggregate demand goes down.

Event C: Causes increase in aggregate demand and in money demand (as income goes up, people want large money holdings). Excess money demand results, with Event *B* consequences. Net impact: no change in aggregate demand, as only at original income and interest rates do *MD* equal *MS*.

14

INFLATION AND UNEMPLOYMENT

KEY TERMS

accelerationist theory theory that unemployment cannot be permanently reduced through inflation.

natural rate of unemployment unemployment rate determined by demand and supply for workers such that employers and workers are paying and receiving the real wages they expected.

Phillips Curve (PC) curve showing trade-off between inflation and unemployment when the public's expected rate of inflation is unchanged.

We are now ready to use our models to explain the business cycle. So far, we have developed both the Keynesian and monetarist models of aggregate demand. Now, we will ask how increases in aggregate demand will affect prices and output. To get our answer, we need to know what causes the short-run aggregate supply curve to shift.

WHAT CAUSES THE SHORT-RUN AGGREGATE SUPPLY CURVE (AS) TO SHIFT?

At full employment, wages and prices are at the full-employment level and everyone is being paid what they expected to be paid. No one is fooled by inflation. Workers are paid the real wage they expected. Savers are paid the real interest they expected. If no one were ever fooled by inflation, the short-run aggregate supply curve would be vertical and would be the same as the long-run aggregate supply curve! The short-run *AS* curve does not have a vertical slope because assumably wages and prices are slow to adjust to an increase in aggregate demand. "Being slow to adjust" *means* someone is being fooled. We will assume in this chapter that the workers are fooled. In this version of the *AS* curve, workers are fooled by inflation into working for a lower real wage than they had anticipated. Another version has inflation causing savers to get less in real interest than they had anticipated. Many other versions exist and, unfortunately, little evidence suggests which, if any, of them is true. The workers getting fooled version is presented because it is easy to understand and the other versions are similar to it. Most likely, a correct version of the *AS* curve has the fooled group being randomly rotated among the many players in the economy. In the workers getting fooled version, along any given short-run *AS* curve, nominal wages (*W*) are held constant.

Along any given short-run *AS* curve, nominal wages (*W*) are held constant. How are these wages set? In a competitive economy, real wages (*W/P*) will be set so the demand and supply for labor are equal. The labor market will then be in equilibrium and the economy at full employment. However, workers must contract ahead of time to work for a money wage (*W*). They will set *W* so that their expected real wage (*W/P*) will be consistent with full employment.

For example, suppose the labor market is in equilibrium when the real wage is $5.00. That is, at a real wage of $5.00, the demand for workers equals the supply of workers and the economy is, by definition, at full employment. If workers expect a price index of 200 (so *P* = 2.00), they will receive a nominal wage of $10.00 at full employment ($10/2.00 = $5.00). The short-run aggregate supply (*AS*) curve associated with a nominal wage of $10 is thereby also the *AS* curve associated with an expected price level of 200. Skip ahead for the moment to Figure 14–2. If full-employment output is 4,000 units, and then *AS*-0 (in Panel A) is the *AS* curve associated with an expected price level of 200 since at full employment (*Q* = 4,000), the actual price level on this curve is 200. Similarly, *AS*-1 in Figure 14–2 is associated with the expected price level of 220.

To find the expected price level associated with each *AS* curve, find the price level at which it intersects the full-employment level of output.

YOU SHOULD REMEMBER

1. Wages are constant along each short-run *AS* curve.

2. Workers must estimate what the future price level will be and then contract for money wages. Money wages will be set so the expected real wage assures workers of being fully employed.

3. The expected price level for each *AS* curve is the price level at which it intersects the full-employment level of output.

4. An increase in the expected price level increases money wages and shifts the *AS* curve up.

THE RELATIONSHIP BETWEEN THE *AS* CURVE AND THE PHILLIPS CURVE

If the aggregate supply curve stays fixed, then a rightward shift in the *AD* curve will increase prices and output and reduce unemployment. To describe the resulting relationship between prices and unemployment, economists use the **Phillips Curve.** There is one Phillips Curve for each aggregate supply curve. It shows how prices and unemployment are inversely related when the *AD* curve shifts and the *AS* curve (and thus wages and the expected inflation rate) stays constant.

Figure 14–1 shows how we draw a Phillips Curve. In Panel A, we have aggregate supply curve *AS*-0. If aggregate demand is *AD*-0, the price level will be 200 and output will be 4,000 units. Assume this corresponds to a 5 percent unemployment rate. In Panel B, this is Point *G*. Now suppose *AD* shifts to *AD*-1. This increase in aggregate demand moves the economy from Point *G* to Point *H*. Output goes up 2 percent to 4,080 units. The price level is now 220. Suppose the 2 percent added output reduced unemployment by one percentage point to 4 percent. (This would correspond to Okun's Law.) We connect Points *G* and *H* to get the Phillips Curve *PC*-0 that is derived from *AS*-0. On the Phillips Curve, price and unemployment are inversely related: When one goes up, the other goes down.

More often, the Phillips Curve has the inflation rate rather than the price level on the vertical axis. We will deal with this below. For now, treat any increase in the price level as the same thing as an increase in inflation. As a study hint, think of the Phillips Curve as the aggregate supply curve drawn backwards, as *less* output means *more* unemployment. So, when the economy moves *up* and *left* of the Phillips Curve, it is because aggregate demand is shifting *up* and *right* along the aggregate supply curve.

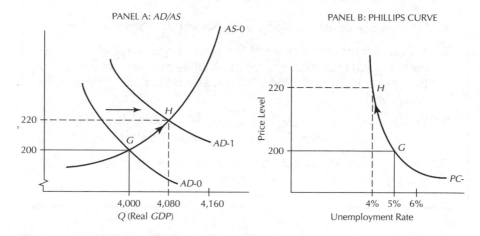

Figure 14–1. The Effect of Supply and Demand on the Phillips Curve

Along the Phillips Curve, *higher* prices result in more output and *less* unemployment because when only *AD* shifts, prices and unemployment move in opposite directions. The rise in prices caused by a rightward shift in *AD* is called **demand-pull inflation:** the shift in *AD* "pulling" the economy up the *AS* curve.

Why does a higher price level result in more output and employment? Assume that workers contract with employers in the short run to work whenever the employers want them to at a certain nominal wage. Workers set this nominal wage based upon what they think the price level is. However, if inflation is higher than expected, they will be "fooled" into working for a lower real wage. Employers will hire more workers at the lower real wage, increasing output and reducing unemployment. So, the more inflation and prices exceed expected levels, the higher will be the level of output and employment and the lower will be the rate of unemployment.

YOU SHOULD REMEMBER

1. The Phillips Curve describes how prices and unemployment are related when aggregate supply is unchanged.

2. When the aggregate supply curve has not changed, higher prices mean less unemployment.

HOW SHIFTS AFFECT THE *AS* CURVE AND THE PHILLIPS CURVE

An increase in costs will shift up the *AS* curve and the Phillips Curve. In Figure 14–2, *AS*-0 is the aggregate supply curve we had in Figure 14–1 (and *PC*-0 is its corresponding Phillips Curve).

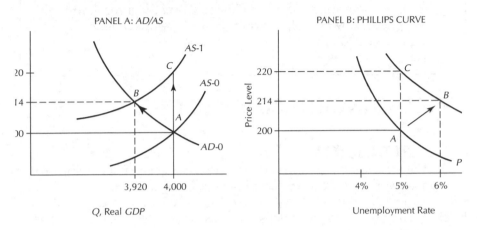

Figure 14–2. The Effect of Stagflation on the Phillips Curve

Let us start in Panel A with *AD*-0 at Point *A*. Suppose wages and other input costs go up such that aggregate supply shifts up to *AS*-1. To have firms produce 4,000 units of output with unemployment equaling 5 percent, prices now must rise to 220 to cover the higher costs. This is Point *C* on *AS*-1 and *PC*-1 (in Panels A and B respectively). However, the economy will go to Point *B*. When output falls to 3,920 units, unemployment rises to 6 percent. So at Point *B* on the Phillips Curve, the price level is 214 and the unemployment rate is 6 percent.

When the *AS* curve shifts up, the economy goes from Point *A* to Point *B*: Prices go up, output goes down, and unemployment goes up. Prices and unemployment move up together: This is called *stagflation*. The increase in prices caused by the *AS* curve shifting up is called **cost-push inflation.**

YOU SHOULD REMEMBER

1. When nominal wages and other costs increase, the aggregate supply curve and the Phillips Curve shift up.

2. If aggregate demand does not change, a higher aggregate supply curve (and a higher Phillips Curve) will result in higher prices, lower output, and more unemployment: This is called stagflation.

VISUALIZING THE BUSINESS CYCLE

• *A RECESSION*

The following describes a typical recession, starting at full employment.

Suppose workers have an expected price level of 220 and set their money wages accordingly: *AS-*0 is the *AS* curve associated with an expected price level of 220, and *PC-*0 is the Phillips Curve associated with an expected price level of 220. See Figure 14–3.

Assume the economy is at full employment with $Q = 4,000$ (shown by the Long-Run Aggregate Supply Curve, *S*-Long Run) and an unemployment rate of 5 percent with *AD-*0 and *AS-*0. The economy will be at *E* in both panels. The *natural rate of unemployment* is, in this case, 5 percent—the rate consistent with output being at its potential or full-employment level. Then the government reduces *AD* from *AD-*0 to *AD-*1. As a consequence, the economy goes from Point *E* to Point *F* in both panels. Prices have fallen to 212, real wages will go up, and employment will fall. Unemployment increases from 5 percent to 8 percent. Output falls 6 percent to 3,760 units. Note that the actual price level (212) is below the price level that workers were expecting (220). Workers will be getting a higher real wage than they had initially expected when contracting with employers for work. The result is that employers will hire fewer workers and the economy will produce less than its full-employment level of output.

Once workers realize the price level has fallen, they will in the long run reduce the money wages they are requesting. In addition, the higher unemployment will force wages down. The *AS* curve will then shift down from *AS-*0 until it reaches *AS-*1 (it may take some time to do this). *AS-*1 is the *AS* curve associated with an expected level of 208. The economy will move from Point *F* to Point *G*. The Phillips Curve will shift from *PC-*0 to *PC-*1: *PC-*1 is the Phillips Curve associated with an expected price level of 208. Prices and unemployment will fall. Unemployment returns to its full-employment level of 5 percent. Output has returned to its full-employment level of 4,000 at a price level of 208.

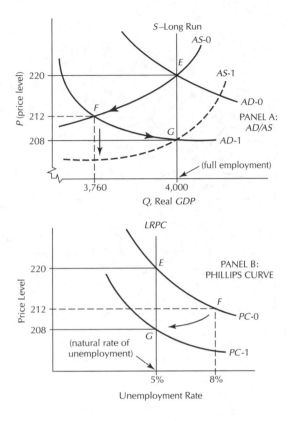

Figure 14–3. The Effect of Recession on the Phillips Curve

YOU SHOULD REMEMBER

1. Recessions are caused mainly by decreases in aggregate demand.

2. The economy returns from a recession back to full employment as wages and prices fall.

3. It is the decline in people's expected price level that causes the Phillips Curve and the aggregate supply curve to shift down.

• *AN EXPANSION*

The following sequence of events describes a typical economic expansion starting at full employment.

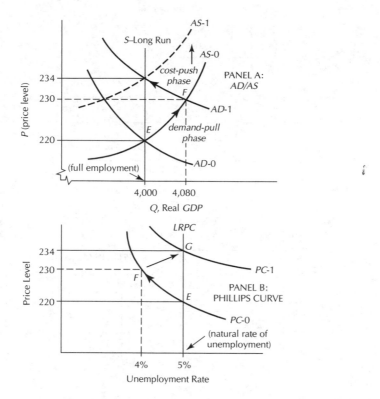

Figure 14-4. The Effect of Expansion on the Phillips Curve

Suppose workers expect the price level to be 220: This corresponds to AS-0 and AD-0 in Figure 14-4. Assuming the economy is in equilibrium at full employment, the initial price level is 220 and unemployment is 5 percent. Then suppose *AD* shifts to *AD*-1. In the short run, the economy shifts from Point *E* to Point *F* in both panels: Prices go up to 230, output goes up 2 percent to 4,080, and unemployment falls to 4 percent. Note that the expected price level (220) is below the actual price level (230), so workers are getting a lower real wage than expected. As a consequence of the low real wage, employers will hire more workers. This is the demand-pull inflation phase of the business cycle (since it is caused by the shift in *AD*).

The higher price level and the tight labor market will cause workers to demand higher nominal wages. *AS* will shift up. Eventually it will reach *AS*-1. The Phillips Curve similarly shifts, from *PC*-0 to *PC*-1. The economy moves from Point *F* to Point *G* as prices rise to 234, output falls back to 4,000, and unemployment returns to its natural level of 5 percent. This is the cost-push phase of the business cycle (since it is caused by the shift in *AS*).

The first phase of the expansion (or recession) was demand-push; the second, cost-push. Note, though, that the cost-push phase is *caused* by the demand-push phase.

YOU SHOULD REMEMBER

1. An expansion in aggregate demand can push output above its full-employment level, but this higher output is not sustainable.

2. The economy returns from overemployment to full employment as prices and costs go up.

3. The increase in people's expected price level causes the aggregate supply curve to shift up.

INFLATION AND THE PHILLIPS CURVE

The Phillips Curve related price levels with unemployment. More often, the Phillips Curve is shown relating inflation to unemployment. To change the above Phillips Curves from price level on the vertical axis to the inflation rate, take the prior year's price level and calculate how much prices have increased. Thus, if the prior year's price level was 200 in Figure 14–4, Point *G* corresponds to a 17 percent rate of inflation, Point *F* to a 15 percent rate of inflation, and Point *E* to 10 percent. In Figure 14–3, if the prior year's price level was 200, Point *E* corresponds to a 10 percent rate of inflation, *F* to 6 percent, and *G* to 4 percent.

Figure 14–5 shows the Phillips Curve *PC*-A associated with Figure 14–4 (with corresponding points) when the prior year's price level was 200 and when the expected price level was 220 (so people were expecting a 10 percent rate of inflation). *PC*-A is associated with *AS*-0. If people initially expected a 17 percent rate of inflation, the Phillips Curve instead would have been *PC*-B.

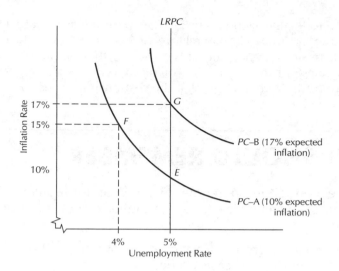

Figure 14–5. The Effect of Inflation on the Phillips Curve

Because the AS curve shifts up when workers expect higher wages, the AD and AS curves have to be *redrawn* each period when there is persistent and expected inflation. Fortunately, the standard Phillips Curve (with the inflation rate on its vertical axis) remains unchanged as long as the expected rate of inflation stays unchanged. But if workers come to expect higher rates of inflation, the PC shifts up.

• *RATIONAL EXPECTATIONS*

Up to now, we have assumed that the business cycle is mainly caused by (1) shifts in aggregate demand combined with (2) slow adjustment in wages and prices, resulting in (3) shifts in real output. Therefore, if the government wants to reduce inflation, the economy will have to pay the cost of reduced output.

Most economists agree that in the long run no trade-off exists between inflation and output. That is, the long-run Phillips Curve should be vertical. Once people come to anticipate inflation, the aggregate supply curve shifts up so that inflation no longer has any impact on output. This leads to the following model of the Phillips Curve:

Unemployment Rate = $N - a$ (Actual Inflation Rate – Anticipated Inflation Rate).

N is the natural rate of unemployment, and a is a positive constant reflecting the trade-off between inflation and unemployment. In the long run, the actual rate of inflation is fully anticipated by the public, so the unemployment rate equals its long-run natural rate. However, if inflation rises faster than anticipated, unemployment falls below its natural rate.

Rational expectation economists reject this version of the Phillips Curve. According to rational expectation economists, the public uses all available information to determine what the inflation rate is likely to be. Fooling people consistently is impossible, for example, by constantly accelerating the rate of inflation. Suppose the government tried accelerating the rate of inflation. Initially, workers and firms might be fooled into increasing their output. However, this will make them worse off since workers will get lower real wages than they expected. However, you cannot fool workers (and other suppliers) forever. They will catch on to the accelerating rate of inflation by adjusting their wages up in the same accelerating fashion. The story ends with the economy returning to full employment.

Rational expectation economists, as we will see in the next chapter, deny that a predictable short-run trade-off exists between inflation and output. If the government announces ahead of time that it is going to cut the rate of inflation (for example, by slowing the growth rate in the money supply) and if people believe this, then the adjustment will take place immediately. On the other hand, if the public does not believe the government, then as inflation reduces, output is likely to fall. Thus, whether a trade-off between inflation and output occurs depends upon the nature of the government and its relationship with the public.

YOU SHOULD REMEMBER

1. In the long run, only the natural rate of unemployment (at full employment) is sustainable. The long-run Phillips Curve is vertical.

2. Along the short-run Phillips Curve, Unemployment Rate = Natural Rate − *a* (Actual Inflation − Anticipated Inflation).

3. Rational expectation economists believe that people anticipate inflation. Consequently, a constantly accelerating inflation would quickly become anticipated and have no effect on output. Similarly, reducing inflation need not reduce output if the public believes that the government will reduce inflation and then acts accordingly.

THE BUSINESS CYCLE

CAN ECONOMIC RECOVERY BE MADE FASTER?

In the Great Depression, it took ten years (from 1929 to 1939) for the economy to return to its 1929 level of real *GDP*, and even this was not a full recovery since the economy would normally have grown 37 percent in ten years. It took over four years for the U.S. economy to fully recover from the 1981–1982 recession. Is there anything our government can do to make recovery go faster?

If you review this chapter's section on "A Recession," you will see that the speed of recovery depends upon how fast the aggregate supply curve shifts down. That is, recovery is faster if wages and other costs fall faster. Four methods of lowering wages and other costs are:

1. *Wage and Price Controls:* The government explicitly tells firms and unions what prices and wages they can set. Milder forms of controls include "jawboning" ("encouraging" firms and unions to cooperate) and wage and price guidelines (with set ranges of price and wage increases).

   In the past, wage and price controls generally have failed in that prices quickly shot up once the controls were removed. The drawbacks include (a) the shortages that result from price ceilings, (b) the impossibility of monitoring cheating in the hundreds of thousands of firms in our economy (see Practical Application, Question 9), and (c) the temptation for the government to increase aggregate demand (and thus the ultimate increase in prices) with the excuse that "price controls will control inflation." As an example of (c), during the wage-price freeze of 1971–1973, the growth rate of the money supply increased from 4.8 percent (in 1970) to 8.1 percent (in 1972).

2. *Tax-Based Income Policy (TIP):* In this untried plan, the government increases taxes on firms and workers who raise prices too much and reduces taxes for those who keep their prices within guidelines. The advantages of this policy are that it (a) rewards those that comply (thus assuring wider compliance) and (b) is more flexible than wage and price controls, allowing goods in demand to go up in price.

   The potential drawbacks of this program include (a) the possibility that higher taxes will shift the aggregate supply curve to the left and raise prices even more, and (b) the fact that changing demand will cause consumers to increase the prices of the goods they want more of and decrease the prices of the goods they want less of. The TIP plan thus taxes those goods people want more of and in effect subsidizes those goods people do not want. This is inefficient, though possibly not as inefficient as wage and price controls.

3. *Supply-Side Incentives for Increasing Output:* By reducing marginal taxes and cutting back on transfer programs, it is possible to shift aggregate supply to the right. This will reduce inflation and increase output. The magnitude of these changes is uncertain. For example, it would take a 5 percent increase in output to reduce inflation by 5.9 percent. We have rarely witnessed such high annual increases in output over long periods of time, and certainly have not seen them result from tax decreases.

4. *Removing Barriers to Lower Prices:* By abolishing minimum wage laws and by reducing the powers of monopolies (including the monopoly power of unions), it may be possible to shift prices down faster. But the political likelihood of such an approach is small.

YOU SHOULD REMEMBER

1. Various methods have been tried or proposed to speed the reduction in wages and prices that is necessary for an economy to recover from a recession.

2. Wage and price controls have been tried in the past, and worked temporarily, but ultimately did not reduce prices below what they would have been.

CAN INFLATION (AT FULL EMPLOYMENT) BE REDUCED?

Some of the above programs have been suggested to reduce inflation when the economy is at full employment. The issue is whether inflation can then be reduced *even if* aggregate demand is not reduced. Proponents of wage and price controls and TIPS argue that by reducing the expectation of higher prices, they will reduce how much of the *AS* curve will shift up, and thus reduce inflation.

Opponents point out that if the *AD* curve does not *also* shift down, the expected price level cannot be permanently reduced: In the long run, people will expect prices to be where the *AD* curve intersects the long-run aggregate supply curve. So, if aggregate demand is unchanged, wage and price controls will not lower price expectations. No matter what type of price controls are used or how heavy the penalties are, no anti-inflation program will work if it does not also shift aggregate demand (by, for example, reducing the growth rate of the money supply). In the long run, people will expect prices to be where the *AD* curve intersects the long-run aggregate supply curve. So if aggregate demand is unchanged (or rising), wage and price controls will not reduce inflationary expectations or inflation. Returning to our bathtub analogy (see Figure 9–5), wage and price controls would then be like trying to keep the bathtub from overflowing by hitting the top of the water. Instead, the tap needs to be turned off.

Suppose, though, that the government does reduce aggregate demand. If the public does not adjust its price expectations down, then a recession will result. In this case, wage and price controls may help the economy by reducing the public's price expectations.

At what speed should inflation be reduced so as to do the least damage to the economy? Reducing aggregate demand quickly to quickly reduce inflation is called going "**cold turkey**." The idea is to break inflationary expectations quickly and abruptly. Reducing *AD* slowly is called **gradualism**. This, it is claimed, allows workers and other suppliers to work out new contracts and reduce wages and costs without the loss in output that has occurred in the past when our economy has gone cold turkey. Both policies depend upon the credibility of our government. If people do not believe the government is really going to reduce aggregate demand (either quickly or slowly), then a recession will result: It will be deep and short under the cold-turkey approach and shallow but long under the gradualist approach.

Finally, we come to those who claim that indexing can make it easier for our economy to live with inflation. All these methods involve *indexing,* whereby a monetary cost or payment is automatically adjusted whenever a specified price index (such as the CPI) changes. These methods include the following. [Note that (1) and (2) are already widespread, (3) is currently in effect, and (4) and (5) have been proposed.]

1. Indexing wages with cost-of-living adjustment (COLA) clauses.

2. Indexing interest rates on mortgages and bonds to change with short-term interest rates or with inflation.

3. Indexing the tax code to avoid bracket creep (so people with the same real income do not get punished by inflation into a higher tax bracket).

4. Indexing the tax code so that inflationary premiums on interest and capital gains are not taxed (since they do not represent real added income).

5. Indexing depreciation costs so that firms can depreciate equipment at current costs and not at historic costs (which do not reflect inflation).

DOES THE PHILLIPS CURVE TELL THE REAL STORY?

The basic idea behind the Phillips Curve is that shifts in aggregate demand are the main cause in the business cycle. An unexpected increase in aggregate demand increases real output and lowers unemployment. In addition, unexpected decreases in aggregate demand reduce real output and increase unemployment. However, business cycles since World War II do not follow this pattern.

The evidence suggests that:

1. Higher rates of inflation, even unexpected increases in inflation, do not result in lower levels of unemployment or higher levels of output.

2. Real interest rates appear to go up with output, suggesting that it is not lower interest rates that stimulate the economy.

3. Unexpectedly higher rates in money growth increase output for one to two years, but not by increasing prices.

4. Most recent business expansions have been led by increases in profitable business ventures. This leads business to borrow and invest more, raising interest rates and output. Alternatively stated, recent business cycles appear to be rooted in shifts of aggregate supply, not in aggregate demand.

This evidence does not rule out the fact that decreases in aggregate demand can seriously harm the economy (as the Great Depression so well proved). It also does not rule out the possibility that the shift in investment profitability is due to some lagged impact of increased money supply (see Question 4 in Chapter 13). What it does suggest is that there are other causes of the business cycle than what is contained in the monetarist and Keynesian models.

YOU SHOULD REMEMBER

1. Wage and price controls will reduce inflation only if they reduce a false impression by the public of where prices are going to be.

2. Some of the main issues are whether inflation should be reduced quickly ("going cold turkey") or slowly (gradualism) and whether people can learn to live with inflation through indexing.

KNOW THE CONCEPTS

DO YOU KNOW THE BASICS?

1. How can you tell what the expected price level is by looking at the *AD/AS* diagram?
2. How can you tell what the expected rate of inflation is by looking at the Phillips Curve?
3. Along a Phillips Curve, how are inflation, unemployment, and output related? What is being held constant?
4. In what sense are workers "fooled" by inflation?
5. How will the economy eventually get to the price level where the *AD* curve intersects the long-run aggregate supply curve?
6. Will a higher rate of inflation always reduce unemployment?
7. What happens to the Phillips Curve when people expect higher rates of inflation?
8. Why must inflation accelerate in order to reduce unemployment below its natural rate?
9. What rate of unemployment and what output level can be sustained in the long run?
10. If wage and price controls worked, how could they help speed the recovery of an economy?

TERMS FOR STUDY

"cold turkey" and gradualism
demand-pull and cost-push
   inflation
expected rate of inflation

long-run Phillips Curve
natural rate of unemployment
Phillips Curve
tax-based income policy (TIP)

PRACTICAL APPLICATION

1. Use the following Phillips Curve schedule and answer the following questions.

Inflation Rate:	20	14	10	8	7	6.5
Unemployment Rate:		3	4	5	6	7	8

   a. If the natural rate of unemployment is 6 percent, what is the expected rate of inflation?

b. If inflation falls from 8 percent to 7 percent, what will happen to unemployment (if expectations about inflation don't change)?

2. Construct the aggregate supply curve associated with the above Phillips Curve schedule, assuming (a) the price level in the prior period was 100, (b) full-employment output is 1,000 units, which corresponds with a 6 percent unemployment rate, and (c) for every 1 percent change in unemployment, output changes 2 percent in the opposite direction (this being one version of Okun's Law). To keep the math simple, assume that every 2 percent change in output equals 40 units of output (2 percent of 2,000).

3. Workers expect inflation to be 20 percent and the economy is fully employed. Then the Fed acts to reduce the inflation rate to 10 percent. What will happen in the short run? In the long run?

4. Describe what is happening in each of the following three graphs. Assume that the initial change (from Point *A* to Point *B*) is caused by a shift in the aggregate demand or aggregate supply curve, and then the economy's self-correcting mechanism operates from Point *B* to Point *C*. For each panel, identify (a) which curve is shifting (*AS* or *AD*), (b) how and why it is shifting, and (c) how the economy gets back to full employment.

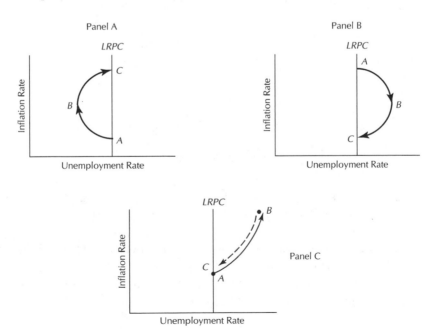

5. What phase of the business cycle (the demand-push or the cost-pull phase of an expansion or a recession) is the economy in when these statements are made?

   a. "Unions have negotiated for lower wages so as to retain their jobs."

   b. "Unemployment has fallen dramatically as inflation has accelerated."

   c. "Firms have been forced by recent wage hikes to raise their prices and produce less."

6. Wage inflation is related to expected inflation by the following equation:

$$\text{Percent Change in Wages} = \text{Expected Rate of Inflation} + \text{Percent Change in Productivity}$$

   If expected inflation is 10 percent and productivity increases by 2 percent, how much will wages change?

7. Use the following graph to answer these questions (assume the economy starts at Point A):

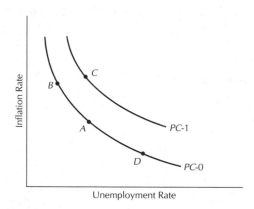

   a. If the Fed increases the growth rate of the money supply, to which point is the economy most likely to move in the short run? In the long run?

   b. If the government decreases government spending, to which point is the economy likely to move in the short run?

   c. Workers come to expect a higher rate of inflation, and they demand higher wages. To which point might the economy move?

8. "Changes in employment and output are caused by how wages and prices change *relative* to each other." Explain.

9. Suppose you own International Widget Works. How could you evade wage and price controls before and after they are enacted?

10. How could wage and price controls appear to be holding down inflation when in fact they are not?

ANSWERS

KNOW THE CONCEPTS

1. The expected price level is where the *AS* curve intersects the long-run aggregate supply curve (i.e., at full employment).

2. The expected inflation rate is where the Phillips Curve intersects the long-run Phillips Curve (at the natural rate of unemployment).

3. More inflation means less unemployment and so more output. The *AS* curve and the expected rate of inflation are held constant along the Phillips Curve.

4. Workers set their wages based upon what they think the price level will be. But if inflation is greater than they expected, they will have been "fooled" into accepting a lower real wage than they wanted.

5. If output differs from the full-employment level of output, workers will adjust their expectations and wages so the *AS* curve shifts the economy along the *AD* curve toward full employment.

6. No. Inflation reduces unemployment only if inflation is higher than expected. If it is lower than expected, unemployment will go up.

7. If people expect higher rates of inflation, they will demand higher wages and raise other factor costs. The Phillips Curve and the *AS* curve will shift up.

8. Because if inflation does not accelerate, the expected rate of inflation will catch up with the actual rate, returning unemployment to its natural level.

9. Only the natural rate of unemployment and the full-employment level of output can be sustained in the long run.

10. Wage and price controls could speed the recovery of an economy if they corrected the mistaken judgment of people as to how high prices and inflation will be. This would cause the *AS* curve to shift more quickly toward full employment.

PRACTICAL APPLICATION

1. a. 8 percent.
   b. Unemployment will rise to 7 percent.

2. See the figure below.

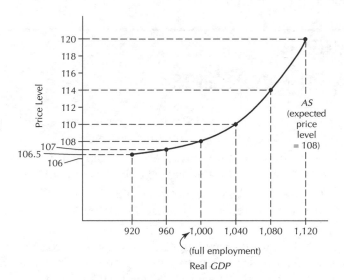

3. Workers will contract for 20 percent higher wages, but when prices go up only 10 percent, employers will find they are paying a higher real wage and so will cut back employment. The economy will go into a recession (as *AD* shifts left). In the long run, both unemployment and lower prices will cause workers to adjust their wages down, so the economy will return to full employment (shifting the *AS* curve right).

4. *Panel A:* From Point *A* to Point *B*, demand-pull inflation (due to the *AD* curve shifting right). From *B* to *C*, cost-push inflation (due to workers finding out inflation is higher than they had expected and raising their wages), and thus pushing up the *AS* curve.

    Panel B: From Point *A* to Point *B*, a demand-pull reduction in inflation (sometimes called "disinflation"). The *AD* curve is shifting left. From *B* to *C*, a cost-push reduction in inflation due to workers finding out inflation is lower than they expected. So they reduce their wages and push down the *AS* curve.

    Panel C: Some event (such as an oil price increase or a worldwide crop failure) has pushed the *AS* curve up and to the left. From Point *A* to Point *B*, the economy experiences a cost-push inflation. From *B* to *C*, there is a cost-push reduction in inflation as workers adjust their wages down so that the *AS* curve shifts right. How far the *AS* curve shifts depends upon whether the long-run *AS* has been reduced.

5. a. Cost-push phase of a recession.

    b. Demand-pull phase of an expansion.

    c. Cost-push phase of an expansion.

6. Wages will go up 12 percent.

7. **a.** *Short run:* to *B*. *Long run:* to *C*.

   b. To *D*.

   c. To *C*.

8. When wages (*W*) rise more quickly than prices (*P*), real wages (*W/P*) are increasing and employment will fall (holding technology and capital constant). When wages rise more slowly than prices, real wages are decreasing, and employment will rise.

9. The trick is to increase your widget price before controls are imposed (since you would not be permitted to increase them after) but also to not lose customers because of your higher price. So you raise your price but offer "special" discounts to your customers (such as coupons, special credit terms, and special volume discounts). Once controls are imposed, you can raise your effective price by cutting back on these discounts. If this is not enough, have your customers pay for some of your costs by picking up the product themselves. Have very strict credit terms or even demand cash in advance for widgets. Have many grades of quality, each with its own price, so you can push up your effective price by reducing the quality in each grade. If your product is in high demand, insist that your customers buy something else from you (at an inflated price) before they can get a widget.

10. If many firms employ the tactics described in Answer 9 above, reported prices will not rise. But the effective price of goods will. So inflation will not be stopped. Note that by evading wage and price controls, firms are actually serving the customers, for otherwise there would be shortages of goods and less output.

15
RATIONAL EXPECTATIONS AND OTHER MODELS OF THE BUSINESS CYCLE

KEY TERMS

neo-Keynesian macroeconomics theory that recessions persist because sticky prices prevent the economy from moving toward full employment.

nominal shocks shocks that change the price level but leave relative prices unaffected. An unanticipated increase in the money supply, for example, is a nominal shock.

rational expectations expectations that are unbiased and based upon the best available information.

rational-expectations macroeconomics theory that the economy is characterized by rational expectations and that business cycles are due to incomplete information.

real business cycle theory the theory that business cycles are caused by changes in productivity—in particular, due to changes in technology and changes in technological knowledge.

real shocks shocks that affect the relative price of goods and inputs. Unanticipated changes in taste, technology, or factor supplies, for example, are real shocks.

shock an unanticipated event.

unbiased forecast a forecast that is neither wrong on average nor systematically wrong.

The business cycle is the movement of the economy above and below the path of potential *GDP*. Business cycle theory is not concerned with economic growth (that is, with how fast the path of potential *GDP* grows). It is concerned with why the economy strays from the path of potential *GDP*.

To illustrate a key issue in business cycle theory, consider the following problem. Suppose the economy is currently at full employment. However, then the money supply is halved and suppose that full employment could only be achieved if all prices and wages were also halved. Almost all economists would expect a recession to result from this event, because prices would *not* be immediately halved. Buy why? No one is made worse off, as halving all prices leaves everyone with the same *real* income as before. However, *not* halving prices makes many worse off as they are thrown out of work in a recession. So why are prices not immediately halved? More generally, why do changes in nominal magnitudes (such as the price level) affect real output?

We will continue to use the workers being fooled model of short-run aggregate supply in this chapter.

RATIONAL-EXPECTATIONS MACROECONOMICS

Rational-expectations macroeconomics is based upon the assumption that people cannot be systematically fooled. Unlike the Keynesian model, it assumes prices and wages are flexible and adjust so markets clear. If markets clear, this means there is no excess demand or supply of any goods or inputs. For macroeconomics, this means that there is no excess supply of labor—that is, no one qualified for a job is unemployed unless they want to be unemployed. However, high unemployment and recession occur because people lack the information necessary to make the work and employment choices necessary to bring the economy to produce up to its potential. In the halving-the-money-supply example presented at the beginning of this chapter, rational expectations say prices *would* be halved if people were well informed. However, if the event was unexpected, it may take time for them to discover what has happened. People looking for work, for example, may be slow to reduce their wage demands and so will be unemployed by their own choosing. So, until wages drop, a recession occurs. The following example illustrates the central ideas of rational-expectations macroeconomics. Suppose that the government wants to stimulate the economy and does so by increasing the money supply by 10 percent. The first time the government does this, it works. However, it works by fooling workers and other suppliers into accepting lower real wages. Now suppose the government does the same thing again ten times in a row. By the tenth time, people will have caught on and will raise their wages and prices. Then the 10 percent increase in the money supply will no longer work: It will increase prices—not output. The logic of this example leads rational-expectations theorists to reject any theory that states that people can be systematically fooled time after time. The rational-expectations theory can be explained by a series of assumptions and results:

ASSUMPTIONS

ASSUMPTION 1: PEOPLE WILL TRY TO MAKE GOOD FORECASTS

Businesses need to forecast how well their goods will sell and at what profit. Workers and consumers need to forecast income and price levels. They try to make the *best forecasts,* as follows.

1. *They make unbiased forecasts.* They do not make **systematic errors** (i.e., they don't repeat the same mistake time after time) when estimating inflation, output, and other economic variables.

2. *They use the available information well.* For example, if the government is following a certain policy (such as stimulating the economy before elections), people notice it.

Rational-expectations theorists believe that people will make **random errors** instead of systematic errors. For example, when people's errors in forecasting inflation rates are random, it is impossible for economists to predict whether people will overestimate or underestimate how high inflation will be.

YOU SHOULD REMEMBER

1. An unbiased forecast will be correct on average and not make the same error year after year.

2. According to rational-expectations theory, people will make unbiased forecasts that use information well.

3. The errors people make will thus be random and unpredictable. Any model that assumes people make systematic errors is rejected.

ASSUMPTION 2: PEOPLE TAKE STEPS TO AVOID BEING FOOLED

To keep things simple, consider only workers. In equilibrium, the demand and supply for workers is equal. Now suppose the government increases the money supply unexpectedly. Money wages will rise and workers will initially assume that this represents an increase in their real wages. So they'll work more, and output and employment will go up. However, they have been fooled: When prices go up, the workers will find that only their nominal wages, not their *real* wages, have increased. They have confused a **real shock** (an unanticipated event that changes real wages or real output) with a **nominal shock** (an unanticipated event that changes all prices and costs equally, ultimately leaving real wages and real output unchanged in the long run).

Workers will take steps to avoid this happening again. They will demand cost-of-living adjustments in their wage contracts. They will become more aware of government policy and inflation. The next time the money supply is increased, real output won't be affected.

Some texts say that the rational-expectations theory assumes flexible prices and wages. This is not quite correct. The rational-expectations theory assumes that prices and wages will become more flexible if the government keeps trying to fool suppliers and workers into increasing output and employment. Being fooled is costly. However, having flexible wages and prices is also costly. People balance these two costs: When the government tries to fool people more often, people will in turn pay the costs of becoming more flexible.

These ideas can be illustrated by Texas Hold'em, a popular poker game. In Texas Hold'em, players see their own two cards. In stages, each stage accompanied by betting, five more cards are revealed to all players. The player who has the best hand (from his two cards and the five common cards) wins. Usually, the more the person bets, the better cards they are holding. Some players are called "rocks": they only bet good cards. If this is known, then savvy players can predict what the rock is holding by the rock's bets. In just the same way, when the government is a rock, acting in a predictable way, investors can place their bets (invest their money) with more certainty. In poker, it is winner take all. In an economy, when more people bet (invest), there are more winners and the economy prospers. However, there are other players (known as maniacs) who frequently bluff (trying to fool others by betting large amounts even when they have bad cards). Maniacs often win in poker as they are unpredictable. However, if the government bluffs frequently, the economy loses: The economy becomes more unpredictable and thus less desirable to work and invest in.

YOU SHOULD REMEMBER

1. A *shock* is an unexpected event. A *real shock* changes the relative prices of goods and inputs. A *nominal shock* changes all prices and costs equally, leaving relative prices unchanged.

2. Workers (and other input suppliers) will produce more when their wages go up only if they believe that their real wages have gone up. Therefore, nominal shocks increase output only when they are mistaken for real shocks (i.e., only if workers are fooled).

3. Workers will avoid being fooled by making their wage payments more flexible (i.e., wages will become more responsive to changes in prices and economic conditions).

RESULTS

RESULT 1: ANTICIPATED SHIFTS IN THE AD CURVE HAVE NO REAL EFFECTS

If workers know what the government is going to do, they will set their wage contracts so that they are fully employed. Consider Figure 15–1. The labor market is in equilibrium when output is at full employment (*FE*). And the *AD* curve is based on what the government is expected to do. What is the expected price level? It is *P*–0, the price level where the *AD* curve (*AD*–0) intersects the long-run aggregate supply curve, *S*–Long Run, at full employment *FE*. People expect the economy to be at full employment and not to systematically be above or below it. So the aggregate supply curve *AS*–A must go through Point *A*.

If *AD* shifts up to *AD*–B and workers have anticipated this, they will raise their wages and the *AS* curve will *also* shift up to Point *B* (to *AS*–B). Anticipated increases in aggregate demand will raise only prices and costs. They have only nominal, not real, effects. (See Practical Application, Question 2.) As an analogy, suppose you are playing poker with someone who always cheats in the last hand of the evening. Once you anticipate this, you can avoid being cheated, by not betting in the last hand.

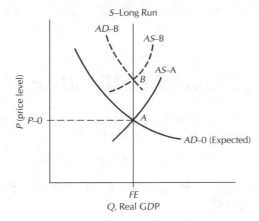

Figure 15–1. Determining That Anticipated Shifts in Supply and Demand Have No Effects on Rational Price Expectations

If the government tries to stimulate the economy (by increasing *AD*) in a way the public anticipates, then it *cannot* increase output. In particular, a policy of always stimulating the economy when there is high unemployment will *not* be effective, since it can be anticipated.

YOU SHOULD REMEMBER

1. In rational-expectations theory, people expect the economy to be at full employment and the price level to be where the *AD* curve intersects the full-employment level of output (on the long-run aggregate supply curve).

2. Anticipated shifts in *AD* will not affect output or relative prices. Only the level of prices and costs will change.

3. The government cannot stimulate output by increasing aggregate demand in any anticipated or predictable manner.

RESULT 2: ONLY UNANTICIPATED SHIFTS IN THE AD CURVE AFFECT REAL OUTPUT

The remarkable conclusion of rational-expectations theory is that shifts in *AD* affect output only when they trick workers and suppliers into increasing output and employment. For example, an unanticipated increase in aggregate demand increases output only because the aggregate supply curve does not shift up with it. (If the poker maniac we described above starts to bluff every hand, you will be fooled into thinking he or she has a good hand until you catch on.)

YOU SHOULD REMEMBER

Unanticipated increases in *AD* increase real output, while unanticipated decreases in *AD* reduce real output.

RESULT 3: FREQUENT AND UNEXPECTED POLICY CHANGES HARM THE ECONOMY

If the government tries to stimulate the economy in any predictable manner (such as when unemployment rises), its policy will become ineffective. On the other hand, if it tries to continually surprise the economy, it may affect output but in negative ways.

For example, every time the government raises the price level to try to fool workers, it is crying wolf. At first, workers respond (by working more). Eventually, they stop responding. Someday, the wolf does come along, and workers do not respond. For example, new technology may raise real wages, but workers, having been fooled by seemingly good wage increases in the past, do not respond. The result is a sluggish economy and lowered output.

Another example of how frequent policy changes can harm the economy is that workers, to cope with the greater uncertainty produced by the policy changes, will demand higher real wages. Also, savers will demand a higher real interest rate. As a result, employment and investment will contract, reducing output and growth. (Returning to Texas Hold'em, most people would demand higher expected winnings to play with a maniac because of the added uncertainty and variance added to the game. If people are risk-adverse, this in turn would reduce the number of poker games they are willing to play.)

YOU SHOULD REMEMBER

1. It is impossible for the government to fool people systematically into increasing output. Eventually, people catch on.

2. The effects of continued changes in government policy will be to dull the economy's responses to real changes and to increase uncertainty.

RATIONAL-EXPECTATIONS MODEL

Rational-expectations theory assumes that people do the best they can collecting information and making plans. The main features of most rational-expectations models include the following:

- People have budget constraints and maximize their utility. People do this by taking into account what they expect in the future.

- Barring unexpected events, people get what they planned.

- The models use explicit equations describing a household's utility function and a business's production functions along with the budget constraint people face now and in the future.

- By using these equations, precise predictions can be made. The level of precision allows one to gauge how much and when an event (such as an increase in taxes) will affect the economy.

- Usually these models have many possible outcomes. However, only one outcome is consistent with people's expectations and plans being met (barring an unexpected event). This is the outcome consistent with rational expectations.

Today, most macroeconomic theorists, even if they call themselves monetarists or Keynesians, use rational-expectations theory. Therefore, current theory differs greatly from the models of the past. For example, most macroeconomic models of the 1950s and 1960s assumed people used an average of past inflation rates to predict what inflation will be. Consequently, in these models, the government can always fool people by increasing inflation above this average level. Believing that most people can be fooled in the same way year after year is difficult. Therefore, rational-expectations economists would reject this assumption. Similarly, they reject any model assuming people can be continually fooled or mistaken.

PROBLEM   Describe why these models would be rejected by rational-expectations economists:

Model A: Economic expansions will tend to occur in election years since the party in power will try to stimulate the economy to increase its chance of being reelected.

Model B: When governments run up a big debt, they will inflate the money supply to reduce the real value of what they owe.

Model C: Expanding the money supply (or increased government spending) will always stimulate the economy.

> *Model D:* The public can easily predict when X occurs. When X occurs, output will grow above its long-run equilibrium level.

SOLUTION *Model A:* If people had this information ("the party in power will try to stimulate the economy"), they would immediately increase wages and prices in election years. The results would be more inflation, not a higher *GDP*. The model would be wrong. ("Stimulate the economy" means to try to increase real *GDP*, usually by expanding the money supply faster or increasing government spending).

> *Model B:* If the model was correct and savers knew this, they would demand a sufficiently high interest rate to offset the effects of the expected inflation. The real value of what the government owes would not change. The model would be wrong.

> *Model C:* If anticipated, expanding the money supply (or increasing government spending) raises prices, not output.

> *Model D:* If the public did not raise wages and prices, the added output would not be worth the added time spent working. So it will pay the public to predict X, raising wages and prices, not output.

AN EXAMPLE OF A RATIONAL-EXPECTATIONS MODEL

Rational-expectations models use equations and advanced math, so presenting one here is difficult. The following model is a very crude and simple model to give you a sense of what these models entail.

Assumptions:

1. People live forever, and the population is fixed at 1,000 persons.

2. Each person has a stock of capital (K) that produces output Q. Let Q be the annual output of K, such that $Q = 0.10K$. That is, capital pays a rate of return of 10 percent.

3. Q can be consumed (as C) or saved. If people save by producing more than they consume ($Q > C$), K increases by $Q - C$ units. If people dissave by consuming more than they produce ($C > Q$), then, on net, K decreases by $C - Q$ units. When K equals 100 units, people discount the

future by 10 percent and will neither save nor dissave. When K is less than 100 units, people discount the future by less than 10 percent and will save to build up K. When K is greater than 100 units, people discount the future by more than 10 percent and will dissave.

4. People trade their Q for the Q of others to get the mix they want. Total trade and measured *GDP* equals the sum of C across all persons. Each unit of C requires k real units of money for trading purposes. As a result, each person's money demand is $M/P = kC$, where M is the nominal money supply per person and P is the price of one unit of C. k equals 0.05.

5. The nominal money supply is fixed by the government at $10 per person. Long-Run Results: In the long run, people neither save nor dissave, so that in the long run, K equals 100 units and $Q = C = 10$.
Per Person: $K = 100$, $C = 10$, and since $M = kPC$, $P = \$20$.
For the Economy: Real *GDP* = 1000 C = 10,000 units.
Each application starts from this point. All terms (M, C, K, Q) are per capita and all persons are exactly alike.

• *APPLICATION ONE:*

Suppose the government surprised people by doubling their cash holdings to $20. This type of event is called a *monetary shock*. What would happen? At the current level of consumption, people would have twice the money they need. While thinking they are richer, they will try to reduce their cash balances by consuming more. C goes up, corresponding to an economic expansion (C being higher than 10 units per person). However, since $C > Q$, capital (K) will become smaller. People did not expect this (since they thought they were richer). Now they discover they are poorer. Because K is below 100 units, people will start saving to get back to the original K. Output (C) will contract.

An important prediction is that the bigger the expansion, the greater the contraction. This is a testable proposition. Evidence suggests that a recession's size is not related to the size of an expansion that preceded it. If this model is valid, it suggests that most contractions and expansions are not caused by changes in the money supply.

• *APPLICATION TWO:*

What would happen if the productivity of capital rose so that, at $K = 100$, it yields 12 percent (and at 12 percent, people will neither save nor dissave at a K of 120)? This type of event—a change in the productivity—is called a *technological shock*. In this case, two things occur. First, output goes up to 12 units (using $Q = rK$, $12 = 0.12 \times 100$). Second, people start saving to build up K (ultimately to 120 units). So C will fall below 12 but will be above its old level of 10. An economic expansion will occur as C rises. Eventually, C will equal 14.4 units (12 percent of the long-run K of 120 units). The price level will fall from \$20 to \$13.89 (as $M = 10$). In this model, technological change leads to an expanding output, an initial higher rate of return, and a downward pressure on prices. The U.S. economy expansion since the mid–1980s matches this pattern.

Actual rational-expectations models are more realistic than this one. Current modeling suggests that technological and fiscal shocks are the best explanation of past recessions and expansions since World War II. However, no current model can explain the severity and length of the Great Depression.

CRITICISMS OF RATIONAL EXPECTATIONS

1. *Expectations are not formed rationally.* If expectations are rationally formed, using all the relevant information available, then forecasts of prices, interest rates, and output should be unbiased (with no systematic mistakes), efficient (use all past information), and consistent (forecasts should not conflict). The bottom line is that errors in forecasts should be unpredictable. If errors are predictable, then people are making systematic mistakes and not learning from them. Surveys of consumers and businesses show they make systematic errors in forecasts. This sort of evidence is not totally persuasive since what matters for the economy is people's forecast about the prices and output that matter most to them and not what they think is happening to the whole economy.

   A more general criticism is that using all information may not be rational. Most people, for example, tie their shoes by habit without thinking about it. While we may not optimally tie our shoes every day, a good job is sufficient for most purposes. We all have various habits and rules of thumb. They save time so we can focus on more important tasks. Similarly, most businesspersons may find that focusing on running their businesses efficiently and using rules of thumb to set prices is more profitable than spending the time and money to get the best information possible about the economy.

2. *Real changes may be needed, particularly in unemployment, to force people to change their expectations.* Suppose the best forecasts predict that if workers do not lower their wages, unemployment will increase. Given the inaccuracy of forecasts, workers should rationally wait and see if unemployment does increase before they agree to a lower wage. Consequently, changes in aggregate demand, even if anticipated, may have real effects.

3. *Because of multiyear contracts, workers may not be able to adjust fully to new information.* Similarly, firms that do business with each other (for example, farmers, fertilizer makers, seed sellers, and tractor makers)

may be better off adjusting their prices infrequently since their prosperity is linked to one another. Thus, institutional impediments may prevent making rapid adjustments even if people's expectations are rationally formed.

4. *Recessions cost too much and last too long to be rational.* A typical recession in recent years reduced *GDP* by 5 percent and lasted ten months (expansion lasted longer, about 50 months). This represents nearly a half trillion dollars in lost *GDP*. Recall that in rational-expectations models, people will spend money to predict and prepare for events. Evidently, predicting and preparing for these past recessions must have cost more than half a trillion dollars. The criticism is that this is not reasonable (half a trillion dollars should buy pretty good forecasts). One response to this type of criticism is that recessions cost less than the output lost since more output can be produced later. A second response is that the government often causes the recessions, and predicting what the government is going to do is not just costly but impossible.

RATIONAL EXPECTATIONS, RANDOM WALK, AND THE STOCK MARKET

One of the most dramatic applications of rational expectations is the stock market in what is called the **efficient-market theory.** The stock market is efficient when all current information is reflected in the prices of stocks. As a consequence, stock market prices change *only* when *unexpected* new information becomes available. Since this new information is by definition unpredictable, stock market prices will follow a **random walk** (around its overall growth-trend line). A random walk is a series of numbers, randomly chosen, so that one cannot predict future numbers from the past. To see how one could form a random walk, suppose we start with a stock at 100 dollars. We toss a die and take its value and subtract 3 from it. We let this be the change in the stock price (so if we roll a 4, the new stock price will be 101 dollars). Over time, the stock will rise an average of 50 cents a toss (the average of the sum of +3, +2, +1, 0, –1, and –2 divided by 6). However, it will have unpredictable ups and downs around this trend line. Indeed, it will form all sorts of formations, have many interesting support levels, all of them useless for predicting future changes.

Overall, the stock market appears to be an efficient market characterized by a random walk. There are some exceptions. So people have found predictable trends, such as the fact that stock prices rise in early January. But these exceptions are often short-lived and not large enough to be profitable once the costs of trading stocks is taken into account.

What are the implications of this model for your own finances? Basically, you should (1) seek to buy a mix of stocks at the lowest cost possible and

(2) hold rather than trade them. By buying a mix of stocks from different industries, you reduce the odds your portfolio will be wiped out by one stock or one group of closely related stocks doing badly (a mix of fifteen to twenty stocks is usually sufficient). Diversity protects you from the risk of losing money when some but not all stocks do very poorly. Other ways to diversify include buying stocks from several nations and buying them at different times (for example, buying 200 dollars worth of stock every month). Buying stocks at the lowest commissions puts more of your money to work. Similarly, if you buy a mutual fund, your best buy is usually a no-load fund (one that does not charge you for buying the fund) that has a low annual expense ratio (usually expressed as a percent of asset value). One type of fund that has a low annual expense mutual fund is an index fund. An index fund buys the set of stocks in a major stock index (such as the Standard & Poor's stock index). As these basically hold the stocks rather than trade them, they often have the lowest expenses. Most other types of mutual funds turn over their portfolio at least once a year, creating considerable costs and creating taxes for you on the capital gains realized each year (thereby reducing the fund's effective long-run return). These expenses add up, which is why on average index mutual funds have beaten out other mutual funds.

REAL BUSINESS CYCLE THEORY

There is a substantial body of evidence suggesting that price surprises and money disturbances do not affect real economic activity. If this is true, then where does the business cycle come from? A clue comes from the fact that changes in investment spending have played a large role in recent business cycles. What is significant is that these increases in investment spending do not appear to come from more money being made available (as the Keynesian and monetarist models suggest). *If* they were caused by more funds being made available, real interest rates would fall in expansions. However, interest rates rise with rising investments. So, by using simple demand and supply analysis, these increases must come from investment projects becoming more profitable.

Real business cycle theorists focus on changes in technology (as well as in technological information) as causing these shifts in profitability. For example, faster computers allow businesses to cheaply monitor their inventories, finances, workers, and other costs. This leads to greater output from the same inputs, and so, to higher profits. With more-profitable investments available, businesses borrow more, raising real interest rates. Both aggregate supply and aggregate demand increase, creating an economic expansion (with an indeterminate effect of prices). On the other hand, suppose corporate takeovers cause managers to focus on company politics and not on managing their firms. The result will be a decrease in profitable investments, causing business to borrow less, leading to lower real interest rates and lower output, creating an economic recession. These expansions and recessions are not mistakes, nor are they the result of sticky prices. Instead, they reflect the adjustments the economy must make to new technology. For example, the rise in oil prices in the 1970s necessitated that many workers in energy-intensive industries lose their jobs, retrain, and find new jobs in other industries. This caused a decrease in output during this adjustment period.

One shortcoming of the real business cycle model is its exclusive focus on technological change. Yet government regulations, taxes, and court rulings have similar effects on the profitability of investments. For example, some economists blame the economic slowdown in the late 1980s and early 1990s in part on the increase in corporate tax rates contained in the Tax Reform Act of 1986.

YOU SHOULD REMEMBER

1. In the real business cycle, changes in the profitability of investments due to technological change cause the business cycle.

2. Technological improvements result in higher output, higher real interest rates, and an uncertain effect on prices.

NEO-KEYNESIAN MACROECONOMICS

Both the rational-expectations and real business cycle theorists believe that markets clear, even in recessions. For example, even in recessions, all those who want to work at prevailing wages do. But owing to mistakes (due to poor information) or the need to shift workers between employers (due to technological shocks), the level of employment is below that capable of producing potential *GDP*. However, once people are aware of what wage and price changes are necessary to achieve full employment, wages and prices adjust quickly.

Neo-Keynesians believe in rational expectations. However, they do *not* believe prices will quickly change to achieve full employment. In terms of the halving-of-money example at the beginning of this chapter, they believe prices will be slow to change even if everyone *is* aware they must be halved to achieve full employment.

The neo-Keynesians also hold that sociological and economic forces keep markets from clearing when the economy turns down. They base this position on Keynes' key insight that prices and wages are slow to change (that is, they are "sticky"). As a result, wages may be set too high, creating massive unemployment. Yet, because wages are slow to change, this high rate of unemployment may persist for years. A logical remedy for the recession is for the government to increase aggregate demand.

Some of the new Keynesian (or neo-Keynesian) macroeconomic models include:

1. *Insiders-Outsiders Model of Labor Unions.* Unions represent current workers ("insiders"), not the workers who lose their jobs ("outsiders"). The result is that insiders may have little incentive to reduce wages, even if many workers lose their jobs. To illustrate, suppose the rate of inflation unexpectedly drops while union wages continue to rise. The real wage will rise and some or many union workers will lose their jobs. However, there is little reason for the remaining workers, especially those whose jobs are protected by seniority, to lower wages. On the contrary, the higher real wages make them better off! So they will keep real wages high. Evidence suggests that unions bargain for lower wages only when the jobs of workers with seniority are threatened—for example, by a plant closing. Similarly, German unions are pushing for higher real wages even if this means the continued massive unemployment of those from the former East Germany.

2. *Credit-Rationing Model.* In this model, banks loan to only the best customers and limit how much they can borrow (that is, they ration credit). So even if interest rates drop as the government pumps more money into the economy and even if businesses become more profitable, banks may not lend the extra money needed to fuel new investment spending. Why would banks ration credit? The reason is that borrowers differ in their creditworthiness. By limiting lending to those lenders with a good track record of paying off past loans and by limiting how much each customer is loaned, banks can reduce the likelihood the customer will default on the loan. Lowering interest rates and making more funds available may bring in less creditworthy borrowers who will end up defaulting on their loans. The same logic applies to high-quality apartments: Lowering rents may bring in only deadbeats and ne'er-do-wells. So even with a large vacancy rate, rents on high-quality apartments may not fall. In effect, the high rents (or, for banks, high interest rates) screen out undesirable clients.

3. *Multiyear-Contracts Models.* Unions typically have three-year contracts, locking them into certain wages. Even unions with COLA clauses (cost-of-living adjustment clauses that adjust wages for changes in inflation) are not fully indexed. That is, inflation will still lower real wages, but not as much as it would have without the COLA clause. Similarly, nonunion employers may have implicit agreements to increase wages at a certain

pace, agreements that restrict employers from lower wages in a recession. Also, retailers changing prices frequently may find themselves losing business to those that change prices less often when customers prefer stores with predictable prices. In all these cases, prices and wages will be slow to change.

4. *Strategic Complementarities.* Two inputs are complements when they are used together in production. For example, complementarity exists between workers and employers. It also exists between firms in the same chain of production (for example, a steel company supplying steel to an auto firm). Suppose that in a given industry workers can be lazy or hardworking and that managers can be lazy or hardworking. If both are hardworking, their joint product is high and both benefit. If both are lazy, their joint product is low and they both get less. However, if one is lazy and the other hardworking, they do not get along and nothing is produced. Further, assume that managers and workers move often between jobs in this industry. The result is likely to be an industry ethos. It could be "work hard" or it could be "work lazy." If everyone (workers and managers) is lazy and one manager (or worker) works hard, the hardworking manager (or worker) will be unproductive and lose his or her job. If everyone is hardworking and one manager (or worker) is lazy, the lazy person will lose his or her job. So we have two possible equilibriums, each one consistent with rational expectations.

Similarly, an economy could have multiple equilibriums, all consistent with rational expectations. A possible role for government policy could be to move the economy from one equilibrium to another, expanding output.

5. *Informational Externalities.* Suppose I have to know the value of General Motors. Fortunately, I do not have to do extensive research. Instead, I just look up GM's stock price, multiply this by its outstanding shares, and derive its market value. This is an example of informational externality. I benefit (in saved research costs) from the information that the stock market freely provides to me.

To illustrate the impact of informational externalities, suppose that all the merchants of a nation are lined up on the same street and are trying to figure out how many goods to stock their shelves with. If they expect good times, they will buy large amounts of goods. If they expect bad times, they will buy few goods. To infer how the economy will turn out, they look out onto the street to see what the others are doing. If one merchant stocks up his or her shelves with lots of goods, the others will quite possibly follow. Because of strategic complementaries, the result may be that the economy does well. On the other hand, all might follow a merchant who puts in only a few goods, resulting in the economy doing poorly. In both cases, expectations are confirmed and thus rational.

What is important to note about all these models is how a recession can create new forces that keep the economy from returning to full employment. The recession creates "ratchets" that keep the economy from sliding back on its own to full employment. The central issue is whether these models accurately pinpoint the causes of lingering downturns. Another issue is whether an increase in aggregate demand, if anticipated, would create more employment in the first two models. For example, when aggregate demand goes up, union insiders could push for still-higher wages and worried bank officials could push up interest rates. In both cases, an anticipated increase in aggregate demand may not create more employment.

YOU SHOULD REMEMBER

1. Neo-Keynesian macroeconomists seek to show that rational expectations can be made consistent with sticky prices and non-clearing markets.

2. Most of their models show how a recession might set up forces that keep prices and wages from adjusting to levels consistent with the full employment of resources. The insider-outsider model of unions shows that insiders, protected by seniority, may not care about those who have lost their jobs.

WHERE DOES BUSINESS CYCLE THEORY STAND TODAY?

Rational expectations is well accepted today by almost all macroeconomists. Most economists agree with its implication that frequent government tinkering with the economy will prove counterproductive. Finally, most also agree that the business cycle rises mainly out of unexpected shocks of some form.

The main disagreements include:

1. The *sources* of the unexpected shocks. Monetarists obviously focus on money, Keynesians focus on aggregate spending, and real business cycle theorists focus on technological and productivity changes. Rational-expectations models allow for a variety of sources but tend to emphasize the government as a key source of macroeconomic instability.

2. *How do shocks cause recessions?* Rational-expectations theorists focus on how poor information leads the public to confuse relative price changes with changes in the price level (as in the example at the beginning of this chapter). Real business cycle models focus on the adjustments that must be made in the wake of technological change, including higher unemployment as the economy shifts output between sectors. Keynesians focus on how prices and wages can be slow to adjust even if people are aware that prices and wages are not at market clearing levels.

3. *Why did the Great Depression last so long?* The simple fact is that we do not know. It is hard to believe that people did not eventually become aware that prices and wages were too high at some point in the 1930s. It is equally hard to believe it was caused by falling productivity. One explanation is that during the Great Depression, the economy was hit by successive waves of bad shocks that kept the economy down. It was a period of protectionism and trade wars, which devastated the export sector of the U.S. economy. Also, the income tax was raised several times and the new social security tax was introduced. Another policy discouraging investments was the passing of the Wagner Act in 1936, which made unions stronger. Also the introduction of many new regulations slowed recovery.

4. *How can we avoid the business cycle?* The government, by adopting a more predictable and stable monetary policy, could reduce the frequency and severity of the business cycle. As the real business cycle model emphasizes, there are forces outside the government's control that can create expansions and recessions. These are unavoidable. If markets *do* clear in recessions, then there is little the government can do. If they do *not* clear, then, as the Keynesians argue, the increasing aggregate demand may stimulate the economy.

KNOW THE CONCEPTS

DO YOU KNOW THE BASICS?

1. Suppose you have the price level forecasts that business leaders have made in the past. How can you tell whether their forecasts are unbiased and without systematic error?

2. Why do rational-expectations economists not expect people to make systematic errors in their forecasts?

3. If forecast errors are random, can one predict when a recession is going to occur?

4. Why do workers supply more labor in response to an unanticipated increase in inflation?

5. Why will workers supply no more labor in response to an anticipated increase in inflation?

6. With rational expectations, why can the government not stimulate the economy out of every recession?

7. How will an expansion caused by an unanticipated fiscal and monetary policy differ from one caused by "real causes," as in the real business cycle?

8. If firms know the price of their output is going up because people have changed their tastes and increased their demand for the firms' output (this being a real shock), how will firms change their output?

9. If firms know the price increase is due to a nominal shock, how will they change output?

10. How can an active discretionary governmental policy that is designed to increase output actually reduce output in the long run?

TERMS FOR STUDY

credit rationing
efficient market theory
insider-outsider model of unions
neo-Keynesian economics

random errors
random walk
rational expectations
real business cycle theory
systematic errors

PRACTICAL APPLICATION

1. If a baseball player has a .300 batting average, why is it unbiased to predict that for every ten times at bat, he or she should have three hits? Why is predicting four hits (out of ten) a biased prediction?
   Note: A .300 batting average means that the player makes a hit 30 percent of the time.

2. Use the following table to answer the questions below. This table shows the supply and demand for labor in an economy.

Real Wage	Labor Supply	Labor Demand
4	70	130
5	80	115
6	90	90
7	100	75
8	110	60

a. What is the real wage (W/P) at full employment?

b. If workers expect a price level of 200 (i.e., $P = 2.00$), what money wage (W) will they want?

c. If workers expect a price level of 200 (and are paid the money wage from (b) above), then what actual price level will cause firms to hire 115 units of labor?
Note: Assume that firms know what the actual price level is.

d. If workers come to expect the price level in (c) above, what wage will they demand? What will happen to output?

3. Suppose the Fed announces "We are *not* going to increase the money supply" and then surprises everyone by increasing it by 20 percent. What will happen? If the Fed does this ten times in a row, what will happen the eleventh time?

4. Continuing Question 3, what will happen the twelfth time the Fed announces "We are *not* going to increase the money supply" if it actually does *not* increase the money supply that time?

5. This problem presents a crude real business cycle model that focuses on the labor market. All households are alike and have 3,000 hours a year available for working (L) or household time (H). Each hour of labor pays a sufficient wage to allow the worker to buy one unit of consumption good C. Consumption good C is combined with a half-hour of home time to create household output Z. (For example, C could be purchased food, which when added to cooking time equals a meal, Z.) Each unit of Z effectively takes one hour of work time plus one-half hour of household time.

a. How many hours will people work? What is the real wage? What is per capita C and Z?

b. A technological shock increases the productivity of work time such that one hour of labor produces two consumption goods. What will happen to work time, real wages, per capital C and Z?

c. A technological shock increases the productivity of home time such that only one-quarter hour of time is needed to change C into Z. (We are returning to the original case where one hour of L produces one C).

d. Work hours and output move together over the business cycle. Which of the two cases better match this result?

6. Why is it unlikely that you will find a ten-dollar bill on the sidewalk? How does this logic apply to the stock market?

7. Does the random-walk model of stock prices predict that no stock newsletter will be able to beat the market consistently?

8. Hundreds of firms are in the fashion industry, making all types of clothing, jewelry, and other fashion accessories. Despite all this competition, only a few colors are offered each year. Firms not producing clothing in the predominant colors have a hard time selling their clothes because customers have a hard time finding accessories and matching clothing. In addition, offering too many colors is costly since stores would have to carry far larger inventories. Which of the models presented in this chapter does the fashion industry seem to reflect? Suppose this year's colors are green and purple, but the public would buy more if this year's colors were red and white. How would a firm, knowing this, take advantage of this information?

9. This problem illustrates the rationale behind credit rationing. Suppose there are two types of borrowers. Half the potential borrowers are "good," who want to borrow $100,000 on projects that will pay back $130,000 in a year. The other half are "bad" borrowers, who want to borrow $100,000 on projects that will pay back $120,000 if they succeed and only $80,000 if they fail (there is half a chance they will succeed). Assume borrowers lose nothing if the project fails. What is the lowest interest rate banks must charge to be sure they only get good borrowers? What will happen to the bank's returns if they lower the interest rate? (Assume they cannot tell who is bad and who is good when making a loan.) Suppose the Fed lowers the discount rate: Will this encourage banks to lend at lower interest rates?

10. The following ad ran on the radio: "Listeners, doesn't it stand to reason that gasoline prices will go up in summer when more people are driving? And doesn't it stand to reason that the best time to buy futures in gasoline is in winter before gasoline prices go up? So listen to reason: Buy a gasoline futures contract in the winter!" (Note: A futures contract guarantees delivery of a commodity at a certain price. If you buy a futures contract guaranteeing a price of $1.00 a gallon and its price then rises to $1.20, you will make 20¢ per gallon. That adds up to a lot when the futures contract is for 42,000 gallons.) What is wrong with the logic of this commercial?

ANSWERS

KNOW THE CONCEPTS

1. First, find out whether the forecasts were correct on average. Then find out whether the errors were systematic (i.e., whether mistakes were repeated).

2. A person making systematic errors is making the same costly mistake again and again. If people are rational, they will avoid past errors.

3. Only recessions that are due to real causes (such as an OPEC oil price increase) can be predicted. Those that are due to unanticipated shifts in the *AD* curve cannot, by definition, be anticipated.

4. When firms offer workers higher money wages and ask them to work more, workers accept since they think they are getting higher real wages (but in fact inflation will reduce their real wages).

5. When workers correctly anticipate inflation, they adjust their wages such that they supply the labor they want and no more.

6. According to rational-expectations theory, government cannot systematically trick workers and suppliers into producing more, and in particular, it cannot systematically do this whenever the economy is in a recession (since its actions can then be anticipated).

7. Fiscal and monetary policy increase aggregate demand, raising inflation and output. *AD* is increased in part by making more funds available for investment, thereby decreasing the real interest rate. In the real business cycle, both the *AD* and *AS* curves are shifted out. Output goes up but inflation may be unaffected. Since the cause of the expansion is new investment opportunity from new technologies becoming available, real interest rates rise.

8. A change in taste that increases the demand for a good means, first, that people are willing to pay more in real terms for the good, and second, that the factors that produced the goods now out of favor are now available to be hired. So the firms will produce more, knowing costs won't rise to offset their profits from producing more.

9. If the increase in price is only nominal, there are no new available factors from out-of-favor goods. So costs will rise to offset the output's higher price. Firms will raise their price, not their output.

10. An active discretionary policy adds uncertainty to the economy and reduces the responsiveness of firms to all price changes, whether they are due to real or nominal shocks.

PRACTICAL APPLICATION

1. The forecast of three hits out of ten times at bat is unbiased in the sense that on average it will be right. Sometimes, the baseball player will hit more, sometimes less. Predicting four hits will be right some of the time, but more often it will be too high. So it is biased.

2. **a.** W/P at full employment is $6.
   b. $W = \$12$ ($\$12/2.00 = \$6$).

    c. Firms will hire 115 units when the real wage is 5. So to make W/P equal to 5, with $W = \$12$, we need a price level (P) of 240 ($\$12/2.40 = \$5$).

    d. Workers will demand a wage of $14.40, since $\$14.40/2.40 = \$6$. Output will return to its full-employment level.

3. The first time this occurs, people will not anticipate the increase in the money supply. Output will increase in the short run. But by the eleventh time, people will anticipate the increase in the money supply, so in the short *and* long run, only prices will increase. Real output will be unaffected.

4. People will expect prices to rise, so the *AS* curve will shift up. But the *AD* curve will be unchanged. So output will fall and prices will rise (there will be a cost-push stagflation). In the long run, output and prices will return to their original levels.

5. a. $L + H = 3,000$. For each hour of L, we need 0.5 hour of H, so $H = 0.5L$. Solving for L ($1.5L = 3,000$), $L = 2,000$ hours a year and $H = 1,000$ hours a year. The real wage is one C per hour of work. Output is 2,000 C per person and 2,000 Z per person.

    b. $L + H = 3,000$. For each hour of L, we need one hour of H, so $H = L$. Solving for L ($2L = 3,000$), $L = 1,500$ hours a year. The real wage rises to 2 C per hour of work. Output is 3,000 C per person and 3,000 Z per person.

    c. For each hour of L, we need 0.25 hour of H to produce one Z. $1.25L = 3,000$, so $L = 2,400$. The real wage remains unchanged. However, due to more hours of work, per capita output rises to 2,400 C and 2,400 Z.

    d. Part *C*. When technological progress occurs in household productivity (rather than in labor productivity), hours of work (L) go up with output (C).

6. If there were an abundance of ten-dollar bills around, people would notice this and pick them up. Economic incentive gets rid of easy ways to make money. In terms of the stock market, if there is an easy way to make money, someone would have discovered it, exploited it, and it would no longer exist. As a result of this logic, economists predict that the stock market is an efficient market characterized by rational expectations.

7. On the contrary, out of the thousands of stock newsletters, random chance says that some will have always been right (just as if you tossed ten coins together 1,000 times, it is almost certain that all ten will be heads in at least one of the tosses). However, according to the efficient-market model, because they were just lucky, the future predictions of these "winning" newsletters will be no better or worse than that of other newsletters.

8. The fashion industry shows strategic complementarity. It pays all firms to produce items that go with the product of other firms (jewelry matching clothing, matching shoes, and so forth). The public may prefer reds and whites, but they prefer reds and whites only if they can get all their fashion needs in these colors. Otherwise, red and white items are not wanted. A large firm, controlling a large segment of the industry, would be needed to produce and sell items in red and white. Thus, a paradox exists. Many small firms lead to less choice and perhaps less-desirable choices, while a few large firms might offer more of what the public wants.

9. The bank would have to charge at a minimum any rate above 20 percent (and no more than 30 percent). This drives away bad borrowers who cannot make the loan pay at, say, 21 percent (as they would have to pay back $121,000 if it succeeds). Lowering the rate below 20 percent will bring in bad borrowers, who on average pay back $100,000—a net rate of return of 0 percent. Suppose the bank lowers its rates to 18 percent. It will on average lend half its money to good borrowers (and get 18 percent) and the other half to bad borrowers (and net 0 percent): They will get only a net 9 percent return on average. Thus, lowering the interest rate from 21 percent to 18 percent lowers its net return from 21 percent to 9 percent! This makes banks keep interest rates high and ration credit.

10. This ad assumes that the people making a living buying and selling futures contracts are unaware that summer exists! Can you imagine a futures trader saying, "Wow, what is this summer thing? No wonder I've been losing money year after year!" I do not think so. The futures price for gasoline will rise in winter in anticipation of higher prices in summer. Any easily available information, such as that hawked in a radio ad or in an investment seminar, will be incorporated into prices until no further profits, barring unexpected events, can be made.

16
OPEN-MARKET MACROECONOMICS

KEY TERMS

exchange rate rate at which the currency of one nation trades for the currency of another. An exchange rate of 200 yen per dollar means one dollar can buy 200 yen.

interest rate parity theory that the real interest rates on equally risky investments in trading nations should be the same after adjusting for expected changes in the values of currencies.

purchasing power parity theory that exchange rates will adjust until a unit of any currency is able to buy the same set of goods and services in all trading nations.

real exchange rate rate at which the goods and services in one country trade for the goods and services of another.

INTRODUCTION

A closed economy is one that does not trade with other nations. Many macroeconomic models assume the economy is closed because such models are easier to understand. An open economy is one freely trading goods and assets with other nations. International trade has become increasingly important in the U.S. economy, growing from 5 percent in 1950 to over 14 percent today. In other nations, it plays an even larger role. Because international trade plays such an important role in our economy, it is important to incorporate it into our macroeconomic models. This makes the models more complicated.

To keep things simple, we will assume that only two nations exist: the United States and Switzerland. In addition, we will discuss international trade from the United States' perspective. Thus, U.S. goods sold in Switzerland are exports and Swiss goods sold in the United States are imports. Finally, instead of saying "goods and services" are traded, we will just refer to "goods" with the "and services" implied.

THE KEY TO UNDERSTANDING WORLD TRADE

The biggest fallacy students make is to assume that nations trade only goods (such as cars and oil). In fact, nations also trade financial assets such as stocks, bonds, and bank loans. The United States sells its goods *and* assets in exchange for other nations' goods and assets.

Exports are the U.S. goods and services sold to foreigners, and imports are the foreign goods and services bought by U.S. citizens. When the United States sells wheat to Switzerland, that wheat is an export. When Switzerland sells its watches in the United States, those watches are imports. *Net exports* is the net of the goods **sold** by the United States and equals the value of exports minus the value of imports.

The United States also trades financial assets, such as stocks and bonds. Equivalent to exported goods are the United States assets purchased by foreigners. Equivalent to imported goods are the foreign assets purchased by United States citizens. **Net foreign investment (NFI)** is the net of the assets purchased by United States citizens and equals the purchase of foreign assets by United State citizens minus the purchase of United States assets by foreigners.

Unless governments intervene, the total amount of goods and assets bought and sold tend to equal each other. We have:

Imports + Foreign Assets Purchased by United States
Citizens = Exports + United States Assets Purchased by Foreigners.

The left-hand side of this equation shows the total dollars used by United States citizens to buy Swiss goods and assets. The right-hand side of this equation is the total dollars Swiss citizens use to buy United States goods and assets. Where did the Swiss citizens get all these dollars? They get dollars by selling goods and assets to the United States! That is why tariffs (a tax on imports) harm export sales. While a tariff may save jobs otherwise taken away by imports, the result is that foreigners have fewer dollars to buy U.S. goods and assets. The result is fewer jobs in the export sector. On net, tariffs decrease employment.

Just as Swiss citizens trade Swiss francs for dollars to buy U.S. goods and assets, United States citizens trade dollars for Swiss francs to buy Swiss goods and assets. The exchange rate is the rate at which one currency is traded for another. For example, 1.31 Swiss francs currently trade for one dollar, so that one hundred dollars buys 131 Swiss francs. The exchange rate goes up or down until the dollar value of the goods and assets the United States sells to Switzerland equals the dollar value of the goods and assets we buy from Switzerland. What would happen if the United States buys more from Switzerland than it sells? That is, what if:

Imports + Foreign Assets Purchased by United States
Citizens > Exports + United States Assets Purchased by Foreigners?

In this case, the United States does not have enough Swiss francs from its sales of goods and assets to Switzerland to pay for the goods and assets it wants to buy from Switzerland. There is a shortage of Swiss francs. As a result, the value of the Swiss franc will go up until the value of what the United States buys equals what it sells (for example, from 1.31 Swiss francs for one dollar to an exchange rate of 1.35). What would happen if the United States sells more than it buys? That is, what if:

Imports + Foreign Assets Purchased by United States
Citizens < Exports + United States Assets Purchased by Foreigners?

Now the United States has more Swiss francs than it needs to buy Swiss goods and assets. There is a surplus of Swiss francs. The value of the Swiss franc will fall until the United States sells what it buys (for example, from 1.31 Swiss francs for one dollar to an exchange rate of 1.25).

YOU SHOULD REMEMBER

1. What a nation sells equals what a nation buys if we include goods and services as well as assets.

2. Exchange rates change until what a nation buys equals what it sells.

3. When a nation sells more than it buys, it has a surplus of foreign currency and the exchange rate for that currency will fall until imports + foreign assets purchased by domestic citizens equals exports + domestic assets purchased by foreigners.

4. When a nation buys more than it sells, it has a shortage of foreign currency and the exchange rate for that currency will rise until the market clears.

THE EXCHANGE RATE

In this section, to keep things simple, we will talk exclusively about the value of a dollar in foreign exchange markets. The value of the dollar is the exchange rate for the dollar: how many units of foreign exchange a dollar can be traded for. For example, if the dollar's exchange rate against the Swiss franc is 2.5, then one dollar can buy 2.5 Swiss francs. (The symbol for the Swiss franc is SwF, so this is quoted as 2.5 SwF/$.) The dollar is said to have appreciated or increased in value if it can buy more Swiss francs than before (say to 3.0 SwF/$). The dollar is said to have depreciated or decreased in value if it can buy fewer Swiss francs than before (say to only 1.3 SwF/$).

1. How to Convert Foreign Prices Into Dollars:

Dollar Price = Foreign Price/Exchange Rate.

If a Swiss watch costs 250 Swiss francs and the exchange rate is 2.5 SwF/$, then the U.S. price will be 100 dollars. When the exchange rate goes up, Swiss goods will be cheaper in the United States. For example, when the exchange rate increases to 5 SwF/$, a Swiss watch costs only 50 dollars

2. How to Convert Dollar Prices Into Foreign Prices:

Foreign Price = Dollar Price × Exchange Rate.

If a Chevrolet costs 20,000 dollars and the exchange rate is 2.5 SwF/$, then the Chevrolet will cost 50,000 Swiss francs. When the exchange rate goes up, United States goods will cost more in Switzerland. For example, when the exchange rate increases to 5 SwF/$, the Chevrolet will cost 100,000 Swiss francs.

What determines the exchange rate? First remember that the exchange rate is the value of a dollar. The second thing to remember is that if foreigners want to buy more goods and assets from the United States, they have to buy more dollars. Therefore, when the rest of the world's demand for U.S. goods and assets increases, the demand for the dollar increases! The result is that the price of the dollar—its exchange rate—increases. Conversely, when U.S. demand for world goods and assets goes up, U.S. citizens have to sell dollars (to get the foreign exchange), the supply of dollars increases, and the value of the dollar falls.

By combining these forces of demand and supply, the value of the dollars is determined by the exchange rate that makes the demand for dollars equal its supply. Recall the basic equation of international trade:

Imports + Foreign Assets Purchased by United States
Citizens = Exports + United States Assets Purchased by Foreigners.

The left-hand side of this equation reflects the supply of dollars (since U.S. citizens are selling dollars to buy the needed foreign currency to purchase foreign goods and assets). The right-hand side reflects the demand for dollars (since foreigners are buying dollars to purchase United States goods and assets). The next section puts this equation into a demand and supply form.

THE DEMAND AND SUPPLY OF THE DOLLAR

The United States has flexible exchange rates. With some exceptions, the government lets the dollar's exchange rate be set by the free market forces of demand and supply.

This section focuses on what determines the Swiss franc price of the dollar. The demand and supply of the dollar as a function of its franc price is shown in Figure 16–1.

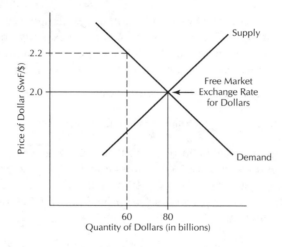

Figure 16–1. Flexible Exchange Rates: Demand and Supply of the Dollar

The main things to note are:

1. The *demand curve is the demand by foreigners for U.S. dollars. Foreigners* (here, Swiss citizens) demand dollars to buy (1) U.S. goods and services, (2) U.S. physical assets (by, for example, building a factory in the United States), and (3) U.S. financial assets (such as stocks, bonds, and Treasury bills).

2. *The demand curve has a negative slope: As the dollar becomes cheaper, Swiss citizens demand more dollars.* When the price of the dollar falls (when it takes fewer francs to buy a dollar), the dollar has **depreciated.** As a result, the franc price of U.S. goods, services, and assets becomes cheaper. For example, at 2.2 SwF/$, a 12,000-dollar Chevrolet costs 26,400 francs; at 2.0 SwF/$, only 24,000 francs. So demand for Chevrolets exported to Switzerland goes up as the dollar depreciates. As the dollar depreciates, the demand for all U.S. exports goes up, as does the demand for U.S. dollars with which to buy them. In Figure 16–1, the quantity of dollars the Swiss want goes from 60 to 80 billion (per year) as the dollar depreciates from 2.2 to 2.0 SwF/$.

3. *The supply curve is the supply by U.S. citizens of dollars in exchange for Swiss francs.* Why would U.S. citizens be willing to give up dollars in order to get Swiss francs? So they can buy Swiss goods, services, and assets. It takes Swiss francs to buy Swiss goods, so U.S. citizens must give up (i.e., supply) dollars to get Swiss francs.

4. *The supply curve has a positive slope.* When the value of the dollar goes up (so one dollar trades for more francs), the dollar has **appreciated.** The positive slope means that as the value of the dollar rises, U.S. citizens want more francs and so are willing to supply more dollars. Why? Because the U.S. price of Swiss goods is then lower. For example, a watch costing 100,000 francs costs 50,000 dollars when the exchange rate is 2 but costs only 45,455 dollars when it is 2.2 SwF/$.

5. *In equilibrium, the demand and supply of dollars are equal.* This occurs in Figure 16–1 at 2.0 SwF/$. At this price, the Swiss want 80 billion dollars (per year) with which to buy U.S. goods, services, and assets. U.S. citizens are willing to supply 80 billion dollars (per year) to buy 80 billion dollars worth of Swiss goods, services, and assets. The **equilibrium exchange rate** has been reached.

YOU SHOULD REMEMBER

1. The exchange rate is the price of one country's currency stated in terms of another's.

2. When the dollar appreciates, its exchange rate has gone up (SwF/$ goes up). When the dollar depreciates, its exchange rate falls (SwF/$ goes down).

3. When the dollar appreciates, import prices fall and the price of U.S. exports to other nations rises.

4. When the dollar depreciates, import prices rise and export prices fall.

5. The demand for the dollar by foreigners reflects their demand for U.S. goods, services, and assets. The supply of dollars to foreigners by U.S. citizens reflects the citizens' demand for foreign goods, services, and assets.

6. At the equilibrium exchange rate, the dollars demanded equal those sold: The dollar value of the goods, services, and assets bought by foreigners and sold by U.S. citizens will be equal.

• *PURCHASING-POWER PARITY*

The theory of purchasing-power parity asserts that exchange rates will adjust until the same unit of currency (here, a dollar) is able to buy the same quantity of a good from all trading nations. To illustrate, suppose steel is the only good traded. Suppose steel sold for $100 in the United States, 200 yen in Japan, and for 50 Swiss francs in Switzerland. No one in the United States would buy Japanese or Swiss steel unless it also sold for $100. This means that the exchange rate with Japan will be 2 yen for every dollar, making the U.S. price of Japanese steel $100. Similarly, the exchange rate with Switzerland will be 0.5 Swiss franc for every dollar. The theory of purchasing-power parity is another form of the law of one price. The law of one price states that with unimpeded trade, identical goods will sell for the same price in all competitive markets (adjusting for differences in transportation and marketing costs).

If nations trade identical goods, then the doctrine of purchasing-power parity states:

$$\text{Exchange Rate} = \frac{\text{Foreign Price Level}}{\text{Domestic Price Level}}$$

where the price level is the price of a basket of traded goods valued at the respective country's prices. For example, if foreign price levels are twice that of the United States, the dollar will be exchanged for 2 units of foreign currency. This will make the dollar price of the basket the same if bought in the United States or if purchased from a foreign nation.

What is relevant for trade is not the exchange rate alone but the *real exchange rate*: the rate at which goods from one nation trade for the goods of another. Suppose that all American cars sold for $20,000 each and all German cars sold for 80,000 euros (the currency of the European Union) and that the exchange rate is 2. (One dollar buys 2 euros. This rate is made up to illustrate this problem. Currently, the exchange rate is one dollar for 0.85 euro.) Then a German car in the United States would sell for $40,000. In a real sense, it takes two U.S. cars to buy one German car, or one U.S. car is "worth" one-half of a German car. The real exchange rate is ½. In general,

$$\text{Real Exchange Rate} = \frac{\text{Exchange Rate} \times \text{Domestic Price}}{\text{Foreign Price.}}$$

In this case, $1/2 = 2 \times \$20,000/\$80,000$.

If nations traded identical goods, the theory of purchasing-power parity predicts the real exchange rate will be one. For example, a ton of steel from the United States would trade for a ton of steel from Japan. Because goods are not identical, actual real exchange rates do not equal one. If the real exchange rate increases, U.S. goods become more expensive to foreigners, reducing the net exports from the United States. Lower real exchange rates make U.S. goods cheaper to foreigners, increasing net exports from the United States.

The theory of purchasing-power parity predicts that if the nation's price level increases relative to the price level in other nations, its exchange rate will fall. For example, if inflation rate in the United State is 10 percent and the Swiss inflation rate is 6 percent, the theory of purchasing-power parity predicts that the exchange rate of the dollar will fall by 4 percent (the percent change in the exchange rate equals the foreign inflation rate minus the United States inflation rate). Exchange rates do not always act as the theory of purchasing-power parity predicts. One reason is that nations do not trade identical goods. Another is that some nations do not allow the free flow of goods and monies. However, the main reason it does not always work is that nations trade both goods and assets. The asset market often drives exchange rates away from purchasing-power parity. However, over long periods, exchange rates do reflect the relative purchasing power of currencies.

YOU SHOULD REMEMBER

1. According to the theory of purchasing-power parity, exchange rates adjust until the same unit of currency can buy the same quantity of a good or service from all trading nations.

2. Exchange Rate = Foreign Price Level/Domestic Price Level, where price levels are the price of a basket of traded goods and services.

3. If purchasing-power parity holds, then the percent change in the exchange rate for a given foreign currency equals the foreign nation's inflation rate minus the United States' inflation rate.

THE MARKET FOR ASSETS

Nations trade more than just goods and services. They also trade financial assets. People buy assets to earn interest[1]. Consequently, if other nations' assets offer higher rates of return, United States citizens are likely to purchase more foreign assets than other nations purchase from the United States.

---

[1] To be more precise, they buy assets to earn interest plus the expected return from the appreciation of the asset (for example, when a stock goes up in value). In this section, we are including the return from the appreciation of the asset in the interest rate..

The market for loanable funds determines the United States interest rate. To keep things simple, assume that the only assets traded between nations are bonds. Savers supply loanable funds. Savers include private savers, the government (when it runs a surplus), and foreign savers. Foreign savers purchase U.S. bonds and this is reflected in the basic equation of international trade as United States assets purchased by foreigners:

Imports + Foreign Assets Purchased by United States
Citizens = Exports + United States Assets Purchased by Foreigners.

Borrowers demand loanable funds. Borrowers include United States private borrowers, the government (when it runs a deficit), and foreign borrowers. Foreign borrowers sell bonds to U.S. citizens and this is reflected in the basic equation of international trade as foreign assets purchased by United States citizens (it could equally as well be called foreign assets sold to U.S. citizens).

The price in the loanable funds market is the real interest rate. Demanders (borrowers) react to a higher real interest rate by demanding (borrowing) less. Suppliers (savers) react to a higher real interest rate by supplying (lending) more.

To illustrate how international markets affect the market for loanable funds, consider the case of a small country. This country can borrow and lend from foreign capital markets at a rate of r_W. r_W is the world real interest rate. To keep the example simple, assume that the nation's savings all go toward domestic investment; it does not buy assets from other nations. Figure 16–2 shows its domestic market for loanable funds.

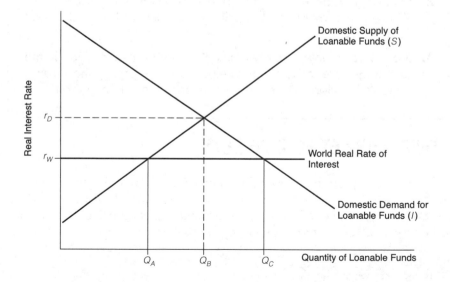

Figure 16–2. The Market for Loanable Funds

Points to Note About Figure 16–2

1. The real interest rate, not the nominal interest rate, is on the vertical axis because the real return matters to savers and borrowers.

2. Higher interest rates make saving more desirable.

3. Higher interest rates make borrowing more expensive, so borrowers borrow less.

4. Without a world capital market, the market would clear at r_D and Q_B.

5. With a world capital market, the country borrows $Q_C - Q_A$ at the world interest rate of r_W. The country's trade deficit equals $Q_C - Q_A$. Domestic savings equals Q_A and savings from abroad equals $Q_C - Q_A$.

6. As a result of world markets, the country can invest more in capital to grow faster. Investment spending equals Q_C.

7. We are assuming that the country uses all of its savings (Q_A) domestically. More generally, $Q_C - Q_A$ is the *net* of foreign savings borrowed and equals the nation's trade deficit.

8. Any factor that increases savings (shifting the S curve right) or decreases domestic investment (shifting the I curve left) decreases the amount the country will borrow from abroad. It also decreases its trade deficit.

9. An increase in the world interest rate will decrease investment from abroad.

PROBLEM How will the following events affect the level of investment in a nation and the amount it borrows from other nations (which equals its trade deficit)? What will be the effect on the equilibrium real interest rate?

Event A: The government runs up a larger than expected deficit (however, private savings is unaffected).

Event B: World interest rates fall.

Event C: The nation raises its corporate income tax rates.

Event D: Foreign investors suddenly begin to worry that the nation will devalue its currency, making it worth less when they get paid back for loans. The world rate of interest to this nation increases as a result.

SOLUTION Event A: Shift demand curve to right (as government borrows more). The interest rate remains unchanged at the world rate; the nation borrows more from the world. The trade deficit increases (as net borrowing from the world increases).

Event B: World interest rate line moves down. The nation borrows more from other nations as it increases domestic investment. The trade deficit increases.

Event C: Shifts demand curve to left (as any given investment now pays a lower after-tax return than before). Interest rates remain unchanged at the world level, but less is borrowed from other nations. The trade deficit decreases.

Event D: Shifts world interest rate line up. The nation borrows less from other nations as interest rates increase and domestic investment falls. The trade deficit decreases.

When the loanable fund market clears, the loanable funds borrowed equal the loanable funds saved. For a nation without international trade, this means $I = S$, where I is investment spending and S is savings (private savings plus the government surplus). For a nation with international trade, this means

$$S + \text{United States Assets Purchased by}$$
$$\text{Foreigners} = I + \text{Foreign Assets Purchased by United States Citizens}$$

or

$$S = I + NFI.$$

To see why the last equation follows from the first, recall that *NFI* equals foreign assets purchased by domestic citizens minus domestic assets purchased by foreign citizens.

Changes in interest rates affect the value of the dollar. When interest rates rise in the United States (compared to the rates paid in the rest of the world), U.S. investments become more attractive. Loanable funds (capital) will flow on net into the United States to purchase U.S. assets. The demand for the dollar will increase and the dollar will appreciate in value. When interest rates fall in the United States (compared to the rest of the world), loanable funds will flow out of the United States, increasing the supply of dollars (as Americans demand more foreign currency with which to purchase foreign assets) and the dollar will depreciate in value.

YOU SHOULD REMEMBER

1. The loanable funds market brings together savers and borrowers, including foreign savers and borrowers. Foreign savers purchase domestic assets. Foreign borrowers sell foreign assets to domestic citizens. Savers supply loanable funds. Savers save more when real interest rates go up. Borrowers demand loanable funds. Borrowers borrow more when the real interest rate goes down.

2. Net foreign investment (*NFI*) equals the value of foreign investment by domestic citizens minus the value of domestic investment by foreigners. If a nation on net borrows from other nations, NFI is negative.

3. Since *NFI = NX =* – trade deficit, when a nation borrows more from other nations (making *NFI* more negative), its trade deficit increases. When it borrows less, its trade deficit decreases.

4. The loanable funds market clears when *S = I + NFI.*

5. When United States interest rises relative to world interest rates, international capital (loanable funds) flows into the United States, increasing the demand for the dollar and causing the value of the dollar to appreciate.

6. When United States interest rates fall relative to world interest rates, international capital will flow from the United States, causing the value of the dollar to depreciate.

• *INTEREST RATE PARITY*

According to the theory of interest rate parity, the same dollar investment in projects with equal risk in different countries should pay the same real rate of return. If one nation pays below the world rate, it will not be able to attract investments and will have to raise its rate to world levels. Suppose you buy a Swiss bond paying a fixed return of 8 percent a year in Swiss francs. What is its rate of return in dollars? If the dollar's exchange rate decreases (if the dollar depreciates), each successive dollar payment will be higher! For example, if the Swiss bond pays 120 Swiss francs per year and the exchange rate goes from 2SwF/$ to 1 SwF/$, the dollar payments will go from 60 to 120 dollars. More generally, we have:

$$\% \text{ return in dollars} = \% \text{ Swiss return} +$$
$$\% \text{ expected rate of depreciation in the dollar}$$

% return in dollars = % Swiss return –
% expected rate of appreciation in the dollar.

The theory of interest rate parity predicts that interest rates on domestic investments will equal the percent return in dollars on foreign investments. For example, if the interest rate on United States bonds is 8 percent while Swiss bonds pay 5 percent in Swiss francs, then investors must expect the exchange rate for the dollar to depreciate 3 percent per year over the life of the bond.

YOU SHOULD REMEMBER

1. The theory of interest rate parity predicts that the same dollar investment in projects with equal risk in different countries should pay the same real rate of return when expected changes in exchange rates are included.

2. When interest rate parity holds, United States interest rates equal foreign interest rates plus the expected rate of depreciation in the value of the dollar.

FACTORS AFFECTING THE EXCHANGE RATE

Table 16–1 summarizes the factors affecting the exchange rate. One new factor is the United States' growth rate relative to foreign growth rate. When real *GDP* rises faster in the United States than in the rest of the world, U.S. citizens want to buy relatively more of all goods, including imports. To buy more imports, U.S. citizens sell more dollars to get foreign currency, causing the value of the dollar to decrease.

Table 16–1. Factors Affecting Value of Dollar

Factor	Change in Factor	Effect on Dollar
Single Factor		
Affecting Demand		
• Foreign demand for U.S. goods and services (i.e., demand for U.S. exports)	Increase	Appreciation
	Decrease	Depreciation
• Foreign demand for U.S. physical assets (such as plants in United States) and financial assets (such as bonds and stocks)	Increase	Appreciation
	Decrease	Depreciation
Affecting Supply		
• U.S. demand for foreign goods and services (i.e., demand for imports)	Increase	Depreciation
	Decrease	Appreciation
• U.S. demand for foreign physical assets and financial assets	Increase	Depreciation
	Decrease	Appreciation
Combined Factors		
• U.S. price level *relative to* foreign price level	Increase	Depreciation
	Decrease	Appreciation
• U.S. interest rates *relative to* foreign interest rates	Increase	Appreciation
	Decrease	Depreciation
• U.S. growth rates *relative to* foreign growth rate	Increase	Depreciation
	Decrease	Appreciation

PROBLEM: Describe how the following events will affect the value (exchange rate) of the dollar.

Event A: The U.S. government runs a large deficit while private savings remain unchanged.

Event B: The U.S. government prints too much money, causing the inflation rate to rise dramatically.

Event C: New management techniques increase the rate of return on U.S. investments.

Event D: A buy-foreign craze hits the United States.

SOLUTION: *Event A:*   Value of dollar up. The government borrows more to finance its larger deficit, causing interest rates to increase. The higher return makes U.S. investments more attractive to foreigners. Foreigners will demand more dollars to buy more U.S. assets, causing the dollar to appreciate.

Event B: Value of dollar down. To maintain purchasing-power parity so that the price of U.S. goods in foreign currency stays the same, the value of the dollar has to fall.

Event C: Value of dollar up. In the loanable funds market, the demand for funds will increase, increasing the real rate of return. Foreigners will demand more dollars, causing the dollar to appreciate.

Event D: Value of dollar down. To buy more imports, U.S. citizens will sell more dollars, reducing their value.

YOU SHOULD REMEMBER

1. Foreigners buy dollars to buy U.S. goods and assets. American citizens sell dollars to buy the foreign currency needed to buy foreign goods and assets. Simple demand and supply applies to determine the value of the dollar, as reflected in the basic equation of international trade:

Imports + Foreign Assets Purchased by United States Citizens = Exports + United States Assets Purchased by Foreigners.

On the left-hand side of the equal sign is the supply of the dollar. On the right-hand side is the demand for the dollar.

2. The exchange rate—the value of the dollar—is the number of units of foreign currency a dollar trades for. Exchange rates change until the United States sells what it buys, including assets.

3. An increase in the U.S. real interest rate (relative to what other nations pay) increases the attractiveness of U.S. investments. This increases the net demand for the dollar, causing the exchange rate to appreciate. A decrease in the U.S. real interest rate decreases the exchange rate.

OTHER EQUATIONS

The basic equation of international trade is:

Imports + Foreign Assets Purchased by United States Citizens = Exports + United States Assets Purchased by Foreigners.

On the left are the goods and assets U.S. citizens purchased from other nations. On the right are the goods and assets foreign citizens purchased from the United States. Because Americans need foreign exchange to buy foreign goods and assets while foreigners buy U.S. goods and assets with dollars, the same equation can be read another way. The left-hand side is the supply of dollars. The right-hand side is the demand for dollars.

Some textbooks make this more complicated by combining terms. If your text does this, I suggest rewriting their equations in the demand and supply form shown above. For example, the basic equation can be rewritten as

$$\text{Net Exports} = \text{Net Foreign Investment}$$

or

$$NX = NFI.$$

This form focuses on net sales and purchases. It states that the net of the goods and services the United States sells to the world equals the net of the assets the United States buys from the world.

Since $S = I + NFI$, we can also write

$$NFI = S - I$$

or

$$NX = S - I.$$

where S equals private savings plus the government surplus. It shows that when a nation saves more than it invests domestically, it has a trade surplus. Why? The excess savings purchases foreign assets. To get the foreign currency to buy the foreign assets, it is necessary for the nation to sell more goods than it buys. Conversely, when a nation invests more domestically than it saves, the nation will have a trade deficit (NX will be negative since imports exceed exports).

Letting T be net taxes (Taxes – Transfer Payments), the above can be rewritten once more as:

$$NX = \text{Private Saving} + G - T - I$$

or

$$NX = \text{Private Savings} + \text{Government Surplus} - I$$

or

$$\text{Government Deficit} = \text{Trade Deficit} + \text{Private Savings} - I.$$

This form emphasizes the twin deficits. If private savings and domestic investment are relatively constant, then an increase in the government's deficit will result in an equal increase in the trade deficit.

FIXED EXCHANGE RATES

Before 1973, most nations had **fixed exchange rates**. Under fixed exchange rates, a government buys and sells its currency at a certain exchange rate against all other currencies. To do this, governments need to accumulate large holdings of other nations' currencies in order to sell them to maintain the value of its own currency. As a result, the demand and supply of the currency *no longer have to be equal* since the government makes up any differences from its reserves of currencies.

In Figure 16–3, Panel A, we show the effects of an **overvalued currency:** The government tries to set the exchange rate *above* its free market level. Here, the U.S. government holds the exchange rate of the dollar at 2.2 SwF/$ while its free market level is 2.0. Supply exceeds demand: Foreigners want 40 billion fewer dollars than U.S. citizens want to supply. In this case, the United States has a **balance-of-payments deficit.** The U.S. government has to buy the 40 billion excess supply of dollars with its Swiss franc reserves. This balance-of-payments deficit reduces the U.S. government's reserves of francs. Eventually, if these deficits continue, the government will have to **devalue** the currency by lowering the official exchange rate. Governments are often forced to do this suddenly, as currency speculators, sensing a coming devaluation, stage a **run on the currency,** demanding that the government exchange its Swiss francs for the speculators' dollars.

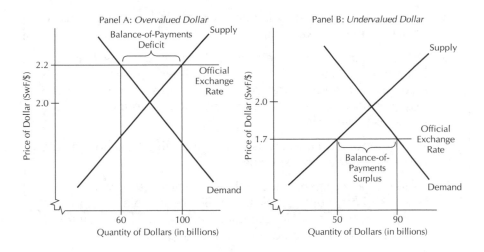

Figure 16–3. The Effect of Fixed Exchange Rates: Overvalued, Undervalued

In Figure 16–3, Panel B, the U.S. government has undervalued the dollar by setting the exchange rate **below** its free market value (at 1.7 instead of 2.0). Now there is an excess demand of 40 billion dollars—the United States has a **balance-of-payments surplus.** Demand exceeds supply: Foreigners want more dollars than U.S. citizens want to supply. To satisfy the excess demand, the U.S. government will hand out dollars for francs, increasing its reserves of francs.

At some point in time, the United States might want to stop accumulating francs. If so, it will **revalue** the dollar by raising its official exchange rate. Note that when a currency is overvalued, dwindling reserves force the government to devalue: no such pressure forces countries to revalue an undervalued currency, since the government can go on accumulating reserves without limit if it wishes.

> Hint: To remember these results, remember that an *excess demand for dollars equals the excess supply of foreign currency.* So an overvalued dollar (relative to Swiss francs) means an excess supply of dollars, an excess demand for francs, and, as a result, decreasing U.S. government reserves of francs. An undervalued dollar means an excess demand for dollars, an excess supply of francs, and a resulting increase in the U.S. government reserves of francs.

YOU SHOULD REMEMBER

1. Under fixed exchange rates, the government buys and sells its currency at a fixed rate.

2. An overvalued currency is one whose fixed exchange rate is above its free market value.

3. When a government overvalues its currency, it will have a balance-of-payments deficit. It will have to run down its reserves of foreign currency. Eventually, its reserves will run out, forcing it to devalue its currency by lowering its official exchange rate.

4. An undervalued currency is one whose fixed exchange rate is below its free market value.

5. When a government undervalues its currency, it will have a balance-of-payments surplus. It will accumulate foreign currency reserves. To avoid accumulating too much, it may revalue its currency by increasing its exchange rate.

RUNS ON CURRENCIES AND CAPITAL FLIGHT

A run on a currency occurs when many people try to sell the currency, causing its exchange rate to fall dramatically. Recently, runs on the currency of Mexico, Brazil, and Indonesia have occurred. In all these cases the countries had borrowed heavily from other countries (net outgoing assets were positive as other countries bought the bonds and stocks in these countries). To some extent, the value of these nations' currency had been increased by the demand for their currency by foreigners in order to buy the nation's stocks and bonds. At some point, foreign investors became less confident in their investments in these countries. In some cases, they worried about the government imposing exchange controls (which prevents the foreign investors from getting the return on their investment out of the country). In other cases, they worried about the future growth of the country. In still other cases, they worried about the government inflating their currency, making the fixed returns on bonds worth less. Whatever the case, foreign investors suddenly try to take their investments out of the country. This is called *capital flight*. To see what would happen, let us suppose this country is Switzerland (which is actually the least-likely country for this to occur in given its history of a stable currency and free markets). Investors would sell Swiss bonds and stocks, causing the bond and stock markets in Switzerland to crash. When they sell these investments, they get Swiss francs. Next, they try to sell the Swiss francs. This will cause the value of the Swiss franc to fall. Panic might set in as other foreign investors, seeing the value of their Swiss investments fall, begin selling. A run on the Swiss franc starts. Switzerland might try to borrow money from other nations (including the International Monetary Fund) to pay off foreign investors and avoid the panic. Sometimes, this tactic has worked.

If the run on the Swiss currency continues, Switzerland will find itself for a period of time without foreign investors to finance its capital spending. Notice that the actual physical capital has not left Switzerland. What has happened is that the *claims* to the future returns of these assets (the Swiss bonds and stocks previously held by foreigners) have now returned to Switzerland. To get Swiss savers to hold this larger stock of assets, the real interest rate will have to be higher. This is the same thing as saying that bonds and stocks will sell for a lower price. As a result of the higher interest rates, investment spending falls and the economy often goes into a recession. To make the Swiss franc more valuable, the Swiss government could run a surplus by spending less or by raising taxes. It could also reduce its money supply (which would cause its prices to fall). Unfortunately, these actions reduce aggregate demand, making the recession worse! Such actions may eventually restore the confidence of the world in its economy, but they come with a terrible cost.

FISCAL AND MONETARY POLICY IN AN OPEN ECONOMY

When an economy is in a recession, a government usually tries to revive the economy by trying to increase aggregate demand. It can stimulate aggregate demand in two ways. First, it can use monetary policy: increasing aggregate demand by expanding the money supply. Second, it can use fiscal policy: increasing aggregate demand by running a deficit. The following are some basic insights of economics as to how effective fiscal and monetary policy will be in an open economy with flexible exchange rates (which means that free market forces set the rates).

1. **In an open economy, monetary policy is more effective.**
    Recall that more money stimulates aggregate demand by getting people to spend the extra money:
    We have:

    Money Supply Up $\rightarrow$ People Spend More $\rightarrow$ Aggregate Demand Up

    The only impact of international markets is that the value of the dollar will fall as domestic prices rise. The real exchange rate should remain unaffected so that output will not be adversely affected.
    Because the United States is a large country, its monetary policy can affect the real exchange rate and the real interest rate. In this case, we might have in the short run:

    Money Supply Up $\rightarrow$ Real Interest Rates Down $\rightarrow$ Net Capital Outflows Up
    (Net Exports Up) $\rightarrow$ Exchange Rate Down $\rightarrow$ Aggregate Spending Up

    The increase in aggregate spending comes from domestic investment going up (due to lower interest rates) and from net export spending going up (due to the reduction in the exchange rate making imports more expensive).

2. **In an open economy, fiscal policy is less effective.**
    Recall that in a closed economy, when the government spends more, this adds to total spending. However, what will happen if the world market fixes interest rates? The government has to borrow (sell bonds) to finance its added spending. If it borrows from U.S. savers, it will have to pay a higher interest rate. Therefore, it will instead choose to borrow at the world rate from foreign savers. How do the foreigners get the dollars to buy the U.S. bonds? They will have to sell more to the United States and/or buy less from the United States. This means net exports will fall by the amount the government's deficit spending increases. Aggregate demand ($= C + I + NX$) will remain unchanged.

We have:

G Up $\rightarrow$ Deficit Up $\rightarrow$ Finance Deficit by Selling to Foreigners $\rightarrow$ To get dollars, they buy less of our exports and sell more imports to us $\rightarrow$ *NX* down by amount deficit up $\rightarrow$ Aggregate Demand unchanged.

What makes net exports go down? The value of the dollar rising! Exchange rates have to rise to make foreigners want less of our goods and more of our government bonds.

KNOW THE CONCEPTS

DO YOU KNOW THE BASICS?

1. What is the difference between physical and financial capital?
2. If the United States has a trade deficit, does that mean the United States is selling more to the world than it is buying back?
3. What makes up the demand for the dollar? The supply for the dollar? The net demand for the dollar?
4. What must change to make sure the number of dollars bought equals the number of dollars sold?
5. Can a nation have a fixed exchange rate, no exchange controls, and an independent monetary policy?
6. When a firm sells a bond, is it supplying or demanding loanable funds?
7. What equations describe equilibrium in the loanable funds market?
8. If the exchange rate rises, what will happen to the price of U.S. exports and to the price of foreign imports into the United States?
9. How are capital flight and a run on a currency related?
10. If a country has a flexible exchange rate, can the government stimulate the economy by lowering interest rates?

TERMS FOR STUDY

appreciation and depreciation
  of a currency
fixed exchange rate
flexible exchange rate

interest rate parity
purchasing power parity
value of the dollar

PRACTICAL APPLICATION

1. For each of the following events, determine whether it is *supply* or *demand* for the dollar that is affected, whether the curve shifts to the *left* or to the *right,* and whether an *increase* or a *decrease* in the value of the dollar results.

   Event A: *Rambo Part IV* sells big in Europe.

   Event B: Americans flock to Britain.

   Event C: American stocks and bonds sell well in Europe.

   Event D: Japan builds a factory in Iowa.

   Event E: American interest rates move above those of other nations.

   Event F: American monetary policy becomes more expansionary, increasing the U.S. price level.

   Event G: Americans buy more French wine.

2. The exchange rate for the dollar is 0.90 British pounds per dollar and 260 yen per dollar.

   a. How many dollars will it take to buy 1 pound? 1 yen?

   b. What will a $12,000 Chevrolet cost in Britain? In Japan?

   c. What will a suit costing 200 pounds cost in the U.S.? A 20,000-yen suit?

3. If the exchange rate for the dollar changes from Question 2's values to 0.80 pounds and 300 yen, then answer questions (a) through (c) above, plus:

   d. How has the dollar appreciated or depreciated against the pound and the yen?

4. A French company has a factory built in Utah. It could (1) have the factory shipped to France or (2) keep the factory in the United States.

   a. How are each of these treated in international trade accounts (goods or assets)?

   b. Does the choice have any effect on the value of the dollar?

5. Two countries, A and B, produce and sell only wheat. In Country A, a ton of wheat sells for 20 Ables. In Country B, it sells for 5 Babels.

   a. If there are no trade barriers or transportation costs, what must the exchange rate be for Ables?

   b. What if the exchange rate is higher?

   c. Lower? (Hint: Use the doctrine of purchasing power parity.)

6. Some economists view trade flows as reflecting capital flows. If so, how will the following events affect the net exports of these countries?

   Event A: New investment opportunities develop in Canada.

   Event B: Sweden imposes higher taxes on its businesses.

   Event C: Poland suffers a crop failure viewed as being a temporary setback.

7. Suppose a British bond pays 15 percent: It costs 1,000 pounds and will pay back 1,150 pounds in one year. The current U.S. rate is 2.0/$ and is expected to increase 5 percent by next year to 2.10/$.

   a. What is the expected rate of return on this bond *in dollars?*

   b. How much would an equivalent U.S. bond have to pay to beat this rate?

8. A nation having a fixed exchange rate has been running a deficit in its balance of payments. It is running short of foreign currency reserves. It wants to get out of this problem.

   a. Has it overvalued or undervalued its currency?

   b. If it changes its exchange rare, will it devalue or revalue its currency?

   c. If, instead, it changes its monetary policy to get rid of this deficit, will it increase or decrease its money supply?

   d. Alternatively, if it changes its fiscal policy, will it raise or lower taxes?

9. China has one of the highest savings rate in the world (currently about 40 percent of *GDP* compared to 10 to 15 percent in the United States if one includes changes in personal wealth). For various reasons, much of China's savings has been used to buy U.S. stocks and bonds (particularly, government bonds). How will this likely affect China's net exports to the United States? Some have condemned China for saving so much and investing in the United States. If China stopped saving and buying U.S. stocks and bonds, would the United States be worse or better off?

10. We assumed in this chapter that foreigners do not want to hold extra dollars. This is not always the case. For example, some foreign governments hold dollars to back up their own currency. In addition, some foreigners prefer to use dollars to back up their own currency. Also some foreigners prefer to use dollars to conduct illegal transactions. Suppose the rest of the world suddenly wants to hold more dollars. How should the following equation be rewritten?

   Imports + Foreign Assets Purchased by United States
   Citizens = Exports + United States Assets Purchased by Foreigners

ANSWERS

KNOW THE CONCEPTS

1. A physical asset is the actual capital, such as a machine or plant. Financial capital is a claim to the output of physical assets.

2. No. The United States is selling more goods than it is buying. However, when currency markets clear, its sale of goods *and* assets equals the goods and assets it is buying back from the world.

3. The demand for the dollar equals the demand by foreigners for U.S. goods and assets since they need dollars to buy these items. The supply of dollars equals the supply by U.S. citizens for foreign goods and assets since they need foreign currency to buy these items. The net demand for the dollar equals demand minus supply. When the currency market for the dollar clears, net exports plus net outgoing assets equals zero.

4. The exchange rate.

5. No, it can have only two of the three. For example, no exchange controls (where money moves freely in and out of the country) plus a fixed exchange rate means it will have to buy and sell dollars to keep the exchange from changing. Consequently, its monetary policy will depend on the exchange rate. With flexible exchange rates, it can have an independent monetary policy because it is not restricted to using its money supply to prop up its currency.

6. They are demanding loanable funds.

7. Demand equals Supply.

$$\text{Domestic Investment} + \text{Government Deficit} +$$
$$\text{Net Foreign Investment} = \text{Private Savings.}$$

$$I + NFI = \text{Private Savings} + \text{Government Surplus} = S$$

8. When the dollar appreciates, the price of U.S. exports to foreigners will go up (as it takes more of their own currency to buy a dollar). The dollar price of imports will fall (as it takes fewer dollars to buy a unit of foreign currency). Net exports will likely fall.

9. To make the answer concrete, suppose there is capital flight from Mexico. Capital flight means foreigners want to hold less of Mexico's financial assets (stocks and bonds). They sell the assets for pesos and then try to sell the pesos for dollars (or for the currency they want). Capital flight causes a run on the peso (*run* as in *to run down*). The value of the peso will fall.

10. If the world markets set the nation's interest rates, most governments can do little to change it (although the U.S. government is large enough to have an effect). This reduces the effect of fiscal policy in open economies.

PRACTICAL APPLICATION

1. *Event A:* Demand, Right, Increase.

Event B: Supply, Right, Decrease.

Event C: Demand, Right, Increase.

Event D: Demand, Right, Increase.

Event E: Demand, Right, Increase.

Event F: Demand, Left, Decrease; Supply Right, Decrease.

Event G: Supply, Right, Decrease.

2. a. 1.11 $/£ and .00384 $/yen.

   b. 10,800 pounds and 3,120,000 yen.

   c. British suit: $222.22. Japanese suit: $79.92.

3. a. 1.25 $/£ and .00333 $/yen.

   b. 9,600 pounds (it is cheaper than in Question 2).
   3,600,000 yen (it is more expensive than in Question 2).

   c. British suit: $250 (it is more expensive than in Question 2).
   Japanese suit: $66.67 (it is cheaper than in question 2).

   d. Against the pound, the dollar has depreciated. Against the yen, the dollar has appreciated. Note the effect on import and export prices!

4. a. When the factory is shipped to France, it is counted as an export. When it keeps the factory in the United States, it is counted as an outgoing *financial* asset. It is the same as if the French firm bought the stock issued to finance the building of the factory.

   b. Both have the same effect on the dollar since both reflect the same increase in the demand for U. S. dollars.

5. a. 0.25 Babels per Able. This assures that Country B's wheat sells for 20 Ables in Country A and that A's wheat sells for 5 Babels in B.

   b. If Ables are overvalued (say at .5 Babels per Able), B's wheat will be cheaper (only 10 Ables). A's citizens will want to import wheat from B and will try to exchange their Ables for Babels. The increase in demand for Babels will increase the value of the Babel and reduce the value of the Able back to 0.25.

   c. If Ables are undervalued (say at 0.1), A's wheat will be cheaper (only 2 Babels). B's citizens will demand A's wheat and thus demand more Ables to buy it with: Ables will appreciate back to 0.25.

6. *Event A:* Canada's net exports will be negative. To get the Canadian dollars to invest in Canada, other nations must sell more to Canada than they buy.

   Event B: Sweden's net exports will be positive as capital leaves.

   Event C: Poland's net exports will be negative as Poland borrows to tide itself over this crisis.

7. **a.** In dollars: you invest $500 today to get $547.62 in one year: a 9.5 percent return. As an approximation, the net U.S. interest rate on foreign bonds equals:

   Net U.S. Interest Rate on Foreign Bonds = Foreign Interest Rate – Expected % Appreciation of Dollar (Against Foreign Currency).

   b. You would invest in the U.S. bond when it pays 9.5 percent or better.

8. **a.** Overvalued.

   b. Devalue.

   c. Decrease.

   d. Raise.

9. China has to export more to the United States than it buys back in order to get the dollars to buy U.S. stocks and bonds. It has a net export balance with the United States. Its current accounts are positive. The savings it invests in the United States helps keep real interest rates low. Some of its savings goes into the private sector, increasing the capital stock, productivity, and future growth rate in the United States. The bulk goes into buying government bonds, allowing the U.S. government to spend more without having to raise taxes. If the government spends the money wisely (to increase current and future productivity), then its effect is positive. With a larger economy, the United States can pay off the bonds and still enjoy more consumption. If the government wastes the money, U.S. wealth will be reduced. But this would not be China's fault, it would be ours. If China stopped investing in the United States, we would likely be worse off; either we would have less growth or we would have to pay right now for wasteful government spending.

10. If the world demands more dollars than they need to buy United States goods and assets, then:

    Imports + Foreign Assets Purchased by United States Citizens = Exports + United States Assets Purchased by Foreigners + Net Exported Dollars.

    As inflation went down in the 1980s, foreign demand for dollar holdings went up, allowing the United States to buy more goods and assets from the world than it sold to the world. In effect, the United States sold paper dollars in exchange for real goods and assets!

17

ELASTICITY

Note: **Microeconomics** studies the factors that determine the relative prices of goods and inputs. (A review of chapters 3 and 4 is suggested.) This chapter describes how economists measure the response of output to changes in prices and income. Chapter 18 examines the factors affecting demand. Then, chapters 18, 19, and 20 describe what determines supply.

To measure the effects of price and income on demand and supply, economists use "elasticities." **Elasticity** is a measure of responsiveness: It equals the percent change in quantity *divided* by the percent change in the variable that caused quantity to change. That is, it measures cause and effect in percentage terms. The effect is in the numerator; the cause is in the denominator.

THE PRICE ELASTICITY OF DEMAND

The **price elasticity of demand** measures the responsiveness of the *quantity demanded* of a good to a change in its *price*. We will use "$E(Q^d, P)$," which stands for the *E*lasticity of the Quantity Demanded with respect to Price changes. Formally, we have:

$$E(Q^{\mathrm{d}},P) = \frac{\text{Percent Change in the Quantity Demanded}}{\text{Percent Change in Price}}$$

where *both* percent changes are expressed as *absolute values,* (that is, as positive numbers).

When $E(Q^{\mathrm{d}},P) > 1$, demand is **elastic:** A given percent change in price causes an even greater percent change in the quantity demanded. Just as an elastic rubber ball bounces a lot when one drops it, so it is when demand is elastic: The quantity demanded "bounces" or responds a lot to price changes.

When $E(Q^{\mathrm{d}},P) < 1$, demand is **inelastic:** A given percent change in price causes a smaller percent change in the quantity demanded. Just as a ball made of an inelastic material like clay does not bounce when one drops it, so it is when demand is inelastic: The quantity demanded does not respond much to price changes.

When $E(Q^{\mathrm{d}},P) = 1$, demand is **unitary elastic:** A given percent change in price causes the same percent change in quantity demanded.

Figure 17-1 shows several demand curves. Panel 1 shows a **perfectly inelastic demand curve** $E(Q^{\mathrm{d}},P) = 0$: Price has no effect on the quantity demanded. Panel 2 shows a **perfectly elastic demand curve** $E(Q^{\mathrm{d}},P) = \infty$: An infinitesimally small increase in price above *P0* reduces demand to 0 and an infinitesimally small decrease in price increases demand to infinity. In Panel 3, at Point *F*, demand curve *C* is more elastic than demand curve *B*, and *B* is more elastic than *A*.

> Note: One can compare elasticities by comparing slopes *only* at the point where the curves go through the same point.

Panel 4 shows a **unitary elastic demand curve** ($P \times Q$ is the same at all points on this type of demand curve). Note that *Q* here represents the quantity of an individual good or service. In the sections on macroeconomics, *Q* stood for real *GDP*—the national quantity of goods and services.

Economists use the following equation to predict the effects of price on output:

$$\begin{array}{c}\text{Percent Change in} \\ \text{Quantity Demanded}\end{array} = -E(Q^{\mathrm{d}},P) \times \begin{array}{c}\text{Percent Change in} \\ \text{Price}\end{array}$$

This equation is an approximation that is accurate for small changes in price.

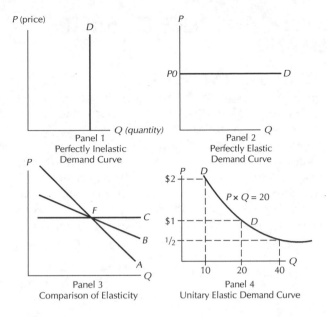

Figure 17–1. The Elasticity of Various Demand Curves

As an example, studies have shown that the price elasticity of demand for candy is 0.5: A 10 percent increase in the price of candy will reduce the amount bought by 5 percent. Its demand is inelastic. On the other hand, studies have shown that the demand for electricity in the long run is elastic: $E(Q^d, P) = 2.0$. A 10 percent increase in the price of electricity will reduce the quantity demanded by 20 percent.

YOU SHOULD REMEMBER

1. Price elasticity of demand is the percentage change in the quantity demanded for every 1 percent change in the price.

2. When demand is more elastic, consumers are more sensitive to price changes, increasing or decreasing their purchases more. When demand is inelastic, consumers are more insensitive to price changes.

3. Demand is elastic when output changes by a greater percentage than price does. Demand is inelastic when output changes by a smaller percentage than price does.

MEASURING THE PRICE ELASTICITY OF DEMAND

MEASURING THE PERCENT CHANGE

If the price goes up 10 percent and the quantity demanded goes down 30 percent, the elasticity of demand is 3.0. However, how do we measure the percent change?

For example, if the price was $10 and now it is $7, by what percent did the price fall? To get the percent change, one divides the change in price ($3) by some base price: either the old price ($10), the new price ($7), or an average of the two ($8.50). The percent changes in price, using these respective bases, are 30 percent, 42.86 percent, and 35.29 percent. Like most texts, we will use the *average* price as the base. If P_0 is the original price and P_1 the new price, and Q_0 and Q_1 the similar quantities, we have:

$$\text{Percent Change in Quantity Demanded} = \frac{Q_1 - Q_0}{(Q_1 + Q_0)/2} \times 100$$

$$\text{Percent Change in Price} = \frac{P_1 - P_0}{(P_1 + P_0)/2} \times 100$$

$E(Q^d, P)$ is the ratio of the absolute value of these two terms. This ratio can be simplified to:

$$E(Q^d, P) = \frac{\text{Change in } Q}{\text{Change in } P} \times \frac{\text{Average } P}{\text{Average } Q}$$

where the "Changes" are stated as absolute values.

Point elasticity is the elasticity at a particular point. Using calculus, it equals the absolute value of the first derivative of quantity with respect to price multiplied by the point's price divided by its quantity.

Example: Calculating the Elasticity of Demand

PROBLEM   At $5, consumers demand 200 records. At $6, consumers demand 160 records. What is the elasticity of demand over this range of prices?

SOLUTION   1.22, or (40/1.00 × $5.50/180). The price increased 18.18 percent, causing the quantity demanded to fall 22.22 percent

MEASURING ELASTICITY ON A STRAIGHT-LINE DEMAND CURVE

A *straight-line demand curve* has several interesting elasticity properties (see Figure 17–2, page 309). First, as one moves down the demand curve, the price elasticity of demand becomes smaller (i.e., more inelastic). Starting at *P0*, demand is perfectly elastic [$E(Q^d,P) = \infty$]; it then falls but remains elastic until halfway down. Halfway down the demand curve (at 1/2 *P0*), $E(Q^d,P)$ equals unity ($= 1$). It then becomes inelastic until at $P = 0, E(Q^d,P) = 0.$

On a straight-line demand curve, the elasticity at a given point equals (1) the length of the demand line below the point *divided* by (2) the length of the line segment above it.

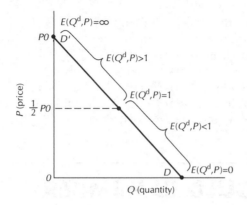

Figure 17–2. The Change in Elasticity Along a Straight-Line Demand Curve

Be sure to notice that all along the straight-line demand curve, the slope is constant but the elasticity changes! So remember that slope and elasticity are not the same thing (and can only be compared where the curves cross, as in Panel 3 of Figure 17–1). Also, because elasticity can change along the same demand curve, when you measure the elasticity of demand, always specify over what range of prices the elasticity was measured.

PROBLEM   What is the price elasticity of demand at point *A* in this diagram?

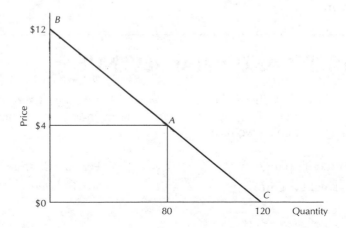

SOLUTION   0.5. The price elasticity is the length from *A* to *C* divided by the length from *B* to *A*. Fortunately, we do not have to calculate these but can instead use geometry. By using the price (vertical) axis, the price elasticity equals the price at *A* ($4) divided by the length from the vertical intercept ($12) to the price at *A*. So price elasticity equals

$$\$4/(\$12 - \$4) =$$
$$\$4/\$8 = 0.5.$$

Alternatively, by using the (horizontal) quantity axis, the price elasticity equals the horizontal intercept (120) minus the quantity at *A* (80) divided by the quantity at *A*. So price elasticity equals

$$(120 - 80)/80 = 40/80 = 0.5$$

Note that this rule works only for straight-line curves. For curved demand curves, draw a straight line tangent to the point *A* for which you are trying to calculate the elasticity, and then calculate the elasticity from the tangent line.

YOU SHOULD REMEMBER

1. The *percent change in price* is usually calculated by dividing the change in price by the average price (and multiplying by 100).

2. The *elasticity of demand over a segment of the demand curve* is the percent change in quantity demanded divided by the percent change in price (both expressed as absolute values).

3. As one goes down a straight-line demand curve, it becomes more inelastic. It is elastic until halfway down, halfway down it is unitary elastic, and then it is inelastic the rest of the way down.

ELASTICITY AND TOTAL REVENUE

Economists use elasticities to tell what will happen to **total revenue** (price times output) when prices change. Total revenue is the same thing as total sales. In particular, we have:

$$\text{Percent Change in Total Revenues} = (1 - E(Q^d, P)) \times \text{Percent Change in Price}$$

Therefore:

1. If $E(Q^d,P) > 1$, price and total revenue are *negatively related*, or when demand is elastic:

   - An increase in price will reduce total revenue.

   - A decrease in price will increase total revenue.

2. If $E(Q^d,P) < 1$, price and total revenue are *positively related*, or when demand is *in*elastic:

   - An increase in price will increase total revenue.

   - A decrease in price will decrease total revenue.

3. If $E(Q^d,P) = 1$, total revenue is the same whether price goes up or down. This result and the following results all assume we are moving along a demand curve and not shifting it! The percent changes in this equation can be positive or negative.

Another version of the above equation is

$$MR = P \times (1 - 1/E(Q^d, P))$$

where *MR* is marginal revenue, the change in the industry's total revenue $(P \times Q)$ when the industry produces and sells another unit of output (or the change in a firm's total revenue if we are talking about a firm). This equation allows us to relate elasticity to total revenue to output. If $E(Q^d, P) > 1$, then $MR > 0$: An increase in output will increase on total revenue. For example, if the price elasticity of demand is 3 and the price is \$12, then increasing output will increase total revenue by \$8 (= \$12 × (1 – 1/3)). If $E(Q^d, P) < 1$, then $MR < 0$: Another unit of output will reduce total revenue. For example, if the price elasticity of demand is 0.75 and the price is \$12, another unit of output will reduce total revenue by \$4 (= \$12 × (1 – 1/0.75)).

Since all these calculations are being done along a demand curve, what happens to total revenue when output goes up is the same thing that will happen when price goes down. So if demand is elastic (>1), a decrease in the price will increase total revenue, or equivalently, an increase in output will increase total revenue. And if demand is inelastic (<1), a decrease in price will decrease total revenue, or equivalently, an increase in output will decrease total revenue.

Examples: Effect of Prices on Total Revenue

PROBLEM The price elasticity of demand for wheat is 0.3. If a bountiful harvest results in 20 percent lower wheat prices, what will happen to the total revenues of farmers?

SOLUTION Total revenue will go down by about 14 percent (0.7 × –20 percent).

PROBLEM An airline is flying at half capacity. If it lowers its airfares by 10 percent, will it increase its profits when $E(Q^d,P) = 2.0$? When
$E(Q^d,P) = 0.6$? Assume it has the same total cost even though it
will have more passengers at the lower price.

SOLUTION When demand is elastic, the airline will increase its profits by lowering its price [when $E(Q^d,P) = 2.0$, its total revenue will go up
10 percent, and since its total costs don't change, its profits go
up]. But when demand is inelastic, its total revenue will fall [by 4
percent when $E(Q^d,P) = 0.6$], as will its profits.

Once again, the straight-line demand curve has some special properties:
Starting from the price at 0 output and decreasing price to half its level, total
revenue increases (this being the elastic portion of the demand curve). Total
revenue peaks halfway down, then falls (in the inelastic portion) as the price
approaches $0. Figure 17–3 shows an example. Do not make the following
common mistake: *Do not confuse total revenue with total profits.* Where
total revenue is highest is almost *never* where profits are highest!

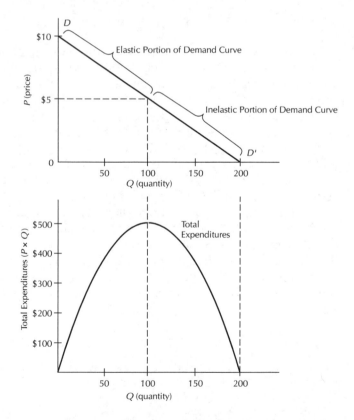

Figure 17–3. Determining Revenue Along the Straight-Line Demand Curve

YOU SHOULD REMEMBER

1. *When demand is elastic,* total revenue and price are negatively related: A fall in price increases total revenue and a rise in price decreases total revenue.

2. When *demand is inelastic,* total revenue and price are positively related: A fall in price decreases total revenue and a rise in price increases total revenue.

3. Going down a straight-line demand curve, total revenue increases as the price falls until halfway down, where total revenue is at a maximum, but as the price falls further, total revenue falls.

4. When demand is elastic, total revenue and output are positively related: Higher output increases total revenue, and lower output decreases total revenue.

5. When demand is inelastic, total revenue and output are negatively related: Higher output reduces total revenue, and lower output increases total revenue.

6. Along a demand curve, when output goes up, price goes down. Since the price elasticity of demand is measured along a demand curve, what is true about an increase in price will be true for a decrease in output. And what is true about a decrease in price will be true for an increase in output.

FACTORS AFFECTING ELASTICITY

PERTAINING TO DEMAND

PRICE ELASTICITY

Most texts list a set of factors that increase the price elasticity of a demand curve. The presence of these factors makes consumers buy even more than otherwise when the price goes down and buy even less than otherwise when the price goes up. In fact, these factors all reflect the effect of one *main factor.*

> When *more* **substitutes** for a good become available, demand becomes *more* elastic.

For example, wheat is a substitute for white bread. A good that has many close substitutes is like a grocery store in a neighborhood with many other grocery stores: If it charges too much, its customers switch to the other stores. If it lowers its prices, it can attract a lot of the other stores' customers. So the demand for its groceries is very elastic. In general, then, the more substitutes a good has, the more elastic its demand will be.

Factors Affecting Price Elasticity

1. *The Fraction of Income Spent on the Good:* The more people spend on a good, the more important it is in their budget. So if its price goes up, they are *more* willing to search long and hard for substitutes.

2. *How Narrowly Defined the Good Is:* "Bread" is a more narrowly defined good than is "wheat product"; "white bread" is more narrowly defined than "bread." The narrower the definition, the *more* substitutes the good is likely to have and thus the more elastic its demand will be. For example, the demand for Fords is more elastic than the demand for automobiles; the demand for automobiles is more elastic than the demand for transportation.

3. *How Easy It Is to Find Out About Substitutes:* The easier consumers can find out about the price and availability of substitutes, the more elastic demand will be. Advertising plays a crucial role in increasing the availability of substitutes to consumers.

4. *How Much Time Is Available to Adjust to Price Changes:* The more time consumers have to find out about substitutes, the more elastic demand becomes.

Those goods consumers consider to be "necessities" usually have inelastic demands. On the other hand, goods considered to be "luxuries" usually have more elastic demands. However, exceptions do occur: The demand for ice cream is far more inelastic (0.1) than the demand for food (0.3).

> # YOU SHOULD REMEMBER
>
> **1.** The more substitutes a good has, the more elastic its demand is.
>
> **2.** The larger the good's share of the consumer's budget, the more likely it is that consumers will seek substitutes when its price goes up. The more information available about substitutes, the easier it is for consumers to find substitutes. The more time consumers have, the easier it is for them to find and adopt the substitutes. The presence of each of these factors increases the elasticity of demand.
>
> **3.** The more narrowly a good is defined, the more elastic its demand is likely to be.

INCOME ELASTICITY

We denote this as $E(Q^d, I)$:

$$E(Q^d, I) = \frac{\text{Percent Change in Quantity Demanded}}{\text{Percent Change in Income}}$$

As you will recall from Chapter 4, a good is a **normal good** if it goes up in demand when income increases $E(Q^d, I) > 0$). Most goods are normal. A good is a **superior good** if it goes up in demand when income increases *and* its share in income also goes up $E(Q^d, I) > 1$). Gourmet food is an example. A good is a **necessity** if it goes up in demand when income increases *but* its share in income goes down ($0 < E(Q^d, I) < 1$). Food is a necessity. A good is an **inferior good** if it goes down in demand when income goes up $E(Q^d, I) < 0$). Examples include cheap red wine and flour for home baking.

If $E(Q^d, I) > 1$, then when income goes up, the good's share of consumers' income goes up. If $E(Q^d, I) < 1$, then when income goes up, its share of consumers' income goes down. In general:

$$\begin{array}{c}\text{Percent Change in} \\ \text{Share of Income}\end{array} = [E(Q^d, I) - 1] \times \begin{array}{c}\text{Percent Change} \\ \text{in Income}\end{array}$$

CROSS ELASTICITY

This measures the responsiveness of the demand for a good to the price of another good. We will denote it as $E(Q^d, Pog)$ where Pog stands for *Price of the Other Good*. It is equal to:

$$E(Q^d, Pog) = \frac{\text{Percent Change in Quantity Demanded}}{\text{Percent Change in Price of Other Goods}}$$

When consumers buy more of Good A when Good B's price goes up, economists say Good A is a **substitute** for Good B (and Good B is a substitute for Good A): $E(Q^d, Pog) > 0$. For example, when hamburger prices go up, consumers buy more hot dogs.

When consumers buy less of Good A when Good B's price goes up, economists say Good A is a **complement** to Good B: $E(Q^d, Pog) < 0$. Complements often are goods that are used together. Thus, for example, when the price of hot dogs goes up, the demand for hot dog buns goes down.

YOU SHOULD REMEMBER

1. The **income elasticity** of a good is the percent change in the quantity demanded of the good for every 1 percent increase in income. Normal goods have positive income elasticities: Most goods normally go up in demand when income goes up. Inferior goods go down in demand when income goes up: They have negative income elasticities.

2. A superior good's income elasticity exceeds unity: Its share of income goes up as income goes up.

3. Goods are substitutes when their cross elasticities are positive: The demand for one goes up when the price of the other goes up. Goods are complements when their cross elasticities of demand are negative: The demand for one goes down when the price of the other goes up.

PERTAINING TO SUPPLY

The **price elasticity of the quantity supplied** measures the responsiveness of the quantity supplied to price changes. It will be denoted as $E(Q^s, P)$. It is defined in the same way $E(Q^d, P)$ was:

$$E(Q^s, P) = \frac{\text{Percent Change in Quantity Supplied}}{\text{Percent Change in Price}}$$

Figure 17–4 shows four supply curves: Curve D is a **perfectly elastic supply curve** $[E(Q^s, P) = \infty]$: A price below *P0* reduces output to zero; a price above *P0* increases output to infinity. Curve A is a **perfectly inelastic supply curve** $[E(Q^s, P) = 0]$: A higher price does not increase output at all. An example would be the supply of authentic paintings by Vincent van Gogh.

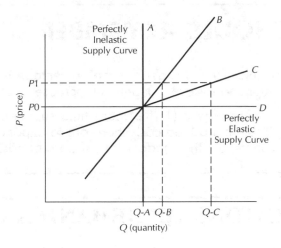

Figure 17–4. The Elasticity of Various Supply Curves

Factors Affecting Supply Elasticity

1. *How Much Time Is Available to Adjust to Price:* A basic rule of economic life is that the faster one wants something done, the more costly it will be. So when the price of a good goes up, firms at first increase output very little. Then firms adjust by hiring more factors and expanding their plants, and new firms enter the industry. With more time to adjust, the supply response becomes larger. For example, in Figure 17–4, an increase of price from *P0* to *P1* will not immediately affect output (*Q-A*); the immediate short-run supply curve is *A.* Given some time, *B* becomes the supply curve and *Q-B* the quantity supplied. With even more time, firms enter the industry and existing firms expand, so the supply curve becomes *C* and *Q-C* the quantity supplied.

2. *How Easy It Is to Store Goods:* When the price of a good drops, firms have to choose between selling it now or putting it into their inventory if they believe the drop in price is only temporary. Therefore, the cheaper it is to store goods, the more elastic the supply will be for *temporary changes in the price.* For example, when the demand for steel tem-

porarily falls, steel manufacturers often store their unsold steel rather than reduce their price.

3. *How Cheap It Is to Increase Output:* To increase output is costly. Typically, if an industry tries to buy more inputs, the price of inputs goes up. Similarly, some production processes are quite costly to set up. The less input costs rise and the smaller set-up costs are, the more elastic the supply curve will be.

YOU SHOULD REMEMBER

1. The supply elasticity of a good is the percentage increase in quantity supplied for every 1 percent increase in price.

2. Supply is more elastic (1) the more time suppliers have to adjust, (2) the less added costs there are to expanding, and (3) in the short run, the cheaper it is to store goods.

INTERACTIONS OF DEMAND AND SUPPLY

Elasticities can be used to predict the effect of events on price.

First, consider an event that shifts the supply curve vertically up by X percent (for example, a 10 percent tax). The percent change in the demand price will approximately equal:

$$\text{Percent Change in Price} = \frac{E(Q^s, P)}{E(Q^d, P) + E(Q^s, P)} \times X \text{ percent}$$

For example, if the price elasticity of demand ($E(Q^d, P)$) is 2.0 and the price elasticity of supply ($E(Q^s, P)$) is 3.0, then a 10 percent tax will increase the price paid by demanders by approximately 6 percent ($= 3/5 \times 10$ percent). If both elasticities are doubled (to 4 and 6, respectively), the impact of taxes on price is the same. What matters for the effect of taxes on prices is the relative size of the demand elasticity to the supply elasticity. The higher the relative size of the supply elasticity, the greater fraction of a tax will be borne by buyers in the form of higher prices.

Second, consider an event that shifts the supply curve horizontally right by X percent (for example, more production facilities are built and brought into operation). The percent change in the price will approximately equal:

$$\text{Percent Change in Price} = -\frac{1}{E(Q^d,\ P) + E(Q^s,\ P)} \times X \text{ percent}$$

For example, if the price elasticity of demand $(E(Q^d,P))$ is 2.0 and the price elasticity of supply $(E(Q^s,P))$ is 3.0, then a 10 percent shift up in supply will decrease the price by 2 percent (1/5 × 10 percent). Doubling both elasticities (to 4 and 6, respectively) halves the impact of the greater supply on price (to a 1 percent decrease in price). Similarly, if the capacity of refineries producing gasoline is cut by 20 percent due to a hurricane, and if the price elasticity of demand for gasoline is 0.2 and the price elasticity of supply of gasoline is 0.3, then the resulting increase in price will be 40 percent (= –1/0.5 × –20 percent). The more inelastic demand and supply are, the more a supply shock will change price.

KNOW THE CONCEPTS

DO YOU KNOW THE BASICS?

1. When economists say the price elasticity of demand for bananas is 2.0, what do they mean?

2. If consumers of a good are very sensitive to its price, is the good's demand elastic or inelastic?

3. If the output demanded is the same regardless of the price, what is the price elasticity of demand?

4. If one demand curve has a steeper slope than another, is the steeper demand curve more inelastic?

5. What is the main factor that increases the elasticity of demand for a good?

6. When will total revenue go up if the price is reduced?

7. If the income elasticity of demand for a good is greater than 1, what will happen to the demand for the good and to the good's share of people's income when income goes up?

8. How can one tell if two goods are substitutes? Complements?

9. Will firms produce where total revenues are highest?

10. If the demand for a good goes up, what will be the immediate supply response? The longer-term supply response?

TERMS FOR STUDY

cross elasticity of demand
elastic, inelastic, unit elastic
income elasticity of demand
normal goods, inferior goods

price elasticity of demand
price elasticity of supply
substitutes, complements
total revenue

PRACTICAL APPLICATION

1. For the following demand curve, calculate the slope and the price elasticity of demand over each price range ($10 to $8, $8 to $6, and so on):

Price	$10	$8	$6	$4	$2	$0
Quantity	0	4	8	12	16	20

Now do the same, but change dollars to cents.

2. **a.** Compare the effect of a $1,000 tax on cars with the effect of a 10 percent tax on cars. Which tax is likely to have the same impact on the demand for cars (in percentage terms) no matter which year it was imposed?

Hint: Inflation has increased the price of cars over time, so the $1,000 represents a smaller percentage of car prices in more recent years.

   b. What does your answer imply about the relative advantages of using slopes or elasticities to predict the impact of a price change?

3. **a.** When the wheat harvest falls by 10 percent due to bad weather, wheat prices go up 40 percent. What is the price elasticity of demand for wheat?

   b. Using this number, what will happen to the wheat bought by consumers if the government raises the price of wheat by 20 percent? What happens to the total revenue of wheat farmers?

   c. Still using the elasticity from (a) above, what will happen to the price of wheat if the government destroys 10 percent of the crop? To the total revenues of wheat farmers?

4. Why will tourists likely have a more inelastic demand curve for restaurant food than will "locals"?

5. Why do merchants often have sales (and cut their prices) on air conditioners in spring and early summer when demand is highest?

6. Select from each of these groups the good that is likely to have the highest price elasticity of demand:

   Group A: Energy, oil, gasoline, Shell gasoline, Bill's Shell Station gas.

Group B: The gasoline bought by those with long commutes to work; the gasoline of those with short commutes.

Group C: Gas bought from Joe, who has no competitors; gas bought from Bill, who has many competitors.

Group D: Eyeglasses from Sid's Glass Emporium in a state that does not permit advertising; eyeglasses from the same store in a state that does permit advertising.

7. When Titantown Bus Company raised its bus fare, its total revenues fell. When Petrogard Bus Company raised its bus fare, its total revenues went up. What can we conclude about the elasticity of demand for each company?

8. Which of these groups do you expect to be complements and which do you expect to be substitutes? What is the likely sign of the cross elasticity of demand?

Group A: Tires and cars.

Group B: Buses and airplanes.

Group C: Coal and oil.

Group D: Hot dogs and hamburgers.

9. In international trade, when the dollar falls (or depreciates), the foreign price of U.S. exports to the other nations falls. At first, total dollars of exports fall, but then they rise—following a J-shaped curve. How does this pattern follow what is known about the elasticity of demand for goods over time?

10. As people earn more income, their food purchases go up but their share of income spent on food goes down. What can we conclude about the income elasticity of food demand?

ANSWERS

KNOW THE CONCEPTS

1. They mean that the quantity demanded will increase 2 percent for every 1 percent decrease in price.

2. Elastic

3. It is perfectly inelastic $[E(Q^d, P) = 0]$.

4. You cannot tell *unless* the two curves cross. At the crossing point, the steeper curve is the more inelastic.

5. The greater availability of substitutes.

6. When the good's demand is elastic.

7. As income goes up, the quantity demanded will go up and the good's share in income will go up.

8. Two goods are substitutes if, when the price of one goes up, the demand for the other also goes up. Two goods are complements if, when the price of one goes up, the demand for the other goes down.

9. No. Firms will produce where profits are highest.

10. The immediate supply response will be a small increase in supply (or perhaps no increase). However, given time, suppliers will increase the quantity supplied.

PRACTICAL APPLICATION

1. The slope is –1/2 at all points. Between $10 and $8, elasticity is 9, and then 2.33 between $8 and $6, then 1.0, 0.43, and 0.11. Changing from dollars to cents does not affect these elasticities, but it changes the slope from –50 to 1/.02. One of the advantages of elasticities is that their value stays the same when the unit of measuring prices or output changes.

2. **a.** Due to inflation, the $1,000 represents a smaller percentage of car prices over time. When cars were sold for $2,000, the $1,000 in added price meant car prices would go up 50 percent: we'd expect a huge decrease in demand. When cars sell for $10,000, this is only a 10 percent increase in price: we expect a smaller decrease in demand. On the other hand, the 10 percent tax would probably have similar impact if imposed today or 30 years ago.

   b. Inflation does not harm the usefulness of elasticities; this is one reason why economists use them.

3. **a.** 0.25 (10 percent/40 percent).

   b. It will decrease by 5 percent (–.25 × 20 percent). Total revenues will rise 15 percent [(1–.25) × 20 percent].

   c. Price will go up 40 percent. (10 percent/.25); total expenditures on wheat will go up 30 percent.

4. Tourists have little time to price shop among substitute restaurants, so their demand curve for any one restaurant is likely to be more inelastic. Tourists also lack the substitute of home-cooked meals.

5. In spring and early summer, more people are seeking to buy air conditioners. This makes the advertising cost *per customer* lower. With more merchants advertising, customers can more easily price shop. So merchants face a more elastic demand curve for their air conditioners. This leads them to cut prices (to increase their total revenues), causing sales to occur at these times.

6. **a.** Bill's Shell Station gas.
   b. Gasoline bought by those with longer commutes (they have more incentive to price shop and to buy fuel-efficient cars).
   c. Bill.
   d. The store in the state that permits advertising.

7. Titantown's demand is elastic; Petrogard's is inelastic.

8. *Group A:* Complements (negative).
   Group B: Substitutes (positive).
   Group C: Substitutes (positive).
   Group D: Substitutes (positive).

9. The elasticity of demand for most goods is more elastic in the long run (when people have time to adjust) then in the short run. When U.S. export prices fall to foreigners, demand is inelastic in the short run, so total dollars from export sales (i.e., total revenue) falls. In the long run, it becomes more elastic, so the same price decrease now results in higher total revenues.

10. The income elasticity is positive (since food purchases went up) but less than unity (since food's share of income went down).

18

THE THEORY OF DEMAND

KEY TERMS

consumer surplus what consumers are willing the pay for a good less what they actually do pay for the good.

income effect effect of change in real income on the quantity of a good demanded.

marginal utility addition to total utility from consuming one more unit of a good.

substitution effect (of a price change) effect on the quantity demanded of a good when its relative price is changed (and real income is constant): A lower relative price increases consumption.

total utility total satisfaction derived from consuming goods and services.

MARKET AND INDIVIDUAL DEMAND

In this chapter, we analyze how one consumer changes his or her demand for a good when the good's price changes. Is this useful for analyzing a whole market with many consumers? The answer is yes. The **market demand curve** for a good is the *horizontal sum* of the demand curves of all consumers. Thus, the effect of price on market demand is the sum of its effects on the demand of the individual consumers.

In Figure 18–1, we derive the market demand curve for records when there are only two consumers, Abe and Bob. Abe's demand curve is D_{ABE} and Bob's demand curve is D_{BOB}. To get the market demand curve for records, we start with some price (say $5). We find out how much each consumer buys at that price. We then add up these amounts. This gives us the quantity demanded "by the market" at that price. For example, at $5, Abe demands 6 records and Bob demands 4: The market demand at $5 is 10 records. We then do this for all prices. The result is a market demand curve (D_{A+B}) that is the horizontal sum of D_{ABE} and D_{BOB}.

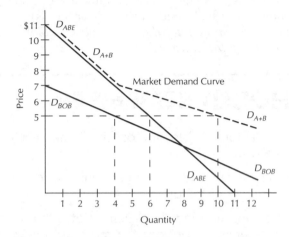

Figure 18–1. How Market Demand Is Affected by Price Changes

YOU SHOULD REMEMBER

1. The market demand curve for a good is the horizontal sum of demand curves for all consumers.

2. Market demand curves sum the effects of price on all consumers.

THE LAW OF DIMINISHING MARGINAL UTILITY

To illustrate the basic theory of demand, assume economists can measure a consumer's satisfaction in "utils." **Total utility** measures a consumer's total satisfaction, or total utils, from a good. When the consumer consumes an additional unit of a good, total utility goes up: Economists call this addition to total utility **marginal utility.**

For example, suppose a consumer eating five units of food has a total utility of 50 utils; adding a sixth unit, total utility increases to 58 utils. The marginal utility of the sixth unit is 8 utils (58 – 50).

The **law of diminishing marginal utility** states that as people consume more of a good in a given period, (1) their total utility goes up, *but* (2)

each added unit of the good adds *less* to their total utility. That is, as more of a good is consumed, its marginal utility declines. This law implies that the seventh unit of food in the example above should have a marginal utility that's less than 8 utils of the sixth unit (perhaps 7 or 5 utils).

Note that as more is consumed, total utility is going up. What is "diminishing" is the addition of total utility.

YOU SHOULD REMEMBER

1. Total utility is the total satisfaction or "utils" one gets from consuming some good.

2. Marginal utility is the addition of total utility from consuming one additional unit of the good.

3. The law of diminishing marginal utility states that as people consume more units of a good, the marginal utility of each added unit declines.

THE LAW OF EQUAL MARGINAL UTILITY PER DOLLAR

Consumers want the highest total utility their income allows them to achieve. **The law of equal marginal utility per dollar** states that the highest utility is achieved when the last dollar spent on all goods yields the same marginal utility. To see why this is true, suppose Emily spends her income on two goods, steak and beans. Currently, she spends all her money buying 10 pounds of steak and 40 cans of beans a week. Steak costs $8 a pound, and beans cost $2 a can. Her weekly income is $160 (note that price × quantity should equal income if Emily spends all her income). Suppose that the last pound of steak bought (the 10th pound) adds 16 utils to Emily's total utility. That is, steak has a marginal utility of 16 ($MU_S = 16$). Suppose that the last can of beans bought (the 40th can) has a marginal utility of 6 ($MU_B = 6$). Is Emily doing the best she can?

To answer this, let's assume that Emily can buy fraction amounts of each item (for example, she can buy one-eighth of a pound of steak or one-third of a can of beans). We need to know the marginal utility of the last dollar spent on each item. To get this figure, we divide marginal utility by price. The marginal utility per dollar for steak is 2 ($MU_S/P_S = 16/8 = 2$), while the marginal utility per dollar for beans is 3 ($MU_B/P_B = 6/2 = 3$). This means that the last dollar spent on steak adds 2 utils to total utility, while the last dollar spent on beans adds 3 utils. Bean dollars offer a higher marginal utility than steak dollars. Therefore, Emily would be better off spending more on beans and less on steak. Taking a dollar away from steak lowers her utility by 2 utils, and spending that dollar on beans raises her utility back up 3 utils, so she is 1 util better off. As Emily buys more beans and less steak, the marginal utility of beans will fall (due to diminishing marginal utility) while that of steak will rise. Eventually, she will be getting the same marginal utility per dollar spent on steak and beans. When she is getting equal marginal utility per dollar, she is maximizing utility. No shift in spending can make her any better off.

PROBLEM   Bill consumes only two goods, steak and beans. At his current consumption level, the marginal utility of steaks is 30 and the marginal utility of beans is 12. Steaks cost $6 a pound, and beans cost $3 a can. Is Bill doing the best he can? If not, how should he change his spending to do better?

ANSWER   In this type of problem, I suggest you use the following table:

Item	Steak	Beans
Marginal utility	30 utils	12 utils
Price	$6	$3
Marginal utility/price	5	4

If the numbers in the last line do not equal, Bill is not doing the best he can. He should spend more on steak and less on beans. In this case, if he spends one more dollar on steak and one less dollar on beans, he can raise his utility by 1 util. He would then continue to do this until achieving equality in the last row (perhaps both offering 4.5 utils per dollar).

Examples: Using the Law of Equal Marginal Utility per Dollar

PROBLEM   In the above example, would Bill be better off buying more steak and beans?

SOLUTION   Yes, he would always be better off with more of everything. However, the essential point is that he is already spending all of his income. So he cannot buy more of both! He has to choose. Using marginal utility per dollar helps him make that choice.

PROBLEM   Bill is getting the highest utility he can. The price of steak is $10, and the price of beans is $3. The marginal utility from steak is 50 utils. What is the marginal utility from beans?

SOLUTION If Bill is getting the highest utility, the MU per dollar must be equal:

$$\frac{MU_s}{P_s} = \frac{MU_B}{P_B}$$

Fill in the numbers you know, and solve for the number you do not know:

$$\frac{50}{10} = \frac{MU_B}{3}$$

The marginal utility of beans is 15.

YOU SHOULD REMEMBER

1. The consumer achieves the highest level of utility when the last dollar spent on each good has the same marginal utility.

2. The marginal utility per dollar for a good is derived by dividing its marginal utility by its price.

3. In equilibrium, relative marginal utilities of goods will equal their relative prices: A good that costs twice as much should have twice the marginal utility.

DERIVING THE LAW OF DEMAND FROM THE LAW OF EQUAL MARGINAL UTILITY PER DOLLAR

The **law of demand** states that the quantity of a good demanded will fall when the price of the good rises. This law can be derived from the law of equal marginal utility per dollar.

We begin with consumers at their highest utility (given their income). With food and clothing as the only two goods they consume, we should have:

$$\frac{MU_f}{P_f} = \frac{MU_c}{P_c}$$

Now assume the price of food goes up from P_f to $P_{f'}$. Holding the amount of food and clothing consumed constant, neither MU_f nor MU_c changes. However, now:

$$\frac{MU_f}{P_{f'}} < \frac{MU_c}{P_c} \quad \text{since } P_{f'} > P_f.$$

Because food now has a lower marginal utility per dollar than clothing, food dollars are worth less than clothing dollars: Consumers will buy more clothing and less food. Buying more clothing reduces MU_c and buying less food increases MU_f. This brings the consumer back to equal MU/P. This supports the law of demand (a higher P_f reduces the quantity of food demanded).

A WARNING AND A REMINDER

A Warning

The law of diminishing marginal utility is sometimes incorrectly used to argue that the rich get less utility out of added income than the poor. However, utility cannot be measured. A greedy rich man, for example, may get more utility from another dollar than a poor ascetic hermit.

A Reminder

The demand curve is the schedule of a good's marginal benefits. Marginal benefits in turn reflect (in dollar terms) the good's relative marginal utility. Thus, the price of a good reflects its marginal value, not its total value. This is why water has a lower price than diamonds. Water has a greater total value but because it is so plentiful, its marginal value is lower.

INCOME EFFECTS AND SUBSTITUTION EFFECTS

When a good's price goes up, two things occur: (1) its relative price goes up *and* (2) consumers' real income goes down (since they can buy less than before). To describe how price changes affect consumers, economists separate the effect of a higher price into these two separate effects:

1. **The Substitution Effect:** The decrease in demand when a good's relative price goes up, holding real income constant. A *higher relative price* for food causes consumers to *buy less* food because the higher price reduces the marginal utility per food dollar. MU_f/P_f. This is true even if the higher price does *not* reduce the real income of consumers. Real income is defined to be "constant" if consumers *can* buy the same amount of food and other goods as before (although in fact they will buy less food).

2. **The Income Effect:** The change in demand when real income changes (holding the *relative* price of the good constant). For a given money income, an *increase* in the actual price of a good will *reduce* real income. This lower real income in itself will *reduce* the quantity demanded of a *normal good.* But it will *increase* the quantity demanded of an *inferior good*.

The total change in the quantity demanded is the sum of these two effects. Table 18–1 summarizes these effects.

Table 18–1. The Effects of a Price Change on Demand

Price Change	Type of Good	Substitution Effect (1)	Income Effect (2)	Net Effect On Quantity (3) = (1) + (2)
Up	Normal	–	–	–
	Inferior	–	+	?
Down	Normal	+	+	+
	Inferior	+	–	?

Note that it is possible for a higher price to increase demand. This occurs with inferior goods *and* when the income effect is strong. (This case is called the **Giffen Paradox,** which has rarely, if ever, been observed.)

Examples: Using Income and Substitution Effects

PROBLEM Suppose the government puts a tax on food. To predict the effect of the tax on food consumption, should one use the substitution effect, the income effect, or both combined?

SOLUTION Use only the substitution effect. Why? Because the nation's income has not changed. The tax merely shifts income from food consumers to those to whom the government gives the tax dollars. (Of course, a poorly designed tax can reduce the real income of a nation, and to the extent it does, economists add in the income effect.)

PROBLEM When oil prices went up, America was importing one-third of its oil. To predict the effect of higher oil prices on oil consumption in the United States, economists added the substitution effect to one-third the income effect. Why one-third?

SOLUTION Because one-third was the fraction of oil the United States imported. This represents the lost income from higher oil prices Americans paid to foreign countries. The other two-thirds was only a transfer of income from oil consumers to domestic oil producers and so did not represent a change in national income.

YOU SHOULD REMEMBER

1. The *substitution effect* of a price change is its effect on the quantity of a good demanded due to its effect on the good's relative price, holding real income constant.

2. The *income effect* of a price change is its effect on the quantity of a good demanded due to the effect of the price change on real income.

3. The net effect of a price change is the sum of its substitution and income effects.

4. Taxes and subsidies do not usually change national income significantly, so their main impact is described by the substitution effect.

CONSUMER SURPLUS

Most of us have had the experience of making a good deal when we bought something for far less than what we were willing to pay. Economists refer to this as the good's **consumer surplus:** It is (1) the maximum amount consumers would pay for a certain amount of a good *minus* (2) the actual dollars they did pay.

In Figure 18–2, we show the demand curve for a consumer (*DD*). The consumer pays $3 for each pizza and buys 10 pizzas a month. The distance between the demand curve [which reflects (1)] and the price line *T* [which reflects (2)] is the unit's consumer surplus. For example, the consumer would have paid up to $7 for the fourth pizza but in fact only paid $3: The consumer surplus for the fourth pizza is $4 ($7 – $3). The total consumer surplus from all 10 pizzas equals $35 [= area of triangle *VTU*, which in turn equals the base (*TU* = 10 pizzas) times the height (*VT* = $7) divided by 2].

Example: Using Consumer Surplus

PROBLEM In a given month, Sue is willing to pay $10 to see one movie, $8 to see a second movie, and $6 to see a third.

A. If the price of a movie is $7, what is Sue's consumer surplus?

B. If the theater owner offers three tickets for $19, will Sue take the deal? What is the most the theater owner could charge for the three-ticket package deal?

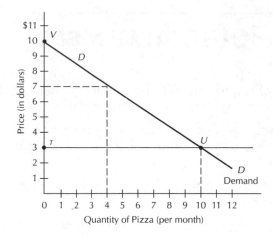

Figure 18–2. Consumer Surplus Shown by Demand Curve

SOLUTION   A. $4 ($3 for the first movie plus $1 for the second). Sue will not go to the third movie.

B. Yes. Now her consumer surplus is $5 ($10 + $8 + $6 – $19), which is better than the surplus that results from buying tickets separately. At most, Sue would pay $20, the amount that would leave her with the same consumer surplus ($4) as the option of buying tickets separately ($4 = $24 of value – $20 package-deal cost).

Note: The theater owner makes more money from Sue with the package deal.

YOU SHOULD REMEMBER

1. Consumer surplus measures the difference between what a good is worth to consumers and what they pay.

2. The demand curve reflects the (marginal) value of each unit of the good to consumers.

APPLICATIONS FOR BUSINESS: PRINCIPLE OF EQUAL MARGINAL BENEFIT PER UNIT

We saw that consumers are best off when they get equal marginal utility per dollar. This is a specific case of a more general and powerful tool for decision making: **the principle of equal marginal benefit per unit.** This principle states that when faced with a limited amount of resources (such as money or time), the decision maker should allocate the units of the resource to different alternative uses such that *its marginal benefit in each use is equal.* This will achieve the highest net benefit of all possible allocations.

Examples: Equal Marginal Benefit per Unit

PROBLEM   A grocery store has limited shelf space. Every product line generates a yearly profit per square foot of shelf space. As the shelf space devoted to any item is increased, its marginal benefit (i.e., its addition to total yearly profits) goes down. How many square feet should the store owner devote to each item?

SOLUTION   The last square foot devoted to each item should have the same marginal benefit (i.e., should add the same amount to the store's profits). Suppose the last square foot devoted to soup adds $100 to the store's profits while the last square foot devoted to cake mixes adds $80. The store should expand the space devoted to soup and contract the space for cake mixes. For example, one more square foot added to soup that's taken away from cakes will add $20 to the store's profits.

PROBLEM   A business has a policy of never borrowing money but instead generates all of its capital by reinvesting its profits. It thus has a limited amount of capital to invest among many projects. Each added dollar of investment in a project will yield a certain annual return, but usually this rate of return per marginal dollar invested tends to fall as more is invested. How much should the firm invest in each project?

SOLUTION   The last dollar in each project should yield the same marginal benefit. If the last dollar in Project A yields a 10 percent return while in Project B it yields a 25 percent return, funds from Project A should be diverted into Project B.

PROBLEM   A business executive has a limited amount of time. Each added hour of time in any task has a certain marginal benefit to the executive. Usually, as more time is devoted to any particular task, its marginal benefit declines. When will the executive be getting the best use of his or her time? Will the most valuable tasks get the most time devoted to them?

SOLUTION   The best use of time will occur when the marginal benefit of the last hour devoted to each task is the same. However, this does not imply that the most time should be devoted to the most valuable task. For example, suppose Task A has a marginal benefit in the first hour of $1,000, in the second hour of $1, and no marginal benefit after that. Task B has a marginal benefit of $3, $2, and $1 for the first, second, and third hour respectively. With five hours, the executive should devote two hours to Task A and three to B. So even though Task A has a higher total benefit ($1,001), less time should be devoted to it.

KNOW THE CONCEPTS

DO YOU KNOW THE BASICS?

1. Why do we add consumers' demand curves together *horizontally* to get the market demand curve?

2. How are total utility and marginal utility related?

3. Does a good with a higher total utility also have a higher marginal utility?

4. What happens to total utility as marginal utility diminishes (as one consumes more of a good)?

5. If the marginal utilities per dollar of two goods are not the same, why will consumers change their consumption pattern?

6. What is the substitution effect of a price increase?

7. What is the income effect of a price increase? How does it differ for normal and inferior goods?

8. Is the marginal utility of a candy bar greater to a poor person or a rich person?

9. Bill has spent $300 for a video recorder. He would have been willing to pay $500. What is his consumer surplus?

10. Even if consumers could still consume the same goods they have been consuming, why will a change in relative prices cause them to change their consumption pattern?

TERMS FOR STUDY

consumer surplus
Giffen Paradox
income effect
law of diminishing marginal utility

law of equal marginal utility
   per dollar
marginal utility
substitution effect
total utility

PRACTICAL APPLICATION

1. Suppose a market has only three consumers. Derive the market demand curve from this table.

Consumer	Quantity Demanded			
	Price			
	$4	$3	$2	$1
A	10	14	18	22
B	0	2	4	6
C	5	6	10	16

2. Use the following table to answer these questions. *TU* stands for total utility.

Units	1	2	3	4	5
TU of Good X	6	10	12	13	13
TU of Good Y	7	11	12	12	11

  a. What is the marginal utility (*MU*) of each unit? (Provide your answer in the form of a table.) Is marginal utility increasing or diminishing?

  b. If the consumer has $7 to spend and both goods cost $1, how many of each should the consumer buy?

  c. If the price of good Y goes to $2 while income remains at $7, what will happen to the amounts demanded?

3. For Bill, clothing has a marginal utility of 20 utils and food has a marginal utility of 20 utils. If clothing costs $4 and food $8, is Bill doing the best he can? If not, what can he do to increase his utility?

4. Suppose food costs $12 and clothing costs $2, and at the highest level of utility, clothing has a marginal utility of 6 utils. What is the marginal utility of food?

5. If you are taking a test that has several questions, how should you allo-cate your time among the questions in order to get the highest score?

6. Mary buys a Cadillac instead of a Chevrolet. The Cadillac costs exactly twice as much as the Chevrolet. What can we conclude about Mary's marginal utility of owning a Cadillac relative to owning a Chevrolet?

7. Mary values one game of golf a month at $40, a second game a month at $30, a third game at $20, a fourth game at $15, and a fifth game at $5. She would never play more than five times a month, even if golf were free. If each game costs $25, how many will she play? If, instead she can join the golf club, pay monthly dues, and play for "free," how much, at most, would she be willing to pay in monthly dues? Suppose she *must* join the club to play golf: How much in monthly dues would she be will-ing to pay?

8. What economic law does the following statement ignore: "Consumers are crazy. They pay little for water, which is highly valuable, and pay a great deal for diamonds, which have little value."

9. Suppose the government taxed food and either (1) gave the tax rev-enues back to Americans in the form reduced income taxes or (2) gave the tax revenues to a foreign government. In which case, (1) or (2), will the demand for food go down more? (Food is a normal good.)

10. Mary has $12 to spend. She buys two beers (which cost $3 each) and three bowls of chili (which cost $2 each). Then the price of beer falls to $2 and chili's price goes up to $3. How will Mary change her consump-tion of beer and chili? Does this event reflect a substitution effect, an income effect, or both?

ANSWERS

KNOW THE CONCEPTS

1. Because economists want to sum the amounts consumers will buy at each price.

2. Marginal utility is the addition to total utility when one more unit of a good is consumed.

3. The total utility and marginal utility of different goods need not be relat-ed. Water, for example, has a high total utility but a small marginal utility.

4. As long as marginal utility is positive, when more of a good is con-sumed, total utility increases.

5. Because consumers will be better off by consuming more of the good that has the higher marginal utility per dollar. By doing this, they will be gaining more utils per dollar than they are giving up.

6. The substitution effect is the decrease in the quantity demanded of a good that results when the good's relative price goes up (holding the consumer's real income constant).

7. The income effect of a price increase is the change in the quantity demanded due to the decrease in real income caused by the price increase. For a normal good, the quantity demanded falls; for an inferior good, it rises.

8. Since utility between persons cannot be objectively compared, it is impossible to say.

9. $200 ($500 – $300) is Bill's consumer surplus.

10. Those goods whose price fell will now have a higher marginal utility per dollar: Consumers will demand more of these goods.

PRACTICAL APPLICATION

1. The market demand curve will be:

Price	Quantity Demanded
$1	44
2	32
3	22
4	15

2. **a.**

Units	1	2	3	4	5
MU of X	6	4	2	1	0
MU of Y	7	4	1	0	–1

There is diminishing marginal utility.

b. When each unit costs $1, the above table is also the marginal utility per dollar. To get the answer, buy goods in the order of highest marginal utility per dollar (so you would buy the first Y, then the first X, then the second X and Y, etc.) until all $7 is spent. The answer will be 4X and 3Y (both having an equal MU/P of 1).

c. To answer what happens when the price of Good Y goes to $2, we construct the MU/P table:

Units	1	2	3	4	5
MU/P of X	6	4	2	1	0
MU/P of Y	3.5	2	.5	0	-.5

Buying in order of *MU/P*, the consumer will buy 3X and 2Y (with an equal *MU/P* of 2). Demand for Good Y falls from 3 units to 2. This illustrates the law of demand.

3. *MU/P* for clothing is 5, for food 2.5. Bill should buy more clothing and less food.

4. From the equality of *MU/P*, $MU_f/\$12 = 6$ utils/\$2. $MU_f = 36$ utils.

5. You should allocate your time so that the last minute spent on each question adds the same number of points to your total score.

6. For Mary, the marginal utility of owning a Cadillac must be twice as high, or higher, as the marginal utility of owning a Chevrolet.

7. At \$25 a game, she will play two games a month (as the rest she values at less then \$25). She would pay \$90 at most in club dues (as she gains a savings of \$25 per game for the first two games and a consumer surplus of \$40 for the three additional games she will play). If she must join to play, she would pay dues of \$110, as the first two games are now worth \$70 (this is now her *gain,* since she otherwise cannot play them). This is one reason why many golf clubs exclude nonmembers: it raises the dues they can charge.

8. This statement ignores the law of diminishing marginal utility. Water's total value is high, but there is so much of it, its marginal utility is low. The opposite is true of diamonds. This is known as the "diamond-water paradox."

9. In case (2), because the loss in real U.S. income is greater, so the income effect reduces food demand more.

10. Mary will buy more beer and less chili. Since she could have bought her old quantities at the new prices, her real income has not changed. So this event reflects the substitution effect only.

19

COST AND OUTPUT

KEY TERMS

economic profit payment received in excess of what is necessary to get something done.

fixed costs costs that neither increase nor decrease as output changes.

law of diminishing marginal returns after some point, as a firm adds more and more units of an input, the input's marginal physical product diminishes (i.e., it adds less to total output than before).

marginal cost addition to total cost due to increasing output by one unit.

marginal physical product (MPP) addition to total output due to increasing an input (such as labor) by one unit.

SHORT- AND LONG-RUN COSTS

How do costs change with output? The answer, which tells how steep the supply curve will be, is found by looking at two time periods:

1. **The short run,** when the firm can change (either increasing or decreasing) some but *not all* of its inputs in order to produce more or less output. Usually, in the short run, the firm meets a higher demand by hiring more labor and buying more materials, but leaves its plant and equipment unchanged.

2. **The long run,** when the firm can change *all* of its inputs, including its plant size and equipment.

SHORT-RUN COSTS

In using marginal analysis (see Chapter 1), we saw that the *most important cost* for making output decisions is marginal cost. **Marginal cost (MC)** is the increase in total cost caused by increasing output by one unit. If six units of output cost $60 and seven units $77, the marginal cost of the seventh unit is $17 ($77 − $60).

• *MARGINAL COST IN THE SHORT RUN*

Economists generally have found that in the short run marginal costs form a U-shaped pattern with output, first falling as output is increased, but then rising. The section of falling *MC* (from 0 to Point *B* in Figure 19–1) is called the section of *increasing marginal returns.* The section of rising *MC* (from *B* and up) is called the section of *diminishing marginal returns.*

Why does the marginal cost curve have this U shape? To see why, assume for simplicity that labor *(L)* is the only input the firm can increase in the short run.

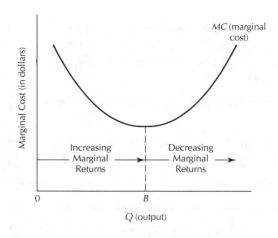

Figure 19–1. The U-Shaped Pattern of Marginal Cost in the Short Run

The **marginal physical product** of labor *(MPP)* is the addition to total output that results when one more unit of labor is added. If ten workers produce twenty shoes and eleven produce twenty-three shoes, the *MPP* of the eleventh worker is three shoes (23 − 20).

MC equals the cost of the added labor needed to produce that unit of output. If an added unit of *L* has an *MPP* of three units, then one added unit of output takes (approximately) one-third of a unit of labor to produce. In general, it takes 1/*MPP* of a unit of *L* to produce one more unit of output. To get the marginal cost of that unit of output, we multiply the wage of labor (*W*) by the labor to produce it, 1/*MPP*:

$$MC = W/MPP$$

For example, if $W = \$12$ and *MPP* is three shoes, it takes one-third of a unit of *L* to produce a shoe: The shoe's *MC* is $4.

MC changes because MPP changes.

In the section of increasing marginal returns, each added worker provides more than the previous worker to total output: *MPP* is going up. So *MC* (or W/MPP) goes down as output is expanded. However, the **law of diminishing marginal returns** states that beyond some level of output, the input's *MPP* declines, such that successive units add less and less to total output. In this section of decreasing marginal returns, *MPP* is going down. So *MC* (or W/MPP) goes up once decreasing returns have set in.

To see why *MC* has this U shape, imagine a large factory fully stocked with equipment and materials. To produce one unit of output will likely take many workers (especially when the factory is based around an assembly line). Thus the first output will have a high marginal cost. However, the successive units of output will take fewer units of labor to produce and thus marginal cost will fall. However, at some point, as the plant reaches its capacity in terms of the number of workers it can use, adding more workers no longer adds as much to output as previously (i.e., we have diminishing returns), so each added unit costs more and more to produce. Hence, *MC* will have a U shape.

Table 19–1 illustrates the relationship between *MC* and *MPP* for a shoe manufacturer when the wage is $12. Up to 3 workers, the firm experiences increasing marginal returns (*MPP* is increasing). The second worker increases output by 4 shoes, so the *MC* of a shoe is $3 ($12/4). However, the third worker has a higher *MC* (5), reducing *MC* to $2.40 ($12/5). Beyond 3 workers, the firm experiences diminishing marginal returns and thus rising marginal costs.

Table 19-1. The Relationship Between Marginal Cost and Marginal Physical Product

Labor Input	Output	MPP	MC (when W = $12)
0	0	—	—
1	3	3	$4.00
2	7	4	3.00
3	12	5	2.40
4	16	4	3.00
5	19	3	4.00
6	21	2	6.00
7	22	1	12.00

YOU SHOULD REMEMBER

1. Marginal costs are the most important costs in making output decisions. Marginal cost is the increase in total cost needed to produce another unit of output.

2. The short-run marginal cost curve relating marginal cost to output usually has a U shape. The section of falling marginal costs reflects increasing *MPP*. The section of rising *MC* reflects decreasing *MPP*.

3. The law diminishing marginal returns states that, beyond some point, as more units of an input are added, its *MPP* falls. This law applies when the amount of other inputs is not changed.

• *MARGINAL COST AND TOTAL COSTS*

The **total cost** *(TC)* of producing output consists of:

1. **total fixed costs** *(TFC)*: the cost of inputs the firm cannot change in the short run (such as plant and equipment) and

2. **total variable costs** *(TVC)*: the total cost of all the inputs (such as workers and materials) the firm *does change* in the short run to produce more. This can be visualized as:

$$TC = TFC + TVC$$

TFC stays the same when output changes. It equals the firm's total cost when output is zero (and thus when *TVC* = 0).

Since *TFC* stays the same as output goes up, both *TVC* and *TC* go up by *MC* when one more unit of output is produced. (Note that this result is true by definition: *MC* is the increase in *TC* due to one more unit of output.)

TVC is the sum of *MC*s. If the marginal cost of the first unit of output is $5, the second unit $4, and the third $3, then the *TVC* of one unit is $5, the *TVC* of two units is $9, and of the three units, $12.

As *MC* is falling in the section of increasing marginal returns, *TVC* increases, but each increase becomes smaller as *MC* becomes smaller. In Figure 19-2 (see page 343), this occurs as output increases to level *B*. Beyond *B, MC* rises, *TVC* increases, and each successive increase becomes bigger. Note that:

1. *MC* is the slope of the *TVC* cost curve.

2. The *TC* curve is the vertical sum of the *TVC* and the *TFC* curves.

3. The *TFC* curve is a horizontal line, since *TFC* is the same when output goes up.

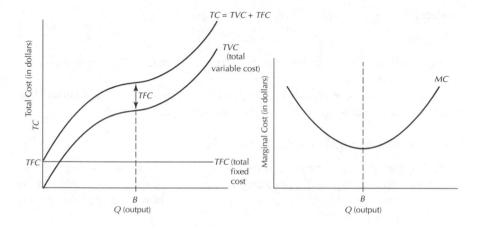

Figure 19–2. The Relationship Between Marginal Cost and Total Cost

---

YOU SHOULD REMEMBER

1. *Total fixed cost* is the total cost of all fixed inputs that stay the same when output is changed. *Total variable cost* is the total cost of all variable inputs that increase or decrease with output.

2. *Total cost* is the sum of total fixed cost and total variable cost.

3. Total variable cost at any level of output is the sum of all marginal costs up to that level of output.

4. Total cost and total variable cost go up by marginal cost.

• *MARGINAL COST AND AVERAGE COST*

Average cost is the cost per unit, or total cost divided by total output. There is an average cost for each type of cost.

Average total cost *(ATC)* equals

$$TC/Q$$

where Q is the number of units of output the firm is producing. We also have:

$$\textbf{Average Variable Cost } (AVC) = TVC/Q$$
$$\textbf{Average Fixed Cost } (AFC) = TFC/Q$$

Since $\qquad\qquad ATC = TC/Q = (TVC + TFC)/Q$

we also have: $\qquad ATC = TVC/Q + TFC/Q$

and finally: $\qquad\quad ATC = AVC + AFC$

Since total fixed cost does not change with output, AFC is always smaller at higher levels of Q.

To understand how AVC and ATC change with output, you must first understand how *average* and *marginal* amounts are related.

How Average and Marginal Costs Are Related

1. If we add a number to a sum that is *smaller* than the sum's average, the average will go *down*. For example, if a five-foot man walks into a room of men whose height is six feet, the average height of the men in the room will go down.

2. If we add a number to the sum *equal* to its average, the average will remain the *same*.

3. If we add a number *larger* than the sum's average, the average will go *up*.

The number being added is the marginal addition. Marginal cost *(MC)* is the number being added to total cost *(TC)*. When the addition (here, MC) exceeds the average (here, *ATC),* the average will go up. For example, suppose a firm is producing 50 units and has an ATC of \$20. If the 51st unit has an MC of \$25, the ATC of 51 units will go up (to \$20.10). In general, the change in ATC as output increases depends on how it relates to the MC of the added output.

(1) If $MC < ATC$, ATC goes down.
(2) If $MC = ATC$, ATC stays the same.
(3) If $MC > ATC$, ATC goes up.

Because MC is also the addition to total variable cost as output increases, the resulting change in average variable cost (AVC) depends also upon how it compares to MC.

(1) If $MC < AVC$, AVC goes down.
(2) If $MC = AVC$, AVC stays the same.
(3) If $MC > AVC$, AVC goes up.

In general, the average cost curve moves toward the marginal cost curve as output increases.

Figure 19–3 shows how *MC* and *AVC* are related. *MC* starts out below *AVC*, so *AVC* falls. Then *MC* begins to rise, but as long as *MC is* below *AVC*, *AVC* falls. At $Q = A$, $MC = AVC$: at this output, *AVC* is *at a minimum!* When $Q > A$, $MC > AVC$ so *AVC* rises as output rises.

The *ATC* curve is the horizontal sum of *AVC* and *AFC*. Since *AFC* is continually falling, the *ATC* curve becomes closer to the *AVC* curve as Q increases. At $Q = B$, $MC = ATC$; at this output, *ATC is at a minimum!* (See Practical Application, Question 2, for a numerical example of these relationships.)

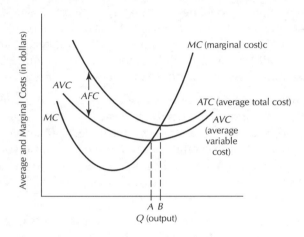

Figure 19–3. The Relationship Between Marginal Cost and Average Cost

YOU SHOULD REMEMBER

1. When output expands, as long as marginal cost is smaller than the average cost, *AVC* falls. *MC* equals *AVC* at the minimum *AVC*. Then *MC* exceeds *AVC* and *AVC* rises.

2. Average cost moves toward marginal cost.

3. Average fixed cost becomes smaller as output expands.

4. At the minimum average total cost, *MC* = *ATC*. At the minimum average variable cost, *MC* = *AVC*.

LONG-RUN COSTS

In the long run, all inputs can be changed. So marginal cost is no longer affected by the law of diminishing marginal product (which assumes some inputs are fixed). When all inputs are increased, economists say the firm has increased its "scale." There are three possible cases:

1. **Economies of scale** (or increasing returns to scale) occur when average total cost falls as output expands. With increasing returns to scale, an increase in *all* inputs leads to a *more* than proportional increase in output (for example, if doubling all inputs triples output). This results in less inputs per unit output and so a lower *ATC* as output expands. Economies of scale mainly occur because of economies from specialization and from better utilization of large capital equipment (for example, a large farm can make better use of a tractor than a one-acre farm).

2. **Constant returns to scale** occur when *ATC* stays the same as output expands. With constant returns to scale, an increase in all inputs leads to a proportional increase in output (for example, doubling all inputs doubles output). This reflects the basic scientific law that if you repeat the experiment, you should get the same results as before. So if 5 workers and 3 machines give you 10 widgets, then another 5 workers and 3 machines should give you another 10 widgets.

3. **Diseconomies of scale** (or decreasing returns to scale) occur when *ATC* goes up as output expands. With decreasing returns to scale, an increase in all inputs leads to a less than proportional increase in output (for example, if doubling all inputs increases output only by 50 percent). Diseconomies of scale often result from the problems and added cost associated with large bureaucracies.

Figure 19–4 shows these three cases.

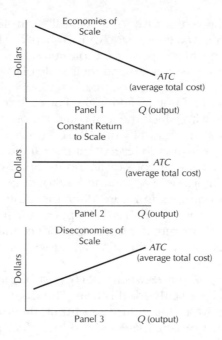

Figure 19-4. The Changing Scales of Cost in the Long Run

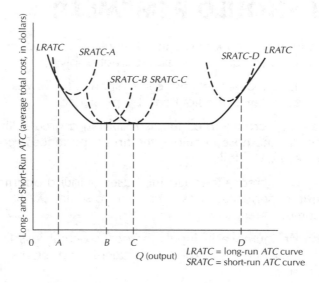

Figure 19-5. Determining the Minimum Efficient Scale in the Short and in the Long Run

Figure 19–5 shows the case for a "typical" firm. Like the short-run *ATC* curve, the long-run *ATC* curve (*LRATC*) is U shaped. The U shape reflects the fact that most firms first experience economies, then constant returns, and finally diseconomies as they expand their scale of operations.

In the long run, the firm has the freedom to vary all inputs and to choose the most efficient technology and scale. For each level of output, there is one optimal scale with which the firm could choose to produce it. The cost of this optimal scale is shown by the *LRATC* curve: The *LRATC* curve shows the lowest *ATC* at which each level of output can be produced. However, in the short run, the firm cannot vary all inputs. So it will face a higher cost if it must produce more or less than the level of output for which its current scale is best. For example, in Figure 19–5, the minimum cost of producing output level *A* is shown by the *LRATC*. Suppose the firm has a plant equal to this scale. In the short run, if it wants to produce more or less, its *ATC* will be *higher*: This is shown by the *SRATC-A* curve. For each output, there is a different *SRATC* curve.

In Figure 19–5, output *B,* where *LRATC* just becomes its smallest, is the **minimum efficient scale** for this firm. The larger a firm's minimum efficient scale is relative to the industry's output, the fewer firms there can be in the industry that can compete and produce efficiently.

YOU SHOULD REMEMBER

1. In the long run, all inputs can be increased so that the law of diminishing marginal returns need not apply.

2. The long-run average cost curve shows the lowest *ATC* at which each level of output can be produced.

3. When an increase in all inputs results in a greater than proportionate increase in output, the firm experiences economies of scale. *LRATC* falls.

4. When an increase in inputs increases output proportionately, the firm experiences constant returns to scale. *LRATC* remains the same.

5. When an increase in inputs increases output less than proportionately, the firm experiences decreasing returns to scale. *LRATC* rises.

PROFITS AND COSTS

Each firm has two types of costs:

1. The **explicit costs** it pays for inputs. These are the costs recorded by accountants.

2. The **implicit costs** of its owners' time and investment in the firm. These costs are measured by what the owners could have earned had they worked and invested in their next-best alternative (the *opportunity costs of their time and capital*). These costs usually are ignored by accountants.

Since accounting profits ignore implicit costs:

Accounting Profits = Total Revenue – Explicit Costs.

Economic profit is the amount paid in excess of what was necessary to get something done. The amount necessary to get something done is its cost, including *both* explicit costs. Thus:

Economic Profits = Total Revenue – (Explicit + Implicit Costs)

Considerable confusion is caused by the term "economic profits." It might be better thought of as "excess profits," because it is the excess over what the business owner needs to be paid in order to produce. Thus, while a business needs to make an accounting profit to stay in business, its economic profit can be zero and it will remain in business!

Example: Calculating Economic Profit

PROBLEM   Jerry was a computer programmer who earned $50,000 a year. He decided to go into business for himself, investing $100,000 of his savings (which had been earning 7 percent in a money market fund). In the first year, his business had $200,000 in revenues and $120,000 in explicit costs. What was his economic profit?

SOLUTION $23,000. Implicit costs equal forgone earnings ($50,000) plus forgone interest ($7,000 = 7 percent of $100,000). $23,000 = $200,000 – ($120,000 + $57,000).

YOU SHOULD REMEMBER

1. A firm has two costs: the *explicit cost* of the inputs it buys and the *implicit cost* of the time and money invested by its owners.

2. *Economic profit* is the excess of revenue over the firm's costs, when costs include explicit and implicit costs.

3. *Accounting profits* ignore implicit costs and so overstate the firm's true economic profit.

KNOW THE CONCEPTS

DO YOU KNOW THE BASICS?

1. Why are average costs lowest in the long run?
2. What is happening to the marginal productivity of workers as marginal costs fall?
3. Why do marginal costs rise?
4. Is the law of diminishing marginal returns true when all inputs are increased together?
5. How is the total variable cost curve derived from the marginal cost curve?
6. How is the total cost curve derived from the total variable cost curve?
7. When $MC < AVC$, how will AVC change when output is increased?
8. How is MC related to AVC and ATC at their respective minimum values?
9. Why does the ATC fall when the firm is experiencing economies of scale?
10. Why would a firm be better off not producing when its economic profits are negative?

TERMS FOR STUDY

accounting profit
average variable, fixed, and
   total costs
constant return to scale
diseconomies of scale
economic profit
economies of scale
explicit costs
implicit costs

law of diminishing marginal
   returns
long and short run
long-run average cost
marginal cost
marginal physical product
total cost
total fixed costs
total variable costs

PRACTICAL APPLICATION

1. Assume $Q = 0$ when $L = 0$ and the wage, W (the cost of L) = \$60. Fill in the following table to answer the question below:

Labor Input (L)	1	2	3	4	5	6	7	8	9
Output (Q)	2	5	9	14	19	23	26	28	29
MPP									
MC of 1 Q									

At what L do diminishing returns set in?

2. Fill in this table.

Q	MC	TVC	AVC	TFC	AFC	TC	ATC
0	—		—	\$112	—		—
1	\$16						
2	14						
3	12						
4	6						
5	12						
6	16						
7	22						
8	30						
9	38						
10	44						

  a. Where do diminishing marginal returns set in?

  b. What is the minimum *AVC*? What is *MC* at that level of output?

  c. What is the minimum *ATC*? What is *MC* at that level of output?

3. Some quick questions:

  a. If *ATC* = $12 at *Q* = 5, what is *TC*?

  b. If *ATC* = $10 at *Q* = 10 and *AVC* = $11 at *Q* = 11, what is the *MC* of the eleventh unit?

  c. If *ATC* = $12 and *MC* = $15, is *ATC* rising or falling?

  d. If *ATC* = $15 and *AVC* = $10 at *Q* = 10, what is *TFC*?

  e. If *TC* = $150 at *Q* = 8 and $180 at *Q* = 9, what is the *MC* of the ninth unit?

4. If one added worker increases output by ten units, how much labor is embodied in each unit of output? If the added worker costs $12,000, what is the marginal cost of one extra unit of output?

5. Answer true or false:

  a. *ATC* falls only when *MC* falls.

  b. At the minimum *AVC*, *AVC* = *MC*.

  c. *ATC* falls when *MC* < *ATC*.

  d. *TC* increases by *MC*.

6. Mary Jones can work in a factory and earn $16,000 a year or, alternatively, be a farmer. Assume that except for monetary reward, she doesn't care which she does. To farm, Mary has to invest her savings of $20,000. The annual cost of seed, fertilizer, etc., is $5,000. She could earn 10 percent annually on her best alternative investment.

  a. What is the total cost of farming (including implicit costs)?

  b. What is the minimum Mary must make in farming to just make it worthwhile?

  c. If her farm revenues are $30,000, what is her economic profit? Her accounting profit? Should she stay in farming?

  d. Answer (c) above for revenues of $20,000.

7. Acme Tables employs workers and machines to produce tables. It has the following production schedule:

Output	Labor Hours	Machine Hours
10	10	5
30	20	10
60	40	20
90	80	40

Between 10 and 30 units of output, does it have increasing, constant, or decreasing returns to scale? If labor and capital costs $10 a unit, what is happening to *ATC*? Do this for the other levels of output.

8. How will computers affect company size and the scale of production?
9. What is wrong with the following statements:
    a. "Even if government spends its money on wasteful projects, it still has worth because it creates jobs."
    b. "Even if the savings and loans did go bankrupt by financing useless office buildings and shopping centers, at least they created jobs."
    c. "Even if one life is prolonged by billions of dollars spent on triple bypass operations for people over age 80, then we should spend it."
10. Consider the cost curves of a trucking firm.
    a. Suppose there is an increase in the price of gasoline. How will each of these cost curves shift up (if they shift at all): *MC, ATC, AVC, AFC?*
    b. Suppose the cost of incorporating and setting up a trucking business goes up. How will each of the above cost curves shift?

ANSWERS

KNOW THE CONCEPTS

1. Because the firm can then select the scale of plant and the amount of equipment that is most efficient for each level of output.
2. *MPP* is increasing, meaning it takes less labor units to produce each unit of output.
3. Because *MPP* decreases due to the law of diminishing marginal returns, each added unit of output requires more labor units to produce, and so, a higher marginal cost.
4. No. It holds true only when some inputs are not increased.
5. *TVC* is the sum of the *MC*s.
6. *TC* is derived by adding fixed costs to *TVC*.
7. *AVC* will fall.
8. *MC* = *AVC* at *AVC*'s minimum. *MC* = *ATC* at *ATC*'s minimum.
9. *ATC* falls since each added unit of output costs less since less added inputs are needed to produce it.
10. Because then it would be better off investing its time and capital elsewhere. Total costs equal the opportunity cost (i.e., the forgone revenues) of the best alternative: If the firm earns less, it's better off with the alternative.

PRACTICAL APPLICATION

1.

Labor Input (L)	1	2	3	4	5	6	7	8	9
Output (Q)	2	5	9	14	19	23	26	28	29
MPP	2	3	4	5	5	4	3	2	1
MC of 1 Q ($)	30	20	15	12	12	15	20	30	60

At $L = 5$, we begin to have diminishing marginal returns (*MPP* falls and *MC* rises).

2.

Q	MC	TVC	AVC	TFC	AFC	TC	ATC
0	—	$ 0	—	$112	—	$112	—
1	$16	16	$16	112	112	128	$128
2	14	30	15	112	56	142	71
3	12	42	14	112	37.33	154	51.33
4	6	48	12	112	28	160	40
5	12	60	12	112	22.40	172	34.40
6	16	76	12.67	112	18.67	188	31.33
7	22	98	14	112	16	210	30
8	30	128	16	112	14	240	30
9	38	166	18.44	112	12.44	278	30.89
10	44	210	21	112	11.20	322	32.20

    a. $Q = 4$.

    b. Minimum $AVC = MC = 12$ at $Q = 5$.

    c. Minimum $ATC = MC = 30$ at $Q = 8$.

3. a. $60 $(Q \times ATC = TC$ since $ATC = TC/Q)$

    b. $21. $Q \times AVC = TVC$ (since $TVC = AVC/Q$). At $Q = 10$, $TC = 100 (10 × $10). At $Q = 11$, $TC = 121 (11 × $11). *MC* equals the increase in *TC*: $21 = $121 – 100.

    c. Rising (because $MC > ATC$).

    d. $30. $Q \times ATC = TC$ (since $ATC = TC/Q$). So $TC = 150 (10 × $15). $TVC = 100 (10 × $10). Since $TC = TFC + TVC$, $TFC = 50.

    e. $30 ($180 – $150).

4. One-tenth of a worker is embodied in each unit of output. So each unit costs one-tenth of $12,000, or $1,200.

5. **a.** False
   b. True.
   c. True.
   d. True.

6. **a.** $23,000: Explicit costs are $5,000. Implicit costs include her forgone earnings of $16,000 plus forgone interest of $2,000 she could have earned had she invested the $20,000 of savings at 10 percent.
   b. $23,000.
   c. Economic profit = $7,000. Accounting profit = $25,000. She should farm.
   d. Economic profit = –$3,000 (i.e., $3,000 loss). Accounting profit = $15,000. She should not farm.

7. Between 10 and 30 units of output, input doubles, and output triples: this is increasing returns to scale. *ATC* falls from $15 to $10. Between 30 and 60, there are constant returns to scale (as both input and output doubles). *ATC* stays at $10. Between 60 and 90. There are decreasing returns to scale (inputs go up 100 percent but output only goes up 50 percent). *ATC* rises from $10 to $13.33.

8. Diseconomies of scale are what keep companies and plants from getting too large. However, computers allow a single manager to do more and monitor more workers. This increase in the span of control allows a smaller bureaucracy to control any given level of output. Or, alternatively stated, the diseconomies of scale will not set in until the firm reaches a larger level of production. So computers will allow a larger scale of production, although one with perhaps fewer workers and managers.

9. All three statements ignore opportunity cost. Statement (a) ignores that there may be more valuable projects the government could spend the money on, Statement (b) ignores that there were more profitable projects that the savings and loan institutions could have lent money to. In both cases, alternative spending would have created about the same employment. Statement (c) ignores that the money spent elsewhere may have saved more lives.

10. **a.** *MC, ATC,* and *AVC* will shift up. *AFC* will remain unchanged.
    b. *AFC* and *ATC* will shift up. *MC* and *AVC* will remain unchanged.

20
COMPETITIVE SUPPLY

KEY TERMS

breakeven price the price at which the firm just covers all its costs.

perfect competition condition that exists when there is enough competition among sellers that no one seller can raise its price without losing all its customers to the other sellers.

shutdown price price below which a firm will shut down.

sunk cost cost that cannot be avoided.

RULES OF BASIC DECISION MAKING

The rules of decision making are of fundamental importance to both businesspeople and economists.

CONCERNING COSTS

Four Main Rules in Making a Decision

1. Pay attention only to costs that actually change as a result of the decision. These costs are the marginal costs of the decision. Similarly, in considering benefits, pay attention only to the change in total benefits.

2. Be sure to include implicit costs in total costs.

3. Ignore sunk costs. These are the costs that are unaffected by the decision, since they already have been either incurred or committed. Because sunk costs are the same no matter what decision is made, they should play no role in the decision-making process.

4. Make the decision that will secure the largest net benefit.

Examples: Application of Decision-Making Rules

PROBLEM Due to cost overruns, a factory has cost, so far, $4 million to build. It will be useless (not even having a scrap value) unless completed, but this will take another $2 million. If completed, the factory will produce future revenues whose present value is worth $3 million to the firm. Should the factory be completed?

SOLUTION Yes. It will produce a revenue worth $3 million, and the marginal cost of completion is $2 million. So the firm will be better off (by $1 million) by completing the factory. The $4 million already spent is sunk cost—not completing the factory won't get rid of the loss, but completing it will make the firm better off by $1 million. If the factory is not completed, the firm will lose $4 million. If it is completed, the firm will lose only $3 million ($3 million in revenue less a total cost of $6 million). So the firm should complete the factory. (This would be true whether the sunk costs were $10 million or $100 million: Sunk costs are ignored in the decision-making process.)

PROBLEM An owner of an apartment complex took out a mortgage to buy the complex. The monthly mortgage payment comes to $300 per apartment. Maintenance and utilities are $250 a month for an occupied apartment and zero for an unoccupied apartment. If the local rents are lower than the owner expected, what is the lowest rent the owner should ever accept?

SOLUTION $250. Any rent above this makes the owner better off by renting (since renting covers at least part of the sunk mortgage costs). However, any rent below this does *not* cover the marginal cost of having the apartment occupied (versus having it empty).

CONCERNING OUTPUT

How much should a firm produce? Should it produce at all? The rules for answering these questions are the same for all firms, whether they are monopolists or competitors.

STEP 1: FINDING THE BEST LEVEL OF OUTPUT

Produce Q where MR = MC.

where MC (Marginal Cost) $=$ Addition to Total Costs (due to one more unit of output)

$$MR \text{ (Marginal Revenue)} = \text{Addition to Total Revenue (due to one more unit of output)}$$

$$\text{Profit} = \text{Total Revenue } (TR) - \text{Total Cost } (TC)$$

$$\text{Addition to Profit (due to one more unit of output)} = MR - MC$$

Using marginal analysis (see Chapter 1), the firm will add to its profits as long as each added unit of output adds more to TR than to TC. This is the same as saying $MR > MC$. The firm will continue to increase Q as long as $MR > MC$, until $MR = MC$, and then it will be at its highest attainable profit.

Note: There may be several Qs where $MR = MC$. One or more may be where profits are the smallest! However, there will be at least one Q where $MR = MC$ *and* profits are highest. In the vicinity of this Q and leading up to it, MR exceeds MC, while at higher levels of output, MC exceeds MR.

Example: Using Marginal Analysis

PROBLEM   Fill in the following table and indicate what is the most profitable level of output.

Output	Price	Total Revenue	Total Cost	MR	MC	Profit	Addition to Profit
0	$45	$ 0	$20	—	—	–$20	—
1	40	40	25	—	—	—	—
2	35	70	35	—	—	—	—
3	30	90	55	—	—	—	—
4	25	100	95	—	—	—	—

SOLUTION

Output	Price	Total Revenue	Total Cost	MR	MC	Profit	Addition to Profit
0	$45	$ 0	$20	—	—	–$20	—
1	40	40	25	$40	$ 5	15	$35
2	35	70	35	30	10	35	20
3	30	90	55	20	20	35	0
4	25	100	95	10	40	5	–30

The optimal level of profit is achievable where $MR = MC$ (at 3, where $MR = MC = \$20$). Up to this output, $MR > MC$, so producing the first and second units of output added to total profits (each unit of output contributed $MR - MC$ to profits). When $MR < MC$, profits fall. (Producing at 3, where $MR = MC$, gives the firm the highest attainable profit; other levels may be as profitable, such as 2, but none are better.)

STEP 2: COMPARING TOTAL REVENUE WITH TOTAL AVOIDABLE COSTS

Shut down when total avoidable costs exceed *TR*.

- *Short-Run Shutdown Rule 1*
  Shut down if: $TR < TVC$ at Q from Step 1.
                         or
                    $P < AVC$ at Q from Step 1.

- *Long-Run Shutdown Rule 2*
  Shut down if: $TR < TC$ at Q from Step 1.
                         or
                    $P < ATC$ at Q from Step 1.

In terms of the rules for decision making, only the costs that *change* should be considered in deciding whether to produce or shut down: These are the firm's total avoidable costs. As long as total revenues cover these costs, the firm is better off staying in business. Otherwise, it should shut down.

Fixed costs are the cost of fixed inputs (inputs that the firm does *not* increase when it wants more output). We will assume that in the *short run*, all fixed costs are *sunk costs*. For example, the plant and equipment are usually considered as sunk costs because most firms either own or have long-term contracts for the use of their plants and equipment. Some inputs are considered fixed in the short run because, while the firm could increase them to produce more output, to do so quickly would prove too expensive. For example, the cost of expanding a factory will be much higher if it has to be done within a month than if it has to be done within a year. Because fixed costs are sunk costs in the short run (only!), firms ignore them in their short-run decision making. Instead, each firm should compare its total revenues with total variable costs. If $TR > TVC$, then at least it is reducing the burden of fixed costs by producing output. If $TR < TVC$, it is adding to its losses and should shut down.

In the long run, all costs, including fixed costs, are avoidable. For example, factories wear out, and at some point firms have to decide whether to rebuild or shut down. If $TR \geq TC$, the firm is making a profit or breaking even and should stay in business. If $TR < TC$, the firm is incurring a loss, which it could avoid by shutting down.

Why in the short run is the shutdown rule $P < AVC$? Multiply both sides by the Q that the firm would otherwise produce: $P \times Q < AVC \times Q$. We then have $TR < TVC$, for the "Short-Run Shutdown Rule" set forth above. The same logic holds for the long run (if $P < ATC$, the firm should shut down).

Example: Deciding to Shut Down

PROBLEM   A firm's most profitable level of output is ten machines a year. But it is only the "most profitable" in the sense that when the firm produces ten machines, it is incurring the smallest loss. Its revenues are $100,000, but its fixed costs are $30,000 and its variable costs are $90,000. Should it shut down in the short run? Should it shut down in the long run (when the fixed cost of $30,000 could be avoided)?

SOLUTION   It should not shut down in the short run (since $100,000 > $90,000). If it *did* shut down in the short run, it would be worse off: It would lose $30,000 in fixed costs instead of $20,000 ($100,000 minus a total cost of $120,000). In the long run, the $30,000 of fixed cost no longer is sunk, perhaps because the plant has worn down and is ready to be replaced. So in the long run, the firm must incur a cost of $120,000 to operate. It will choose instead to shut down (since $100,000 in revenues < $120,000 in costs).

HOW COMPETITIVE FIRMS MAKE DECISIONS CONCERNING COSTS AND OUTPUT

We will now describe how competitive firms determine how much output to produce and whether to shut down or not. An industry is perfectly competitive when no single firm can raise its price without losing all of its customers. For example, if a farmer tries to sell wheat at $3.51 when the market price is $3.50, no one will buy from that farmer.

Economists describe firms in perfectly competitive industries as being **price takers.** Price takers take the current market price as given, knowing their individual actions have no influence on it.

Conditions Leading to Perfect Competition

1. Many firms are in the industry.

2. Buyers do not care which firm they buy from. They regard all firms as producing similar (homogeneous) products.

3. Buyers are informed enough to know who has the lowest price.

4. Firms can easily enter or exit the industry.

5. Condition 4 (ease of entry) is more important than Condition 1 (many firms). For example, if there are few firms in an industry, but easy and quick entry of new firms, then should any or all of the few firms try charging too much, new firms will enter the industry and push the price back down. Empirical evidence shows that **ease of entry** is more important than the number of firms for creating competition.

While few industries are perfectly competitive, the result from assuming perfect competition applies to all industries to the degree they face competitive pressures over time. Thus, the model of perfect competition is very useful for predicting the effects of demand and cost changes.

Since each price-taking firm has no discernable effect on market prices, the demand curve facing each price taker is *perfectly elastic* (see Chapter 17)—straight horizontal line at the market price. In Figure 20–1, Panel A shows the demand facing one firm in an industry. Panel B shows the industry's demand curve. The market price is $10 (where supply equals demand). Notice that the single firm's output is very small compared with the industry's output. It is so small that changing the amount it produces does not affect price.

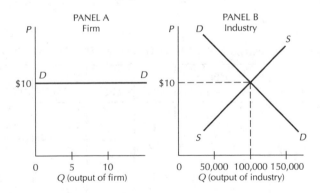

Figure 20–1. Determining the Effect of One Firm on Industry Demand

YOU SHOULD REMEMBER

1. In a competitive industry, no single firm has any influence on price.

2. In a competitive industry, each firm is a price taker: We show this by a horizontal demand curve facing each firm.

3. A set of conditions for a competitive industry is many firms, homogeneous product, well-informed buyers, and easy exit and entry. Few firms but easy entry also leads to competition.

RULES OF SUPPLY

• *SHORT RUN*

Short-Run Rule 1: Produce at the Q where P = MC.

The competitive firm can sell all it wants at the market price (P). So the marginal revenue from an added unit of output is P: $MR = P$ for price takers. Using marginal analysis, the firm expands output as long as $P > MC$ and produces at the output (Q) where $P = MC$.

Now let's apply this rule to Table 20–1. What is the best level of output when $P = \$30$?

Table 20–1. Determining Profits with the Rule of Short-Run Supply

Output	Total Revenue	Marginal Revenue (= P)	MC	TVC	AVC	TC	Profit
0	$ 0	—	—	$ 0	—	$ 15	–$15
1	30	$30	$40	40	$40	55	– 25
2	60	30	30	70	35	85	– 25
3	90	30	20	90	30	105	– 15
4	120	30	10	100	25	115	5
5	150	30	25	125	25	140	10
6	180	30	30	155	25.83	170	10
7	210	30	41	196	28	211	– 1
8	240	30	60	256	32	271	– 31

Profits are highest ($10) at $Q = 6$ where $P = MC = \$30$.

Short-Run Rule 2: Shut down when P < Minimum AVC.

The firm should shut down if TR < TVC at its best level of Q. If P is less than the firm's *minimum AVC*, then certainly P < AVC at all levels of output. Multiplying each side of P < Minimum AVC by Q, we have TR < TVC, which means the firm should shut down. (Note that the minimum AVC is found where the MC curve crosses the AVC curve.)

At what price will the firm in Table 20–1 shut down? The firm's **shutdown price,** the price at which it just covers its variable costs, is $25. At a price any lower, it will shut down.

PLOTTING A FIRM'S SHORT-RUN SUPPLY CURVE

In Table 20–1, what Q should the firm produce if P = $41? Q should be 7 (where MC = $41). At P = $60, Q = 8 (where MC = $60). At P = $20, Q = 0, since the firm should shut down at any price below $25. In general, the **short-run supply curve** for a competitive firm is identical to the section of its marginal cost curve above its shutdown price (i.e., the section of the MC curve above where it crosses the AVC curve).

The short-run supply curve for a firm (a different firm than shown in Table 20–1) is represented by the darkened line in Figure 20–2.

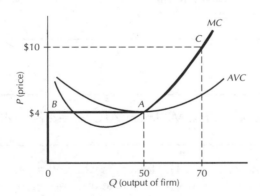

Figure 20–2. The Short-Run Supply Curve of a Competitive Firm

Key Procedure for Plotting Firm's Short-Run Supply

1. Start at the top of a graph.

2. Put a straight edge horizontally across the graph. This represents the horizontal demand curve the single competitive firm faces.

3. Go across until you intersect the rising section of the firm's *MC* curve: The firm will supply the amount on the quantity axis at the price on the price axis. (For example, at Point *C* in Figure 20–2, at a price of $10, 70 units of output will be supplied.)

4. Continue down the *MC* curve until you reach the bottom of the *AVC* curve—this is the firm's minimum *AVC* (at Point *A*, where the firm will supply 50 units). The firm will shut down below this price ($4). So draw a straight line to the price axis (from Point *A* to *B*), and then draw a line down the axis (from *B* to 0) to show that below $4, no output will be "supplied."

YOU SHOULD REMEMBER

1. Price equals marginal revenue for price takers.

2. In the short run, the firm will shut down if the price of output is below its minimum average variable costs.

3. If the firm produces at all, it will produce where price equals marginal cost.

4. The MC curve above minimum AVC (where AVC = MC) is the firm's short-run supply curve.

• *LONG RUN*

Rule: Produce when $P \geq$ Minimum ATC where $P = $ MC.

Our logic is the same as above: The best Q is where $P = MC$. However, if P falls below the firm's minimum *ATC,* then the firm, no matter what Q it produces, cannot cover its costs. It should shut down.

Figure 20–3 shows the long-run supply curve for a single firm: its *MC* curve above its *minimum* average *total* cost. The firm's long-run supply curve goes up from 0 to *E* (the long-run shutdown price being $8), over to Point *D* (at $8, the firm supplies 60 units), and then up the *MC* curve through Point *C*. Note that in the long run, the firm's **breakeven price** (the price at which its total revenue equals its total cost) is also its shutdown price. (*Proof:* long-run shutdown $P = $ Minimum *ATC*, and if both sides are multiplied by the Q at the shutdown price, we have $TR = TC$.) Note that the Minimum *ATC* can be found where the *MC* curve intersects the *ATC* curve.

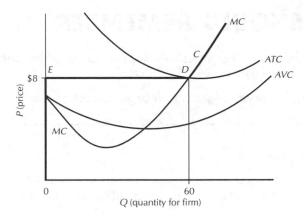

Figure 20–3. The Long-Run Supply Curve of a Competitive Firm

YOU SHOULD REMEMBER

1. In the long run, the firm should produce when $P \geq$ Minimum *ATC* and where $P = MC$.

2. The *MC* curve above minimum *ATC* (where *ATC* = *MC*) is the firm's long-run supply curve.

THE CONSTRUCTION OF THE INDUSTRY'S SHORT-RUN SUPPLY CURVE

• *SHORT RUN*

Recall the definition of short run: In the short run, firms have fixed factors that they cannot vary. Let us now add a second condition: Time is too short for new firms to enter or exit the industry. Because there are a fixed number of firms in the short run, any increase in supply can come only from the existing firms. So the industry's supply curve is the horizontal sum of the supply curves of all the firms in the industry. For example, if there are 10,000 firms that are all like the one in Table 20–1, then at a price of $25, 50,000 units will be supplied; at $30, 60,000 units. Note that the supply curve reflects *marginal cost*.

YOU SHOULD REMEMBER

1. In the short run, the industry's supply curve is the horizontal sum of the supply curve of all firms.

2. The supply curve reflects the marginal cost of output.

• LONG RUN

In the long run, firms can enter or exit the industry and will do so according to the profits that can be earned. When all firms are alike:

If profit > 0, firms will enter the industry.

If profit < 0, firms will exit the industry.

If profit = 0, the industry will be in long-run equilibrium.

In the long run, *economic profits* equal zero. Recall that economic profits are the excess over what is needed to pay a firm to produce. Thus, when economic profits are positive, new firms are willing to enter the industry. When economic profits are negative, firms will leave. Note that when economic profits are zero, *accounting profits* are positive and equal to the **normal profits** that compensate owners for their implicit costs.

YOU SHOULD REMEMBER

1. The entry and exit of firms cause economic profits to equal zero in the long run.

2. In the long run, accounting profits will be positive and equal to the return to owners for their implicit costs.

• FROM SHORT RUN TO LONG RUN

To show how an industry reacts to an increase in demand, we will examine an industry in which all firms, both entering and existing, have the same cost curves.

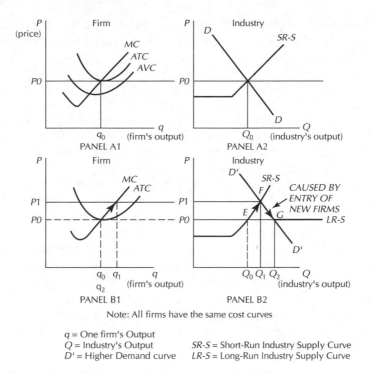

Figure 20–4. Comparing the Impact of Increased Demand in the Short Run and Long Run for One Firm Versus the Industry

In Panels A1 and A2 of Figure 20–4 (see above), we show the industry initially in long-run equilibrium. At price $P0$, $P0$ = Minimum ATC = MC (Note that output is being produced at the *lowest average cost*.) Each firm supplies q_0 and industry supply is Q_0. Assuming we start with 10,000 firms, Q_0 = 10,000 × q_0. *SR-S* is the industry's short-run supply curve. It's the horizontal sum of the MC curve (above minimum AVC) of all 10,000 firms.

In Panels B1 and B2, we show the effects of an increase in demand (from DD to $D\,'D\,'$). In the short run, the price rises to P_1. Each firm produces q_1 units of output and industry output expands to Q_1 (10,000 × q_1). Each firm is making a profit (since $P > ATC$ at q_1).

In the long run, these profits attract new firms into the industry, increasing the industry's output supplied. New firms enter until the last firm to enter causes all firms to just break even. The long-run supply curve will be *LR-S*. In the long run, Q_2 will be supplied. Each firm will produce q_0, breaking even in the long run. Our assumption that all firms have the same costs assures that in the long run, output will be supplied at PO since this is the minimum ATC of all firms. Any higher price will cause new firms to enter. As we shall see in the next section, an industry's supply need not be horizontal as shown here.

This pattern of response has been observed numerous times. First demand goes up. Price goes up (from Point E to Point F) and this encourages each firm to produce more (increasing Q from Q_0 to Q_1). Initially, the industry is very profitable. Eventually, new firms enter and their competition pushes the initial price increase back down (from F to G) as well as expands total output even more (from Q_1 to Q_2). Profits return to 0. An example of this pattern occurred when hand-held calculators were introduced. At first, they were high priced (over $100). The initial firms making them made large profits. But soon, large numbers of competitors entered the industry, bidding the price down and expanding output.

Alternatively what if demand goes down? Price goes down (but no further down than the short-run shutdown price). The industry bears large losses and eventually some firms shut down. The exit of firms pushes output down even more, allowing the remaining firms to raise prices. Profits return to zero. Recently, the fall in the price of oil caused many oil-producing firms to suffer large losses. Output only slowly contracted, though, as oil wells were slowly shut down. Eventually, the industry recovered, but at a lower level of production.

Note that output changes much more in the long run (due to the entrance or exit of firms) than in the short run: *Supply is more elastic in the long run than in the short run.*

YOU SHOULD REMEMBER

1. When demand changes, the greatest change in price will occur in the short run. The long-run entry or exit of firms will diminish or eliminate the initial change in prices.

2. In the short run, all firms can suffer losses or enjoy profits. In the long run, profits and losses are eliminated.

3. Supply is more elastic in the long run.

PLOTTING AN INDUSTRY'S LONG-RUN SUPPLY CURVE

In Figure 20–5, Panel A shows the supply curve (SS) for a competitive industry when (1) all firms are equally efficient and (2) the industry can buy all the inputs it wants at the same price. The long-run supply curve is perfectly elastic, with firms entering when the price exceeds $8 or exiting when the price falls below $8. This is a **constant-cost industry.** Changes in demand do not affect the long-run supply price (of $8).

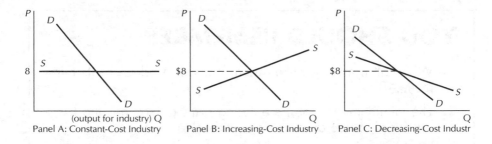

Figure 20–5. Determining the Long-Run Supply Curve for Various Types of Competitive Industries

Panel B shows an **increasing-cost industry.** If all firms are equally efficient, then the only cause of the rising supply price (as output increases) can be rising prices of some of the inputs the industry employs. For example, construction prices usually go up during economic expansions as building firms bid up the price of building materials. Another reason for increasing costs is that the new firms entering the industry are less efficient than the existing ones.

When all firms are alike, the long-run price will be P = Minimum ATC = MC. (Referring to Figure 20–3, each firm will be at Point D.) When firms differ in efficiency, in the long run, the least-efficient firm in the industry will break even (being at Point D) but others will make a profit (Point D being lower on their MC curve). When firms differ in efficiency the supply price at each level of output equals the Minimum ATC of the least-efficient firm in the industry.

Panel C shows the long-run supply curve of a **decreasing-cost industry.** Minimum ATC falls when the industry expands if the greater output allows more specialization and economies in the supply of inputs: This reduces the price of inputs. For example, expanding sales of video recorders allowed for economies of scale in the production of video recorder components and caused the price of video recorders to fall.

> # YOU SHOULD REMEMBER
>
> **1.** When all firms are alike, each firm will produce at its minimum *ATC*.
>
> **2.** The minimum *ATC* of the entering firms determines the long-run supply price as output expands.
>
> **3.** Increasing costs are caused by rising factor prices or less-efficient firms entering the industry.
>
> **4.** Decreasing costs are caused by economies of scale that reduce the cost of inputs.

EFFECTS OF COSTS ON SUPPLY

Increases in fixed costs (such as the cost of plant and land) and variable costs (such as wages and price of raw materials) affect output and prices as follows:

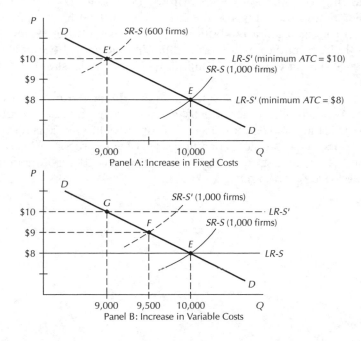

Figure 20–6. Effects of Costs on Supply

Increase in Fixed Costs

Panel A of Figure 20–6 shows a constant-cost industry. Initially, there are 1,000 firms producing 10 units of output each, with a resulting short-run supply curve of SR-S (1,000). Since this is also the long run, each firm's minimum ATC is $8 and so the long-run supply curve is LR-S. Demand equals supply at P = $8. Then fixed costs go up (for example, the interest payments on the money firms owe increase). *The* MC *curve is unaffected by changes in fixed cost.* (Recall that MC is the change in TVC when output increases by one unit: Changing TFC has no effect on MC.) So SR-S is unchanged: In the short run, neither output nor price is affected (at Point E). But firms are losing money. In the long run, some will exit the industry. The industry's long-run supply curve will shift up (to LR-S ´) to reflect in increase at ATC from $8 to $10. Price will go up to $10 and output will fall to 9,000 (at E ´) Be careful! Each remaining firm still has its old MC curve: All that has happened is that the shutdown price has gone up. So each *remaining* firm will produce more, being higher on their MC curve. (If, for example, each firm produces 15 units of output, there will be 600 firms left in the industry.)

Increase in Variable Costs

In Panel B of Figure 20–6, start out as before, at P = $8 and Q = 10,000. Then let variable costs increase (for example, wages go up). An increase in variable costs shifts up each firm's shutdown price *and* MC curve. The industry's supply curve, both short- and long-run, will shift up. This is shown by the shift to SR-S ´ and LR-S ´.

In the short run (with 1,000 firms), the industry will be where the SR-S ´ curve (the sum of the 1,000 MC ´ curves) equals demand. P = $9 and Q = 9,500 at Point F. In the long run, firms exit the industry and output is where the new LR-S ´ intersects demand at $10 (Point G): Output falls to 9,000 units.

Change in Demand

In the short run, an increase in demand always increases price and output (since MC is rising). In the long run, an increase in demand will not affect the price in a constant-cost industry; it will raise it in an increasing-cost industry; it will lower it in a decreasing-cost industry. (Check this by drawing a new demand curve to the right of DD in Figure 20–5.)

YOU SHOULD REMEMBER

1. Changes in fixed costs have no effect on price or output in the short run in competitive industries.

2. Increases in variable costs increase price and reduce output in the short run. In the long run, price increases even more and output falls even more than they did in the short run as firms exit the industry.

3. In the long run, increases in fixed costs raise prices and lower industry output. But the fewer remaining firms will produce more than before.

COMPETITION BIDS PRICE DOWN TO COST

This chapter can be summarized in the following rule: competition bids price down to cost. In the short run, competition bids the price down to marginal cost, because marginal cost is the relevant short-run cost. In the long run, competition bids the price down to the minimum average total cost, the cost that is relevant in the long run.

To apply this rule, suppose demand increases. In the short run, the price goes up because marginal cost is rising. In the long run, the new price will be determined by what happens to minimum average total cost. As we will see, in a constant-cost industry, price remains constant. In a rising-cost industry, the price rises. In a decreasing-cost industry, price decreases.

Next, apply the rule to cost changes. Suppose variable cost increases exist (for example, wages go up). This increases marginal cost and average cost, so the price will go up in both the short and long runs. Next, suppose the cost of an input fixed in the short run increases. In the short run, this does not affect marginal cost (which reflects variable costs), so the price remains unchanged. In the long run, this raises average total cost, so the price rises.

SHORT AND LONG RUNS

To better learn this material, mentally separate the short-run material from the long-run material. Next, assume that each production facility (a plant if the good is manufactured or a store if the product is retailing) is individually owned. Call each of these a firm. In the short run, a firm has fixed capital and equipment. Because of diminishing marginal product, each added unit of output requires more workers than the previous unit. As a result, marginal cost rises. Since price equals marginal cost, the supply price of goods rises as output goes up. In the long run, the firm can add machines and equipment. Say the best mix of capital and labor is one machine and one worker producing one unit of output. To produce another unit, the firm just adds another unit of labor and capital. Its costs will not rise (unless wages or the price of a capital goes up as the industry expands). It still faces diminishing marginal product (for example, one machine, two workers, 1.5 units of output). But this does not affect its cost as it expands because it is hiring more labor and more capital. A competitive industry's supply price will be constant if input costs remain constant as the industry expands. Its supply price will increase (decrease) if input costs increase (decrease) as the industry expands.

Here is the breakdown between short and long run for a competitive industry:

- Short Run
  Output only from variable inputs
  Variable Inputs have diminishing marginal productivity
  Diminishing marginal productivity causes rising marginal cost
  Firm Output: Price = Marginal Cost
  Supply Price = Marginal Cost
  Industry Output (if all firms alike): Number of Firms × Firm Output

- Long Run
  Output from adding new firms
  Firm chooses mix of inputs to product output at lowest cost per unit
  Supply Price = Minimum Average Total Cost
  Industry Output: Number of firms increase (or decrease) until industry output drives demand price down (or up) to minimum average total cost.

AUCTION THEORY

This chapter describes how costs determine the prices when an industry is competitive. In the short run, prices reflect marginal costs. In the long run, they reflect the lowest average total cost of producing the good.

But what determines the price of goods like art and land that already exist and do not need to be produced to bring to market? For these goods, economists use auction theory (however, auction theory applies to all goods). Auction theory describes what happens when buyers compete for a limited number of goods. Markets can be thought of as auctions, where buyers and sellers put in bids. Actual auctions include English auctions such as eBay (where buyers bid the price higher and higher, with the highest bidder getting the good), Dutch auctions (where the auctioneer starts with a high price and then decreases the price until the first bid), and sealed auctions (where buyers submit sealed bids, the highest one getting the good). The revenue equivalence theorem states that under certain general conditions, all of these auctions will yield the same price (or revenues if more than one good is offered for sale). Assume there are N items for sale and there are many more buyers, each of whom purchases only one item. According to the revenue equivalence theorem, the auction will reward the items to the N buyers who value the items the most. The price will reflect slightly more than the value of the $N + 1$th highest bidder. This is what happens where the demand curve crosses a vertical supply curve.

One interest application of the auction theory is the winner's curve. If buyers have to estimate what an item is worth, then it is likely that the winning bidder is the one with the most optimistic estimate. As a result, the winning bidder often pays more than the item turns out being worth—hence, the curse. To illustrate, suppose a teacher put a jar with $10 of nickels up for bid. Students must guess what the jar holds. Students bid for the jar (assume they have sufficient cash with them to match what they think the jar is worth). The "winner" is likely to be a student who estimates that the jar holds more than $10.

Another application of auction theory is the second-price action. In the second-price auction, the winner pays the second highest bid for the item. The advantage of this structure is that the bidders are more willing to reveal and bid what they think the item is worth. Bidding how much one values the item at has no cost (since the winning bidder only pays the next highest bid) and bidding below what the item is worth may result in the loss of a good deal. As a result, this type of auction gets to the strike price quicker than an English auction (where it pays to bid less than what you think an item is worth).

KNOW THE CONCEPTS

DO YOU KNOW THE BASICS?

1. Why does a firm increase Q when $MR > MC$?
2. What will a firm lose if it shuts down in the short run? When can it reduce this loss by producing?
3. What will the firm lose if it shuts down in the long run? When will it do better by producing?
4. If a competitive firm can sell 1 widget at $10, at what price will it be able to sell 1,000 widgets? How many widgets can it sell at $10.01?
5. What is the competitive firm's supply curve in the short run? Long run?
6. How do you find the industry's short-run supply curve?

7. How do you describe the long-run supply of the least efficient firm in an industry?

8. Does industrial output increase more in the short run or long run when demand goes up? Why?

9. When do fixed costs affect the industry's supply?

10. What forces determine how prices will change in the long run when demand goes up?

TERMS FOR STUDY

breakeven price
constant-cost industry
decreasing-cost industry
increasing-cost industry
marginal analysis
marginal cost
marginal revenue

perfect competition
price taker
profit
short and long run
short-run and long-run supply
shutdown price
sunk cost

PRACTICAL APPLICATION

1. In Table 20–1, the fixed cost is $15. Redo the table assuming the fixed cost is $35.

   a. Does the change in fixed costs affect marginal cost?

   b. Does it affect the optimal level of output (in the short run)?

2. Some quick questions:

   a. At $Q = 8$, a firm's profit is $40. At $Q = 9$, its *MR* is $60 and its *MC* is $55. What is its profit at $Q = 9$?

   b. At $Q = 7$, a firm's profit is $70, and at $Q = 8$, it's $75. The marginal cost of the eighth unit of output is $12. What is its marginal revenue?

   c. At $Q = 9$, a firm's profit is $100; at $Q = 10$, it's $90. What do we know about the tenth unit's marginal revenue and cost?

3. Answer true or false. Assume the firm is a price taker.

   a. The firm should always produce more when $P > ATC$.

   b. The firm should always produce more when $P > AVC$.

   c. The firm should always produce more when $P > MC$ and $P > AVC$.

   d. In the short run, the firm should always shut down when it's incurring a loss.

   e. In the long run, the firm should always shut down when it's incurring a loss.

4. An airline has signed a long-term contract to rent planes at a cost of $200,000 per month. In a given month, suppose each plane can make 100 flights. Each flight costs $5,000 in labor, gas, and other variable costs. What is the minimum total dollar amount of fares per flight that the airline should accept rather than cancel the flight?

5. Use the following table to answer the questions.

Output	1	2	3	4	5	6	7	8
MC	3	2	1	2	3	4	5	6

   a. What is the minimum AVC? (Recall that TVC is the sum of the MCs and AVC is the average MC.) What is this firm's short-run shut-down price?
   b. What is this firm's short-run supply curve (for prices from $1 to $6)?
   c. If the firm's fixed cost is $9, what is its long-run supply schedule?

6. Suppose there are 100 firms in an industry. Each has the following cost schedules:

Output	1	2	3	4	5	6	7
MC	3	2	1	2	3	4	5
AVC	3	2.50	2.00	2.00	2.20	2.50	2.86
AFC	9	4.50	3.00	2.25	1.80	1.50	1.29

   Answer the questions below using the following demand curve for the industry.

Price	$2	3	4	5	6
Q Demanded	940	860	780	700	620

   a. What is the industry's short-run supply schedule?
   b. What will price and output be in the short run? How much will each firm produce? What will the profit be?
   c. Allowing for entry and exit, what will the long-run supply curve be?
   d. How much will each firm produce in the long run? How many firms will there be? What will their profit be?

7. We begin this problem by assuming that the industry in Questions 5 and 6 above is in the long-run equilibrium. Then demand falls, decreasing by 210 units at each price level. (For example, at $5, demand falls from 700 units to 490 units.)

a. In the short run, what will happen to price and output? What is the output and profit of each firm?

b. In the long run, what will happen to price and output? How many firms will be in the industry? What will their profit be?

8. What are the long-run effects of an output tax of $1 per unit on a constant-cost industry? On an increasing-cost industry? On a declining-cost industry?

9. Assume that oil refineries (which convert oil into gasoline, heating oil, and other fuels) are in a competitive industry. Suppose oil refineries only produced gasoline. If demand for gasoline goes up, why does the price of gasoline go up in the short run? What will happen to refineries' profits? Next, suppose oil refineries can choose to produce gasoline or heating oil. Further, oil refineries are operating at capacity so that an increase in gasoline production means less heating oil is produced. Why will the price of gasoline go up when the demand for gasoline goes up?

10. Suppose all firms in a competitive industry only have fixed costs (cruise ships are somewhat like this). Each firm produces exactly 100 units a year, and the fixed cost in per year terms, is $100,000. What is the long-run price of output? What determines price in the short run? How sensitive will the price be to fluctuations in demand? Answer the same questions for a competitive industry where all firms have only variable cost. Each firm has a variable cost of $1,000 a unit.

ANSWERS

KNOW THE CONCEPTS

1. Because the firm adds to its profits by producing more when $MR > MC$.

2. If the firm shuts down, its short-run loss will equal TFC. If the firm produces, its short-run loss will equal $TFC - (TR - TVC)$. So if $TR > TVC$, the firm will reduce its short-run loss by producing.

3. Long-run shutdown loss equals zero. So the firm should produce only when $TR > TC$.

4. $10. At $10.01, it won't be able to sell any.

5. The short-run supply curve is the MC curve above its intersection with the AVC curve (i.e., above the minimum AVC). The long-run supply curve is the MC curve above its intersection with the long-run ATC curve (i.e., above the minimum ATC).

6. Take the horizontal sum of the supply curves of all firms.

7. The least-efficient firm will just break even. It will make no profit. It will supply output at its minimum *ATC* (since for profits to equal zero, *P* = minimum *ATC*).

8. Output increases more in the long run because new firms enter, increasing total supply.

9. Fixed costs affect the industry's supply curve only in the long run. An increase in fixed costs shifts the long-run supply curve up.

10. The industry's price will go up when demand goes up if new suppliers are less efficient than current suppliers and/or input prices go up when the industry demands more inputs. The price will stay constant if all firms are equally efficient and the industry can get all the inputs it needs at a constant price. The price may go down if input prices go down when more inputs are demanded.

PRACTICAL APPLICATION

1. **Table 20–1. With Fixed Cost of $35**

Output	Total Revenue	Marginal Revenue (= *P*)	MC	TVC	AVC	TC	Profit
0	$ 0	—	—	$ 0	—	$ 35	–$35
1	30	$30	$40	40	$40	75	– 45
2	60	30	30	70	35	105	– 45
3	90	30	20	90	30	125	– 35
4	120	30	10	100	25	135	– 15
5	150	30	25	125	25	160	– 10
6	180	30	30	155	25.83	190	– 10
7	210	30	41	196	28	231	– 21
8	240	30	60	256	32	291	– 51

a. No, *MC* is not affected. (*MC* is the change in *TC*: Each entry in the *TC* column has gone up 20 but the *change* in *TC* is still the same.)

b. No. The optimal level of output is not affected. The firm still produces 6 units of output (the firm loses the least—$10—at *Q* = 6; note that if the firm shuts down, it loses more—$35).

2. a. $45.

 b. $17.

 c. *MC* exceeds *MR* by $10. All answers are from the following equation:

$$\text{Change in Profit} = MR - MC.$$

3. a. False.
   b. False.
   c. True.
   d. False.
   e. True.
4. $5,000.
5. a. Minimum AVC = $2 (at Q = 4, also at Q = 3). The shutdown price is $2. The AVC and AFC schedule for this firm is given in the answer to Question 6, below.
   b. The supply curve is obtained by finding the Q at which $P = MC$. The firm's short-run supply schedule is:

Price	$1	2	3	4	5	6
Firm's Q	0	4	5	6	7	8

   c. Its minimum ATC is $4 at Q = 6. It's long-run supply schedule is:

Price	$1	2	3	4	5	6
Firm's Q	0	0	0	6	7	8

6. a. The industry's short-run supply schedule is:

Price	$1	2	3	4	5	6
Firm's Q	0	400	500	600	700	800

   b. Supply equals demand at P = $5 and Q = 700. Each firm produces 7 units of Q making a profit of $6 (*TR* of $35 less $9 of fixed costs and $20 of variable costs; recall that *TVC* is the sum of the *MC*s and the *TFC* = $9).
   c. In the long run, P = minimum ATC = $4. So the supply curve will be horizontal at $4 in the long run.
   d. At $4, output demanded will be 780 units. Each firm will produce 6 units. There will be 130 firms (780/6). Profit will equal zero.

7. a. With 130 firms (from Question 6, above), the industry's supply curve in the short run (i.e., 130 × firm's short-run Q) and demand curve will be:

Price	$1	2	3	4	5	6
Industry Q Supplied	0	520	650	780	910	1,040
Q Demanded	—	730	650	570	490	410

Demand equals supply at $3 (with $Q = 650$). Each firm will produce 5 units at a loss of $5.

b. Firms will exit the industry until in the long run, $P = \$4 =$ minimum *ATC*. At $4, 570 units will be demanded. Each firm will produce 6 units, so there will be 95 firms (570/6).

8. In all cases, output declines and the producers add $1 to their unit cost (*ATC*) to derive the price consumers pay. In the constant-cost industry, the suppliers' *ATC* is the same at lower outputs as it was originally, so the price paid by the consumer goes up by $1. In the increasing-cost industry, decreased output has a lower *ATC*, so the price goes up, but by *less* than a dollar. In the decreasing-cost industry, decreased output raises *ATC*, so the price goes up by *more* than a dollar.

9. In competitive industries, when demand goes up, the price goes up in the short run because marginal cost is rising (making the supply curve positively sloped). The higher price, while reflecting a higher marginal cost, can be above the average cost of producing the good (recall that average costs rise slower than marginal cost). So profits go up (Profits = (Price – Average Total Cost) × Output). This is particularly true of oil refineries that have a large fixed cost and a physical capacity such that, beyond a certain point, marginal costs rise rapidly. This makes the short-run supply curve of gasoline fairly steep. As a consequence, the price of gasoline is very sensitive to shifts in the demand curve. If refineries also produce heating oil, there is another cost of producing gasoline: the foregone revenue from producing heating oil. When the demand for gasoline goes up and more gasoline is produced, less heating oil is produced. As a consequence, the price of heating oil goes up, increasing the opportunity cost of producing gasoline.

10. The long-run price will be $1,000 (the average cost). In the short run, supply is fixed (equaling the number of firms times 100). As a result, in the short run, price is purely demand-determined. If the demand curve shifts $100 down, the price will fall $100. If the demand curve shifts up $100, the price will rise $100. The price will be very sensitive to demand in this industry. Further, this type of industry tends to be boom or bust. In the second type of industry, the long-run and short-run price will be $1,000, no matter if the demand curve shifts up or down. Price will be insensitive to demand. This will be a stable industry.

21
ASYMMETRIC INFORMATION

KEY TERMS

asymmetric information when one person knows more than another, making it hard for them to do business with each other. If they had otherwise done business, then asymmetrical information is the cause of a *market failure*.

moral hazard once two people agree to a contract, the risk that one of them will act to the detriment of the other. For example, after a business pays an insurance company for fire insurance, the firm burns down the property as it is worth less than it was insured for.

principal-agent problem the dual problem of (1) the principal who hires the agent setting up a contract so that the agent will do what the principal wants, and (2) the agent setting up the contract so that the principal will pay for the work the agent does.

lemon problem because sellers know the quality of their product more than buyers, there may be an adverse selection of poor quality goods being sold.

adverse selection when, due to poor information, "bad" products (or buyers) are selected. For example, sellers of junk cars will seek out uninformed buyers and try to pass off their cars as good. This reduces the value of truly good cars. As another example, buyers who are sick will seek to buy health insurance from sellers who can't tell who is sick. As a result, the premiums of insurance policies may be too expensive for someone who is currently healthy.

signals action taken by person to signal or reveal relevant information. An example is a student who joins many clubs in college to reveal to employers that they will be good managers.

market failure when markets fail to produce and allocate goods efficiently (and in particular, when mutually advantageous trades are not made).

In many competitive markets, goods are standardized, and buyers know what they are getting. In markets where products differ from one another, brand names often let buyers know what they are getting. Similarly, in many markets, suppliers get paid in cash and have no further obligations to the buyer, so sellers know what they are being paid and the cost of what they are selling.

However, in many other markets, buyers and sellers are not sure what they are getting. Because one person knows more than another, not all mutually beneficial trades will take place. For example, suppose buyer B would be willing to pay $100 for a high-quality used DVD player and seller S has a high-quality used DVD player she would be willing to sell for as little as $40. The joint benefit of this trade is $60. However, the trade may not take place because buyer B does not know that seller S's DVD player is of high quality. As a result, buyer B may walk away from the deal, leaving both B and S worse off. The failure to make mutually advantageous trades is a *market failure* associated with asymmetric information.

Asymmetric information can lead to market failure. Market failure due to asymmetric information usually involves four elements:

1. One person (the buyer or seller) benefits from not revealing information relevant to the other person the buyer or seller could be trading with (for example, a seller of a low-quality DVD player gets a higher price by not revealing its quality from buyers).

2. The other party cannot easily find out the information on his or her own.

3. As a result, some buyers and sellers do not trade, resulting in a market failure.

4. Often market mechanisms arise that seek to profit by getting buyers and sellers together who otherwise would not have traded due to their differences in information.

PROBLEM

a. B is willing to buy good X for $12 and seller S is willing to sell it for $20. They do not trade ("trade" here meaning trading the good for money). Is this a market failure?

b. B is willing to buy a high-quality good for $18 and a low-quality good for $12. B buys the good from seller S for $15, thinking it is high quality, and finds out later it is low quality. The good costs seller S $10. Is this a market failure?

c. The next day, B values another high-quality good for $18 but, being uncertain as to its quality, does not buy it from seller S who offers it for $15. The good is a high-quality good that cost seller S $10. Is this a market failure?

d. How could someone profit from the situation in part c?

SOLUTION

a. No. If made, the trade would not be mutually advantageous. If seller S would be willing to sell it for $7 (or any price below $12) and the trade did not take place, it would be a market failure.

b. Yes. The source of market failure is not the absence of trade, as the trade did take place. The source of the market failure is the absence of a mutually advantgeous trade (as buyer B lost from the deal).

c. Yes. If the trade had been made, both parties would have been better off. But it was not made. That makes it a case of market failure.

d. Whenever demand price is higher than supply price and trade does not take place, one can make a profit (up to the differences in prices by getting buyer and seller together). In this example, a middle person could buy the DVD from the seller at $11, find a way to convince the buyer it is high quality and sell it for $17. The middle person would make a $6 profit. The maximum profit that could be made in this situation (ignoring the costs of getting buyer and seller together) is $8 (the demand price minus the supply price, $18 − $10). Market failure is often an opportunity for profit.

ADVERSE SELECTION

A classic case of adverse selection involves health insurance. The first element is that there is an incentive on the part of buyers to lie about their health in order to pay smaller premiums. Second, it is often too expensive for the insurance company to determine the real health status of those buying their policies. The result is that people with potentially higher health costs will be more willing to buy the insurance. Instead of insuring a random selection of the population, the insurance company will end up insuring an adverse selection of customers: those who will prove, on average, more costly. As a result, it will have to charge a higher price for its policy. The third element is that a market failure will occur (1) if people who are healthy cannot afford to buy health care insurance at these higher rates, and (2) if it would be mutually profitable for insurance companies to sell them a policy if it could tell that these customers are healthy.

The following simple example illustrates this result. Assume that half the population is healthy and that their average health care costs are $1,000 a year. Assume the other half of the population is unhealthy and that their average cost of health care is $3,000 a year. Because any individual's actual health care costs will vary substantially around these average amounts, people in both groups are willing to pay their average costs plus 10 percent because they do not want to face the risk of unexpectedly high health care costs. Assume this extra 10 percent covers the insurance firm's costs and provides them with a reasonable profit. Suppose the health insurance company offers a policy covering all health care costs for a year at $1,100. All persons will buy the policy, resulting in the insurance company having to pay out an average of $2,000 per customer in health care costs. This is unprofitable. Suppose it then instead charges $2,200 a year (this covering the average cost of all the population plus 10 percent). Now only the "unhealthy" half of the population will buy the policy. This is an example of adverse selection. This adverse selection runs the insurance company's average cost up to $3,000. To make a profit, the insurance company will end up charging $3,300 for the policy. The unhealthy will buy the policy, and the insurance company will earn a reasonable profit. The market failure occurs for the healthy half of the population who do not buy health insurance (as it is only worth $1,100 to them and has a price of $3,300). This is a market failure in the sense that if the insurance company could identify who is healthy, it could offer them a policy at $1,100 that would be a mutually beneficial trade between the company and the healthy buyers.

The fourth element is that market institutions often reduce the extent of market failure by getting buyers and sellers together. For example, many employers offer health insurance to their employees. Because workers are not usually selected by their lack of health, more people can afford to buy health insurance from their employers. Similarly, insurance companies are always seeking ways to distinguish between healthy and unhealthy persons. It may be possible in the future to use medical tests to accurately measure what a person's likely health care costs will be. This will result in people being able to buy health insurance at a cost that reflects their likely future health care costs. This would be the efficient solution from an economic point of view. However, it may not be what many people consider a fair solution. In particular, it would mean that people born with health defects will face very high insurance prices.

Another example of adverse selection is buffet restaurants. Buffet restaurants charge the same price regardless of how much one eats. Buffet-style meals are cheaper to produce because a large amount of food can be prepared at one time in advance (for example, it takes about the same time to prepare ten steaks as it does one). Because everyone pays the same price, people who are big eaters are more likely to go to a buffet restaurant. This runs up the average cost of a meal. There will be a market failure if small eaters do not eat at the buffet restaurant because they find the price of the meal too high, even though they would be willing to pay a price that adequately covers the cost of the food they do eat. One market institution that addresses this problem is the cafeteria, where food is also prepared in advance but people pay by how much they eat. But this is not a perfect solution as it is costly for a cafeteria to individually price out food. Other market institutions that address this problem are buffets offering only healthy food. If big eaters usually avoid healthy food while small eaters prefer healthy food, this allows small eaters to have buffet-style meals at a price reflecting their eating style.

Similarly, adverse selection explains in large part why the interest rate charged on payday loans far exceeds those charged by banks and credit cards. A payday loan is where the lender (whose store is usually located in shopping malls) lends workers money for a few days, and workers agrees to pay back the loan plus interest out of their next paycheck. Because people who are good credit risks can get loans at far lower rates, some of the persons taking out payday loans are high credit risks. Some of them do not repay the loan. Given the small amount of money lent and the high cost of collecting from those who do not pay back the loan, the interest rates on the payday loans have to be high to cover the loan's costs. The asymmetric information is that the lender does not know who the good credit risks are (a good credit risk is someone who promptly pays back the loan). As a result, those who are good credit risks may not take out the loan due to its high interest rates. If the lender knew they were good credit risks and would have offered an interest rate that was mutually acceptable, then this would not be an example of a market failure.

YOU SHOULD REMEMBER

1. There are four elements to adverse selection. First, some customers are more expensive than others to do business with; the costly customers have an incentive to not reveal who they are. Second, it is too expensive for sellers to tell who the costly customers are. Third, as a result, the seller ends up with mainly costly customers and has to charge a high price. Fourth, market institutions often arise that seek to profit by correcting the asymmetry in information.

2. Market failure will arises when customers who have lower costs (1) are priced out of the market and (2) would have paid a price acceptable to the seller otherwise. Market failure also occurs when customers do not get what they want due to a lack of information.

3. Market solutions to this failure include identifying which customers have low costs.

THE MARKET FOR LEMONS

Just as high-cost customers can drive out low-cost customers, poor-quality products can drive out high-quality products. The market for used cars illustrates this. If you buy a new car and then turn around the next day to sell it, its price will have fallen by several thousand dollars. Even though it is the same car as a new car, it is worth a lot less! Why? The reason is that buyers of used cars cannot easily judge the quality of the car. And even though your car may be in mint condition, other similar cars are being offered by sellers who are selling their car because they know their cars have higher repair costs and do not run well (these bad cars are known as "lemons"). Buyers of used cars, knowing that a large fraction of used cars are lemons, pay less for them.

The existence of asymmetrical information (in this case, informed sellers and uninformed buyers) results in lower prices for used cars. This in turn reduces the incentive for sellers of good cars to sell their cars. Fewer good cars increase the fraction of used cars that are lemons being offered for sale. In some cases, it is possible that lemons will drive all good cars out of the used car market. While this is possible, what is more likely is that owners of good cars will delay reselling their cars. This will increase the ratio of good cars to lemons as cars get older. As a result, good cars will fetch a higher relative price as they get older and so, if one has a good car, it pays to wait.

The four elements of asymmetric information are present in the used car market. The first element is that informed sellers of poor quality cars have an incentive to lie about the quality of their cars (because they then can get a higher price). The second element is that it is expensive for buyers to find out about the quality of used cars. The third element is a market failure: Some sellers of good cars cannot find a mutually advantageous price for their car. The fourth element is that market institutions will arise that try to correct the asymmetric information. One way is for sellers to offer a warranty to sellers guaranteeing the car for a certain period. Another way is the existence of brand name used car dealers (such as CarMax) that inspect and guarantee the cars they sell. Similarly, new car dealers offer used cars that they certified to be fully inspected and in good shape.

PROBLEM

There are two types of one-year-old cars: lemons (with high repair costs) and cherries (with low repair costs). Buyers are willing to pay $10,000 for a lemon and $20,000 for a cherry.

a. Suppose that half the cars sold are lemons. If buyers cannot tell lemons from cherries, what price are they willing to pay for a used car (assuming they are willing to pay the expected or average value)?

b. Suppose another brand of car is more reliable such that only one fourth of the cars are lemons. If the other values are the same, what price will buyers be willing to pay for a used car?

c. How would reducing the fraction of lemons affect the price of new cars?

SOLUTION

a. $15,000. $15,000 = ½ × $10,000 + ½ × $20,000.

b. $ 17,500. $17,500 = ¼ × $10,000 + ¾ × $20,000.

c. Comparing b to a, one can see that more reliable cars will have better resale value. This increases the value of the car to new car buyers and, correspondingly, the price consumers are willing to pay for more reliable cars.

MARKET SIGNALING

When asymmetrical information causes some people to withdraw from a market, they have an incentive to engage in activities that send a "market signal" indicating that they have the traits other people want. For example, a car dealer offering a one-year warranty on a used car is sending a signal to buyers that the car dealer's car is of better quality. Similarly, employees may engage in community service to signal that they are good management material.

Market signaling is effective if *only* those who have better traits can engage in it. To illustrate this, consider a company that offers higher quality goods but can't get a price reflecting the higher quality because buyers cannot easily tell that the company's goods are high quality. This is a market failure if buyers would be willing to pay a mutually agreeable high price if they did know the company's quality. One solution is for the company to establish a brand name. This may involve selling at a low price for a sufficient length of time until the market comes to recognize the company's high quality. Once the company has established its brand name, its brand name becomes an asset. In turn, most customers expect high quality from the company since the company has an incentive to not cut back on its quality because this would reduce the value of an expensively acquired asset (its brand name). Another way to create a brand name is to have expensive ads, featuring expensive celebrities endorsing the company's product. Customers would expect the company to offer higher quality products because the company cannot afford to waste the ads on a poor-quality product that few will buy again. Note that for expensive advertising to work, it must have the key feature of a market signal: It must be so costly that the poor-quality companies cannot afford to use it.

Education may be a market signal. Assume that some workers are high-productivity workers and that others are low-productivity workers. Assume further that employers cannot tell which is which (the reason usually given for this odd assumption is that workers are in teams). Finally, assume education does not affect the productivity of workers (that is, it only serves to signal which workers are which). Education can provide such a market signal only if high-productivity workers find it profitable to get an education. Suppose the lifetime productivity is Y for high-productivity workers and X for low-productivity workers. Further, suppose education cost C_Y for high-productivity workers and C_X for low-productivity workers such that $C_X > C_Y$ (the reason usually given for this is that X workers are also less productive in getting an education so that it takes them longer). The conditions for only high-productive workers to get educated are:

1. $Y -$ Average$(X, Y) > C_Y$ and

2. $Y - X < C_X$

where Average(X, Y) is the productivity of the average worker in the population. If high-productivity workers (and only high-productivity workers) get an education, they will earn a lifetime income worth Y. If no one gets an education, they will earn the average productivity (Average(X, Y)). If only one high-productivity worker gets an education, the increase in lifetime pay is $Y -$ Average(X,Y). If this pay covers the cost of education, workers will get the education. This is condition 1. As more go to college, this difference gets wider, until it equals $Y - X$ when all (and only) high-productivity workers get an education. Condition 2 makes sure no low-productivity worker gets an education. While the first low-productivity worker would increases lifetime earnings by $Y - X$, this does not cover their cost of education (C_X). Condition 2 is necessary because if low-productivity workers do get an education, education cannot be a market signal, and no one would get an education.

PROBLEM

There are equal numbers of two types of workers, Y and X. Y workers are more productive, producing a lifetime output worth $400,000. X workers are less productive with a lifetime output worth $300,000. Employers cannot, without a market signal, tell them apart. What is the most that education can cost workers Y such that they still get an education? What is the minimum an education must cost workers X so that none of them get an education?

SOLUTION

If none get an education, the average lifetime pay will be $350,000. If education separates Y from X workers, it will increase by $50,000 the lifetime pay of the first Y to get an education.

Thus, education has to cost $50,000 or less for a Y worker to want to get an education. When more Y workers get an education, the pay for X workers will fall to $300,000. If one X worker got an education, it would increase that worker's lifetime earnings by $100,000. No X will get an education as long as education costs more than $100,000.

In this example, when no one gets an education, all workers are paid the average productivity (low-productivity workers getting more than they produce and high-productivity workers getting less). If this does not affect overall productivity or hours of work (such that all workers have jobs and work the same hours as they would at a higher or lower wage), then this is not a market failure. All mutually advantageous trades are taking place. In this case, education would be an economic waste because it does not raise the productivity of workers; instead, at a great cost, it just reallocates pay from low- to high-productivity workers. There are two objections to the idea that the only role for education is to signal employers which workers are more productive. One is that employers can directly observe the productivity of most workers in less time than it takes for a worker to get a college education. Two is that education, if it is only a market signal, is a very expensive signal (a college education often costs over $100,000 in direct costs and foregone income). It seems that alternative and cheaper signals would arise (such as achievement tests).

YOU SHOULD REMEMBER

1. Sellers of higher quality products have an incentive to use costly market signals to indicate that their products are better quality.

2. For a market signal to be credible, it must be too costly for low-quality products to use and sufficiently costly that high-quality producers investing in it would not want to risk losing their investment by cutting the quality of their products.

3. Brand names are one type of market signal. Education may be another.

MORAL HAZARD

Moral hazard is the risk that one party to a contract will change his or her behavior to the detriment of the other party of the contract. An example is people with insurance who take more risk because they know they are protected by the insurance. As a result, the insurance company gets more claims. For example, a person with fire insurance is less likely to buy a fire extinguisher. A more extreme example is a person with car insurance who deliberately lets her car be stolen because she can get more from the insurance company than by selling it. Other examples include people who overbuild in flood planes because they have flood insurance and people who do not secure their property in a hurricane because they believe the government will pay for all damages.

Moral hazard raises the cost of insurance and can result in market failure when some people don't buy policies that have become too expensive due to the added costs from moral hazards.

Moral hazard is an example of asymmetric information. Buyers of the insurance have an incentive to not tell the insurance company that they will act in a risky way that could prove costly to the insurance company.

This may seem to not be a problem if everyone was equally abusive. In this case, there is no adverse selection, and the added cost would just be added to the policy's cost. Yet from the economic point of view, moral hazards can result in market inefficiency. This is because insurance rates typically reflect the average cost of all policyholders rather than the costs incurred by the owner of a policy. As a result, each policyholder bears only a fraction of the cost they impose on the company (and, eventually, on all other policy holders). This leads to excessive costs. To illustrate, suppose all holders of a health insurance policy could get procedure X. They value it at $400 and it costs the insurance company $1,000. Suppose the insurance company passes on the cost to customers in the form of higher rates. Each individual will get the procedure as it is worth $400 to them and the cost of their getting the procedure costs them very little (their policy will go up by $1,000 divided by the number of policyholders). However, because everyone acts this way, the net effect is that all policyholders will be worse off by $600 ($1,000 in higher insurance costs minus the $400 value of the policy).

Moral hazard can result in market failure when policyholders run up costs in excess of benefits such that some people drop the policy. It is also a problem when people differ in the propensity to engage in costly activity. Moral hazard occurs when a person has a costly characteristic because of the nature of the contract, while adverse selection occurs when costly characteristics exist independent of the contract and vary over the population.

Insurance companies seek to avoid moral hazard problems in several ways. One way is to insure less than 100 percent of the risk. For example, most auto insurance companies will pay less than the resale value of a car if it is in an accident or is stolen. Similarly, fire insurance companies rarely insure the full value of a building. Also, health insurance companies have deductibles that impose some fraction of the health care costs on the person incurring the cost.

PROBLEM

A state required car insurances to pay the full blue book value for cars. What happened to auto thefts? Why?

SOLUTION

Auto thefts went up. People whose car was worth less than its blue book value found it profitable to leave their cars where they would be stolen and then collect on the insurance.

PROBLEM

What happens to the number of businesses that burn up when the economy goes into a recession?

SOLUTION

The number of fires goes up. When a recession causes the value of the business to fall, at some point its value as a going business falls below the amount for which it was insured. The moral hazard occurs if business owner then burns it down (or, more innocently, neglects its upkeep such that the risk of fire increases).

YOU SHOULD REMEMBER

1. Moral hazard and adverse selection are both causes of market failure.

2. Moral hazard occurs when people take more risks because they are insured for the losses. For example, people with health insurance may take less care of themselves knowing the insurance company will pay for a large fraction of their health care costs. The added costs of these risks add to the expense of the insurance, leading some to not buy it. This creates the market failure.

PRINCIPAL-AGENT PROBLEMS

Many studies indicate that paying workers piece rate (that is, by the amount they produce) instead of by the hour significantly increases worker productivity and worker pay. Yet few firms use piece rates. The human resource literature gives many reasons why, but a key reason is the difficulty in charging a piece rate when the firm modernizes the plant. After modernization, workers will produce more due to the modernization even if they do not work harder. For the firm to earn the full return of its cost of the modernization, it must reduce the piece rate. On the other hand, workers may not trust the firm to set the new piece rate so that they are fairly rewarded for their added effort. The dissatisfaction that this creates often leads the firm to give up on piece rates and instead pay an hourly rate.

The history of piece rates reflects the complexity of what is known as the principal-agent problem. In the principal-agent problem, the principal's and the agent's interests differ, and as each cannot easily monitor what the other is doing, the result can be that less than optimal work is done.

In the case of piece rates, the principal is the employer, and the agent is the worker. The employer wants the best effort (which is defined below) from the worker. Because it is too expensive to monitor workers fully, workers may not give the employer their best effort. In the principal-agent literature, workers will shirk if not offered sufficient incentive.

The goal is to set up a mutually efficient contract between the principal and the agent. There is a demand and supply curve for the worker's effort. The demand price on the demand curve reflects the marginal benefit the employer gains from each added unit of effort. The supply price on the supply curve reflects the marginal cost of effort to the worker (in foregone time, energy, and effort). The worker's best effort is the level where the demand and supply curve cross: where the last dollar of effort yields the firm one dollar of benefit. This is where the joint benefit is highest.

What would a contract between employer and workers look like where the workers are giving their best effort? First, on the margin, the workers must be paid at least a dollar for the last unit of effort; otherwise, they will not supply the effort. Second, the workers must be better off (or at least as well off) working for this firm as for other firms. Third, the firm has to be better off (or at least as well off) with these workers as with other potential hires. That is, the contract must be efficient and mutually advantageous.

At this point, the economic literature has some good news and some bad news. The good news is that economists know what this "perfect" contract is (at least in the case where everyone can tell what the future will be and no one is adverse to risk). The firm pays each worker its total profit, and, in return, each worker pays the firm a hiring fee to hire them. The hiring fee equals the firm's profit minus the worker's cost of working (including the cost of their best effort). Workers will give the best effort as on the margin;

the last dollar of effort will increase their pay (the total profits of the firm) by one dollar. The firm in return will be able to hire the worker at a competitive price as workers compete to get the job by bidding the hiring fee up until the difference between profits and the hiring fee equals the minimum salary for which they are willing to work. The bad news is that this "perfect" contract is impossible! It would involve billions of dollars being traded between each worker and the firm.

Put another way, the principle-agent problem is a problem because it is hard to solve. The nature of capitalism is that people try to solve problems by trying various arrangements until, through competition, the best and most productive arrangement emerges. Let us now consider why, in the context of the principal-agent context, some of the arrangements might be optimal in the "second-best" sense: not as good as the "perfect" contract but close enough to be useful.

The most common contract is to pay workers by the hour. One way to motivate workers with hourly pay is to pay them more than they can get elsewhere. In turn, if workers are caught shirking (not putting forth their best effort), they are fired. Knowing that they may be fired and that they will lose a valuable job, workers have an incentive to police themselves and not shirk. The higher wage may not only pay for itself in higher productivity but also in the reduced need for the firm to monitor workers closely (for example, it may be able to hire fewer managers per worker). This is an example of an efficiency wage, a wage deliberately set above market levels to encourage workers to work harder.

PROBLEM

> Assume a worker gains $10,000 in leisure time by goofing off on the job. They can earn $50,000 elsewhere. If the worker goofs off, there is a 5 percent chance the boss will catch the worker and fire them. Assume that if the worker is fired, the worker values the loss of every dollar in annual pay above $50,000 at $10 (because the worker will lose the added dollar this year, next year, and for every year he planned to have otherwise worked for his current employer). What is the minimum the firm must pay in annual pay to encourage the worker to not shirk? Assume the worker is risk-neutral (only caring about averages).

SOLUTION

> $70,000. The benefit of shirking is $10,000 a year. The average cost of shirking, in a year, is 5 percent, of what the worker will lose if fired (this is the "average" of 95 times not having any cost and of 5 times losing their job). The minimum loss that will leave the worker indifferent between shirking and not shirking will be $200,000 (as 5 percent of $200,000 is $10,000). The annual addition to their salary above $50,000 must be $20,000 (working back-

wards, the worker will value losing the annual $20,000 premium at ten times its value). Their salary equals $50,000 plus $10,000/(0.05 × 10).

PROBLEM

How will this premium (the pay over and above $50,000) change (a) if the probability of being caught and fired rises to 20 percent, and if instead (b) the worker plans to stay with the firm for a shorter period of time so that every dollar of lost annual pay is only worth five times its value?

SOLUTION

For (a), the premium will fall to $5000 ($10,000/(0.20 × 10). Employers can pay less when improvements in monitoring technology make it easier to catch shirkers. For (b), the premium rises to $40,000. The shorter the job horizons of workers, the more expensive it is to motivate them to work hard. This is in part why many firms opposed legislation mandating that they give workers advance warning of a plant closing.

Besides hourly pay, many workers receive some form of profit sharing. Most economists are skeptical of profit sharing because each worker only receives a small fraction of the total profits. For example, if there are 1,000 workers and a worker, by one dollar more of extra effort, increased the company's profits by $20, that worker would only get 2 cents ($20/1,000) in extra pay. On the other hand, it is cheap to tell other workers to work hard (as they bear the cost), so profit sharing may encourage workers to monitor each other. This is why profit sharing among members of a small work team is often an effective tool to motivate workers.

Profit sharing can be made more effective if there is a cut-off level where workers only get paid the bonus when profits rise above a certain level. This will increase productivity because workers will work hard enough to make the cut-off level.

One problem with profit sharing is that profits are partially determined by luck and in part by the efforts of the workforce. This uncertainty makes it less attractive to workers if they do not like wide swings in their pay from year to year. To reduce the element of luck, some firms replace profit sharing with bonuses based upon some formula that is more directly related to worker effort (for example, some index of the quantity and quality of the goods being produced).

The principal-agent problem also exists outside the workplace. Patients (as principals) hire doctors (the agents) to look out for their interest. However, doctors have their own interests. For example, a doctor may recommend an operation that they would not themselves undergo in similar circumstances. Home sellers (as principals) hire real estate agents (the agents) to sell their home. The agent has an incentive to sell the home as fast as possible (thereby reducing their workload) and so may underprice the home to sell it quickly.

YOU SHOULD REMEMBER

1. Principal-agent problems involve a principal who hired the agent to do some task. The problem arises when it is impossible to monitor directly whether the agent is making the best effort in doing what the principal wants.

2. Piece rates and profit sharing are methods that try to tie the agent's interest to the interest of the principal.

3. An efficiency wage is a wage above market wage that increases workers productivity. If workers shirk and get caught, they will suffer by being fired and then having to work at a firm paying a lower wage. This motivates them to not shirk and to be more productive.

KNOW THE CONCEPTS

DO YOU KNOW THE BASICS?

1. What is market failure? What are some of the causes of market failure?
2. What are the four elements usually present when there is asymmetric information?
3. How and when does asymmetric information cause market failure?
4. How and when does adverse selection raise costs?
5. What is the moral hazard problem for insurance companies?
6. How does moral hazard lead to market failure?
7. How might an expensive advertising campaign be a market signal?
8. What is a necessary condition for a market signal to work?
9. How might paying a higher wage solve, at least partially, the principal-agent problem between employers and workers? How might this save the employer money?

10. When will profit sharing be effective in motivating workers to work harder?

TERMS FOR STUDY

adverse selection
asymmetric information
efficiency wage
lemon problem
market failure

market signaling
moral hazard
principal-agent problem
shirking

PRACTICAL APPLICATION

1. John's daily productivity depends upon his skill, his time on the job, and the effort he makes. Suppose that in a given day of work, he has a choice of how much effort (E) to expend. The following table shows the cost to John of expending each added unit of effort and the corresponding benefit to the firm of the added unit of his effort:

E John's Effort	Marginal Benefit to Firm of Added Unit Effort	Marginal Cost to John of Added Unit of Effort
1	$50	$5
2	$40	$10
3	$30	$15
4	$20	$20
5	$10	$25

a. What is John's best effort level?

b. If the firm pays John by the hour (and there is no way they can monitor his effort level), how much effort will he put forth?

c. Suppose the firm can observe John's effort, what price should they be willing to pay (assuming they pay the same price for each unit)? How might the firm increase its profits by paying a different price for each unit of effort?

d. Suppose that the firm cannot observe John's effort but offers him 50 percent of its profits (the increase in profits from more E is assumed to equal the marginal benefit to the firm of more E). How much E will John put forth?

e. Suppose the firm has five workers and it splits all its profits among all five workers such that each gets a fifth of its profits. How much effort will each worker put forth? Suppose instead that workers are in a team and the team gets the full profits? How many units of effort will the team, as a group, be willing to supply?

2. There are nine people in a town. Person 1 eats $1 of food at a meal, person 2 eats $2 of food at a meal, and so forth (so person 9 eats $9 of food at a meal). Each person is willing to pay a price equal to twice the cost of food they eat (so that person 2 will pay up to $4 to eat at a restaurant). Burr's Buffet cannot tell who will eat what amount so it charges the same price to all persons. Assume Burr will set its price so that the value of the meal to its marginal customer (this is, the meal's demand price) equals its average meal cost. (If Burr is a monopoly, it would charge a price exceeding its average cost. However, if there is competition in the restaurant business, this assumption produces the competitive outcome that in the long run price reflects average cost). What will the price of meal be and how many people will eat at Burr's? What is the market failure in this case?

3. If a computer is good, customers value one year of its services at $1,000 and a second year at $1,000. Assume that if the computer is good, 10 percent of its customers will sell it after one year. If it is bad, it goes bad at the end of the first year: Customers value one year of the bad computer's service at $1,000 and a second year at $0. If it is bad, all customers will sell it after one year. Assume that 20 percent of the computers are bad and that 80 percent are good. Assume customers cannot tell whether a computer is good or bad so that computers sell for its average value (accounting for the mix of good and bad computers).

   a. What is the price of a one-year-old computer? (Assume price reflects its average value.) Next calculate the price of a new computer? Assume the price of a new computer reflects its value to the marginal customer who plans to sell it in one year.

   b. Suppose a better brand of computers only has 10 percent bad computers? What will its used and new price be?

4. In a small town, there are two people who paint homes. Jim does a bad job such that when customers find out (too late) how bad his work is, they do not use him again. Mary does a good job such that customers come back to Mary. Both charge the same price for painting a house and make a $400 profit from each job. The value to Mary of repeat business is $1,000 as it allows her to work year-round. New customers, without a market signal, cannot tell who is better. If one person advertises and the other does not, new customers go to the person who advertises (if both advertise, half go to each). What must advertising cost (per new customer) at a *minimum* (!) for it to be worthwhile for Mary to purchase?

5. Suppose the federal government insures deposits at savings and loan banks and charges a premium that did not vary with the risk of loans. What type of asymmetrical information problem will likely be the result of this policy?

6. A salesperson if lucky can sell $200,000 if she works hard, and if the salesperson is lucky but does not work hard she will sell $150,000. If she is unlucky, she can sell $150,000 if she works hard and $100,000 if she does not work hard. The added effort and time to work hard costs the salesperson $25,000 (that is, she must get a minimum $25,000 extra to work hard). The employer cannot tell if the salesperson is lucky or not, nor can the employer tell if the salesperson is working hard. The salesperson, if she quits, could earn $60,000 every year at another firm (without having to work hard at that firm). Compare the following pay packages for their cost to the firm and for their ability to motivate the worker:

    Plan A: Pay the salesperson $90,000 every year and demand hard work.

    Plan B: Pay the salesperson what they sell.

    Plan C: Pay the salesperson $60,000 plus 60 percent of what she sells (but this bonus can be no more than $30,000).

    Plan D: Pay the salesperson $60,000 plus 60 percent of what she sells over $100,000.

7. The Smiley Face Fire Insurance Company was insuring $100,000 homes for 90 percent of their value (that is, $90,000). Its premium was $900 a year. It decides to offer a new fire insurance policy that pays $120,000 when the $100,000 home burns. It increases its premium to $1,200. If it was breaking even on its old policy, will it make or lose money on the new policy?

8. The interest rate one pays on a loan depends on one's credit record (which is available from one of the major credit reporting companies). The worse one's credit record, the higher the interest rate. What would happen if the government outlawed credit reports?

9. Workers in large workplaces (with over 1,000 workers at one location) get paid more than they do in smaller work places. If workers are similar in skill and quality, why might an employer with a large workplace pay more?

10. Health insurance is often provided by large employers to their workers. The employer can provide the insurance at a reasonable cost because it does not have an adverse selection of workers. Does the same logic apply to an employer whose workers usually stay in the job a short time?

ANSWERS

KNOW THE CONCEPTS

1. Market failure occurs when a mutually advantageous trade does not take place. As a result, the market does not efficiently allocate goods and services. It can be caused by asymmetric information, monopoly, externalities, public goods, and poorly organized markets.

2. Asymmetric information occurs when one person knows more than another. One element is that one person has an incentive to not reveal information that is relevant to the person they are trading with. The second element is that the other person cannot easily find out this information. The third element is that they do not make a mutually advantageous trade. When this occurs, the market is said to have "failed." The fourth element is that people (often intermediaries) make a profit by finding ways to get people trading who were prevented from doing so by the asymmetry in their information.

3. Asymmetric information is harmful when it causes people to not make mutually advantageous trades. The harm is the net benefit lost. The main reasons asymmetric information leads to market failure are adverse selection and moral hazard.

4. Adverse selection can occur when some customers can cost a seller (such as an insurance firm) more than others and the seller can't tell who the costly customers are. As a result, the seller must charge a price that covers the average cost of its customers. This in turn attracts only the higher cost customers, raising the average cost and the price. The result is that low-cost customers are shut out of the market.

5. Even if insurance companies could avoid adverse selection, they face the likelihood that customers will take more risks because they are covered for all or most of their losses. This raises the cost of the insurance and makes it less attractive when all customers take more risks. When only some of the customers take more risks, this makes the insurance less attractive (too costly) to those who do not take added risks.

6. In the case of insurance, when buyers of the policies take more risks because they are insured, this is called a moral hazard. It will result in an increase in the cost of the policy. This results in two social losses. First, there are the people who would have otherwise bought the policy but now find it too costly. This is a market failure. Second, those who continue to hold the policy may find the increase in premiums exceeds the value they gained from acting in a more risky manner (recall the example of people getting procedure X with health insurance). This is a loss because the cost exceeds the benefit.

7. If only producers of high-quality items can afford to advertise, then advertising could serve as a market signal to customers that the good is high quality. For example, producers of high-quality items might make more profit (perhaps due to greater customer loyalty) and are the only firms that can afford to pay for advertising. In turn, advertising lets them charge a higher price or attract more customers.

8. The market signal must be profitable to those who are more productive (or who offer higher quality goods or services), and just as important, it must not be profitable to those who are less productive (or who offer lower quality).

9. Wages that exceed market wages mean the worker will lose wealth if fired from the job. This may give them the incentive to exert more effort and be more productive so as to avoid being fired. If the worker is not worse off changing jobs, then it would pay to shirk as there is no cost to being caught (assuming the person gains utility from shirking).

10. If one's efforts substantially increase one's share of profits, then profit sharing will likely motivate workers. This applies mainly to heads of corporations and in firms with few workers. When one's share is small, profit sharing may motivate workers to monitor other workers. This can occur, for example, when goods are team produced.

PRACTICAL APPLICATION

1. **a.** Effort Level 4 (where the marginal benefit of the last unit of effort just covers its cost). Recall that cost is the minimum one needs to be paid to supply something, so if John is paid $20 a unit, he is willing to supply four units, not three.

   b. He will supply zero units of effort, as the first unit costs him $5 to supply and he gets no reward. An efficiency wage could motivate John to supply some level of effort, but only if the firm could monitor effort.

   c. If effort is discrete (as shown), it would make the most by paying $15 a unit and get three units of effort (the added cost of the fourth unit would be the increase in cost from paying $15 for three units ($45) to $20 for four units ($80), or $35). This is not worth the added marginal benefit of $30. However, there is no reason to pay the same price for each unit. If it pays $5 for the first unit, $10 for the second, and so forth, up to $20 for the fourth unit, the firm will make the highest possible profit and get four units of effort. Alternatively, it could simply pay John a bonus of $50 ($5 + $10 + $15 + $20) if John supplies four units of effort.

d. John gets half the marginal benefit to the firm for each added unit of effort. Thus, he gets $25 for the first unit, $20 for the second, $15 for the third, and $10 for the fourth. He will supply three units (whose benefit to Joe is $15 and covers his cost of $15).

e. Now each worker gets one-fifth of the company's marginal benefit for each added unit of effort. The first unit adds $10 to their pay, the second unit adds another $8. Workers will only supply one unit (as it adds $10 to their pay and costs them only $5 to supply; they will not supply the second unit as it only adds $8 to their pay and costs them $10 to supply). As a team member, each worker gets one-fifth of their effort plus one-fifth of the effort of each and every team member. Thus, each member gets the full marginal benefit to the firm assuming all team members put forth that unit of effort. Because they are a team and know each other, they can police each other to all supply the same level of effort. They will choose to supply, as a team, four units of effort per worker.

2. To do this problem, start with customer 9, calculate the demand price and the supply price, and work down until the two are equal. If Burr charges $18, only person 9 will eat at Burrs. The price of the meal will be $18 and the average cost of a meal will be $9. If it charges $16, persons 8 and 9 will eat at Burr's, and the average cost will be $8.50. Continuing, one will find that the demand price will equal the supply price (the average cost) when it charges $6, with customers 3 through 9 eating at its restaurant. The market failure is that customers 1 and 2 find Burr's price too high, yet, if Burr knew what they would eat, the opportunity for mutually beneficial trade exists. In particular, customer 2's demand price of $4 exceeds the $2 cost, but he does not eat at Burr's. This is a social loss of $2 (which, for this missed trade, equals its demand price minus its supply price). Customer 1's demand price of $2 exceeds the cost of $1, and she does not eat at Burr's. This is a social cost of $1.

3. a. For every 100 customers, 80 of them will have good computers. Of these, 8 (10 percent of 80) will sell their computer after one year. The other 20 customers will have bad computers, and all of them will sell their computers. Thus, 8/28ths of the used computers sold will be good and worth $1,000. The rest are worthless. The used price will be the average value or $286 (= 8/28 × $1,000). Those buying a new computer for only a year will pay $1,000 plus the resale price of $286 (ignoring time discounting): $1,286.

b. For every 100 customers, 90 of them will have good computers, and 9 of them will sell them after one year. All 10 bad computers will be sold after one year. The used price will be 9/19ths of $1,000 or $474. The computer's average value to a one-year buyer is $1,000 plus $474 or $1,474. Better quality means a higher sales price.

4. The value of a new customer to Jim is $400. For advertising to be a market signal, the price of advertising must exceed $400 per customer to make advertising not worthwhile for Jim. If the advertising per new customer costs more than $400 but less than $1,400, it will be worthwhile to Mary. Firms that advertise will, in this case, be those that have higher quality and repeat business.

5. There will be a moral hazard problem. Savings and loan banks that make riskier loans can charge borrowers a higher interest rate and, in turn, pay savers a higher interest rate. Savers will put their money in savings and loan banks paying a higher rate because they are protected if the loans turn out bad. This is an example of the moral hazard problem: Those who are insured from loss take greater risks. The result in the 1980s was a loss to government (who insured the banks) that exceeded $150 billion due to bad loans granted by savings and loan banks.

6. If the salesperson does not work hard, she will be willing to work for this firm if she gets $60,000 or more. If she does work hard, she must get $85,000 or more ($60,000 for foregone opportunities plus $25,000 for added effort). In addition, she will only work hard if that results in $25,000 (or more) in pay that she would get if she did not work hard.

   Plan A: She will not work harder as working hard does not increase her pay (she might work hard if the firm could monitor her effort, but it cannot).

   Plan B: The worker will earn $50,000 more if she works harder, which more than covers her cost. This is the problem with Plan B: The firm pays the worker far too much compared to other firms— $200,000 in unlucky years and $150,000 in lucky years.

   Plan C: The worker will earn 60 percent of the added $50,000 more in pay if she works hard. This amount, $30,000, covers her cost of $25,000, so she will work hard. However, the firm pays the worker too much: $180,000 in lucky years ($60,000 plus 60 percent of $200,000) and $150,000 in unlucky years ($60,000 plus 60 percent of 150,000).

   Plan D: The worker works more because the extra pay from working hard (60 percent of the $50,000 in added sales due to working hard) covers the cost of working hard. It is also cheaper than plans B and C. It costs the firm $120,000 in lucky years ($60,000 plus 60 percent of $100,000) and $90,000 in unlucky years ($60,000 plus 60 percent of $50,000).

7. Let f be the fraction of homes that burn down. Ignoring other costs, the firm will break even if $900 = f × $90,000. So f must equal 0.01. Under the new policy, it will break even if $1,200 = f × $120,000. Thus, if f remains at 0.01 (that is, if one percent of the homes burn down a year), it will break even. But will f remain the same? Under the old policy,

homeowners had an incentive to maintain their homes to prevent fires as the homeowner would lose $10,000 if their home burned down. Under the new policy, they gain $20,000 if their home burns down! This gives them less incentive to take steps to prevent a fire. As a result, f is likely to be higher and the Smiley Face Fire Insurance Company will now lose money.

8. If the government outlawed credit reports, lenders cannot tell which customers are more likely to pay back their loans. They would then face an adverse selection problem. The customers least likely to pay back their loans will be the most willing to borrow. This will push up interest rates. More honest customers will be priced out of the loan market because they will find interest rates too high.

9. It is usually more costly to monitor workers in a large workplace. An employer with a large workplace might pay more to encourage workers to monitor their own effort. Workers with higher wages don't want to get fired and so will try not to shirk and to do a good job. The higher way, in turn, allows the employer to spend less on supervisors and other methods of monitoring workers. Small employers usually can quickly look over workers and tell what the workers are doing. Thus, they do not need to pay an efficiency wage.

10. The same logic does not apply to firms with transitory employment. Recall that adverse selection occurs when customers know their likely health care costs and the insurer does not. In this case, the firm can be thought of as the insurer. A large firm that retains workers will likely hire most of its workers when they are young and before most people become aware of their long-term health status. Because people when they are young do not know their long-term health care costs, they will not adversely select working at large firms providing health insurance. This is not the case of employers with a transitory workforce. If it cannot discriminate in favor of young workers, and if it provides health insurance, it will likely get an adverse selection of workers who have high health care costs. As higher health care costs are paid for out of wages, the resulting low wages will drive away those who are healthy. They will end up working for employers not offering health insurance.

22
MONOPOLIES

KEY TERMS

monopoly the only seller of a good that has no close substitutes.

price discrimination the selling of the same good at different prices.

price searchers buyers or sellers having large enough shares of a market such that when they buy or sell more, they change the market price.

A firm is a **monopoly** (sometimes called a pure monopoly) when (1) it is the only firm selling the good, (2) it has no current or potential rivals, and (3) its good has no close substitutes. Unlike the customers of a perfectly competitive firm, the customers of a monopolistic firm cannot go elsewhere.

A **price searcher** is any buyer or seller who influences price. When a seller is a price searcher, the seller can lower the market price by selling more. In contrast, a perfectly competitive firm is a **price taker** ("taking" the price as given) since the competitive firm can sell all it wants without depressing the market price. Each price taker faces a horizontal demand curve for output; a price searcher faces a downward-sloping demand curve.

A monopoly is one of several types of price searchers that we shall discuss in this chapter and the next.

WHY DO MONOPOLIES EXIST?

Monopolies (and other types of price searchers) exist because of barriers to entry and cost advantages.

BARRIERS TO ENTRY
Barriers to entry keep potential competition away so that a monopoly can make a profit in the long run without worrying about new rivals coming on the scene. The main barriers to entry are:

1. *Legal Restrictions:* The government limits entry into many industries (such as telephone and electricity) and occupations (e.g., by the licensing of doctors and dentists).

2. *Patents:* The government provides barriers to entry to inventors and artists for a certain number of years by granting them patents and copyrights. This prohibits others from copying their ideas.

3. *Control of Strategic Resources:* The ownership of a strategic resource needed to produce a good prevents rivals from entering. For example, most of the world's diamond mines are controlled by DeBeers.

COST ADVANTAGES

A firm may have a monopoly because no one else can produce the good as cheaply. This may be due to:

1. *Economies of Scale:* If economies of scale are so large that a firm can produce all the output of an industry and still have falling average costs, then it will be able to underprice any potential rival, driving the rival out of the business.

2. *Technological Superiority:* By investing in research, a firm may be able to keep ahead of rivals by being able to produce the good at a lower cost than they can.

YOU SHOULD REMEMBER

1. A monopoly is the only seller of a good.

2. A price searcher will reduce the market price for its good when it sells more. A monopoly and other types of price searchers face a downward-sloping demand curve for their output.

3. Monopolies are protected from competition by barriers to entry or by having lower costs.

BASIC ELEMENTS

MARGINAL REVENUE

A monopoly faces a downward-sloping demand curve: To sell more, it must lower its price. Consider Table 22–1.

Table 22–1. The Effect of Price on Marginal Revenue

Demand Curve		Revenue	
Price	Quantity Demanded	Total Revenue $(P \times Q)$	Marginal Revenue
$10	1	$10	$10
9	2	18	8
8	3	24	6
7	4	28	4
6	5	30	2
5	6	30	0
4	7	28	–2
3	8	24	–4
2	9	18	–6
1	10	10	–8

The first two columns show the demand curve facing the monopoly firm. As it sells more, price falls.

$$\text{Total Revenue} = \text{Price} \times \text{Quantity}$$

Marginal revenue is the change in total revenue due to one more unit of output.

Facts About Marginal Revenue

1. Marginal Revenue = Price – Loss from Price Cut on Prior Output.
   For example, the fourth unit of output in Table 22–1 has a price of $7. So the firm generates $7 in earnings from it. However, to sell the fourth unit, the firm had to cut the price by $1, so it lost $3 on the first three units of output. Therefore, it generated $4 in earnings (which equals the *MR* of the fourth unit).

2. *MR* < *P* whenever the firm has to cut its price to sell more. So for all price searchers, *MR* < *P*! (This is true regardless of the shape of the demand curve, as long as it is downward-sloping.)

3. The firm will *never* produce where *MR* is negative. This will lower its total revenue and its profits.

4. Total revenue is largest at the level of output at which *MR* = 0. Up to this point, each added unit of output increases the firm's total revenue (since *MR* > 0). However, do not confuse total revenue with total profit: The firm will not produce where total revenue is highest but rather where total profit is highest.

5. When demand is elastic, more output increases total revenue, and so $MR > 0$. In general we have:

Table 22–2. How Elasticity of Demand Affects Marginal Revenue

ELASTICITY OF DEMAND	MARGINAL REVENUE
Elastic (>1)	Positive
Unitary Elastic (= 1).	Zero
Inelastic (< 1)	Negative

6. Because of 3 and 5 above, a firm will never produce where the firm's demand is inelastic. Remember that we are talking about the demand curve *facing the firm*! For example, farmers produce where the market demand for wheat is inelastic. This does not contradict what we just said, because the demand curve facing *each* farmer is *perfectly* elastic.

7. If the demand schedule is a downward-sloping straight line, then (a) the marginal revenue curve is twice as steep as the demand curve (for example, in Table 22–1, for every $1 fall in price, *MR* falls $2) and (b) the *MR* curve intersects the bottom axis at half the output the demand curve does. In Figure 22–1, the demand curve intersects the horizontal axis at $Q = 10$, while the *MR* curve hits it at $Q = 5$. Remember that this is true only of *straight-line demand curves*!

8. The total revenue curve shows the total revenue at each level of output. *MR* is the slope of the total revenue curve: It is the "rise" in *TR* over the "run" of one more *unit*.

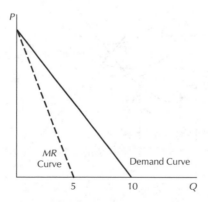

Figure 22–1. The Effect of Demand on Marginal Revenue

YOU SHOULD REMEMBER

1. Marginal revenue is the increase in total revenue from selling another unit of output.

2. $MR = P$ – Loss from Price Cut on Prior Output.

3. Price > Marginal Revenue (for all but the first unit of output).

4. Monopolies will produce only where $MR \geq 0$ and the firm's demand curve is elastic.

THE OUTPUT DECISION

Short-Run Rule: Produce where $MR = MC$ if $P \geq AVC$.
Long-Run Rule: Produce where $MR = MC$ if $P \geq ATC$.

By following these rules, the firm will maximize its profits (at $MR = MC$) and shut down only when it cannot cover its avoidable costs. Note that P, AVC, and ATC are all evaluated *at the output* the firm would produce (the Q where $MR = MC$) if it produces at all.

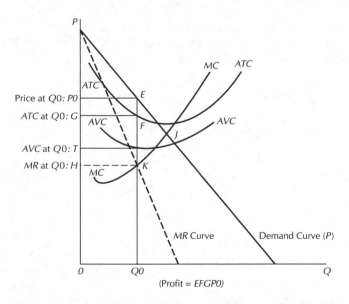

Figure 22-2. The Demand and Cost Curves of a Monopoly

Figure 22–2 shows the demand and costs curves facing a monopoly. The monopoly will maximize its profits at $Q0$ (the Q where $MR = MC$). $P0 > AVC$ at $Q0$ ($AVC = I$ at $Q0$) so it will produce in the short run. $P0 > ATC$ at $Q0$ ($ATC = G$ at $Q0$), so it produces in the long run. Its profits will be the average profit per unit ($P - ATC$) times output: $P0 - G \times Q0$ (or area $GFEPO$).

If its fixed costs were higher such that the ATC at $Q0 > P0$, it would shut down in the long run but produce in the short run. In the short run, a monopoly *can* make a loss. In Figure 22–3, the optimal output level (if output is to be produced) is at $Q = 3$ ($MR = MC = \$4$). In the short run, the firm will not shut down because $P = \$7$ exceeds its AVC of $6. It is making a loss of $15 ($TR = 3 \times \$7 = \$21$ less $TC = 3 \times \$12 = \$36$ equals a loss of $15). However, in the long run, it will shut down since P = $7 does not cover its ATC of $12.

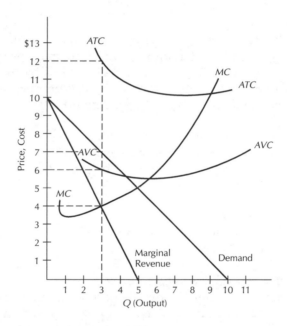

Figure 22-3. Visualizing a Monopoly's Shut-Down in the Long Run

FALLACIES AND FACTS

• *FALLACIES*

"Monopolies charge the highest price they can get."

The highest price comes from producing just one unit of output. As long as MR > MC, a monopoly will profit by selling more—which requires it to lower its price.

"Monopolies always make a profit."
In the short run, monopolies can incur losses, like other firms.

"Monopolies produce where they make the highest average profit per unit."
A firm making the highest profit per unit is *not* making the highest profit. It should produce more. For example, suppose the first unit of output adds $3 to profits; the next, $2; the third, $1; and the fourth subtracts $1 from profits. The highest average profit ($3) is from producing one unit. However, the *highest profit* ($6) is from producing three units (its average profit per unit of output is then only $2). A firm should always produce more when the additional output adds to profits, even if it adds less to profits than the average profit and thus lowers average profits.

• FACTS

Monopolies do not necessarily produce at the lowest average cost.
With perfect competition, in the long run, firms must produce at their lowest average cost (or be driven out of the business by those who do). Monopolies have no such competition. They may produce where *ATC* is falling, is at its minimum, or is rising (depending upon where $MR = MC$).

Monopolies produce only where demand is elastic.
Only over the range of output where demand is elastic is $MR > 0$. Since $MC > 0$, it can only be over this range that the profit-maximizing condition can hold: $MR = MC$.

Price exceeds marginal cost.
$P > MR$. Since $MR = MC$ at the monopolist's profit-maximizing level of output, it follows that $P > MC$.

A monopoly does not have a supply curve.
A supply curve tells how much firms will produce at each price. However, the monopoly is not a price taker: The monopoly sets its own price. A supply curve showing the quantity a monopoly will produce at a given price is *impossible to construct* because the same price on different demand curves will elicit different quantities from a monopoly. For example, while a monopoly will usually supply more when the price goes up, the opposite can happen. (See Practical Application, Question 5.)

Monopolies produce less than competitive firms when costs are the same.
If an industry has the same costs regardless of whether it has many firms or just one firm, then total industrial output will be greater when the industry is competitive (with many firms) than when it is monopolized by one firm. When there is only one firm, the one firm, operating as a monopoly, will see industry's demand curve as its own, such that its $MR < P$. When

there are many firms, each firm's share of total output will be so small that each firm's $MR = P$. Thus competitive firms will produce until $P = MC$, while a monopoly will stop short at a smaller output, where $P > MR = MC$. For example, if both marginal cost and average cost are \$2 in Table 21–1, the monopoly would produce 5 units of output (where $MR = MC = \$2$). If the same monopoly is replaced by many competitive firms with the same \$2 average and marginal cost, they will produce 9 units of output (where $P = MC = \$2$). Be careful! Both monopolies and competitive firms produce where $MR = MC$. The *difference* is that when the monopoly produces more, its price falls: its $MR < P$.

YOU SHOULD REMEMBER

1. To get the highest profits, a monopoly will produce where $MR = MC$ and will shut down if it cannot cover its avoidable cost. In the short run, it will shut down if at its best output, $P < AVC$; in the long run, if $P < ATC$.

2. For a monopoly, price exceeds marginal cost.

PRICE DISCRIMINATION

So far, we have assumed the monopoly sells all its output for the same price. But the monopoly may be able to charge a different price for different units. This is called **price discrimination** if the differences in price do *not* reflect cost differences (such as transportation costs). Recall that:

$$MR = P - \text{Loss on Prior Units from Price Cuts.}$$

By charging different prices, the monopoly does not have to cut its price on its prior output. As a result, its MR will be greater.

However, to charge different prices, it is *essential* that buyers cannot *resell* their purchases. Otherwise, the buyers who can buy at the lower price will resell to all other buyers, thereby destroying the ability of the monopoly to charge less to some but not all buyers.

Price discrimination results in:

1. More profits (because of the higher MR).

2. More output (because of the higher MR).

Perfect price discrimination occurs when the monopoly gets the demand price for *each* unit. In Table 22–1, the perfect price discriminator would sell the fourth unit for $7, the fifth for $6, the sixth for $5, and so forth. Thus, the monopoly does not lose from cutting its price on its prior output! Its $P = MR$. It produces the same output that a competitive industry would with its costs. For example, if its average and marginal cost is $2 at all levels of output, the monopoly would produce 9 units (as would a competitive industry).

TWO MAIN METHODS OF PRICE DISCRIMINATION

Method One: Volume Discounts

With volume discounts, customers pay less per unit when they buy more. If these discounts do not reflect a cost saving to the seller, then they are a form of price discrimination.

Example: More Profits from Volume Discounts

PROBLEM   A firm has a monopoly on a special spring water, which it produces at an average cost and marginal cost of $0 (i.e., it has no costs). Each customer's demand price for one quart of spring water is $4; for the second quart, $3; third, $2; fourth, $1; fifth, $–1. How much should the firm charge if it charges the same price for all units? How can it enhance its profits by using volume discounts?

SOLUTION   If it charges the same price for all units, its best profit per customer is $6 (at $P = 2 for three quarts). However, if it uses volume discounts, charging the demand price for each unit ($4 for the first quarter, $3 for the second, and so on), it will sell 4 quarts to each customer and will have a $10 profit per customer.

Some examples of volume discounts include the "frequent flier" bonuses offered by airlines, the "builders' discount" offered by building supply companies, and "buy two, get one free" offers.

Method Two: Segregated Markets

The monopoly may be able to segregate and separate markets and charge a different price in each. This will increase profits if the different markets have different elasticities of demand. Without segregating its markets, at its optimal output the monopolist's demand curve has an elasticity that equals a certain average of the elasticities in each separate market. However, by separating its markets, it will pay the monopoly to (1) raise prices in those markets that have the more inelastic demands and (2) lower prices in those markets with the more elastic demands.

The basic rule of making the most profits from separate markets is to (1) sell to each until the last unit sold in each has the *same* marginal revenue and (2) have $MR = MC$.

Example: Benefits of Price Discrimination

PROBLEM   Without separating two markets, a firm's $MR = \$15$, an average of Market A's MR of $25 and Market B's MR of $5. How can the firm gain by separating the two markets?

SOLUTION   By separating the two markets, the firm can withdraw one unit of output out of Market B (losing $5) and sell it to Market A (gaining $25), and so on net increase its total revenues by $20. The firm should continue doing this until both markets have the same MR (*and* an MR equal to its MC).

Examples of ways businesses segregate markets (and offer those with more elastic demand curves lower prices) include senior citizen discounts on drugs and travel, cents-off coupons (so that only those with coupons get a low price), special subscription rates for college students, and lower rentals by apartment owners only to new tenants.

YOU SHOULD REMEMBER

1. Price discrimination is the selling of the same good at different prices. Price differences reflecting only cost differences do not represent price discrimination.

2. Perfect price discrimination is when the seller prices each unit of output at its demand price.

3. For price discrimination to work, it must be difficult for buyers to resell to one another.

4. If a firm can sell its output at different prices in separate markets, it should allocate its output so that the last unit sold in each has the same marginal revenue and $MR = MC$. By doing this, the firm will charge more to those with inelastic demands and less to those with elastic demands.

5. All forms of price discrimination raise total output and increase total profits.

TAXES AND MONOPOLIES

LUMP-SUM TAX

A **lump-sum tax** is a tax that is the same no matter what the monopoly produces. Just as a change in fixed costs has no effect on *MC*, a lump-sum tax has no effect on *MC* and so has no effect on the monopoly's optimal output (where *MR = MC*) or price.

In contrast, a lump-sum tax will raise prices and reduce output in the long run in a competitive industry.

The lump-sum tax will force a monopoly to shut down in the short run if it exceeds *TR – TVC*, and in the long run if it exceeds *TR – TC*.

UNIT TAX

A **unit tax** is a tax per unit of output (for example, a $1-per-unit-output tax). It increases *MC*. So it has the same effect as an increase in wages or other variable costs. A unit tax *reduces output and raises prices* in both the long and short run.

The increase in price will be *less* than the increase in the unit tax for a straight-line demand curve.

Examples: Effect of Unit Tax on Monopoly

PROBLEM   A monopoly has the demand schedule shown in Table 22–1. Both its average cost and marginal cost are $4 for all units of output. The government then imposes a $2 unit tax on the monopoly's output. How much will its price go up?

SOLUTION   By $1. Before the tax, the monopoly had the highest profit by producing 4 units of output (whose *MR = MC* = $4) and then selling them at a price of $7. The tax increases the firm's effective *MC* to $6, so the firm will produce 3 units of output (whose *MR* = $6) and will sell them at a price of $8.

The price will go up more than the tax when the demand curve has a constant elasticity. For any demand curve, the relationship between marginal revenue and price is $MR = P(1 - 1/E)$. For a constant-elasticity demand curve, E stays the same for all Q. A monopoly will produce where $MR = MC$, so:

$$MC = P(1 - 1/E), \text{ or}$$
$$P = MC/(1 - 1/E).$$

If $E = 3$, for example, the $1 - 1/E$ term equals 2/3 and $P = MC/(2/3)$ or $P = 1.5\ MC$ since $1/(2/3)$ equals 1.5. If the before-tax *MC* remains the same, a tax of $10 per unit will increase the price 1.5 times the tax, in other words, by

$15. Note that this method works only if *MC* remains the same while *Q* falls. If *MC* does not remain constant, one has to use calculus to solve the problem.

PROBLEM A monopoly faces a constant-elasticity demand curve with an elasticity of 4. At all *Q*, it is $MC = ATC = \$24$. What price will it charge customers? If the government imposes a unit tax of $12 on the firm, what price will the monopoly charge?

ANSWER $P = MC/(1 - 1/4) = 4/3 \times MC$. Before the tax, its price will be $32 (solve $P = 4/3 \times \$24$). After the tax, its price will be $48 (solve $P = 4/3 \times \$36$). The price increases by $16 ($4/3 \times \$12$).

YOU SHOULD REMEMBER

1. An increase in fixed costs or a lump-sum tax will not affect a monopoly's output or price. The only exception is if the increase is so large that it forces the monopoly to shut down.

2. An increase in variable costs or a unit tax will decrease a monopoly's output and raise its price.

KNOW THE CONCEPTS

DO YOU KNOW THE BASICS?

1. What causes price to exceed marginal revenue for a monopoly?

2. Why does $P = MR$ for a competitive firm?

3. If a monopoly finds itself in an inelastic portion of a demand curve, how will it change its output?

4. Can monopolies make losses?

5. Does a monopoly produce where it makes the highest profit per unit of output?

6. Why does a monopoly not produce where $P = MC$?

7. How does price discrimination increase *MR*?

8. If a firm sells in different markets, in which ones should it charge a higher price?

9. How will a lump-sum tax affect a monopoly's output?

10. When will a monopoly's behavior differ from that of a competitive industry when a lump-sum tax is imposed?

TERMS FOR STUDY

marginal revenue   price discrimination
monopoly   price searcher
perfect price discrimination

PRACTICAL APPLICATION

1. A monopoly is currently producing 10 units of output. At $Q = 10$, $P = \$14$, and $MC = \$12$. At $Q = 9$, $P = \$15$. Should it have produced the tenth unit of output?

2. A monopoly that has both a constant average cost and marginal cost of $5 faces the following demand curve:

Quantity	1	2	3	4	5	6	7	8
Demand Price	$9	$8	$7	$6	$5	$4	$3	$2
Marginal Revenue								

    a. Fill in the marginal revenue of each unit.

    b. How many units will the monopoly produce?

    c. What is its profit?

3. If the monopoly in Question 2 above is a perfect price discriminator, then:

    a. What is the marginal revenue of each unit?

    b. How many units will the monopoly produce?

    c. What is its profit?

4. a. What lump-sum tax would shut down the monopolist in Question 2 (assuming it does not price discriminate as in Question 3)?

    b. What would be the effect of a smaller lump-sum tax?

    c. What would the effect of a $2 unit tax be on price and output?

5. While an increase in demand will usually cause a monopoly to produce more, this need not always be true, as this question shows.

    a. Suppose a monopoly can sell one widget at $4, two at $3, and three at $2, and that its marginal cost for each unit is $1. How many widgets will it produce?

b. Now suppose the demand curve shifts up so the monopoly can sell one unit at $10, two at $5, and three at $3. How many widgets will it produce now?

6. The following are examples of price discrimination. Indicate which group has the higher elasticity of demand:

   a. Drugstores give senior citizens a discount of 10 percent on their prescriptions.

   b. Children under 12 get into movies for half price.

   c. A grocery store offers "double couponing." For example, a 50¢-off coupon is worth $1 off.

7. A price ceiling of *P* makes the marginal revenue also equal to *P* for outputs from zero to the output corresponding to *P* on the demand curve. Suppose a monopoly can sell one unit of output for $20, two units for $18, three for $16, and so forth (it has to lower its price by $2 to sell each added unit). The marginal and average cost for all units of output is $6.

   a. What price will the monopoly charge? How many units will it produce?

   b. If the government imposes a price ceiling of $16, how many units will it produce? Of $10? Of $6?

   c. What will happen if it imposes a price ceiling of $4?

8. What is wrong with the following statements?

   a. "If a monopoly is making a loss where *MR* = *MC*, then it can raise its price to get rid of its loss."

   b. "Monopolies tend to be in markets where demand is inelastic."

   c. "Monopolies react to an increase in demand by raising price, not output."

9. In Market A, one unit sells for $10 and the quantity demanded goes up one unit for every $2 price decrease. In Market B, the demand price for one unit is $6 and the quantity demanded goes up one unit for every $1 price decrease. If you were a price discriminator with a constant marginal cost of $2, what price would you charge in each market?

10. The Computer Chip Company (CCC) sells its CCC-400-DX chip (for use in personal computers) for $500. It takes the same chip, cuts off part of it to make it less powerful, and sells it for $200 as the CCC-400-SX chip. Is this a form of price discrimination? Why?

ANSWERS

KNOW THE CONCEPTS

1. Because the demand curve facing a monopoly is downward sloping, to sell another unit of output, a monopoly has to reduce P for all its output. $MR = P$ – Loss due to price cut on prior output. So $MR < P$.

2. The competitive firm can sell all it wants without reducing its price. So $MR = P$ since it has no loss due to price cutting.

3. In the inelastic portion of the demand curve, the monopoly can cut output and increase total revenue. Since less output also lowers total cost, profits will go up. So the monopoly decreases output until demand is no longer inelastic.

4. Yes, in the short run.

5. No. As long as added output adds *anything* to profit, even when it adds less than the average profit, it should be produced.

6. A monopoly has to lower its price to sell more, and this causes a loss on its prior output. Its $MR < P$, and so it will stop production before $P = MC$ since then $MR < MC$.

7. Because the firm does not cut the price on prior output when it practices price discrimination (or does not cut it as much as when it sells all output at the same price), the MR of added output is higher.

8. In the markets with more inelastic demands (and lower marginal revenues).

9. If it does not cause the monopoly to shut down, it will not affect its output (or price) at all.

10. A lump-sum tax (or change in fixed cost) has no effect on monopoly output. In a competitive industry, it will reduce output in the long run.

PRACTICAL APPLICATION

1. No. $MR = \$5$ ($\$14 \times 10 - \$15 \ 9$). Since $MR < MC$, the firm should not produce the tenth unit of output.

2. **a.** Since MR is the increase in TR, we have:

Quantity	1	2	3	4	5	6	7	8
Demand Price	$9	$8	$7	$6	$5	$4	$3	$2
Marginal Revenue	$9	7	5	3	1	−1	−3	−5

   b. $Q = 3$ (where $MR = MC = \$5$; $Q = 2$ also gives the same profit).

   c. Profit = \$6 (\$21 − \$15).

3. a. Same as the demand price: 1, \$9; 2, \$8; 3, \$7; etc.

   b. $Q = 5$.

   c. Profit = \$10 ($TR = \$9 + 8 + 7 + 6 + 5 = \$35$ and $TC = 5 \times \$5 = \$25$).

4. a. Any lump-sum tax exceeding its profits of \$6.

   b. No effect on MR or MC and so none on P or Q.

   c. Q would be reduced to 2 units (where MR = new MC of \$7); the price would be increased by \$1 to \$8.

5. a. It will produce two widgets ($MR > MC$ for the first (\$4 > \$1) and second unit (\$2 > \$1) but $MR < MC$ for the third (\$0 < \$1)).

   b. One widget. When demand goes up, in this case, supply goes down!

6. Price discriminators lower the price for those with more elastic demands. Senior citizens are more price sensitive to drug prices because drugs make up a sizable proportion of their budget. Most children have less money and so are more sensitive to prices. And people who use coupons are usually willing to shop around for the lowest prices.

7. Without a price ceiling, the MR for the first unit of output is \$20, for the second \$16, for the third \$12, and so forth, decreasing by \$4 for each added unit of output.

   a. $P = \$14$ and $Q = 4$ (with an $MR = 8$). Producing a fifth unit will add \$4 to total revenue but \$5 to total cost, so the monopoly stops at the fourth unit.

   b. If the price ceiling is \$16, it is above what the monopoly would charge, so it has no effect. So, $P = \$14$ and $Q = \$4$. But with a price ceiling of \$10, the $MR = P$ for all Q from 0 to 6, so the monopoly charges \$10 and produces $Q = 6$. With $P = \$6$, it produces 8 units (as $MR = \$6$ for 0 through 8 units).

   c. It would shut down at $TC > TR$.

8. a. If $MR = MC$, the monopoly is making its best profit. A higher (or lower) price will only make it worse off.

   b. Monopolies will always be in the elastic region of the demand curve (where $MR > 0$).

   c. An increase in demand changes MR. It usually—but not always—increases it. If it does increase MR, the monopoly will increase output.

Output	1	2	3	4	5	6
MR-Market A	$10	6	2	–2	–6	–10
MR-Market B	$ 6	4	2	0	–2	– 4

9. You would change the price at the Q where $MR = \$2$. This price is $6 in Market A and $4 in Market B.

10. This is a form of price discrimination, since the difference in price is not cost-related (in fact, the SX chip is more expensive to make). Evidently, the demanders of more computer power have a more inelastic demand for chips.

23
BETWEEN MONOPOLY AND COMPETITION

KEY TERMS

cartel an arrangement among sellers in a market to jointly set prices and output.

monopolistic competition market like that of perfect competition (many sellers, easy entry and exit, and perfect information), except that each seller sells a closely related but not identical product.

oligopoly market with few sellers and medium to high barriers to entry.

perfectly contestable markets markets with unimpeded and costless entry and exit of firms.

We have described markets that are perfectly competitive (in Chapter 20) and, at the other extreme, markets controlled by monopoly (in Chapter 22). We will now describe some of the in-between cases. We begin with the most competitive case and progress to increasingly monopolistic cases.

There are two forces pulling at any market. One force is the pull of the monopoly profits that could be earned if all firms *colluded* by agreeing to charge a high price. The other force is the pull of the profits that one firm could make if it *competed* with other firms by cutting its price to get more business. *The force of collusion leads the market to monopoly; the force of competition leads it toward perfect competition.*

Example: When Is Competition Likely to Occur?

PROBLEM   Suppose a professor puts a dollar down on a table once every minute until one student in the class raises his or her hand: That student gets all the money on the table. How will the class get the greatest amount of money?

SOLUTION The class will get the most by colluding and agreeing to wait until the professor runs out of money (and then divide the money). However, each student has an incentive to cheat by raising his or her hand and taking it all (this being a form of competition). What is more, each student knows that if he or she does not raise his or her hand, someone else will. As can be predicted, the competitive result (a hand being raised early) becomes more likely (1) the more students there are, (2) the less students know each other, and (3) the less likely the losing students will or can retaliate against the student getting the money.

As we shall see, the same forces are at work in the marketplace to make the competitive results come about.

YOU SHOULD REMEMBER

The two main forces affecting firms are (1) the pull of collusion, which increases industrial profits if all firms act collusively like a monopoly and (2) the pull of competition, which rewards an individual firm with more profits when it cuts its price.

PERFECTLY CONTESTABLE MARKETS

NATURE
The central feature of this type of market is that any firm can enter or exit costlessly. There are no legal barriers, nor are there any start-up costs. There can be one firm, a few firms, or many firms.

RESULT
Output and prices will be at the competitive level. Economic profit $= 0$; $P = MC$ in the short run, and $P = MC =$ Minimum ATC in the long run.

EXPLANATION
If any firm makes an economic profit, another entering firm can undercut its price and take away its business. Either this will occur or the firm, knowing this, will set its price as low as it can. The minimum price is the minimum of the firm's long-run ATC curve.

EXAMPLE

An airline has all the flights between two major cities. At first glance, it would seem this airline would act as a monopoly. However, it may be quite easy for another airline to enter this market should the first airline charge any price exceeding its cost. If so, the first airline will charge the competitive price.

YOU SHOULD REMEMBER

1. No matter what the market structure, the cheaper entry is, the more competitive prices and output will be.

2. In perfectly contestable markets (those with costless entry and exit), prices and output will be the same as set by perfect competition. In the long run, $P = MV = $ Minimum ATC.

MONOPOLISTIC COMPETITION

NATURE

The nature of monopolistic competition is the same as the nature of perfect competition (many firms, easy entry and exit, and perfect information) *except* that firms sell similar but not identical products. (For example, restaurants compete with one another, but do not serve the same fare.)

Each seller practices **product differentiation,** trying to differentiate its product from its competitors by advertising, service, quality, and/or location.

Each seller has a range of customers, some very loyal to its product and others, not. As a consequence, due to product differentiation, each seller faces a downward-sloping demand curve.

Examples include most retail establishments (including dress shops, restaurants, and grocery stores) in large cities.

RESULTS

Each firm is like a small monopoly: it faces a downward-sloping demand curve and produces where $MR = MC$ but $P > MC$. In the short run, the firm can make a profit or loss.

In the long run, any economic profits are bid away by new firms entering. So in the long run, we still have $MR = MC$. We also have $P = ATC$ (Economic profits $= 0$ when $P = ATC$). But $P >$ Minimum ATC due to product differentiation (and the resulting downward-sloping demand curve).

Since the firm does not produce at minimum ATC, it has **excess capacity** (more could be produced at a lower cost).

EXPLANATION

Figure 23-1, Panel A, shows the short-run results (before any new firms can enter this market). The firm faces a downward-sloping demand curve, its more loyal customers willing to pay the higher prices. Like a monopoly, it chooses to produce where $MR = MC$ but $P > MC$. Here, the firm produces 100 units, $MR = MC = \$10$, and the price is $\$15$. Its ATC is $\$11$, so it makes a $\$400$ economic profit ($P = \$15$ less $ATC = \$11$ equals $\$4$ profit per unit $\times$ $\$100$).

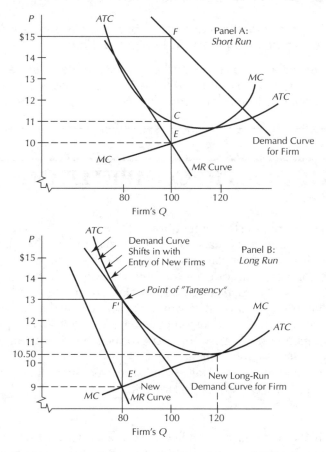

Figure 23–1. Monopolistic Competition: A Comparison of Short-Run and Long-Run Results

Because of free entry, new firms will enter, offering similar (but not identical) products. This reduces the demand for the firm's output. Entry continues. The firm's demand curve keeps shifting left, until the firm makes no economic profit: Panel B shows the long-run results. The long-run (and lower) demand curve just touches the ATC curve at Point F'. This

tangency (the demand curve just touching the *ATC* curve) is what differentiates monopoly from monopolistic competition.

$P = ATC = \$13$ and the firm makes no economic profits. The firm produces 80 units of output, $MR = MC = \$9$. The firm's excess capacity is 40 units (since it could produce 120 units at its minimum *ATC* of $\$10.50$).

EXAMPLE

Two gas stations are located on the opposite ends of a small town. If both charge the same price, customers will go to the station closer to their homes. However, if one station charges more than the other, its share of the town's business falls until only those living next to the station use it. In the short run, the two stations are likely to set the same price, each getting about half the business and making a good profit. However, this will attract new gas stations. Each new gas station splits the market further. Entry continues until profits go to 0. These will have excess capacity in that the original two stations could have served the whole town.

The two gas stations could have lowered their prices to prevent the entry of the new competitors (this is called **limit pricing**). If entry were quick and easy, they would have done so (giving the result of perfectly contestable markets). However, if entry is slow and costly, they may be better off with higher prices and more profits now, even if it means more competition and less profits in the future.

YOU SHOULD REMEMBER

1. Monopolistic competition is like perfect competition except for product differentiation.

2. Each firm faces a downward-sloping demand curve. If the industry is profitable, entry will shift each firm's demand curve to the left until it just touches and is tangent to its *ATC* curve.

3. The long-run result will be no profits, $P > MC$ and $P = ATC >$ Minimum *ATC* (i.e., excess capacity).

4. Limit pricing is the practice of lowering one's price, making less profits now, but also discouraging the entry of new competitors.

OLIGOPOLY

NATURE

In an oligopoly, there are few firms, and new firms face high (or medium) barriers to entry (often because existing firms have large economies of scale and can, if need be, drive new firms out of business with a costly price war).

There is **mutual interdependence** because the actions of one seller significantly affect the others. This is in contrast to competition, where the actions of any one firm have no effect on the market price or the sales of other firms. With mutual interdependence, one firm cutting its price can take away a large part of another firm's business. The goods can be identical or differentiated.

Examples of oligopolies include the automobile, the cigarette, the mainframe computer, and the breakfast cereal industries.

RESULTS AND EXPLANATION

The results are indeterminate because they depend upon how each firm acts. Figure 23–2 shows one of, say, four firms in an oligopoly. If all firms charge the same price, we will assume that each gets one-quarter of the quantity demanded. This is shown on the *DD* ("acting alike") demand curve for one of these firms. If all firms charge $10, each will sell 100 units (and total industry-wide demand will be 400 units). If all firms charge $9, each will sell 117 units (total industry-wide demand being 468). However, if the other three firms charge $10, then the demand curve facing this one firm is *dd* ("acting alone"). At $10, it sells 100 units (as above). However, when it charges $9 (and the others still charge $10), it gets some of the other firms' customers, selling 150 units.

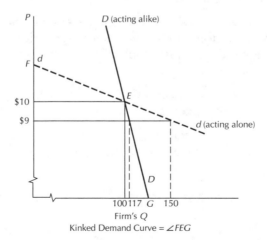

Figure 23–2. Oligopolies: Showing Indeterminacy

So if the firm does charge $9, it will sell 117 units if others also cut their price to $9. It will sell 150 units if they do not. Instead, it will sell somewhere between 117 and 150 units when the others cut their price (but not all the way down to $9.) So the results are *indeterminate* because of mutual interdependence.

This indeterminacy makes it very difficult to model or predict how oligopolies will act. For example, suppose two contractors are bidding to build a bridge for the city. Each can build it at a cost of $5 million and each knows the city will pay up to $12 million to have it built. Each has to submit a sealed bid (i.e., a bid that the other cannot see) at the same time: the lowest bid gets the contract. What will the winning bid be? If they collude, it will be $12 million. If they compete, it will be $5 million. If they partially collude, the bid may be between $5 million and $12 million. The results are indeterminate because what one contractor does affects the other.

An oligopolic firm faces a **kinked demand curve** when (1) other firms maintain their price when it raises its price but (2) other firms match its price cuts. In Figure 23–2, the kinked demand curve would be *FEG*.

The same demand curve is shown in Figure 23–3. Beneath it is the marginal revenue curve *FEHIJ*. From 0 to 100 units of output, the *MR* curve from demand curve *dd* applies (this being the *FH* segment of the *MR* curve). From 100 on, the *MR* curve from the demand curve *DD* applies (this is *IJ*). Since this curve is lower, there is a vertical segment at 100 units between *I* and *H* (between $4 and $8).

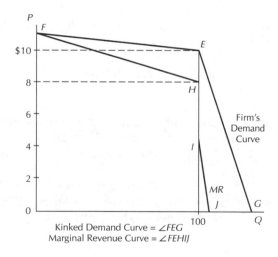

Figure 23–3. Oligopolies: Comparing the Kinked Demand Curve with the Marginal Revenue Curve

If marginal cost at $Q = 100$ falls between $4 and $8, the firm will produce 100 units and charge $10. This makes the output and price of the oligopolistic firm facing a kinked demand curve inflexible with respect to changes in cost. Falling marginal costs will not reduce prices until costs fall below $4; rising marginal costs will not increase the price until it goes above $8.

In the long run, economic profits can be made since entry is costly. Depending upon the degree of collusion or competition, the results can be monopolistic or competitive. The main forces affecting this outcome are discussed later in this chapter in the section on "cartel cheating."

YOU SHOULD REMEMBER

1. In oligopolies, what one firm does has a large impact on the sales of the other firms. This mutual interdependence makes the price and outcome difficult to predict.

2. A kinked demand curve for each firm results when it raises its prices alone but the other firms retaliate by cutting their prices when it lowers its price. This can result in the same price and output over a wide range of costs.

SPECIAL MODELS OF OLIGOPOLIES

To get specific results, we need to specify how oligopolistic firms will react to one another. These are some of the models.

• *DOMINANT-FIRM OLIGOPOLY*

NATURE
In this industry, one firm dominates the market and many other small firms compete for the remaining fraction of the market. There is limited entry, so the dominant firm does not worry about the smaller firms taking away most of its business.

An example was OPEC when Saudi Arabia dominated the oil industry and was willing to cut back on its oil production to drive up oil prices. (Due to changing times, this seems no longer to be the case.)

RESULTS
The dominant firm sets its price to maximize profits, taking into account the effect of its price on the supply of the many other small firms. Like a monopoly, it can make a profit in the long run, with $P > MC$ and $P >$ Minimum ATC. But unlike a monopoly, it controls only a fraction of the market and so sets its price lower than a monopoly would.

EXPLANATION

Since there are many small firms which act competitively, the dominant firm has to take into account what the small firms will supply at each price. The dominant firm then figures out how much it can sell by subtracting the small firms' supply from market demand. With this information, the dominant firm sets its price where $MR = MC$. Consider Table 23–1.

Table 23–1. Dominant-Firm Oligopoly: Determining Dominant Firm's Residual Demand Schedule

Price	$9	$8	$7	$6	$5
Market Q	700	750	800	850	900
Supply of Other Firms	300	250	200	150	100
Q of Dominant Firm	400	500	600	700	800
Dominant Firm's TR	$3,600	$4,000	$4,200	$4,200	$4,000
MR (per 100)	$600	$400	$200	$ 0	–$200
MC (per 100)	$200	$200	$200	$200	$200

The first row shows the quantity demanded (Q) in the market at each price. The second row shows how many units the small firms (i.e., the "other firms" in the industry) will supply at each price. The third row shows the difference: This is the dominant firm's **residual demand curve,** showing how much the dominant firm can sell at each price. The last row shows that it will produce 600 units, since here $MR = MC$. It will sell its output at a price of $7 at a marginal cost (per 100 units) of $200, or an MC of $2 per unit. Other firms will produce 200 units.

Some conclusions about dominant-firm oligopoly are:

1. *The more elastic the supply of other firms, the more elastic the demand facing the oligopolistic firm.* This will reduce the price it sets. For example, suppose the quantity supplied by the small firms at each price in Table 22–1 increased by 50 percent (so, for example, at $7 they supplied 300, and at $6, 225 units). The market price would fall to $6 and the firm would then produce 625 units. (Work this out! Note that lowering the price from $7 to $6 increases the firm's TR by $250. This raises its output by 125 units, so its MR per unit becomes $2, which equals its per-unit MC.)

2. *The smaller the total industrial output the dominant firm has (at any given price), the more elastic the residual demand curve will be.* The result will be a lower price.

YOU SHOULD REMEMBER

1. A dominant-firm oligopoly is one where one firm dominates the industry. It acts monopolistically but the many others act competitively. The dominant firm sets its price $P > MC$.

2. The dominant firm faces a residual demand curve: At each price, it can sell the market output less what the other firms sell.

3. The more elastic the supply of other firms and the smaller the dominant firm's share of total output, the lower the market price.

• *PRICE LEADERSHIP OLIGOPOLY*

NATURE

One firm dominates the industry. There are few firms, and the other firms have found it to their advantage to set their prices equal to that of the dominant firm (which is thus the **price leader**).

The price leader often gets its position by being able and willing to punish firms that undercut its price. This it does with a **price war**. The price war inflicts losses on all, but the lesson learned (not the cut prices) pays off in the long run. The willingness to suffer losses (which in the short run may seem irrational) is a **credible threat** when it results in greater long-run profits.

RESULTS

Like the dominant firm, the price leader faces a residual demand curve. Its MR = its MC and $P > MC$ and $P >$ Minimum ATC. However, if the price leader charges too much, the other firms may *not* follow its lead and may instead charge a lower price. The price leader, knowing this, will take this into account by setting a lower price. Note that in the dominant-firm model, the other firms are already charging their lowest price, so the dominant firm does not worry about the price being undercut.

YOU SHOULD REMEMBER

1. Price leadership occurs when one firm sets the price and all other firms follow.

2. The price leader will set the price to maximize its profits, taking into account the fact that a lower price increases the odds that other firms will follow and not undercut its price.

3. The price leader often holds its position by making the credible threat of a price war if the other firms try to undercut its price.

• *CARTEL*

NATURE
A cartel has an explicit and sometimes even a formal (and legal) agreement to set prices and output centrally. Cartels are illegal in the United States, but several illegal cartels have existed (with short life spans). In Europe, cartels are legal. A cartel is like an oligopoly: a few firms in an industry with high barriers to entry. OPEC is, of course, the most famous example of a cartel.

RESULTS
The cartel acts to maximize the profits for the whole industry. It therefore acts like a monopoly: $P > MC$. Output need not be at the minimum ATC.

Cartels and oligopolies both suffer from the **cartel cheating problem:** the tendency for each member to try to cut its price. As a consequence, an important part of the cartel's function is to police its members and make sure they charge the cartel price and not less.

EXPLANATION
The cartel will make the largest profit by treating the industry's demand curve as its demand curve, and then allocating output to the firms with the lowest cost. It sets $MR = MC$ at the same output and price a monopoly would.

One way a firm can cheat on a cartel is by secretly giving its customers a lower price. For example, using the illustration at the beginning of the oligopoly section, suppose the cartel sells 400 units at $10. Assume the average and marginal cost of output is $6. There are four firms and each gets to sell 100 units. Their joint profit is $1,600. If they cut their price to say, $9, their joint profit falls (to $1,404; $TR = \$9 \times 468$ less $TC = \$6 \times 468$). At $P = \$10$, each firm gets $400 in profits. All firms are worse off if all cut their price to $9 (each earns a smaller profit of only $351, the joint profit divided among the four firms).

However, suppose only one firm cuts its price for all its customers to $9: Its sales will increase to 150 units and its profits will go up from $400 to $450 ($3 profit per unit $\times$ 150). So, it pays firms to cheat if they can get away with it.

Because $P > MC$, it pays each firm to seek new customers by offering them lower prices (while maintaining the same price for old customers). However, customers become adept at playing one firm off another, with the result that when many firms practice price cutting, the cartel will break apart (as most have eventually done). An example of this cheating process occurred when OPEC collapsed as each oil-exporting nation cut its price in order to earn more profits, with the result that oil prices collapsed.

Another form of cheating is **nonprice competition,** where firms compete by offering better quality and service and by advertising more. The results of this type of cheating, if left unchecked, will be that the added costs of the extra service and quality will eventually rise until they wipe out much if not all the cartel's profits.

YOU SHOULD REMEMBER

1. Cartels are oligopolies with explicit agreements to set prices and outputs centrally. They will act like a monopoly, with the same price and output.

2. Cartels and all other types of oligopolies suffer from cheating. Each firm can profit from cutting its price (but only if the others do not).

3. Another from of cheating is nonprice competition, which increases the cost of all its members. Forms of nonprice competition include advertising, better service, and better quality.

GAME THEORY AND OLIGOPOLY

The theory of games is used to understand how people interact when each person's actions significantly affect the others. We will cover game theory in detail in the next chapter. This section will show how game theory applies to oligopoly.

As an example, suppose two airlines exist. If Airline One cuts fares, Airline Two will lose business. Similarly, if Airline Two cuts fares, Airline One will lose business. If both cut fares, they will both be worse off if ticket sales do not increase substantially.

A payoff matrix shows the payoffs from each possible strategy. Continuing our example, the top shows Airline One's set of possible choices: charging high fares or charging low fares. On the left are Airline Two's choices. In each box is what happens to each airline's profits when they select the respective choices:

		Airline One's Choices	
		High Fares	Low Fares
Airline Two's Choices	High Fares	1 gets $100 2 gets $100	1 gets $120 2 gets –$20
	Low Fares	1 gets –$20 2 gets $120	1 gets $30 2 gets $30

If the two airlines collude, they would both charge high fares. However, what if they cannot collude? Each airline might choose the *maximum strategy:* For each choice, the airline decides the *worst* that could happen, and then chooses the choice that is the best of these worsts. For Airline One, the worst that will happen if it charges high fares is that Airline Two will charge low fares and One loses $20; the worst if it chooses low fares is that it gains $30. So it chooses the best of the worst: low fares. Airline Two does the same analysis and also charges low fares. This is a stable result, as both choices coincide.

This is a simple example. However, it explains, for example, why all cigarette companies advertise heavily even when it does not increase total cigarette sales (to see how, put Low Ad Budget where High Fares is and High Ad Budget where Low Fares is).

If a game is played over and over, each side learns what the other can do. The best strategy that often arises is called "tit for tat." In this strategy, each airline does what is *jointly* best for both (here, charge high fares). However, if one airline lowers its fare, the other retaliates in the next round (and one round only) by lowering its fare. They then return to high fares unless the other airline lowers fares again. Eventually, both do what is best for both: charge high fares.

FORCES THAT PROMOTE COMPETITION

Cheating is a form of competition: It destroys collusion. Forces that promote cheating promote the competitive results.

In the hand-raising example at the beginning of this chapter, we saw that (1) the greater the number of firms, (2) the less that firms know about what the other firms are doing, and (3) the less likely that firms can retaliate (for example, with a price war), the *more likely cheating will occur* and the more likely prices and output will be at the competitive level.

Competition will also be greater when it is difficult to detect whether firms are cutting their prices. Detection will be more difficult and competition more likely: (1) when prices are not public knowledge but instead are privately set between buyers and sellers, (2) the more output demand varies from year to year (so when sales go down, other firms do not know if a price cutter is the cause), (3) when there are many types of products (varying in quality and service), and (4) when there is frequent innovation with new products and improvements.

Cheating is also more likely when it pays more: when price greatly exceeds marginal cost. Then another sale will bring more profits. Often, this occurs when an industry has high fixed costs, low variable costs, and excess capacity due to a fall in demand. At such times, cartels (such as OPEC) tend to break apart as each firm finds the temptation to go its own way too great to resist.

Cheating is also more profitable the *more elastic the industry's demand curve is.* A more elastic demand increases the gain in sales from price cutting.

YOU SHOULD REMEMBER

1. Price cutting (or cartel cheating) is a force for competition. It benefits society and consumers.

2. Price cutting is more likely: (1) the harder it is to detect, (2) the less it is punished, (3) the more it pays, and (4) the more elastic demand is.

3. Collusion is less likely in industries with varying demand, heterogeneous products, frequent innovations, and excess capacity.

KNOW THE CONCEPTS

DO YOU KNOW THE BASICS?

1. What force pushes an industry toward monopoly?

2. What force pushes an industry toward lower prices?

3. With free and costless entry into a market with only one firm, at what level will the price be set?
4. Why does a monopolistic competitor face a downward-sloping demand curve?
5. How is monopolistic competition like perfect competition?
6. What is the source of indeterminacy for whether an oligopoly will act competitively or monopolistically?
7. Why do farmers help each other out, while in other industries businesses are glad to see their rivals go out of business?
8. When and why does it pay a firm to undercut the industry's price?
9. How do price wars serve to discipline an industry?
10. Why is the competitive result more likely when firms can undercut a collusively set price level more easily?

TERMS FOR STUDY

cartel
cartel cheating problem
collusion
credible threat
dominant-firm oligopoly
limit pricing
monopolistic competition

mutual interdependence
oligopoly
perfectly contestable markets
price leadership
price war
product differentiation

PRACTICAL APPLICATION

1. Identify which type of market (perfect competition, perfectly contestable markets, monopolistic competition, and oligopoly and its various types) these conditions most likely describe.

   a. Few firms and high barriers to entry.

   b. A Dairy Board that tells dairies how much milk to produce and requires all milk be sold to it.

   c. Many restaurants in a town, each serving a slightly different menu. It is easy to enter the restaurant business.

   d. One major firm dominates the computer industry but many small firms actively compete.

2. Use the following table (which shows the demand curve for a given market) to answer the questions below:

Quantity Demanded	1	2	3	4	5	6	7
Demand Price	$10	9	8	7	6	5	4

    a. What price and output would a monopoly have if it has a constant average and marginal cost of $4 per unit?

    b. If there are two firms (with $AC = MC = \$4$), what price and output will they set if they collude successfully?

    c. Given that the price in (b) has been set, how will it pay one of the firms to cut its price?

    d. If both firms continue to cut prices, what price will emerge?

3. In the table in Question 2, suppose one firm has a marginal cost of $2. It is the sole firm in the industry. New firms can enter, but their marginal and average costs equal $5.

    a. Without the threat of entry (if new firms cannot enter), what price would the firm set?

    b. With the threat of entry, what price will it set? (This is called limit pricing.)

4. Suppose a firm of entry faced a kinked demand curve that is described by this table. Answer the questions below.

Quantity	1	2	3	4	5	6	7	8	9	10
Price	$20	19	18	17	16	15	12	9	6	3

    a. Where is the "kink" in this demand curve? What are other firms doing above the kink? Below it?

    b. If this firm has a constant $MC = AC$ of $3, what output and price will it choose?

    c. How far can its MC go before it raises its price?

    d. How much can its MC fall before it lowers its price?

5. Two drug companies, Company A and Company B, produce drugs in the same field of medicine. Each can choose to spend little *or* a lot on research. If only one spends more, it will produce better drugs more often and will make large profits. However, if both spend more, the result is that each makes the other's drugs obsolete more quickly, with less profits for both. The following shows their payoff matrix:

		Drug Company A's Choices	
		Spend Little	Spend a Lot
Drug	Spend Little	A gets $200	A gets $300
Company		B gets $200	B gets $ 50
B's			
Choices	Spend a Lot	A gets $ 50	A gets $100
		B gets $300	B gets $100

    a. What will be the result if they collude?

    b. What will be the result with a maximum strategy?

    c. What will happen if this game is played over and over?

6. A professor offers to split $1,000 among all students getting the highest score on a test. The test is to be multiple choice. Before the test, all the students meet and agree to answer all questions with "B." Identify if the following promotes collusion (all students answering "B") or competition (some students putting down the correct answers):

    a. The teacher publicly announces each student's score.

    b. Students live with each other in the same dorm.

    c. The brightest students are also the most athletic, and thus able to protect themselves against reprisals if they get caught putting down the right answers.

    d. A few students are "loners" and "unsocial."

    e. The class is very large.

7. A leading industrialist complains, "These young upstart firms in our industry are cutting prices. They have no community spirit or integrity. They just cause trouble and losses." As a consumer, would you agree?

8. On a street corner, enough newspapers are sold to yield a profit of $100 a day. One newspaper vendor could handle these sales. If other jobs pay a daily wage of $20, how many newspaper vendors will locate on this street corner? (Assume sales are evenly divided between vendors.) How is this excess capacity?

9. In an industry with high fixed costs and low variable costs, why will a fall in demand increase price-cutting pressures?

10. How does the football rivalry between two schools differ from the rivalry between two businesses?

ANSWERS

KNOW THE CONCEPTS

1. The promise of monopoly profits.

2. Competition and the profits to be made from undercutting the industry's price whenever $P > MC$.

3. The perfectly competitive price level of $P = $ Minimum ATC.

4. Product differentiation results in its customers differing in their loyalty to (or liking for) its product. A higher price drives away those less loyal and a lower price attracts new customers.

5. As in a perfectly competitive market, profits encourage entry, and the competition from the new entrants drives economic profits to zero in the long run.

6. The source of indeterminacy is that each firm does not know how its rivals will react when it changes its price.

7. Because there are so many farmers, there is no mutual interdependence. So by helping another farmer stay in business, each farmer is not hurting himself or herself. However, when there are few rivals, one going out of business helps the others: There is mutual interdependence in this case.

8. Whenever $P > MC$, it pays to get some extra sales (by offering new customers a lower price).

9. A price war can serve to punish firms that undercut the industry's collusively set price. Of course, a price war can also signal the movement toward greater competition.

10. More firms will undercut the price, and the rewards from acting collusively will be smaller and more short term. This makes the competitive outcome more likely.

PRACTICAL APPLICATION

1. a. Oligopoly.
   b. Cartel.
   c. Monopolistic competition (and perhaps perfectly contestable markets).
   d. Dominant-firm oligopoly.
2. a. $MR = MC = 4$ at $Q = 4$ and $P = \$7$.

b. Same as **a.** Output has to be distributed between them. Most likely each will get 2 units of Q.

c. Each firm initially produces 2 Q. If it gets a new customer (not already in the market), it could sell another unit at $6 and add $2 to its profit (increasing its profits from $6 to $9). If it could attract a current customer of the other firm, it could charge, say, $6.95 and add $4.95 to its profit.

d. The competitive price of $4 will emerge.

3. a. $MR = MC = \$2$ at $Q = 5$ and $P = \$6$.

b. Its limit price will be $5, and Q will equal 6.

4. a. Between 6 and 7 Q. Above $15, only this firm is raising its price: below $15, other firms are matching its price cuts.

b. For $Q = 6$, $MR = 10$. For $Q = 7$, $MR = -6$. So $Q = 6$ and $P = \$15$.

c. To increase P, $MC > \$10$.

d. Even if $MC = 0$, this firm will not cut its price.

5. a. Both will spend a little.

b. Both will spend a lot, this being the best of the worst.

c. Both will spend a little.

6. a. Collusion.

b. Collusion.

c. Competition.

d. Competition.

e. Competition.

7. The upstarts are promoting competition, which is good from the consumer's point of view.

8. Five vendors will locate on the corner. This is an excess capacity of four, since one could do the job alone.

9. Given high fixed costs, the industry will likely have a high price (at least in the long run). Given low variable costs, it will have a low MC. A fall in demand usually results in excess capacity. And with excess capacity, each firm will be looking for ways to use it. One way is to seek new customers by cutting price.

10. In football, there is only one winner. In competition, there can be many winners, with each firm taking a certain fraction of the market.

24
GAME THEORY

Game theory is the study of how people behave in situations where one's actions affect the actions of others. We applied game theory in the previous chapter to oligopolies. However, game theory has far wider applications. It is really the theory of coordination. Game theory extends the tools of economic analysis to any situation where humans have to coordinate their actions with one another, whether in the family, in the workplace, in social groups, or among nations.

An important feature of game theory is that people are rational in making their choices (that is, their preferences are well ordered). A second key feature is that a person has to take into account the reaction of others. This does not occur with the model of perfect competition where each firm takes the price as given. For example, a wheat farmer growing more wheat does not have to worry about price retaliation from neighbors. On the other hand, one airline adding more flights has to worry about how the other airlines might react.

COOPERATION

If we see people cooperating with each other to do some task for a long period, what can we infer?

1. Each person is better off in the group (and cooperating) than he or she would be not in the group. The value of leaving the group is called the **threat point**. Each person's payoff for being in the group has to exceed the threat point.

2. The "game" must be a positive-sum game. That is, the group members, by cooperating, must produce more together than they can apart. Since the sum of the group's output exceeds the sum of the threat points, the group remains stable.

3. Noncooperation by any individual must not pay (at least for the majority of players). Noncooperation is any action that benefits the individual but worsens the group. If it becomes widespread, the group would dissolve, no matter how mutually advantageous the group was.

Two types of games exist. Noncooperative games are games where players cannot enter into binding and enforceable contracts before playing the game. Cooperative games allow for binding and enforceable contracts. In noncooperative games, one result may be that people do cooperate even in the absence of a binding contract. Thus, the term *noncooperative* in *noncooperative game* refers to the ground rules of the game, not the outcome.

YOU SHOULD REMEMBER

1. Game theory is about how people come to cooperate with each other.

2. In most games, only a few players exist such that one player's actions will cause other players to react. Players therefore have to take into account the reactions of others.

3. If we observe people cooperating, we can infer that cooperation pays.

NONCOOPERATION

Economic efficiency is achieved when all mutually advantageous trades take place. If people do not cooperate when it is mutually advantageous for them to do so, then economic efficiency is not being achieved. The essential question is then: Why do people not always cooperate even when it pays?

The following game played between Alice and Bob is an example of a prisoner's dilemma game. It shows why people may not cooperate even when it is in their joint interest. This is a noncooperative game because no one can bind the other ahead of time to a certain action. The basic game is as follows. Alice and Bob are coworkers working on a project. *Cooperation* occurs when both help each other: this produces the biggest joint product, which Bob and Alice share. *Noncooperation* occurs when one deliberately hurts the productivity of the other (for example, by withholding important information). The firm gives a bonus to a worker when he or she does better than the other worker. As a result, hurting the other pays, assuming the coworker does not also hurt you. However, if both harm each other, they get the lowest joint payoff, which they also share. The payoff table is as follows, the first term being Bob's payoff and the second, Alice's payoff. All payoffs are in thousands of dollars.

First Term: Bob's Payoff		Alice	
Second Term: Alice's Payoff (noncooperation)		Harm Bob (cooperation)	Help Bob
Bob	Harm Alice (noncooperation)	15, 15	30, 10
	Help Alice (cooperation)	10, 30	25, 25

Points to Note

1. *Cooperation* is when Alice and Bob help each other. Cooperation makes them jointly better off (with a total of $50,000).

2. *Noncooperation* (hurting the other) by Alice and Bob makes them jointly worse off (jointly sharing $30,000).

3. When Alice is cooperative but Bob is not, she gets only $10,000 while he gets $30,000. For Bob, noncooperation appears to pay.

4. If Alice and Bob could somehow enforce cooperative behavior, they would do this.

5. For a dilemma to occur with a noncooperative solution, it must pay for one person to be noncooperative (here, to hurt the other). Otherwise, people would always cooperate. Suppose no bonus was given for being better. Then, if Alice hurt Bob while Bob helped Alice, each would get $20,000 (their share of the joint product of $40,000). The result would be that no gain is made from noncooperation.

The remarkable result is that each, by being selfish and rational, chooses not to cooperate and both end up worse off. A **dominant strategy** for each player exists when, no matter what the other does, one is better off taking the same action. For example, if Bob hurts Alice, Alice is best off if she hurts

Bob also (raising her pay from $10,000 to $15,000). If Bob helps Alice, Alice is best off if she hurts Bob (raising her pay from $25,000 to $30,000). "Hurting Bob" is Alice's dominant strategy. "Hurting Alice" is also Bob's dominant strategy. The "best" strategy gives the "worst" result!

In the prisoner's dilemma game, players do not bear the full cost of their actions. In the game above, when Bob hurts Alice, he reduces the total payoff from $50,000 to $40,000, yet he gains $5,000 (increasing his payoff from $25,000 to $30,000). If he bore the full cost of his actions, hurting Alice would give him a payoff of $15,000 (a decrease of $10,000): He would be worse off hurting Alice. Therefore, when players bear the cost their actions impose on everyone, they will make the right choice, maximizing the total payoff.

This game suggests noncooperation is more likely to occur when it is difficult to punish those who do not act cooperatively. Two basic methods can enforce cooperation. One is by contract that penalizes persons for not cooperating. The other is repeated play. Repeated play allows players to punish others for not cooperating.

NASH EQUILIBRIUM

The prisoner's dilemma has a unique solution because both players have the same dominant strategy. When more choices are added, the chances that all persons will have the same dominant strategy become less likely. John Nash suggested the following solution that often works. If a set of strategies with the property states that no player can benefit by changing his or her strategy while the other players keep their strategies unchanged, that set of strategies constitutes a **Nash equilibrium.** To underline the importance of this concept, whenever we see people cooperating in the same way over a long period of time, inferring that their strategies reflect a Nash equilibrium is plausible. Why? Because people keep doing things the same way when not changing does pay.

Nash equilibrium is self-reinforcing. If every player *expects* the other players to choose the Nash equilibrium, then each player *will* choose the Nash equilibrium. Expected behavior matches actual behavior. Thus, Nash equilibrium is consistent with rational expectations.

Suppose three levels of cooperation (none, half, full) are available for Bob and Alice with the following payoffs (in $1,000s):

First Term: Bob's Payoff		Alice's Levels of Cooperation		
Second Term: Alice's Payoff		None	Half	Full
Bob's Levels	None	30, 30	80, 20	90,10
of	Half	20, 80	50, 50	110, 40
Cooperation	Full	10, 90	40, 110	80, 80

In this game, no dominant strategy exists. Consider Alice's case. If Bob does not cooperate, Alice is best off not cooperating. If Bob is half-cooperative, Alice is best off not cooperating. However, when Bob is fully cooperative, Alice is best off giving half cooperation. So no single choice will make Alice best off no matter what Bob chooses. Similarly, Bob also does not have a dominant strategy.

The game does have a Nash equilibrium. To find a Nash equilibrium (and more than one may exist), start with any pair of choices and see if both players are worse off if one or the other moves away from it (assuming the other does not change). For example, suppose both Alice and Bob are fully cooperating. Alice is better off giving half cooperation. Therefore, this is not a Nash equilibrium. Consider both giving half cooperation. Alice is better off not cooperating. After trying all other combinations, we are left with neither cooperating. Alice is worse off giving more cooperation, assuming Bob gives none. Similarly, Bob is worse off doing anything differently assuming Alice continues to be uncooperative. So the upper left-hand corner is a Nash equilibrium. Neither will cooperate.

PROBLEM   People can drive big cars or small cars. Assume that people care only about accident costs and that accident costs are proportional to the combined weight of the cars crashing. Accidents between cars happen at random. When everyone drives small cars, the joint crash costs are lowest (and are the same for both cars). When everyone drives large cars, the joint crash costs are highest (and the same for both cars). However, when a large car crashes into a small car, almost all of the costs of the accident are borne by the small car. The payoff matrix is as follows:

First Term: Car B's Crash Costs		Car A	
Second Term: Car A's Crash Costs		Small	Large
Car B	Small	15, 15	30, 10
	Large	10, 30	25, 25

a. What is the cooperative solution to this game?

b. What will be the dominant strategy for all players?

SOLUTION **a.** This is another version of the prisoner's dilemma. The cooperative solution is for everyone to drive a small car, making accident costs the lowest.

b. The dominant strategy for all persons is to drive a big car. If the other person drives a big car, then driving a big car is also best (lowering accident costs from 30 if driving a small car to 25). If the other person is driving a small car, then driving a big car is best (lowering accident costs from 15 if driving a small car to 10). Everyone will drive a big car.

YOU SHOULD REMEMBER

1. The prisoner's dilemma is a game where (1) when all cooperate, the joint payoff is greatest, (2) when all do not cooperate, the joint payoff is lowest, and (3) when one person does not cooperate, that person gets the highest payoff.

2. The dominant strategy, one where the same action is always best no matter what others choose, in the prisoner's dilemma is not to cooperate.

3. When a dominant strategy does not exist, a Nash equilibrium often exists. In a Nash equilibrium, each person's strategy does the best for him or her assuming the others keep their strategy the same.

SEQUENTIAL GAMES

In the games above, all players make their choice at the same time. In sequential games, one player moves first and the others react. The resulting choices can differ because the first player's choice has *commitment value* in that the other players know exactly what choice the first player made.

Let us repeat the multiple-choice game between Alice and Bob that had the payoff matrix:

First Term: Bob's Payoff		Alice's Levels of Cooperation		
Second Term: Alice's Payoff		None	Half	Full
Bob's Levels	None	30, 30	80, 20	90,10
of	Half	20, 80	50, 50	110, 40
Cooperation	Full	10, 90	40, 110	80, 80

As you recall, the Nash equilibrium is that both offer no cooperation. Let us now suppose that Alice makes her choice first and that she cannot change her mind later. What choice will Alice make? To solve a sequential game, we begin at the end. For every action Alice makes, we examine what is best for Bob to do. If Alice chooses none, Bob will choose none and Alice's payoff will be $30. If Alice chooses half, Bob will choose none and Alice's payoff will be $20. If Alice chooses full, Bob will choose half and Alice's payoff will be $40. Next, Alice chooses the best of these: She will give full cooperation (getting $40), and Bob will react by giving only half (getting $110).

In this game, the person who goes second does better (for example, if Bob goes first, Alice gets $110,000). More often, in sequential games, the person going first does better. Similarly, in some industries, the leader going first dominates the market and earns the most. Therefore, sometimes going first pays. In other industries, the leader spends billions developing its technology; others then copy the technology at no cost and go on to dominate the industry by undercutting the leader's price. Sometimes, going second pays.

COORDINATION GAMES

Some games lead to cooperative solutions. However, as we will see, they need not lead to the best cooperative solution. Consider the following game (whose form is called the battle of the sexes). Alice and Bob have two choices, choice X or choice Y. In this game, Alice and Bob are productive only if they both do the same thing. Thus, they must cooperate to be productive. As an example, suppose that to be productive, they must share data using the same spreadsheet program (brand X or brand Y). The payoff table (in $1,000) is:

First Term: Bob's Payoff		Alice	
Second Term: Alice's Payoff		Brand X	Brand Y
Bob	Brand X	20, 30	0, 0
	Brand Y	0, 0	30, 20

Two Nash equilibriums exist: both chose X or both chose Y. A key feature of this game is that which choice is made matters to each player. (Alice is better off if X is the joint choice, while Bob is better off if Y is the joint choice.) As a result, being noncooperative (even irrationally stubborn) may benefit a player who will then get his or her way. For example, Bob could insist on Brand Y. If Alice is equally as stubborn, a long period of battle having zero productivity could occur. Ultimately, one will give in to the other.[1] Social customs may arise in organizations to avoid such wasteful battles by selecting one person to make the choice (and reap the rewards). For example, a common custom is to let senior managers make the choice. Suppose the custom is that Bob makes the choice. The next payoff table shows a potential problem with this custom. Suppose the technology of the spreadsheet programs changes so that one program is better than the other. We might have a payoff table as follows:

| First Term: Bob's Payoff | | Alice | |
Second Term: Alice's Payoff		Brand X	Brand Y
Bob	Brand X	20, 60	0, 0
	Brand Y	0, 0	30, 20

Brand X is the better program (producing a total of $80,000 compared with $50,000 for Y). However, Bob will choose Y (paying him $30,000 instead of $20,000). How does the corporation insure that Bob will make the right choice? One way is to allow transfers (for example, both Alice and Bob get a base salary of $20,000 and Bob gets profits for all the rest). Alternatively, Alice and Bob could share power and rewards (each getting 40 for choosing X instead of 25 for Y).

---

[1] In the battle of the sexes version of the game, the players are a married couple who get no value going anywhere alone. However, the husband prefers going to the fights (choice Y), and the wife prefers going to the opera (choice X).

YOU SHOULD REMEMBER

1. In the battle of the sexes game, cooperation pays, but multiple Nash equilibriums exist. Noncooperation does not pay.

2. If joint payoffs are not shared, a costly battle may have to establish who will make the choice.

3. Transfer payments make it more likely that the highest joint payoff will be selected.

4. Solve sequential games by going backward. The results can differ because the second player to go knows what the first one did.

GAMES AND PAY

In the games above, the form of the payoff affects how people cooperate. Consider the use of rank in setting pay. By using rank, the person who does best gets the most pay, the person who is next best gets the next highest pay, and so forth. As we have seen, if workers can hurt the productivity of other workers (as in the first game in the chapter), a prisoner's dilemma is created, encouraging noncooperation. On the other hand, sharing of total payoffs tends to lead to the cooperative solutions. An example is profit sharing (often combined with team production). Why then do many firms use rank pay? The benefit of rank pay is that it discourages workers from cooperating. Why would a firm want this? Because the Nash equilibrium preferred by workers might be one where everyone is lazy! A rank pay system discourages this and may prove profitable, providing workers cannot do too much harm. Some firms put workers into teams and then reward individual teams with rank payoffs.

KEYNESIAN GAMES

Suppose many players in an economy play the following game whose payoff is as follows:

First Term: Bob's Payoff		Alice	
Second Term: Alice's Payoff		Choice X	Choice Y
Bob	Choice X	20, 20	0, 0
	Choice Y	0, 0	30, 30

With many players, the Nash equilibrium will be that they all choose X or they all choose Y. Since Y is more productive (producing a total of $60,000), it is the preferred choice. If there were only two players, it would be the joint choice. However, with many players, this need not be the case. Suppose players had to choose between X and Y before their productivity was known and they all choose X. Suddenly, it becomes known that Y is more productive. If just one player goes to Y, they will be unproductive. The result could be that coordination among many players leads to a less-than-optimal choice. Arranging for all of them to change (especially if the gains of changing are uneven) is just too costly. This type of coordination problem shows why certain technical standards may gain dominance when, in some sense, they are not the best. The prime example usually given is the QWERTY keyboard for typing (the letters coming from the upper left-hand corner of the keyboard). The QWERTY keyboard was designed in the nineteenth century with the letters chosen to slow the typist to keep the mechanical keys from jamming. QWERTY became the standard keyboard used by everyone. August Dvorak devised a new keyboard in the 1930s that, it was claimed, allowed people to type faster and was easier to learn. According to the usual QWERTY story, the Dvorak keyboard was not adopted because it would require the coordination of the typing industry (for example, revising typing courses, producing new keyboards, and so forth). Old technology being locked in is called *path dependency*. Path dependency occurs when, once started along a certain path, an economy becomes locked into an inferior technology. Unfortunately, for the advocates of path dependency, the QWERTY story turned out to be false (the QWERTY keyboard is as fast as any other). They have yet to produce a major example of path dependency.

This type of thinking forms part of the new Keynesian economics, which puts Keynesian ideas into a rational-expectations framework. The goal is to explain why such persistent slumps in the economy as the Great Depression could exist. The basic idea is that multiple equilibriums exist, that the economy could slip into an inferior equilibrium, and that through path dependency could be stuck there.

To illustrate a game that can lead to a slump, suppose that all players are employers and they can choose to invest in technology X or technology Y. Technology X requires low investment in capital and in training workers. Technology Y requires high investment in capital and in training workers. Technology Y, if widely used, has the higher payoff. The drawback to using technology Y is that Y is too costly to use when not enough highly trained workers are readily available in the labor market. Suppose 40 percent of the workforce has to be highly trained for Y to be the more profitable technology. This leads to two possible equilibriums. If less than 40 percent of the workforce is trained in Y, X will be more profitable and everyone will use X. If more than 40 percent of the workforce is trained in Y, then Y is the more profitable technology and everyone will use Y. The result is a coordination game like those above where everyone selects X or everyone selects Y.

This example can be used to explain economic expansions and slumps. Assume everyone is using X. Then technology Y is discovered. The market anticipates that everyone will switch to Y, and investors invest in the switch, anticipating (rationally) the positive outcome. The economy grows, the stock market soars, and productivity rises. At this point, perhaps due to new information, the market comes to believe that the magic 40-percent mark will not be made. Therefore, everyone stops investing, and the 40-percent mark is not made. Suddenly, firms that had invested in Y go bankrupt, over-trained workers find themselves out of jobs, and the economy goes into a recession. This is a version of the post-Walrasian story of expansion and recession. Most post-Walrasian models have common features: (1) Investments create externalities that make other firms more profitable (here, creating a supply of trained workers). (2) Some critical level of economy-wide investment must be obtained for it to be profitable for individual firms. (3) Expectations about the attainability of the critical level affect the level of economic activity.

EVOLUTIONARY GAMES

So far, the players have been intelligent and rational and have learned their economics well. Suppose, instead, that players start out making random choices, observe the results, and by learning, adopt simple rules of thumb to play. To illustrate the results, let players meet at random to play the following game and let each choose by using a coin toss whether or not to cooperate:

First Term: Player B's Payoff		A	
Second Term: Player A's Payoff		Not Cooperate	Cooperate
B	Not Cooperate	15, 15	30, 10
	Cooperate	10, 30	25, 25

With many players, one-half the tosses will say to cooperate and one-half will say to not cooperate. One-fourth will be in pairings where both cooperate, one-fourth in pairings where neither cooperates, and one-half in pairings where only one cooperates. Of those choosing cooperation, half will meet with cooperators and half will meet with noncooperators. So, of those choosing cooperation, 50 percent will make $25 and 50 percent will make $10. Of those not cooperating, 50 percent will make $15 and 50 percent will make $30. Suppose people use the following rule of thumb: I will keep on with my current strategy if I make the average or more, otherwise, I will change. The average person makes $20 (1/4 × $10) + (1/4 × $15) + (1/4 × $25) + (1/4 × $30). In the next turn, half of the noncooperators will choose cooperation and half of the cooperators will choose noncooperation. The basic odds remain unchanged, and the game will continue like this forever.

Now suppose people meet randomly the first time, but if they want, they can continue with the current partner using the same strategy. (For example, if an honest worker finds an honest employer, he or she stays in the current job). The result will be that, after the first round, the cooperating pairs will remain paired and the others will be randomly paired. Those in the noncooperative pairings in the first round will now both choose to be cooperators. Those in the mixed pairings will both choose to be noncooperators. Thus, we have the same half-and-half pairings as before. Again, one-quarter of this group will become permanently paired as cooperators. As the game continues, the honest pairings will dominate and all persons will eventually end up in an honest pairing.

This is an example of an evolutionary game. People do not start out as honest or dishonest, but they learn. Because honesty pays, people learn to be honest as the game evolves. Of course, not all games end up with all persons being honest (for example, our first version did not).

PROBLEM In the game above, suppose that cooperating pairs break up after a randomly determined number of turns in the game (similar to normal turnover in the job market). Will everyone continue to be cooperative?

SOLUTION No. Suppose everyone but you is cooperative. You could cheat (not cooperate) your long-time partner just before the end and get more. This would cause your pairing to break up, but then you would be paired with other cooperators and cheat them too. Therefore, noncooperation will pay for at least some people. In a similar way, a crook does better when everyone else is honest.

Evolutionary game theory gets its name because it has been applied to evolution. Why, for example, do most predatory animals cooperate with the other members of their pack? Obviously, animals do not read game theory books to plot strategies. Yet, they will learn certain behaviors that prove to be productive. Most likely, cooperation results in more food, as a pack of animals is more likely to kill a larger prey with a lower probability of injury. The simple rule of thumb—does this mean more food for me—could lead animals to cooperate.

KNOW THE CONCEPTS

DO YOU KNOW THE BASICS?

1. Why does a perfect competitor not have to worry about the reactions of others?

2. Why does a monopoly not have to worry about the reactions of others?

3. How could you change the payoff in the prisoner's dilemma game so the cooperative solution is always chosen?

4. Why would repeated play lead to the cooperative solution in the prisoner's dilemma?

5. Why can we infer a Nash equilibrium usually occurs when we see people cooperating in a similar pattern over time?

6. Why are transfer payments important for getting decision makers to make the most productive decision all the time?

7. Why do people become cooperative in evolutionary games?

8. How can an inferior technology become the norm?

9. Why, when there are many players, will similar players be treated equally?

10. Why is the core of a game, assuming one exists, stable?

TERMS FOR STUDY

allocation
cooperative and noncooperative
  games
core
dominant strategy

evolutionary games
game
Nash equilibrium
path dependency

PRACTICAL APPLICATION

1. Alice and Bob are at a strange auction. The item up for auction is $20. The rules are that no one can bid twice in a row and that the highest bidder gets the $20. Also, and this is very strange, the highest bidder *and* the next highest bidder have to pay their bids. For example, if Bob bids $5, Alice bids $6, and Bob then passes, Alice gets the $20 and pays $6 to the auctioneer and Bob pays the auctioneer $5. Both have $100 to bid. What is the optimal strategy?

2. Only two commercial airlines fly from an airport: Alice Airline and Bob Airline. They fly the same route at the same time. It costs each only $100 per passenger to fly, no matter how many passengers they fly. The government requires that Alice announce her price and then lets Bob follow her in naming his price. Alice cannot collude with Bob nor can either change the price once it is announced. Assuming customers have no brand loyalty (that is, they will buy from whoever has the lowest price), what is Alice's optimal strategy?

3. If in question 2, Alice and Bob can change their fare whenever they want, what fare are they likely to end up charging when the demand for seats is $P^D = 500 - 0.1Q$?

4. At a recent U.S. Open, one of the four major golf tournaments, the pro finishing first won $625,000 while the second-place player won $370,000. The winnings continue to fall quickly, so that the pro coming in tenth won only $78,863. What is the advantage to the Professional Golf Association (PGA), which runs the tournaments, of having such a steep pay scale? Why not, instead, let the top five finishers share the same prize? How does the steepness of the pay scale affect the willingness of golfers to collude?

5. The CEO of a company makes the following announcement to the vice presidents, "In five years, I'm going to step down and one of you five will become CEO. I will let each of you run a division of the company, and the one making the highest profit will get my job." What is the advantage of this type of contest compared with grooming a favorite for the position? What is the disadvantage? Why will the CEO's pay be much larger than that of the vice presidents?

6. A newly married couple finds they are playing the following game. Each can choose to invest in the relationship (doing things that make the other person happy) or not. If only one person invests in the relationship, that person is worse off (because of all the effort in making the other happy) and the other is better off. The payoff matrix is in *utils*, a measure of utility. If both invest, the joint payoff is highest.

First Term: Husband's Payoff	Wife		
Second Term: Wife's Payoff		Not Invest	Invest
Husband	Not Invest	100, 100	250, 50
	Invest	50, 250	200, 200

a. Which choice makes the couple better off jointly?
b. If this is a noncooperative game (each person makes an irrevocable choice), what would the outcome be?
c. If this is a cooperative game, what would the outcome be?

d. Suppose divorce is possible. Does it make a difference if divorce requires mutual consent or if divorce is no-fault (where either party can get a divorce without the other's consent)?

7. Alice and Bob, who do not know each other, want a ticket to the hit show "Economics!" Only two tickets are left. One ticket is for a front-row seat, and the other is in the back row. Both Alice and Bob value the front-row ticket at $100 and the back-row ticket at $50. Either ticket costs $20. If they go to the box office, each has an equal chance of getting the front-row ticket. If one goes to a ticket agent (who has special contacts) and pays a fee of $10, he or she will get the front-row ticket. If both go to the ticket agent, each paying a fee of $10, they have an equal chance of getting the front-row ticket.

   a. What type of game is this? What will the noncooperative solution be?

   b. Does the existence of the ticket agent make society better or worse off?

8. A zero-sum game occurs when all the wins and losses always add up to the same number, the number usually being zero. Tossing a penny and then the loser paying the winner one dollar is an example of a zero-sum game. The net winnings (plus one dollar for the winner, minus one dollar for the loser) is zero. A positive-sum game occurs when the joint payoff from cooperating is largest. A negative-sum game occurs when the joint payoff from cooperating is not the largest. In terms of the dollars won and lost, are the following games positive-, zero-, or negative-sum games?

   a. The futures market in wheat.

   b. The stock market.

   c. Paying taxes to the government.

   d. A union calls a strike.

9. Two firms dominate a market. Each faces three choices. They can remain their current size (not expand), they can make a small expansion, or they can make a large expansion. If both firms make a large expansion, the excess output wipes out their profits. The following shows the payoff matrix:

First Term: B's Payoff Second Term: A's Payoff		Company A		
		Not Expand Expansion	Small Expansion	Large
Company B	Not Expand	36, 36	30, 40	18, 36
	Small Expansion	40, 30	32, 32	16, 24
	Large Expansion	36, 18	24, 16	0, 0

    a. What choice will the firms make if they have to commit at the same time (assume they cannot contract with each other)?

    b. What choice will they make if Company A makes the first choice and, then, Company B follows.

10. The government is one of the largest debtors in the economy. It can reduce the size of this debt by inflating the currency but only if savers are unprepared for inflation. If savers are prepared, they will lend the government less and demand higher interest rates. The economy is best off when the government does not inflate and the public does not prepare. Suppose the payoff matrix looks like this:

First Term: Savers's Payoff Second Term: Government's Payoff		Savers	
		Prepare	Not Prepare
Governmnent	Inflate	30, 30	20, 60
	Not Inflate	60, 20	50, 50

    a. If this is a noncooperative game, what will the outcome be?

    b. Some economists call for the government to precommit itself to not inflating (for example, by using a gold standard or by a fixed growth rate). How will this affect the economy? Why is a commitment necessary?

ANSWERS

KNOW THE CONCEPTS

1. A perfect competitor is so small relative to the market that it has no perceptible effect on price, no matter what it does. Thus, it does not have to worry about its effects on price and, thus, on how others will react.

2. A monopoly does have to worry about buyers buying less when it raises the price. However, the buyers themselves take the monopoly's price as given. Thus, there is no strategic behavior on the part of buyers. On the other hand, if only a few buyers exist, they could refuse to buy unless the monopoly lowers the price sufficiently. In this case, we would have a game.

3. Let each player's payoff reflect the marginal impact of his or her actions on the total payoff. In this way, all players will internalize the collective costs of their actions.

4. Studies have shown that a tit-for-tat strategy results in the highest payoff in actual games. It does so by eventually leading to joint cooperative behavior. The strategy is as follows. Cooperate until the other player does not cooperate. Then, for one turn, do not cooperate (this is the tit-for-tat). Then start over. This punishes noncooperation and rewards cooperation.

5. If people are rational, we can assume each is doing what is optimal for that person. Every person must think that any other action will result in a loss. What is more, each player's actions are likely to be based upon the expectation that other people will act similarly. This describes a Nash equilibrium.

6. Transfer payments can be used to reward people for making the socially optimal choice. Without such payments, the person making the choices (perhaps the boss) may be better off making a choice that enriches himself or herself at the expense of the organization.

7. They cooperate when experience shows them cooperation gives better results. Not all players will have the same experience, so some may end up not cooperating.

8. When the choice of technology was made, people may not have been aware of all the future benefits and costs of the choice. Consequently, they could end up with an inferior technology. They may be stuck with it when it requires the coordinated actions of many people to change.

9. Allocations in the core tend to end up treating similar people similarly. Suppose person A and person A´ are exactly alike, but the current allocation gives a lower payoff to A´. A´, being similar to A, can bid to replace A (accepting slightly less than A). This goes on until A and A´ get the same. At that point, the allocation is stable and in the core.

10. If an allocation is in the core, no one can find a better allocation. This makes the core stable.

PRACTICAL APPLICATION

1. The optimal strategy is for only one of them to enter the auction, bid a dollar, and get the $20 (assume bids are in dollar increments). If Bob bids first, then Alice should not enter the action. To see why, suppose Bob bids the dollar and Alice bids $2. Bob is best off bidding $3, as he then nets $17 ($20 − $3) as compared with losing $1 if he did not bid (which he has to pay given that the two top bids paid). Alice is now best off bidding $4 since netting $16 is better than losing $2. This continues. For how long, though? Suppose Bob gets to a bid of $19. Alice is better off bidding $20. Although she nets nothing, this is better than losing $18 if she did not bid. This goes on until Bob runs out of money (Alice bids $100 and he cannot come up with $101). Alice loses $80, and he loses $99. Alice, knowing this, is best off not bidding after Bob has made his bid. Similarly, if Alice goes first, Bob is best off not bidding.

2. Whoever charges the lowest price gets all the business. Alice's best strategy is to name a price of $100 and just cover her cost. If she names any higher price, say $150, Bob can name a lower price, say $148, and get all the flights.

3. A fare of $300 will maximize their joint profits ($MR = 500 − 0.2Q$ and $MC = 100$ (solve for Q and the optimal price). Because they are free to retaliate, they can punish one another for deviating from $300. For example, a simple strategy of matching prices will do this (since then each shares the smaller joint profits). Since they know this, the Nash equilibrium will be that each sets a price of $300. The FAA is looking into requiring airlines, once they post a price, to honor it for a fixed period. As this and the game in question 2 show, the effect of this rule could lead to lower prices.

4. The goal of the PGA is to get the best effort out of its players. Since the PGA cannot monitor effort, it has to set the schedule of winning to reward effort. If it paid the same to the five finishers, none of the five would have any incentive to expend more effort than necessary to get into the top five. Consider the following case. Suppose the top five players are all equally skilled such that if they all apply their maximum effort, each has an equal chance of winning. Suppose also that applying maximum effort costs each an extra $50,000 of effort. If the five collude, they could each save the $50,000 by applying less-than-maximum effort. To discourage collusion, the top prize has to be large enough to make each player better off not colluding. In this case, the top prize has to be $250,000 more than the average of the five top prizes. Why? The cost of maximum effort is $50,000. The benefit is a one-fifth chance (since the other players will also not collude) at the top prize. The top prize has to be at least $250,000 more to make the benefit of not colluding worth-

while. This gives rise to the steep winning schedule. Rank tournaments are used to get people to apply the most effort, but the prize has to be large. In addition, as we have seen, it has to be in a situation where one player cannot harm the production of the other.

5. As in golf, this ranking game gets the vice presidents to make their best effort. The top pay must be sufficiently high enough to cover the joint-effort cost of all five executives, assuming they have an equal chance of winning. Otherwise, the contest is not worth entering. The drawback of the game is that the vice presidents have no incentive to cooperate with each other. If they must cooperate, then grooming a favorite will be better. It will not get the best effort from the nonfavorites, but it will avoid the costs of no cooperation.

6. **a.** Both investing in the marriage gives the couple their highest joint payoff.

   b. The dominant (and Nash) choice for each is not to invest. For example, if the wife invests, the husband is best off not investing. If the wife does not invest, the husband is best off not investing. The husband will not invest. Since the wife faces the same payoffs, she also will not invest.

   c. One way to get the optimal joint payoff is to make some form of contract (such as a prenuptial agreement). Alternatively, repeated play can lead to the optimal payoff.

   d. If divorce is no-fault, then if either gets less than the cooperative payoff, he or she can leave the marriage. Suppose one spouse is a non-investor and the other is an investor. The investor can threaten to leave the marriage and get the cooperative payoff in another marriage. The noninvestor, knowing this, will optimally choose to invest also. On the other hand, when mutual consent is required, the non-investor could refuse to let the other leave. This makes the outcome of both not investing more likely.

7. **a.** This is a prisoner's dilemma game. If neither goes to the agent, the expected value for each is $55 (0.5 chance of getting the $100 plus 0.5 chance of getting the $50 ticket minus $20 to buy the ticket). The joint payoff of going to the agent is $45 (subtracting another $10 for the agent's fee). The payoff matrix is:

First Term: Bob's Payoff		Alice	
Second Term: Alice's Payoff		Go to Agent	No Agent
Bob	Go to Agent	45, 45	70, 30
	No Agent	30, 70	55, 55

The dominant solution for each is to go to an agent.

b. The ticket agent is a social waste. Both Bob and Alice end up in the same situation as they were without the agent (half a chance at getting the good ticket) except they are worse off by the $20. Some people have likened this situation to the hiring of lawyers to settle a dispute. If one hires a lawyer, he or she increases the odds of winning. If neither hires a lawyer, or both hire a lawyer, they probably have about the same chance of winning. Since both will hire a lawyer, they jointly are worse off.

8. a. A zero-sum game (or a slightly negative-sum game, once commissions are taken into account). In a futures contract, one person agrees to buy at a certain price and the other agrees to sell at the same price. The dollars gained by the buyer equal the dollars lost by the seller and vice versa.

b. A positive-sum game when stocks increase. Holders of stocks will gain if the investments underlying the stocks increase in value. Of course, if stock prices decrease, it becomes a negative-sum game.

c. It can be a positive-sum game if the government puts the tax dollars to more valued use than the taxpayers would have done. It is a negative-sum game if the government wastes the tax dollars.

d. A negative-sum game. Whatever the final contract, the same terms could have been achieved without the costs of the strike. Since both the firm and the union suffer the costs of the strike, they are on net worse off having the strike. So why do strikes occur? One answer is that they occur by mistake. If that were the case, strikes would be random events. The evidence suggests otherwise. For example, a company that has had one strike is more likely to have another one. Some economists have suggested that strikes do produce some value (such as making workers happier with the wage gains they do get).

9. a. The Nash equilibrium is that each makes a small expansion.

b. A will have a large expansion and B will not expand. Work the answer backward. If A chooses to not expand, B then chooses a small expansion and A's payoff is $30. If A chooses a small expansion, B then chooses a small expansion and A's payoff is $32. If A chooses a large expansion, B chooses not to expand and A's payoff is $36. A is best off choosing a large expansion and B, given this, chooses not to expand.

10. a. The government inflates and savers prepare, making both worse off.

b. If the government precommits and savers do not prepare, then more will be lent and borrowed and both sides will be better off (with a joint payoff of 100 versus 60). This is why chairmen of the Federal Reserve Board always sound boring and look honest: savers are more likely to believe them.

25
EFFICIENCY AND REGULATION

THE COMPETITIVE PROCESS

Society has to answer three questions about how it is going to use and allocate its scarce resources:

1. *What goods are going to be produced?*
2. *How are these goods to be produced?*
3. *Who should get these goods?*

The unique point about the competitive economy is that it tends to reward (with profits) firms that answer questions 1 and 2 correctly. Firms that market and produce the right goods efficiently are profitable. Those that do not, make losses and go out of business. The main way to make economic profits in a competitive economy is to *innovate:* to find new and more valued goods to produce or to find less-expensive ways to produce goods. Profits lead others to copy the innovator and ultimately bring the innovation's full benefit to consumers in the form of cheaper prices for the same goods or better goods for the same price. In the long run, the pursuit of profits will cause economic profits to be bid back to zero.

YOU SHOULD REMEMBER

1. Economic profits in a free and competitive economy come from innovation.

2. Economic profits reward firms for finding new and better ways to make and market their goods.

3. Competition bids economic profits back to zero, passing the benefits of innovations on to consumers.

THE EFFICIENCY OF COMPETITIVE MARKETS

Efficiency is one of the main concerns of economists. Why should anyone care about efficiency? Because when an economy is efficient, it is getting the best value for the least cost. A loss in efficiency is the equivalent of the destruction that results from war. However, some people say that an equitable distribution of income is more important than efficiency as an economic goal and are willing to sacrifice some efficiency to get greater equality. However, even here, it is better for everyone concerned, poor and rich alike, that greater equality be achieved at the lowest possible loss in efficiency. So even those concerned about equality should be concerned about efficiency.

Suppose an economy has the marginal benefits (MB) and marginal costs (MC) shown in Table 25–1. The good involved is lunchboxes. How many lunchboxes should the economy produce to maximize its net benefits?

Table 24–1. Determining the Optimal Production Rate

Quantity	1	2	3	4	5	6
MB	$6	$5	$4	$3	$2	$1
MC	$1	$2	$2.50	$3	$4	$5

Using marginal analysis, the first lunchbox should be produced, because it adds $6 to total benefits and only $1 to total cost. Similarly, the second and third lunchboxes add more to benefits than to costs ($MB > MC$) and so increase net benefits. On the fourth lunchbox, $MB = MC$: This is the optimal number of lunchboxes, the number that maximizes society's net benefits.

If the lunchbox industry is competitive, the *socially optimal quantity* of lunchboxes will be produced. To see why, recall that the demand curve is the marginal benefit curve: The demand price (P^d) equals the value that consumers place on the marginal lunchbox, so $MB = P^d$. For example, consumers will pay $4 for the third lunchbox because that is the marginal value it adds to their utility. Also, the supply curve is the marginal cost curve: The supply price (P^s) equals the cost of the marginal lunchbox, so $MC = P^s$. Since demand equals supply in competitive markets, it follows that $P^d = P^s$ and $MB = MC$: The optimal number of lunchboxes will be produced.

Economists measure the gain in net benefits by the **total surplus** from producing a good. Each unit of the good contributes to net benefits the difference between *MB* and *MC*. For example, the first lunchbox added $5 to net benefits ($6 − $1) and the second, $3 ($5 − $2). The total surplus when $Q = 4$ is $9.50 ($5 + 3 + 1.50 + 0).

The surplus going to consumers is the **consumer surplus:** the amount consumers would pay for the good less what they actually did pay for the good. For $Q = 4$, the consumer surplus is $6 (the total value of $6 + 5 + 4 + 3 less the payment of $12 for all 4 units).

The surplus going to producers is the **producer surplus:** what producers are paid less their marginal costs. For $Q = 4$, this equals $3.50 (the price of $3 × 4 minus the sum of *MC*s of $1 + $2 + $2.50 + $3, or $12 − $8.50).

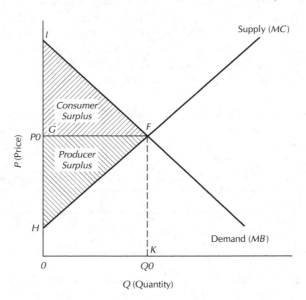

Figure 25–1. Visualizing Consumer and Producer Surplus

The total surplus is largest when $MB = MC$ and demand equals supply. In Figure 25–1, at the competitive level of output ($Q0$), (1) the consumer surplus is the area below the demand curve but above the price ($P0$): Area *GFI*,

(2) the producer surplus is the area below the price (*P0*) and above the supply curve: Area *HFG*, and finally, (3) the total surplus is the sum of (1) and (2): Area *HFI*.

An economy is **allocatively efficient** when all possible reallocations of goods (and inputs) will make someone worse off. Alternatively stated, an economy is allocatively efficient when no additional mutually beneficial trades can be made between any two persons (or groups). This occurs when marginal benefit equals marginal cost: at the competitive industry's price and output.

YOU SHOULD REMEMBER

1. A free and competitive economy maximizes net benefits.

2. Consumer surplus measures the excess of a good's total value over what was paid for the good.

3. Producer surplus measures the excess of producers' total revenue over their marginal costs.

4. Allocative efficiency exists when there are no more mutually beneficial trades to be made between people. A competitive economy is allocatively efficient when $P = MC = MB$.

THE SOCIAL LOSS FROM MONOPOLY

Because $P > MC$ for a monopoly, this means that the last unit of output is worth more than it costs. Thus, the economy would be better off if monopolies produced more. For example, if $P = \$24$ and $MC = \$10$ for the next unit of output, a monopoly could produce but does not; the loss to the economy is $14. The marginal cost of $10 reflects the value of what the resources could produce elsewhere in the economy. Pulling these resources away from what they otherwise would be producing and instead producing the monopoly good would benefit consumers by $24 and cost the economy $10 less of goods elsewhere, for a net gain of $14. Consider Table 25-2.

Table 25–2. Determining Social Loss

Quantity	4	5	6	7	8	9	10
Demand Price	$16	$15	$14	$13	$12	$11	$10
Marginal Revenue	—	$11	$ 9	$ 7	$ 5	$ 3	$ 1
Marginal Cost	$ 9.50	$ 9	$ 9	$ 9.50	$10	$11	$13

The monopolist will produce 6 units of output (since $MR = MC = \$9$ at $Q = 6$). But to secure the largest net social benefit, 9 units should be produced. At $Q = 9$, marginal benefit *to consumers,* as reflected by the demand price (P^d), equals marginal cost ($11). The social loss from monopoly is the loss in net benefits because monopolies produce too little. If 9 and not 6 units of output were produced, this would add $5.50 to society's net benefits (the sum of $P^d – MC$, or $3.50 for the seventh unit, $2 for the eighth, and $0 for the ninth). Thus, the social loss from monopoly is $5.50.

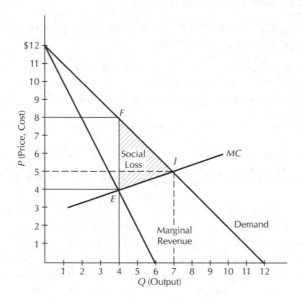

Figure 25–2. Determining Social Loss from Monopoly

In Figure 25–2, the monopolist produces 4 units of output where $MC = MR = \$4$ $P = \$8$. As long as the value consumers place on output (shown by the demand curve) exceeds marginal cost, society would be better off with more produced. The net benefit to society is greatest when $Q = 7$ where $P = MC = \$5$. The social loss from monopoly is the sum of the differences between P and MC between 4 and 7 units: Area *EFJ*. Using the formula for finding the area of a triangle, we have 1/2 (base × height) or 1/2 (7 − 4) ($8 − $4), or a loss of $6 (1/2 × 3 × $4).

It is important to remember that a monopoly causes a social loss because it produces too little, not because it is making a large profit. In fact, if the monopoly is a perfect price discriminator (see Chapter 22), it will produce as much as competitive firms and thus cause no social loss. Yet it will be making its largest possible profit!

YOU SHOULD REMEMBER

Because $P > MC$ for the last unit of output, monopolies could increase the net benefit to society by producing more (until $P = MC$). The social loss from monopoly is the total net gain from the added output that should have been produced as measured by this added output's excess of P^d over MC.

REGULATING MONOPOLY

• *PRICE CEILINGS*

A price ceiling on a monopoly can, if correctly placed, increase its output. For the range of output where the price ceiling is below the price on the demand curve (P^d), the monopoly will regard the ceiling price as its marginal revenue: MR = ceiling price. Why? Because like the perfectly competitive firm, if the monopoly produces more in this range of output, its price— the ceiling price—does not fall. In Table 25–2, a price ceiling of $11 would cause the monopoly to produce 9 units. This particular price ceiling (P^c) is socially optimal since P^c equals MC at the intersection of the MC curve and the demand curves (so $P^c = P^d = MC$). A lower or higher ceiling will cause less than 9 units to be produced. For example, if $P^c = $13, Q = 7; if $P^c = $950, Q = 7. If the ceiling is too low, the monopoly will shut down (e.g., if P^c is below $9).

A monopoly facing the demand and cost curves in Figure 25–3 would produce 3 units of output (where $MR = MC = $4) at a price of $7. A price ceiling of $5 would give the monopoly an effective demand curve that is horizontal between A and B and then from B to D. Along the horizontal segment, the monopoly's new MR equals P! The monopoly will produce 5 units of output.

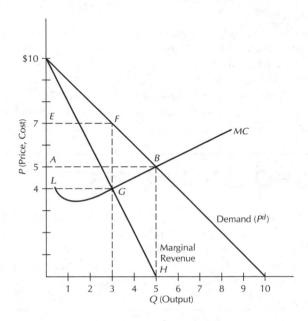

Figure 25–3. The Effect of Price Ceiling on Monopoly

Key Procedures for Drawing *MR* Curves with Price Ceiling

1. At the ceiling price (P^c), draw a horizontal line to the demand curve. Along this line, $MR = P^c$.

2. For output whose $P^d < P^c$, the old *MR* curve is still valid.

3. At the output where $P^d = P^c$, the *MR* curve is a vertical line connecting P^c with the old *MR* (below it).

For example, with a price ceiling of $7, the *MR* curve runs horizontally from *E* to *F*, down from *F* to *G*, then along the old *MR* curve from *G* to *H*. The firm would produce 3 units of output (since $MR = MC$ at $Q = 3$). A price ceiling of $4 will also elicit a monopoly output of 3 units (the *MR* curve would be *LGH*). Any price ceiling above $7 would not affect output (since it is above the price the monopoly would freely choose to charge). A price below $4 would reduce the monopoly output below its freely chosen level of 3 units. This would make society worse off (since less would be produced).

• *DO REGULATIONS WORK?*

The above analysis of price ceilings provides the central rationale for the public regulation of monopolies. Certain industries are regarded as having such large economies of scale that one firm can meet all the demand and still not achieve its most efficient scale. These industries will tend to be natural monopolies, since the first firm in the industry can expand and eliminate any potential competition and yet still make monopoly profits (assuming, of course, entry is costly so that the industry is not a perfectly contestable market). In these industries, economies of scale produce falling *MC*. Some economists consider railroads and such public utilities as electricity and water natural monopolies (but this is disputed by others).

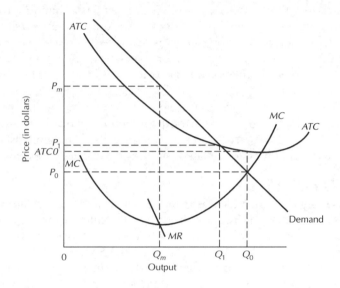

Figure 25-4. The Cost Curve of a Natural Monopoly

Figure 25–4 shows the cost curve of a natural monopoly. Its efficient scale of output (where the *ATC* curve bottoms out) is larger than the market, allowing it to drive out any competitors. Its price will be P_m. From a social point of view, though, its output should be Q_0, where $MC = P^d = P_0$. However, if this ceiling price is imposed, the price will not cover the monopoly's cost ($ATC_0 > P_0$). The monopoly will go out of business. The alternative is to subsidize the monopoly or allow it to charge a price equal to its average total cost (P_1).

The Limits of Price-Ceiling-Type Regulations

1. Usually, the government guarantees regulated industries such as public utilities a certain return on their costs. Thus, regulated firms have less incentive to hold down costs. In fact, often the more costs they have, the higher the price and profit they are allowed.

   For example, regulatory agencies have allowed many electric companies to make consumers pay for their huge losses from nuclear power plants. Other studies suggest that regulated utilities pay their workers about 30 percent too much and spend too much on plant and equipment.

2. The **capture hypothesis** postulates that regulatory agencies tend to be "captured" by the industry they regulate and act in the industry's behalf rather than the consumers'. Regulators are often drawn from the industry, later returning as consultants or employees. So they may be inclined to favor the industry. Also, the industry itself has a much more focused interest than the general public does in seeking favorable regulations.

Often, when a regulatory agency is "captured," a price ceiling becomes a price floor forced upon consumers (such as utility rates).

For example, regulation of the trucking industry limited entry and raised fares. Between 1940 and 1970, the number of licensed carriers declined; in addition, trucks were prohibited by government regulations from carrying freight on return trips. When the industry was deregulated in the late 1970s, truck fares declined significantly. Similarly, when the airline industry was deregulated, air fares fell about 30 percent.

• ANTITRUST

If a monopoly does not have economies of scale, then an alternative to regulation is to break the monopoly up into smaller firms. The Sherman Antitrust Act (1890) outlawed any contracts or conspiracies leading to monopoly. The Clayton Act (1914) reinforced the Sherman Act by outlawing specific practices, such as price discrimination (in particular, larger firms getting a lower price from suppliers than smaller firms), tying contracts (contracts that force buyers buying one item to buy another item from the firm), and interlocking directorates (where the same persons serve on the boards of directors of several firms in the same industry). In addition, the Celler-Kefauver Act (1950) prohibited mergers that would lead to greater monopolizing of an industry.

The drawbacks of antitrust policy are that (1) a firm may be dominant in an industry because it is more efficient, and breaking up the firm reduces efficiency and (2) some of the outlawed practices (such as price discrimination and "predatory" price cutting) may at times make society better off. For example, the Robinson-Patman Act (1936), in the name of protecting society from monopoly, outlawed discounts for large purchases and special concessions to any favored set of buyers. The real purpose of this law was to discourage grocery and department store chains from competing with local stores. Thus, the law promoted the monopoly of less efficient local merchants.

VERTICAL INTEGRATION

Imagine a stream going from a fertilizer maker to a farmer growing wheat and then flowing on to a mill that grinds the wheat and from there on to a cereal maker and finally to the customer eating the cereal. Vertical integration occurs when one firm combines several or all of these steps. For example, the cereal company could integrate downstream by buying and operating the mill. Alternatively, the fertilizer company could integrate upstream by buying and operating the farm.

The gains from vertical integration include (1) the stability and efficiencies that come from combining operations, (2) preventing the leakage of private information (for example, a new way to apply fertilizer so it works better), and (3) reducing transaction costs. *Transaction costs* include the time and expense of negotiating, writing, and enforcing contracts. It also reduces *opportunistic behavior* when one person seeks his or her private gain at the expense of the joint good. For example, suppose the cereal maker wants farmers to grow a special type of wheat that is of value only to the cereal maker (because the wheat goes snap, crackle, and pop). The cereal maker could act opportunistically by either not buying all the wheat (if demand for the cereal falls) or paying a lower price (claiming the farmers did not grow it right even when the farmers did). The farmers could act opportunistically by not spending as much money as needed to grow the wheat correctly. One way to prevent opportunistic behavior is through contracts and reputation. Another way is vertical integration: the cereal company runs its own farms.

The costs of vertical integration include (1) *agency costs,* the costs of slack effort on the part of employees and managers and the costs needed to deter slack effort, (2) *influence costs,* the costs employees spend influencing the distribution of benefits within a firm, and (3) the reduction in innovations because innovators collect less of the benefits of their innovations within a firm than if they owned their own firm. Most of these costs are avoided by using independent suppliers. These suppliers are likely to have lower costs because of the discipline of the marketplace.

VERTICAL INTEGRATION AND ANTITRUST

Antitrust laws have been used to break up the vertical integration of firms. Economists usually oppose this because vertical integration almost always increases the efficiency of the firm.

What if one of the firms on the stream of goods going from raw material to final product is a monopoly? Economic theory shows that vertical integration makes the monopoly more efficient, increasing the monopoly's output, and this makes society better off by increasing the net benefit from the good. Using antitrust to break up a vertically integrated monopoly just makes the monopoly worse! Consider the following cases:

1. *Using vertical integration to undo some of the effects of monopoly.* Suppose a beer distributor sells beer competitively at $50 a barrel. The distributor buys beer from several local breweries. Because of its monopsony market power, it pays the breweries $30 for each barrel. This is inefficient because the last barrel produced has a marginal cost of $30 but is worth $50 to consumers. If the beer distributor vertically integrates by buying the breweries, more beer would be produced. Another example is the major car companies wanting to open their own car distributorships. Several states have outlawed this form of vertical integration (requiring instead a local ownership of distributorships). Studies have shown that the outlawing of this vertical integration significantly increases car prices.

2. *Using vertical integration to promote price discrimination.* Price discrimination always increases output and makes society better off. Unfortunately, monopolies are not always able to practice price discrimination because the low-price buyer can resell to the high-price buyer, making it impossible to sell at the high price. Suppose the monopoly is a pharmaceutical firm that owns a drug that both cures acne and reduces the cost of making floor polish. If it could, it would sell at a high price to those with acne and at a low price to floor polish makers. However, it cannot price discriminate, so it sets its price somewhere in between. What would happen if the company vertically integrated by buying the floor polish company? It could produce floor polish at a lower cost and, at the same time, it could charge those with acne the high price. The effect would be a greater output of the drug and a lower welfare loss.

3. *Vertical integration to acquire information.* Vertical integration allows for the sharing of critical information. Consider the case of an aluminum company that buys all the bauxite from several local firms. It wants to expand, and the success of its expansion depends upon the availability of low-cost bauxite. The bauxite firms would have an incentive to tell the aluminum company that they can supply the increased demand at a low cost, even if they cannot. The aluminum company could be better off buying the bauxite firms to find out what the true costs will be. In this way, it avoids economically wasteful investment.

PROBLEM   Along the rivers of Germany in the eighteenth century, robber barons taxed shipping coming down the rivers. If several robber barons are on a single river, each taxing the most he can, what will the effect be of combining their operations? Which would make Germany better off?

SOLUTION   When each robber baron imposes his tax, he does not care how the tax affects the tax revenues of the others. One set of taxes will maximize their joint profits. However, each baron, by acting independently, will set the tax higher than this, because none cares that the reduced business (due to the tax) will harm the taxes collected by the robber barons downstream. If the barons vertically integrated by combining their operations, the overall tax would be lower and yet total shipping would be greater. Because of the added shipping, the total taxes collected would be greater. German business and the robber barons are better off with vertical integration (eventually, this did occur). The same argument applies to any two monopolies on the same stream of production. For example, when Microsoft Windows added a browser, two monopolies were combined, to the net benefit of consumers.

YOU SHOULD REMEMBER

1. Vertical integration has the benefit of coordinating different levels of production, keeping important information private, and reducing the cost of transacting with many independent suppliers. It has the disadvantage of replacing private suppliers with bureaucrats (increased agency and influence costs and less innovations).

2. Vertical integration by a monopoly makes it more efficient and increases its output. Most economists oppose using antitrust laws to break up vertical integration.

IS MONOPOLY BAD?

Monopoly, oligopoly, and monopolistic competition often exist because (1) as with innovations, someone has to be first and thus, by definition, a "monopoly," (2) they have economies of scale that allow them to produce at a lower cost than if the industry were made up of many firms, and (3) because customers prefer buying brand names and having a smaller range of choice. Perfect competition in these cases may be too costly and not desirable. For "perfect" competition to exist in the restaurant business, all restaurants in a town would have to serve the same food. Most consumers would reject perfect competition and instead favor variety even if it meant higher restaurant prices. A good brand name is something a seller wants to protect with quality controls—and something consumers also value because they then can be more certain of what they are buying. The fact that consumers choose brand names over generic brands shows that they do not want perfect competition in all products. In addition, competition can wipe out an innovator's profit too quickly and discourage further research and inventiveness (this is recognized in our patent and copyright laws).

Nevertheless, when a monopoly makes its profits from withholding output, it causes social harm. Interestingly, some economists contend that our government is the main source of monopoly in our economy. It supports cartels for various agricultural products (including milk and peanuts), it prevents foreign competition with tariffs and quotas, and supports unions that hold a monopoly on the supply of labor inputs to certain industries.

WHEN WON'T A COMPETITIVE ECONOMY BE EFFICIENT?

Even without monopoly, competitive firms will not produce the socially optimal level of output when the price does not reflect all the marginal benefits of the good or when marginal costs do not reflect the full cost of producing the good. This occurs when some of the benefit or cost of the good is borne by someone *other* than those buying and selling it. An example is when a firm does not have to pay for the damage its pollution causes. Another example is when viewers receive a television station's signals but don't pay for the benefit. We will cover this issue in detail in Chapter 29.

YOU SHOULD REMEMBER

1. A price ceiling imposed upon the price of a good produced by a monopoly can, if it is not placed too low, cause the monopoly to produce more of the good. The price ceiling eliciting the greatest output is equal to the price where the demand curve and the marginal cost curve intersect.

2. Natural monopolies occur when the efficient scale of production is large relative to the market size of the industry. As a result, only one (or a few) firms will dominate the industry and will tend to act monopolistically.

3. Government regulations, such as those on electric utilities, seek to effectively put a price ceiling on monopoly goods. The capture hypothesis suggests that regulations will tend over time to favor the industry over the consumers as the regulatory agencies are "captured" by the industries they control.

4. Antitrust seeks to break up firms and to discourage practices believed by lawmakers to encourage monopoly.

KNOW THE CONCEPTS

DO YOU KNOW THE BASICS?

1. How can a firm profit by finding a more valuable good to produce?
2. Who ultimately gets the economic profits in a competitive economy?
3. What is the contribution to net benefits of the last unit of a good produced in a competitive economy?
4. In Figure 25–1, what area represents the total value of $Q0$ units of output?
5. In Figure 25–1, what area represents the total cost of producing $Q0$ units of output?
6. What is Area *IFH* in Figure 25–1?
7. Why is a minimum-wage law not allocatively efficient when it prevents workers from getting a job?
8. How does a monopoly create social losses?
9. Will a price ceiling always cause a monopoly to produce more?
10. When might a competitive economy produce too much of a good (from a social point of view)?

TERMS FOR STUDY

allocative efficiency	producer surplus
capture hypothesis	total surplus
consumer surplus	

PRACTICAL APPLICATION

1. Imagine that the government has created rules so that all firms in an economy are monopolies. Assume all consumers are alike and all own equal shares in the monopolies. As a result, all monopoly profits are earned by the consumers who have to pay monopoly prices. Are people in this economy better off or worse off because each firm is a monopoly and is making a profit?
2. Suppose consumers suddenly want fewer action movies and more romances than are now being produced. Describe how profits will play a role in getting movie producers to switch.
3. Use this table to answer these questions.

Quantity	1	2	3	4	5	6
Demand Price	$14	$12	$10	$8	$6	$ 4
Supply Price	$ 4	$ 6	$ 7	$8	$9	$10

    a. What level of output will yield the largest net benefit?

    b. In a competitive economy, what level of output would be produced and sold?

    c. What is the consumer surplus? The producer surplus? Their sum? And what is the net benefit?

4. Suppose a price ceiling of $4 is placed on the good in Question 3.

    a. What will be the net benefit? The consumer and producer surplus?

    b. Show that the price ceiling on the price in a competitive industry is inefficient, using (1) marginal analysis, (2) consumer and producer surplus, and (3) allocative efficiency.

5. Using the table from Question 3, assume the firms in the industry establish a monopoly.

    a. What output will they produce?

    b. What will the social loss be (as compared to when the firms acted competitively)?

6. A price ceiling on the price in an industry monopolized by one firm can be efficient. In Question 5, what price ceiling will maximize social output?

7. Using the table from Question 3, what is the social cost of a tax of $6? (Hint: How much will output and social surplus go down by?)

8. Federal water in western states is sold to farmers for $10 an acre-foot (which is enough water to cover an acre with a foot of water), while it is sold to California cities for $200 an acre-foot. Why is this inefficient?

9. Using Question 3's table, suppose the government subsidized output by $6 a unit and that the economy is competitive. What level of output will be produced? Will society be better off or worse off because of the subsidy? By how much?

10. Suppose the government restricts all families to owning only one car. Why would this be allocatively inefficient?
Hint: Assume one person values one car at $12,000 and would value a second at $7,000. A second person values one car at $5,000. What trade would make both of these persons better off when people are allowed to own more than one car?

ANSWERS

KNOW THE CONCEPTS

1. In the long run, a set of inputs costing $10 will produce $10 of output. A firm that finds a good to produce that consumers value at $12 can make a $2 profit. In the long run, though, the price will return to $10, so consumers get the "profit" in the form of a $12 good costing them only $10.

2. Consumers, in the form of lower prices.

3. The last unit just covers its cost: It adds nothing to net benefits. However, up to the last unit, each additional unit increases net benefits.

4. The area under the demand curve: *OIFK*.

5. The area under the supply curve: *OHFK*.

6. *IFH* is the difference between the area under the demand curve and the area under the supply curve. It is the net benefit of *Q0* units of output or the total surplus.

7. If employers would have to hire workers whom the minimum wage prevents from working, then the minimum wage has prevented a mutually beneficial trade from taking place. So it is not allocatively efficient.

8. A monopoly could produce more output whose value (i.e., price) exceeds its cost, but it does not because its *MR* < *P*. The social loss comes from the fact that it could produce more (*not* from the fact it makes a large profit).

9. No. A low enough price ceiling can cause a monopoly to produce less or even shut down.

10. When the producers of the good do not bear all of the cost of producing the good.

PRACTICAL APPLICATION

1. Everyone is worse off even though they share in the monopoly profit. This is because consumers lose more in consumer surplus than the monopoly gains in profits. Recall that monopolies make a profit by reducing output. Thus, if all firms are monopolies, then all firms would produce less, and, as a consequence, per capita output and income would be less.

2. Initially, action movies will make losses and romances will make profits. The producers who switch first will make profits. The profits reward those producers who produce the goods consumers want. The losses

penalize those who do not. Of course, when public tastes change again, movie producers will again switch to making the movies the public demands.

3. a. 4.

b. 4.

c. Consumer surplus: $12. Producer surplus: $7. Their sum: $19. Net benefit of 4 units: $19 (the same as the sum of consumer and producer surpluses).

4. a. Only 1 unit will be produced. The net benefit from 1 unit will be $10. Consumer surplus: $10. Producer surplus: $0.

b. (1) Marginal analysis: The second, third, and fourth units have $MB \geq MC$ and should be produced.

(2) The consumer plus producer surplus is bigger at $Q = 4$ ($19 versus only $10).

(3) There are consumers who are willing to pay producers at least their cost or more for the second, third, and fourth units of output. The price ceiling prevents these mutually beneficial trades so it is not allocatively efficient.

5. Use the following table:

Quantity	1	2	3	4	5	6
Demand Price	$14	$12	$10	$8	$6	$ 4
Supply Price	$ 4	$ 6	$ 7	$8	$9	$10
Marginal Revenue	14	10	6	2	-2	-6

a. The monopoly will produce 2 units of output (recall that the supply price equals the MC: for the first 2 units of output, $MR > MC$).

b. The social loss is $3 ($3 loss from not producing the third unit plus $0 for the fourth).

6. The price ceiling should be set, where $P^d = MC$, $P^c = 8.

7. Sellers will add $6 to their price, resulting in 2 units of output being produced. The social surplus of 2 units is $16, while the optimal social surplus (at $Q = 4$) is $19. So society is worse off by $3 (the difference between MB and MC of the units not produced because of the tax—in this case, units 3 and 4).

8. This policy is inefficient because the total benefit from the water could be increased by reallocating it to its highest value use. By withdrawing an acre-foot from farming (where it is put to $10 worth of use) and sending it to cities (where it is worth $200), society is better off by $190. Part of the loss from not reallocating the water is reflected in the fact that California cities are spending huge sums to get more water while water-intensive crops (rice and soybeans) are being grown in the desert!

9. Competitive suppliers will cut the price below their costs by $6, so output will expand to 6 units (where the sixth unit's *MC* of $10 less $6 equals the demand price of $4). Society is worse off. While consumers may gain from the lower price, they lose because the resources to produce units 5 and 6 should have produced more valued goods elsewhere (recall that marginal cost reflects opportunity cost). The social loss from producing unit 5 is $3 (its *MB* is $6 and its *MC* is $9) and from unit 6, $6. So society is worse off by $9.

10. Suppose Owner A values his car at $5,000. Owner B values her car at $12,000 and would pay $7,000 for a second car. These two owners could be better off if Owner A could sell Owner B his car (say at $7,000). So restricting the number of cars a person can own is not allocatively efficient.

26
FACTOR DEMAND AND PRODUCTIVITY

KEY TERMS

marginal factor cost (MFC) addition to total cost when one additional unit of an output is employed.

marginal revenue product (MRP) addition to total revenue when one additional unit of an input (such as labor or capital) is employed.

monopsony input buyer that faces a higher input price as it employs more inputs.

Note: "Inputs" and "factors" are the labor, capital, materials, and land that a firm employs to produce output.

Why does Mike Myers make more than $19 million a movie? Because his presence in a film adds that amount (or more) to the movie's revenues. Without him, the movie studio would have a harder time financing and marketing the film and would likely sell fewer tickets. So his salary is *derived* from what his employer (the movie studio making his films) earns from its customers for his output.

So it is with all inputs, whether they are labor, land, or capital. Their value is derived from how much they add to the value of the final product. This chapter describes the forces that determine the *derived* demand for all inputs. Chapter 27 will show how the analysis applies to labor markets, and Chapter 28 will cover the markets for land, capital, and entrepreneurship.

HOW TO MEASURE PRODUCTIVITY AND PROFITS

A firm wants to know how many units of an input it should hire. Suppose the firm wants to know how much labor it should hire. The firm will use marginal analysis.

Using Marginal Analysis to Make Input Hiring Decisions

1. The firm wants to maximize its profits:

$$\text{Profits} = \text{Total Revenue} - \text{Total Cost}$$

The firm breaks the hiring decision into steps of hiring one more unit of labor at a time. The "unit" of labor could be an additional hour of work or an additional work year, depending upon what is convenient for the firm to add.

2. The *marginal benefit* of one more unit of labor is the amount it adds (by increasing output) to total revenue:

Marginal Revenue Product (MRP) = *Increase in Total Revenue Due to One More Unit of Input* (here, due to one more worker being hired)

3. The *marginal cost* of one more unit of labor is the amount it adds to total cost:

Marginal Factor Cost (MFC) = *Increase in Total Cost Due to One More Unit of Input* (here, the added cost of employing another worker— including wage and fringe benefit costs)

4. As long as each additional worker adds more to revenue than to cost, profits go up. So the firm will continue to hire as long as:

$$MRP \geq MFC.$$

5. It will maximize its profits and hire enough workers so that:

$$MRP = MFC.$$

Firms can be price takers (perfectly competitive) or price searchers (such as monopolies) in the markets in which they sell their output: This affects how they value the output a worker produced (the *MRP*). They also can be price takers or price searchers in the market in which they buy inputs: This affects how they value the cost of an added worker (the *MFC*). We will now study the four possible cases.

YOU SHOULD REMEMBER

1. Marginal revenue product (*MRP*) is the addition to total revenue due to employing an additional unit of an input.

2. Marginal factor cost (*MFC*) is the addition to total cost due to employing an additional unit of an input.

3. The firm will maximize profits by hiring until *MRP* = *MFC*.

DETERMINING MARGINAL BENEFIT BY MARGINAL REVENUE PRODUCT

CASE ONE: PRICE TAKER IN AN OUTPUT MARKET

A perfectly competitive firm (i.e., a price taker) can increase output and still sell it at the same price. So if $P = \$10$ and a worker adds four units to total output, the worker adds $40 to the firm's total revenue—this is the worker's *MRP*. For a price taker,

$$MRP = \text{Price} \times MPP.$$

MPP is the **marginal physical product** of the input: how much the added input increases total *physical* output.

Table 26–1 shows the *MRP* for a price-taking firm whose price is $4. The *MPP* schedule shows diminishing marginal returns (or diminishing *MPP*) throughout.

Table 26–1. The Marginal Revenue Product for a Price-Taking Firm

Units of Input	1	2	3	4	5	6	7
Output	8	15	21	26	30	33	35
MPP	8	7	6	5	4	3	2
MRP = P × MPP	$32	$28	$24	$20	$16	$12	$ 8

The third input, for example, adds 6 units to total output (21 – 15). Each unit sells for $4, so the third unit adds $24 to total revenue (check this out by directly calculating the change in total revenues).

Using marginal analysis, if marginal factor cost is $20, the firm will hire 4 units of input. If *MFC* then falls to $16, the firm will hire 5 units. As a consequence, we have this result: *The MRP schedule is the derived demand curve for the input.*

Figure 26–1 shows the derived demand for labor by this firm when *P* = $4.

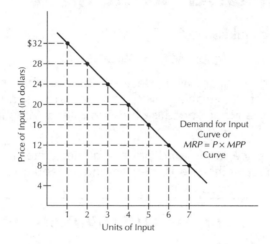

Figure 26–1. Derived Demand Curve for a Price-Taking Firm

The derived demand curve is negatively sloped because of the law of diminishing marginal returns. (See Chapter 19.) Thus, the other inputs are being held constant when the firm calculates the marginal worth of an added worker.

CASE TWO: PRICE SEARCHER IN AN OUTPUT MARKET
As a price searcher (such as a monopoly) sells more, the market price of its good goes down. So *MR* < *P*.

Suppose another worker adds four units to output, and these four units sell for a total of $40 (or at an average price of $10 each). However, to sell these four units, the price searcher had to cut its price. Assuming this price cut reduced its revenues on its prior output by $28, these four units added $12 to total revenue ($40 – $28) and had an average marginal revenue of $3 each. So we have *MRP* of a price searcher:

$$MRP = MR \times MPP.$$

Here, *MR* = $3 and *MPP* = 4, so *MRP* = $12.

Note that the formula $MRP = MR \times MPP$ also applies to price takers, since $MR = P$ for a price taker. Because $MR < P$ for a price searcher, a price searcher will place a *lower* value on inputs and hire fewer of them (other things being equal).

The price searcher's derived demand curve for an input (its *MRP* curve) slopes downward because of (1) diminishing *MPP* and (2) falling *MR*.

YOU SHOULD REMEMBER

1. For a price taker, $MRP = P \times MPP$.

2. For a price searcher, $MRP = MR \times MPP$.

3. For a price taker, *MRP* declines as the firm hires more because of diminishing *MPP*. For a price searcher, *MRP* declines even more because besides falling *MPP*, its *MR* also falls as it hires more.

4. For both price takers and price searchers, the marginal revenue product schedule is the demand schedule for the input.

• *FACTORS SHIFTING THE DERIVED DEMAND FOR AN INPUT*

Table 26–2 shows how various factors change the demand for an input.

Table 26–2. Factors Shifting the Derived Demand for Inputs

Factor	Shift in Factor	Shift in Derived Demand
1. Demand for output (change in *P* and *MR*)	Increase Decrease	Increase (to right) Decrease (to left)
2. Change in productivity	MPP Up MPP Down Industry-wide increase	Increase Decrease Up if demand elastic; down if inelastic
3. Price of substitute input	Price Up Price Down	Uncertain Uncertain
4. Price of complementary input	Price Up Price Down	Decrease Increase

An increase in output demand *that raises price and marginal revenue* increases the amount of input firms want to hire. An increase in *MPP* increases what firms are willing to pay for each input.

An industry-wide increase in productivity (and not just at the firm level) has an uncertain effect on labor demand. When all firms become more productive, the same set of inputs produces a higher output. *If demand is elastic,* this higher output will increase the industry's total revenues and thus what firms pay for inputs. *If demand is inelastic,* this higher output will reduce total revenues and input demand.

How does an increase in the price of another input, such as an increase in the cost of machinery, change labor demand? First, the machine's higher price raises the cost and price of output, which in turn reduces output demand (this is the **output effect**). Second, when labor and machinery are substitutes (such that one input can to some degree replace the other), then the firm, to *produce a given amount of output*, will use more labor and less machinery (this is the **substitution effect**). So the output effect of a higher machine price reduces labor demand, while the substitution effect increases it. The net effect is uncertain.

Complements are inputs used closely together. When the price of one goes up, less of both will be used. So the output effect and this effect reinforce each other. For example, most highly skilled workers have jobs that use much energy. When energy prices went up, the demand for highly skilled workers went down, even in those industries where output didn't fall.

• *FACTORS AFFECTING THE ELASTICITY OF DERIVED DEMAND*

By what percentage will labor demand go down when wages go up by 1 percent? To find out, economists use the elasticity of labor demand.

$$\textbf{Elasticity of Input Demand} = \frac{\text{\% Change in Quantity of Input Demanded}}{\text{\% Change in Input's Price}}$$

Note that both percent changes are stated as absolute values. For example, the elasticity of labor demand in many industries is 0.5: A 10-percent wage increase reduces the quantity of labor demanded by 5 percent.

Labor demand is more elastic when the quantity of labor demanded goes down *more* when wages go up. Input demand will be *more elastic:*

1. *When* MPP *Falls Less:* When *MPP* falls less as more of the input is employed, the input demand schedule is thus flatter and more elastic. When *MPP* falls quickly, it is more inelastic. For example, if a bakery needs only one truck driver to make deliveries, the *MPP* of added truck drivers falls quickly. So its demand for truck drivers is inelastic: A lower wage for truck drivers will not increase the number of truck drivers it hires.

2. *When the Demand for Output Is More Elastic:* When an input's cost goes up, so does the price of output. So the more elastic output demand is, the more output and thus input employed will fall when the price of output (and wages) go(es) up. For example, the growing competition from foreign car makers has made the demand for U.S. cars, and thus the demand for U.S. auto workers, more elastic.

3. *When It Is Easier to Substitute Other Inputs:* The more close substitutes there are for an input in the production process, and the more readily available these substitutes are, the more firms will replace the input when the input's price goes up. For example, a greater ability for firms to easily hire nonunion workers makes the demand for unionized labor more elastic.

4. *When the Input's Initial Share of Total Cost Is Larger:* The larger its share, the more a given increase in the input's price increases the price of output in percentage terms. And the more price goes up (in percentage terms), the more output and thus inputs employed will fall. As an *approximation,* we have:

% Change in Price = Input's Share × % Change in Input's Price

For example, labor costs represent about 25 percent of a car's total cost. So a 10-percent wage increase will increase car prices about 2.5 percent. However, if labor's share were 90 percent the price would go up 9 percent—and labor demand would fall more. An exception to (4) (and this approximation) occurs when inputs have close substitutes, but this is rare for such major inputs as capital and labor.

YOU SHOULD REMEMBER

1. The demand curve for an input is shifted by changes in the demand for output, by changes in the price of other inputs, and by changes in productivity.

2. When input demand goes down more when its price rises, its demand is more elastic. When the quantity of an input demanded is insensitive to price changes, its demand is inelastic.

3. The demand for an input will be more elastic when (1) its *MPP* curve is flatter, (2) the demand for output is more elastic, (3) it has close substitutes, and (4) its share of total cost is larger.

DETERMINING MARGINAL COST BY MARGINAL FACTOR COST

CASE THREE: PRICE TAKER IN AN INPUT (FACTOR) MARKET

Most firms, even large firms, employ only a small fraction of the total work-force. So almost all firms are price takers in the markets in which they buy inputs: They can hire what they want at a constant price. Even firms that are monopolies in the markets in which they sell are usually price takers in hiring.

$$MFC \text{ for Price Takers} = \text{Price of the Factor}$$

Labor's *MFC* is its wage (including fringe benefits and training costs).

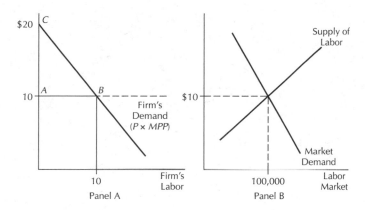

Figure 26–2. Demand and Supply of Labor from the Point of View of a Price Taker in an Input Market

Figure 26–2 shows the demand and supply for labor from the firm's (Panel A) and input market's (Panel B) point of view. At a wage of $10 an hour, the firm in Panel A hires 10 workers and the market in Panel B hires 100,000 workers. The market demand curve reflects the sum of firms' demands (but takes into account that as all firms hire and produce more, the price of out-put falls). The supply curve of labor shows that at higher wages, more per-sons want to work.

CASE FOUR: PRICE SEARCHER IN AN INPUT (FACTOR) MARKET: MONOPSONY

The vast majority of factor markets are competitive. However, in some cases, there is a **monopsony**, a firm so dominant in a factor market that its hiring decisions affect the input's market price. A monopsony in the labor market, for example, has to pay a higher wage if it wants to employ more workers.

The cost of an added worker is the worker's wage *plus* the cost of paying a higher wage to all its previously hired workers. Or in general:

MFC for Price Searcher = Price of the Factor *plus* Added Cost of Paying Higher Price to Already Hired Inputs

Example: MFC for a Monopsony

PROBLEM   A firm has hired nine workers at $400 a week. To hire a tenth worker, it must pay $410 a week. Suppose the tenth worker's *MRP* is $450. Should the firm hire the tenth worker?

SOLUTION   No. The worker would cost $410 plus the added pay of $10 each for the other 9 workers: The worker's *MFC* is $500 ($410 + 9 × $10). Since *MFC* > *MRP*, the worker should not be hired.

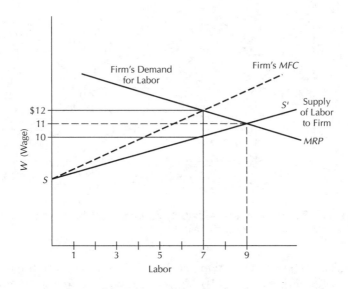

Figure 26–3. Demand and Supply of Labor from the Point of View of a Monopsonist

Figure 26–3 shows the demand and supply for workers of a monopsony. *SS´* is the supply curve facing this firm: It is upward sloping (instead of flat like that of the price taker). *MFC* exceeds the wage. When the supply curve is a straight and upward-sloping line, *MFC* rises twice as fast as the supply curve. The *MRP* curve is the firm's demand curve for labor. This firm will hire until *MRP* = *MFC* at $12, paying a wage of $10 to 7 workers. If this firm were forced to act competitively, it would hire more workers (9) at $W = MRP = \$11$.

YOU SHOULD REMEMBER

1. A price searcher in its output market can be a price taker in its input market.

2. For price takers in the input market, *MFC* = Price of Input.

3. For a price searcher in the input market, *MFC* = Price of Input Plus Added Cost of Paying Higher Wages to Already Hired Inputs.

4. For the price searcher, *MFC* > Price of Input.

THE FOUR CASES COMBINED

Table 26–3 summarizes the chapter. In the table, the price of the input is *W* (the wage of the input). From a social point of view, an input should continue to be hired until its marginal benefit to consumers ($P \times MPP$) falls to its marginal cost to suppliers (the supply price, *W*). When $P \times MPP = W$, the socially optimal level of employment is achieved. Perfectly competitive firms will hire the socially optimal level of employment. A monopoly hires fewer inputs because it values the marginal benefit of another input ($MR \times MPP$) less than consumers do ($P \times MPP$) since it has to cut its price to sell more (so that $MR < P$). Similarly, a monopsony hires less than the socially optimal amount because its marginal cost of another input (*MFC*) is higher than the input's supply price (*W*) since it has to raise its wage to hire more (so that $MFC > W$).

Table 26–3. Marginal Analysis of Input Decisions

	Marginal Benefit of Input	Marginal Cost of Input	Source of Inefficiency
Society	$P \times MPP$	W	—
Competitive firm, input and output markets	$P \times MPP$	W	none
Monopoly	$MR \times MPP$	W	$P > MR$ as $MR = P - |\Delta P| \times Q_{old}$
Monopsony	$P \times MPP$	$MFC > W$	$MFC > W$ as $MFC = W + \Delta W \times L_{old}$
Monopoly and monopsony	$MR \times MPP$ $MFC > W$	$MFC > W$	$P > MR$ and

Figure 26–4 shows all four cases. It shows what will be the demand (DD') and supply (SS') curves of labor if this industry is fully competitive (firms being price takers in both input and output markets): Case 1 and Case 3. DD' reflects P times MPP, while SS' reflects the wage (W) at different levels of employment. A fully competitive industry will be at Point A.

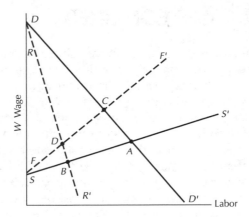

Figure 26–4. The Four Cases Combined

Suppose only one firm produces all the output in this industry. It would be a monopoly (Case 2), so it values each added worker's output at its MR, not its price: $MRP = MR \times MPP$. Its "demand" curve for labor (that is, its marginal benefit curve) is shown by RR'. If it is still a price taker in hiring workers (Case 3), it will be at Point B.

Now suppose there is only one firm that is a price taker in the output market (perhaps because it competes in international markets) but is a monopsony (perhaps because it is the major employer in a small town): this is Case 1 and Case 3. *DD´* is its demand curve for labor (as *P* is given). However, it is not aware that as it hires more, wages go up. It sees the marginal factor cost of labor as the *FF´* curve. It will be at Point *C*. Note that the wage it pays is *below* this point on the *SS´* curve (as *MFC > W* in this case)!

If the one firm is both a monopoly and a monopsony (Case 4): Its marginal benefit and marginal cost of labor curves are *RR´* and *FF´*, so it will be at Point *D*. Once again, the wage it pays will be below Point *D*. It hires the fewest workers and pays the lowest wage of all possible combinations.

EFFICIENCY

We will now examine why input markets are efficient when firms are price takers in both their output *and* input markets. Our example will involve workers, but it also applies to land and capital.

Each price taker will hire labor until:

Wage = Price × Marginal Physical Product ($W = P \times MPP$).

Suppose that for all firms, $W = \$10$ and $P = \$2$ with $MPP = 5$. To show that this is optimal, we have to show that total output will be reduced when firms hire a different number of workers than they currently are hiring. Suppose one worker is taken from Firm A and given to Firm B. In Firm B, the worker's $MPP < 5$ (due to diminishing MPP); in Firm A, an MPP of 5 will be lost. So total output will fall. Obviously, this is inefficient.

Workers want to be with the firm paying them the highest wage (other things being equal). The desire for high wages causes workers to allocate themselves to firms efficiently (since they will go where they are most valued). In the above case, the worker would not want to work for Firm B, since Firm B would pay less than $10 while Firm A pays $10. So the worker will stay with Firm A, as is efficient.

When all factors are paid this way, we will have, for any two inputs, for example, capital (K) and labor (L):

$$\text{Wage} = P \times MPP \text{ of } L$$
$$\text{Capital Rental} = P \times MPP \text{ of } K$$

Or (solving out P)

$$\frac{MPP \text{ of } L}{\text{WAGE}} = \frac{MPP \text{ of } K}{\text{Capital Rental}}$$

Capital's cost is calculated as an hourly "rental" so that it is expressed in hourly terms, as worker's wages are expressed.

This is the criterion for maximizing profits. Recall the principle of *equal marginal benefit per unit.* (See Chapter 18.) The firm can hire several inputs. It should hire each until the last dollar spent on each yields the same marginal benefit. The marginal benefit per dollar of any input is $MR \times MPP$/Input Cost. When this is equal for all inputs, the firm is getting the most output for its money. The above expression meets this criterion (after canceling out the MR terms).

Example: Making Hiring Decisions

PROBLEM   An added worker costs $10,000 a year. An added machine costs $20,000 a year. The marginal worker adds 50,000 units to total output. The marginal machine adds 80,000 units. How can the firm produce more at its current total cost?

SOLUTION   It can produce more by hiring more workers and fewer machines. The worker adds 5 units per dollar (50,000/$10,000), the machine, 4 (80,000/$20,000). So, for example, getting rid of one machine and using the $20,000 savings to buy two workers will on net increase output by 20,000 units (–80,000 from one less machine but + 100,000 from two workers). So at the same total cost, the firm can produce 20,000 more units of output. The firm will continue to hire more units of labor (lowering labor's *MPP*) and fewer units of capital (increasing capital's *MPP*) until both yield the same marginal addition to output *per dollar* cost.

YOU SHOULD REMEMBER

1. When firms are price takers in both the markets they sell in and the markets they buy factors in, inputs will be allocated to their most valued use.

2. Firms will hire inputs until the marginal physical product of each per dollar cost is the same. This will give it the most output for a given cost (and equivalently, the least cost for a given output).

INCOME ALLOCATION

When a firm is a price taker and pays all inputs according to Input Price = Output Price × *MPP* of Input, the total revenue of the firm will be fully (not more nor less) spent in the long run on the factors it employs. The proof of this assertion is beyond the scope of this book, but its implications are important and so are discussed here.

Consider again Table 26–1. Suppose the wage is $16. The firm will hire 5 workers. But the firm's total revenue will be the sum of the revenues added by each worker (*TR* = Sum of *MRP*s): $32 + $28 + $24 + $20 + $16 = $110. However, the firm spends only $80 on workers (5 × $16). So it has a $30 "surplus." However, this surplus is what will be paid for capital inputs and land inputs when they are paid their marginal revenue product. So the firm itself makes no economic profit or loss in the long run. In terms of Figure 26–2, Panel A, labor is paid $100 and other inputs receive the area equal to triangle *ABC* (or 1/2 of base times height: $50). *TR* is $150.

YOU SHOULD REMEMBER

1. When all factors are paid their marginal value (P × *MPP*), total revenue will equal total costs in the long run.

2. The surplus of each factor will be the income of other factors, and vice versa.

KNOW THE CONCEPTS

DO YOU KNOW THE BASICS?

1. When American textile workers lose their jobs, why are consumers and not their employers responsible?

2. What is the benefit of hiring one more worker? The cost?

3. When will the firm stop hiring more workers?

4. When will a firm that is a price taker in both its output and input market stop hiring?

5. Is the following true: "Monopolies are also price searchers (monopsonies) in their input markets."

6. Why do monopolies not hire enough workers from a social point of view?

7. Why does labor cost more than its wage to a monopsony?

8. What rule should firms follow to allocate workers to their most valued use?

9. "If there were no workers, no output could be produced. So workers deserve more than their marginal worth." Comment.

10. How does marginal physical product differ from marginal revenue product?

TERMS FOR STUDY

complements and substitutes
  in the production process
elasticity of input demand
marginal factor cost (*MFC*)
marginal revenue product (*MRP*)
monopsony

output effect
price taker and price searcher
  in input market
price taker and price searcher
  in output market

PRACTICAL APPLICATION

1. The federal government owns 95 percent of the land in Alaska. If it cut back its holding to 90 percent, this would double the land available for private development. It has been argued that this would lower Alaskan land prices (which is true) and that "the lower price of land would make Alaskans poorer." Why is the assertion in quotes wrong?

2. If a firm can hire 100 workers at $100 per worker per week and 101 workers at $101, what is the cost of worker number 101?

3. Use the following table to answer these questions. Assume the firm is a price taker in all markets.

Labor Units	1	2	3	4	5	6	7	8
MPP	20	18	16	14	12	10	8	6

    a. If the firm hires 4 workers, how much is it producing (assuming $Q = 0$ when it hires no workers).

    b. If the wage is $12 and the price of output is $1, how many workers should the firm hire?

c. Answer the same question for $W = \$24$ and $P = \$2$; $W = \$36$ and $P = \$3$; $W = \$48$ and $P = \$4$. (You will find that only the *ratio of wages to prices (W/P)* matters for employment decisions.)

d. If $W = \$35$ and $P = \$2$, how many workers should the firm hire (if it can hire only whole labor units).

4. Indicate whether the following events will increase, decrease, or have an uncertain effect on the quantity of labor demanded by U.S. automobile manufacturers.

Event A: Demand for U.S. cars falls.

Event B: Wages of auto workers go up.

Event C: Price of machinery goes up. (Machinery and auto workers are complements.)

Event D: Price of machinery goes up. (Machinery and auto workers are substitutes.)

Event E: Total productivity goes up in U.S. auto making. Demand for U.S. cars is elastic.

5. A firm can sell fifty widgets for $5 each and fifty-two for $4.90 each. When it hires another worker, its output goes up from fifty to fifty-two units. The firm can hire all the workers it wants at $8.

a. Should it hire this worker?

b. If instead fifty firms were producing one widget each, would one of them hire this worker?

6. This problem illustrates the substitution effect. The widget industry can produce one widget with one of two technologies. Technology A uses two units of labor and three units of capital, while Technology B uses three units of labor and two units of capital.

a. If wages are $2 and capital cost is $1.50 a unit, which technology will the widget industry use?
Hint: Which costs less per widget?
How many workers per unit of output will the industry employ?

b. If wages are still $2 but capital cost is $2.50, which technology will the widget industry use? How many workers per unit of output will it employ?

c. What was the substitution effect?

7. Continuing with Question 6 above, we will now show the output effect. The demand curve for widgets is:

Demand Price	$8	$8.50	$9	$10	$11	$12
Output Demand	400	375	350	300	250	200

   a. When wages are $2 and capital cost is $1.50, what is the cost per widget? Assuming the cost per widget equals the price per widget (as it does in the long run in a competitive industry), how many widgets will be demanded?

   b. When wages are $2 but capital cost is $2.50, what is the cost per widget? Output demand?

   c. What is the output effect?

   d. How many units of labor were demanded in (a)? in (b)?
Remember: Labor Demand = Output Demand × Labor per unit of output.

8. One hour of labor costs $10 and an hour of machine time costs $30. The *MPP* of an hour of labor is 30 added widgets. The *MPP* of an hour of machine time is 120 widgets. How can the firm produce more at the same cost?

9. Before 1975, professional baseball players had restrictive reserve clauses that required the team acquiring a player's contract to pay a large sum to the owner of the team losing the player (this sum had to be large enough to compensate owners for their loss).

   a. Suppose a player had an *MRP* of $500,000 annually but was being paid only $100,000. How did the system keep a player from getting what he was worth? Which case does this reflect?

   b. After 1975, players (with a certain level of seniority) could become free agents, selling their services to the highest bidder. What would this do to this player's wage (assuming he is worth $500,000 to all teams)? Will this bankrupt baseball?

10. A firm can hire one worker at $100 per day, two workers at $110 per worker per day, three workers at $120 per worker per day, and so forth (each added worker adding $10 to all workers' daily wage). The *MRP* for all workers is $200.

   a. How many workers will it hire? What wage will it pay?

   b. If the input market were competitive, such that there were many firms, each hiring only *one* worker, how many would be hired? What wage would they be paid?

ANSWERS

KNOW THE CONCEPTS

1. While the news media often blames employers for plant closings and firings, the employers are only reflecting the desires of consumers: Here, consumers no longer want to buy American-made textiles. The demand for labor is a *derived demand!*

2. The benefit is the addition to total revenue (the marginal revenue product, or *MRP*). The cost is the addition to total cost (the marginal factor cost, or *MFC*).

3. When workers no longer add more to total revenue than to total cost: when $MRP = MFC$.

4. When Price of Output × Marginal Physical Product = Price of Input (from $MRP = MFC$).

5. No. Almost every firm, monopoly or competitor, is a price taker in the markets in which it buys factors.

6. For the last worker hired by a monopoly we have $MR \times MPP$ = Wage. But the value of the worker's output to consumers is Price of Output × *MPP*. Since $P > MR$ for a monopoly, society would gain (as its marginal benefit exceeds the marginal cost) from more employment.

7. A monopsony has to raise its wage to all its workers to hire one more worker. So its cost of another worker is:

   Wage + Added Cost of Higher Wage for Workers Already Hired

   So, its $MFC >$ Wage.

8. Workers should be allocated to the job where they have the *highest* marginal worth: where Wage = Price of Output × *MPP* is highest. This is exactly what competitive markets do.

9. The same is true for capital, for land, and for materials. However, if they all get more than their marginal worth, total costs will exceed total revenues by several times. So the position taken in the quote is an economic impossibility. At the level of the whole economy, it says that all inputs should get more than they produce.

10. *MPP* is the addition to total output due to an added input. *MRP* is the addition to total revenue due to an added input. The first is a physical measure, the second, a monetary measure.

PRACTICAL APPLICATION

1. The fact that private land is so costly in Alaska tells us it has a high marginal physical product. So more land would raise total Alaskan output a great deal. Alaskans as a whole would be better off. Sometimes it is easy to forget the simple fact that more inputs mean more output.

2. $201.

3. **a.** 68. Total Output = Sum of *MPP*s.
   b. 5 workers.
   c. As long as $W/P = 12$, the firm will hire 5 workers.

    d. 2 workers. The first worker adds $40 to total revenue and the second worker adds $36 to total revenue. Both cost less, $35, so the firm hires both. But the third worker would add $32 to *TR* but would cost $35, so the third worker should not be hired.

4. *Event A:*   Decrease (shift demand for labor curve to left).

    Event B: Decrease (move along demand for labor curve).

    Event C: Decrease (shift to left).

    Event D: Uncertain effect. Data suggest that it would decrease labor demand.

    Event E: Increase (shift to right).

5. a. No. the worker adds $4.80 to total revenue (52 × $4.90 – 50 × $5) and $8 to total cost.

    b. Yes. The worker adds $9.80 (2 × $4.90) less 10¢ lost on the first unit of output, or $9.70, to total revenue.

6. a. Technology A (because it costs less). The industry will use two units of labor per unit of output. (Technology A costs $8.50, while B costs $9.)

    b. Technology B. The industry will use three units of labor per unit of output. (A costs $11.50 and B costs $11.)

    c. The substitution effect was the one-unit increase in labor per unit of output due to the higher price of capital.

7. a. $8.50. $Q = 375$.

    b. $11.00. $Q = 250$.

    c. The output effect is the reduction in demand by 125 units (from 375 to 250) caused by the higher price of capital.

    d. 750 (375 × 2) and 750 (250 × 3), respectively.

    Note that the higher price of capital has two effects on labor demand: Its output effect is negative (as *Q* falls from 375 to 250) but its substitution effect is positive (as labor per unit of output increases from 2 to 3). In this case, these effects exactly offset one another.

8. The marginal product per dollar for labor is 3 (30/$10) and for capital, 4 (120/$30). The firm is getting more value per dollar spent on capital, so it should use more capital and less labor. For example, if it got rid of 3 worker hours (losing 90 units of output) and used the $30 to buy one machine hour (gaining 120 units of output), it could increase output by 30 units (120 – 90) with no change in cost.

9. a. If the player is sold, the acquiring team has to pay a one-time payment worth the value of the stream of $400,000 annual profits to the old team's owner. So they can afford to pay only $100,000 to the player. This is Case 4—a monopsony—where workers are paid less than they are worth and the owner keeps the difference.

    b. The player's salary will be bid up to $500,000. This covers what he adds to the team's revenue. Baseball is not being bankrupted by the higher salary, since added revenues cover added costs.

10. a. The firm is a monopsony. The first worker's *MFC* is $100, the second worker's *MFC* is $120, the third, $140, and so on. It will hire 6 workers (the sixth worker having an *MFC* of $200) and pay a wage of $150.

    b. Each firm, because it hires only one worker, does not care that paying a higher wage raises the hiring cost of other firms. It cares only about its benefits and its costs. So a new firm will hire a worker if the worker's *MRP* covers his/her wage. So there will be 11 firms, hiring 11 workers, at a wage of $200.

27

WAGES, LABOR MARKETS, AND UNIONS

KEY TERMS

compensating wage differentials differences in money wages compensating for differences in nonmonetary aspects of work (e.g., working conditions and fringe benefits).

economic rent any payment to a factor in excess of its opportunity cost.

full wage total monetary value of a job (per period); the sum of money wages plus the monetary value of all the nonmonetary aspects of work.

human capital the skills and ability acquired through investment in schooling and on-the-job training.

WORKERS AND JOBS

Why do workers of the same ability earn different wages? Why do doctors earn more than schoolteachers? How do unions affect wages? To answer these questions, this chapter presents two labor market models and their modifications.

MODEL 1: WORKERS ALIKE, JOBS ALIKE

ASSUMPTIONS

1. All workers are equally skilled.

2. All jobs are exactly alike in terms of amenities, fringe benefits, and so forth.

3. Competition exists among employers (there are no monopsonies) and workers (there are no unions).

4. Workers are well informed about what jobs pay.

5. Workers can change jobs easily and employers can change workers easily.

These assumptions will be modified as we move toward more realistic cases.

RESULTS

1. The wage level will be set so the labor market clears.

2. All firms pay the same wage.

EXPLANATION

Figure 27–1 shows the demand and supply for workers in a given labor market. The equilibrium wage is $8, where the demand for workers (70 jobs) equals the supply (70 workers).

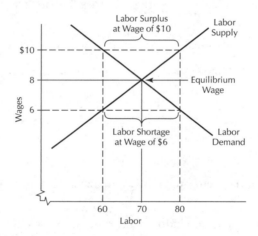

Figure 27–1. The Effect of Labor Demand and Supply

If wages are too high, there will be a surplus of workers. At a wage of $10, for example, there is a surplus of 20 workers. The surplus workers will bid wages down.

If wages are too low, there will be a shortage of workers. At a wage of $6, there is a shortage of 20 workers. Employers who cannot get enough workers will bid wages up.

If one firm pays a wage below the market, all its workers will quit and no others will apply. The firm must raise its wage or go out of business. If it pays a wage above the market, it will have a surplus of applicants. This surplus will alert the employer to the fact that the firm is paying too much. It will lower its wage or be underpriced in the output market and driven out of existence by competing firms.

Note how each assumption listed earlier is necessary for this result. All workers are equally skilled, so employers value all workers equally and can pay each the same wage. All jobs are alike in nonmonetary (or nonpecuniary) aspects, so workers compare wages alone and go to the job paying the highest wage. Workers are informed and can easily change jobs. Employers are not restrained by unions from lowering wages and can replace their workers easily if workers demand wages that exceed the market level.

IMPLICATIONS

1. A firm can determine how its wages compare to what other firms are paying by looking at its resignation rate and its application rate. When resignations are high and applications few, it is paying too little.

2. Competition among workers forces wages down. Competition among employers forces wages up. (This is an example of the "invisible hand" moving people by self-interest to outcomes that are actually in the economy's interest.)

3. Any factor that *increases the demand* for workers will increase wages

$$\text{Wage} = \text{Price of Output} \times \text{Marginal Physical Product}$$

Any factor that increases demand for output (and thus its price) or *MPP* will increase labor demand (and thus wages). For a nation as a whole, wages will be higher when:

a. The nation has more capital per worker.

b. The nation has better technology, managerial skills, and know-how.

c. The nation has abundant natural resources.

When workers in one industry become more productive (because of an innovation or perhaps more capital), the benefits spill over into other industries. As the industry expands, drawing workers from other areas of the economy, wages elsewhere will rise. This phenomenon is sometimes referred to as "a rising tide lifting all ships": Workers benefit from the higher productivity and wages of others.

4. Any factor that *decreases the supply* of workers will increase wages.

In the thirteenth century, the Black Plague wiped out one-third of Europe's population, but left the capital, land, and technical know-how intact. Real wages doubled in many areas. Besides plague, war, and pestilence, some of the factors affecting the supply of labor include:

a. Population.

b. Labor-force participation rate. (This is the fraction of the population that wants to work and is working or seeking a job.)

c. Hours of work per worker.

To get work hours supplied, we multiply $(a) \times (b) \times (c)$. In the next section, we'll discuss the factors affecting (c).

YOU SHOULD REMEMBER

1. When workers are alike in skills and jobs are alike in amenities, all jobs will pay the same wage.

2. At equilibrium wage, the quantity of workers demanded equals the quantity supplied.

3. Factors increasing worker productivity increase wages: More capital, more natural resources, and better technology all increase a nation's wage level.

4. Factors decreasing the supply of workers increase wages; a smaller population, a smaller fraction of persons who work, and fewer hours of work per worker all increase a nation's wage level.

• *HOURS OF WORK FOR AN INDIVIDUAL*

In this century, real wages have risen. As a result, males have worked fewer hours (in 1900, the average work week was 55 hours; today it is 37 hours) while females have worked more (their labor-force participation rate increased from 21 percent in 1900 to over 54 percent today). To understand these divergent results, the main thing to remember is that a person's decision to supply *more* hours of work is also a decision to demand *less* leisure.

An *increase* in the real wage has two effects:

1. ***The Substitution Effect:*** Economists divide the time of workers between work and leisure. Work is any activity for which the worker gets paid. Leisure time includes the remaining hours for which the worker does not get paid. Thus, leisure may involve a great deal of effort and energy (for example, cleaning a home or taking care of children) and yet it is not "work" by this definition.

A higher real wage increases the reward for working and thereby increases the opportunity cost of leisure time. This higher relative cost of work time, by itself, will cause workers to *substitute* (i.e., give up) some leisure time in order to work longer hours so as to get the greater amount of goods the higher wage now buys.

2. ***The Income Effect:*** Leisure is a normal good (see Chapter 18). So when income goes up, people usually want to "buy" more leisure and work less.

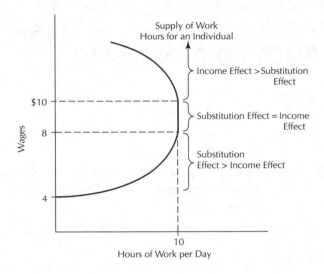

Figure 27–2. The Backward-Bending Supply Curve of Labor

YOU SHOULD REMEMBER

1. One more hour of work means one less hour of leisure time. Therefore, the supply of work hours is the mirror image of the demand for leisure hours.

2. A higher wage has two effects. The substitution effect increases work hours because the higher wage makes leisure time more expensive. The income effect reduces work hours because higher income increases the demand for leisure time.

3. The net effect of a wage increase depends upon which effect is stronger. When the income effect dominates, a higher wage means workers want to work fewer hours and a lower wage means workers want to work more hours. When the substitution effect dominates, a higher wage means workers want to work more hours and a lower wage means less hours.

The net effect of higher wages depends upon whether the substitution effect or the income effect is stronger. Figure 27–2 shows a typical backward-bending supply curve of labor for a worker. In Figure 27–2, the worker works only if wages exceed $4. From $4 to $8, the substitution effect dominates the income effect as higher wages elicit more hours of work. For $8 to $10, the two effects precisely offset each other: In this wage range, the supply of hours for this worker is perfectly inelastic. From $10 up, the income effect dominates the substitution effect as higher wages result in fewer work hours.

For males, the income effect has dominated the substitution effect: Higher real wages have reduced their hours of work. For females, the opposite has been true.

MODEL 2: WORKERS ALIKE, JOBS DIFFERENT

ASSUMPTIONS
Assumptions 1, 3, and 4 of Model 1, *plus:*

2´. Jobs differ in their working conditions. Some are pleasant, some dangerous, and so forth.

5. Workers place the same value on amenities and disagreeable working conditions.

Assumption 2´ means workers now will compare not only wages but working conditions as well. Assumption 5 assures that all workers place the same value on any particular job's working conditions and so are willing to accept the same money wage for that particular job.

RESULTS
The **full wage** of all jobs will be equal. Money wages will vary to compensate workers for the nonmonetary differences between jobs.

EXPLANATION
Full wages are the full monetary value workers place on working in a given job. Full wages serve the same role as money wages did in Model 1: Any job whose full wage is too high will have a surplus of applicants, and any job whose full wage is too low will have a shortage of workers. Only when all jobs pay the same full wage will the labor market be in equilibrium: No workers will want to change jobs.

Those jobs with disagreeable aspects will have to pay a higher money wage; those jobs with positive nonmonetary aspects will be able to pay a lower money wage. These **compensating wage differentials** compensate workers for differences in working conditions. For example, garbage collectors are paid reasonably well because their job is unpleasant.

IMPLICATION

Employers with better working conditions can pay lower money wages. This gives an incentive to employers to provide pleasant working conditions. Employers will improve working conditions as long as the dollar savings from lower wages cover the employers' cost of providing better working conditions.

EXTENSION

We can modify Assumption 5 by assuming (more realistically) that workers differ in the value they place upon many amenities. For example, the extra pay differential workers would demand to work on a high-rise construction project most likely will vary widely from worker to worker. If so, workers in any given job will have the same or _higher_ full wage than they can get elsewhere. Those workers getting higher full wages in their current job than they can earn elsewhere are earning economic rents. An **economic rent** is any payment in excess of opportunity cost (here, it's the excess in full wages over what the worker can get elsewhere). In Models 1 and 2, all jobs paid the same full wage in equilibrium so that no workers received any economic rents.

YOU SHOULD REMEMBER

1. When workers are alike in skill and taste but jobs differ, than all jobs will pay the same full wage.

2. Differences in money wages will compensate for differences in nonmonetary aspects of work. These wage differentials are called compensating wage differentials.

OTHER MODELS OF DIFFERENCES IN WAGES

In the above models, workers were equally skilled and were considered interchangeable by employers. Now let's modify this assumption.

• HUMAN CAPITAL

Human capital is the set of skills that a worker acquires through schooling and experience that improve the worker's productivity and income. The cost of schooling includes its direct costs (such as tuition and books) plus its forgone cost (mainly what could have been earned had one not been in school). The benefit of extra schooling is the value of the increase in future earnings that occurs as a result of the extra schooling.

How do we know that more schooling will lead to higher wages? In the short run, we do not know for certain. For example, a particular skill may suddenly no longer be in demand. However, in the long run, people will not bear the cost of learning a skill unless it pays to do so. Thus, higher wages in the long run compensate workers for the costs of schooling and training.

• *NONCOMPETING GROUPS*

Certain skills and attributes, either natural or acquired, may be in high demand. The workers who have these skills will earn more than those who do not. Those who do not have the skills may not be able to get them (at least not quickly). So an economy can have **noncompeting groups**— whole groups of workers who have special skills and earn economic rents. For example, when oil prices went up, the salaries of experienced oil geologists quadrupled. They earned much more than they could get in any alternative career.

• *SPECIAL SKILLS*

Entertainers, professional athletes, and top managers often have unique skills that make them special. They earn salaries far greater than what they could earn elsewhere. Their high salaries are mostly economic rents and not a compensating differential nor a reflection of opportunity costs. For example, a movie star making $400,000 a year who otherwise would have made $40,000 as a salesperson is earning an economic rent of $360,000.

• *EFFICIENCY WAGES*

In efficiency-wage models, paying a higher wage itself makes workers more efficient. There are several ways this can occur, and we will focus on the shirking model of efficiency wages. In this model, the firm can only sporadically monitor what workers are producing. So there is opportunity for workers to shirk on the job. However, to keep productivity up, the firm has to motivate workers to not shirk. To do this, the firm (1) pays wages that are higher than what workers can get elsewhere, so workers will suffer a great loss if fired, (2) periodically and unexpectedly monitors workers to see if they are shirking or not, and (3) fires them when caught shirking. If the wage premium is worth more to workers than the cost of working hard, then they will not shirk. One piece of evidence in favor of this model is that similar workers in large plants earn 10 percent higher wages than they do in smaller plants. It may be that monitoring is more difficult in larger work places so that a higher wage premium is needed to discourage shirking.

YOU SHOULD REMEMBER

1. The fact that education is costly means that in the long run educated workers must be paid more (or they will not become educated).

2. Whole groups of workers can earn economic rents if there are no other competing groups of workers to bid down their wage.

3. A single worker can earn an economic rent as a result of having a skill or other attribute that is unique.

DISCRIMINATION

Discrimination occurs when workers with the same ability as other workers are denied well-paying jobs or receive less pay because of their race, sex, or other characteristics not related to productivity.

Suppose brown-eyed workers get lower pay than blue-eyed workers. Why would employers ever hire blue-eyed workers when they cost more? Why then do not all workers get the same full wage, as in Model 1 or 2? Some possible explanations of this are:

1. Customers refuse to deal with brown-eyed workers.

2. Coworkers may refuse (or demand a wage premium) for working with brown-eyed workers. If employers cannot keep brown-eyed workers separate from other workers, employers will hire them only when they work for less.

3. Employers may themselves dislike brown-eyed workers. If there are enough unprejudiced coworkers and employers and thus enough jobs for brown-eyed workers from nondiscriminatory employers, then brown-eyed workers will get the same pay. This suggests that a group will be more discriminated against the larger the group and the smaller the fraction of unprejudiced employers.

4. Employers may find it too costly to discover a worker's true ability. Employers may find, for example, that height is a good "cheap screening device" for selecting managers. They may believe that tall people make "natural leaders." So tall children, knowing this, become leaders early, acquiring skills that later will reinforce the employers' belief that they deserve high-paying leadership jobs.

Some economists believe that the forces of competition and profit seeking will, with time, wear down the barriers caused by discrimination. Laws against discrimination may speed this process. However, these laws may fail if employers avoid hiring minorities because they fear the lawsuits that may result if they dismiss a minority worker.

YOU SHOULD REMEMBER

1. The key to understanding discrimination is understanding why employers would ever hire workers of the same ability at higher wages than those discriminated against.

2. The lower wages caused by discrimination may reflect the employers' distaste (or prejudice), the customers' distaste, or the distaste of other workers.

3. Discrimination may reflect its use as a cheap screening device by employers; widespread discrimination may result in a self-fulfilling prophesy.

UNIONS

UNIONS IN PRICE-TAKING FIRMS

A union has a monopoly on the supply of labor to the firms it has organized. Figure 26–3 shows the industry's demand for labor (*DD*) and the workers' supply of labor (*SS*). If the union wants the most members, it will set the wage at $6. It it wants the biggest total wage payments (Wages × Man-hours), it will set the wage at $7, employment being at 70 workers where the union's marginal revenue curve intersects the axis. If it wants the most profits (the total difference between wages and supply costs), it will set the wage at $10 (for a profit of $160): This is at the point the marginal revenue curve intersects the supply curve.

Whatever the union's goals (and they can certainly be other than those above), if the union wants higher wages, it must accept the fact that it will then have fewer members. Unions in the 1970s, for example, pushed their wages up from 12 percent to 25 percent higher than nonunion wages. Union employment and membership fell as a result.

Unions achieve a higher wage by (1) prohibiting employers from paying a lower wage (say, by setting wages at $10 in Figure 27–3) and (2) limiting the supply of workers in the industry (say to 40 in Figure 27–3). Craft unions, which represent workers with a certain type of skill, typically try to restrain entry into the profession. For example, the American Medical Association helped close down many medical schools at the beginning of this century. Industrial unions, which represent all types of workers in the same industries, more often set wages (although a few seek to limit entry and training also).

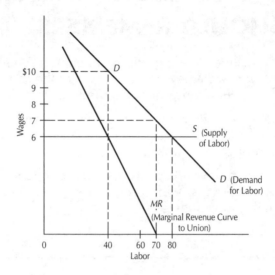

Figure 27–3. Unions: Visualizing the Wage/Employment Trade Off

Some unions try to raise wages by limiting how much each worker produces. Although the same goal could be achieved by reducing the number of workers, a union in a declining industry may feel pressured to keep its current members employed. Limiting productivity will prove useful in increasing labor demand only when the price elasticity of output demand is inelastic (see Chapter 26).

Unions have two effects on nonunion wages:

1. **The Spillover Effect:** In Figure 27–3, if the union increases the wage from $6 to $10, 40 workers will be out of work. They will spill over into the nonunion sector and lower wages there.

2. **The Wage-Threat Effect:** Nonunion firms, to avoid being unionized, may raise their wages. Note that when this effect predominates, both union and nonunion workers will lose jobs.

YOU SHOULD REMEMBER

1. Unions face a trade-off between employment and wages when they organize a competitive industry.

2. Unions may achieve higher wages by setting a minimum wage; by restricting labor supply; and, when output demand is inelastic, by reducing productivity.

3. Unions have two effects on nonunion wages. First, those losing jobs in the union sector will spill over into the nonunion sector, lowering nonunion wages. Second, nonunion employers, to avoid the threat of being unionized, may pay a higher wage.

UNIONS AND EFFICIENCY

Unions are a monopoly. They are the only suppliers of labor to unionized employers. Like all monopolies, unions act to cut their output (which is employment) and raise its price (the wage). As with all monopolies, the result is that unions reduce the social welfare (as measured by the triangle between the demand and supply curve of labor over the range it cuts employment).

Some studies suggest that the cost of higher wages may be partially offset by some cost-saving offsets allowed by the presence of a union. Some of the offsets include:

1. *Reducing turnover.*

   Higher wages reduce turnover costs. In addition, unions appear to reduce turnover even further than accounted for by their higher wages. One model suggesting why is the *exit-voice* model. In a nonunion firm, a worker with a legitimate grievance may be afraid to voice his or her complaint, fearing retaliation from management. This leaves only one choice if the problem is serious enough: to exit (quit) the firm. On the other hand, a worker in a union firm has a grievance procedure where he or she can voice complaints without fear of retaliation. Therefore, the union firm will have lower turnover costs, having replaced exit with voice.

2. *Better training of workers.*

   In some industries, such as construction, workers work for many employers, often on a week-to-week basis. In these industries, the union usually sets up an extensive training program where workers can learn their trade. If the same industry were nonunion, none of the employers would provide training because of the short time workers are with them. Studies have shown that in some cases, union firms construct buildings at a lower cost than nonunion firms did because of their better-trained workforce.

3. *Encouraging workers to invest in firms.*
Unions usually make it harder for firms to fire workers. Therefore, workers know they will be with the firms for a long period. In turn, they will invest more in the unique skills needed by their particular firms because they know they will get a return on their investment. In general, the union is able to police written and unwritten agreements between the workers and management (such as paying the pension promised).

Unions also have added costs (other than higher wages). Unions pose what is called the *hold-up problem* for the firm. Suppose a firm is planning to make a major investment that will increase the productivity of all its inputs, including its workforce. However, this investment will pay only if the union does not push up wages to match the increase in productivity. The union might say it would not push up wages. However, once the firm makes the investment, the union could go ahead and push up wages anyway, knowing the firm will not fire workers because they are now more productive due to the firm's investment. This type of opportunistic behavior is called *the hold-up problem*. The potential of being held up will keep firms from making needed investments. Evidence suggests that this is a serious problem. Union firms are less likely to invest in capital and in research and development. In addition, unionized firms grow slower than nonunion firms, a fact also suggesting the existence of underinvestment.

UNIONS AND MONOPSONISTIC EMPLOYERS

Unions may face employers who act as a monopsony. In this case, over some range of wages, it is possible for unions to get both higher wages *and* more employment.

Whenever a monopoly (here, the union) faces a monopsony (the employers), we have a **bilateral monopoly.**

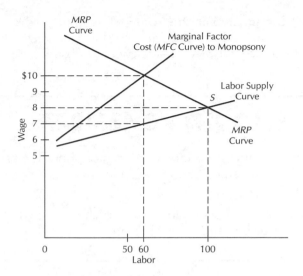

Figure 27–4. The Effect of a Union on Monopsony Employers

Figure 27–4 shows the marginal revenue product (*MRP*) of labor to the monopsony, the supply curve (*SS*), and it marginal factor cost (*MFC*) to the monopsony. If employers were competitive and workers were not in a union, the wage would be $8 and employment 100. If workers are not in a union but the employers are monopsonistic, the monopsony will pay a wage of $7 and hire 60 workers (where *MFC* = *MRP* = $10).

But when the workers are represented by a union, the union can present a wage the monopsony must pay.

Key Procedure for Finding Employment for a Bilateral Monopoly

1. Start at the monopsony wage and employment where *MFC* equals *MRP* ($7 and 60 workers).

2. Draw a horizontal line across the graph at whatever union wage you want (as long as it is above 1's level).

3. Employment will be where this line intersects the labor supply curve (*SS*) or the marginal revenue product curve (*MRP*), whichever comes first.

4. The highest employment will be at the point the supply curve intersects the *MFC* curve.

Starting at $7, as the wage goes up to $8, employment moves from 60 to 100 along the *SS* curve. At $8, the industry has the highest employment. Then going up from $8, employment falls as we move up and inward on the *MFC* curve. At $10, for example, 60 workers will be employed.

What wage the union will choose depends upon its bargaining power and its goals. It is possible for the union to get higher wages and more employment, but in actuality, the union could choose a wage that reduces employment.

YOU SHOULD REMEMBER

1. Unions, facing a monopsonist (a monopoly buyer of labor) can increase employment *and* wages (this does not mean they will).

2. The highest level of employment is at the wage where the supply of labor intersects the *MRP* curve.

THE MINIMUM WAGE

In Chapter 3, we saw that the effect of a minimum wage, like that of any other price floor, is to create a surplus of workers. Studies have shown that for every 10 percent increase in the real minimum wage, teenage employment falls between 1 percent and 3 percent. In addition, we saw above that employers offer better working conditions when they can offer and attract workers at a sufficiently lower money wage. However, the minimum wage (because it prevents lower wages) discourages firms from offering better working conditions. Some studies suggest that the minimum wage causes firms to cut back on working conditions (including on-the-job training) to such a degree that the minimum wage reduces full wages.

Theoretically, a minimum wage could have the same effect of increasing employment as a union could, *when* employers are monopsonistic. However, almost all low-skilled workers can work in a wide range of jobs, so their employers are not monopsonists. So while the monopsonist argument is often used to justify the minimum wage, it has little basis in fact—especially since a minimum wage reduces, not increases, employment.

Another justification given for a minimum wage is that it helps the poor. But studies show that most workers whose income falls below the poverty level earn substantially more than the minimum wage. (Most minimum-wage workers are middle-class teenagers.) Thus, a higher minimum wage cannot substantially help the poor.

KNOW THE CONCEPTS

DO YOU KNOW THE BASICS?

1. How can an employer tell if it is paying its workers too little (compared to other firms)?

2. If a firm lowers its wages, what will happen to the firm's application and resignation rates?

3. Are workers worse off when they work in dangerous jobs with disagreeable working conditions?

4. Why do employers give their workers fringe benefits?

5. What is the main cost of a college education?

6. Will a higher wage always make workers work more?

7. When can unions raise both wages and employment?

8. Why is it costly for employers to not hire workers that are discriminated against?

9. What keeps a union from raising wages too much?

10. If nonunion firms are not worried about being unionized, how will a higher union wage affect nonunion wages?

TERMS FOR STUDY

backward-bending supply
  curve of labor
bilateral monopoly
compensating wage differential
economic rent
efficiency wage

full wages
human capital
income and substitution effects
  on work hours
noncompeting groups

PRACTICAL APPLICATION

1. Using Model 2, suppose (a) Job A has dangerous working conditions, which workers would be willing to pay a minimum of $2 an hour to remove and (b) Job B has a better fringe benefit program, which workers would pay up to $1 an hour to get. How will the hour money wages compare between these two jobs? Which job will workers prefer to take?

2. Why do barbers in India earn less than U.S. barbers, even when both have the same equipment and know-how?

3. Why does attendance in MBA programs go up during recessions?

4. How will the following events affect a worker's hours of work?

   Event A: The worker inherits $500,000.

   Event B: A male worker's wage goes up. (Assume that his income effect is stronger than his substitution effect.)

   Event C: A female worker's wage goes up. (Assume that her substitution effect is stronger than her income effect.)

5. If the government stopped subsidizing the cost of college and fewer people went to college as a result, what would be the short-run and long-run impact on the earnings of college graduates?

6. Unions tend to demand higher wages the more inelastic the demand for labor is (because then the trade-off between wages and employment is lessened). How will the following factors affect union wage demands (other things being equal)?

   a. The demand for output is highly elastic.

   b. Labor represents a small fraction of total cost.

   c. It is easy to substitute capital for labor.

   d. The union controls only a small fraction of the industry.

7. Which of the following best explains why American workers are paid more than workers in Mexico?

   a. American unions.

   b. The minimum wage.

   c. American workers are more productive.

8. Use the following table to answer these questions. The table shows weekly wages and the supply of labor at that wage.

Workers	1	2	3	4	5	6	7	8
Wages	$100	125	150	175	200	225	250	275
MRP	$400	375	350	325	300	275	250	225

   a. If firms in the industry are price takers in this factor market, how many workers will they hire? At what wage?

   b. If this industry is a monopsony (having only one employer or a cartel of a few employers), then how many workers will the monopsony hire?

   Hint: Calculate the monopsony's *MFC.*

9. How will the following events affect the likelihood that workers will shirk?

   Event A: A recession makes jobs scarce.

Event B: Computers allow the firm to constantly monitor workers.

Event C: Workers plan to be in the job only a short time.

10. Professional accountants recently raised the requirement to get a license to practice accounting from having a college degree to having a master's degree (they also have to pass a rigorous exam). How would this impact the wage and number of accountants? How would it benefit new accountants? Old accountants?

ANSWERS

KNOW THE CONCEPTS

1. When its resignation rate is too high and its application rate is too low.

2. Its application rate should fall and its resignation rate should rise.

3. No. Workers in dangerous jobs are getting the same or higher full wage than they could get elsewhere. Their higher money wage compensates for the poor nonmonetary aspects of the job.

4. With higher fringe benefits, employers can attract workers while paying lower wages. If the reduction in wages covers the fringe benefits' cost, employers will offer them.

5. Forgone earnings, i.e., the amount that could have been earned if instead of going to school the person had worked.

6. No. If the income effect (higher wages making leisure more desirable) dominates the substitution effect (higher wages making leisure more expensive), workers will work less.

7. When the union faces a monopsony.

8. Because those discriminated against are cheaper to employ. By hiring these workers, the firm can make more profits and become more competitive.

9. With higher wages, there will be less employment.

10. It will lower nonunion wages as unemployed union workers spill over into the nonunion sector looking for jobs.

PRACTICAL APPLICATION

1. Job A must pay $3 more than Job B. This compensates the workers for having the $2 dangerous working conditions and for not having the $1 better fringe benefits. Workers will then have the same full wage in both

jobs: They'll take either one. Note that *only* in equilibrium are workers indifferent between jobs.

2. The opportunity cost of being a barber is higher in the United States. Thus, all jobs benefit from the fact that in the United States, there is more capital, know-how, and resource per worker.

3. A major cost of schooling is forgone earnings. In a recession, this cost is reduced. So more people continue their schooling (unless they believe the earnings of MBA holders is also going to be depressed in the future).

4. *Event A:*   Hours of work will decrease.

   Event B: Hours of work will decrease.

   Event C: Hours of work will increase.

5. In the short run, an increase in the cost of college would reduce the number of people getting a college education. Wages of college graduates would remain unchanged until their numbers dwindled (which could take years). In the long run, the stock of college graduates would fall, increasing the wages of college graduates as their fewer number increased their marginal product. Ultimately, the cost of going to college would once again pay for itself, but (a) college graduates would earn more to justify the higher cost of college and (b) there would be fewer college graduates, so they will have a higher marginal product to cover their higher cost.

6. **a.** Reduce wage demands.

   b. Increase wage demands.

   c. Reduce wage demands.

   d. Reduce wage demands (the smaller the fraction of the industry a union controls, the more elastic the demand for union output will be because of the competition from the nonunion firms).

7. Answer (c). Americans earn more because they produce more.

8. **a.** The industry will hire 7 workers at a wage of $250.

   b. The following table shows the monopsony's *MFC*.

Workers	1	2	3	4	5	6	7	8
Wages	$100	125	150	175	200	225	250	275
MRP	$400	375	350	325	300	275	250	225
MFC	$100	150	200	250	300	350	400	450

The *MFC* is the increase in total cost. For example, for a monopsony hiring all workers, 3 workers cost $450 (3 × $150) and 4 cost $700 (4 × $175): hiring the fourth worker increases total cost by $250. The monopsony will hire until *MRP* equals *MFC* or 5 workers at a wage of $200.

9. *Event A:*   Decrease shirking, because workers will lose more if fired.

  Event B: Decrease shirking, because workers are more likely to get caught.

  Event C: Increase shirking, because loss of good pay is less if worker is only going to be in the job a short time.

10. The impact would be to reduce the number of accountants over time and thus raise the wages of those who are accountants. Old accountants would benefit. New accountants would get higher wages, but only to offset their higher costs of becoming accountants, so they would not benefit (or would benefit by less than those who are already accountants).

28
RENT, INTEREST, AND PROFITS

KEY TERMS

capital human-made resources of production useful for more than one year.

economic profit excess of revenues over costs (including the opportunity cost of owner's time and investments).

economic rent payment (usually in annual terms) to factor in perfectly inelastic supply.

interest payment for the use of funds over a period of time.

Economic rent is a payment to any factor in perfectly inelastic supply. In other words, economic rent has *no* impact on supply. As noted in Chapter 27, economic rent is also any payment in excess of a factor's opportunity cost. This is an equivalent definition. Why? Because once a factor receives its opportunity cost, any added payment leaves its supply unchanged.

Economic profit is the excess of total revenues over costs (including the opportunity costs of the owner's time and investment). Economic profit is like a rent, except competition eliminates economic profits in the long run. (Note, however, that a monopoly does not face competition and thus can earn long-run economic profits.)

Interest is a payment for the use of funds over a period of time. These funds may finance the production of **capital**, a durable human-made resource of production that yields a return over several years. The income from capital is called its **yield** or **return,** and is stated as a percent of the original investment. So if a $2,000 machine yields $200 a year, its **rate of yield** or its **rate of return** is 10 percent ($200/$2000 $\times$ 100).

At one time, "rent" was defined as the return on land and "interest" as the return on capital. However today, economists recognize that all factors can earn rents, interests, *and* profits. For example, suppose an actor invests $100,000 in acting lessons. The alternative interest he could have earned on the $100,000 is 10 percent. Without acting lessons, he would have earned $20,000 a year in some other profession. With lessons, skill, and luck, he earns $70,000 a year as an actor. Of the $70,000, $20,000 compensated him for the opportunity cost of his time and is the "wage" portion of his compensation. His interest income on his investment in acting lessons is $10,000 (10 percent of $100,000). And $40,000 is an economic rent (the payment in excess of his opportunity cost of $30,000).

ECONOMIC RENT

Economic rent is any payment that does not affect the supply of the input. As a consequence, economic rent is a *purely demand-determined payment.* For example, suppose a farm grows a given amount of cotton and nothing else. Suppose cotton costs (in fertilizer, labor, and other nonland costs) $5,000 to grow. Any payment for this farm's annual crop in excess of $5,000 is an economic rent (because above $5,000, cotton will be grown regardless of how high the price is). If the crop is worth $12,000, for example, the economic rent is $7,000 ($12,000 − cost of $5,000). When cotton demand falls and the crop's price falls to $7,000, economic rent falls by an equal amount, to $2,000. When demand goes up and the crop's price goes up to $20,000, economic rent rises to $15,000.

Some factors earn economic rents because they are more efficient. Figure 28–1 shows the supply cost (or the nonland cost) of growing cotton on different land. We assume each acre of land grows the same amount of cotton but at different costs. As we move from left to right on the supply-of-land curve, we move from the most efficient land to the least efficient land. The first acre put into production grows the crop at a cost of $2,000. The 80,000th acre's cost of growing the crop is $7,000. Demand equals supply at Point *B*: 100,000 acres will be cultivated, each acre producing $12,000 worth of cotton. The best land has a growing cost of $2,000 and so earns an economic rent of $10,000. The 80,000th acre earns an economic rent of $5,000 ($12,000 − $7,000). The 100,000th acre put into production has a growing cost of $12,000: It earns no economic rent. The 100,000th acre of land represents **marginal land.** Most land's nonland cost is just covered by what it produces. If land sells for ten times its economic rent, then the first acre would sell for $100,000, the 80,000th acre for $50,000, and the 100,000th acre, the marginal land, for zero dollars.

Total economic rent received from all land is the sum of all rents, or Area *ABC*. This area is the producer's surplus (see Chapter 25) for cotton farmers.

Now let's consider several propositions about taxes and rents:

1. *A tax only on economic rent* will not affect the supply or allocation of the factor. The most profitable use for the factor before the tax is still its most profitable use after the tax. So the tax does harm efficiency: Resources are still allocated to their best use.

2. *A price ceiling on economic rent* will not affect supply but will affect the allocation of the factor. Suppose three people want an apartment: A will pay $800 for it, B will pay $600, and C will pay $400. Without a price ceiling, A will get the apartment. But with a price ceiling of, say, $300, A or B or C may get it. There is no assurance that the apartment will go to the person who most values it (A). From an economic point of view, price ceilings on economic rent are allocatively inefficient.

3. *A tax on the actual rent* from land that exceeds its *economic* rent will reduce the supply of productive land. For example, in Figure 28–1, a tax of $5,000 an acre will reduce the after-tax return on land to $7,000 and acreage to 80,000 acres.

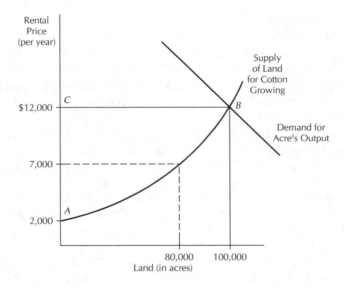

Figure 28–1. Determining Land Rent

YOU SHOULD REMEMBER

1. Economic rent is a payment to a factor whose supply is fixed. Economic rent is purely demand-determined: It goes up or down by the change in what consumers pay for the factor's output.

2. A tax on economic rent affects neither the supply of resources nor how they are used.

3. Rent provides an incentive to allocate resources to their most efficient and productive use. Price ceilings on rent remove this incentive.

INTEREST

Most business firms borrow to finance their investments. **Investment** is the *addition* firms make to their current capital stock. Their current capital includes their plants, equipment, special know-how (technology), and any other durable man-made inputs. Capital has a productive life beyond a year, while "materials" are used up within the year.

Interest is the price the firm pays to borrow funds. If it pays $1,000 a year to borrow $5,000, its interest rate is 20 percent. On the other hand, the investment's yield (or return) is its payoff. If a $5,000 investment pays back $1,500 a year, its rate of return (rate of yield) is 30 percent. To maximize profits and wealth, a firm should borrow when the rate of return on its investments exceeds the interest rate.

Examples: How to Maximize Profits and Wealth

PROBLEM   An investment costs $6,000 and pays back $1,500 a year forever. The interest rate is 10 percent (for simplicity, we assume the firm can both borrow and lend at this rate). Should the firm make the investment?

SOLUTION   Yes. The project yields a rate of return of 25 percent ($1,500/$6,000 × 100), which exceeds the interest rate of 10 percent. By borrowing $6,000 and then paying back $600 (10 percent of $6,000) a year in interest, the firm will increase its profits by $900 a year ($1,500 return − $600 in interest payments).

PROBLEM   If the above project returns $500 a year (instead of $1,500), should the firm make the investment?

SOLUTION   No. The interest rate (10 percent) exceeds the project's yield
(8.33 percent). The firm would be better off lending the $6,000 at
10 percent and earning $600 a year (instead of this project's
return of only $500).

How do we calculate an investment's _yield_ (also called its _internal rate of
return_)? For a given investment, estimate its current costs and its future
benefits. Next, set up the net present value formula for the investment (the
present value of its future benefits minus its current costs), letting the interest rate be a variable (say, the letter _i_). Finally, plug in different values for the
interest rate until you find one for which the net present value of the investment is zero. The interest rate that causes the net present value of the
investment to equal zero is the investment's _yield._ Fortunately, most financial calculators and spreadsheet programs have routines that will solve for
the yield.

If the investment's yield exceeds the market rate of interest you can borrow at, then you should make the investment. Why? You can pay off the loan
out of the yield and have the difference left over as profit (this is usually
true, but some exceptions are covered in finance courses). For example, if
an investment yields 12 percent and you can borrow at 8 percent, the difference, 4 percent, is pure profit.

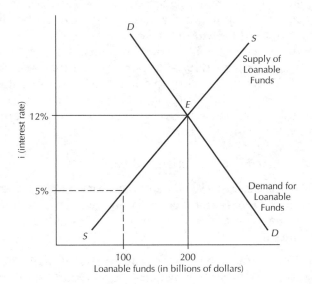

Figure 28–2. The Demand and Supply of Loanable Funds

One role of interest rates is to assure that only the most productive projects are financed. A **usury law** sets a price ceiling on the interest rate

charged on loans. A **usury ceiling** prevents the efficient allocation of capital.

Suppose the usury ceiling is 5 percent. In Figure 28–2, $100 billion will be saved. However, that is only one-half of what would have been invested and saved at the market rate of 12 percent if not for the usury ceiling. Thus, usury laws *reduce total savings and total investment!* Furthermore, projects paying less than 12 percent may be financed. For example, if a project paying 12 percent is pushed aside for one paying 7 percent, the economy will lose the 5 percent difference. As a result, usury ceilings can reduce economic growth, reduce total investment, and misallocate capital.

What factors determine the market rate of interest? Recall that when savers buy a bond, they are lending money to the firm that issued the bond. The interest rate on any particular bond (or other loan) is determined by the following factors.

Factors That Determine the Market Rate of Interest

1. *Real Rate Interest:* Most people prefer a dollar's worth of consumption today over the same amount of consumption in a year. So it is necessary to pay them *more* in a year to get them to give up a dollar's worth of consumption today. The real rate of interest reflects this extra payment. If in order to save $1,000 in real goods today, savers must be paid $1,100 in real goods in a year, then the real rate of interest is 10 percent. This "pure" rate of interest reflects people's time preference for the present over the future.

2. *Premium for Default Risk:* The issuer of the bond may not pay back the loan or bond (i.e., may **default**). If savers anticipate a high risk of default, a high interest rate will be offered.

3. *Risk Premium for Interest Rate Changes:* Most bonds pay a fixed rate of interest. When interest rates go up, the value of these bonds falls. To compensate savers for this risk, bonds may carry an added risk premium. Since longer-term bonds and loans are more exposed to this risk, they typically pay a higher interest rate. The **normal yield curve** for bonds is for bonds with greater maturity (i.e., longer terms) to pay higher interest rates.

   A recent trend has been for bonds and loans to pay a variable interest rate (usually based upon the three-month U.S. treasury bill rate). These bonds have little interest rate risk and so usually pay less interest.

4. *Inflationary Premium:* Savers want more dollars back in interest when they expect inflation: They then can get the *real* interest rate they want. For example, the savers in (1) above want to be paid $1,100 in real goods in a year. If they expect prices to go up 10 percent, they will want 10 percent more dollars, or $1,210, so they can still buy $1,100 worth of real

goods. If r is the real interest rate and p is the expected rate of inflation, then i, the nominal interest rate quoted on the bond market, will equal:

$$i = r = p + (r \times p).$$

Here, i = 21% [.21 = .10 + .10 + (.10 × .10)]. Usually the $r \times p$ term is so small that it is ignored. In this case, we write $i = r + p$.

5. *Premium for Administration Costs:* Interest also has to cover the cost of administering the loan. For small loans (such as those on credit cards), this cost can be significant.

YOU SHOULD REMEMBER

1. Interest is a payment to savers for giving up current consumption and lending the resulting savings.

2. A firm borrows as long as its investment projects have a higher (or the same) rate of return as the market rate of interest.

3. The supply of loanable funds reflects how much people want to save. The demand reflects the expected rates of return on investment projects.

4. Investments represent *additions* to the current capital stock.

5. The interest rate is the real rate of interest, *plus* a premium for default risk, *plus* a risk premium for possible changes in the value of the loan (or bond), *plus* an inflationary premium, *plus* a premium to cover administrative costs.

MAKING INVESTMENT DECISIONS

Firms making an investment decision have to compare current costs with future returns. The main method of doing this is using present value.

The Steps in Making an Investment Decision

Step 1: Calculate the present value of returns.
The present value (PV) of a return of R dollars in N years is:

$$R/(1 + i)^n,$$

where i is the market interest rate stated as a decimal number (see Chapter 13). **Present value** is the *discounted* value of the R dollars: It is the amount one would borrow today at i percent to pay back R dollars in N years.

Take the returns for each future year, calculate their present values, and then add them together. The resulting number—the present value of the returns—is the amount that can be borrowed today and paid back with the returns.

Step 2: Calculate the cost.

If the firm is buying capital now, there is no need to discount. However, if costs are incurred over several years, these costs will have to be discounted just as returns are.

Step 3: Invest if present value of returns ≥ cost.

If a project costs $500 and has returns whose present value is $700, the firm can borrow $700, invest $500 to pay off the $700 loan, and have $200 left over as a profit. (Recall that the $700 present value is the amount the returns can be used to borrow against.)

Examples: Using Present Value to Make an Investment Decision

PROBLEM A machine costs $2,000. It lasts two years and has no scrap value. In the first year, it produces $990. In the second year, it produces $1,210. Should the firm invest in the machine, if the interest rate is 10 percent?

SOLUTION No. *Step 1*: PV = $990/1.10 + $1,210/1.21 = $1,900. *Step 2*: Cost = $2,000. *Step 3*: PV < Cost.

PROBLEM You can buy or lease a car for one year. If you buy the car, you pay $10,000 now and can sell it for $8,640 in one year. You can lease it for one year for $2,600 (which has to be paid now). In both cases, you have the same maintenance and gas costs. When the interest rate is 20 percent, should you buy or lease?

SOLUTION Lease. Find out the *PV* of buying the car for one year. It is $10,000 less the *PV* of getting back $8,680 in one year: $10,000 − $8,640/1.20, or $2,800. Here, leasing is cheaper since it costs only $2,600.

VALUE OF AN ASSET

The value of a piece of land is the present value of all its future rentals. Similarly, capital's value is the present value of all its future rentals. If an asset's yearly "rental" is R per year and if the asset lasts forever, then its present value—when the interest rate is *i* percent—is shown by the following:

$$PV = R/i,$$

where *i* is stated as a decimal. So an asset paying $200 a year forever is worth $2,000 when the interest rate is 10 percent. (One could borrow $2,000 at 10 percent and pay back $200 a year forever.) However, if the interest rate fell to 5 percent, the asset would be worth $4,000 ($200/0.05).

ECONOMIC PROFITS

Economic profits are residual payments. They are the excess of total revenues over total costs (including the costs of the owner's time and capital). Unlike economic rents, economic profits disappear in the long run when subjected to competitive pressures. Economic profits are "quasi-rents," because they are like economic rents except that they disappear with competition.

> Note: We are talking about *economic profits*. Recall that accounting profits ignore the opportunity cost of an owner's time and investment and do not disappear in the long run.

Economic profits arise from several sources:

1. *Innovation:* An entrepreneur discovers a cheaper way to produce an existing good or finds a more valued use for existing resources (e.g., by discovering a new and more valuable good to produce with these resources). Either way, entrepreneurs earn on economic profits until competitors copy their methods and bid their profits away.

2. *Monopoly:* By reducing output produced from its competitive level of production, a monopoly can earn economic profits.

3. *Risk Bearing:* In many industries, only a fraction of those entering will ever succeed (i.e., the restaurant industry). It seems reasonable, then, that the few winners must earn more than their costs. Otherwise, no one would be willing to bet their resources in these risky enterprises.

A central role of economic profits is to tell producers what goods consumers want them to produce. Economic profits signal what goods consumers want more of, while losses signal what goods consumers want less of.

YOU SHOULD REMEMBER

Economic profits are rents that can be bid away by competition. They arise from innovation, risk bearing, and the reduction of output due to monopoly.

KNOW THE CONCEPTS

DO YOU KNOW THE BASICS?

1. Economists sometimes refer to economic rent as a payment to a factor that no one can produce more of. How does this match our definition?

2. Is the "rent" paid on an apartment purely an economic rent?

3. If a factor's payment is totally an economic rent and its demand curve shifts down 50 percent, what will happen to the factor's payments? To its supply?

4. Why do interest rates reflect "the public's impatience and capital's productivity"?

5. Who are the lenders and borrowers of a bond?

6. Why do bonds with longer maturities normally pay more?

7. Why does a price ceiling on rents or interest lead to allocative inefficiencies and lower output?

8. How can a college student earn an economic profit by his or her choice of study?

9. How does risk lead to profits for some?

10. What two roles do all factor payments play?

TERMS FOR STUDY

economic profit	rate of return
economic rent	real (or pure) rate of interest
inflationary premium	risk premium
interest	usury premium
marginal land	

PRACTICAL APPLICATION

1. There are five plots in a town that are suitable for locating gas stations. The nonland cost (in annual terms) of developing and operating the first plot is $10,000. For the second plot, the cost is $20,000, for the third plot, $30,000, and so forth.

   a. If each location generates $100,000 in annual revenues, what is each plot's economic rent? Is any plot marginal?

   b. If each location generates $40,000 in annual revenues, what is each plot's economic rent? Is any plot marginal?

2. Assume that initially the economy is in equilibrium in all markets such that all goods cost a dollar to produce, sell for a dollar, and have a marginal benefit of a dollar.

   a. Firm A discovers a new product that proves popular and makes huge profits. How are consumers better off?

   b. Instead of the above, Firm B discovers a way to produce its current output at 10¢ a unit and makes huge profits. If it does not lower its price, how are consumers better off?

3. A firm has four possible projects in which it can invest. Their rates of return are 15 percent, 12 percent, 10 percent, and 7 percent. What will determine how many of these projects it finances? Does it matter whether the firm has to borrow to finance the projects, or whether the firm has to finance the projects from its own funds?

4. A college town has two types of renters: townspeople and students. There are 200 student renters who are willing to pay $500 a month for an apartment. Of the renters who are townspeople, 100 are willing to pay $600 for an apartment and another 150 townspeople are willing to pay $400. There are 240 identical apartments in the town.

   a. What is the free market rent?

   b. What would the rent be if there were no students?

   c. Who causes high rents, apartment owners or renters?

   d. A rent control law imposes a rent ceiling of $300. Suppose that at this low rent, no apartment owner will bother renting to students unless there is no one else to whom he or she can rent. Who gains from the rent ceiling? Who loses?

5. Suppose there are five drug companies all working on finding a cure for cancer. Each one has a one-in-five chance of finding the cure and being able to patent it. It costs $100 billion for each company to do cancer research. Assume firms will do the research if expected profits (the probability of getting the cure times the profits from the cure) cover research cost. What must the profits from the cure be? What would hap-

pen if drug companies were forced to sell drugs at cost, including their research cost?

6. Which of the following is the best example of someone collecting an economic rent:

   a. A landlord who rents an apartment at an amount just covering his or her cost.

   b. A student who buys a ticket for $10 but would have paid $15.

   c. An auto dealer who sells a car for $12,000 and would have taken $10,000.

7. A firm has a project returning $1,000 a year in perpetuity (i.e., forever). Assume the market rate of interest is 5 percent.

   a. What is the present value (*PV*) of the returns from this project?

   b. What is the maximum cost the firm will bear to build this project?

   c. If the project cost $5,000, what will happen to the firm's value?

8. Many people like the idea of owning and operating a small inn. Some economists have called innkeeping a "capital consumption industry," because they think more is invested in inns than is ever earned. Suppose this is true, how could this occur?

9. Suppose all farmland is good only for farming and is of equal quality. Will a reduction in farm aid reduce agricultural output?

10. How will the following events affect the interest rate that a bond pays and the price of the bond?

   Event A: An increase in the expected rate of inflation.

   Event B: A growing confidence that the firm issuing the bond will survive and prove creditworthy.

   Event C: A growing concern that future bond prices will prove more variable.

ANSWERS

KNOW THE CONCEPTS

1. The quantity of a "nonreproducible" factor cannot be increased. So its supply is inelastic and it thus earns rent.

2. No. Some, if not most, of an apartment's rent is a return on improving the property (by building the apartments) and a compensation for maintenance.

3. The factor's payment will fall 50 percent and its supply will be unchanged.

4. The supply of loanable funds reflects the impatience of savers: The more impatient they are, the less they supply. The demand for loanable funds reflects the productivity of capital. The more productive capital is, the more firms demand. Thus, the equilibrium interest rate is influenced by both these factors.

5. Firms borrow money by issuing bonds. The savers who purchase the bond are lending their money to firms.

6. Because they are exposed for a longer period of time to the risk of their value falling (due to interest rates rising, greater inflation, or default).

7. With a price ceiling, owners no longer have an incentive to allocate their resources to their most valued use. So a price ceiling results in the misallocation of resources.

8. If a student can anticipate before others do which fields of study will pay better, then by choosing to major in a well-paying field he or she can make a profit. However, in the long run, other students will perceive the field's value and compete its profits away.

9. Without profits for some, none would be willing to risk money. Profits for some make up for the losses of others.

10. Factor payments give an incentive to people (1) to supply the factor (*except* for economic rent) and (2) to allocate the factor to its most valuable use.

PRACTICAL APPLICATION

1. **a.** Plot 1: $90,000. Plot 2: $80,000. Plot 3: $70,000. Plot 4: $60,000. Plot 5: $50,000. No plot is marginal.
   b. Plot 1: $30,000. Plot 2: $20,000. Plot 3: $10,000. Plot 4: $0. Plot 5: Will not have a gas station (unless it is already built and its cost a sunk cost). Plot 4 is marginal.

2. This problem illustrates how an innovative economy is always moving in the direction of greater output and making people better off.
   a. For firm A to sell any output, it must offer consumers more marginal benefit per dollar than they are getting elsewhere. So, for their money, consumers are now getting a higher marginal benefit and so *more* total benefit: they are better off.
   b. Firm B uses fewer resources to produce its goods, which are now released to produce more elsewhere. The total output of other goods goes up, their prices fall, and consumers are better off.

3. The market interest rate determines how many projects it will build. If the rate is 11 percent, the firm will undertake only the first two projects (paying 15 percent and 12 percent). Even if the firm can finance all four

projects with its own funds, it would never invest in the projects paying 10 percent and 7 percent. When the interest rate is 11 percent, it would be better off to lend the funds out and earn 11 percent.

4. **a.** $500.

   b. $400.

   c. Renters.

   d. Those who gain are the 240 townspeople who pay less rent than they would have paid otherwise. Those who lose are the apartment owners and students who cannot find an apartment.

5. Profits must equal or exceed $500 billion to have each firm's expected profits cover the $100 million cost. This reflects a return on risk bearing. If drug companies could recover only their own research costs, none would do cancer research.

6. **c.** The dealer earns a $2,000 rent.

7. **a.** $20,000.

   b. $20,000.

   c. It will go up $15,000. (For example, the firm could borrow $20,000 today and pay its loan from the project's returns. After deducting the $5,000 cost, it will have added $15,000 to its current value.)

8. There are three possible reasons. The first is that people get some nonmonetary utility out of being an innkeeper. So they are willing to suffer a monetary loss if this nonmonetary utility covers this loss. A second reason is that inn buyers, perhaps because they are new, are ignorant of the likely losses they will suffer. A third reason is if inn buyers are "risk seekers": people willing to lose on average in order to have a small chance of winning a lot of money (such as when people buy lottery tickets). Since few inns have made a lot of money, this is an unlikely reason. In any case, beware of investments that everyone just loves.

9. No. Farmland prices will fall enough to keep farms in production, since farms have no alternative uses. As long as farm prices cover the nonland costs of farmers, output will stay the same. (Note: if farmland does have alternative uses, farm output will fall.)

10. The interest rate and the price of a bond are *inversely* related.

    Event A: Increase interest rate; reduce bond price.

    Event B: Reduce interest rate; increase bond price.

    Event C: Increase interest rate; reduce bond price.

29
PUBLIC CHOICE AND EXTERNALITIES

SOCIAL OPTIMALITY AND FREE MARKETS

Without fraud, misinformation, *and* externalities, people, left alone, will select the best goods to consume and produce them in the most efficient manner. This follows from the fact that free trade allows people to reallocate goods and inputs to their most valued use.

However, in the presence of externalities, the free market may *not* produce the socially optimal quantities of goods. Externalities lead to **market failure**—from a social point of view, the market produces with too much or too little of a good.

There are two types of externalities. **Negative externalities** result when activities impose uncompensated costs on people. This means that a good's **social cost** (the cost borne by everyone to produce the good) exceeds its **private cost** (the cost borne by those producing the good). For example, a steel firm dumping its waste in a stream may harm the health of those downstream. Here, steel's social cost exceeds its private cost because the firm does not pay for the harm its dumping does to others. When a good has *negative externalities*, producers pay only a fraction of the good's total cost. Therefore, they will produce *too much* of the good from a social point of view.

Positive externalities result when an activity benefits people who do not pay for those benefits. This means that a good's **social benefit** (the benefit to everyone) exceeds its **private benefit** (the benefit received by the good's producers). For example, a farmer's apple trees may allow local honey producers to raise more bees. Here, an apple tree's social benefit exceeds its private benefit because bee producers do not pay for the benefits they get from the tree. When a good has *positive externalities,* producers only get a fraction of its total social benefits and so will produce *too little* from a social point of view.

YOU SHOULD REMEMBER

1. Externalities occur when an activity's social costs and benefits are not borne privately by those producing the good.

2. In free markets, too much of a good with negative externalities is produced. Too little of a good with positive externalities is produced.

SOLUTIONS TO MARKET FAILURES CAUSED BY EXTERNALITIES

ASSIGN PROPERTY RIGHTS

Assigning property rights to all of a good's benefits gives owners the right to the property's benefits; the owners then have the incentive to use the property wisely. A major property right is the right of people to sue for the damage done to them by others. For example, polluters will bear the cost of their pollution when citizens can sue for the damages done to them.

The absence of clear ownership rights results in the **problem of the commons.** In England, commons were unowned areas where any farmer could graze field animals. No farmer expected to benefit from saving grazing land for future use, because other farmers coming along would get the benefit instead. As a result, farmers overgrazed and destroyed the commons. On the other hand, an owner would have had an incentive to maintain that land and prevent overgrazing. Just as the unowned commons were abused in the past, currently oceans are overfished and public timberlands are overcut since without property rights, no one has an incentive to maintain the future value of these unowned resources.

ENCOURAGE LOWER TRANSACTION COSTS

According to the **Coase Theorem,** people can get rid of any market failure by bargaining among themselves if *transaction costs are low*. What's more, the distribution of property rights does not affect this outcome. Consider the following example.

A factory dumps its waste into a nearby stream. This costs the people downstream $20,000 in damages each year. To clean up its waste, the factory would have to spend $12,000 annually. From a social point of view, society would be better off cleaning up the waste since the benefits exceed the costs.

What would happen if the factory has the right to dump unclean waste into the stream? Without transaction costs, the downstream citizens could (and would) get together and pay the factory $12,000 not to pollute.

Now suppose the factory does not have the right to dump without the downstream citizens' permission. In this case, it will also not pollute because its dumping costs would be $20,000 (to compensate the downstream citizens for damages) while cleanup costs are only $12,000.

Thus, in both cases, the outcome—no pollution—is the same regardless of who has the property rights to the stream.

The presence of high transaction costs can cause this socially optimal result not to occur. For example, when the factory has the right to dump, it may be too costly for downstream citizens to get together and pay the factory not to pollute. One way to lower transaction costs would be to allow for class-action suits against polluters, rather then requiring each person to go to court individually.

GOVERNMENT TAXES AND SUBSIDIES

Taxes on negative externalities and subsidies for positive externalities can correct market failures.

Panel A of Figure 29–1 shows the case when producing widgets results in negative externalities. Due to pollution, the social marginal cost (*SMC*) is $4 per unit above the private marginal cost (*PMC*). In a free market, firms produce 50 widgets and sell them at $10. The marginal social *and* private benefit is $10 *but* the widget's social cost is $14: Too much is being produced. Ideally, the government could impose a $4 tax per widget: This would raise widget's private cost to its true social cost. Firms would then produce 35 widgets and sell them at a price of $12. At this output, social marginal benefit equals social marginal cost.

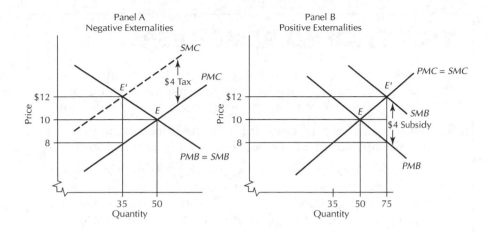

Figure 29–1. How Taxes and Subsidies Correct Negative and Positive Externalities

Panel B shows the case when there is a positive externality in the consumption of widgets (but no negative externalities). Due to the uplifting effect of widget consumption, its consumers benefit others by $4 for each unit they consume. In a free market, 50 widgets are consumed at a price of $10. However, the fiftieth unit's social marginal benefit ($14) exceeds its social *and* private marginal cost of $10. More should be produced. With a subsidy of $4 per unit, suppliers will treat the social marginal benefit curve (*SMB*) as their new demand curve. They will produce 75 units at a price of $12.

GOVERNMENT REGULATION

Government regulation tells firms what they can and cannot do. For example, all firms may have to install a certain type of pollution control.

The limits of regulation are that:

1. Because most regulations apply to all firms regardless of their individual costs and benefits, regulations can be inefficient. For example, all cars in the United States have about $1,000 worth of pollution-control equipment, whether they are used in Los Angeles or in Utah. Yet in Utah, pollution is so low that the marginal benefit of less car pollution is negligible.

2. Standardization in regulations does not allow for individual tastes. For example, in certain communities, citizens would prefer to breathe polluted air rather than suffer the loss of jobs caused by the imposition of pollution standards.

YOU SHOULD REMEMBER

1. When no one owns a resource, no one has an incentive to maintain its value, since anyone can get the benefits of the upkeep. The lack of property rights leads to market failure.

2. The Coase Theorem states that without transaction costs, the socially optimal amount of each good will be produced.

3. Cures for market failures include (a) assigning property rights, (b) lowering transaction costs, (c) imposing government taxes (for negative externalities) and subsidies (for positive externalities), and (d) imposing government regulations.

4. Government regulations, when made standard for all, result in added costs.

PUBLIC GOODS

A pure **public good** is a good that people can consume without reducing what others consume. Examples include (up to a point) the services of a lighthouse, a musical concert, and national defense. Basically, a public good is a special case of a positive externality.

Two central aspects of public goods are:

1. The marginal benefit of a public good is the sum of its benefits to everyone. Figure 29–2 shows A's demand curve for the public good and B's demand curve. For the fourth unit, A will pay $5 and B, $7. So the social demand for the fourth unit is $12. The **social demand curve** is the *vertical* sum of the individual demand curves.

2. Public goods will *not* be optimally supplied by the free market when *the cost of exclusion* is high. **Exclusion cost** is the cost of excluding a potential consumer of a good (especially a public good) or from enjoying the benefits of the good.

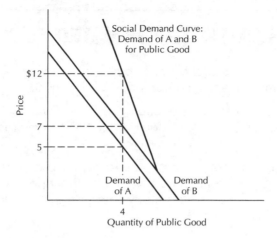

Figure 29–2. Comparing Social Demand and Marginal Benefit of a Public Good

When exclusion costs are high, there is a **free-rider problem.** A free rider enjoys the benefits of the public good without paying for it. When enough people are free riders, the public good is not supplied. Therefore, everyone, including the free riders, is then worse off.

For example, suppose roads are paid for with voluntary contributions. While any one driver might like well-maintained roads, his or her contribution will have little effect. So why should the driver contribute? There is little added benefit for the cost. However, if most drivers thought like this, there would be few roads. However, if noncontributors can be excluded from using the roads (for example, by collecting tolls), the free-rider problem is eliminated.

An example of a public good whose exclusion cost is low is a concert: Free riders are easily excluded by allowing only those who buy tickets to hear the concert. On the other hand, it is impossible to exclude any citizens from the benefits of national defense. Thus, all nations pay for national defense with taxes.

YOU SHOULD REMEMBER

1. One person's consumption of a pure public good does not decrease anyone else's consumption of that good.

2. The marginal benefit of a public good is the sum of its benefits to all person's. Its social demand curve is the vertical sum of all individual demand curves.

3. When exclusion costs are high, the free-rider problem results. Free riders get a public good's benefit without paying any of its cost. When there are too many free riders, too little of the public good is produced.

AN APPLICATION: POLLUTION CONTROL

Pollution is costly (in terms of health, aesthetics, and so forth). Getting rid of it is also costly. Socially, society wants to minimize this sum:

Total Cost = Pollution Cost + Pollution-Abatement Costs

The socially optimal level of pollution is the level that minimizes this total cost. Note that the optimal level of pollution is *not* zero when the cost of achieving zero pollution exceeds its benefits.

Getting rid of pollution is a public good—this suggests that government action is needed to reduce pollution to its optimal level. Marginal analysis is used to derive the optimal level of pollution. The control variable will be tons of pollution per year. The *marginal benefit* of more pollution is the *marginal reduction in pollution-abatement costs*. Figure 29–3 shows the marginal benefit (*MB*) schedule of more pollution. To see why the *MB* curve for pollution has a negative slope, start at 90 tons. The ninetieth ton of pollution costs nothing to get rid of (so this will be the level of pollution without government intervention). If the government acts to reduce pollution, we move left. Moving left, the *MB* curve measures the marginal cost of getting rid of each additional unit. For example, it costs only $10 to get rid of the seventieth ton, while it costs $40 to get rid of the thirtieth ton. Since the marginal cost of getting rid of pollution goes up as more is eliminated, the *MB* curve (which shows the marginal cost saved) rises as we move left and falls as we move right.

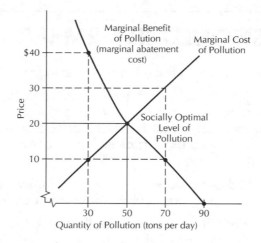

Figure 29-3. Determining the Socially Optimal Level of Pollution by Comparing Marginal Benefit and Marginal Cost

The marginal cost (*MC*) schedule shows the marginal cost of pollution. This is the damage an additional unit of pollution does to people's health and property. The thirtieth ton, for example, harms society by $10, and the seventieth ton, by $30.

In a sense, the *MC* curve is society's supply curve for pollution while the *MB* curve is society's demand curve. However, the *MB* curve is not a demand "for pollution." Rather, it is a demand to keep the cost of reducing pollution down.

The socially optimal level of pollution occurs where marginal benefit equals marginal cost: at 50 tons. Too *little* pollution, say 30 tons, costs more to get rid of than it is worth (e.g., getting rid of the thirtieth unit costs $40 but is only worth $10). On the other hand, too *much* pollution is also harmful. For example, getting rid of the seventieth unit costs $10 buts saves society $30 in health costs. *Not* getting rid of the seventieth unit makes society worse off.

The government can get firms to produce the optimal amount of pollution by (1) imposing a tax equal to the public's marginal cost of pollution or (2) restricting pollution to 50 units through regulations.

Regulations are not generally favored by economists, because changing technology and tastes can make the regulated level either too low or too high from a social point of view. However, given that the government is going to regulate the amount of pollution allowable, the most efficient method to achieve this aim is to allow producers to buy and sell the rights to pollute. In this way, those producers with the lowest cost of pollution abatement will be the ones to reduce pollution. (See Practical Application, Question 7.)

YOU SHOULD REMEMBER

1. Pollution is socially costly, but so is getting rid of pollution.

2. The marginal benefit of a unit of pollution is the pollution abatement cost saved by not reducing pollution by one unit. The marginal cost of pollution is its social cost. More pollution should be allowed as long as marginal benefit exceeds marginal cost.

3. One method of reducing pollution is to impose a tax on polluters equal to the marginal social cost of pollution.

4. Another method of reducing pollution is to regulate how much each firm can pollute. This is most efficiently done if firms are allowed to trade their rights to pollute.

PUBLIC CHOICE

We have modeled the choices by firms and households on the assumption that they act in their own interest. It seems reasonable to assume that government bureaucrats and politicians also act in their own self-interest. Yet, it is commonly assumed government always acts in the public interest. For example, some economists have in the past proposed government spending, regulations, and taxes that, if applied optimally, would enhance the welfare of the United States. However, they did not predict how the public sector would actually use these monies and powers. The results were often disappointing. For example, agencies that are supposed to regulate industries in the public interest often end up regulating them in the industry's interest. As an example, the FDA has raised the cost of developing new drugs so much that current drugs face little competition. As another example, before the airline industry was deregulated, the FAA set monopoly-like fares that averaged 33 percent above the market rate.

However, now many economists are trying to understand how governments act. The theory of public choice analyzes how decisions are made in the public sector.

To understand public choice, we have to compare it to private choice. Public choice and private choice are similar, as (1) both are motivated by self-interest, (2) both face trade-offs due to scarcity, (3) and both involve competition (for example, political parties compete for office and government bureaucrats compete for government funds). On the other hand, public choice differs from private choice, as (1) most government goods are furnished free, without charge, (2) the payment for government goods is through taxes, which you pay whether you like it or not or go to jail, and (3) the choice of government goods is in large part determined by voting. With private goods, consumers vote with their dollars for exactly the goods they want. With public goods, each voter has to choose between two parties, both offering a package of "goods." With private goods, consumers vote frequently and producers quickly find out what consumers want. However, with the "package deals" offered by political parties and with the secret ballot, it is often hard to discern which part of the package voters are actually attracted to.

Because voters face package deals set before them by politicians, a central issue of public choice is whether the votes on these "deals" reflect the true preferences of consumers. The **voting paradox** states that *how* a majority will vote on a set of issues can depend on the order in which the issues are presented. They may vote for A over B. And for B over C. And yet, they may vote for C over A! (See Practical Application, Question 5, for an example.) Since how a majority will vote can depend on the *order* of the issues, who controls the public agenda matters a great deal. In particular, economists expect government agencies to set the public agenda to favor their interests. As one example, budget cutting in most government agencies usually results in the most popular and necessary programs being cut first. In this way, public officials try to create a crisis in which their funding will be restored.

Related to the voting paradox is Kenneth Arrow's famous "impossibility theorem," which states that it is not generally possible to sum a population's preferences into a "social preference function" that could be used to guide government policy. This means that statements such as "Policy X is the best for society" are meaningless.

The **median voter model,** another model of public choice, predicts that when two people are running for office, they will position themselves near the opinions of the median voter. The median voter is the voter at the fiftieth percentile. If one candidate gets too far from the median, the other candidate will win the election. Suppose we have 100 voters. The first feels that government spending should be $1, the second voter wants $2 spent, and so forth. The median voter wants $50 to be spent. Suppose one candidate for office favors $60. The other candidate merely has to promise to spend $59 and will win with 59 percent of the vote. So both candidates, if they want to win, will promise to spend $50, giving each an equal chance at winning. Any other position will lose.

DEALING WITH SPECIAL INTERESTS

Unfortunately, the median voter model does not explain why so many laws favor only a small minority of the population. To explain this, public choice theorists point out that one way to achieve a majority is to combine many special interest groups by promising each something they feel strongly about.

This is called **logrolling**—the trading of votes to get legislation favoring only a minority passed. For example, farmers in the farm states may want a price-support program. The textile mill owners in southern states want a tariff on foreign textiles. To get their bills passed, the farm-state representatives and the southern-state representatives agree to vote for each other's bills. With this type of trading, the "log" of bills gets pushed through Congress.

Such special-interest legislation benefits only a small fraction of the population but costs everyone (in higher taxes and prices). This is socially harmful when it costs the nation more than it benefits the special interests. For example, consumers paid $150,000 per year for every job saved by the auto import quota imposed by our government. Yet, the jobs saved only paid $30,000. (What is worse, the $150,000 would have created three or more jobs elsewhere.)

To see why such **pork-barrel legislation** gets passed (along with the dynamics of logrolling), suppose we hypothetically offered each congressional representative a special program that is worth $10,000 to his or her district but that costs taxpayers *nationally* $30,000. The conditions are that they must vote for a whole log of programs, such that only representatives who vote for the log of programs get a special program. The nation would be better off without any of these programs. However, all representatives may vote for the log of programs. By joining the logroll, their district gets $10,000. By refusing, the log of programs may still pass. If it passes, the district does not benefit but still pays higher taxes. However, by joining, the *addition* to taxes for the district from having its program included is very small. (For example, with 500 districts, the $30,000 total cost of adding its program to the log is only $600 [$30,000/500].) So each representative will vote for the whole log of programs.

If special-interest legislation is so prevalent, why do voters not oppose it? The model of **rational voter ignorance** states that voters rationally do not have any incentive to make fully informed votes. This follows because one person's vote has little effect on an election's outcome. Since it is very costly to become informed about public issues, rational voters, balancing a large cost against a small likely benefit, will be ignorant voters.

On the other hand, special-interest groups benefit from legislation that focuses benefits upon them. They can concentrate their efforts on key legislators. Because the legislation's costs are diffuse (perhaps only a few dollars per voter), few in the public have an incentive to oppose it.

The existence of logrolling shows why, in public-opinion polls, the public dislikes Congress but generally likes their local congressperson. They like the "pork" their district is getting but do not like having to pay for all the other districts' pork. However, if they vote in a congressperson who opposes all such special-interest legislation, they lose their local benefits but still have to pay for those going to all the other districts.

Legislation can result in rents (and profits) to special-interest groups. However, **rent seeking** by seeking favorable legislation can be costly (e.g., in contributions to campaigns). In the extreme, rent-seeking behavior will use up all the benefits of the legislation. From a social point of view, rent seeking produces a net social loss, in that it increases costs without any corresponding benefit to society.

One solution to exploitative special-interest group legislation is to require more than a majority vote, and in the extreme, **unanimity.** However, as the consent of more is needed, society runs into the **hold-out problem.** For example, suppose a program is worth, after deducting its costs, $100 million to the nation. If unanimity (the consent of everyone) was needed, then one representative could hold out by demanding, say, $50 million for his or her district in exchange for his or her consent. Since each representative has an equal incentive to be a holdout, any legislation, productive or not, would be difficult to pass. Thus, as a greater proportion of votes is needed for passage, society gains by having less special-interest legislation but loses by having less legislation in the public good.

Another solution is for legislation to be considered only at the government level (local, state, or national) at which its benefits are felt. In this way, those benefiting will also have to pay its costs. In addition, the smaller the area legislation covers, the greater the freedom citizens have of moving away. To see why the ability to move is important, suppose citizens can move at will between cities at no cost. Then each city would have to provide the optimal amount of social services (parks, sewers, etc.) at the lowest price (i.e., taxes) per unit of service, or be bid out of existence as its citizens move to cities offering the optimal package of services and taxes. Therefore, smaller governments and greater mobility of citizens and firms between cities, states, and nations produce better government. (This result is called the **Tiebout Hypothesis.**)

YOU SHOULD REMEMBER

1. The voting paradox is that different results can be voted for, depending upon the order in which issues are presented to voters.

2. In two-person races, both candidates will try to take positions close to the median voter's positions.

3. During logrolling, representatives vote for each other's special-interest legislation.

4. The optimal level of government services and taxes occurs when (a) governments compete with each other and (b) citizens can freely and at low cost move from one governing unit (such as city or state) to another.

KNOW THE CONCEPTS

DO YOU KNOW THE BASICS?

1. Does the existence of an externality imply a market failure?

2. How does voting differ from using market prices as a means of allocating resources in the economy?

3. Why does the absence of private-property rights lead to the overuse and poor maintenance of the property?

4. Why would a market failure never occur if all transactions were costless?

5. When will society be better off with more pollution?

6. Why do private goods not suffer from the free-rider problem?

7. Why is the average voter underinformed?

8. What determines whether a public good will be underproduced without government intervention?

9. How can special-interest groups gain benefits at a greater expense of the whole economy?

10. How does the international mobility of citizens and multinational firms improve government?

TERMS FOR STUDY

Coase Theorem
exclusion cost
holdout problem
logrolling
median voter
negative externality
paradox of voting

positive externality
private good
problem of the commons
public good
rational ignorance of voters
unanimity

PRACTICAL APPLICATION

1. Use the following to answer the questions below:

Quantity	1	2	3	4	5	6	7
MSB	$10	$8	$6	$4	$3	$2	$ 1
MSC	$ 1	$2	$3	$4	$6	$8	$10

MSB is the marginal social benefit of the good; *MSC*, the marginal social cost.

a. If there are no externalities, how many units of this good should be produced? How many will be produced?

b. If there are positive externalities so that each buyer gets one-half of the social benefit of the good, how many units should be produced? Will be produced? What would the government have to do to get the optimal amount produced?

c. If there are negative externalities so that each seller pays half the social cost of the good, how many units should be produced (assume there are no positive externalities)? Will be produced? What should the government do to get the optimal amount produced?

2. To illustrate why oceans will be overfished, suppose a professor puts twenty beads on her desk and promises the class that she will double the number of beads on the desk every five minutes. Any student can come up any time and take any number of beads. At the end of the class, she will pay 10 cents a bead.

a. What policy is best for the class as a whole?

b. What policy is best for each student?

c. How would property rights help?

3. There are fifty farmers in a valley. Each year the valley floods, destroying all crops. A dam can be built at $2,000 for each foot in height (this cost is an annualized cost). The first foot saves *each* farmer $100 per year in damages, the second foot saves each farmer an additional $90 in damages, the third, $80; and so on.

a. Suppose the dam is three feet high. What is the social benefit of one more foot?

b. What is the socially optimal height of the dam?

c. Suppose forty of the farmers get together and agree to share costs: How high will their dam be? Why are the remaining ten farmers "free riders"?

4. Mr. Jones lives next to Mrs. Smith in an apartment building with thin walls. Mrs. Smith sings opera, which she values at $20 a day. Mr. Jones hates Mrs. Smith's singing and would pay up to $30 a day for her to stop singing.

a. What type of externality is this?

b. What will happen if the apartment contract states that anyone can sing if they want?
Hint: Use the Coase Theorem and assume no transaction costs.

c. What will happen if the apartment contract states that to sing, one must get permission from his or her neighbors?

5. Smith, Jones, and Parker each have a vote on the city council. They are to vote on which of three projects are to be built. Their ranking of these projects (with 1 being the one they want most and 3 the least) is as follows.

	Project A	Project B	Project C
Smith	1	2	3
Jones	3	1	2
Parker	2	3	1

The projects are brought up in pairs.

a. Between Projects A and B, which will win?

b. Between Projects B and C, which will win?

c. Between Projects C and A, which will win?

d. How does this illustrate the voting paradox?

6. Why might smaller school districts produce better schools?

7. In Smogville, the government will allow only 6 units of pollution. There are two firms, Widget International and Smokestack, Inc. The government can either (1) have the same standards for both, allowing each 3 units of pollution or (2) give each firm the right to pollute 3 units and allow the right to be sold to the other company. Without pollution controls, each would put 6 units of pollution into the air. The marginal abatement costs (*MAC*, the cost of reducing pollution by one unit) are:

Units of Pollution	1	2	3	4	5	6
MAC of Widget	$100	$ 90	$ 80	$ 70	$ 60	$50
MAC of Smokestack	$500	$400	$300	$200	$100	$80

a. What will the total abatement cost of option (1) be?

b. In option (2), how many units of pollution will Smokestack, Inc., buy from Widget International? What is the total abatement cost in this case?

c. Why is option (2) more efficient?

8. Why do Democrats running in primaries usually sound more liberal than they do in the main election? (Assume that Democratic voters are more liberal on average than the general population.)

9. A polluting firm argues, "If I have to pay for the damage my pollution causes, this will raise my costs and the social cost of my products." Is the firm correct?

10. Apply the theory of public choice to the following issues:

   a. What will happen to social security as the fraction of population collecting it increases? (Think of social security recipients as a special interest group).

   b. What is a disadvantage for the European Economic Community of having central control over all members?

   c. Why do government agencies often cut the most popular programs when their revenues are cut?

11. In a large apartment house, all tenants had to pay for their own utilities. The rent was $500. Each tenant used $200 of water and electricity a month, yielding a total cost of $700. Then, the apartment owner decided to pay for all utilities and adjusted the rents to reflect the *average cost* for all apartments. Each apartment owner can now use as much water and electricity as he or she wants. How does the new rent compare with $700?

ANSWERS

KNOW THE CONCEPTS

1. No. Market failures occur only in the absence of clear property rights and when there are high transaction costs.

2. Because consumers make choices among many goods and because they directly benefit from their market choices, consumers send a more frequent and informed "signal" to producers than they do when voting.

3. Without property rights, those who maintain the property will not necessarily benefit. So they have no incentive to keep the property up or prevent its overuse.

4. Because those harmed by a negative externality could get together and pay those responsible for it to stop. Similarly those helped by a positive externality could get together and pay those responsible to produce more.

5. When the marginal cost of getting rid of it is greater than the marginal benefit from getting rid of it.

6. Because when one person consumes a private good, others are by definition excluded from enjoying it.

7. Because the likelihood of affecting the outcome is small. So the benefit of voting correctly is small.

8. Too little of the good will be produced without government intervention if the cost of excluding free riders is high. When exclusion costs are low, free riders can be forced to pay: The optimal amount will be produced.

9. Because the per taxpayer cost of special interest legislation is so low that it does not pay anyone to oppose it.

10. Mobility forces nations to compete for citizens and businesses. This pushes them toward offering the optimal mix of public goods and taxes.

PRACTICAL APPLICATION

1. **a.** Four units should be and will be produced.
   b. Four units should be produced. Three units will be produced. The government would have to establish a subsidy of $2 per unit.
   c. Four units should be produced. Five units will be produced. The government should impose a tax of $3 per unit.

2. **a.** The class should wait until the end of the period to "harvest" the beads.
   b. Each student should rush up and grab all twenty beads immediately. If he or she does not, someone else will.
   c. If one of the students owned the beads, he or she would allow their value to grow to its highest level because he or she would be assured through property rights of getting this value.

3. **a.** The marginal social benefit of the fourth foot is $3,500 (50 farmers × $70 marginal benefit to each).
   b. Seven feet high [the seventh foot's marginal social benefit is $2,000 (50 × $40)]. Its marginal cost is $2,000.
   c. Six feet high (the sixth foot is worth $2,000 to the forty farmers). The remaining ten farmers are free riders since each is getting $450 in benefits ($100 + $90 + ... + $50) at no cost. On the other hand, the forty farmers had to pay $300 each for the same benefit.

4. **a.** A negative externality.
   b. Mr. Jones will pay Mrs. Smith $20 at a minimum and up to $30 for her to stop singing. She will agree not to sign.
   c. Mrs. Smith will offer Mr. Jones $20 to give his permission to sing, but Mr. Jones will refuse.

5. **a.** Project A.
   b. Project B.
   c. Project C.
   d. If Project A is compared with Project B, and then the winner (A) with Project C, C will win. However, if B is compared with C, and then the winner (B) compared with A, A will win. So a different agenda pro-

duces a different outcome. (How would you pair the choices so B would win?)

6. Parents have greater mobility between smaller school districts. This forces school districts to compete for students and thus do a better job. In the last twenty years, school districts have been merged and enlarged. According to some economists, the resulting loss in competition is partly to blame for the higher administrative cost per pupil and the lower student performance observed over the same period. (Of course, these results also have many other causes.)

7. **a.** Each firm will get rid of its fourth through sixth unit of pollution. The total abatement cost will be $560.

   b. Smokestack will buy two of Widget's rights to pollute. The first saves it $200 and cost Widget only $80. A price between $200 and $80 will benefit both. The second saves Smokestack $100 and cost Widget $90. Once again, at some price between these numbers, both benefit by the trade. The third is not worth it: it saves $80 but cost Widget $90. The total abatement cost (with Widget getting rid of 5 units of pollution and Smokestack just 1) will be $430.

   c. Because the firms with the lowest cost of getting rid of pollution will be the ones getting rid of the pollution.

8. By using the median-voter model, the median voter in the Democratic primary will be more liberal than in the general election. So Democratic candidates will be more liberal in the primary than in the general election (just as Republican candidates are usually more conservative-sounding in the primaries).

9. No. Its pollution is a cost to society, whether it pays it or someone else does. Forcing it to pay this cost does not change the total social cost. Furthermore, as it cuts back its production, the marginal social cost of the good it produces will *fall* (see Panel A of Figure 28–1).

10. **a.** The retirees become more numerous, it becomes more costly to subsidize them (currently, they are getting about $40,000 more than they ever put in). So voters have more of an incentive to oppose it. As social security becomes more costly, it most likely will be cut back.

    b. Central control has advantages. However, when different democratic nations can have different rules, one way they compete is by offering better laws and better services for the taxes they collect. Too much central control stifles these incentives.

    c. By threatening to cut popular programs, government bureaucrats are acting in their own interest. The result is that the spreading will soon be restored.

11. Because one renter's added utility cost is spread over all renters, the social (actual) utility cost is higher than the private cost. For example, if there are 50 apartments and I use $50 more electricity, my bill only goes up $1. So renters now use more water, gas, and electricity than before. Rents will have to exceed $700 to cover this added cost (studies show that unmetered apartments use 30 percent more gas and electricity). Renters are worse off because they end up paying for more utilities than they wanted.

30
GOVERNMENT SPENDING AND TAXATION

In 1998, the federal government spent over $6,100 per person, while state and local governments spent around $2,800 per person. This represents 29 percent of *GDP*. Total taxes (federal, state, and local) were $9,717 per person, representing 31.5 percent of *GDP* (note that this is per person, not per taxpayer). The federal government collected 65.5 percent of this. The state and local level collected the remaining 34.5 percent. Income taxes accounted for 48 percent of federal taxes, followed by social security (33 percent), and corporate taxes (11 percent).

This government spending went for (1) goods and services (such as defense, highways, education, and police services) and (2) transfer payments. Transfer payments are payments made to individuals without any service or goods being required in exchange. Examples are welfare payments, social security payments, and unemployment compensation.

Income support (including social security and welfare programs) represented 46 percent of the federal budget, followed by defense at 16 percent, and net interest (paid on the federal debt) of 14.7 percent. At the state and local level in 1996, 33 percent of the combined budgets went for education, followed by 16 percent for income support and over 7 percent for fire and police protection.

COST-BENEFIT ANALYSIS OF GOVERNMENT SPENDING

From the standpoint of efficiency, government spending on goods and services should be undertaken only when benefits exceed costs. One method to achieve this goal is to require governments to analyze the costs and benefits of each program. Unfortunately, the ability of government officials to do this accurately may be limited. For example, one study showed that the actual costs of government projects were on average two to three times higher than the government's projected cost. Also, benefits are often difficult to measure.

The common emphasis on employment rather than efficiency in government spending is detrimental to the economy. Suppose there are two projects using only labor. Both yield $100,000 in benefits but one takes two workers and the other ten. Which is better? The one with two workers, because its opportunity cost is lower. To see why, recall that the only way to increase income per person is to increase output per person (see Chapter 27). That is, when *fewer* persons—and less employment—are needed to produce a given amount of output, per capita income goes *up*!

YOU SHOULD REMEMBER

1. When the costs of government projects exceed their benefits, our economy becomes less efficient.

2. Efficiency, not employment, is the means by which the highest output and income per person is achieved.

THE ECONOMICS OF TRANSFER PAYMENTS

Transfer payments can be either (1) cash or (2) payments-in-kind (that is, in the form of specific goods and services). Examples of payments-in-kind include free schooling, free medical care, and free food.

If the government gives someone $10,000 in free education, what is the impact of this spending? First, it replaces what the person would have spent anyway on education (say this is $8,000). Second, the difference between what the person would have spent and what the government supplied increases the amount spent on education. In this example, the difference is $2,000. So the $10,000 in free education increases the amount spent on education not by $10,000 but by $2,000. *An in-kind payment increases total spending on the in-kind good by less than the in-kind payment.*

What is the $10,000 in free education worth to the person getting it? If the person had been given $10,000 in cash (instead of $10,000 in education) and spent it all on education, then the person valued the free education at least as much as $10,000, since he or she was willing to pay that amount for education. However, if the person would have spent only part of it on education (say, only $8,000), then the person values the education by less than $10,000. Why? Because the $2,000 in extra education was not worth $2,000 to the person (or it would have been spent on education and not on something else). To the recipients, *in-kind payments are worth less than (or at best the same as) the same amount paid in cash.*

If the government's goal is to increase the utility of recipients, then all transfer payments should be in cash and not in kind.

YOU SHOULD REMEMBER

1. The total quantity of a good demanded will increase by less than any in-kind payment made in the form of that good.

2. In-kind payments are worth less than their cash equivalent.

TAXATION

Most people when asked how much they pay in taxes, will tell you what they pay in *income* taxes. Yet the income tax represents only 48 percent of federal taxes and about one-third of all taxes (including state and local taxes). The rest of federal taxes is made up of payroll (or Social Security) taxes (33 percent), the corporate tax (11 percent), and many other smaller taxes. Local and state taxes are evenly divided between property tax, income tax, sales (or excise) tax, and other taxes. Most taxes are **direct taxes** on persons or legal entities such as corporations (such as personal and corporate income taxes) but some are **indirect taxes** on goods and services (such as sales or excise taxes, and tariff duties on imports).

To understand the impact of taxes, you need to know what the **marginal tax rate** is. It is the percentage of taxes paid on *added* income. For example, if Joe's income goes up from $30,000 to $40,000 and he is in the 28-percent tax bracket (this is his marginal tax rate), he must pay $2,800 in extra taxes (or 28 percent of the added $10,000). The **marginal tax rate,** not the average rate, *affects incentives* to work and invest, since it determines the marginal benefit of working and investing. The **average tax rate** is the percentage of total income paid in taxes. For example, in 1998, a single person making $40,000 would have paid $7,852 in federal taxes, or an average tax rate of 19.6 percent. However, the marginal tax rate would have been 28 percent. Suppose a job requiring a move offers $2,000 more in pay. However, this is only worth $1,440 after 28 percent in taxes are deducted. If the annualized moving costs exceed $1,440, taking the job is not worth moving. Because of the complexity of the tax codes, I suggest using one of the tax software programs to find your marginal tax rate. After calculating your current taxes, add $1,000 to your income and let the program calculate how much your taxes increase. For example, if they are $330 higher, your marginal tax rate is 33 percent ($330 / $1,000 × 100).

A **progressive tax system** is one under which, as persons earn more, their average tax rate rises. Under a **proportional tax system,** everyone pays the same average tax rate. With a **regressive tax system,** as persons earn more, their average tax rate falls.

In a progressive tax system, the marginal tax rate is higher than the average tax rate (recall that when the marginal exceeds the average, the average rises). In a proportional system, the average and marginal tax rates are the same at all levels of income. In a regressive tax system, the marginal tax rate is below the average rate. See Practical Application, Question 2, for an example. Be careful! It is not necessarily true that the rich pay less taxes in a regressive tax system: They may pay more while still paying a smaller percent of income. Also, in a progressive tax system, it is possible for the marginal tax rate to go down over some ranges of income, but as long as the marginal tax rate exceeds the average rate, the average rate will go up with income.

YOU SHOULD REMEMBER

1. The marginal tax rate (the tax rate on added income) affects incentives.

2. In a progressive tax system, people with more income pay a higher percent of their income in taxes. The marginal tax rate exceeds the average tax rate, causing the average rate to rise as income goes up. In a regressive system, people with more income pay a smaller percent of their income in taxes. The marginal tax rate is below the average rate, causing the average rate to fall.

EQUITY IN TAXES

Since most people would like to pay less taxes, their basic notion of what is fair and equitable often coincides with what produces less taxes. Other less biased principles of **equity** include:

1. **Horizontal Equity:** Equals should pay equal taxes. If two persons are exactly alike, consistency requires that both should pay the same tax. For example, consider the double taxation of corporate income. It is commonly argued that it is "fair" to tax corporations at the same rate as individuals. However, the income from corporations that is paid out in dividends is first taxed at the corporate level and then taxed at the personal level. Thus, dividend income is taxed at a higher rate rather than at the same rate as other income. The principle of horizontal equity holds that dividend income should be taxed only once (say, by allowing corporations to deduct their dividends as expenses).

2. **Vertical Equity:** Unequals should pay different taxes. If Smith and Jones earn different incomes, then it seems right they should also pay different taxes.

3. **Benefits Principle:** People should pay taxes in proportion to the benefits they receive from the government. For example, taxes on gasoline are paid for by drivers, who benefit from good roads; these taxes support road construction and maintenance. The rationale for this principle is that, except for helping the poor, it is not right to benefit one group of people at the expense of others—those who get the benefit from a government program should pay for it. The same principle is used to condemn stealing and slavery.

4. **Ability to Pay Principle:** People who are able to pay more taxes should pay more. This implies that people who earn more should pay more. However, this result is consistent with some regressive tax systems, depending on what the vague term "ability to pay" means, so it is not a useful criterion. Note that this principle is inconsistent with the benefits principle.

TAXES AND EFFICIENCY

Taxes distort economic decisions. One criterion of selecting taxes is to choose those that distort decisions the least. To measure the distortions caused by taxes, economists measure their **deadweight loss** (also called **the excess burden of taxation**). Taxes impose a burden upon the private sector (the buyers and sellers of goods) exceeding the tax revenue collected. The deadweight loss is the excess of the private sector's burden over the tax revenues collected. The excess burden of the tax on a good (or its dead-weight loss) is the excess of its cost to buyers and sellers over the tax rev-enues collected.

In Figure 30–1, we show the demand and supply for labor in an economy with 100 million workers. Without any tax, each worker will work 2,000 hours at a wage of $4. With a 40-percent tax rate, workers must be paid more in before-tax wages to get the same after-tax wages. The after-tax wage labor supply schedule is *SS* (the same one as when there are no taxes). The before-tax wage schedule is *S ′S ′*.

Key Procedure for Showing Effects of Taxes

1. The impact of a tax can be represented by shifting the demand curve down or supply curve up. It does not matter which is used. We will shift the supply curve up.

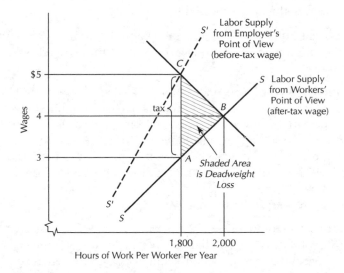

Figure 30–1. Tax on Wages Compared with Deadweight Loss

2. The original supply curve (which reflects what suppliers must be paid) is also the after-tax curve. In Figure 30–1, *SS* shows the wages workers get after taxes.

3. Next, we construct the supply curve showing the supply price *including taxes*. We *add* the tax vertically to the original supply curve to get the new supply curve including taxes. For example, if the supplier's price is $10 and the tax is $2, the supply price including taxes is $12. Thus, the supply curve including taxes is $2 above the original supply curve. In

Figure 30–1, the vertical distance between $S'S'$ and SS equals the taxes workers pay.

In Figure 30–1, labor supply drops to 1,800 hours per worker, the before-tax wage is $5, the after-tax wage is $3 (60 percent of $5), and taxes are $2 (40 percent of $5). Total tax revenues are $3,600 per worker ($2 × 1,800 hours) The cost of the tax to workers and producers is $3,600 in the taxes they paid plus the lost surplus measured by the area of triangle *ABC. The deadweight loss is Area ABC.* It is equal to $200 per worker. (The area of a triangle is 1/2 of base × height, or 1/2 × $2 × 200 hours.) The deadweight loss for every dollar of taxes collected is 5.5 cents ($.055 = $200/$3,600). One study suggests that the actual deadweight loss is 30 cents per tax dollar collected. Other studies show varying deadweight losses.

The $200 deadweight loss represents the loss in social net benefits that no one gets. It occurs here because people are working less than is socially optimal.

PROBLEM Suppose that for each person in the economy, the demand and supply of annual hours of work (L) is:

$$W^D = \$24 - 0.005\,L$$

$$W^S = \$2 + 0.005\,L$$

where W^D is the before-tax marginal value of an hour of work to an employer and W^S is the after-tax labor supply of a worker.

a. How many hours, and at what wage, will each person work?

b. If a $2 an hour tax is imposed, what is the new hours of work? What are the total taxes? What is the deadweight loss? What is the deadweight loss per dollar of taxes collected?

SOLUTION **a.** Solving $W^D = W^S$ for L, we have $22 = 0.01L$ and $L = 2,200$ with $W = \$11$.

b. Solving $W^D - \$2 = W^S$ for L, $L = 2,000$, $W^D = \$14$ and $W^S = \$12$. Total taxes are $4,000 ($2 times 2,000 hours). The deadweight loss is the area between the demand and supply curve between 2,000 and 2,200 hours. The area equals $200 (0.5 × base × height = 0.5 × 200 × $2). The deadweight loss per tax dollar collected is ten cents ($200/$2,000 = $0.10).

The more inelastic demand and supply are, the smaller the deadweight loss from a given tax. Note that when demand and supply are more inelastic, output will fall less when a given tax is imposed. So the less a tax changes output, the smaller the deadweight loss is likely to be. For example, a tax on a good whose supply is perfectly inelastic will not affect its output at all, so there is no distortion or deadweight loss.

YOU SHOULD REMEMBER

1. The deadweight loss (or excess burden) of a tax is the private sector's loss less the taxes collected.

2. The deadweight loss is less the more inelastic demand and supply are.

MAJOR DISTORTIONS IN OUR CURRENT TAX CODES

By taxing some activities and not others, our tax codes redirect resources away from their most efficient use. Some of the major distortions in our current codes are caused by:

1. *The Use of Historical Costs for Depreciation:* Businesses can deduct depreciation expenses only on the basis of the historical cost of assets. However, inflation increases the replacement cost of assets. As a result, using historical costs *understates* costs, *overstates* profits, and thus *increases* the effective tax rate on true profits.

2. *Allowing Homeowners to Deduct Mortgage Interest Payments:* Since homeowners can deduct these payments without having to also record the implicit rental of their homes and the change in their homes' value as a source of income, homes, in effect, become businesses that can deduct expenses and yet do *not* have to report income—a very good deal! Tax laws thus favor homeownership over business investment. See Practical Application, Question 6.

3. *Allowing Tax-Free Bonds:* While the federal government taxes most interest income, it does not tax the interest income from state and municipal bonds. As a result, capital is diverted from private investment into state and municipal projects.

Because of their competitive advantage, tax-free bonds pay a lower interest rate. When should someone buy a tax-free bond? If the person's marginal tax rate is t and a municipal tax-free bond pays i percent and a corporate bond pays r percent, then the municipal bond should be bought when:

$$i\% > (1-t)\,r\%.$$

Example: Comparing Tax-Free Bonds with Other Bonds

PROBLEM   If a municipal bond pays 9 percent and the corporate bond pays 10 percent and a person is in the 40 percent tax bracket, should the person buy the municipal bond?

SOLUTION   Yes. The after-tax return on the corporate bond is 6 percent (10 percent − 4 percent taken away in taxes), so the municipal bond pays more (9 percent) in after-tax dollars. The corporate bond would have to pay 15 percent before it would pay the same in after-tax income as the municipal bond ($15\% = i\%/(1 - t)$ or 9%/.6).

   4. *Taxing Inflation-Caused Capital Gains:* Current tax laws tax all the price appreciation of certain assets (such as stock and land) as capital gains. However, part of an asset's price increase just reflects inflation. This part of its price rise is *not* real income (since it merely maintains the real value of the asset), yet it is taxed. Suppose Mr. Jones buys a stock at $100 and a year later sells if for $110. In the same year, prices go up 6 percent. However, $6 of the price increase was not real income: Only the $4 is a true capital gain. If Mr. Jones pays a 20 percent tax on capital gains, he will pay a tax of $2 on the price increase of $10. However, this is an effective tax rate of 50 percent on the true capital gain (.50 = $2/$4).

All these distortions add to the deadweight losses of taxes. It is probably impossible to have a tax that does not distort the economy in some way. Nevertheless, the deadweight loss can usually be reduced when (1) all types of income are treated equally and (2) taxes are imposed only upon true real income, removing the distortions caused by inflation on replacement value and the price of assets.

YOU SHOULD REMEMBER

1. Whenever the government taxes one type of income and not another, a distortion results. People will invest less in earning the taxed income and more in earning the untaxed income. Too little will be invested in earning the taxed income.

2. When inflation is not properly accounted for, a distortion results. Inflation increases the effective tax rate of corporate profits because business firms can write off only historical costs. Inflation reduces the effective tax rate on homes because it increases the interest rate and thus the tax write-off on new fixed-rate mortgages and on all variable-rate mortgages.

SOME SPECIAL TAXES

Some economists have proposed the following taxes as being better than our current taxes.

THE VALUE-ADDED TAX (VAT)

The **value-added tax** is a tax on a company's "value added" (the difference between its sales and what it buys from other firms). Each firm reports what it sells and also what it has bought and pays a certain percentage of the difference in taxes. By reporting on what it has bought and *from whom*, the tax authorities can see if other firms are correctly reporting their sales. So while VAT is like a sales tax, tax cheats are more easily caught with a VAT.

THE FLAT TAX

The **flat tax** is a proportional tax. In 1998, a flat tax of 20 percent would have collected the same revenues the income tax collected. The flat tax has the advantage of reducing the marginal tax rate and increasing economic activity. A deduction is usually proposed so it does not affect the poor too severely.

The **Laffer curve** suggests that as the marginal tax rate increases, total tax revenues first increase and then fall when the marginal rate becomes excessive (see Chapter 11). The flat tax (or a less progressive tax) is one way to take advantage of this result: By getting rid of excessively high marginal tax rates, more tax revenues might be collected.

THE CONSUMPTION TAX

Unlike the income tax a **consumption tax** taxes people only on their consumption spending. As with the income tax, people would report their income. However, they would also report their savings, i.e., what they have *added* to their assets and savings accounts. Then they would deduct their savings from their income and pay taxes only on their consumption. This has the advantage of rewarding savings, which in turn will be used to finance more investment and thus increase economic growth. Individual retirement accounts (IRAs) are a step in the direction of a consumption tax.

COMPARING TAXES

Which is better: an income tax or a consumption tax? One criterion is efficiency: Which tax system introduces the least distortion into the economy? A distortion occurs to the extent that relative market prices differ from the relative marginal costs of goods. For example, the same percent sales tax on goods X and Y will not be distorting as it does not change the price of good X *relative* to the price of good Y ($P_X/P_Y = P_X(1 + t)/P_Y(1 + t) = MC_X/MC_Y$). (Note: This assumes relative marginal costs do not change with output.)

This is why a sales tax is usually more efficient than a "sin" tax, which taxes only a few goods (such as liquor and gasoline) with high tax rates.

A consumption tax is more efficient than an income tax for the choice between consuming and saving. In an efficient economy, the price of consuming a dollar today ($1) is the foregone consumption in the future achieved by saving ($1 plus after-tax interest). The social cost of $1 of consumption is the foregone production in the future ($1 plus before-tax interest). An income tax makes the after-tax interest fall below the before-tax interest and thus distorts the choice of how people allocate their consumption spending over time. A consumption tax does not tax interest so that the after- and before-tax interest rates are the same.

When comparing tax systems, the comparison should be revenue-neutral. It is revenue-neutral when both tax systems collect the same tax revenue. For example, a 6 percent tax on all goods is usually more efficient than a tax on only a few goods that collects the same total tax revenues. On the other hand, a 6 percent tax on all goods will be less efficient than a 1 percent tax on only a few goods, and it is certainly less efficient than no tax on any goods. But this is neither a fair nor a useful comparison. Similarly, comparing a 30 percent income tax with a 30 percent consumption tax is not a useful comparison as the consumption tax will collect less in tax revenues (since consumption is usually less than income).

TAX INCIDENCE AND TAX SHIFTING

The persons paying a tax are not necessarily those who bear the tax. For example, the corporate income tax may reduce wages (so that workers bear the tax) or raise prices (so that consumers bear the tax). This is the problem of **tax incidence:** Who bears the tax? Because of **tax shifting** (through higher prices or lower costs), the burden of the tax need not be borne by those who pay it.

For example, suppose the international supply of capital is perfectly elastic to the United States at a 10 percent interest rate and that out nation borrows extensively from other countries. Who then bears the incidence of a corporate income tax (assuming there are only two factors, labor and capital)? The answer is that labor will bear the corporate income tax. Any reduction in capital's return below 10 percent (due to the corporate income tax) will cause an exit of capital from the United States until capital's *after-tax* rate of return rises back to 10 percent. Capital will not suffer. However the reduction in capital will reduce wages until workers fully bear the tax.

As a general rule of thumb, the burden of taxation falls upon those with more inelastic demand and supply. More poetically, "The bears feast on those who run the slowest." For example, landowners can do little to avoid rising property taxes, while companies who are free to move their plants from state to state are often able to bargain for large tax reductions.

YOU SHOULD REMEMBER

1. A value-added tax is like a sales tax, but it is easier to catch tax evaders with a VAT tax.

2. A consumption tax encourages savings since it does not tax income that is saved. Only once the income is spent is it taxed.

3. Who pays a tax and who bears the tax can be entirely different because of tax shifting.

4. Those with more elastic supplies and demands will bear more of a tax.

KNOW THE CONCEPTS

DO YOU KNOW THE BASICS?

1. If you give a poor family 100 pounds of cheese, will the family's consumption of cheese go up by 100 pounds?

2. Would senior citizens prefer free food or the equivalent amount in cash?

3. In a progressive tax system, Mr. Smith pays 20 percent of his income in taxes. Is his marginal tax rate greater than, equal to, or less than 20 percent?

4. Is it always true that in all regressive tax systems the rich pay less taxes than the poor?

5. How does the deadweight loss reflect lost net benefits?

6. "The less a tax affects people's behavior, the more efficient it is." Is this true? If so, why?

7. How does inflation affect the allocation of capital between building homes and building plants and equipment?

8. Why do municipal and state bonds pay a lower interest rate than do corporate bonds?

9. Why will a VAT tax of 8 percent have the same effect as a sales tax of 8 percent?

10. "We would be better off if the government required employers to double the number of workers needed to do each job." Is this true?

TERMS FOR STUDY

ability-to-pay principle
average tax rate
benefits principle
deadweight loss (or excess
   burden) of tax
direct and indirect taxes
horizontal equity

marginal tax rate
payments-in-kind
progressive, proportional, and
   regressive tax systems
tax shifting and tax incidence
transfer payments
vertical equity

PRACTICAL APPLICATION

1. In Freedonia, Mrs. Clark earns $50,000 and pays $20,000 in taxes. Mrs. Smith, her neighbor, earns $100,000 and pays $30,000 in taxes. Is Freedonia's tax system progressive, regressive, or proportional?

2. Three countries have the following marginal tax rates:

Marginal Tax Rate	Countries		
Income Levels	Country A	Country B	Country C
0–$10,000	10%	20%	30%
$10,000–$20,000	20%	20%	20%
$20,000–$30,000	30%	20%	10%

   a. What type of tax system does each country have?

   b. What taxes will a person earning $15,000 pay in each country? What is the person's average tax rate? Marginal tax rate?

   c. What taxes will a person earning $25,000 pay in each country? What is the person's average tax rate? Marginal tax rate?

3. What principle of equality applies to these situations.

   a. A property tax that pays for city improvements.

   b. The equal taxation of income from wages and the interest earned on a corporate bond.

   c. The bank robber, who when asked why he always robbed banks, answered "Because that's where the money is."

4. Mrs. Fearn is a schoolteacher. Her average tax rate is 20 percent and her marginal tax rate is 50 percent. She has to decide whether to teach summer school. She would earn $2,000, but she would have to give up summertime activities that she values at $1,200. Should she teach summer school?

5. Suppose a poor family spends 10 percent of its income on cheese. The family's income is $6,000. The government gives the family $2,000 in free cheese.

   a. How will this affect the family's total cheese consumption?

   b. Is the family better off by $2,000 or by less than $2,000?
   Assume the family cannot resell the cheese.

6. Suppose the government imposes a large tax on white bread.

   a. Will the revenue collected from this tax be greater in the first year it is imposed or in the third year, after people have had time to adjust? (Assume the population does not grow.)

   b. Will the deadweight loss be greater in the first year or in the third year?

   c. Who will bear more of this tax: Mr. Jones who sincerely believes that "white bread is essential for health" or Mrs. Smith who regards brown bread as an equal to white bread?

7. Suppose a municipal bond pays 8 percent and a corporate bond of the same maturity and degree of risk pays 12 percent.

   a. What tax bracket do you have to be in to be just willing to buy the municipal bond?

   b. Who would buy municipal bonds in a regressive tax system: the rich or the poor?

8. Steve values a painting at $15,000 and the painting costs $12,000. However, the government imposes a $4,000 tax on the painting. What is the deadweight loss of this tax?

9. Use the following table to answer the questions below:

Quantity	1	2	3	4	5	6
Demand Price	$11	$8	$6	$4	$2	$1
Supply Price	$1	$2	$3	$4	$5	$6

   a. What will the price and quantity bought and sold be?

   b. The government imposes a $10 tax. Derive the supply curve including the tax. What will the price and quantity bought and sold be?

   c. How much did the demand price of the good go up? How much did the supply price, net of taxes, go down? What is the demander's burden of the tax (what percentage of the unit tax is their price increase)? The supplier's burden?

10. Which of the following are transfer payments?

   a. Unemployment compensation paid to a laid-off worker.

   b. Money the government pays to buy buses.

    c. Salary received by postal workers.

    d. Money given by parents to their child as a present.

11. Since individuals pay income tax on dividends that are paid out of after-tax profits made by corporations, corporate profits are taxed twice.

    a. Is the corporation income tax horizontally equitable?
(To answer this, assume the income and corporate tax rates are 30 percent and two businesses, one a corporation and the other not, both make $100,000.)

    b. Is it vertically equitable?

    c. Is it justified under the ability-to-pay argument if capital is in perfectly elastic supply to the United States?

ANSWERS

KNOW THE CONCEPTS

1. No. It will go up only by the difference between 100 pounds and how much cheese the family had been buying before.

2. The cash.

3. Greater than 20 percent.

4. No. In a regressive tax system, the rich can pay more taxes but less in percentage terms.

5. The lost consumer and producer surplus is the loss in net benefits to society.

6. Yes. The more inelastic demand and supply are, the less people will change and the smaller the deadweight loss.

7. Inflation raises the tax on the profits from plants and equipment and lowers it on homes. Thus, it pushes the allocation of capital toward homes.

8. Because corporate bonds, to compete, have to pay more in before-tax interest to give savers the same after-tax interest that tax-free municipal and state bonds pay.

9. A good's final price is the sum of the value added by those making and selling the good. So an 8 percent tax on one is the same as an 8 percent tax on the other.

10. No. Output per worker would be cut in half, as would income per person.

PRACTICAL APPLICATION

1. Mrs. Clark's average tax rate is 40 percent. Mrs. Smith, who earns more, has an average tax rate of 30 percent. Freedonia's tax system is regressive.

2. **a.** Country A has a progressive tax system; B has a proportional tax system; C has a regressive tax system.

   b. In Country A: $2,000 in taxes, an average tax rate of 13.3 percent, and a marginal tax rate of 20 percent.

   In Country B: $3,000 in taxes, an average tax rate of 20 percent, and a marginal tax rate of 20 percent.

   In Country C; $4,000 in taxes, an average tax rate of 26.7 percent, and a marginal tax rate of 20 percent.

   c. In Country A: $4,500 in taxes, an average tax rate of 18 percent, and a marginal tax rate of 30 percent.

   In Country B: $5,000 in taxes, an average tax rate of 20 percent, and a marginal tax rate of 20 percent.

   In Country C: $5,500 in taxes, an average tax rate of 22 percent, and a marginal tax rate of 10 percent.

3. **a.** The benefits principle.

   b. Horizontal equity.

   c. The ability-to-pay principle.

4. It is the *marginal* tax rate that affects Mrs. Fearn's choice. The $2,000 more in income will be taxed at a 50 percent rate, leaving her with $1,000 after taxes. This will not cover her $1,200 opportunity cost of teaching, so she should not teach.

5. **a.** Cheese consumption will go up by $1,400.

   b. The family is better off by less than $2,000. If given $2,000 in cash, the family would have bought $800 in cheese (10 percent of $8,000) and preferred other goods to cheese for the remaining $1,200. So the remaining $1,200 in cheese the family would not have bought, if given the choice, is worth less than $1,200 to the family. The family is better off, but by less than $2,000.

6. **a.** Tax revenues will be less in the third year as compared with the first. Recall that in the long run, both demand and supply become more elastic. In this case, in the long run, demanders will find substitutes for white bread and suppliers can more easily exit the white bread industry. (This is equivalent to holding constant where the demand and supply curve cross but rotating the curves so they are closer together. In other words, the demand curve rotates counterclockwise and the supply curve rotates clockwise.) In three years, output (and thus tax revenues) will fall more.

b. The deadweight loss will be more in three years, compared with one, because Q will be less in three years (compared with level in one year). Recall that with straight-line demand and supply curves, the deadweight loss equals $0.5 \times$ Tax $|\Delta Q|$. $|\Delta Q|$, the change in Q expressed as a positive number, is greater in the third year.

c. Mr. Jones will bear more of the tax because his demand for it is more inelastic since he has fewer good substitutes for white bread.

7. a. The "breakeven" tax bracket is the one with the tax rate t where $(1 - t) \times 12\% = 8\%$. So $t = 33.3\%$. If one is in this tax bracket or higher, the municipal bond should be bought.

b. In a regressive tax system, the poor will have the higher marginal tax rates and so will buy municipal bonds.

8. $3,000. Steve will not buy the painting, since with the tax added on, it costs $16,000 and Steve values it at only $15,000. So the government collects no tax revenue. However, Steve is worse off by the lost consumer surplus of $3,000 ($15,000 value – cost of $12,000). The deadweight loss is $3,000.

9. a. 4 units at $4.

b.

Quantity	1	2	3	4	5	6
Demand Price	$11	$8	$6	$4	$2	$1
Original Supply Price	$1	$2	$3	$4	$5	$6
Supply Price— Including Taxes	$11	$12	$13	$14	$15	$16

Suppliers will produce and sell one unit at a before-tax price of $11 (the price paid by demanders) and an after-tax price of $1 (the amount received by suppliers).

c. The demand price goes up $7 (from $4 to $11). The supply price falls $3 (from $4 to $1). The demanders bear 70 percent of the tax, while the suppliers' burden is 30 percent.

10. (a) and (d) are transfer payments.

11. a. No. The unincorporated business pays $30,000 in income taxes. However, the same business incorporated pays much more. To the corporate taxes of $30,000 we add, if its after-tax income is paid out as dividends, another $21,000 in income taxes.

b. No, it is not vertically equitable, as an unincorporated business making more will pay the same tax as the incorporated business. In the case above, it will have to make $170,000 to pay the same total tax ($51,000).

   c. No. If capital is in perfectly elastic supply to the United States, which is a useful approximation, then the burden of the corporate income tax falls on workers and consumers. It is hard to argue that these persons are more able to pay than the general public, as the two groups are probably identical.

31
INTERNATIONAL TRADE

KEY TERMS

absolute advantage ability to produce a good with fewer inputs.

comparative advantage ability to produce a good at a lower *relative* cost.

exports goods and services sold by domestic citizens to other nations.

imports goods and services that are bought by domestic citizens and are produced by other nations.

law of comparative advantage nations are better off when they produce goods they have a comparative advantage in supplying.

We are all traders. For example, as workers, we trade our time and effort for the goods and services our wages buy. In studying international trade, remember that *what is true about trade is true about international trade.* These truths are:

Trade is mutually beneficial. Two people do not exchange goods and services unless *both* expect to benefit. Just because one person "profits" from trade, it does not mean the other "loses": Both sides profit or they would not trade.

Exports are what you sell and imports are what you buy. Workers export time and effort and import purchased goods and services. Nations **export** goods in order to buy **imports.** Sometimes you hear the claim that "Exports are good and imports are bad." In other words, this claim says it is better for a nation to give away (i.e., sell) more than it takes back (i.e., buys)! Instead, a smart nation tries to get the *most* back for what it sells.

The cheaper imports are, the better off a nation is. The more a person gets back for what he or she gives away, the better off the person is. It is the same for nations. When a nation's imports cost less, a given amount of its exports then buys more imports.

Inflows of monies tend to equal outflows. Have you ever worried about whether California sells more to the rest of the United States than it buys back? Or about your town's trade imbalance? No one worries about these issues, because people don't sell goods except to buy back other goods. The same is true for world trade. Nations *sell* to the United States to get the dollars to buy from the United States. The U.S. export industry would be devastated if U.S. citizens stopped buying imports.

In recent years, the United States has had a serious trade imbalance. It is importing more goods than it exports. However, nations also trade assets (such as stocks and bonds). When one adds in these other items, it turns out that what the U.S. spends on other nations' goods *and* assets just about equals what they spend on our goods and assets! For example, in 1990, the United States imported $92 billion more goods than it exported. However, the United States spent only $3 billion more on foreign goods *and* assets than foreigners bought from the United States (this difference is reflected in the change in U.S. official reserve assets). So the flows of monies in and out of the United States are about equal.

YOU SHOULD REMEMBER

1. People do not trade unless both sides expect to benefit.

2. Imports are what a nation gets back in exchange for giving away exports.

3. The cheaper imports are, the more a nation gets back in trade.

WHEN WILL A NATION BENEFIT FROM TRADE?

Recall that the relative price of Good A is the amount of Good B that has to be given up to get one more unit of Good A. When Good A costs $12 and Good B costs $6, the relative price of Good A is 2 (since two units of B have to be given up to buy one unit of A). So,

$$\text{Relative Price of A} = P_a / P_b$$

where P_a is the price of Good A and P_b, the price of Good B.

Two nations should trade whenever the relative prices of goods (before trade) are different. To show this, assume there are only two goods: food and clothing. Assume food sells for $20 a unit and clothing for $10 a unit (so the relative price of food is 2). Then Martians land and quote the following prices: Food is 6 Blops a unit and clothing is 2 Blops per unit. Their relative price for food is 3.

Should we humans trade with the Martians? The answer is yes: The Martians have a different relative price (3 instead of our 2). They value food more highly than we do. So we can benefit by specializing in food production and buying clothing from them. For each two units of clothing we stop producing (which cost $10 each to produce), we can produce one unit of food (at a cost of $20), sell it to the Martians (for 6 Blops), and buy back three units of clothing (worth $30)! By giving up producing two units of clothing (and producing food instead), we get three units of clothing back!

However, if the Martian prices were 4 Blops for food and 2 Blops for clothing, both humans and Martians have the same relative prices and there would be no gains from trade.

On the other hand, if Martian prices were 2 Blops for food and 2 Blops for clothing, their relative price for food would be 1. This is lower than our relative price for food. So we humans would gain by specializing in producing clothing and buying food from the Martians. By producing one less unit of food, we could produce two more units of clothing and trade them for two units of food.

It does not matter which way relative prices differ—what matters is that they differ! Remember, we are talking about relative price differences *before* trade takes place. After trade, relative prices tend to become the same.

Why do relative prices (before trade) differ between nations? The main reasons are (1) differences in relative costs of producing goods, due to differences in labor, capital, and technology, (2) differences in taste, and (3) differences in natural resources and climate.

WHAT GOODS SHOULD A NATION TRADE?

A nation should sell those goods that other nations value at a higher relative price than it does. A nation should buy those goods that other nations are willing to sell at a lower relative price than it has. Buy low, sell high!

In the example above, our relative price for food was 2. When the Martians' relative price was 3, we sold (exported) food. When it was 1, we bought (imported) food.

YOU SHOULD REMEMBER

1. Differences in before-trade relative prices make trade beneficial.

2. When relative prices differ, a nation can always get more of one good without giving up the consumption of the other.

3. Relative price (as compared with the other nations' relative prices) determines which goods to produce and export and which goods to import.

4. A nation should produce more of the good that it has a lower relative price of producing and should export that good.

5. A nation should produce less of the good that it has a higher relative price of producing and should import that good.

THE LAW OF COMPARATIVE ADVANTAGE

The **law of comparative advantage** summarizes the main points of the two preceding sections. It states that a nation should compare its relative prices before trade. The nation should then *export* those goods that it can produce at a *lower* relative price than other nations and *import* those goods that it otherwise would have to produce at a *higher* relative price. The nation can have *more of all goods* by doing this. (So will the other nations trading with it!) How is this possible? Because when each good is produced by those nations with the lowest relative price of producing it, more of all goods can be produced.

To show this, suppose there are "units of resource" (part labor, part capital, and part land) that nations use to produce food and clothing. The following table shows what this unit can produce in the United States and France:

Table 31–1. Illustrating the Law of Comparative Advantage

Country	Output of 1 Unit of Resource		Relative Price of Food
	Food	Clothing	
United States	5	or 10	2
France	2	or 8	4

For example, 1 unit of resource can produce 5 units of food *or* 10 units of clothing in the United States. Here, the price of food in the United States is one-fifth of a unit of resource; the price of clothing is one-tenth of a unit of resource. So the relative price is 1/5 divided by 1/10, or 2. For every unit of food produced, the United States must give up 2 units of clothing.

In this example, the United States has an **absolute advantage** in producing food *and* clothing: It can produce more food or more clothing with a unit of resource than France can. Even though the United States is more efficient in each, it still gains by trading with France! Why?

The United States has a **comparative advantage** in producing food: It has a lower relative price of producing food (2 versus France's 4). Just invert the relative price of food to get the relative price of clothing: It is one-half a unit of food for the United States and one-fourth a unit of food for France: France has the comparative advantage in producing clothing. According to the law of comparative advantage, the United States should produce and export food; France should produce and export clothing.

To show how this will increase world output, start with no trade. Then the United States moves 1 unit of resource from producing clothing and reallocates it to producing food. France moves 2 units out of food production into clothing. The net result is shown in Table 31–2.

Table 31–2. Impact of Transfer of Resources

Transfer	Impact on Food	Impact on Clothing
In U.S.		
1 unit		
from clothing		−10
to food	+5	
In France		
2 units		
to clothing		+16
from food	−4	
New Impact on World Output	+1	+6

With more of both goods, there will be some mutually acceptable trading terms that will make both nations better off.

The **terms of trade**—the relative price that goods trade at—will fall between the before-trade relative prices. So food's relative price after trade will fall between 2 and 4. Supply and demand will determine its final relative price.

YOU SHOULD REMEMBER

1. Each country should produce more of the good that it has a lower relative price of producing.

2. World output will be increased when all nations produce those goods that they have a comparative advantage in producing.

3. By trading, two countries can both end up with more than they had before trade.

4. The terms of trade for a good will fall between the before-trade relative prices of both countries.

GRAPHICAL ANALYSIS OF COMPARATIVE ADVANTAGE

Note: This section is for those who have been required to graph the effects on international trade. Other readers may not benefit from this section (as it repeats the prior material in this chapter).

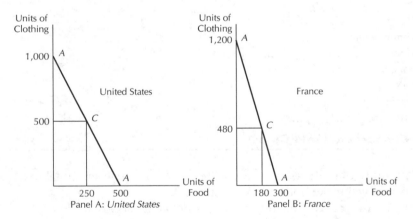

Figure 31–1. Comparing Benefits of Trade: Before-Trade Possibilities

To show the benefits of trade, we begin with the production possibility curves for the United States and France, based upon Table 31–1. We will assume the United States has 100 units of resources and France has 150. Figure 31–1 shows the before-trade production possibility curves: This also shows the consumption possibilities when there is no trade. For example, the United States can have 1,000 units of clothing and no food (when all 100 units of resources produce clothing) or 500 units of food and no clothing, or some combination of each shown by line *AA*. The absolute value of the slope equals the relative price of food (for the United States, 2; for France, 4). Assume for the sake of illustration that each country consumes at Point *C* (e.g., the United States consumes 500 units of clothing and 250 units of food).

Now we introduce trade. Let the world terms of trade be 3. The United States will produce all food and no clothing: It will be at Point *D* in Figure 31–2. Then it starts to sell each unit of food for 3 units of clothing. As it does so, it moves up and to the left on Line *DE*. It can stop at any point and consume food and clothing at any point on this line. Because of trade, the U.S. consumption possibility curve (*DE*) is above its production possibility curve (*AA*). It can get more of *both* goods.

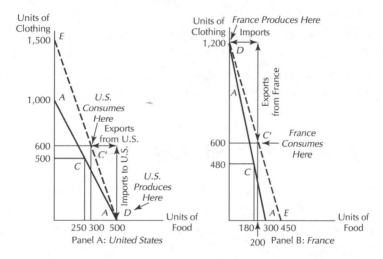

Figure 31–2. Comparing Benefits of Trade: After-Trade Possibilities

If its new consumption is at Point *C′*, it has 600 units of clothing (instead of 500) and 300 units of food (instead of 250). How does it do this? It produces 500 units of food and sells (exports) 200 units to buy (import) 600 units of clothing.

France will specialize in producing clothing (at Point *D* in Panel B of Figure 31–2). It can then sell each unit of clothing for one-third a unit of food: It can consume on Line *DE*. If it chooses Point *C′*, it will export 600 units of clothing in exchange for 200 units of food. It too will have more food and clothing with trade than it did without trade.

Key Procedure for Graphing Effects of Trade*

1. For each country, calculate how much of the good on the vertical axis it could produce if it devoted all of its resources to producing that good and none of the other. Do the same for the good on the horizontal axis. Plot these points on the respective axes and connect them: the connecting line is the *production possibility curve.*

2. Each country produces only the good it has a lower relative cost of producing. Plot this point. Then assume the country sells all it produces and buys the other good at the world's terms of trade: Plot this point. Then connect these two points. This is the country's *consumption possibility curve.* If plotted correctly, it will be above and to the right of the production possibility curve (plotted in step 1).

3. Each country will select some combination of the two goods to consume: this combination will be shown by a point on its consumption possibility curve.

4. A nation's imports will be equal to its consumption of the good it does *not* produce (as plotted in step 3).

5. A nation's exports equals the difference between the total output of the good it produces and the amount it consumes.

YOU SHOULD REMEMBER

1. Without trade, a nation can consume only along its production possibility curve.

2. With trade, a nation will specialize in producing one good. It will export that good, and import the other.

3. The absolute value of the slope of the production possibility curve equals the before-trade relative price of the good on the bottom axis. The absolute value of the slope of the consumption possibility curve equals the terms-of-trade relative price for the good on the bottom axis.

4. By producing the good whose before-trade relative price is less than the terms-of-trade price, a nation can consume more of both goods.

---

*Note: This procedure applies only to straight-line production curves.

THE EFFECT OF TARIFFS AND QUOTAS

Tariffs are a tax on imports. One study estimated that tariffs (and other trade restrictions) cost every American $500 annually in the form of higher prices.

Figure 31–3 shows the effect of trade. *DD* and *SS* are the *domestic* demand and the *domestic* supply for clothing in the United States (that is, the demand and supply of the nation's citizens). Without trade, the price of clothing is $10. Assume the world price of clothing is $6. The world's supply curve is *W-S*. At $6, consumers will buy 700 units of clothing, domestic producers will produce 300 units, and the United States will import the remaining 400 units.

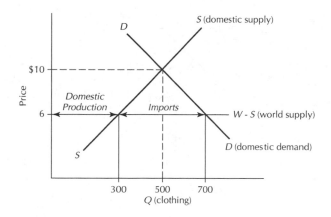

Figure 31–3. Effects of World Trade in a No-Tariff Situation

Figure 31–4 (see page 578) shows the effect of a $2 tariff on clothing imports. The domestic price of clothing will rise to $8. Consumers will buy 600 units (down from 700), domestic producers will produce 400 units (up from 300), and imports will be 200 units (down from 400). *The effect of a tariff on a good is to reduce the good's consumption, increase its domestic production, and reduce imports.*

From a social point of view, what has happened?

1. Area *A* is the *cost of inefficient production.* This is how much over and above the $6 world price the United States is paying in added production costs for the added domestic output of 100 units (from 300 to 400). Area *A* = $100 (remember, the area of a triangle equals 1/2 base × height).

2. Area *B* is the *tariff revenues* collected. Area *B* = $400.

3. Area *C* is the *lost consumer surplus* caused by the fall in consumption from 700 to 600 units. Area *C* = $100.

4. Area *E* is the *added profits* to producers because of clothing's higher price. Area *E* = $700.

5. Areas *A* + *B* + *C* + *E* = the *total loss to consumers* because of the higher price. This Area = $1,300.

The *social* loss is Area *A* plus Area *C*. Consumers lose Areas *A* + *B* + *C* + *E*. However, the government gets Area *B* in taxes and producers get Area *E* in profits. On net, Areas *A* and *C* are *a deadweight loss:* No one benefits from this loss. Consumers lose *more* than others gain. Consumers lose $1,300, and the government and producers gain $1,100, so the deadweight loss is $200.

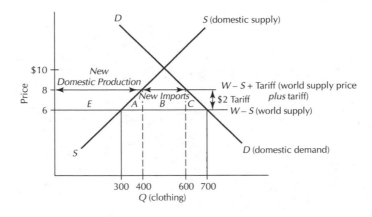

Figure 31–4. Effects of a $2 Tariff on World Trade

A **quota** is a limit on the amount of imports. If set correctly, it has the same effect on output and consumption as a tariff. In Figure 31–4, a quota limiting imports to 20 units of food will push food prices up to $8.

All areas will be the same except for Area *B:* The government will not collect any tariff revenues. Where does this $400 of lost tariff revenues go? Usually, the government gives importers a certain quota so the importers get the $400 (since they can buy 200 units at $6 and sell them for $8). With the U.S. "voluntary export quotas" on Japanese automobiles, the Japanese auto firms get the implicit tariff revenues (which is one reason they are happy to "volunteer" to limit exports)!

YOU SHOULD REMEMBER

1. A tariff raises domestic prices, reduces consumption, increases domestic production, and reduces imports.

2. Consumers lose more than others gain: The difference is the deadweight loss of the tariff.

3. A quota can have the same effect as a tariff, except that the government does not collect any tax revenues.

TRADE AND UNEMPLOYMENT

In the examples above, trade caused the United States to shift production away from clothing and into food. In this shift, workers became temporarily unemployed in the clothing industry until they could find jobs in the food industry. However, then all workers earned a higher real wage. So while unemployment is costly, it results in everyone being better off.

This is *not* the case if some workers *specialize* in the clothing industry and are thus unable to transfer their skills to food production. Those workers will *lose* by having to produce clothing at lower wages or by becoming unemployed. The same will be true of other workers specializing in clothing production. Nevertheless, since the nation as a whole benefits from free trade, it is possible to compensate "losers" for their losses and for everyone to be better off.

Several economic studies have shown that the total cost borne by workers who are thrown out of work because of foreign trade is on average $5,000 per worker. Yet the cost to consumers of protecting one job with a quota or tariff is, in most studies, between $100,000 and $200,000 a job. Tariffs are a very expensive and very inefficient method of "job protection." As another example, Americans, due to a tariff on sugar imports, pay $100 more per family of four per year for sugar, which goes to benefit only 11,400 sugarcane growers in this country!

ARGUMENTS FOR TARIFFS

Protection from Cheap Foreign Labor: This is a fallacious argument. A country benefits from trade whenever it has a *comparative* advantage in some goods, even when it does not have absolute advantage in any good (see the example of France above).

The United States is quite capable of competing with low-wage countries, because it has more capital and skilled labor. In a sense, it has *cheap* skilled labor compared with "low-wage" nations. The worry over competition from cheap foreign labor is misplaced. The United States faces its greatest competition from the more advanced countries, such as Japan and Germany.

Protection of American Way of Life, Self-Sufficiency, and Military Preparedness: Any of these goals, if desirable, is far cheaper to achieve by subsidies.

Protection of Infant Industries: Some argue that tariffs should be used to protect beginning (or "infant") industries from competition until they can grow and become profitable. However, this makes sense only if the present value of future profits makes up for the current losses to consumers due to the higher prices caused by the tariff. Thus, those infant industries which want tariff protection should be required to pay back later in higher taxes the current cost to consumers of the tariff protection. In this way, only those industries which truly believe that they have a valid case for a tariff will seek tariff protection. Most likely, the number of valid cases would prove to be small.

Bettering the Terms-of-Trade: This is one of the few possibly valid arguments for tariffs. If the United States has monopsony power so that when it buys less, the world price of an imported good falls, then some tariff can make the United States better off. But this assumes that other nations will not retaliate with higher tariffs. If they do, all nations will likely be worse off.

Strategic Trade Policy: Recently, the United States has been using the threat of higher tariffs and quotas as a lever to force other countries to lower their tariffs. In some cases, we have been successful. However, far too often, U.S. citizens end up paying forever the higher prices caused by a tariff that did little but evoke other countries to slam more tariffs on us.

YOU SHOULD REMEMBER

1. Tariffs are a very expensive form of job protection. There are far cheaper ways to help workers in their transition between jobs.

2. The only two possibly valid reasons for tariffs are to protect infant industries and to better the world terms of trade. However, both reasons apply only in limited circumstances.

FACTOR PRICE EQUALIZATION

One of the effects of international trade is to make factor prices more equal across nations. This follows the **factor price equalization theorem:** with free trade, the real earnings of similar factors will become equal in the long run. Over the last forty years, the differences between capital's real rate of return in the major trading nations have become relatively small. However, more important, beginning in the 1970s, there has been a strong trend toward the equalization of real wages for labor around the world. For example, real wages in Korea have been growing 9 percent annually and are converging on the real wages of similar low-skill workers in the United States (which have been stagnant). This was not always the case. After World War II, U.S. unskilled labor benefited from the United States having the most capital per worker in the world. Now, capital moves freely between nations, so this advantage no longer exists. In effect, international trade has had the same impact on low-skilled workers in the United States as an increase in their supply would. From the viewpoint of those who favor greater equalization in international income and care about the world's poor, this has been a positive trend. From the point of view of an American low-skilled worker with low aptitude for reading and math, this has not been a windfall.

Some suggest that the solution is to lock up the borders. This would only make the United States worse off. A more positive solution would be to make U.S. workers more productive. This could include providing better education and on-the-job training, along with increasing domestic savings and structuring the tax codes to be more favorable to productive investments.

One of the main benefits of free trade is that it brings the forces of competition into the nation. Competition forces people to improve—or to step aside and let their betters do their jobs. With free trade, everyone has the incentive to improve. With free trade, the crisis caused by factor price equalization gives the above solutions a chance of being applied. With tariffs, the likely results are complacency and economic stagnation.

> # YOU SHOULD REMEMBER
>
> According to the factor price equalization theorem, free trade causes real factor prices of various nations to converge over time.

KNOW THE CONCEPTS

DO YOU KNOW THE BASICS?

1. Mary buys a car from Joe's Car Sales. Joe is the only dealer in the area and makes a big profit from the sale. Does Mary benefit or lose from her purchase?

2. If Japan sold imports to the United States, but did not buy any exports from the United States, would the United States be worse off?

3. When will two nations not benefit from trade?

4. "Cheap imports are hurting the U.S. economy." Is this true?

5. How are farmers (who export a large volume of their output) hurt by tariffs on imports?

6. Which goods should a nation specialize in producing when it trades with other nations?

7. According to the law of comparative advantage, how can the world produce the greatest output?

8. Who benefits from tariffs? Who loses? How do the total losses compare with total benefits?

9. Why would foreign producers prefer a quota over a tariff that had the same impact?

10. "Everyone should do what he or she is best at." Is that true?

TERMS FOR STUDY

absolute advantage	law of comparative advantage
comparative advantage	relative price
exports	tariffs
factor price equalization	terms of trade
imports	quotas
infant industries	

PRACTICAL APPLICATION

1. Peru can produce 16 units of corn or 8 units of wheat with a unit of resource. Mexico can produce 12 units of corn or 4 units of wheat.

   a. Which country has the absolute advantage in producing each good?

   b. What is the relative price of wheat in each country? Of corn?

    c. If these are the only countries in the world, which should produce wheat? Corn?

    d. In what range will the terms of trade for wheat fall?

2. Suppose Santa Claus was real and gave gifts to children at Christmas.

    a. Who would benefit?

    b. Who would be hurt?

    c. Would our nation on net be better or worse off?

    d. From a social point of view, does the dumping of goods by foreign nations harm our nation?

    Note: "Dumping" is the selling of imports below cost. Santa Claus is guilty of dumping.

3. The United States spends billions of dollars subsidizing the export of goods from the United States. Does this help or hurt the United States?

4. In science fiction literature, robots are often banned from Earth because they "can do everything better, leaving nothing for humans to do."

    a. Would robots cause humans to have nothing to do?

    b. Which tasks would humans perform?

    c. Would humans be better or worse off?

5. Countries Y and Z have the following production possibility schedules for food and clothing:

Country Y Food	0	4	8	12
Clothing	12	8	4	0

Country Z Food	0	4	8	12
Clothing	36	24	12	0

    a. Before trade, what is the relative cost of food in each country?

    b. With trade, which country will produce food? Clothing?

    c. Show the consumption possibility schedule for both countries when the terms of trade for food is 2.

6. There are two towns on a hill called High and Low for their respective position on the hill. While High's merchants can send goods for free to Low (as it's downhill all the way), Low's merchants have to pay dearly to ship goods up to High. One day the merchants of Low get together and proclaim that they want "a level playing field" because it is "unfair" that High's merchants ship for free. So, in the interest of "fair trade," Low requires all merchants from High to take their goods down the hill,

then back up, and then back down. Are the people of Low better or worse off now that trade is "fair"?

7. Assume that the world price of oil is $15 per barrel. At that price, the United States imports 400 million barrels a day and consumes 600 million barrels a day. The government then imposes a $5-per-barrel tax on oil imports. For every $1 increase in oil prices, domestic consumption goes down 20 million barrels a day while domestic production goes up 40 million barrels a day.

   a. What will the new oil price be (assume the world supply is perfectly elastic at $15)?

   b. What will the new consumption, domestic production, and import levels be? How much will the government collect in taxes?

   c. What will be the cost of inefficient production, the loss in consumer surplus, and deadweight loss? (Use the triangle formula of 1/2 × change in price × change in quantity for both the loss of efficiency and the loss in consumer surplus.)

   d. Why, from an efficiency point of view, would a $5 tax on *all* oil be better than the $5 tax on oil imports?

8. Suppose trade follows this pattern: The United States buys cars from Japan, Japan buys oil from the Middle East, and the Middle East buys machinery from the United States. What then is wrong with reciprocity legislation requiring *each* country to buy from the United States exactly the amount it sells to us? (This type of trading pattern is called *multilateral trade*, as opposed to *bilateral trade* between two nations.)

9. Use the following table:

Price of Clothing	$8	$7	$6	$5	$4	$3	$2
Domestic demand	100	200	300	400	500	600	700
Domestic supply	900	800	700	600	500	400	300

   a. Without trade, what will the price of clothing be?

   b. If the world price of clothing is $6, what will happen? If it is $2?

   c. Construct a table of this country's demand for clothing imports (which is its *excess demand for clothing at each price*) and its supply of clothing exports (which is its *excess supply of clothing at each price*).

10. Use this table:

Price of Clothing	$5	$4	$3	$2	$1
Other nations' demand	1,300	1,400	1,500	1,600	1,700
Other nations' supply	2,600	2,400	2,200	2,000	1,800

a. What is the excess supply curve of other nations for clothing? (Give your answer in the form of a table.)

b. Using the table in Question 9 above, what will the world price of clothing be? How much will the United States import from other nations?

ANSWERS

KNOW THE CONCEPTS

1. Mary benefits, or she would not have bought the car.

2. The United States would be better off: It would have the imports without having to pay for them.

3. When their relative prices are the same.

4. No. Cheap imports mean the United States is getting back more for the exports it sells.

5. Tariffs reduce foreign sales to the United States. This means foreigners have fewer dollars with which to buy U.S. goods. In turn, this reduces foreign demand for U.S. agricultural products.

6. The goods that have relative prices that are lower than their world terms-of-trade relative prices.

7. When each country produces the goods it has the lowest relative price of producing, world output will be maximized.

8. The gainers are (a) producers and factors of production that are specialized in producing the good the tariff is imposed upon and (b) the government. The losers are consumers (including the nonspecialized factors producing the good). Total losses exceed total benefits.

9. Because a quota allows the producers, rather than the government, to benefit from the higher price.

10. No. Everyone should do what he or she has a *comparative* advantage in doing, not what he or she has an absolute advantage in doing. What is true for nations is also true for people.

PRACTICAL APPLICATION

1. a. Peru has the absolute advantage in both goods.

   b. For wheat: Peru, 2; Mexico, 3.

      For corn: Peru, 1/2; Mexico, 1/3.

   c. Peru should produce wheat. Mexico should produce corn.

    d. Between 2 and 3.

2. a. Consumers of toys.

    b. Factors specialized in toy production.

    c. Better off: The factors released from toy production could produce other goods. So, the nation could have more toys *and* more other goods.

    d. No. Dumping makes the United States better off.

3. It hurts the United States. It is the equivalent of giving away goods without getting anything back.

4. a. No. Unless the robots have the same relative price of doing things as humans do, they (or their owners) would want to trade with humans.

    b. Humans would perform those tasks that they have a lower relative price performing than robots have.

    c. Humans would be better off.

5. a. Y: 1. Z: 3.

    b. Y will produce food. Z will produce clothing.

    c.

Country Y	Food	0	4	8	12
	Clothing	24	16	8	0

Country Z	Food	0	6	12	18
	Clothing	36	24	12	0

6. Both the people of High and Low are worse off. Some of the goods that were mutually advantageous to produce and trade are now too expensive to make. Further, resources that would have been used to produce useful goods are now used to lift High's goods down, up, and down the hill. Only Low's merchants will benefit—but at the greater cost to Low's consumers. Remember, trade takes place because trading partners are *not* equal—each has some advantage the other does not. Otherwise, why trade?

7. a. $20 (World price of $15 + $5 tariff).

    b. *Consumption:* 500 million barrels a day ($5 price rise reduces consumption by 5 × 20 million from 600 million).

        Domestic Production: 400 million barrels a day. (Domestic production was 200 million; it goes up by 5 × 40 million to 400 million.)

        Imports: 100 million barrels a day (consumption of 500 million less domestic output of 400 million).

        Taxes: $500 million a day ($5 × 100 million barrels imported).

c. *Cost of Inefficient Production:* $500 million a day (1/2 × price change of $5 × change in domestic oil production of 200 million).
   Consumer Surplus Loss: $250 million a day (1/2 × price change of $5 × change in consumption of 100 million).
   Deadweight Loss: $750 million a day (sum of the above).

d. A tax on all oil has no cost of inefficient production (since domestic supply will remain at 200 million barrels). There is only the consumer surplus loss of $250 million a day. Also, more tax revenue will be collected, because all oil is taxed: tax revenues will be $2,500 million a day ($5 × 500 million barrels a day consumed). So the tax on all oil has a lower deadweight loss per tax dollar. For the import tax, the deadweight loss was $1.50 per tax dollar collected. For the all-inclusive tax, it is 10 cents per tax dollar collected.

8. With more countries specializing in the goods they have a comparative advantage in supplying, world output and the welfare of the United States will be greater. However, multilateral trade means the United States will have trade surpluses with some (here, the Middle East) and trade deficits with others (here, Japan). Forcing reciprocity will reduce the gains from comparative advantage and make the United States worse off.

9. a. $4.

b. At $6, the U.S. will export 400 units of clothing. At $2, the United States will import 400 units of clothing.

c.

Price	Exports	Imports
$8	800	—
7	600	—
6	400	—
5	200	—
4	0	0
3	—	200
2	—	400

10. a.

Price	Excess Supply to U.S.
$5	1,300
4	1,000
3	700
2	400
1	100

b. The world price will be $2. Other nations will have an excess supply of 400 units of clothing at $2. This matches the United States' excess demand of 400 units of $2. The United States will import 400 units.

APPENDIX

WEB SITES FOR ECONOMICS

The following sites are good for doing research about recent topics:
Policy Research (good links to other groups doing policy research):
www.ontheissues
EconLinks (up-to-date data and easy-to-read economic analyses):
econlinks.com
Brookings Institute (more in-depth research): *www.brook.edu*

The following sites provide links to other web sites about specific topics:
Mining Company: *economics.miningco.com/finance/economics*
WebEc: *www.helsinki-fi/webec*

The following sites provide data:
Economagic: *www.economagic.com*
Statistical Resources: *www.stat-usa.gov*

The following sites provide governmental data:
Bureau of Economic Analysis (*GDP* data): *www.bea.doc.gov*
Bureau of Labor Statistics (unemployment, *CPI*): *www.bls.gov*
Federal Reserve Board (money, interest rates): *www.federalreserve.gov*
Census: *www.census.gov*

This site searches for government agency web pages about the topic you specify:
www.firstgov.gov

This site searches for data from federal agencies about topics you specify:
www.fedstats.com

INDIFFERENCE CURVE ANALYSIS

Some texts use indifference curves to present the theory of demand. An indifference curve shows the various combinations of goods that yield the same level of utility to a consumer. The name *indifference* refers to the fact that the consumer does not care which combination of goods he or she gets if they are all along the curve. That is because they all yield the same utility. These curves are sometimes called utility curves.

FROM THEORY TO CURVE

Why do indifference curves look like they do? The answer comes from economic theory. Consider what it means to say that Good X and Good Y are both goods. It means that more of one makes you better off. So if I give you more of Good X (so that you are moving horizontally to the right in the indifference diagram), you are moving to a higher utility. The same is true if I give you more of Good Y (so that you are moving vertically up). This implies three things. First, higher utility curves are higher! That is, as you move up and to the right, your utility should be going up. Second, each indifference curve should have a negative slope. Why? Because if you get more of one good, you have to have less of the other or you will be moving to a higher indifference curve. Third, the curves cannot cross. Higher is higher. At all points, more of both goods should always move you to a higher curve. When curves cross, this will not occur at all points (draw it and see). More importantly, if you cross curves, you lose the whole predictive power of indifference curve analysis. That is, you will get your answer marked wrong. The law of demand gives indifference curves their concave (bowed-in) shape. The absolute slope shows how many units of Y a person is willing to pay for another unit of X. The law of demand says that as you get more X, its demand price should fall. So as you move to the right along an indifference curve, its slope should be getting flatter.

AN INDIFFERENCE CURVE

Figure A–1 shows one indifference curve.

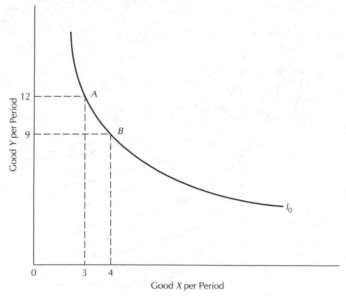

Figure A–1. An Indifference Curve

Points to Note About Figure A–1:

1. The consumer gets the same utility at point A (12 Ys and 3 Xs) that he or she does at point B (only 9 Ys but 4 Xs).

2. The consumer is indifferent between point A and point B.

3. All points above I_0 make the consumer better off.

4. All points below I_0 make the consumer worse off.

5. A consumer who is at point A is willing to trade 3 units of Y to get the fourth unit of X (moving from point A to B).

6. At point A, the consumer's demand price for 1 more X is 3 Y: A lower price would make him or her better off; a higher price worse off.

7. The slope of I_0 between points A and B is (approximately) –3.

8. The demand price for X equals the positive value of the slope (i.e., 3). The demand price is not in dollars but in units of Y.

9. As you move to the right on I_0, the slope becomes flatter. This reflects the law of demand. The demand price for X falls as the consumer has more X.

MANY INDIFFERENCE CURVES

For every level of utility is a separate and distinct indifference curve. Figure A–2 shows several of the curves.

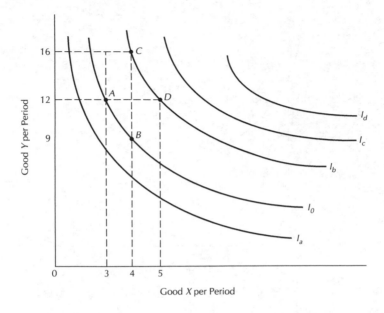

Figure A–2. Many Indifference Curves

Points to Note About Figure A–2:

1. Indifference curves are like height lines on a map: A given line shows a given height, and higher lines show the consumer reaching greater heights of satisfaction.

2. Curve I_a shows a lower level of utility than curve I_0.

3. Curve I_b shows a higher level of utility (as do I_c and I_b).

4. Point C shows a higher level of utility than point B because the consumer has more Y (16 instead of 12 units) and the same amount of X (4 units).

5. Point D shows a higher level of utility than point A because the consumer has more X (5 units instead of 3) and the same Y (12 units).

6. Indifference curves do not cross or touch: A higher curve must always show a higher utility.

7. Crossing curves is a no-no! A definite no-no. I mean it! If you do, I will tell Mom!

BUDGET CONSTRAINT

The budget constraint shows the combinations of goods the consumer can buy with his or her current income. It is a constraint because the consumer could buy less than his or her income but not more! That is, no borrowing! We assume the consumer spends all his or her income on goods X and Y. These assumptions keep the analysis simple and give reasonable predictions. Figure A–3 shows the budget constraint for a consumer who earns $100 a day, where the price of Y is $10 and the price of X is $20.

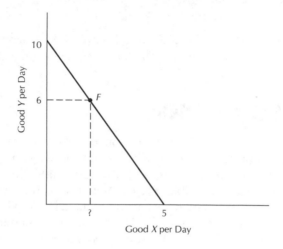

Figure A–3. Budget Constraint Facing Consumer

Points to Note About Figure A–3:

1. At any point on the budget constraint, the consumer's spending is $100.

2. If the consumer buys only good Y and no X, he or she can buy 10 units of Y (= income divided by the price of Y): This is the vertical intercept.

3. If the consumer buys only good X and no Y, he or she can buy 5 units of X (= income divided by the price of X): This is the horizontal intercept.

4. The slope of the budget constraint is –2 (a rise of –10 as X runs 5 units from 0 to 5).

5. The consumer must give up 2 units of Y to get 1 more unit of X.

6. The supply price of X is 2; the price is in units of Y, not in dollars.

7. The supply price equals the price of X divided by the price of Y.

8. How many units of X can the consumer buy if he or she is at point F? To solve this, solve for how much the consumer is spending on good Y (6 units cost $10 each so he or she is spending $60 on Y). Subtract this from income to get $40 being spent on good X. Good X costs $20 per unit, so this $40 buys 2 units of X. So the question mark can be replaced with 2.

9. An increase in income will move the whole budget constraint up and to the right without changing its slope.

10. An increase in the price of X would leave the vertical intercept unchanged but would cause the curve to become steeper, moving the horizontal intercept to the left.

11. An increase in the price of Y would leave the horizontal intercept unchanged but would cause the curve to become flatter, moving the vertical intercept down.

UTILITY MAXIMIZATION

The indifference curves show what the consumer wants: The higher the better. The budget constraint shows what the consumer can get. So given that the consumer is on budget constraint, the consumer tries to get to the highest indifference curve possible. Figure A–4 shows the results. Point E shows the highest level of utility the consumer can achieve given his or her income and the prices of goods X and Y. The consumer is said to be in equilibrium at point E: The consumer does not want to move because any move off point E along the budget constraint makes him or her worse off. Figure A–4 shows the consumer demanding 3 units of good X.

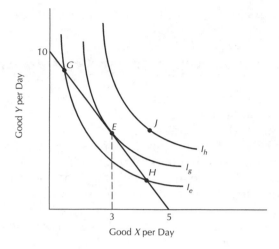

Figure A–4. Utility Maximization

Points to Note About Figure A–4:

1. I_g is the highest indifference curve the consumer can get.

2. The consumer would prefer to be at point J, but he or she does not have enough income to reach that point.

3. The consumer could be at point G or point H, but these have a lower utility than he or she can achieve at point E.

4. If, at any point on the budget constraint, the indifference curve cuts through the budget constraint (such as at point G or H), the consumer can move to a higher curve.

5. At point E, where the highest achievable utility is reached, the indifference curve does not cut through the budget constraint. Instead, it is tangent (that is, it just touches the curve once).[1]

6. At point E, the demand price for good X (the positively stated slope of the indifference curve) equals its supply price (the positively stated slope of the budget constraint). The consumer is in equilibrium.

7. At point G, the demand price exceeds the supply price: The consumer moves toward more X.

---

[1] There are two exceptions to this tangency condition. First, the indifference curve may not be nice and smooth as we show it. It may be jagged. At point E, it may not be tangent, but the highest curve will still touch the budget constraint once while lower curves will cut through the budget constraint. Second, the consumer may be in a corner, such that he or she buys all of one good and none of the other. For example, if the demand price for X exceeds the supply price of X at all points, the consumer will buy all X. Tangency will not be achieved. But the not-cut-through condition will hold.

8. At point *H*, the supply exceeds the demand price: The consumer moves toward less *X*.

SHOWING THE EFFECTS OF LOWER PRICE

The income and substitution effects of a lower price can be illustrated in various ways with indifference curve analysis. We will choose one of the more common ways. The substitution effect is shown by changing the slope along a given utility curve. The change in slope is due to the change in price. The substitution effect is now defined as the change in the demand for good *X* due to a change in the price of *X*, holding the consumer's utility level constant. The income effect is shown by changing utility curves such that one is at the same slope on each curve. The income effect is now defined as the change in the demand for good *X* as a result of the resulting change in utility, holding the price constant.

Figure A–5 shows these two effects when we lower the price of good *X* from $20 to $10; the price of *Y* is still $10 and the consumer's income is $100.

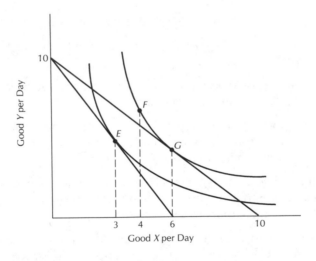

Figure A–5. Slope Same at Points *E* and *F*

Points to Note About Figure A–5:

1. Total effect of lower price: Point *E* to point *G*, demand for *X* up 3 units.

2. Income effect: Point *E* to point *F*, income effect increases *X* demanded by 1 unit.

3. Substitution effect: Point *F* to point *G*, substitution effect increases *X* demanded by 2 units.

SPECIAL CASE

If an event changes prices but lets the consumer still buy what he or she bought before, we say there is no income effect. That is, if the consumer does not change, he or she will have the same utility as before. However, the new prices, no matter what they are, will allow the consumer to move to a higher utility. The direction and extent of the move will be mainly determined by the substitution effect (although there is a small, very small, income effect). In Figure A–4, the consumer had $100 in income and the price of X was $20 a unit and the price of Y was $10 a unit. The consumer bought 4 units of Y (show this) and 3 units of X. Figure A–6 shows the effect when the price of good X falls to $10 but income falls by $30. With $70, the consumer can still buy 3 units of X (costing $30) and 4 units of Y (costing $40).

The new budget constraint goes from point X = 0, Y = 7 to point X = 7, Y = 0. The consumer can still buy, if he or she wants, at point E. Now the old indifference curve cuts through this new budget constraint. So we know the consumer can move to a higher utility. In this case, any place along the line segment between E and K will yield a higher utility than before. Exactly where depends on where the new tangency point will be (not shown). We see in Figure A–6 that when the consumer moves to segment EK, more X will be demanded. This is a substitution effect.

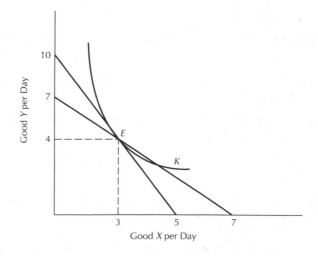

Figure A–6. Special Case

THE EASY CASE

To make the use of indifference curves easier, here is a simple trick. Suppose we are interested in good X only. We assume the consumer spends all his income on good X and on other goods. Now here is the trick: Define ach unit of other goods so that each unit costs $1. Now let us look at what this does for us. Mr. Consumer spends $200 a week on X and other goods. The price of X is $40 a unit. Figure A–7 shows the results.

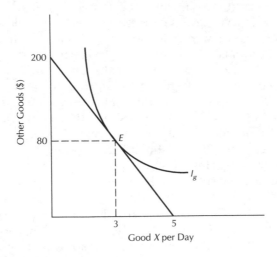

Figure A–7. The Easy Case

Points to Note About Figure A–7:

1. The vertical intercept is his dollar income. Why? Because $200 buys 200 units of other goods.

2. He buys 80 units of the other goods. Why? He is spending $120 on good X (3 × $40), so he is spending $80 on the other goods.

3. The difference between the vertical intercept and $80 is the amount he is spending on good X ($120).

4. The slope of the budget constraint, stated as a positive number, is the supply price of good X in dollars (here, it is $40).

5. The slope of the utility curve (stated as a positive number) is the demand price for good X in dollars!

By using the convention that other goods cost $1, we have gotten rid of the relative price and can substitute the actual price. This makes this type of graph much easier to use. I suggest you repeat the previous two sections, letting good Y be all other goods.

GLOSSARY

absolute advantage ability to produce a good with fewer inputs

accelerationist theory theory that unemployment cannot be permanently reduced through inflation

accounting profits profits ignoring implicit costs. Equals total revenue less explicit costs

actual or realized investment total investment spending, including unsold output put into inventory

added buyer effect a lower price for a good attracts new buyers into a market, increasing its quantity demanded

adverse selection when, due to poor information, "bad" products (or buyers) are selected. For example, sellers of junk cars will seek out uninformed buyers and try to pass off their cars as good. This reduces the value of truly good cars

aggregate demand total real quantity of goods and services demanded in an economy

aggregate demand curve a curve showing how the aggregate quantity demanded increases as the price level of all goods and services falls

aggregate supply total real quantity of goods and services demanded in an economy

aggregate supply curve (long run) a vertical curve showing in the long run that the aggregate quantity supplied equals the full-employment level of output when costs have time to adjust to price changes, no matter what the price level

aggregate supply curve (short run) curve showing how the aggregate quantity supplied increases in the short run when prices go up but factor costs do not change

allocative efficiency (also termed "Pareto efficiency") when no possible trade or reallocation of goods and inputs will make some better off without making others worse off

appreciation when it takes more of another nation's currency to purchase a nation's currency

assets what people own or what other people owe them

asymmetric information when one person knows more than another, making it hard for them to do business with each other. If they had otherwise done business, then asymmetrical information is the cause of a *market failure*

average tax rate percent of income paid in taxes

backward-bending supply curve of labor a curve showing that as real hourly wages go up, workers first supply more and then fewer hours of work

balanced-budget multiplier number that a change in government spending must be multiplied by to get resulting change in *GDP when* taxes increase the same amount as government spending

balance-of-payment account account made up of two accounts that keep track of goods, services, and assets flowing in and out of a nation. See also **capital account** and **current account**

barter trade without money

bilateral monopoly market where a monopsony and monopoly deal with each other

bond a certificate of indebtedness. Usually pays a predetermined stream of payments for a prespecified number of years

breakeven price price at which the firm just covers its costs

built-in stabilizers government spending that automatically increases and taxes that automatically decrease when *GDP* falls

business producers of goods and services

Cambridge *k* the fraction of income people want to hold in money balances. When the demand for money equals its supply, *k* is the inverse of velocity (so that $MV = PQ$ can be rewritten as $M/k = PQ$ or as $M = kPQ$

capital stock of plants, equipment, inventory, and other resources of production useful for more than one year

capital account account keeping track of physical and financial assets flowing on net into a country

capture hypothesis hypothesis that regulatory agencies tend to be "captured" by the industry they regulate and act on the industry's behalf rather than the customers'

cartel an arrangement among sellers in a market to jointly set price and output

cartel cheating problem all collusive agreements suffer from the tendency of each member to cut its price and take a bigger share of the market

classical economics a school of economics emphasizing the forces that clear markets. In particular, it emphasizes the importance of real variables (such as relative prices, capital stock, labor supply, and technology) in determining the real output and the importance of the money supply in determining nominal variables (such as price level)

Coase theorem theory that people can get rid of any market failure by bargaining among themselves when transaction costs are low

collusion attempt, either explicit or implicit, to not compete

commodity money a widely traded good valued both for its use as a medium of exchange and for itself. The main example is gold

comparative advantage ability to produce a good at a lower relative cost

compensating wage differentials differences in money wages compensating for differences in nonmonetary aspects of work (such as differences in working conditions and fringe benefits)

complementary inputs inputs used closely together. When the price of one goes up, less of both will be used even if output is unchanged

complements two goods that go together (such as peanut butter and jelly). When the price of one goes up, the quantity demanded of the other goes down

constant-cost industry industry with perfectly elastic long-run supply curve

constant returns to scale when long-run average total cost stays the same as output expands. Results when a given increase in all inputs increases output in the same proportion

consumer surplus what consumers are willing to pay for a good minus what they do pay

consumption household spending on consumption goods and services

consumption function function showing consumption at different levels of disposable income

consumption goods goods and services that are consumed or used up within the year, such as food and electricity. (Although in practice, many goods counted as consumption goods last longer, such as dresses, cars, and toasters)

contradictory gap See *GDP* **gap**

control variable variable that decision maker can increase or decrease to get the best net benefit or profit. For example, a control variable for a firm is the output that it produces

cost-push inflation inflation caused by upward shift in the aggregate supply curve. Usually a reaction to demand-pull inflation

credible threat threat that in the short run seems irrational (as it harms the person making it) but is credible because it results in long-run profits. An example is a dominant firm's threat to cut its price and drive out of business any competitor charging less than it does

cross elasticity of demand responsiveness of the quantity demanded to a change in the price of *another* good. Percent change in quantity demanded of a good due to a 1 percent increase in the price of another good

crowding out decreases in private investment spending (which is mainly financed by borrowing) due to increases in government borrowing (that push up interest rates)

current account account keeping track of goods and services flowing on net out of a country

cyclical unemployment unemployment due to downturns in the economy

deadweight loss loss to society without offsetting gains

deadweight loss of a tax total loss to producers and consumers from a tax minus tax revenues collected. Also termed "excess burden of a tax"

debt financing selling bonds to raise money. This form of financing obligates the firm to make fixed payments to bond holders

decreasing-cost industry an industry with a long-run supply curve that is downward sloping

"deficits do not matter" theory that equilibrium income will be the same if government spending is paid for with taxes or borrowings

deflation decrease in price level

deflationary gap see *GDP* **gap**

demand curve any downward-sloping curve that shows a greater quantity of a good demanded at a lower price, provided that other determinants of demand (such as income and prices of other goods) are held constant

demand-pull inflation inflation caused by rightward shift in aggregate demand curve

depreciation decline in the value of an asset over a given time, usually a year. (For calculating national income, depreciation is called the "capital consumption allowance")

depreciation (of a currency) when the value of a currency goes down (i.e., it takes less of another nation's currency to purchase it)

desired or planned investment total investment spending that businesses *want* to make. It does *not* include unwanted inventory accumulation

discount rate interest rate the Federal Reserve System charges banks that borrow funds from it

discretionary economic policy changing economic policy to actively affect the economy

discrimination workers not getting the same well-paying jobs or getting less pay than others with the same ability because of their race, sex, or other characteristic not related to productivity

diseconomies of scale when long-run average total cost goes up as output expands. Results when a given increase in all input results in a smaller than proportional increase in output

disinflation decrease in rate of inflation

disposable income after-tax income available for consumption spending and saving by households

dominant strategy a strategy better than every other strategy for a player regardless of what the others in the game do

economic profit payment in excess of what is necessary to get something done. Economic Profits = Total Revenue – (Explicit + Implicit Costs)

economic rent any rent to a factor in excess of its opportunity cost. Also, payment to factor in perfectly inelastic supply

economics study of how people choose among alternative uses of their scarce resources

economics of sale when a long-run average total cost falls as output expands. Results when a given increase in all inputs results in a more than proportional increase or output

effectiveness lag time it takes for government action to affect economy

efficiency when people produce all that can be, given their resources. To produce more of one good, an efficient economy must produce less of other goods and is on its production possibility curve

elastic demand when a given percent in price causes a greater percent decrease in the quantity demanded, decreasing total revenue

elasticity responsiveness of one variable to the change in another, both changes expressed as percents. The elasticity of Q with respect to P is the percent change in Q for every 1 percent change in P

equation of exchange $MV = PQ$, or money times velocity equals price times output

equilibrium in aggregate demand when spending equals income

equilibrium price price at which the quantity demanded equals the quantity sold. Also termed the "market clearing price"

equity financing selling stocks to raise money. The firm pays stockholders by paying dividends and by increasing the value of the firm

exchange rate rate at which one currency is exchanged for another. When one Euro trades for 1.1 dollars, it takes $1.10 to buy one Euro

expansionary gap see *GDP* **gap**

explicit costs dollar costs actually paid out

exports goods and services sold by domestic citizens to other nations

factor of production any input used to produce output (the main factors being land, labor, and capital)

Federal Open Market Committee (FOMC) arm of Federal Reserve System that oversees buying and selling of government bonds by the Federal Reserve Bank of New York for the purposes of regulating the money supply

Federal Reserve System institution that regulates money supply and operations of banking system. Controlled by Board of Governors. Also called "the Fed"

fiat money a money not backed by gold or any other valuable good. For example, the dollar

final good good produced for final use and not for resale within the year

fiscal policy policy involving government spending and taxation

fixed costs costs that neither increase nor decrease as output changes

fixed exchange rate exchange rate set and supported by a nation's government, which buys and sells its currency at that rate

flexible exchange rate an exchange rate that is set by free market forces without government intervention. Also called "floating exchange rate"

foreign exchange rate the price of one nation's currency in terms of another nation's currency

45-degree line a valuable reference line since all points on this line have the same value on the vertical and horizontal axes

fractional reserve banking banking system where banks lend money out they owe their depositors

free good good that is not scarce; good whose supply exceeds demand at a zero price

free-rider problem while everyone benefits from a public good, each tries to be a free rider by not paying for it. As a result, the good may not be supplied in a free market

frictional unemployment unemployment due to the normal workings of an economy

full-employment deficit what the deficit *would be* if the economy were at full employment (also called the "active" or "structural" deficit)

full-employment level of output output where the demand and supply for labor (and other factors) are equal, there being neither a shortage nor a surplus of workers. Also termed "potential output"

full wage total monetary value of a job (per period); the sum of money wages plus the monetary value of all nonmonetary aspects of work

game theory the study of how people behave in situations where one's actions affect the reaction of others

GDP gap between actual and full-employment output. When output is above its full-employment level, there is an "inflationary" or "expansionary" gap; when it is below, a "deflationary" or "contractionary" gap

Giffen good good whose demand decreases when price goes down. The good must be an inferior good for this to occur

government debt total accumulated borrowings of the government

government deficit excess of government spending over taxes collected (for a year)

government surplus excess of taxes over government spending (for a year)

graph visual presentation of how two variables are related to each other

gross domestic product (GDP) market value of final output produced within borders of nation

gross national product (*GNP*) market value of all final output produced by a nation's resources (including resources located abroad)

holdout program whenever the consent of a higher percent of people is needed, each person has a greater incentive to hold out his or her consent, with the result that less is achieved

households owners of all factors in the economy. Households provide the services of labor, land, capital, and ownership to businesses

human capital knowledge and skills that make people more productive. Created by natural ability and on-the-job training

implementation lag time it takes for the government to implement its policy and take action

implicit costs costs incurred because of alternative opportunities given up. For a firm, these include the costs of its owners' time and investment

imports goods and services that are bought by domestic citizens and are produced by other nations

income highest level of sustainable consumption. Income minus consumption equals addition to wealth

income effect effect on the quantity demanded of a good when real income changes

income effect of a price change a lower price for a good is like giving consumers more income. Some of this "income" may go for buying more units of the good, increasing its quantity demanded

income elasticity of demand percent change in quantity demanded for every 1 percent change in income

income velocity see **velocity**

increasing-cost industry industry with rising long-run supply curve

inelastic demand when a given percent increase in the price causes a smaller percent decrease in the quantity demanded, increasing total revenue

inferior good a good that people demand less of when their income goes up

inflation rise in general level prices. Usually refers to persistent rise in prices over time

inflation rate percent increase in price level over a year

inflationary gap see *GDP* **gap**

inflationary premium addition to real interest rate to compensate savers for expected loss in purchasing power from inflation

inflationary premium effect of money supply growth higher and expected growth rates in the money supply increase interest rates

injections any form of spending other than consumption. Includes investment and government spending

innovation finding a better way to do something, including a cheaper way to produce a good or a more valued good to produce

input see **factor of production**

interest payment for use of funds over a certain period of time

interest rate parity when capital flows between nations until all nations pay the same interest rates, adjusting for the risk of default and the risk that the nation's currency will depreciate

inverse relationship see **negative relationship**

joint products two goods produced together because it is difficult to produce them separately (e.g., leather and beef)

Keynesian economics a school of economics based upon the macroeconomic theory of John Maynard Keynes. It emphasized how changes in the components of aggregate spending (especially investment) affect aggregate demand and the resulting change in real output due to sticky prices and wages. This school attributes many recessions to a decline in investment spending

kinked demand curve hypothetical demand curve that an oligopolic firm faces when other firms maintain their price when it raises its price but match its price when it lowers its price

labor force all persons employed or unemployed

labor productivity output per labor, measured by dividing real *GDP* by total hours

Laffer curve curve showing that as the marginal tax rate increases, total tax revenues first increase and then fall as the marginal rate becomes excessive

law of comparative advantage nations are better off when they produce goods they have a comparative advantage in supplying

law of demand quantity demanded and price are inversely related—more is demanded at a lower price, less at a higher price (other things being equal)

law of diminishing marginal returns after some point, as a firm adds more and more units of an input, the input's marginal physical product diminishes (i.e., it adds less to total output than before)

law of diminishing marginal utility as people consume more of a good in a given period, its marginal utility declines

law of diminishing returns after reaching a certain level of employment and holding other inputs constant, a firm will find that each added worker increases output less than the previous worker did. Output rises, but at a diminishing rate

law of equal marginal utility per dollar the highest utility is achieved when the last dollar spent on each good has the same marginal utility

law of increasing relative cost as more of a good is produced, its opportunity cost rises

law of one price see **purchasing power parity**

law of supply quantity supplied and price usually are directly related—more is supplied at a higher price, less at a lower price (other things being equal)

leakage any allocation of income that is not directly spent on goods and services. Includes taxes and savings

lemon problem because sellers know the quality of their product more than buyers, there may be an *adverse selection* of poor quality goods being sold

liabilities what people owe others

lifecycle model consumption consumption spending is a function of people's expected future income and spending, including the effects of age and retirement

liquidity ease with which an asset (such as a stock or bond) can be converted into cash

liquidity effect of money supply growth when people do not expect higher inflation, an increase in the money supply reduces interest rates and increases investment spending

liquidity trap John Maynard Keynes asserted that when interest rates were so low as to make bonds unattractive to savers, any increase in the money supply would go into savings (being "trapped" there) instead of being spent. As a result, monetary policy would be totally ineffective for stimulating aggregate spending

logrolling the trading of votes to get positions favorable only to minority interest groups voted in

long run period when firm can change all inputs, including its plant size and equipment. Also, period when firms can enter or exit an industry

long-run neutrality of money see **neutrality of money**

M1 measure of the money supply counting only cash held by the public plus checking accounts

macroeconomics study of the economy as a whole, including the causes of the business cycle, unemployment, and inflation

marginal analysis solving economic problems by using small steps and evaluating the costs and benefits of each marginal step

marginal benefit increase in total benefit due to one more unit of output, labor, or other control variable being increased

marginal cost addition to total cost due to increasing output by one unit

marginal factor cost (*MFC*) addition to total cost when one additional unit of an input is employed

marginal physical product (*MPP*) addition to total physical output due to an added unit of an input

marginal propensity to consume (*MPC*) added consumption spending due to $1 more of disposable income

marginal propensity to save (*MPS*) added savings due to $1 more of disposable income

marginal revenue increase in total revenue due to additional unit of output

marginal revenue product (*MRP*) addition to total revenue when one additional unit of an input (such as labor or capital) is employed

marginal tax rate percent of additional income paid in taxes

marginal utility addition to total utility from consuming one more unit of a good

marginal value value of least importance that a unit of a good (or resource) is currently being put to; the loss suffered due to one less unit of the good

market failure when markets fail to produce and allocate goods efficiently (and in particular, when mutually advantageous trades are not made)

market for loanable funds market where savers and borrowers get together, savers supplying their savings—the loanable funds—to borrowers demanding the funds. The price of loanable funds is the interest rate

median voter model when two people are running for office, they will position themselves near the opinions of the median voter

microeconomics study of factors determining the relative prices of goods and inputs

minimum efficient scale level of output where long-run average total cost achieves its minimum

Monetarist economics a school of macroeconomics emphasizing the effect of money supply upon aggregate demand. Velocity is usually assumed to be predictable over the long run, which allows one to use the quantity theory ($MV = PQ$) to make predictions. This school believes that large and unexpected declines in the money supply will usually cause a recession

monetary base essentially all the cash in the economy. The sum of bank reserves and currency held by the public. Also termed "high-powered money"

monetary policy policy determining level and growth rate of the money supply

money the medium of exchange, what people use to pay for goods and services

monopolistic competition market like that of perfect competition except sellers sell a closely related but not identical product

monopoly only seller of a good with no close substitutes

monopsony a firm so dominant in a factor market that its hiring decisions affect the input's market price. Faces higher input price as it employs more

moral hazard once two people agree to a contract, the risk that one of them will act to the detriment of the other. For example, after a business pays an insurance company for fire insurance, the firm burns down the property as it is worth less than what it was insured for

mutual interdependence when one firm's actions affect another firm's in the same industry significantly, and vice versa

Nash equilibrium a situation where persons interacting with each other choose their best strategy given the strategies that all the other persons have chosen

national savings private savings of households plus government surplus

natural monopoly industry having such large economies of scale that one firm can meet all the demand and still not achieve its most efficient scale

natural rate of unemployment level of unemployment when people's expectations about prices match the actual level of prices. (Occurs at full employment when government and union interventions are absent)

natural resources productive inputs provided by nature such as land, minerals, and water

negative externalities activities imposing uncompensated costs upon others. Also termed "external diseconomies."

negative relationship X and Y are negatively related if when X goes up, Y goes down and vice versa. (Also called an inverse relationship)

Neoclassical (or new classical) economics a school of economics emphasizing the forces which clear markets (as did the classical economists) but also the transitory effects of the money supply on real variables (such as real output and employment). In the long run, neoclassical economists believe that real output is independent of predictable and systematic changes in aggregate demand

Neo-Keynesian economics a school of macroeconomics using rational expectations along with Keynesian economics. This believes that predictable changes in aggregate demand will affect real output in the short run and that prices and wages do not change quickly to clear all markets

net exports exports minus imports

foreign investment the purchase of foreign assets by domestic residents minus the purchase of domestic assets by foreigners. For the United States, net foreign investment usually has had a negative value

net investment addition to the capital stock of the nation. Equals gross investment minus depreciation

neutrality of money in the long run, a larger money supply has no effect on output or on relative prices

Nominal *GDP* *GDP* valued at prices belonging to the same period goods were produced in (referred to also as *GDP* in current dollars)

nominal interest rate actual rate of interest; the extra *money* borrowers have to pay back to lenders, in excess of the loan amount, expressed as percent per year of the loan

nominal money supply dollar amount of money

nominal shock shock changing the price level but leaving relative prices unaffected. (An example is an unanticipated increase in the money supply)

nominal value value of goods in terms of their prices at the time they were produced and sold. Also called "value in terms of current dollars"

nominal wage hourly money earnings

nonprice competition competition between goods on aspects other than price (such as quality and service)

nonpricing rationing any method of equating supply and demand other than price. Its two main forms are waiting lines and discrimination

normal good a good that people demand more of when their income goes up

normal profits long-run accounting profits in an industry, just covering the owner's implicit costs

Okun's law for every 2 percent real *GDP* is below its potential full-employment level over a year's time, the unemployment rate will increase by 1 percent

oligopoly market with few sellers and medium to high barriers of entry

open market operation main method government changes money supply. The buying and selling of government securities by the Federal Open Market Committee (FOMC)

opportunity cost value of best alternative that had to be given up in order to undertake a given course of action

overvalued currency currency whose exchange rate is above its free market equilibrium rate

Pareto efficiency when resources and goods are allocated so that the only way to make one person better off is to make someone else worse off

path dependency when once started along a certain path, an economy becomes locked in to an existing technology, even if better ways of doing things exist

payment-in-kind payment in goods or services rather than in money

perfect competition whenever there is enough competition that no one seller can raise its price without losing all its customers to other sellers

perfect price discrimination when seller charges a different price for each unit of the good that is equal to the unit's demand price

perfectly contestable markets markets with unimpeded and costless entry and exit of firms

permanent income expected average value of future earnings

permanent-income hypothesis consumption spending is a constant fraction of peoples' permanent income

Phillips curve curve showing trade-off between inflation and unemployment when the public's expected rate of inflation is unchanged

physical capital the stock of equipment and structures used to produce goods and services

positive externalities activities creating benefits for others who do not pay for the benefits. Also termed "external economies"

positive relationship X and Y are positively related if when X goes up, Y goes up. When X goes down, Y goes down

precautionary demand for money money demand due to money holdings allowing people to meet unforeseen expenses

present value value of future dollars in terms of what they are worth today. The loan amount one could borrow today and pay back with future dollars

price ceiling law imposed by the government prohibiting the price from going above a certain level

price discrimination the selling of the same good at different prices. See also **perfect price discrimination**

price elasticity of demand percent change in quantity demanded for every 1 percent change in price (both percent changes stated as absolute values)

price elasticity of supply percent change in quantity supplied for every 1 percent change in the price

price floor law imposed by the government prohibiting the price from falling below a certain level

price index cost of a market basket of goods in a given year expressed as a percent of its cost in some base year. When the index is 140, the basket cost 140 percent of its base-year cost

price searchers buyers or sellers having large enough shares of a market such that when they buy or sell more, the market price changes

price takers buyers or sellers whose individual actions have no effect on market price (and thus they "take" the market price as given)

principal-agent problem the dual problem of (1) the principal who hires the agent setting up the contract so that the agent will do what the principal wants, and (2) the agent setting up the contract so that the principal will pay for the work the agent does

private cost cost borne by those producing a good

problem of the commons abuse of resource when no one owns it and thus no one has an incentive to keep it up

producer surplus what producers are paid less their marginal cost

production possibility curve graph showing combinations of goods an individual, firm, or an economy is capable of producing. Also termed "production possibility frontier"

rogressive tax system tax system under which those with higher incomes are subject to higher marginal and average tax rates

public good good whose consumption by one person does not diminish its consumption by others (e.g., national defense)

purchasing power parity when exchange rates between nations change so that goods, both domestic and imported, sell for the same price. Also called the "law of one price" because different units of the same good tend to sell for the same price in any given market

quantity demanded maximum quantity of a good buyers are willing and able to buy at a given price (during a fixed period of time)

quantity supplied maximum quantity of a good sellers are willing and able to supply at a given price (during a fixed period of time)

quantity theory of money theory that uses the equation of exchange ($MV = PQ$) to make predictions by assuming that the annual change in velocity is small and predictable

quota a limit on the amount of an import

random error unpredictable error or mistake

rational expectations expectations that are unbiased and based upon the best available information

real business cycle theory theory that main causes of the business cycle are from real sources (such as changes in tax rate and technology) rather than shifts in aggregate demand

real exchange rate rate at which goods in one country are exchanged for goods of another country

real *GDP* *GDP* valued at prices from a given year (currently, from 1972, also known as *GDP* in constant dollars)

real interest rate percent increase in purchasing power (i.e., in real goods and services) that borrowers pay back to lenders. Equals the nominal rate of interest minus the expected rate of inflation

real money money expressed in terms of what it can buy. Derived by dividing nominal money supply by a price index

real shocks shocks affecting the relative price of goods and inputs, e.g., unanticipated changes in taste, technology, or factor supplies

real value measure of value removing the effects of inflation. The value of a good (or goods) in terms of their price from some given year (called the "base year"). Also called "value in terms of constant dollars"

real wage hourly earnings of workers stated in real terms (equals money wage divided by price index)

real wealth effect increase in aggregate demand due to lower price level (the lower price level increasing the real value of nominal assets, especially money, causing people to spend more). Also called the "real balance effect"

recession when output falls for two consecutive quarters

recognition lag time it takes for the government to recognize that something is wrong with the economy

relative price Good A's relative price tells how much of Good B must be given to get one more unit of Good A

rent see economic rent

rent-seeking activity costing resources and time with the object of obtaining resources or laws having economic rents; considered socially wasteful, as this activity adds nothing to total output

required reserve ratio fraction of their deposits banks must keep at the Federal Reserve Bank

savings foregone consumption (that is usually invested)

scarcity condition that exists when current resources are inadequate to provide for all of people's wants

self-correcting mechanism means by which an economy gets to full employment without government intervention

shift in autonomous spending initial shift in spending that occurs at a given level of income

shift in demand change in demand curve such that a different quantity is demanded at each price. Curves shift only when some variable *other than price* changes. Also called "change in demand"

shock an unanticipated event. See also **real shocks**

shortage quantity demanded exceeds quantity supplied (caused by price being below market equilibrium price)

short run period when the firm can change (either increasing or decreasing) some but *not all* of its inputs

shutdown price price below which a firm shuts down

signals action taken by a person to signal or reveal relevant information. An example is a student who joins many clubs in college to show employers they will be good managers

slope how much the variable on the vertical (or side) axis changes when the variable on the horizontal (or bottom) axis increases by one unit

social benefit benefit all persons get from a good

social cost cost all persons pay for a good

speculative demand for money money demand due to money holdings being safer than many other assets

spending multiplier number by which an initial increase in spending must be multiplied to get the resulting change in total spending

spill-over effect higher union wages causing those losing their jobs in union plants to seek jobs in nonunion plants, forcing nonunion wages down

stagflation inflation and recession occurring at the same time

structural unemployment unemployment caused by changes in demand or technology seriously affecting certain industries, occupations, or areas of the country so that only with very high costs can workers relocate and/or retrain for new careers

substitute inputs two inputs that to some degree can replace one another. When price of one goes up, the firm uses more of the other input per unit of output

substitute products two alternate goods that could be produced with the same (or very similar) set of inputs. (Examples are gasoline and heating oil)

substitutes two goods that compete with each other (such as butter and margarine). When the price of one goes up, the quantity demanded of the other also goes up

substitution effect of a price change a lower relative price means a lower opportunity cost of buying the good, which encourages buyers to buy more of the good (holding real income constant)

sunk costs costs that cannot be avoided

supply curve curve showing relationship between price and quantity of a good that suppliers are willing to supply. Usually upward sloping; the exception is in a decreasing cost industry

supply-side economics theory emphasizing the negative of government taxation on aggregate supply

surplus quantity supplied exceeds quantity demanded (causes by price exceeding market equilibrium price)

tariff tax on imports

tax-based income policy (TIP) policy calling for the government to increase taxes on firms and workers who raise prices too much and reduce taxes for those who keep their prices within guidelines

tax incidence who actually pays a tax

tax multiplier number that a tax change must be multiplied by to get resulting change in *GDP*. A tax multiplier of −5 implies that a $200 increase in taxes will reduce *GNP* by $1,000

tax shifting shifting tax one pays onto others. For example, firm raising its price shifts tax onto consumers

technological progress change in the methods of producing things that results in more output being produced from the same quantity of inputs. Alternatively stated, change resulting in the same quantity of output being produced with less input

terms-of-trade relative price for goods offered in marketplace

theory of public choice economic theory of how governments act

Tiebout hypothesis theory that smaller governments and greater mobility of citizens and firms between cities, states, and nations produce more efficient government

total quality management (lean production) production process focused upon customer satisfaction, the reduction of waste (waste being any production activity not directly contributing to customer's satisfaction), and product reliability

total revenue total sales (usually per year)

total surplus excess of the total value of a quantity of a good over its total cost; sum of the difference between demand price and supply price across all units of a good being bought and produced. Equals the consumer surplus plus the producer surplus

total utility total satisfaction derived from consuming goods and services

trade off when satisfying *more* of one need means satisfying *less* of another

transaction demand for money money demand due to money holding's allowing people to buy and sell goods more easily

transfer payment payment for which no goods or services are received in return. Examples include gifts and food stamps

unbiased forecast forecast that is neither wrong on average nor systematically wrong

undervalued currency currency whose exchange rate is below its free market equilibrium rate

unemployment rate percent of the labor force that is unemployed One is unemployed if actively seeking work or waiting to be recalled or to report to a job

unitary demand when a given percent increase in price causes the exact same percent decrease in the quantity demanded, leaving total revenue unchanged

value added value of a business's output minus its purchases from other businesses

valued-added tax (VAT) tax on a company's value added

variable cost cost of all inputs the firm increases in the short run to produce more

velocity number of times an average dollar is used in a year to buy final goods and services (also called "income velocity")

voting paradox how a majority will vote on a set of issues can be changed by altering the order issues are presented in

wage-threat effect higher union wages causing nonunion employers to also pay higher wages to reduce threat of being unionized

wealth net value of all the assets a person owns (including the value of his or her skills, i.e., the value of all future earnings)

LIST OF ABBREVIATIONS

%Δ	the percent change in	*MRP*	marginal revenue product
AD	aggregate demand, aggregate demand curve	*MRS*	marginal rate of subs
		MS	money supply
AFC	average fixed cost	*MSB*	marginal social benefit
APC	average propensity to consume	*MSC*	marginal social cost
		MU	marginal utility
AS	aggregate supply; aggregate supply curve	*NFI*	net foreign investment
		NI	national income
ATC	average total cost	*NNP*	net national product
AVC	average variable cost	*NX*	net export spending (foreign)
C	consumption spending (household)	*P*	price level
		PC	Phillips curve
COLA	cost-of-living adjustments	P^d	demand price
CPI	consumer price index	*PMC*	private marginal cost
DI	disposable income	*PPI*	producer price index
DOL	Department of Labor	*PQ*	price × output, or nominal *GDP*
FOMC	federal open market committee	P^s	supply price
G	government spending	*PV*	present value
GNP	gross national product	*Q*	output, total income and spending, real *GDP*
$GDP	nominal *GDP*		
I	investment spending	*QD*	quantity demand
i	interest rate	*R*	required reserve ratio
M	nominal money supply	*S*	national savings
MB	marginal benefit	*SMC*	social marginal cost
MC	marginal cost	*S-Long Run*	long-run aggregate supply curve
MD	nominal money demand		
MFC	marginal factor cost	*T*	taxes
M/P	real money supply	*TC*	total cost
MPC	marginal propensity to consume	*TFC*	total fixed cost
		TR	total revenue
MPP	marginal physical product	*TVC*	total variable cost
MPS	marginal propensity to save	*V*	velocity (or *$GDP/MD*)
MR	marginal revenue	*VMP*	value of marginal product

ELEMENTS OF ACCOUNTING

Every business is interested in two things:

1. *How much is the firm currently worth?* The answer to this question is given in its balance sheet.

2. *How much did the firm make last year?* The answer to this question is given in its income statement.

THE BALANCE SHEET

A company's worth is

Net Worth = Total Assets − Total Liabilities

A company's **total assets** is the value of all it owns. This includes its holdings of cash, its current inventory of goods and materials, as well as its land, plant, and equipment.

Total liabilities is everything the firm owes others. Most firms borrow to buy their assets; the amount a firm still owes its creditors is part of its liabilities. Another common liability is what a firm owes its workers when the workers retire and start drawing on their pensions.

Net worth is the answer to the question "How much is the firm currently worth?" Net worth equals the excess of what the firm owns over what it owes.

THE INCOME STATEMENT

A company's net income is:

Net Income = Total Revenues − Total Cost

Total revenues equal total sales. Unlike national income accounting, most firms do not count unsold output as part of its revenues (the exception is when the firm takes several years to build a good, such as a ship; in this case, future revenues from the yet-to-be-sold and uncompleted ship may be allocated over the years it takes to build).

Total cost includes all material and labor cost used to produce the current period's sales. In addition, the firm's machinery and plant has been worn down; the cost of this wear and tear is depreciation.

Net income after taxes is the amount "the firm made last year." Net income after taxes represents an addition to the firm's net worth.

HOW TO OVERSTATE PROFIT

Firms sometimes try to overstate their profits in several ways:

1. *Understate Depreciation:* By overstating how long a machine will last or by understating how much its value has depreciated, firms increase their reported profits. For example, some computer-leasing firms once pretended that their computers would last ten years while in fact technological progress was making them obsolete within three years.

   Inflation increases the value of wear and tear, so by ignoring inflation (and instead valuing depreciation on the basis of the equipment's original cost), the firm overstates its profits.

2. *Overstate the Value of Increased Inventory:* Suppose a firm cannot sell all its output. That may indicate that its output may never be sold. In this case, the firm should add the cost of producing this unsold output to the current period's cost. However, a firm might "pretend" this excess output will eventually be sold and wait to record the cost of producing it to the time when it will be sold. This increases the firm's current reported profits.

3. *Ignore New Liabilities:* When certain liabilities are incurred, some part of them should be reported and/or recorded as a cost in the income statement. However, some firms have ignored such liabilities (examples are potential lawsuits and increases in retiree health-care liabilities).

4. *Overstate Sales:* A firm sometimes gets new sales by lending buyers money to buy the firm's goods. The firm then records these as sales without taking into account that some of its buyers will likely not be able to pay back what they borrowed. A manufacturer of bowling alley equipment pulled this trick and nearly went bankrupt when bowling alley after bowling alley folded. However, it had a wonderful income statement up to that point.

Note that for income-tax purposes, firms try to *understate* profits, using the opposites of these techniques.

SOURCES OF ECONOMIC DATA

Some of the major sources of economic data are listed below: Some you can get free; some are available at most libraries. You are encouraged to at least get the money supply data from the St. Louis Federal Reserve Bank (see below)

1. *Barron's*
    National Business and Financial Weekly
    World Financial Center
    200 Liberty Street
    New York, NY 10281

weekly

If you are or intend to be a business professional, you should read this and *The Wall Street Journal* (see below).

2. *Economic Trends*
    Federal Reserve Bank of Cleveland
    P.O. Box 6387
    Cleveland, OH 44101

monthly, free

Supplies charts on most major economic variables, along with helpful commentary.

3. *National Economic Trends*
    The Federal Reserve Bank of St. Louis
    P.O. Box 442
    St. Louis, MO 63166-0422

monthly, free

National Economic Trends supplies charts and data on *GDP*, prices, costs, spending, and inventories.

4. *Statistical Abstract of the United States*
    Superintendent of Documents
    U.S. Government Printing Office
    Washington, DC 20402

yearly

This has over 1,500 tables on subjects ranging from population, to finance, to foreign commerce, and data on almost every aspect of our economy that is collected by our government. It is a good place to begin any research project, as it tells you where to go for more information.

5. *Survey of Current Business*
    Superintendent of Documents
    U.S. Government Printing Office
    Washington, DC 20402

monthly

This has too much detail for most persons, but is perfect for anyone who must keep up with the details of our economy.

6. *U.S. Financial Data*
    The Federal Reserve Bank of St. Louis
    P.O. Box 66953
    St. Louis, MO 63166–6953

weekly

U.S. Financial Data is one of the best sources of monetary statistics reported in both chart and percent change form. Interest rates and other financial data are also presented.

7. *The Wall Street Journal*
    200 Burnett Road
    Chicopee, MA 01021

daily

No list would be complete without mentioning *The Wall Street Journal*. The editorial page is an on-going lesson in economics.

BUSINESS CYCLE INDICATORS

Each month, the U.S. Department of Commerce publishes a series of economic indicators, including the widely followed leading, coincident, and lagging indicators. These are designed, respectively, to lead, coincide, and lag the business cycle. The components of each indicator are given in Table A–1. These components can be thought of as describing the business cycle.

Table A–1. Components of Business Cycle Indicators

Leading Index Components
1. Average weekly hours in manufacturing
2. Average weekly initial claims for unemployment insurance
3. Manufacturers' new orders, consumer goods and materials, adjusted for inflation
4. Vendor performance: percent of index measuring firms receiving slower deliveries
5. Contracts and orders for plant and equipment, adjusted for inflation
6. Index of new private housing units authorized by local building permits
7. Change in manufacturer's unfilled orders for durable goods, adjusted for inflation
8. Percent change in sensitive material prices, smoothed
9. Money supply, M2, adjusted for inflation
10. Index of consumer expectations

Coincident Index Components
1. Employees on nonagricultral payrolls
2. Personal income less transfer payments, adjusted for inflation
3. Index of industrial production
4. Manufacturing and trade sales, adjusted for inflation

Lagging Index Components
1. Average duration of unemployment in weeks
2. Ratio of manufacturing and trade inventories to sales, adjusted for inflation
3. Percent change in manufacturing labor cost per unit output, smoothed
4. Average prime rate charged by banks
5. Commercial and industrial loans outstanding, adjusted for inflation
6. Ratio of consumer installment credit outstanding to personal income
7. Percent change in Consumer Price Index for services, smoothed

Before a recession, stock prices and the real money supply almost always decline (both of these being the most reliable indicators of what is to come). New orders, new businesses being formed, and housing permits decrease: an indication that aggregate demand is falling. Businesses typically cut back on the hours of work of their employees. Other indicators of an impending recession are a wider difference between commercial paper rates and Treasury bill rates, and an inverted yield curve.

During a recession, firms move to cut back on their number of employees. Real sales and production fall.

At the end of the recession, the lagging indicators fall, thus predicting the end is in sight. Unemployment usually peaks *after* output has hit bottom. This is because firms typically do not let go of valued employees until they must, so changes in employment lag after changes in output. Interest rates also hit bottom after the economy has.

The opposite process occurs during an expansion. One popular rule of thumb is that the economy will turn (going into recession or expansion) when the leading indicators change direction for two consecutive months.

REVIEW AND ADDITIONAL MATERIAL

THE GEOMETRY OF PROFIT-MAXIMIZING

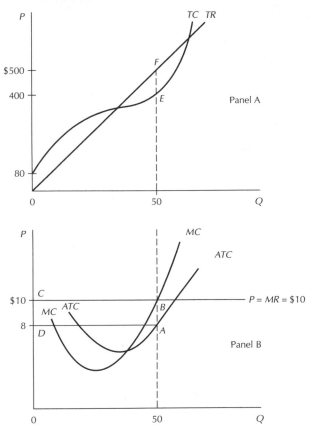

Figure A–8. Determining Profit Maximization

This material presents the graphical approach to analyzing the selection of the best output so as to maximize profits. It shows the relationship between total revenue and cost to marginal revenue and cost and how they should appear at the optimal level of output (where profits are maximized).

Figure A–8, Panel A, shows how total revenue and total costs increase with output for a competitive firm. As Q goes up 1 unit, TR increases by P; so TR is a straight line with a slope of P $(= MR)$. TC starts out at TFC (of $80) and increases by MC: The slope of the TC curve is MC.

The firm wants to select Q to maximize its profits, which is the vertical distance between TR and TC. When TR and TC are smooth lines curved in the manner shown, they will be furthest apart at the output level where both their slopes are the same: The firm will be maximizing profits at this output. In addition, since the slope of TR is MR and the slope of TC is MC, we have $MR = MC$ when the firm is maximizing profits. This occurs in Figure A–8 at an output of 50, where the vertical distance $TR - TC$ is biggest (and equal to $100). F and E are $100 apart. The firm's profit is $100.

Panel B shows the same conditions in marginal terms. At 50 units of output, P $(= MR)$ $= MC$ at $10 and $Q = 50$. Area $ABCD$ equals $100, the firm's profit. This area equals the base (output DA, or 50) times the height (AB or $P - ATC$ at $Q = 50$ is the average profit per unit of output, $2).

$$\text{Output} \times \text{Average Profit} = \text{Total Profit}$$

An increase in fixed costs shifts the TC curve up but leaves its slope at each Q unchanged. So the optimal Q stays the same. If fixed costs go up $100 (to $180), the TC curve will just touch the TR line at Point F. In Panel B, the ATC curve will intersect MC at Point B.

Some other points:

1. A straight line drawn from the origin to any point on the TC line (in Panel A) has a slope equal to the ATC of the corresponding level of output (Slope = Rise/Run or $ATC = TC/Q$).

2. The straight line to TC with the smallest slope has a slope equal to the minimum ATC.

3. The area under the MC curve up to a given Q equals that Q's TVC (since TVC = sum of MCs).

4. A review:
   Profit $= TR - TC = P \times Q - ATC \times Q$
   Profit $= (P - ATC) \times Q$.
   Profit $= TR - TFC - TVC$.
   TVC = Sum of MCs.
   $TC = TFC + TVC = TFC + $ Sum of MCs.
   MC = Change in TC = Change in TVC (when Q goes up 1).
   MR = Change in TR (when Q goes up 1).
   TR = Sum of MRs.

Change in Profit (when Q goes up 1) $= MR - MC$.
Profit $=$ Area between MR and MC curve $- TFC$

THE ALGEBRA OF INCOME DETERMINATION IN THE KEYNESIAN MODEL

If you are called upon to solve for equilibrium income from algebraic (or numerical) formulas for the Keynesian model, use this procedure:

Key Procedure for Solving for Equilibrium Output

1. Write the consumption function (C) as a function of Q. Be sure to include the effect of taxes, if any.

2. Write the expression for total spending ($D = C + I + G$) using the consumption function from Step 1 and the expressions for I and G.

3. Write the income $=$ spending equation, or $Q =$ the equation from Step 2.

4. Collect terms. Solve for Q.

For example, suppose consumption spending has the following functional form:

$$C = 100 + .8Q$$

This equation indicates that consumption equals $100 when output and income is 0, and that consumption spending increases $.80 for every $1 increase in Q. The $100 is called autonomous consumption spending, and 0.8 is the marginal propensity to consume (MPC). As it stands, this equation is in the form required by Step 1. Suppose we have:

$$C = 500 + .8(Q - T)$$

$Q - T$ is disposable income, where T is the tax revenue that the government collects. If $T = \$500$, we substitute this amount into this equation, and then rewrite the equation in the following manner:

$$C = 100 + .8Q$$

The equation is not in the form required by Step 1.

Example: Income in a Simple Economy

PROBLEM   What is equilibrium income and output (Q), when $C = 100 + .8Q$ and $I = \$400$? ($G = T = NX = 0$).

SOLUTION   Following the steps in the key procedure, we have:

1. $C = 100 + .8Q$

2. $D = 100 + .8Q + 400$. (Recall that $D = C + I$.)

3. $Q = 100 + .8Q + 400$.

4. Collect terms: $Q = 500 + .8Q$
    Solve: $.2Q = 500$
    $$Q = 500/.2$$
    $$Q = 2,500$$

Example: Equilibrium Income with Government Sector Added

PROBLEM   What is Q, when $C = \overline{C} + b(Q - T)$, $I = \overline{I} + iQ$, $G = \overline{G} + gQ$, and $\overline{T} = T + tQ$?

Note: the terms with bars over them are the autonomous, or fixed, components of the equation. For example, investment spending equals I when $Q = 0$; then, as Q increases by \$1, I increases by $\$i$. Government spending increases by $\$g$ for every \$1 increase in Q, and taxes increase by $\$t$ for every \$1 increase in Q.

1. $C = \overline{C} + b(Q - \overline{T} - tQ) = \overline{C} - b\overline{T} + b(1 - t)Q.$

2. $D = \overline{C} - b\overline{T} + b(1 - t)Q + \overline{I} + iQ + \overline{G} + gQ.$

3. $Q = \overline{C} + b\overline{T} + b(1 - t)Q + \overline{I} + iQ + \overline{G} + gQ.$

4. Combine terms: $Q = (\overline{C} - b\overline{T} + \overline{I} + \overline{G}) + [b(1 - t) + i + g]Q.$

    Solve $\{1 - [b(1 - t) + i + g]\}Q = (\overline{C} - b\overline{T} + \overline{I} + \overline{G})$

    $$Q = \frac{\overline{C} - b\overline{T} + \overline{I} + \overline{G}}{1 - [b(1 - t) + i + g]}$$

In the first line of Step 4, the term in front of Q on the right-hand side of the equation is the Marginal Propensity to Spend, *MP*Spend (the increase in total spending when national income increases by one dollar). A dollar added to spending is spent and respent according to the multiplier process formula:

$$1 + MPSpend + MPSpend^2 + MPSpend^3 + \dots$$

which equals the spending multiplier: the spending multiplier is $1/(1 - MPSpend)$.

To get equilibrium Q, sum all the terms not multiplied by Q in Step 2 (this sum equals total spending when $Q = 0$) and then multiply this sum by the spending multiplier, $1/(1 - MPSpend)$. In effect, the spending at $Q = 0$ is multiplied by the spending multiplier to get equilibrium national income. This yields the equation in Step 4, with autonomous spending in the numerator and $(1 - MPSpend)$ in the denominator.

SUMMARY OF MACROECONOMIC MODELS

The following chart summarizes the results we have derived in Chapters 7 through 15. Each entry shows the effect of an increase in the fiscal or monetary variable mentioned; the effect of a decrease would be the opposite of the effects shown (for example, an increase in the money supply increases the price level, so a decrease in the money supply decreases the price level). Long-run results assume that the economy begins at full employment.

Table A–2. Summary of Macroeconomic Models

	Aggregate Demand	Effect on Aggregate Supply	Price Level	Output[1]
Keynesian Model *(Chapters 9, 11, 13)* Government spending up	+	0	+	+
Government taxation up	–	0	–	–
Autonomous consumption, investment, or net export spending up	+	0	+	+
Money supply up[2]	+	0	+	+

	Aggregate Demand	Effect on Aggregate Supply	Price Level	Output[1]
Monetarist Model *(Chapter 13)* Money supply up				
Short-run	+	0	+	+
Long-run	+	+	+	0
Government borrowing[3]	+	0	+	+
Money demand up Short-run	–	0	–	–
Long-run	–	–	–	0
Rational-Expectations Model *(Chapter 16)* Anticipated increases in aggregate demand	+	+	+	0
Unanticipated increases in aggregate demand	+	0	+	+
Government borrowing up "deficits do not matter"	0	0	0	0
Constantly changing government policies	?	–	?	–
Technological innovation	+	+	?	+
Supply-Side Economics *(Chapter 11)* Marginal tax rates up	0	–	+	–

[1] Once the economy reaches its capacity, output can no longer be increased in any of these models. Also, in the long run, output will remain unchanged *unless* aggregate supply is affected. Because monetary policy has no effect on aggregate supply, it has no effect on output in the long run. On the other hand, fiscal policy (government spending and taxing) can change aggregate supply because taxes affect the incentive to work while government projects may enhance the productivity of the economy or, alternatively, waste the economy's resources.

[2] In the simple Keynesian model, an increase in the money supply only increases aggregate demand if it reduces interest rates, thereby stimulating investment spending and the economy.

[3] In the simple Monetarist model, more government borrowing only increases aggregate demand if it increases interest rates, thereby causing people to reduce their desired money holding (which in turn increases total spending).

INDEX

BARRON'S
Business Review

More titles in this series—

Accounting, 5th Ed.
Peter J. Eisen
ISBN 978-0-7641-3547-7
408 pp.

Finance, 5th Ed.
A. A. Groppelli and E. Nikbakht
ISBN 978-0-7641-3420-3
500 pp.

Business Law, 4th Ed.
R. W. Emerson
ISBN 978-0-7641-1984-2
611 pp.

Management, 3rd Ed.
P. J. Montana and B. H. Charnov
ISBN 978-0-7641-1276-8
468 pp.

Business Statistics, 4th Ed.
D. Downing and J. Clark
ISBN 978-0-7641-1983-5
481 pp.

Marketing, 3rd Ed.
Richard L. Sandhusen
ISBN 978-0-7641-1277-5
464 pp.

Economics, 4th Ed.
Walter J. Wessels
ISBN 978-0-7641-3419-7
516 pp.

Operations Management
J. K. Shim and J. G. Siegel
ISBN 978-0-7641-0510-4
624 pp.

Barron's Educational Series, Inc.
250 Wireless Blvd.
Hauppauge, NY 11788
Order toll-free: 1-800-645-3476
Order by fax: 1-631-434-3217

In Canada:
Georgetown Book Warehouse
34 Armstrong Ave.
Georgetown, Ont. L7G 4R9
Canadian orders: 1-800-247-7160
Order by fax: 1-800-887-1594

(#88) R12/07

Please visit **www.barronseduc.com** to view
current prices and to order books

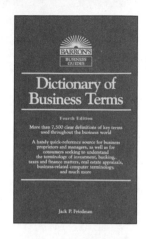
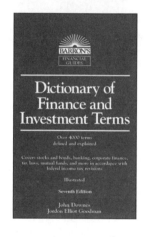